PARIS
2006

Rick Steves, Steve Smith & Gene Openshaw

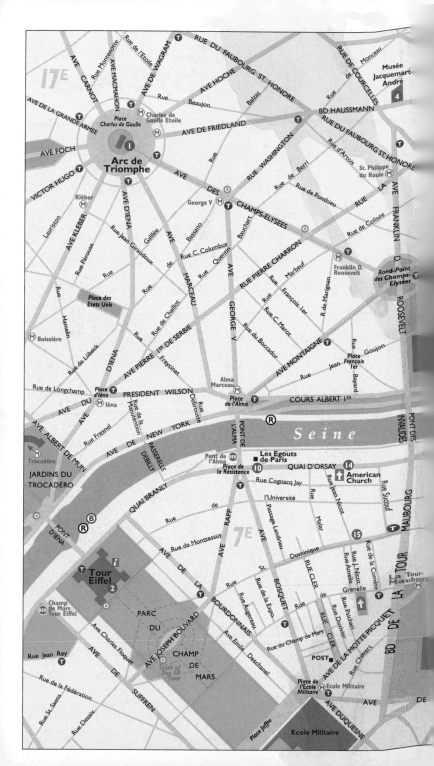

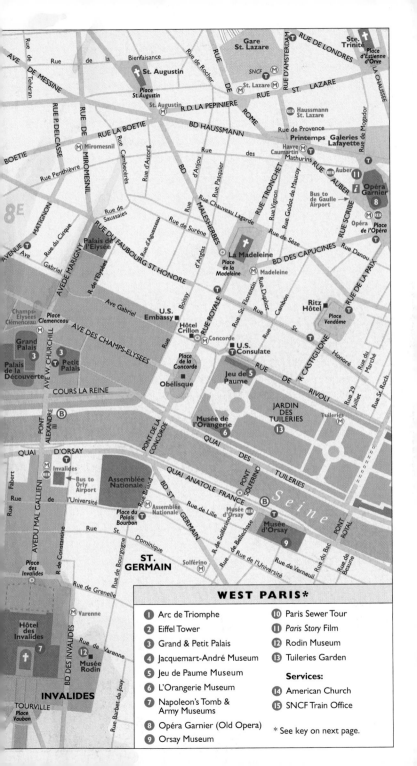

WEST PARIS*

1 Arc de Triomphe
2 Eiffel Tower
3 Grand & Petit Palais
4 Jacquemart-André Museum
5 Jeu de Paume Museum
6 L'Orangerie Museum
7 Napoleon's Tomb & Army Museums
8 Opéra Garnier (Old Opera)
9 Orsay Museum
10 Paris Sewer Tour
11 *Paris Story* Film
12 Rodin Museum
13 Tuileries Garden

Services:

14 American Church
15 SNCF Train Office

* See key on next page.

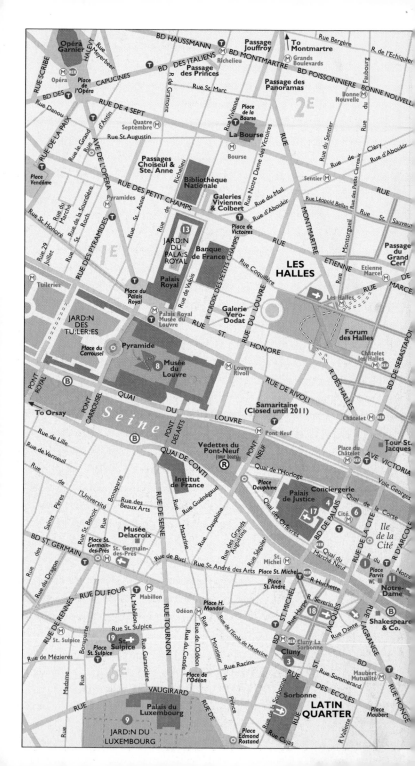

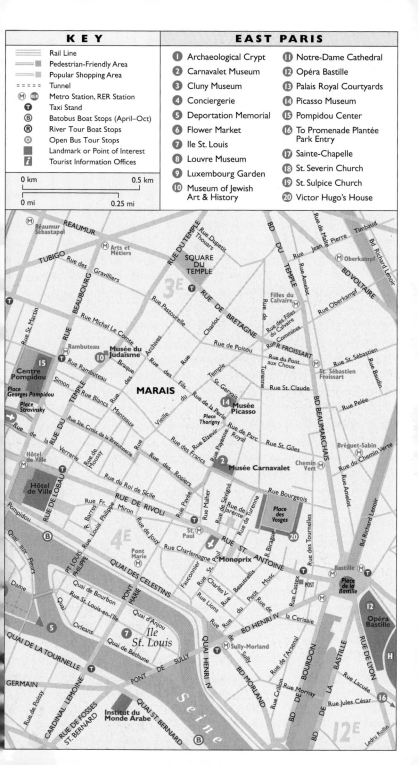

K E Y

Rail Line
Pedestrian-Friendly Area
Popular Shopping Area
Tunnel
Ⓜ ⓇⒺⓇ Metro Station, RER Station
Ⓣ Taxi Stand
Ⓑ Batobus Boat Stops (April–Oct)
Ⓡ River Tour Boat Stops
Ⓞ Open Bus Tour Stops
 Landmark or Point of Interest
𝒊 Tourist Information Offices

0 km   0.5 km

0 mi   0.25 mi

E A S T   P A R I S

1 Archaeological Crypt
2 Carnavalet Museum
3 Cluny Museum
4 Conciergerie
5 Deportation Memorial
6 Flower Market
7 Ile St. Louis
8 Louvre Museum
9 Luxembourg Garden
10 Museum of Jewish Art & History
11 Notre-Dame Cathedral
12 Opéra Bastille
13 Palais Royal Courtyards
14 Picasso Museum
15 Pompidou Center
16 To Promenade Plantée Park Entry
17 Sainte-Chapelle
18 St. Severin Church
19 St. Sulpice Church
20 Victor Hugo's House

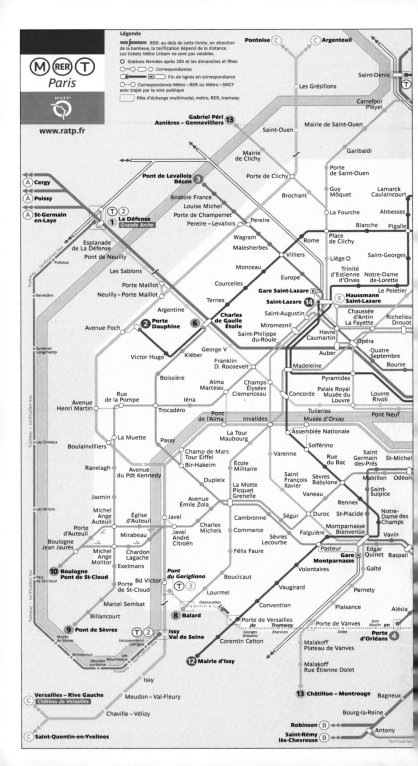

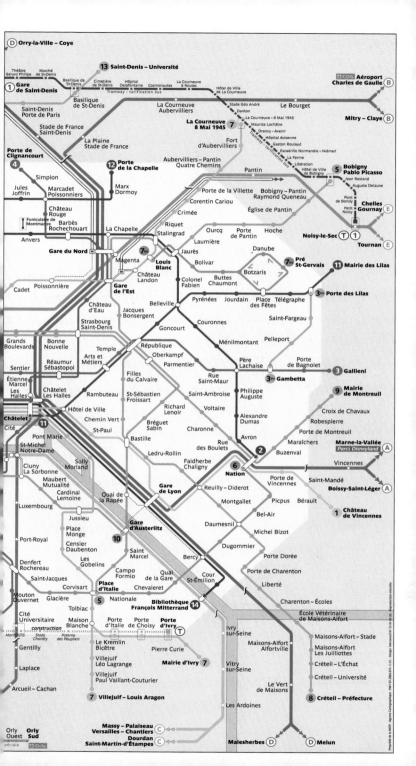

For a complete list of Rick Steves' guidebooks, see page 6.

Avalon Travel Publishing
1400 65th Street, Suite 250
Emeryville, CA 94608

Avalon Travel Publishing is an imprint of Avalon Publishing Group, Inc.

Printed in the United States of America by Worzalla
First printing November 2005
Distributed by Publishers Group West

Portions of this book were originally published in *Rick Steves' Mona Winks,* © 2001, 1998, 1996, 1993, 1988 by Rick Steves and Gene Openshaw; *Rick Steves' France, Belgium & the Netherlands* © 2002, 2001, 2000, 1999, 1998 by Rick Steves and Steve Smith; and in *Rick Steves' France* © 2005 by Rick Steves and Steve Smith.

ISBN(10) 1-56691-730-1
ISBN(13) 978-1-56691-730-8
ISSN 1522-3299

For the latest on Rick's lectures, guidebooks, tours, and public television series, contact Europe Through the Back Door, Box 2009, Edmonds, WA 98020, tel. 425/771-8303, fax 425/771-0833, www.ricksteves.com, or rick@ricksteves.com.

Europe Through the Back Door Managing Editor: Risa Laib
ETBD Editors: Cameron Hewitt, Kevin Yip, Jennifer Hauseman
Avalon Travel Publishing Series Manager: Patrick Collins
Avalon Travel Publishing Project Editor: Madhu Prasher
Research Assistance: Kristin Kusnic
Copy Editor: Mia Lipman
Indexer: Carl Wikander
Production & Typesetting: Patrick Barber, Holly McGuire
Cover Design: Kari Gim, Laura Mazer
Interior Design: Jane Musser, Laura Mazer, Amber Pirker
Maps & Graphics: David C. Hoerlein, Laura VanDeventer, Lauren Mills, Mike Morgenfeld
Front cover images: front image, the Seine River © Richard I'Anson / Lonely Planet Images; back image: Arc de Triomphe © Dominic Bonuccelli
Front matter color photos: p. i, @ Alex Bartel/PHOTOFILE; p. viii, Place du Tertre © FOLIO, Inc.

Rick Steves'

PARIS
2006

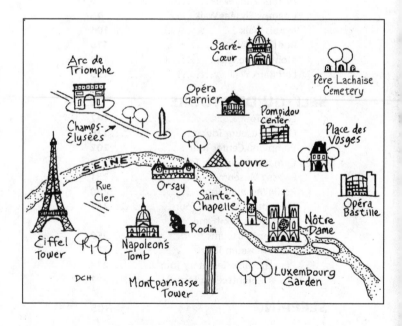

AVALON
TRAVEL

CONTENTS

TRANSPORTATION CONNECTIONS 399

DAY TRIPS

FRENCH HISTORY 478

APPENDIX

INDEX 499

Paris Map Overview

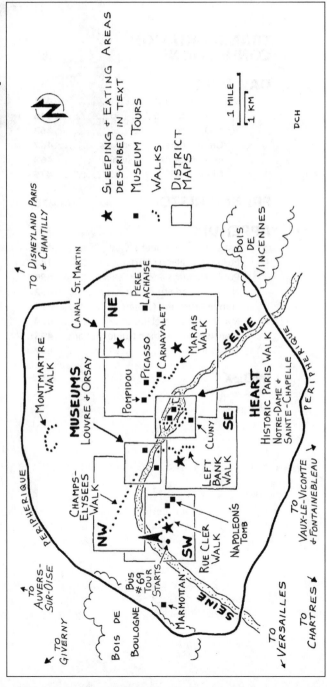

INTRODUCTION

Paris—the City of Light—has been a beacon of culture for centuries. As a world capital of art, fashion, food, literature, and ideas, it stands as a symbol of all the fine things that human civilization can offer. Come prepared to celebrate, rather than judge, the cultural differences, and you'll capture the romance and joie de vivre that Paris exudes.

Paris offers sweeping boulevards, chatty crêpe stands, chic boutiques, and world-class art galleries. Sip decaf with deconstructionists at a sidewalk café, then step into an Impressionist painting in a tree-lined park. Climb Notre-Dame and rub shoulders with the gargoyles. Cruise the Seine, zip up the Eiffel Tower, and saunter down the avenue des Champs-Elysées. Master the Louvre and Orsay museums. Save some after-dark energy for one of the world's most romantic cities.

This Information Is Accurate and Up-to-Date

This book is updated every year. Most publishers of guidebooks that cover a city from top to bottom can afford an update only every two or three years (and even then, it's often by e-mail or fax). Since this book is selective, covering only the sights that make the top week or two in Paris, I can update it in person each summer (plus do a winter checkup). The telephone numbers, hours, and prices of the places listed in this book are accurate as of mid-2005. Even with annual updates, things change. Still, if you're traveling with the current edition of this book, I guarantee you're using the most up-to-date information available in print. For the latest, visit www .ricksteves.com/update. Also at my Web site, you'll find a valuable list of reports and experiences—good and bad—from fellow travelers who have used this book (www.ricksteves.com/feedback).

Use this year's edition. People who try to save a few bucks by

traveling with an old book are not smart. They learn the serious-
ness of their mistake...in Paris. Your trip costs about $10 per wak-
ing hour. Your time is valuable. This guidebook saves lots of time.

About This Book

Rick Steves' Paris is a personal tour guide in your pocket. Better yet,
it's actually three tour guides in your pocket: The co-authors of this
book are Steve Smith and Gene Openshaw. Steve has been traveling to France—as a guide, researcher, and devout Francophile—
every year for the last 20 years. Gene and I have been exploring
the wonders of the Old World since our first "Europe through
the gutter" trip together as high-school buddies almost 30 years
ago. Together, Steve, Gene, and I keep this book up-to-date and
accurate. For simplicity, from this point on, "we" will shed our
respective egos and become "I."

The chapters in this book are organized in the following way:

Orientation includes tourist information, public transportation basics, and easy-to-read maps. The "Planning Your Time"
section offers a suggested schedule with thoughts on how best to
use your limited time.

Sights provides a succinct overview of Paris' most important
sights. They're arranged by neighborhood and include ratings:
▲▲▲—Don't miss; ▲▲—Try hard to see; ▲—Worthwhile if you
can make it; No rating—Worth knowing about.

The **Self-Guided Walks** cover six of Paris' most intriguing
neighborhoods: Historic Paris (Notre-Dame and Sainte-Chapelle),
the Champs-Elysées, the Marais, rue Cler (near the Eiffel Tower),
Montmartre, and the Left Bank.

The **Self-Guided Tours** lead you through Paris' most fasci-
nating museums and sights: the Louvre, Orsay, Pompidou Center,
Carnavalet, Picasso, Rodin, Marmottan, Napoleon's Tomb and
Army Museums, Cluny, and Père Lachaise Cemetery. The Bus
#69 Sightseeing Tour gives an inexpensive overview of the city.

Sleeping is a guide to my favorite hotels in three cozy neighborhoods, from swinging deals to cushy splurges, all with tips
geared to make you feel at home.

Eating offers good-value restaurants ranging from inexpensive eateries to romantic bistros, arranged by neighborhood, plus a
listing of "Grand Cafés."

Paris with Children includes my top 10 recommendations to
help keep your kids (and you) happy in Paris.

Shopping helps you shop painlessly and enjoyably, without
letting it overwhelm your vacation or ruin your budget. Read up
on Paris' great department stores, neighborhood boutiques, flea
markets, outdoor food markets, and arcaded, Old World shopping
streets.

Nightlife is a guide to entertainment and evening fun, with music, bus and taxi tours, and the best night walks and river cruises. You'll also find information on how to easily translate *Pariscope*, the weekly entertainment guide.

Transportation Connections lays the groundwork for your smooth arrival and departure, covering connections by train and plane, with detailed information on Paris' two major airports, an airport nearby, and Paris' six train stations.

Day Trips covers nearby sights: the great châteaux of Versailles (includes self-guided tour), Vaux-le-Vicomte, Fontainebleau, and Chantilly; Chartres' majestic cathedral (includes self-guided tour); the Impressionist retreats of Claude Monet's Giverny and Vincent van Gogh's Auvers-sur-Oise; and, *finalement*, Disneyland Paris. For longer stays, I list accommodations near most of these sights.

The **French History** chapter takes you from Celtic times to the present.

The **appendix** is a traveler's tool kit, with a pronunciation guide, a climate chart, telephone tips, French survival phrases, and a handy almanac of resources.

Throughout the book, when you see a ✪ in a listing, it means that the sight is covered in more depth in one of my self-guided walks or tours—a page number will tell you where to look to find more information.

Browse through this book and choose your favorite sights. Then have a *fantastique* trip! Traveling like a temporary local, you'll get the absolute most out of every mile, minute, and euro.

PLANNING

Trip Costs

Five components make up your trip costs: airfare, surface transportation, room and board, sightseeing/entertainment, and shopping/miscellany.

Airfare: Don't try to sort through the mess. Find and use a good travel agent. A basic round-trip U.S.–Paris flight costs $600–1,100 (even cheaper in winter), depending on where you fly from and when. Always consider saving time and money in Europe by flying "open jaw" (flying into one city and out of another).

Surface Transportation: For a typical one-week visit, allow about $60 for Métro tickets and a couple of day trips. Add an additional $100 if you opt for taxi rides to and from the airport (or less than half that by taking a shuttle, airport bus, or the RER).

Room and Board: You can easily manage in Paris on $120 a day per person for room and board. A $120-a-day budget allows $10 for breakfast, $15 for lunch, $30 for dinner, and $65 for lodging (based on 2 people splitting the cost of a $130 double room).

That's doable. Students and tightwads can do it on $50 ($25 per bed, $15–25 for meals and snacks).

Sightseeing and Entertainment: Get the Paris Museum Pass, which covers most sights in the city (for more information, see page 38). You'll pay about $22 for a one-day pass, $43 for a three-day pass, and $65 for a five-day pass. (While you can buy the pass through some U.S. travel agents, it's easy and cheaper to buy in Paris.) Without a Museum Pass, figure an average of $8 per major sight (Rodin Museum-$6, Louvre-$10) and $6 for minor ones. Assume that bus tours and splurge experiences (concerts in Sainte-Chapelle) cost about $30. An overall average of $20 a day works for most. Don't skimp here. After all, this category is the driving force behind your trip—you came to sightsee, enjoy, and experience Paris.

Shopping and Miscellany: Figure $3–4 per ice-cream cone, coffee, or soft drink. Shopping can vary in cost from nearly nothing to a small fortune. Good budget travelers find that this category has little to do with assembling a trip full of lifelong and wonderful memories.

When to Go

Late spring and fall have the best weather and the biggest crowds. May, June, September, and October are by far the toughest months for hotel hunting. Summers are generally hot and dry; if you wilt in the heat, look for a room with air-conditioning. It's fairly easy to find rooms in summer, and though many French businesses close in August, you'll hardly notice. Paris makes a great winter getaway. Airfares are cheap, the cafés are cozy, and the city feels lively but not touristy. The only problem—weather—is fixed by dressing correctly. Expect cold and rain, but not snow. For more information, see the climate chart in the appendix.

Travel Smart

Your trip to Paris is like a complex play—easier to follow and really appreciate on a second viewing. While no one does the same trip twice to gain that advantage, reading this book in its entirety before your trip accomplishes much the same thing.

Design an itinerary that enables you to hit museums and festivals (see page 491) on the right days. Note the days when sights are closed. Sundays have the same pros and cons as they do for travelers in the U.S. Special events and weekly markets pop up, sightseeing attractions are generally open, shops and banks are closed, public transportation options are fewer, and there's no rush hour. Saturdays are virtually weekdays.

Popular places are even more popular on weekends and inundated on three-day weekends. Expect big crowds around the major

holidays and book rooms in advance for the entire weekend (see page 305 for list). Many sights close on the actual holiday.

Plan ahead for laundry, Internet stops, and picnics. Mix intense and relaxed periods. Every trip (and every traveler) needs at least a few slack days. Pace yourself. Assume you will return.

Reread this book as you travel, and visit local tourist information offices. Buy a phone card or mobile phone and use it for reservations and confirmations. Be positive, and don't let one rude Parisian ruin your day. Ask questions. Most locals are eager to point you in their idea of the right direction. Those who expect to travel smart, do.

RESOURCES

French Tourist Offices in the U.S.

France's national tourist offices in the U.S. are a wealth of information (unlike their counterparts in Paris; see page 24). Before your trip, request any specific information you may want (such as city maps and schedules of upcoming festivals). Note that tourist information offices are abbreviated "TI" in this book.

French Government Tourist Offices: To ask questions and request tourist material, call 410/286-8310. One brochure and the *France Guide* magazine are free; additional brochures are $0.50 each, with a handling fee of $2 per order. Orders will arrive in 2–3 weeks; rush delivery is an extra $4. You can download many brochures free of charge at www.franceguide.com.

Their offices are in:

New York: 444 Madison Ave., 16th floor, New York, NY 10022, tel. 212/838-7800, fax 212/838-7855, Mon–Fri 10:00–16:00, closed Sat–Sun.

California: 9454 Wilshire Blvd. #310, Beverly Hills, CA 90212, tel. 310/271-6665, fax 310/276-2835, Mon–Fri 9:00–16:00, closed Sat–Sun.

Rick Steves' Guidebooks, Public Television Show, and Radio Show

Rick Steves' Europe Through the Back Door gives you budget-travel skills, such as minimizing jet lag, packing light, planning your itinerary, traveling by car or train, finding rooms, changing money, avoiding rip-offs, buying a mobile phone, hurdling the language barrier, staying healthy, taking great photographs, using a bidet, and much more. The book also includes chapters on 38 of my favorite "Back Doors," including one on Paris.

Country Guides: These annually updated books offer you the latest on the top sights and destinations, with tips on how to make your trip efficient and fun. Here are the titles:

Rick Steves' Best of Europe
Rick Steves' Best of
  Eastern Europe
Rick Steves' England
  (new in 2006)
Rick Steves' France
Rick Steves' Germany
  & Austria

Rick Steves' Great Britain
Rick Steves' Ireland
Rick Steves' Italy
Rick Steves' Portugal
Rick Steves' Scandinavia
Rick Steves' Spain
Rick Steves' Switzerland

City and Regional Guides: Updated every year, these focus on Europe's most compelling destinations. Along with specifics on sights, restaurants, hotels, and nightlife, you'll get self-guided, illustrated tours of the outstanding museums and most characteristic neighborhoods.

Rick Steves' Amsterdam,
  Bruges & Brussels
Rick Steves' Florence
  & Tuscany
Rick Steves' London
Rick Steves' Paris

Rick Steves' Prague
  & the Czech Republic
Rick Steves' Provence
  & the French Riviera
Rick Steves' Rome
Rick Steves' Venice

Rick Steves' Phrase Books: In Europe, a phrase book is as fun as it is necessary. This practical and budget-oriented series covers French, German, Italian, Spanish, Portuguese, and French/Italian/German. You'll be able to make hotel reservations over the phone, chat with your cabbie, and bargain at street markets.

And More Books: *Rick Steves' Europe 101: History and Art for the Traveler* (with Gene Openshaw) gives you the story of Europe's people, history, and art. Written for smart people who were sleeping in their history and art classes before they knew they were going to Europe, *101* helps Europe's sights come alive.

Rick Steves' Easy Access Europe, geared for travelers with limited mobility, covers London, Paris, Bruges, Amsterdam, and the Rhine River.

Rick Steves' Postcards from Europe, my autobiographical book, packs 25 years of travel anecdotes and insights into the ultimate 2,000-mile European adventure.

My latest book, *Rick Steves' European Christmas*, covers the joys, history, and quirky traditions of the holiday season in seven European countries.

Public Television Show: My series, *Rick Steves' Europe,* keeps churning out shows (more than 60 at last count), including several featuring the sights in this book.

Radio Show: My new weekly radio show, which combines call-in questions (à la *Car Talk*) and interviews with travel experts,

Begin Your Trip at www.ricksteves.com

At www.ricksteves.com you'll find a wealth of **free informa-tion** on destinations covered in this book, including fresh European travel and tour news every month and helpful "Graffiti Wall" tips from thousands of fellow travelers.

While you're there, the **online Travel Store** is a great place to save money on travel bags and accessories designed by Rick Steves to help you travel smarter and lighter, plus a wide selection of guidebooks, planning maps, and DVDs.

Traveling through Europe by rail is a breeze, but choosing the right railpass for your trip—among hundreds of options—can drive you nutty. At www.ricksteves.com, you'll find **Rick Steves' Annual Guide to European Railpasses**—your best way to convert chaos into pure travel energy. Buy your railpass from Rick, and you'll get a bunch of free extras to boot.

Travel agents will tell you about mainstream tours of Europe, but they won't tell you about **Rick Steves' tours.** Rick Steves' Europe Through the Back Door travel company offers more than two dozen itineraries and 300 departures reaching the best destinations in this book...and beyond. You'll enjoy the services of a great guide, a fun bunch of travel partners (with group sizes in the twenties), and plenty of room to spread out in a big, comfy bus. You'll find trips to fit every vacation size, from week-long city getaways to longer cross-country adventures. For details, visit www.ricksteves.com or call 425/771-8303, ext. 217.

airs on public radio stations. For a schedule of upcoming topics, an archive of past programs, and details on how to call in, see www .ricksteves.com/radio.

Other Guidebooks

For most trips to Paris, this book is all you need. But if you'd like more information, you may want to buy an additional guidebook. Both the readable *Paris Access* guide and the more scholarly *Michelin Green Guide* are well-researched. Of the multitude of other guide-books on France and Paris, many are high on facts and low on opinion, guts, or personality. If you'll be traveling elsewhere in France, *Rick Steves' France 2006* would come in handy.

Recommended Books and Movies

To get the feel of Paris past and present, consider reading some of these books or seeing these films:

Non-Fiction: For a better understanding of the French, check out *French or Foe* or *Savoir-Flair!* (both by Polly Platt).

The Course of French History (by Pierre Goubert) provides a good, succinct summary of French history. Other possibilities include: *A Moveable Feast* (Ernest Hemingway), *A Corner in The Marais* (Alex Karmel), *Is Paris Burning?* (Larry Collins), *A Traveller's History of Paris* (Robert Cole), *Travelers' Tales: Paris* (James O'Reilly), *Paris: The Collected Traveler* (Barrie Kerper), *Culture Shock: France* (Sally Taylor), *Paris to the Moon* (Adam Gopnik), *The Piano Shop on the Left Bank* (Thaddeus Carhart), *Paris Was a Woman: Portraits from the Left Bank* (Andrea Weiss), *Marling Menu-Master for France* (William Marling), and *The Paris Mapguide* (Michael Middleditch).

Fiction: *City of Darkness, City of Light* (Marge Piercy), *Le Divorce* and *Le Mariage* (both by Diane Johnson), *Americans in Paris: A Literary Anthology* (Adam Gopnik), *Inspector Maigret* series (George Simenon), *Sandman* (J. Robert Janes), *Murder in the Marais* (Cara Black), *Murder in Montparnasse* (Howard Engel), *Les Misérables* and *The Hunchback of Notre-Dame* (both by Victor Hugo), *A Tale of Two Cities* (Charles Dickens), and the *Madeline* children's series (Ludwig Bemelmans).

Flicks: *Amélie* (a charming young waitress in central Paris searches for love and the meaning of life), *Blue/White/Red* (a stylish trilogy of films based on France's national motto: Liberty, Equality, and Fraternity), *Camille Claudel* (biography of the talented sculptor and mistress of Auguste Rodin who tries to escape from Rodin's shadow), *French Kiss* (Meg Ryan and Kevin Kline on a romantic romp through Paris, Cannes, and the French countryside), *Gigi* (charming '50s musical of a young girl coming of age and her relationship with a wealthy bachelor bored with the high life in Paris in the early 1900s), *Les Miserables* (a Frenchman trying to escape his criminal past flees from a determined police captain and becomes wrapped up in the revolutionary battles between the rich and the starving), *The Moderns* (a struggling American artist living in the expatriate community of 1920's Paris becomes involved in a plot to forge paintings), *The Phantom of the Opera* (a disfigured musical genius, hiding in the Paris Opera House, terrorizes the cast and crew while promoting a young protegé whom he trains and loves), *The Red Balloon* (a small boy chases his balloon through the streets of Paris), and *Ridicule* (a nobleman realizes that survival in the opulent court of Louis XVI depends on a quick wit and an acid tongue).

Maps

The black-and-white maps in this book, drawn by Dave Hoerlein, are concise and simple. Dave, who is well-traveled in Paris, designed these maps to help you quickly orient and painlessly

navigate. The color city maps (and handy Métro map) at the front of this book will get you most places you'd want to go.

While Paris is littered with free maps, they don't show all the streets. For an extended stay, I prefer the pocket-size, street-indexed *Paris Pratique* or Michelin's *Paris par Arrondissement* (each about €7, sold at newsstands and bookstores in Paris). Before you buy a map, look at it to make sure it has the level of detail you want.

PRACTICALITIES

Red Tape: You need a passport, but no visa or shots, to travel in France. It's a good idea to bring photocopies of your identity papers if the originals are lost or stolen. You are required to have proof of identity on you at all times in France.

Time: In Paris—and in this book—you'll use the 24-hour clock. It's the same through 12:00 noon, then keep going: 13:00, 14:00, and so on. For anything over 12, subtract 12 and add P.M. (14:00 is 2:00 P.M.).

France is six/nine hours ahead of the East/West Coasts of the U.S.

Business Hours: Most shops are open Monday through Saturday (10:00–19:00) and closed Sunday, though many small markets, *boulangeries* (bakeries), and street markets are open Sunday mornings until noon. On Mondays, some businesses are closed until 14:00, and possibly all day. Saturdays are like weekdays (but most banks are closed).

Shopping: Shoppers interested in customs regulations and VAT refunds (the tax refunded on large purchases made by non-EU residents) can refer to page 386.

Discounts: While discounts aren't listed in this book, students with International Student Identification Cards, teachers with proper identification, and youths under 18 or even 26 often get discounts—but you have to ask.

Watt's Up? If you're bringing electrical gear, you'll need a two-prong adapter plug and a converter. Travel appliances often have convenient, built-in converters; look for a voltage switch marked 120V (U.S.) and 240V (Europe).

News: Americans keep in touch in Europe with the *International Herald Tribune* (published almost daily via satellite). Every Tuesday, the European editions of *Time* and *Newsweek* hit the stands with articles of particular interest to European travelers. Sports addicts can get their fix from *USA Today*. Good Web sites include www.europeantimes.com and http://news.bbc.co.uk.

Exchange Rate

I've priced things throughout this book in euros.
1 euro (€) = about $1.20
 Just like the dollar, the euro is broken down into 100
cents. You'll find coins ranging from 1 cent to 2 euros, and bills
from 5 euros to 500 euros. To roughly convert prices in euros
to dollars, add 20 percent to French prices: €20 is about $24,
€45 is about $55, and so on.

MONEY

Banking

Bring plastic (ATM, credit, or debit cards), along with several
hundred dollars in hard cash as an emergency backup. Traveler's
checks are a waste of time and money.

The best and easiest way to get cash in euros is to use French
cash machines, labeled *point d'argent* or *distributeur des billets* (the
French call these *D.A.B.*—day-ah-bay). You'll find these cash
machines all over France—they're always open and provide quick
transactions. Before you go, verify with your bank that your card
will work, inquire about fees (can be up to $5 per transaction), and
alert them that you'll be making withdrawals in Europe; otherwise, the bank may not approve transactions if it perceives unusual
spending patterns. Bring an extra card in case one gets demag-
netized or gobbled up by a machine.

Just like at home, credit or debit cards work easily at larger
hotels, restaurants, and stores. Visa and MasterCard are more
commonly accepted than American Express. Note that restaurants
and smaller businesses often require or prefer payment in cash.
Smart travelers function with hard cash and plastic cards.

You should use a money belt (a pouch with a strap that you
buckle around your waist like a belt and wear under your clothes).
Thieves target tourists. A money belt provides peace of mind and
allows you to carry lots of cash safely.

Don't be petty about getting money. Withdraw a week's worth
of cash, stuff it in your money belt, and travel!

Tips on Tipping

Tipping in France isn't as automatic and generous as it is in the
U.S., but for special service, tips are appreciated, if not expected.
As in the U.S., the proper amount depends on your resources, tipping philosophy, and the circumstance, but some general guide-
lines apply.

Damage Control for Lost or Stolen Cards

If you lose your credit, debit, or ATM card, you can stop people from using your card by reporting the loss immediately to the respective global customer-assistance centers. Call these 24-hour U.S. numbers collect: Visa (tel. 410/581-9994), MasterCard (tel. 636/722-7111), and American Express (tel. 336/393-1111).

Have, at a minimum, the following information ready: the name of the financial institution that issued you the card, along with the type of card (classic, platinum, or whatever). Ideally, plan ahead and pack photocopies of your cards—front and back—to expedite their replacement. Providing the following information will allow for a quicker cancellation of your missing card: full card number, whether you are the primary or secondary cardholder, the cardholder's name exactly as printed on the card, billing address, home phone number, circumstances of the loss or theft, and identification verification (your birth date, your mother's maiden name, or your Social Security number—memorize this, don't carry a copy). If you are the secondary cardholder, you'll also need to provide the primary cardholder's identification verification details. You can generally receive a temporary card within two or three business days in Europe.

If you promptly report your card lost or stolen, you typically won't be responsible for any unauthorized transactions on your account, although many banks charge a liability fee of $50.

Restaurants: At cafés and restaurants, the service charge is included in the bill *(service compris)*, though it's customary to tip 5 percent extra for good service (for details, see page 341). If you order a meal at a counter, don't tip.

Taxis: To tip the cabbie, round up. For a typical ride, round up to the next euro on the fare (to pay a €13 fare, give €14); for a long ride, round to the nearest €10 (for a €75 fare, give €80). If the cabbie hauls your bags and zips you to the airport to help you catch your flight, you might want to toss in a little more. But if you feel like you're being driven in circles or otherwise ripped off, skip the tip.

Special Services: Tour guides at public sites and tour-bus drivers often hold out their hands for tips after the tour; since I've already paid for the tour, I don't tip extra—but some tourists do give a euro or two, particularly for a job well done. I don't tip at hotels, but if you do, give the porter a euro for carrying bags and leave a couple of euros in your room at the end of your stay for the maid if the room was kept clean. In general, if someone in the service industry does a super job for you, a tip of a couple of euros is appropriate...but not required.

When in Doubt, Ask: If you're not sure whether (or how much) to tip for a service, ask your hotelier or the tourist information office; they'll fill you in on how it's done on their turf.

TRANSPORTATION

Transportation concerns within Paris are limited to the subway (Métro), buses, and taxis, all covered extensively in the Orientation chapter. Connections to day-trip destinations are covered in those chapters. You don't want to drive in Paris. If you have a car, stow it (for suggestions on parking, see page 416). For information on connecting Paris with the rest of France and with London on the Eurostar train, see page 414.

For all the specifics on transportation throughout France by train or car, see *Rick Steves' France 2006*.

COMMUNICATING

The Language Barrier and That French Attitude

You've no doubt heard that Parisians are "mean and cold and refuse to speak English." This is an out-of-date preconception left over from the days of Charles de Gaulle. Parisians are as friendly as any other people, and no more disagreeable than New Yorkers. Like many big cities, Paris is a massive melting pot of international cultures; your evening hotel receptionist is just as likely to speak French with an accent as not. And without any doubt, Parisians speak more English than Americans speak French. Be reasonable in your expectations: Waiters are paid to be efficient, not chatty. And Parisian postal clerks are every bit as speedy, cheery, and multilingual as ours are back home.

The biggest mistake most Americans make when traveling in France is trying to do too much with limited time. Hurried, impatient travelers who miss the subtle pleasures of people-watching from a sun-dappled café often misinterpret French attitudes. By slowing your pace and making an effort to understand French culture, you're much more likely to have a richer experience. With five weeks' paid time off each year, your hosts can't comprehend why anyone would rush through a vacation.

Parisians take great pride in their customs, clinging to their belief in cultural superiority despite the fact that they're no longer a world superpower. Let's face it: It's tough to keep on smiling when you've been crushed by a Big Mac, Mickey-Moused by Disney, and drowned in instant coffee. Your hosts are cold only if you decide to see them that way. Polite and formal, the French respect the fine points of culture and tradition. In France, strolling down the street with a big grin on your face and saying hello to

strangers is a sign of senility, not friendliness (seriously). Parisians think that Americans, while friendly, are hesitant to pursue more serious friendships. Recognize sincerity and look for kindness. Give them the benefit of the doubt.

Communication difficulties are exaggerated. To hurdle the language barrier, bring a phrase book (or use the French Survival Phrases near the end of this book), a small English/French dictionary, a menu reader, and a good supply of patience. In transactions, a small notepad and pen minimize misunderstandings about prices; have vendors write the price down. If you learn only five phrases, learn and use these: *bonjour* (good day), *pardon* (pardon me), *s'il vous plaît* (please), *merci* (thank you), and *au revoir* (goodbye). The French place great importance on politeness. Begin every encounter with *"Bonjour, madame/monsieur"* and end every encounter with *"Au revoir, madame/monsieur."*

The French are language perfectionists—they take their language (and other languages) seriously. Often they speak more English than they let on. This isn't a tourist-baiting tactic, but timidity on their part to speak another language less than fluently. Start any conversation with, *"Bonjour, madame/monsieur. Parlez-vous anglais?"* and hope they speak more English than you speak French.

Telephones

Smart travelers learn the phone system and use it daily for making hotel/restaurant reservations, verifying hours at sights, and phoning home.

Tips: For the police, dial 17. In a medical emergency, dial 15.

When spelling out your name on the phone, you'll find that some letters are pronounced differently in French: *a* is pronounced "ah," *e* is pronounced "eh," and *i* is pronounced "ee." To avoid confusion, say "*a*, Anne," "*e*, euro," and "*i*, Isabelle."

Types of Phones

You'll encounter various kinds of phones in France.

French **pay phones** take insertable phone cards (see details below). Simply take the phone off the hook, insert the prepaid card, wait for a dial tone, and dial away.

Hotel room phones are fairly cheap for local calls, but pricey for international calls, unless you use an international phone card (see below).

American mobile phones work in Europe if they're GSM-enabled, tri-band (or quad-band), and on a calling plan that includes international calls. With a T-Mobile phone, you can roam using your home number, and pay $1–2 per minute for making or receiving calls.

Some travelers buy a **European mobile phone** in Europe. For about $125, you can get a phone that will work in most countries once you pick up the necessary chip (about $30) per country. Or you can buy a cheaper, "locked" phone that only works in the country where you purchased it (about $100, includes $20 worth of calls). If you're interested, stop by any European shop that sells mobile phones; you'll see prominent store window displays (Phone House is popular). Don't buy a monthly contract—buy prepaid calling time instead (as you use it up, buy additional minutes at newsstands or mobile-phone shops). If you're on a budget, skip mobile phones and use phone cards instead.

Paying for Calls

You can spend a fortune making phone calls in France...but why would you? Here's the skinny on different ways to pay, including the best deals.

French phone cards come in two types: phone cards that you insert into a pay phone (*télécarte*, best for local calls), and phone cards that come with a dial-up code and can be used from virtually any phone (*carte à code*, best for long-distance and international calls). Look for these cards at any post office and most newsstands and tobacco shops *(tabacs)*, which you'll find everywhere in Paris, including at train stations and airports. Either type of phone card works only in France.

A *télécarte* (tay-lay-kart) is inserted in a public phone to make calls. The *télécarte* represents the efficient, convenient card-operated system that has replaced coin-operated public phones throughout Europe. There are two denominations: *une petite* costs about €7; *une grande* about €15. While you can use a *télécarte* to call anywhere in the world, it's only a good deal for making local calls.

A *carte à code* (cart ah code), which isn't inserted into a phone, comes with a dial-up code that can be used from nearly any phone, including the one in your hotel room (if it's set on "pulse," switch it to "tone"). Cards are marked as national (for France), international, or both, but all work for calls inside and outside the country. You get a better rate if your card corresponds with the type of call you're making; tell the vendor where you'll be calling most often (e.g., *"pour les Etats-Unis"*), and he'll pick the best value. If you're not sure what kind of calls you'll make, buy one that does both. *Le Ticket de Téléphone, 365-Universel,* and *Kosmos* seem like the most common calling-card brands, with denominations in €7, €10 (sometimes), and €15 amounts. They're all good values—my €15 international card lasted for four weeks of regular calls home (about 15 cents a minute).

These *carte à code* cards all work the same way and are simple to use, once you learn the rules (English instructions provided).

Scratch to get your code. Dial the free number (usually 4 digits beginning with a 3). After you dial, the message tells you to enter your code, and then press (*touche*, pronounced toosh) the pound key (#, *dièse*, dee-ehz) or the star key (*, *étoile*, eh-twahl). At the next message, dial the number you're calling, again followed by pound or star (you don't have to listen through the entire sales pitch). Minimize calling phone numbers beginning with 08—they'll incur an additional charge. While per-minute rates are much cheaper with a *carte à code* than with a *télécarte*, it's slower to use (more numbers to dial)—so local calls are quicker with a *télécarte* from a phone booth.

Dialing direct from your hotel room without using a *carte à code* is usually quite expensive for international calls, but it's convenient. I always ask first how much I'll be charged. Keep in mind that you might have to pay for local and occasionally even toll-free calls.

Receiving calls in your hotel room is often the cheapest way to keep in touch with the folks back home—especially if your family has an inexpensive way to call you (either a good deal on their long-distance plan, or a prepaid calling card with good rates to Europe). Give them a list of your hotels' phone numbers before you go. As you travel, send your family an e-mail or make a quick payphone call to set up a time for them to call you, and then wait for the ring.

U.S. calling cards (such as the ones offered by AT&T, MCI, or Sprint) are the worst option. You'll nearly always save a lot of money by paying with a French phone card.

How to Dial

Calling from the U.S. to France, or vice versa, is simple—once you break the code. The European calling chart on page 486 will walk you through it. Remember that France time is six/nine hours ahead of the East/West Coasts of the U.S.

Dialing within France: France has a direct-dial 10-digit telephone system. There are no area codes. To call to or from anywhere in France, including Paris, you dial the 10 numbers directly. All Paris numbers start with 01.

Dialing International Calls: To call France from another country, start with the international access code (00 if you're calling from another European country; 011 from the U.S. and Canada), dial France's country code (33), and then drop the initial 0 of the 10-digit local number and dial the remaining nine digits. For example, the phone number of a good hotel in Paris is 01 47 05 49 15. To call it from home, dial 011 33 1 47 05 49 15.

To dial out of France, start your call with its international code (00), then dial the country code of the country you're calling,

then the number you're calling. For example, to call my office in the U.S., I dial 00 (France's international access code), 1 (U.S. country code), then 425/771-8303 (my area code plus local number).

If you have difficulty making international calls, recheck your prefix numbers (drop the zero/keep the zero?, etc.) by referring to the calling chart in the appendix.

E-mail and Mail

E-mail: E-mail has caught on among hoteliers; today, very few lack an e-mail address, and most prefer to receive bookings online rather than by fax or phone. Many travelers set up a free e-mail account with Yahoo, Microsoft (hotmail), or Google (gmail). Hotels often have computers in their lobby—usually with slow Internet connections—for guests to use. The terminals may be free or operated with coins or a telephone card.

For high-speed Web access, ask at your hotel for the nearest Internet (an-ter-net) café. Post offices that offer Internet access *(cyberposte)* charge less than the cafés; buy a chip-card (for about same prices as phone cards), and you're in business.

The current rage is wireless access, called *Wi-Fi* (wee-fee), available to laptop users for a minimal fee at Internet cafés and some post offices and hotels.

Mail: French post offices are sometimes called PTT, for "Post, Telegraph, and Telephone"—look for signs for *La Poste*. Hours vary, though most are open weekdays 8:00–19:00 and Saturday morning 8:00–12:00. Stamps and phone cards are also sold at *tabac* (tobacco) shops. It costs about €0.90 to mail a postcard to the U.S. While you can arrange for mail delivery to your hotel (allow 10 days for a letter to arrive), phoning and e-mailing are so easy that I've dispensed with mail stops altogether.

TRAVELING AS A TEMPORARY LOCAL

We travel all the way to Europe to enjoy differences—to become temporary locals. You'll experience frustrations. Certain truths that we find "God-given" or "self-evident," such as friendly waiters, ice in drinks, bottomless cups of coffee, hot showers, and bigger being better, are suddenly not so true. One of the benefits of travel is the eye-opening realization that there are logical, civil, and even better alternatives.

Paris is an understandably proud city. To enjoy its people, you need to celebrate the differences. A willingness to go local ensures that you'll enjoy a full dose of Parisian hospitality.

If there is a negative aspect to the image the French have of Americans, it is that we are big, aggressive, impolite, rich,

loud, superficially friendly, and a bit naive. Americans tend to be noisy in public places, such as restaurants and trains. Our raised voices can demolish France's reserved and elegant ambience. Talk softly. While the French look bemusedly at some of our Yankee excesses—and worriedly at others—they nearly always afford us individual travelers all the warmth we deserve.

Judging from all the happy postcards I receive from travelers who have used this book, it's safe to assume you'll enjoy a great, affordable vacation—with the finesse of an independent, experienced traveler. Thanks, and *bon voyage!*

BACK DOOR TRAVEL PHILOSOPHY
From *Rick Steves' Europe Through the Back Door*

Travel is intensified living—maximum thrills per minute and one of the last great sources of legal adventure. Travel is freedom. It's recess, and we need it.

Experiencing the real Europe requires catching it by surprise, going casual..."Through the Back Door."

Affording travel is a matter of priorities. (Make do with the old car.) You can travel—simply, safely, and comfortably—nearly anywhere in Europe for $100 a day, plus transportation costs (allow more for Paris). In many ways, spending more money only builds a thicker wall between you and what you came to see. Europe is a cultural carnival, and, time after time, you'll find that its best acts are free and the best seats are the cheap ones.

A tight budget forces you to travel close to the ground, meeting and communicating with the people, not relying on service with a purchased smile. Never sacrifice sleep, nutrition, safety, or cleanliness in the name of budget. Simply enjoy the local-style alternatives to expensive hotels and restaurants.

Extroverts have more fun. If your trip is low on magic moments, kick yourself and make things happen. If you don't enjoy a place, maybe you don't know enough about it. Seek the truth. Recognize tourist traps. Give a culture the benefit of your open mind. See things as different but not better or worse. Any culture has much to share.

Of course, travel, like the world, is a series of hills and valleys. Be fanatically positive and militantly optimistic. If something's not to your liking, change your liking. Travel is addictive. It can make you a happier American as well as a citizen of the world. Our Earth is home to six billion equally important people. It's humbling to travel and find that people don't envy Americans. They like us, but, with all due respect, they wouldn't trade passports.

Globe-trotting destroys ethnocentricity. It helps you understand and appreciate different cultures. Regrettably, there are forces in our society that want you dumbed down for their convenience. Don't let it happen. Thoughtful travel engages you with the world—more important than ever these days. Travel changes people. It broadens perspectives and teaches new ways to measure quality of life. Many travelers toss aside their hometown blinders. Their prized souvenirs are the strands of different cultures they decide to knit into their own character. The world is a cultural yarn shop. And Back Door travelers are weaving the ultimate tapestry. Come on, join in!

ORIENTATION

Many people fall in love with Paris. Some see the essentials and flee, overwhelmed by the big city. With the proper approach and a measure of patience, you'll fall head over heels for Europe's capital city.

This orientation to the City of Light will illuminate your trip. The day plans—for visits of one to seven days—will help you prioritize the many sights. You'll tap into Paris' information sources for current events. Most importantly, you'll learn to navigate Paris by Métro, bus, taxi, or on foot.

Paris: A Verbal Map

Paris (population of city center: 2,150,000) is split in half by the Seine River, divided into 20 *arrondissements* (proud and independent governmental jurisdictions), circled by a ring-road freeway (the *périphérique*), and speckled with Métro stations. You'll find Paris easier to navigate if you know which side of the river you're on, which *arrondissement* you're in, and which Métro stop you're closest to. If you're north of the river (the top half of any city map), you're on the Right Bank (Rive Droite). If you're south of it, you're on the Left Bank (Rive Gauche). The bull's-eye of your Paris map is Notre-Dame, which sits on an island in the middle

Paris Arrondissements

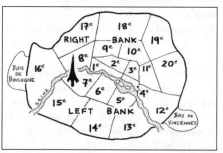

of the Seine. Most of your sightseeing will take place within five blocks of the river.

Arrondissements are numbered, starting at the Louvre and moving in a clockwise spiral out to the ring road. The last two digits in a Parisian zip code are the *arrondissement* number. The abbreviation for "Métro stop" is "Mo." In Parisian jargon, Napoleon's tomb is on *la Rive Gauche* (the Left Bank) in the *7ème* (7th *arrondissement*), zip code 75007, Mo: Invalides.

Paris Métro stops are used as a standard aid in giving directions, even for those not using the Métro. As you're tracking down addresses, these words and pronunciations will help: Métro (may-troh), *place* (plahs—square), *rue* (roo—road), *avenue* (ah-vuh-noo), *boulevard* (boo-luh-var), and *pont* (pohn—bridge).

Planning Your Time

In the planning sections below, I've listed sights in descending order of importance. Therefore, if you have only one day, just do Day 1; for two days, add Day 2; and so on. When planning where to plug in Versailles, remember that the palace is closed on Mondays and especially crowded on Sundays and Tuesdays—try to avoid these days if possible. For other itinerary considerations on a day by day basis, check the "Daily Reminder" on page 21.

Paris in One, Two, or Three Busy Days

If you want to fit in Versailles on a three-day visit, try the afternoon of the second day (easier) or the third day.

Day 1

Morning: Follow this book's Historic Paris Walk, featuring Ile de la Cité, Notre-Dame, the Latin Quarter, and Sainte-Chapelle.

Afternoon: Tour the Louvre.

Evening: Cruise the Seine River, take the "Paris Illumination" nighttime bus tour, or follow the "Floodlit Paris Taxi Tour" (in the Nightlife chapter, page 393).

Day 2

Morning: Follow this book's Champs-Elysées Walk from the Arc de Triomphe down the grand avenue des Champs-Elysées to Tuileries Garden.

Midday: Cross the pedestrian bridge from the Tuileries Garden, then tour the Orsay Museum.

Afternoon: Tour the Rodin Museum or Napoleon's Tomb, or visit Versailles (take the RER suburban train direct from Orsay).

Evening: Enjoy the Trocadéro scene and a twilight ride up the Eiffel Tower.

Daily Reminder

Monday: These sights are closed today—Jeu de Paume, Orsay, Archaeological Crypt, Rodin, Marmottan, Catacombs, Carnavalet, Victor Hugo's House, Montmartre Museum, Giverny, and Versailles; the Louvre and Eiffel Tower are more crowded because of this. Napoleon's Tomb is closed the first Monday of each month (except July–Sept). Some small stores don't open until 14:00. Street markets such as rue Cler and rue Mouffetard are dead today. Some banks are closed. It's discount night at most cinemas.

Tuesday: Many museums are closed today, including the Louvre, Picasso, Cluny, Maritime, and Pompidou, as well as the Grand Palais and the châteaux of Chantilly and Fontainebleau. The Eiffel Tower, Orsay, Versailles, and Giverny are particularly busy today.

Wednesday: All sights are open (Louvre until 21:45). The weekly *Pariscope* magazine comes out today. Most schools are closed, so many kids' sights are busy. Some cinemas offer discounts.

Thursday: All sights are open except the Sewer Tour. The Orsay is open until 21:45. Department stores are open late.

Friday: All sights are open (Louvre until 21:45) except the Sewer Tour. Vaux-le-Vicomte has candlelight visits (June–Aug). Afternoon trains and roads leaving Paris are crowded; TGV train reservation fees are higher.

Saturday: All sights are open except the Jewish Art and History Museum. The fountains run at Versailles (July–Sept), and Vaux-le-Vicomte hosts candlelight visits (May–mid-Oct); otherwise, avoid weekend crowds at area châteaux and Impressionist sights. Department stores are jammed. The Jewish Quarter is quiet.

Sunday: Some museums are free the first Sunday of the month—and therefore more crowded (e.g., Louvre, Orsay, Rodin, Pompidou, Cluny, and Picasso). Several museums offer reduced prices or free admission on Sundays (Orsay, Cluny and Rodin—other than first Sun of the month, when they're free). Napoleon's Tomb is open until 19:00 in summer. Versailles is more crowded than usual today, but the garden's fountains are running (early April–early Oct). Most of Paris' stores are closed on Sunday, but shoppers will find relief in the Marais neighborhood's lively Jewish Quarter and in Bercy Village, where many stores are open. Look for organ concerts at St. Sulpice and possibly other churches. The American Church often hosts a free evening concert at 17:00 or 18:00 (Sept–May only, but not every week). Many recommended restaurants in the rue Cler neighborhood are closed for dinner.

Day 3
Morning: Take this book's Marais Walk.
Afternoon: Stay in the Marais and tour your choice of sights: the Picasso Museum, Carnavalet Museum, Pompidou Center, or Jewish Art and History Museum. (Or visit Versailles, if you haven't already.)
Evening: Take this book's Montmartre Walk, featuring the Sacré-Cœur basilica.

Paris in Five to Seven Days Without Going In-Seine

Day 1
Morning: Follow this book's Historic Paris Walk, featuring Ile de la Cité, Notre-Dame, the Latin Quarter, and Sainte-Chapelle. If you enjoy medieval art, visit the Cluny Museum.
Afternoon: Tour the Opéra Garnier (English tours available), consider the *Paris Story* film (for a good video orientation), and end your day enjoying the glorious rooftop view at Galleries Lafayette department store.
Evening: Cruise the Seine River, take the "Paris Illumination" nighttime bus tour, or follow this book's "Floodlit Paris Taxi Tour" (in the Nightlife chapter, page 393).

Day 2
Reversing the morning and afternoon activities on this day also works well, because the Champs-Elysées Walk leaves you near the Louvre—but most people have more energy for museums in the morning.
Morning: Tour the Louvre (arrive 20 min before opening). Have coffee or lunch at Café le Nemours.
Afternoon: Follow this book's Champs-Elysées Walk from the Arc de Triomphe downhill along the incomparable avenue des Champs-Elysées to Tuileries Garden.
Evening: Enjoy dinner on Ile St. Louis, then a floodlit walk by Notre-Dame.

Day 3
Morning: Tour the Orsay Museum (arrive 15 min before opening).
Midday: Tour the Rodin Museum (picnic or café lunch in gardens).
Afternoon: Visit Napoleon's Tomb, then take this book's Rue Cler Walk and relax at Café du Marché.
Evening: Take this book's Montmartre Walk, featuring the Sacré-Cœur basilica.

Day 4

Morning: Catch the RER suburban train to arrive early (no later than 9:00) at Versailles. Tour the palace's interior.

Midday: Have lunch on Versailles' market square.

Afternoon: Take the shortcut from the market square to Versailles' gardens, and visit Le Hameau and Trianon palaces. Return to Paris with some time for shopping.

Evening: Shop and enjoy a leisurely dinner.

Day 5

Morning: Follow this book's Marais Walk and tour the Carnavalet Museum (free). Have lunch on place des Vosges or rue des Rosiers.

Afternoon: Depending on your interest, tour two of the following three sights—the Pompidou Center, Picasso Museum, or the Jewish Art and History Museum.

Evening: Enjoy the Trocadéro scene and a twilight ride up the Eiffel Tower.

Day 6

Morning: Take an Impressionist escape to Giverny or Auvers-sur-Oise.

Afternoon: Follow this book's Left Bank Walk (featuring art galleries, boutiques, historic cafés, and grand boulevards), mix in some shopping (see "Sèvres-Babylone to St. Sulpice" in the Shopping chapter, page 379), then relax in the Luxembourg Garden or at a nearby café (see "Les Grands Cafés de Paris," page 364).

Evening: Join the parade along the Champs-Elysées (which offers a different scene at night than the daytime walk you enjoyed on Day 2). If you haven't hiked to the top of the Arc de Triomphe yet, consider doing it by twilight.

Day 7

Choose from:

　　More shopping and cafés

　　Montmartre and Sacré-Cœur (by day)

　　Marmottan or Jacquemart-André museums

　　Day trip to Chartres

　　Day trip to Vaux-le-Vicomte and Fontainebleau

　　Day trip to Disneyland Paris

Evening: Night bus or boat tour (whichever you have yet to do).

OVERVIEW

Tourist Information

Paris tourist offices (abbreviated **TI** in this book) have long lines, offer little information, and charge for maps. This book, the *Pariscope* magazine (described below), and one of the freebie maps available at any hotel (or in the front of this book) are all you need. Paris' TIs share a single phone number: 08 92 68 30 00 (from the U.S., dial 011 33 8 92 68 30 00).

If you must visit a TI, there are several locations: **Grands Magasins** (Mon–Sat 9:00–18:30, closed Sun, near Opéra Garnier at 11 rue Scribe), **Pyramides** (daily 9:00–19:00, at Pyramides Métro stop between the Louvre and Opéra), **Gare de Lyon** (Mon–Sat 8:00–18:00, closed Sun), **Montmartre** (daily 10:00–19:00, place du Tertre), and at the **Eiffel Tower** (May–Sept daily 11:00–18:42, closed Oct–April). Both **airports** have handy information offices (called ADP) with long hours and short lines (see Transportation Connections chapter, page 399).

Pariscope: The weekly €0.40 *Pariscope* magazine (or one of its clones, available at any newsstand) lists museum hours, art exhibits, concerts, festivals, plays, movies, and nightclubs. Smart tour guides and sightseers rely on this for the latest listings (see page 388).

Other Publications: The American Church (see below) distributes a free, handy, and insightful monthly English-language newspaper called *Paris Voice*, which has useful reviews of concerts, plays, and current events (available at the American Church and about 200 locations throughout Paris, www.parisvoice.com). Also look for an advertisement paper called *France-U.S.A. Contacts*, with information on housing and employment for the community of 30,000 Americans living in Paris (free, pick it up at the American Church and elsewhere, www.fusac.fr). For a complete schedule of museum hours and English-language museum tours, get the free *Musées, Monuments Historiques, et Expositions* booklet from any museum.

Web Sites: Paris' TIs all share an official Web site (www.parisinfo.com) offering practical information on hotels, special events, museums, children's activities, fashion, nightlife, and more. Two other Web sites that are entertaining and at times useful are www.bonjourparis.com (which claims to offer a virtual trip to Paris—featuring interactive French lessons, tips on wine and food, and news on the latest Parisian trends) and the similar www.paris-anglo.com (with informative stories on visiting Paris, plus a directory of over 2,500 English-speaking businesses).

American Church and Franco-American Center: This interdenominational church—in the rue Cler neighborhood,

facing the river between the Eiffel Tower and Orsay Museum—is a nerve center for the American émigré community. The worship service at 11:00 on Sunday, the coffee hour after church, and the free Sunday concerts (generally Sept–May at 17:00 or 18:00—but not every week) are a great way to make some friends and get a taste of émigré life in Paris (reception open Mon–Sat 9:30–13:00 & 14:00–22:30, Sun 9:00–14:00 & 15:00–19:00, 65 quai d'Orsay, Mo: Invalides, tel. 01 40 62 05 00, www.acparis.org). It's also a good place to pick up copies of *Paris Voice* and *France-U.S.A. Contacts* (described above).

Arrival in Paris
For a comprehensive rundown on Paris' train stations and airports, see the Transportation Connections chapter on page 399.

Helpful Hints
Heightened Security *(Plan Vigipirate):* You may notice an abundance of police at monuments, on streets, and on the Métro, as well as security cameras everywhere. You'll go through quick and reassuring airport-like security checks at many major attractions. This is all part of Paris' anti-terror plan. The police are helpful, the security lines move quickly, and there are fewer pickpocket problems than usual on the Métro.

Theft Alert: Although the greater police presence has scared off some pickpockets, these troublesome thieves still thrive—particularly on Métro and RER lines that serve high-profile tourist sights. Wear a money belt, put your wallet in your front pocket, loop your day bag over your shoulders, and keep a tight grip on your purse or shopping bag. Muggings are rare, but do occur. If you're out late, avoid the dark riverfront embankments and any place where the lighting is dim and pedestrian activity is minimal.

Street Safety: Parisian drivers are notorious for ignoring pedestrians. Look both ways (many streets are one-way) and be careful of seemingly quiet bus/taxi lanes. Don't assume you have the right of way, even in a crosswalk. When crossing a street, keep your pace constant and don't stop suddenly. By law, drivers must miss pedestrians by one meter—a little more than three feet (1.5 meters in the countryside). Drivers carefully calculate your speed and won't hit you, provided you don't alter your route or pace.

Watch out for a lesser hazard: *merde.* Parisian dogs decorate the city's sidewalks with 16 tons of droppings per day. People get injured by slipping in it.

Paris Museum Pass: This worthwhile pass, covering most sights in Paris, is available at major Métro stations, TIs, and museums.

Tips for Tackling the
Self-Guided Tours in This Book

Sightseeing can be hard work. This book's self-guided tours are designed to help make your visits to Paris' finest museums meaningful, fun, fast, and painless.

The opening times of sights can change without warning. Pick up the latest listing of museum hours at a TI. (Museums also distribute a free, up-to-date *Musées, Monuments Historiques, et Expositions* booklet with this information.) Don't put off visiting a must-see sight—you never know when a place will close unexpectedly for a holiday, strike, or restoration.

To get the most out of the self-guided tours, read the tour the night before your visit. When you arrive at the sight, use the overview map to get the lay of the land and the basic tour route. Expect a few changes—paintings can be on tour, on loan, out sick, or shifted at the whim of the curator. To adapt, pick up any available free floor plans as you enter, ask an information person to glance at this book's maps to confirm they're current, or if you can't find a particular painting, just ask any museum worker. Point to the photograph in this book and ask, *"Où est?"* (oo ay; meaning, "Where is?").

The tours in this book cover only the highlights. Many sights rent audioguides (€3–5, dry but worthwhile) that supplement this information. While most readers will find this book's tours more interesting, eager students take advantage of both types of tours and learn even more. (If you bring along your own pair of headphones and a Y-jack, two people can share one audioguide

For detailed information, see page 38.

Museum Strategy: When possible, visit key museums first thing (when your energy is best) and save other activities for the afternoon. Remember, most museums require you to check daypacks and coats, and important museums have metal detectors that will slow your entry. The Louvre, Orsay, and Pompidou are open on selected nights (see "Paris at a Glance," page 40), making for peaceful visits with fewer crowds.

Public WCs: Carry small change for pay toilets, or walk into any sidewalk café like you own the place and find the toilet in the back. The restrooms in museums are free and the best you'll find. Modern, sanitary street-booth toilets provide both relief and a memory (coins required, don't leave small children inside unattended). Keep toilet paper or tissues with you, as some toilets are poorly supplied.

Bookstores: There are many English-language bookstores in Paris where you can pick up guidebooks (at nearly double

and save.) Guided tours in English (usually €6 and widely ranging in quality) are most likely to occur during peak season.

Museums have their rules; if you're aware of them in advance, they're no big deal. Keep in mind that many sights have "last entry" times 30 to 60 minutes before closing. Guards usher people out before the official closing time.

Cameras are normally allowed, but no flashes or tripods (without special permission). Flashes damage oil paintings and distract others in the room. Even without a flash, a handheld camera will take a decent picture (or buy postcards or posters at the museum bookstore). Video cameras are usually allowed.

For security reasons, you're often required to check even small bags. Many museums have a free checkroom at the entrance. These are safe. If you have something you can't bear to part with, be prepared to stash it in a pocket or purse. If you don't want to check a small backpack, carry it (at least as you enter) under your arm like a purse...and hope guards don't notice.

At the museum bookshop, scan the postcards and thumb through the biggest guidebook (or skim its index) to be sure you haven't overlooked something that you'd like to see. If there's an on-site cafeteria, it's usually a good place to rest and have a snack or light meal. Museum WCs are free and generally clean.

And finally, every sight or museum offers infinitely more than the few stops covered in this book. Use these tours as an introduction—not the final word.

their American prices). Most carry this book. My favorite is the friendly **Red Wheelbarrow Bookstore** in the Marais neighborhood, run by charming Penelope and Abigail (daily 10:00–19:00, 22 rue St. Paul, Mo: St. Paul, tel. 01 42 77 42 17). Others include **Shakespeare and Company** (some used travel books, daily 12:00–24:00, 37 rue de la Bûcherie, across the river from Notre-Dame, Mo: St. Michel, tel. 01 43 26 96 50; see page 82 in Historic Paris Walk), **W.H. Smith** (Mon–Sat 10:00–19:00, closed Sun, 248 rue de Rivoli, Mo: Concorde, tel. 01 44 77 88 99), **Brentanos** (Mon–Sat 10:00–19:00, closed Sun, 37 avenue de l'Opéra, Mo: Opéra, tel. 01 42 61 52 50), and **Village Voice** (near St. Sulpice Church at 6 rue Princesse, tel. 01 46 33 36 47).

Bike Rental: Fat Tire Bike Tours runs tours (see page 37) and also rents bikes (€2/hr, €15/24 hrs, includes helmets and locks, credit-card imprint required for deposit, ask for their suggested bike route map, daily 9:00–19:00, south of Eiffel

Tower at 24 rue Edgar Faure, tel. 01 56 58 10 54).

Parking: Most of the time, drivers must pay to park curbside (buy parking card at tobacco shops), but not at night (19:00–9:00), all day Sunday, or anytime in August, when most Parisians are on vacation. There are parking garages under Ecole Militaire, St. Sulpice Church, Les Invalides, the Bastille, and the Panthéon for about €20–25 per day (it's cheaper the longer you stay). Some hotels offer parking for less—ask. See also "Parking in Paris" on page 416 of the Transportation Connections chapter.

Tobacco Stands (Tabacs): These little kiosks—usually just a counter inside a café—sell cards for parking meters, public-transit tickets, postage stamps, and...oh yeah, cigarettes. For more on this slice of Parisian life, see page 118 in the Rue Cler Walk. To find one anywhere in Paris, just look for a *Tabac* sign and the red, cylinder-shaped symbol above some (but not all) cafés.

Getting Around Paris

For such a sprawling city, Paris is easy to navigate. Your basic choices are Métro (in-city subway), RER (suburban rail tied into the Métro system), public bus, and taxi. (Also consider the hop-on, hop-off bus and boat tours, described under "Tours" on page 34.) You can buy tickets and passes at a tabac (tobacco stand—described above) and at most Métro stations. While the majority of Métro stations have staffed ticket windows, smaller stations might discontinue this service as the Métro system converts to automated machines.

Public-Transit Tickets: The Métro, RER, and buses all work on the same tickets. (Note that you can transfer between the Métro and RER on a single ticket, but combining a Métro or RER trip with a bus ride takes two tickets.) A **single ticket** costs €1.40. To save 30 percent, buy a *carnet* (kar-nay) of 10 tickets for €10.70 (that's €1.07 per ticket—€0.33 cheaper than single tickets). It's less expensive for kids (ages 4–10 pay €5.35 for a *carnet*).

If you're staying in Paris for even just a few days, consider the **Carte Orange** (kart oh-RAHNZH), which pays for itself in 15 rides. For about €16, you get free run of the bus and Métro system for one week, starting Monday and ending Sunday. Ask for the Carte Orange *hebdomadaire* (ehb-doh-mah-dair) and supply a passport-size photo. Larger Métro stations have photo booths. The month-long version costs about €51—request a Carte Orange *mensuelle* (mahn-soo-ehl, good from the first day of the month to the last, also requires photo). These passes cover only central Paris. You can pay more for passes covering regional destinations (such as Versailles), but for most visitors, this is a bad value (instead, buy

individual tickets for longer-distance destinations). Despite what some Métro agents say, Carte Orange passes are definitely not limited to residents; if you're refused, simply go to another station or a tabac to buy your pass.

The overpriced **Paris Visite** passes were designed for tourists and offer minor reductions at minor sights (1 day-€9, 2 days-€14, 3 days-€19, 5 days-€28), but you'll get a better value with a cheaper *carnet* of 10 tickets or a Carte Orange.

By Métro

In Paris, you're never more than a 10-minute walk from a Métro station. Europe's best subway allows you to hop from sight to sight quickly and cheaply (runs daily 5:30–00:30 in the morning). Learn to use it. Begin by studying the color Métro map at the beginning of this book.

Pickpockets: Thieves dig the Métro. Be on guard. For example, if your pocket is picked as you pass through a turnstile, you end up stuck on the wrong side (after the turnstile bar has closed behind you) while the thief gets away. Stand away from Métro doors to avoid being a target for a theft-and-run just before the doors close. Any jostling or commotion—especially when boarding or leaving trains—is likely the sign of a thief or a team of thieves in action. Make any fare inspector show proof of identity (ask locals for help if you're not certain). Never show anyone your wallet.

How the Métro Works: To get to your destination, determine the closest "Mo" stop and which line or lines will get you there. The lines have numbers, but they're best known by their end-of-the-line stops. (For example, the La Défense/ Château de Vincennes line, also known as line 1, runs between La Défense in the west and Vincennes in the east.) Once in the Métro station, you'll see blue-and-  white signs directing you to the train going in your direction (e.g., "*direction:* La Défense"). Insert your ticket in the automatic turnstile, pass through, reclaim your ticket, and keep it until you exit the system. Fare inspectors regularly check for cheaters and accept absolutely no excuses.

Transfers are free and can be made wherever lines cross. When you transfer, look for the orange *correspondance* (connections) signs when you exit your first train, then follow the proper direction sign.

Even though the Métro whisks you quickly from one point

Métro Basics

- The same tickets are good on the Métro, RER (within the city), and city buses (but not to transfer between Métro/RER and bus).
- Save money by buying a *carnet* of tickets or a Carte Orange.
- Find your train by its end-of-the-line stops.
- Insert your ticket into the turnstile (brown stripe down), retrieve it, and keep it until the end of your journey.
- Beware of pickpockets.
- Transfers *(correspondance)* within the Métro or RER system are free.
- At the end of your trip, choose the right exit *(sortie)* to avoid extra walking.
- Dispose of used tickets to avoid confusing them with fresh ones.

Key Words for the Métro and RER

French	Pronounced	English
direction	dee-rek-see-ohn	direction
ligne	leen-yuh	line
correspondance	kor-res-pohn-dahns	transfer
sortie	sor-tee	exit
carnet	kar-nay	cheap set of 10 tickets
Pardon, madame/monsieur.	par-dohn, mah-dahm/mes-yur	Excuse me, lady/bud.
Je descend.	juh day-sahn	I'm getting off.
Donnez-moi mon porte-monnaie!	duh-nay-mwah mohn port-moh-nay	Give me back my wallet!

Etiquette

- When waiting at the platform, get out of the way of those exiting the train. Board only once everyone is off.
- Avoid using the hinged seats near the doors when the car is jammed; they take up valuable standing space.
- In a crowded train, try not to block the exit. If you're blocking the door when the train stops, step out of the car and to the side, let others off, then get back on.
- Talk softly in the cars. Listen to how quietly Parisians can communicate and follow their lead.
- On escalators, stand on the right, pass on the left.

to another, be prepared to walk significant distances within stations to reach your platform (most noticeable when you transfer). Escalators are common, but they're often out of order. To limit excessive walking, avoid transferring at these sprawling stations: Montparnasse-Bienvenüe, Chatelet-Les Halles, Charles de Gaulle-Etoile, Gare du Nord, and Bastille.

Before taking the *sortie* (exit) to leave the Métro, check the helpful *plan du quartier* (map of the neighborhood) to get your bearings, locate your destination, and decide which *sortie* you want. At stops with several *sorties,* you can save lots of walking by choosing the best exit.

After you exit the system, toss or tear your used ticket so you don't confuse it with your unused ticket—they look virtually identical.

By RER

The RER (Réseau Express Régionale; air-ay-air) is the suburban arm of the Métro, serving destinations farther out of the center (such as Versailles, Disneyland Paris, and the airports). These routes are indicated by thick lines on your subway map and identified by the letters A, B, C, and so on. Some suburban routes are operated by France's railroad (SNCF) and are called **Transilien**; they function the same way and use the same tickets as the RER. On Transilien trains (but not RER trains), railpasses are accepted; show your pass at a ticket window to get a free ticket to get through the turnstiles.

Within the city center, the RER works like the Métro, but can be speedier (if it serves your destination directly) because it makes fewer stops. Métro tickets are good on the RER when traveling in the city center. (You can transfer between the Métro and RER systems with the same ticket.) But to travel outside the city (to Versailles or the airport, for example), you'll need to buy a separate, more expensive ticket at the station window before boarding. Unlike in the Métro, you need to insert your ticket in a turnstile to exit the RER lines. Also unlike the Métro, not every train stops at every station along the way; check the sign over the platform to see if your destination is listed as a stop (*"toutes les gares"* means it makes all stops along the way), or confirm with a local before you board.

By City Bus

Paris' excellent bus system is worth figuring out. Remember, even though buses use the same tickets as the Métro and RER, you can't use a single ticket to transfer between the systems—or even to transfer from one bus to another. One ticket buys you a bus ride anywhere in central Paris—but if you leave the city center (shown

Key Buses for Tourists

Of Paris' many bus routes, these are some of the most scenic. They provide a great, cheap, and convenient introduction to the city.

Bus #69 runs east–west between the Eiffel Tower and Père Lachaise Cemetery by way of rue Cler (recommended hotels), quai d'Orsay, the Louvre, and the Marais (recommended hotels). For more information, see Bus #69 Sightseeing Tour on page 297.

Bus #87 also links the Marais and rue Cler areas, but stays mostly on the Left Bank, connecting the Eiffel Tower, St. Sulpice, Luxembourg Garden (more recommended hotels and restaurants), St. Germain-des-Prés, the Latin Quarter, the Bastille, and Gare de Lyon.

Bus #24 runs east–west along the Seine riverbank from Gare St. Lazare to Madeleine, Place de la Concorde, Orsay Museum, the Louvre, St. Michel, Notre-Dame, and Jardin des Plantes, all the way to trendy Bercy (cafés and shops).

Bus #63 is another good east–west route, connecting the Marmottan Museum, Trocadéro (Eiffel Tower), pont de l'Alma, Orsay Museum, St. Sulpice, Luxembourg Garden, Latin Quarter/Panthéon, and Gare de Lyon.

as zone 1 on the diagram on board the bus) or transfer to another bus, you must validate a second ticket.

Buses don't seem as romantic as the famous Métro and are subject to traffic jams, but savvy travelers know that buses can have you swinging through the city like Tarzan in an urban jungle. Anywhere you are, you can generally see a bus stop, each one complete with all the information you need: a fine city bus map, route maps showing exactly where each bus that uses this stop goes, a frequency chart and schedule, a *plan du quartier* map of the immediate neighborhood, and a *soirées* map explaining night service, if available. While the Métro shuts down about 00:30 in the morning, some buses continue much later.

Enter buses through the front door. Punch your ticket in the machine behind the driver, or pay the higher cash fare. When you reach your destination, push the red button to signal you want a stop, then exit through the rear door. Even if you're not certain you've figured out the system, do some joyriding (outside of rush hour: Mon–Fri 8:00–9:30 & 17:30–19:30). For information on some of Paris' most scenic and convenient routes, see the sidebar. Handy bus-system maps *(plan des autobus)* are available in any Métro station (and in the €7 *Paris Pratique* map book sold at newsstands). Major stops are displayed on the side of each bus. The handiest bus

Key Bus Routes

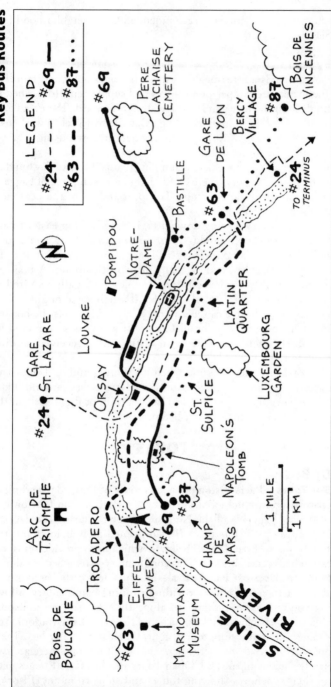

routes are listed for each recommended hotel neighborhood (see Sleeping chapter).

By Taxi

Parisian taxis are reasonable, especially for couples and families. The meters are tamper-proof. Fares and supplements (described in English on the rear windows) are straightforward. There's a €5.20 minimum. A 10-minute ride (e.g., Bastille to Eiffel Tower) costs about €10 (versus €1.07 to get anywhere in town using a *carnet* ticket on the Métro or bus).

Higher rates are charged at night (19:00–7:00), all day Sunday, and to either airport. There's a €1 charge for each piece of baggage and for train station pickups. To tip, round up to the next euro (minimum €0.50).

You can try waving down a taxi, but it's often easier to ask for the nearest taxi stand (*"Où est une station de taxi?"*; oo ay oon stah-see-ohn duh taxi). Taxi stands are indicated by a circled "T" on good city maps, and on many maps in this book. A taxi can fit three people comfortably, and cabbies are legally required to take up to four for a small extra fee (though some might resist). Groups of up to five can use a *grand taxi,* which must be booked in advance—ask your hotel to call. If a taxi is summoned by phone, the meter starts as soon as the call is received, adding €3–6 to the bill.

Taxis are tough to find when it's raining and on Friday and Saturday nights, especially after the Métro closes (around 00:30 in the morning). If you need to catch a train or flight early in the morning, book a taxi the day before.

TOURS

By Bus

Bus Tours—Paris Vision offers bus tours of Paris, day and night (advertised in hotel lobbies). I'd take a Paris Vision tour only at night (see page 393 of the Nightlife chapter); during the day, the hop-on, hop-off bus tours (listed immediately below) and the Batobus (see "Boat Tours," below)—which both provide transportation between sights as well as commentary—are a better value.

Hop-on, Hop-off Bus Tours—Double-decker buses connect Paris' main sights while providing running commentary, allowing you to hop on and hop off along the way. You get a disposable set of ear plugs (dial English and listen to the narration). You can get off at any stop, tour a sight, then catch a later bus. These are ideal in good weather, when you can sit up top. There are two nearly equal companies: L'Open Tours and Les Cars Rouges; pick up their brochures showing routes and stops from any TI or on

their buses. You can start either tour at just about any of the major sights, such as the Eiffel Tower (both companies stop on avenue Joseph Bouvard).

L'Open Tours uses bright yellow buses and provides more extensive coverage (and slightly better commentary) on four different routes, rolling by most of the important sights in Paris. Their Paris Grand Tour (the green route) offers the best introduction. The same ticket gets you on any of their routes within the validity period. Buy your tickets from the driver (1 day-€25, 2 days-€28, kids 4–11 pay €12 for 1 or 2 days, allow 2 hours per tour). Two or three buses depart hourly from about 10:00 to 18:00; expect to wait 10–20 minutes at each stop (stops can be tricky to find—look for yellow signs; tel. 01 42 66 56 56, www.paris-opentour.com).

Les Cars Rouges' bright red buses offer largely the same service, with only one route and just nine stops, for a bit less money (2 days: adult-€23, kids 4–12-€12, tel. 01 53 95 39 53, www.carsrouges .com).

Do-It-Yourself Bus Tour—Paris' cheapest "bus tour" is to simply hop on city bus #69 and follow my self-guided commentary (see Bus #69 Sightseeing Tour, page 297).

By Boat

Seine Cruises—Several companies offer one-hour boat cruises on the Seine (by far best at night).

Two companies are convenient to the rue Cler hotels: **Bateaux-Mouches** has the biggest, open-top, double-decker boats and tour groups by the dozens (departs from pont de l'Alma's right bank, €7, kids 4–12 pay €4, daily 10:00–22:30, tel. 01 40 76 99 99); **Bateaux Parisiens** has smaller, covered boats with handheld audioguides and only one deck (€9.50, kids 4–11 pay €4.50, discounted half-price if you have a valid France or France–Switzerland railpass—does not use up a day of a flexipass, leaves from right in front of the Eiffel Tower, tel. 08 25 01 01 01). Both companies depart every 20–30 minutes (April–Oct daily 10:00–22:30; Nov–March there are fewer boats and they stop running earlier).

The smaller, more intimate **Vedettes du Pont Neuf** are closer to the Marais and Luxembourg area hotels. They depart only once an hour from the center of pont Neuf (2/hr after dark), but they come with a live guide giving explanations in French and English (€10, tip requested, kids 4–12 pay €5, tel. 01 46 33 98 38).

Hop-on, Hop-Off Boat Tour—**Batobus** allows you to get on and off as often you like at any of eight popular stops along the Seine: Eiffel Tower, Champs-Elysées, Orsay/place de la Concorde, the Louvre, Notre-Dame, St. Germain-des-Prés, Hôtel de Ville, and Jardin des Plantes. Safety-conscious glass enclosures turn the boats into sweltering greenhouses on hot days (1 day-€11, 2 days-€13,

boats run mid-April–Oct 10:00–19:00, June–Aug until 21:00, every 15–20 minutes, 45 min one-way, 90 min round-trip, worthless narration). If you use this for getting around—sort of a scenic, floating alternative to the Métro—this can be worthwhile. But if you just want a guided boat tour, Batobus is not as good a value as the regular tour boats described above.

Low-Key Cruise on a Back Canal—Canauxrama runs a lazy 2.5-hour cruise on a peaceful canal without the Seine in sight. Tours start from place de la Bastille and end at Bassin de la Villette (near Mo: Stalingrad). During the first segment of your trip, you'll pass through a long tunnel (built at the order of Napoleon in the early 19th century, when canal boats were vital for industrial transport). Once outside, you glide (not much faster than you can walk) through sleepy Parisian neighborhoods and slowly climb through four double locks as a guide narrates the trip in French and English (€14, departs at 9:45 and 14:30 across from Opéra Bastille, just below boulevard de la Bastille, opposite #50—where the canal meets place de la Bastille, tel. 01 42 39 15 00). The same tour also goes in the opposite direction (from Bassin de la Villette to place de la Bastille). Picnics are welcome.

By Foot

Paris Walks—This company offers a variety of excellent two-hour walks, led by British or American guides. Tours are thoughtfully prepared, relaxing, and humorous. Don't hesitate to stand close to the guide to hear (generally 2 tours per day, €10 each, private tours available, tel. 01 48 09 21 40 for recorded schedule in English, also posted at www.paris-walks.com, paris@paris-walks.com, run by Peter and Oriel Cane). Tours focus on the Marais (4/week), Montmartre (3/week), medieval Latin Quarter (Mon), Ile de la Cité/Notre-Dame (Mon), the "Two Islands" (Ile de la Cité and Ile St. Louis, Wed), *Da Vinci Code* sights (Wed), and Hemingway's Paris (Fri). Ask about their family-friendly tours. Call a day or two ahead to learn their schedule and starting point. Most tours don't require reservations, but specialty tours (such as the *Da Vinci Code* tour) require advance reservations and prepayment with credit card (not refundable, even if you cancel months in advance).

Context Paris—This organization, already well-established in Rome, has recently expanded to the City of Light. Their "intellectual by design" walking tours are led by docents (historians, architects, and academics) and cover both museums and neighborhoods, often with a fascinating theme (explained on their Web site). Try to book in advance, since groups are small and can fill up (limited to 6 participants, generally 3 hours long and €50 per person plus admissions, tel. 06 13 09 67 11, www.contextparis.com, info@contextparis.com). They also offer private tours.

Private Guides—For many, Paris merits hiring a Parisian as a personal guide. **Arnaud Servignat** is an excellent licensed local guide (€150/half day, €250/day, also does car tours of the country-side around Paris for a little more, tel. 06 68 80 29 05, www .arnaud-servignat.com, arnaud.servignat@noos.fr). **Elizabeth Van Hest** is another highly likeable and capable guide (€170 maxi-mum/half day, €260/day, tel. 01 43 41 47 31, e.van.hest@noos.fr). **Paris Walks** or **Context Paris** can also set you up with one of their guides; some Paris Walks guides are trained to work with families (both companies described above).

By Bike and Segway

Fat Tire Bike Tours—Hit the road with a younger crowd for frol-icking four-hour guided rides in English through Paris. Daytime tours feature more history (€24, March–Nov daily at 11:00, June–July also at 15:00); nighttime tours, more lively fun (€28, April–Oct nightly at 19:00). For all tours, meet at the south pillar of the Eiffel Tower, then go to the Fat Tire office to pick up bikes (24 rue Edgar Faure, Mo: Dupleix, tel. 01 56 58 10 54, www.fattirebiketoursparis .com; cash only, up to 26 people per group, no bikes or reservations needed, helmets available upon request at no extra charge).

Fat Tire's pricey **Segway Tours**—on futuristic, stand-up motorized scooters—are novel in that you learn to ride a Segway while exploring Paris (€70, up to 8 per group, daily April–Oct at 10:30 and 18:30, plan on spending nearly an hour getting used to the machine, reservation required for this tour, www.parissegwaytours .com).

Excursions from Paris

Many companies offer bus tours to regional sights, including all of the day trips described in this book. **Paris Vision** offers mass-pro-duced, full-size bus and minivan tours to several popular regional destinations, including the Loire Valley, Champagne region, D-Day beaches, and Mont St. Michel. Minivan tours are more expensive but more personal, given in English, and offer conve-nient pickup at your hotel (€130–200/person). Their full-size bus tours are multilingual and cost about half the price of a minivan tour—worthwhile for some travelers simply for the ease of trans-portation to the sights (about €60, destinations include Versailles and Giverny). Paris Vision's full-size buses depart from 214 rue de Rivoli (Mo: Tuileries, tel. 01 42 60 30 01, www.parisvision.com).

SIGHTS

The sights listed in this chapter are arranged by neighborhood for handy sightseeing. When you see a ✪ in a listing, it means the sight is covered in much more depth in one of my walks or self-guided tours. This is why Paris' most important attractions get the least coverage in this chapter—we'll explore them later in the book.

Paris Museum Pass: In Paris, there are two classes of sightseers—those with a Paris Museum Pass, and those who stand in line. Serious sightseers save time and money by getting this pass.

Most of the sights listed in this chapter are covered by the pass (see list below). Notable exceptions are: the Eiffel Tower, Montparnasse Tower, Marmottan Museum, Opéra Garnier, Notre-Dame treasury, Jacquemart-André Museum, Jewish Art and History Museum, Grand Palais, La Grande Arche de La Défense, Jeu de Paume, Catacombs, *Paris Story* film, Montmartre Museum, Dalí Museum, Museum of Erotic Art, and the ladies of Pigalle.

The pass pays for itself with three admissions and gets you into most sights with no lining up to buy tickets (1 day-€18, 3 consecutive days-€36, 5 consecutive days-€54, no youth or senior discount). It's sold at museums, main Métro stations (including Ecole Militaire and Bastille), and TIs (even at airports). Try to avoid buying the pass at a major museum (such as the Louvre), where supply can be spotty and lines long.

The pass isn't activated until the first time you use it (you write the starting date on the pass). Think and read ahead to make the most of your pass. You could spend a day or two at the beginning or end of your Paris visit seeing free sights (e.g., Carnavalet and Victor Hugo's House) and sights that don't accept the pass (e.g., Eiffel Tower). Validate your pass only when you're ready to tackle the covered sights on consecutive days. The free directory

Paris Sights

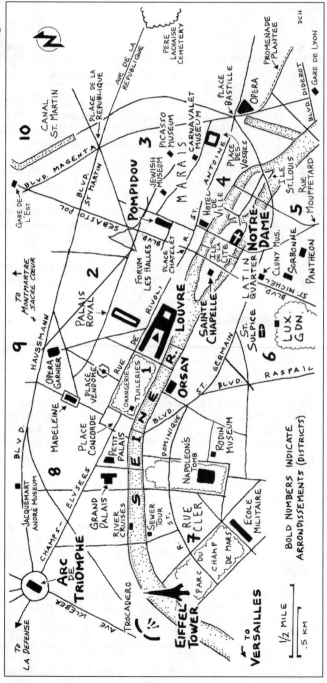

Paris at a Glance

▲▲▲**Louvre** Europe's oldest and greatest museum, starring *Mona Lisa* and *Venus de Milo*. **Hours:** Wed–Mon 9:00–18:00, closed Tue. Most wings open Wed and Fri until 21:45.

▲▲▲**Orsay Museum** Nineteenth-century art, including Europe's greatest Impressionist collection. **Hours:** June 20–Sept 20 Tue–Sun 9:00–18:00; Sept 21–June 19 Tue–Sat 10:00–18:00, Sun 9:00–18:00; Thu until 21:45 year-round, always closed Mon.

▲▲▲**Eiffel Tower** Paris' soaring exclamation point. **Hours:** March–Sept daily 9:00–24:00, Oct–Feb daily 9:30–23:00.

▲▲▲**Arc de Triomphe** Triumphal arch with viewpoint, marking start of Champs-Elysées. **Hours:** Outside always open; inside open April–Sept daily 10:00–23:00, Oct–March daily 10:00–22:00.

▲▲▲**Sainte-Chapelle** Gothic cathedral with peerless stained glass. **Hours:** March–Oct daily 9:30–18:00, Nov–Feb daily 9:00–17:00.

▲▲▲**Versailles** The ultimate royal palace, with a Hall of Mirrors, vast gardens, a grand canal, and smaller palaces. **Hours:** April–Oct Tue–Sun 9:00–18:30, Nov–March Tue–Sun 9:00–17:30, closed Mon. Gardens open early (7:00, 8:00 in winter) and smaller palaces open late (12:00).

▲▲**Notre-Dame Cathedral** Paris' most beloved church, with towers and gargoyles. **Hours:** Church open daily 7:45–19:00; tower open July–Aug Mon–Fri 9:00–19:30, Sat–Sun 9:00–23:00, April–June and Sept daily 9:30–19:30, Oct–March daily 10:00–17:30; treasury open daily 9:30–17:30.

▲▲**Sacré-Cœur** White basilica atop Montmartre with spectacular views. **Hours:** Daily 7:00–23:00.

▲▲**Napoleon's Tomb** The emperor's imposing tomb, flanked by army museums. **Hours:** April–Sept daily 10:00–18:00, summer Sun until 19:00, Oct–March daily 10:00–17:00, closed first Mon of month except July–Sept.

▲▲**Rodin Museum** Works by the greatest sculptor since Michelangelo. **Hours:** April–Sept Tue–Sun 9:30–17:45; Oct–March Tue–Sun 9:30–16:45, closed Mon.

▲▲**Marmottan Museum** Untouristy art museum focusing on Monet. **Hours:** Tue–Sun 10:00–18:00, closed Mon.

▲▲**Pompidou Center** Modern art in colorful building with city views. **Hours:** Wed–Mon 11:00–21:00, closed Tue.

▲▲**Jacquemart-André Museum** Art-strewn mansion. **Hours:** Daily 10:00–18:00.

▲▲**Cluny Museum** Medieval art with unicorn tapestries. **Hours:** Wed–Mon 9:15–17:45, closed Tue.

▲▲**Carnavalet Museum** Paris' history wrapped up in a 16th-century mansion. **Hours:** Tue–Sun 10:00–18:00, closed Mon.

▲▲**Jewish Art and History Museum** Displays history of Judaism in Europe. **Hours:** Mon–Fri 11:00–18:00, Sun 10:00–18:00, closed Sat.

▲▲**Deportation Memorial** Monument to Holocaust victims, near Notre-Dame. **Hours:** April–Sept daily 10:00–12:00 & 14:00–19:00, Oct–March daily 10:00–12:00 & 14:00–17:00.

▲▲**Champs-Elysées** Paris' grand boulevard. **Hours:** Always open.

▲▲**Picasso Museum** World's largest collection of Picasso's works. **Hours:** April–Sept Wed–Mon 9:30–18:00; Oct–March Wed–Mon 9:30–17:30, closed Tue.

▲**Père Lachaise Cemetery** Final resting place for some of Paris' most illustrious dead. **Hours:** Mon–Sat 8:00–18:00, Sun 9:00–18:00.

▲**Luxembourg Garden** Sixty-acre park right out of an Impressionist painting. **Hours:** Daily dawn to dusk.

▲**Catacombs** Underground tunnels lined with bones. **Hours:** Tue–Sun 10:00–17:00, closed Mon.

▲**Paris Sewer Tour** The lowdown on Paris plumbing. **Hours:** May–Sept Sat–Wed 11:00–17:00, Oct–April Sat–Wed 11:00–16:00, closed Thu–Fri.

that comes with your pass lists the current hours of sights, phone numbers, and the price kids pay.

The pass isn't worth buying for children and teens, as most museums are free for those under 18 (teenagers may need to show proof of age). Of the museums that charge for children, some allow kids in free if their parent has a Museum Pass, while others charge admission, depending on age (the cutoff age varies from 5 to 18). If a sight is free for kids, they can skip the line with their passholder parents.

Included sights you're likely to visit (and admission prices without the pass): Louvre (€8.50), Orsay Museum (€7.50), Sainte-Chapelle (€7), Arc de Triomphe (€8), Napoleon's Tomb/Army Museums (€7), Conciergerie (€7), Panthéon (€7), Sewer Tour (€4), Cluny Museum (€5.50), Pompidou Center (€7), Notre-Dame tower (€7), Paris Archaeological Crypt (€3.50), Picasso Museum (€5.50), Rodin Museum (€5), L'Orangerie Museum (when it reopens, about €7), Maritime Museum (€9). Outside Paris, the pass covers the Palace of Versailles (€7.50, plus its Trianon châteaux-€5), Château of Fontainebleau (€5.50), and Château of Chantilly (€8).

Tally up what you want to see—and remember, an advantage of the pass is that you skip to the front of most lines, which can save hours of waiting, especially in summer. Note that at a few sights (including the Louvre, Sainte-Chapelle, and Notre-Dame's tower), everyone has to shuffle through the slow-moving baggage-check lines for security.

To use your pass at sights, boldly walk to the front of the ticket line, hold up your pass, and ask the ticket-taker: *"Entrée, pass?"* (ahn-tray pahs). You'll either be allowed to enter at that point or you'll be directed to a special entrance. For major sights, such as the Louvre, Orsay, and Versailles, we've identified passholder entrances on the maps in this book.

With the pass, you'll pop freely into sights that you're walking by (even for a few minutes) that otherwise might not be worth the expense (e.g., the Conciergerie or Archaeological Crypt).

Museum Tips: The Louvre and many other museums are closed on Tuesday. The Orsay, Jeu de Paume, Rodin, Marmottan, Carnavalet, Archaeological Crypt, Catacombs, Petit Palais, Victor Hugo's House, Montmartre Museum, and Versailles are closed Monday. Some museums offer reduced prices on Sunday. Most sights stop admitting people 30–60 minutes before closing time, and many begin shutting down rooms 45 minutes before.

For the fewest crowds, visit very early, at lunch, or very late. Most museums have slightly shorter hours October through March. French holidays (on Jan 1, May 1, July 14, Nov 1, Nov 11, and Dec 25) can really mess up your sightseeing plans.

The best Impressionist art museums are the Orsay (see tour

Paris Sightseeing Modules

Paris is a big, sprawling city, but its major sights cluster in convenient zones. Grouping your sightseeing thoughtfully can save you lots of time and money. Here's how Paris' sights, walks, shopping opportunities, and other attractions are arranged:

Near the Tuileries Garden: Louvre, Orsay, Jeu de Paume, and L'Orangerie museums; Palais Royal's courtyards; and shopping stroll from place de la Madeleine (see Shopping chapter, page 374).

Historic Core of Paris: Historic Paris Walk, including Notre-Dame, Paris Archaeological Crypt, Deportation Memorial, Ile St. Louis, Sainte-Chapelle, and Conciergerie; flower market, Paris *Plage,* and in-line skating.

Southwest Paris: Eiffel Tower (located in Champ de Mars park); Maritime Museum, Napoleon's Tomb, Rodin and Marmottan museums; Sewer Tour; and Rue Cler Walk.

Southeast Paris: Latin Quarter; Cluny Museum; St. Germain-des-Prés and St. Sulpice churches; Luxembourg Garden and Jardin des Plantes park; Panthéon; Montparnasse Tower; Catacombs; and Left Bank Walk.

Northwest Paris: Arc de Triomphe and Champs-Elysées Walk; Opéra Garnier; *Paris Story* film; Jacquemart-André and Fragonard Perfume museums; Petit and Grand Palais; Grande Arche de La Défense; and shopping at Galeries Lafayette and Passages Choiseul and Ste. Anne.

Northeast Paris: Pompidou Center; Jewish History, Picasso, and Carnavalet museums; Victor Hugo's House; Promenade Plantée Park; Père Lachaise Cemetery; Marais Walk; traffic-free street market on rue Montorgueil; and markets at Bastille and place d'Aligre.

North Paris (Montmartre): Sacré-Cœur basilica; Dalí and Montmartre museums; Montmartre Walk; Moulin Rouge, Museum of Erotic Art, and Pigalle; and Puces St. Ouen flea market (see Shopping chapter, page 374).

on page 176), Marmottan (page 251), and L'Orangerie (slated to reopen in the spring of 2006).

Many museums also host optional temporary exhibitions that are not covered by the Paris Museum Pass (generally €3–5 extra). You can find good information on many of Paris' sights on the French TI's official Web site: www.parisinfo.com.

Near the Tuileries Garden

Paris' grandest park, the Tuileries Garden, was once the private property of kings and queens. Today, it links the museums of the Louvre, L'Orangerie, Jeu de Paume, and the Orsay. And across from

the Louvre are the tranquil, historic courtyards of the Palais Royal.
▲▲▲Louvre (Musée du Louvre)—This is Europe's oldest, biggest, greatest, and second-most-crowded museum (after the
Vatican). Housed in a U-shaped, 16th-century palace (accentuated
by a 20th-century glass pyramid), the Louvre is Paris' top museum
and one of its key landmarks. It's home to *Mona Lisa*, *Venus de
Milo*, and hall after hall of Greek and Roman masterpieces, medieval jewels, Michelangelo statues, and paintings by the greatest
artists from the Renaissance to the Romantics (mid-1800s).

Touring the Louvre can be overwhelming, so be selective. Focus
on the **Denon Wing** (south, along the river): Greek sculptures,
Italian paintings (by the likes of Raphael and da Vinci), and—of
course—French paintings (neoclassical and Romantic). For extra
credit, tackle the **Richelieu Wing** (north, away from the river), with
works from ancient Mesopotamia (today's Iraq), as well as French,
Dutch, and Northern art; or the **Sully Wing** (connecting the other
2 wings), with Egyptian artifacts and more French paintings.

Cost: €8.50, €6 after 18:00 on Wed and Fri, free on first Sun
of month, covered by Museum Pass.

Hours: Wed–Mon 9:00–18:00, closed Tue. Most wings open
Wed and Fri until 21:45. Galleries start closing 30 minutes early.
The last entry is 45 minutes before closing. Tel. 01 40 20 51 51,
recorded info tel. 01 40 20 53 17, www.louvre.fr.

Location: At Palais Royal-Musée du Louvre Métro stop.
(The old Louvre Métro stop, called Louvre-Rivoli, is farther from
the entrance.)

❂ See Louvre Tour on page 147.

Palais Royal Courtyards—Across from the Louvre are the pleasant courtyards of the stately Palais Royal. Although the palace is
closed to the public, the courtyards are open. As you enter, you'll
pass through a whimsical courtyard filled with stubby, striped columns and playful fountains (with fun, reflective metal balls) into
another, curiously peaceful courtyard. This is where in-the-know
Parisians come to take a quiet break, walk their poodle, or enjoy
a rendezvous—surrounded by a serene arcade and a handful of
historic restaurants.

While tranquil today, this was once a hotbed for political
activism. The palace was built in the 17th century by Louis XIII,
and eventually became the headquarters of the powerful Dukes
of Orléans. Because the Dukes' digs were off-limits to the police,
some shockingly free thinking took root here. This was the
meeting place for the debating clubs—the precursors to political parties. During the Revolution, palace resident Duke Phillip
(nicknamed "Phillip Egalité" for his progressive ideas) advocated a
constitutional monarchy, and actually voted in favor of beheading
Louis XVI—his own cousin. Phillip hoped his liberal attitudes

Near the Tuileries Garden

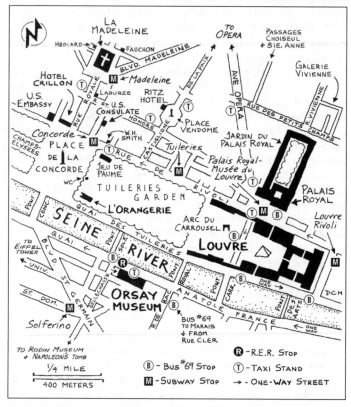

would spare him from the Revolutionaries, but he too was guillotined. His son, Louis-Phillippe, grew to become France's first constitutional monarch (r. 1830–1848). The palace's courtyards were a riotous social and political scene, filled with lively café culture, revolutionaries, rabble rousers, scoundrels, and...Madame Tussaud's first wax shop (she used the severed heads of guillotine victims to model her sculptures).

Exiting the courtyard at the side facing away from the Seine brings you to the Galleries Colbert and Vivienne, good examples of shopping arcades from the early 1900s.

Cost, Hours, Location: Courtyards are free and always open. The Palais Royal is directly north of the Louvre on rue de Rivoli (Mo: Palais Royal-Musée du Louvre).

▲**L'Orangerie Museum (Musée de l'Orangerie)**—This Impressionist museum, lovely as a water lily, is due to reopen (hopefully) sometime in the spring of 2006. (For the latest, ask at any Paris TI.) When it opens, you can step out of the tree-lined,

sun-dappled Impressionist painting that is the Tuileries Garden, and into L'Orangerie (loh-rahn-zheh-ree), a little *bijou* of select works by Utrillo, Cézanne, Renoir, Matisse, and Picasso. On the ground floor, you'll find a line of eight rooms dedicated to these artists. Downstairs is the finale: Monet's water lilies. The museum's collection is small enough to enjoy in a short visit, but complete enough to see the bridge from Impressionism to the Moderns. And it's all beautiful (likely €7, covered by Museum Pass, located in Tuileries Garden near place de la Concorde, Mo: Concorde). If L'Orangerie hasn't reopened and you need a Monet fix, visit the Marmottan Museum (described under "Southwest Paris," below).

Jeu de Paume (Galerie Nationale du Jeu de Paume)—This museum hosts rotating exhibits of top contemporary artists (€6, not covered by Museum Pass, Tue 12:00–21:30, Wed–Fri 12:00–19:00, Sat–Sun 10:00–19:00, closed Mon, on place de la Concorde, just inside Tuileries Garden on rue de Rivoli side, Mo: Concorde).

▲▲▲Orsay Museum (Musée d'Orsay)—The Orsay boasts Europe's greatest collection of Impressionist works. It might be less important than the Louvre—but it's more purely enjoyable.

The Orsay, housed in an atmospheric old train station, picks up where the Louvre leaves off: the second half of the 19th century. This is art from the tumultuous times that began when revolutions swept across Europe in 1848, and ended with the outbreak of World War I in 1914. Begin on the ground floor, featuring conservative art of the mid-1800s—careful, idealized neoclassicism (with a few rebels mixed in). Then glide up the escalator to the late 1800s, when the likes of Manet, Monet, Degas, and Renoir jolted the art world with their colorful, lively new invention, Impressionism. (Somewhere in there, *Whistler's Mother* sits quietly.) You'll also enjoy the works of their artistic descendents, the post-Impressionists (van Gogh and Cézanne) and the Primitives (Rousseau, Gauguin, Seurat, and Toulouse-Lautrec). On the mezzanine level, waltz through the Grand Ballroom, Art Nouveau exhibits, and Rodin sculptures.

Cost: €7.50, €5.50 after 16:15 and on Sun, free at 17:00, free on first Sun of month, covered by Museum Pass. English-language tours usually run at 11:30 daily except Sun, cost €6, take 90 min, and are also available on audioguide (€5). Tours in English focusing on the Impressionists are offered Tue at 14:30 (€6, sometimes also on other days).

Hours: June 20–Sept 20 Tue–Sun 9:00–18:00, Sept 21–June 19 Tue–Sat 10:00–18:00, Sun 9:00–18:00, Thu until 21:45 year-round, always closed Mon. Last entry 1 hour before closing, Impressionist galleries start closing at 17:15. Tel. 01 40 49 48 14, www.musee-orsay.fr.

Location: Above the RER-C stop called Musée d'Orsay; the

nearest Métro stop is Solferino, three blocks south of the Orsay. From the Louvre, it's a lovely 15-minute walk through the Tuileries and across the pedestrian bridge to the Orsay.

○ See Orsay Museum Tour on page 176.

Historic Core of Paris: Notre-Dame, Sainte-Chapelle, and More

○ Many of these sights are covered in detail in the Historic Paris Walk (plus map) on page 70. If a sight's covered in the walk, I've only listed its essentials here.

▲▲**Notre-Dame Cathedral (Cathédrale Notre-Dame de Paris)**—This 700-year-old cathedral is packed with history and tourists. With a pair of 200-foot-tall bell towers, a facade studded with ornate statuary, beautiful stained-glass rose windows, famous gargoyles, a picture-perfect Seine-side location, and textbook flying buttresses, there's a good reason that this cathedral of "Our Lady" *(Notre Dame)* is France's most famous church.

Check out the facade: Mary with the Baby Jesus (in rose window) above the 28 Kings of Judah (statues that were beheaded during the Revolution). Stroll the interior, echoing with history. Then wander around the exterior, through a forest of frilly buttresses, watched over by a fleet of whimsical gargoyles. The long line to the left is to climb the famous tower (see below).

Cost, Hours, Location: Free, daily 7:45–19:00; treasury-€2.50, not covered by Museum Pass, daily 9:30–17:30; ask about free English tours, normally Wed and Thu at 12:00, Sat at 14:30; Mo: Cité, Hôtel de Ville, or St. Michel; clean toilets in front of church near Charlemagne's statue.

Tower: You can climb to the top of the facade between the towers, and then to the top of the south tower, 400 steps total (€7, covered by Museum Pass, July–Aug Mon–Fri 9:00–19:30, Sat–Sun 9:00–23:00, April–June and Sept daily 9:30–19:30, Oct–March daily 10:00–17:30, last entry 45 min before closing, arrive early to avoid long lines).

See page 74.

Paris Archaeological Crypt—This is a worthwhile 15-minute stop with your Museum Pass. You'll visit Roman ruins, trace the street plan of the medieval village, and see diagrams of how early Paris grew, all thoughtfully explained in English.

The first few displays put the ruins in their historical context. Three models show the growth of Paris—from an uninhabited riverside plot; to the Roman town of Lutèce; to an early-medieval city, with a church that preceded Notre-Dame. A fourth model shows the current Notre-Dame surrounded by buildings, along with the old, straight road—the rue Neuve de Notre-Dame—that led up to the church (and ran right down the center of the museum). The

ruins in the middle of the museum are a confusing mix of foundations from all these time periods, including parts of the old rue
Neuve de Notre-Dame.

Press the buttons on the display cases to light up a particular section, such as the medieval hospital (along the far side of
the museum), a well-preserved Gallo-Roman paved room, and
a Roman building with "hypocaustal" heating (narrow passages
through which hot air was pumped to heat the room).

Cost, Hours, Location: €3.50, covered by Museum Pass,
Tue–Sun 10:00–18:00, closed Mon, enter 100 yards in front of
cathedral.

▲▲**Deportation Memorial (Mémorial de la Déportation)**—
Climb down the steps into this memorial to the 200,000 French
victims of the Nazi concentration camps. As Paris disappears
above you, this monument draws you into the victims' experience.
Once underground, you enter a one-way hallway—studded with
tiny lights—commemorating the dead, leading you to an eternal
flame.

Cost, Hours, Location: Free, April–Sept daily 10:00–12:00
& 14:00–19:00, Oct–March daily 10:00–12:00 & 14:00–17:00. It's
at the east tip of the island Ile de la Cité, behind Notre-Dame and
near Ile St. Louis (Mo: Cité).

See page 79.

Ile St. Louis—The residential island behind Notre-Dame is known
for its restaurants (see Eating chapter), great ice cream, and shops
(along rue St. Louis-en-l'Ile).

See page 79.

Cité "Métropolitain" Stop and Flower Market—On place Louis
Lépine, between Notre-Dame and Sainte-Chapelle, you'll find
an early-19th-century subway entrance and a flower market (that
chirps with a bird market on Sun).

▲▲▲**Sainte-Chapelle**—The interior of this 13th-century chapel
is a triumph of Gothic church architecture. Built to house Jesus'
Crown of Thorns, Sainte-Chapelle is jam-packed with stained-
glass windows, bathed in colorful light, and slippery with the
drool of awe-struck tourists. Ignore the humdrum exterior and
climb the stairs into the sanctuary, where more than 1,100 Bible
scenes—from the Creation to the Passion to Judgment Day—are
illustrated by light and glass.

Cost, Hours, Location: €7, €10.50 combo-ticket covers
Conciergerie, both covered by Museum Pass. Open March–Oct
daily 9:30–18:00, Nov–Feb daily 9:00–17:00. Mo: Cité.

See page 85.

▲**Conciergerie**—Marie-Antoinette was imprisoned here, as were
Louis XVI, Robespierre, Marat, and many others on their way to
the guillotine. Exhibits with good English descriptions trace the

history of the building and give some insight into prison life. You can also relive the drama in Marie-Antoinette's cell on the day of her execution—complete with dummies and period furniture.

Cost, Hours, Location: €7, €10.50 combo-ticket covers Sainte-Chapelle, both covered by Museum Pass, April–Sept daily 9:30–18:00, Oct–March daily 10:00–17:00.

See page 91.

Paris *Plage* (The Beach)—The Riviera it's not, but this newly developed faux beach—built along a two-mile stretch of the Seine on the Right Bank—is a fun place to stroll, play, and people-watch on a sunny day. Each summer since 2002, the Paris city government has shut down the embankment's highway and trucked in potted palm trees, hammocks, lounge chairs, and 2,000 tons of sand to create a colorful urban beach. You'll also find climbing walls, a swimming pool, trampolines, *boules*, a library, beach volleyball, badminton, and Frisbee areas in three zones: sandy, grassy, and wood-tiled. As you take in the playful atmosphere, imagine how much has changed here since the Middle Ages...when this was a grimy fishing community.

Cost, Hours, Location: Free, mid-July–mid-Aug daily 7:00–24:00, no beach off-season; on Right Bank of Siene, just north of Ile de la Cité, between pont des Arts and pont de Sully.

Skaters Gone Wild—Thousands of in-line skaters take to the streets Fridays at 22:30 and summer Sunday afternoons as police close off various routes in different parts of downtown (ask at your hotel or a TI). It's serious skaters only on Friday evenings, but anyone can roll with Paris on Sundays.

Southwest Paris: Eiffel Tower Neighborhood

▲▲▲**Eiffel Tower (La Tour Eiffel)**—It's crowded and expensive, but this 1,000-foot-tall ornament is worth the trouble. Visitors to Paris may find *Mona Lisa* to be less than expected, but the Eiffel Tower rarely disappoints, even in an era of skyscrapers.

Built a hundred years after the French Revolution (and in the midst of an industrial one), the tower served no function but to impress. Bridge-builder Gustave Eiffel won the contest for the 1889 Centennial World's Fair by beating out such rival proposals as a giant guillotine. To a generation hooked on technology, the tower was the marvel of the age, a symbol of progress and human ingenuity. Indeed, despite its 7,000 tons of metal and 50 tons of paint, the tower is so

well-engineered that it weighs no more per square inch at its base than a linebacker on tiptoes. Not all were so impressed, however; many found it a monstrosity. The writer Guy de Maupassant routinely ate lunch in the tower just so he wouldn't have to look at it.

Delicate and graceful when seen from afar, the Eiffel Tower is massive—even a bit scary—from close up. You don't appreciate the size until you walk toward it; like a mountain, it seems so close but takes forever to reach. There are three observation platforms, at 200, 400, and 900 feet; the higher you go, the more you pay. Each requires a separate elevator (and line) so plan on at least 90 minutes if you want to go to the top and back. While being on the windy top of the Eiffel Tower is a thrill you'll never forget, the view is actually better from the second level.

A TI/ticket booth is between the Pilier Nord (north pillar) and Pilier Est (east pillar). The stairs (yes, you can walk up to the 2nd level) are next to the Jules Verne restaurant entrance (allow $300 per person for the restaurant, reserve 3 months in advance). As you ascend through the metal beams, imagine being a worker, perched high above nothing, riveting this giant erector set together.

The top level (900 feet) is tiny. And, because fewer visitors pay the extra money to go all the way, it's less crowded. All you'll find here are wind and grand, sweeping views. The city lies before you, with a panorama guide. On a good day, you can see for 40 miles.

The second level (400 feet) has the best views, because you're closer to the sights (walk up stairway to get above netting). There's also a cafeteria and WCs. While you'll save no money, consider taking the elevator up and the stairs down (5 min from 2nd level to 1st, 5 min more to ground) for good exercise and views.

The first level (200 feet) has exhibits, a post office (daily 10:00–19:00, cancellation stamp will read Eiffel Tower), a snack bar, WCs, and souvenirs. Read the informative signs (in English) describing the major monuments, see the entertaining free movie on the history of the tower, and don't miss a century of fireworks—including the entire millennium blast—on video. Then consider a drink or a sandwich overlooking all of Paris at the snack café (outdoor tables in summer) or at the city's best view bar/restaurant, Altitude 95 (see page 351).

Seeing It All: If you don't want to miss a single level, here's a plan for getting the most out of your visit. Ride the lift to second level, then immediately line up and catch the next lift to the top. Enjoy the views on top, then ride back down to the second level. Frolic there for a while and take in some more views. When you're ready, hike down the stairs (no line) or line up for the lift to the first level. Explore the shops and exhibits on this level, have a snack, and take the stairs or lift back to earth.

Cost and Hours: It costs €4 to go to the first level, €7.50 to

Southwest Paris: Eiffel Tower Neighborhood

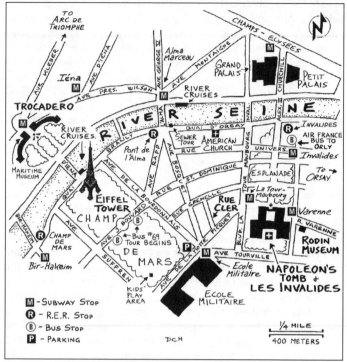

the second, and €11 to go to the top (not covered by Museum Pass).
You can skip the lift and climb the stairs to the first or second level
for €4, or €3 if you're under 25 (March–Sept daily 9:00–24:00,
Oct–Feb daily 9:30–23:00, last entry 1 hour before closing, shorter
lines at night, Mo: Bir-Hakeim or Trocadéro, RER: Champ de
Mars-Tour Eiffel, tel. 01 44 11 23 23, www.tour-eiffel.fr).

Tips: To avoid most crowds, go early (by 8:45) or late in the
day (after 18:00, after 20:00 May–Aug, last entry 1 hour before
closing); weekends are worst. Ideally, you should arrive with some
light and stay as it gets dark.

To pass the time in line, pick up whatever free reading material is available at the tourist stands at ground level. I liked the
wonderful *Eiffel Tower Gazette*, a free newspaper featuring a century of Eiffel Tower headlines.

Before or after your tower visit, you can catch the Bateaux-
Parisiens boat (near the base of the tower) for a Seine cruise.

Best Views: The best place to view the tower is from Trocadéro
Square to the north; it's a 10-minute walk across the river, a
happening scene at night, and especially fun for kids. Consider

arriving at the Trocadéro Métro stop for the view, then walking toward the tower. Another delightful viewpoint is the long, grassy field, Le Parc du Champ de Mars, to the south (great for dinner picnics). However impressive it may be by day, the tower is an awesome thing to see at twilight, when it becomes engorged with light, and virile Paris lies back and lets night be on top. When darkness fully envelops the city, the tower seems to climax at the top of each hour...for 10 minutes. (It's been doing this since the millennium festivities, when it was wired with thousands of special lights.)

National Maritime Museum (Musée National de la Marine)— This extensive museum houses an amazing collection of ship models, submarines, torpedoes, cannonballs, *beaucoup* bowsprits, and naval you-name-it—including a small boat made for Napoleon. You'll find some English information on the walls. The free audioguide is a godsend for *Master and Commander* types; kids like the museum either way (adults-€9, kids-€7, covered by Museum Pass, Wed–Mon 10:00–18:00, closed Tue, on left side of Trocadéro Square with your back to Eiffel Tower, www.musee-marine.fr).

▲Paris Sewer Tour (Les Egouts de Paris)—Discover what happens after you flush. This quick, fascinating, and slightly stinky visit (a perfumed hanky helps) takes you along a few hundred yards of underground water tunnels in the world's first underground sewer system. Pick up the helpful English self-guided tour, then drop down into Jean Valjean's world of tunnels, rats, and manhole covers (Victor Hugo was friends with the sewer inspector when he wrote *Les Misérables*). You'll pass well-organized displays with helpful English information detailing the evolution of this amazing network. Over 1,500 miles of tunnels carry 317 million gallons of water daily through this underworld. It's the world's longest sewer system—so long, they say, that if laid out straight, it would stretch from Paris all the way to Istanbul.

It's surprising to see how much work goes into something we take for granted. Sewage didn't always disappear so readily. In the Middle Ages, wastewater was tossed from windows to a center street gutter, then washed into the river. In castles, sewage ended up in the moat. In the 1500s, French Renaissance King François I moved from château to château (he had several) when the moat muck became too much.

Don't miss the slideshow, fine WCs just beyond the gift shop, and occasional tours in English.

Cost, Hours, Location: €4, covered by Museum Pass, May–Sept Sat–Wed 11:00–17:00, Oct–April Sat–Wed 11:00–16:00, closed Thu–Fri, located where pont de l'Alma greets the Left Bank, Mo: Alma-Marceau, RER: Pont de l'Alma, tel. 01 53 68 27 81.

▲▲Napoleon's Tomb and Army Museums (Tombeau de Napoleon et le Musée de l'Armée)—The emperor lies majestically dead

inside several coffins under a grand dome—a goose-bumping pilgrimage for historians. Napoleon is surrounded by Europe's greatest military museum, the Hôtel des Invalides, which provides interesting coverage of Napoleon and World War II. The dome glitters with 26 pounds of gold.

Cost, Hours, Location: €7, covered by Museum Pass, April–Sept daily 10:00–18:00, summer Sun until 19:00, Oct–March daily 10:00–17:00, closed first Mon of every month except July–Sept; Mo: La Tour-Maubourg or Varenne, tel. 01 44 42 37 72, www.invalides.org.

○ See Napoleon's Tomb and Army Museums Tour on page 259.

▲▲**Rodin Museum (Musée Rodin)**—This user-friendly museum is filled with passionate works by the greatest sculptor since Michelangelo. You'll see *The Kiss, The Thinker, The Gates of Hell*, and many more.

Well-displayed in the mansion where the sculptor lived and worked, exhibits trace Rodin's artistic development, explain how his bronze statues were cast, and show some of the studies he created to work up to his masterpiece (the unfinished *Gates of Hell*). Learn about Rodin's tumultuous relationship with his apprentice and lover, Camille Claudel. Mull over what makes his sculptures some of the most evocative since the Renaissance. And stroll the gardens, packed with many of his greatest works (including *The Thinker*). The beautiful gardens are ideal for artistic reflection...or a picnic (which you're welcome to bring in).

Cost, Hours, Location: €5, €3 on Sun, free first Sun of month, covered by Museum Pass. You'll pay €1 to get into the gardens only—which may be Paris' best deal, as many works are on display there. April–Sept Tue–Sun 9:30–17:45, closed Mon, gardens close 18:45; Oct–March Tue–Sun 9:30–16:45, closed Mon, gardens close 17:00. It's near Napoleon's Tomb, 77 rue de Varenne, Mo: Varenne, tel. 01 44 18 61 10, www.musee-rodin.fr.

○ See Rodin Museum Tour on page 240.

▲▲**Marmottan Museum (Musée Marmottan Monet)**—In this private, intimate, untouristy museum, you'll find the best collection anywhere of works by Impressionist headliner Claude Monet. Follow Monet's life through over a hundred works, from simple sketches to the *Impression: Sunrise* painting that gave his artistic movement its start—and a name. You'll also enjoy large-scale canvases featuring the water lilies from his garden at Giverny.

Cost, Hours, Location: €7, not covered by Museum Pass, Tue–Sun 10:00–18:00, last entry is 17:30, closed Mon, 2 rue Louis Boilly, Mo: La Muette, tel. 01 44 96 50 33, www.marmottan.com. To get to the museum from the Métro stop, follow the brown museum signs six blocks down chaussée de la Muette through

the park; pause to watch kids play on the old time, crank-powered carousel.

○ See Marmottan Museum Tour on page 251.

Post-Museum Stroll: Wander down one of Paris' most pleasant (and upscale) shopping streets, the rue de Passy (2 blocks up chaussée de la Muette in opposite direction from La Muette Métro stop).

Southeast Paris: Left Bank

○ For more information, see the Left Bank Walk on page 135, the Historic Paris Walk (which dips into the Latin Quarter) on page 70, and the "Sèvres-Babylone to St. Sulpice" shopping stroll on page 379.

▲**Latin Quarter (Quartier Latin)**—This Left Bank neighborhood, just opposite Notre-Dame, was the center of Roman Paris. But the Latin Quarter's touristy fame relates to its intriguing, artsy, bohemian character. This was perhaps Europe's leading university district in the Middle Ages, when Latin was the language of higher education. The neighborhood's main boulevards (St. Michel and St. Germain) are lined with cafés—once the haunts of great poets and philosophers, now the hangout of tired tourists. While still youthful and artsy, much of this area has become a tourist ghetto filled with cheap North African eateries. Exploring a few blocks up or down river from here gives you a better chance of feeling the pulse of what survives of Paris' classic Left Bank.

○ See Left Bank Walk on page 135.

▲▲**Cluny Museum (Musée National du Moyen Age)**—This treasure trove of Middle Age (Moyen Age) art fills old Roman baths, offering close-up looks at stained glass, Notre-Dame carvings, fine goldsmithing and jewelry, and rooms of tapestries. The star here is the exquisite *Lady and the Unicorn* tapestry series: In five panels, a delicate, as-medieval-can-be noble lady introduces a delighted unicorn to the senses of taste, hearing, sight, smell, and touch.

Cost, Hours, Location: €5.50, €4 on Sun, free first Sun of month, covered by Museum Pass, Wed–Mon 9:15–17:45, closed Tue, near corner of boulevards St. Michel and St. Germain; Mo: Cluny-La Sorbonne, St. Michel, or Odéon; tel. 01 53 73 78 16, www.musee-moyenage.fr.

○ See Cluny Museum Tour on page 277.

St. Germain-des-Prés—A church was first built on this site in A.D. 452. The church you see today was constructed in 1163 and is all that's left of a once sprawling and influential monastery. The colorful interior reminds us that medieval churches were originally painted in bright colors. The surrounding area hops at night with venerable cafés, fire-eaters, mimes, and scads of artists (free, daily 8:00–20:00, Mo: St. Germain-des-Prés).

Southeast Paris: Left Bank

▲**St. Sulpice Organ Concert**—Since it was featured in *The Da Vinci Code*, this grand church has become a trendy stop among the book's fans. But the real reason to visit is to see and hear its intimately accessible organ. For pipe-organ enthusiasts, this is one of Europe's great musical treats. The Grand Orgue at St. Sulpice Church has a rich history, with a succession of 12 world-class organists (including Charles-Marie Widor and Marcel Dupré) going back 300 years. Widor started the tradition of opening the loft to visitors after the 10:30 service on Sundays. Daniel Roth continues to welcome guests in three languages while playing five keyboards at once. (See www .danielrothsaintsulpice.org for his exact dates and concert plans.)

The 10:30 Sunday Mass is followed by a high-powered 25-minute recital at about 11:35. Then, just after noon, the small, unmarked door is opened (left of entry as you face the rear). Visitors scamper like sixteenth notes up spiral stairs, past the 19th-century Stairmasters that five men once pumped to fill the bellows, into a world of 7,000

The Da Vinci Code in Paris

Dan Brown's novel about a Harvard cryptologist on the hunt for the Holy Grail has become an international bestseller, a pop-culture craze, and a hot conversation topic. This work of fiction—encrusted with real and invented historical information—has sold millions of copies and been translated into 44 languages, flooding bookstores from Paris to Beijing. The movie version (starring Tom Hanks and Audrey Tatou...a.k.a. *Amélie*) was filmed in Paris in 2005 and is due out in 2006.

Since most of the novel is set in Paris, *Da Vinci Code* fans flock to the various sights described in the novel. Several tour companies (such as Paris Walks, page 36) have even put together special walking tours to satisfy this curiosity. While *The Da Vinci Code* may be a good read, it's not accurate either as history or a good travel guide. There just isn't that much to actually see, and Mr. Brown took a lot of creative license in his storytelling. Still, tours do their best to make something of these stops along the Grail trail:

The Louvre's Grand Gallery, near Leonardo's *Virgin of the Rocks:* "Renowned curator, Jacques Sauniere," the book begins, "staggered through the vaulted archway of the museum's Grand Gallery," fell to the parquet floor, smeared a cryptic clue in his own blood, and died. This starts the hunt, as protagonist Robert Langdon and police officer Sophie Neveu follow clues hidden in art, history, and religious lore to solve the murder and, ultimately, find the Holy Grail.

The Louvre's Salle des Etats: Langdon and Neveu find clues in Leonardo's *Mona Lisa*.

The Louvre Pyramid and Arc du Carrousel: Pursued by the police and fearing wrongful arrest, they escape the Louvre and drive off into the night.

Ritz Hotel on Place Vendôme: Langdon's address in Paris.

St. Sulpice Church: Home to the astrological clock—a line on the floor that calibrates sunbeams with the calendar—that Dan Brown incorrectly calls the "rose line." (For more on St. Sulpice, see the Left Bank Walk, page 143.)

Inverted Pyramid in the Carrousel du Louvre: The final stop on your quest is a shopping mall. You'll find the Holy Grail (says Brown) embedded in modern concrete under an inverted glass pyramid, just next to Virgin Records.

pipes. Here, they watch the master play during the next Mass. You'll generally have 30 minutes to kill (there's a plush lounge) before the organ plays; visitors can leave at any time. If late or rushed, show up around 12:30 and wait at the little door. As someone leaves, you can slip in, climb up, and catch the rest of the performance (church open daily 7:30–19:30, Mo: St. Sulpice or Mabillon). Tempting boutiques surround the church (see Shopping chapter, page 374), and Luxembourg Garden is nearby.

○ For more on St. Sulpice, see Left Bank Walk on page 135.

▲**Luxembourg Garden (Jardin du Luxembourg)**—This lovely 60-acre garden is an Impressionist painting brought to life. Slip into a green chair and ponder pondside, enjoy the radiant flower-erbeds, go jogging, or take in a chess game or puppet show (park open daily dawn until dusk, Mo: Odéon, RER: Luxembourg). Notice any pigeons? The story goes that a poor Ernest Hemingway used to hand-hunt (read: strangle) them here.

○ For more on the garden and nearby sights, see Left Bank Walk (page 135). Also see kid-friendly activities at the garden (page 371), "Les Grands Cafés du Paris" (page 364), and the Panthéon mausoleum (see below).

If you enjoy the Luxembourg Garden and want to see more green spaces, you could visit the more elegant Parc Monceau (Mo: Monceau), the colorful Jardin des Plantes (Mo: Jussieu or Gare d'Austerlitz, RER: Gare d'Austerlitz), or the hilly and bigger Parc des Buttes-Chaumont (Mo: Buttes-Chaumont).

▲**Panthéon**—This dramatic, neoclassical monument celebrates France's illustrious history and people, balances Foucault's pendulum, and is the final home to many French VIPs. In 1744, King Louis XV was gravely ill and prayed to St. Genevieve. (After saving Paris from the Franks, she'd become the city's patron saint.) Louis recovered, and thanked Genevieve by replacing her ruined church with a more fitting tribute. By the time the church was completed (1791), however, the secular-minded Revolution was in full swing,

and the church was converted into a secular mausoleum honoring the "Champions of French liberty"—Voltaire, Rousseau, Descartes, and others. The Revolutionaries covered up the church's windows (as you can see from outside) to display grand, patriotic frescoes. On the entrance pediment (inspired by the ancient Pantheon in Rome), they carved the inscription, "To the great men of the Fatherland."

Step inside the vast building (360' by 280' by 270'), and you'll see an altar to liberty—the **Monument to the National Convention**.

Dedicated to the political body that opposed the monarchy during the Revolution, it's inscribed with the familiar motto, "Live free or die." Working clockwise around the church-like space, you'll see monuments tracing the celebrated struggles of the French people: A martyred St. Denis picking up his head, St. Genevieve calming Paris amid Attila's onslaught (6th century), St. Louis as king and crusader, Joan of Arc and her exploits, and so on.

Foucault's pendulum swings gracefully at the end of a 220-foot cable suspended from the towering dome. It was here in 1851 that the scientist Léon Foucault first demonstrated the rotation of the Earth. Stand a few minutes and watch the pendulum's arc (appear to) shift as you and the earth rotate beneath it.

The **crypt** holds a pantheon of greats, including French writers Victor Hugo and Emile Zola and the discoverers of radium, Polish-born Marie Curie and her French husband, Pierre. An **exhibit** explores the building's fascinating history (good English descriptions). And you can climb 206 steps to the **dome gallery** for fine views of the interior as well as the city (accessible only with an escort, who leaves about every hour—see schedule as you enter).

Cost, Hours, Location: €7, covered by Museum Pass, daily 10:00–18:30, last entry 17:45, English tours many days at 11:00 and 13:00. Mo: Cardinal Lemoine.

Montparnasse Tower (La Tour Montparnasse)—This 59-story superscraper is cheaper and easier to ascend than the Eiffel Tower, with the added bonus of one of Paris' best views—the Eiffel Tower is in sight, and Montparnasse Tower isn't. Buy the €3 photo guide to the city, then go to the rooftop and orient yourself. As you zip up 56 floors in 38 seconds, watch the altitude meter above the door. At the top, enjoy the surreal scene with a man in a box and a helipad surrounded by the window-cleaner track. Then scan the city, noticing the lush courtyards hiding behind grand streetfronts. Downstairs, you'll find fascinating historic black-and-white photos and a plush little theater playing *Paris Like Never Seen* (free, 12 min, shows continuously). You'll float past unseen visual delights, spiraling down the Eiffel Tower as the French narration explains, "Paris is radiant and confident, like a lover who finally took her blouse off."

Cost, Hours, Location: €8.50, not covered by Museum Pass, April–Sept daily 9:30–23:30, Oct–March daily 9:30–22:30, last entry 30 min before closing, disappointing after dark, entrance on rue de l'Arrivée, Mo: Montparnasse-Bienvenüe. The tower is an efficient

stop when combined with a day trip to Chartres, which begins at the Montparnasse train station.

▲**Catacombs**—These underground tunnels contain the anonymous bones of six million permanent Parisians. In 1785, the Revolutionary Government of Paris decided to relieve congestion and improve sanitary conditions by emptying the city cemeteries (which traditionally surrounded churches) into an official ossuary. The perfect locale was the many miles of underground tunnels from limestone quarries, which were, at that time, just outside the city. For decades, priests led ceremonial processions of black-veiled, bone-laden carts into the quarries, where the bones were stacked into piles five feet high and as much as 80 feet deep behind neat walls of skull-studded tibiae. Each transfer was completed with the placement of a plaque indicating the church and district from which that stack of bones came and the date they arrived.

From the entry, a spiral staircase leads 60 feet down. Then you begin a one-mile subterranean walk. After several blocks of empty passageways, you ignore a sign announcing: "Halt, this is the empire of the dead." Along the way, plaques encourage visitors to reflect upon their destiny: "Happy is he who is forever faced with the hour of his death and prepares himself for the end every day." You emerge far from where you entered, with white-limestone-covered toes, telling anyone in the know you've been underground gawking at bones. Note to wannabe Hamlets: An attendant checks your bag at the exit for stolen souvenirs. A flashlight is handy. Being under 6'2" is helpful.

Cost, Hours, Location: €5, not covered by Museum Pass, Tue–Sun 10:00–17:00, ticket booth closes at 16:00, closed Mon, 1 place Denfert-Rochereau, tel. 01 43 22 47 63. Take the Métro to Denfert-Rochereau, then find the lion in the big traffic circle; if he looked left rather than right, he'd stare right at the green entrance to the Catacombs.

Northwest Paris: Champs-Elysées, Arc de Triomphe, and Beyond

▲▲**Champs-Elysées**—This famous boulevard is Paris' backbone, with its greatest concentration of traffic. From the Arc de Triomphe down the avenue des Champs-Elysées, all of France seems to converge on place de la Concorde, the city's largest square. While the Champs-Elysées has become a bit globalized, a walk here is a must.

To reach the top of the Champs-Elysées, take the Métro to the Arc de Triomphe (Mo: Charles de Gaulle-Etoile) then saunter down the grand boulevard (Métro stops every few blocks: Charles de Gaulle-Etoile, George V, Franklin D. Roosevelt).

○ See Champs-Elysées Walk on page 95.

Northwest Paris: Champs-Elysées, Arc de Triomphe, and Beyond

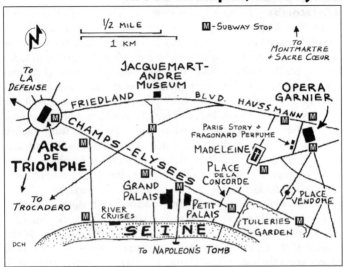

▲▲▲**Arc de Triomphe**—Napoleon had the magnificent Arc de Triomphe commissioned to commemorate his victory at the battle of Austerlitz. The foot of the arch is a stage on which the last two centuries of Parisian history have played out—from the funeral of Napoleon to the goose-stepping arrival of the Nazis to the triumphant return of Charles de Gaulle after the Allied liberation. Examine the carvings on the pillars, featuring a mighty Napoleon and excitable Lady Liberty. Pay your respects at the Tomb of the Unknown Soldier. Then climb the 284 steps (you'll pass an interesting little museum) to the observation deck up top, with sweeping skyline panoramas and a mesmerizing view down onto the traffic that swirls around the arch.

Cost, Hours, Location: Outside—free, always open. Inside—€8, under 18 free, covered by Museum Pass, April–Sept daily 10:00–23:00, Oct–March daily 10:00–22:00. Mo: Charles de Gaulle-Etoile, use underpass to reach arch.

✪ See Champs-Elysées Walk on page 95.

▲**Opéra Garnier**—This grand theater of the belle époque was built for Napoleon III and finished in 1875. From the avenue de l'Opéra, once lined with Paris' most fashionable haunts, the newly restored facade suggests "all power to the wealthy." And Apollo, holding his lyre high above the building, seems to declare, "This is a temple of the highest arts."

While the building is huge, the actual auditorium seats only 2,000. The real show was before and after the performance, when

the elite of Paris—out to see and be seen—strutted their elegant stuff in the extravagant lobbies. Think of the grand marble stairway as a theater itself. As you wander the halls and gawk at the decor, imagine the place filled with the beautiful people of its day. The massive foundations straddle an underground lake (creating the mysterious world of the *Phantom of the Opera*). Visitors can peek from two boxes into the actual red-velvet opera house to view Marc Chagall's colorful ceiling (1964) playfully dancing around the eight-ton chandelier. Note the box seats next to the stage—the most expensive in the house, with an obstructed view of the stage... but just right if you're here only to be seen.

The elitism of this place prompted President François Mitterand to have a people's opera house built in the 1980s, symbolically on place de la Bastille, where the French Revolution started in 1789. This left the Opéra Garnier home only to ballet and occasional concerts (usually no performances mid-July–mid-Sept, check performance schedule at information booth inside). While the library/museum is of interest to opera buffs, anyone will enjoy the second-floor grand foyer and Salon du Glacier, iced with decor typical of 1900.

Cost, Hours, Location: €7, not covered by Museum Pass, daily 10:00–17:00, July–Aug – until 18:00, closed during performances, 8 rue Scribe, Mo: Opéra, RER: Auber, www.opera-de -paris.fr.

Tours: There are English tours of the building on most afternoons (€10, includes entry, 90 min, call to confirm, tour ticket window at opposite end of entry from regular ticket booth).

Nearby: American Express, a TI, and the *Paris Story* film (see below) are on the left side of the Opéra, and the venerable Galeries Lafayette department store (top-floor café with marvelous views) is just behind. Across the street, the illustrious Café de la Paix has been a meeting spot for the local glitterati for generations. If you can afford the coffee, this offers a delightful break.

***Paris Story* Film**—This entertaining film offers a good and painless overview of the city's turbulent and brilliant past, covering 2,000 years in 45 fast-moving minutes. The theater's wide-screen projection and cushy chairs provide an ideal break from bad weather and sore feet, and the movie's a fun activity with kids. It makes a good first-day orientation.

Cost, Hours, Location: €8, kids-€5, family of 4-€21, not covered by Museum Pass. Individuals get a 20 percent discount with this book in 2006 (no discount on family rate). The film shows on the hour daily 9:00–19:00. Next to Opéra Garnier at 11 rue Scribe, Mo: Opéra, tel. 01 42 66 62 06.

Fragonard Perfume Museum—Near Opéra Garnier, two perfume shops masquerade as museums. Either location will teach you

Best Views over the City of Light

Your trip to Paris is played out in the streets, but the brilliance of the City of Light can only be fully appreciated by rising above it all. Take some time to marvel at all the man-made beauty, seen best in the early morning or around sunset. Many of the viewpoints I've listed are free or covered by the Museum Pass; otherwise, expect to pay about €8. Here are some prime locations for soaking in the views:

Eiffel Tower: It's hard to find a grander view of Paris than on the the tower's second level. Go around sunset and stay after dark to see the tower illuminated; or go in the early morning to avoid the midday haze (not covered by Museum Pass, see page 49).

Arc de Triomphe: Without a doubt, this is the perfect place to see the glamorous Champs-Elysées (if you can manage the 284 steps). It's great during the day, but even better at night, when the boulevard positively glitters. Use your Museum Pass to see it at both times (see page 60).

La Grande Arche de La Défense: This is your best bet for a view of Paris from outside the center. Take the elevator up for a good perspective on the city, its suburbs, and the surrounding forests (not covered by Museum Pass, see page 64).

Notre-Dame's Tower: This viewpoint is brilliant—you couldn't be more central—but it does require climbing 400 steps and is usually crowded with long lines (try to arrive early). Up high on the tower, you'll get an unobstructed view of gargoyles, the river, the Latin Quarter, and Ile de la Cité (covered by Museum Pass, see page 71).

a little about how perfume is made (ask for the English handout), but the one on rue Scribe smells even sweeter—it's in a beautiful 19th-century mansion (both free, daily 9:00–18:00, at 9 rue Scribe and 30 rue des Capucines, tel. 01 47 42 04 56, www.fragonard .com).

▲▲**Jacquemart-André Museum (Musée Jacquemart-André)**— This thoroughly enjoyable museum showcases the lavish home of a wealthy, art-loving, 19th-century Parisian couple. After wandering the grand boulevards, you now get inside for an intimate look at the lifestyles of the Parisian rich and fabulous. Edouard André and his wife Nélie Jacquemart—who had no children—spent their lives and fortunes designing, building, and then decorating this sumptuous mansion. What makes the visit so rewarding is the excellent audioguide tour (in English, free with admission, plan on spending an hour with the audioguide). The place is strewn with paintings by Rembrandt, Botticelli, Uccello, Mantegna, Bellini, Boucher, and Fragonard—enough to make a painting gallery famous.

Steps of Sacré-Cœur in Montmartre: Join the party on Paris' only hilltop. Walk uphill or take the funicular, then hunker down on the Sacré-Cœur's steps to enjoy the sunset and territorial views over Paris. Stay in Montmartre for dinner, then see the view again after dark (free, see page 68).

Galeries Lafayette in Opéra District: Take the elevator to the top floor of this department store for a stunning overlook of the old Opéra district. Sit at the breezy café to take it all in (free, see page 377).

Montparnasse Tower: The top of this awful glass skyscraper has some of the best views in Paris—featuring the Eiffel Tower...not the Montparnasse Tower. Zip up the elevator to the 56th floor, then walk to the rooftop (not covered by Museum Pass, disappointing after dark, see page 58).

Pompidou Center: Take the escalator up and admire the beautiful cityscape along with the exciting modern art. There may be better views over Paris, but there are none better from a museum (covered by Museum Pass, see page 202).

Trocadéro Square: This is *the* place to see the Eiffel Tower. Come day or night (when the tower is lit up) for a look at Monsieur Eiffel's festive creation. Consider starting or ending your Eiffel Tower visit here (free, see page 51).

Bar at Hôtel Concorde-Lafayette: This otherwise unappealing hotel is noteworthy for its 33rd-floor bar, where you can sip wine and enjoy a stunning Parisian panorama (free elevator, pricey drinks, see page 64).

Cost, Hours, Location: €9, not covered by Museum Pass, daily 10:00–18:00, elegant café, at 158 boulevard Haussmann, Mo: Miromesnil or St Philippe de Roule, tel. 01 45 62 11 59, www.musee-jacquemart-andre.com/jandre.

Petit Palais (and its Musée des Beaux-Arts)—The free museum is scheduled to reopen after renovation in the spring of 2006. When it does, you'll find a broad collection of paintings and sculpture from the 1600s to the 1900s. To some, it feels like a museum of second-choice art, as the more famous museums in Paris have better collections from the same periods. Others find a few diamonds in the rough from Monet, Renoir, Boudin, and other Impressionists; some interesting Art Nouveau pieces; and a smattering of works from Dutch, Italian, and Flemish Renaissance artists (Tue-Sun 10:00-17:40, closed Mon, across from Grand Palais, avenue Winston Churchill, just west of place de la Concorde, tel. 01 40 05 56 78).

Grand Palais—This grand exhibition hall, built for the 1900 World's Fair, is busy with generally worthwhile temporary exhibits. Get details on the current schedule from TIs or in *Pariscope* (€10.50, €9 after 13:00, not covered by Museum Pass, Mon and Thu–Sun 10:00–20:00, Wed 10:00–20:00, closed Tue, avenue Churchill, Mo: Rond Point or Champs-Elysées).

View from Hôtel Concorde-Lafayette—For a remarkable Parisian panorama, take the Métro to the pedestrian-unfriendly Porte Maillot stop, then follow the Palais de Congrés signs to the glass-and-steel tower. (If you're strapped for time, the skies are clear, and the sun's about to set, spring for a taxi.) Take the free elevator in the rear of the lobby to the 33rd floor, walk up one flight, and enter a sky-high world of semicircular booths, glass walls, pricey drinks (€6 espresso, €8 beer and wine), and jaw-dropping views (best before dark, bar open 17:30–2:00 in the morning, rooms start at €400, 3 place du General Koenig, tel. 01 40 68 50 68, www.concorde-lafayette.com).

▲La Défense and La Grande Arche—Beam yourself out to this *Star Wars*–like complex of glass towers and men in power-suits to contemplate the future of Paris and experience a dramatic contrast of old and new. A business and shopping center, La Défense was first conceived nearly 60 years ago to create a U.S.-style forest of skyscrapers to accommodate the business needs of the modern world. Today, La Défense is home to 150,000 employees and 55,000 residents.

La Grande Arche is the centerpiece of this ambitious complex. Inaugurated in 1989 on the 200th anniversary of the French Revolution, it was dedicated to human rights and brotherhood. The place is big—38 floors holding offices for 30,000 people on more than 200 acres. They say that Notre-Dame Cathedral could fit under its arch.

The complex at La Défense is an interesting study in 1960s land-use planning, directing lots of business and development away from downtown and allowing central Paris to retain its more elegant feel. This makes sense to most Parisians, regardless of whatever else they feel about this controversial complex.

For an interesting visit, take the Métro to the La Défense stop and start with La Grande Arche—take the elevator to the top for great city views and rooms with displays on the Arche's construction. Then stroll among the glass buildings to the Esplanade de la

Défense Métro station, and return home from there. After enjoying the elegance of downtown Paris' historic, glorious monuments, it's clear that man can build bigger, but not more beautiful.

Cost, Hours, Location: La Grande Arche elevator-€7.50, kids-€6, family deals, not covered by Museum Pass, daily 10:00–19:00, July–Aug until 20:00, RER or Mo: La Défense, follow signs to La Grande Arche, tel. 01 49 07 27 57. The entry price includes art exhibits and a film on the Arche's construction.

Northeast Paris: Marais Neighborhood and More

✪ To connect these sights with a fun, fact-filled stroll leading from place de la Bastille to the Pompidou Center, take the Marais Walk on page 106.

▲▲**Pompidou Center (Centre Pompidou)**—One of Europe's greatest collections of far-out modern art is housed in the Musée National d'Art Moderne, on the fourth and fifth floors of this colorful, exoskeletal building. (Renovation will condense the art collection to one floor, but the museum will remain open.) Ahead of its time, this 20th-century art is still waiting for the world to catch up with it. After so many Madonnas-and-children, a piano smashed to bits and glued to the wall is refreshing.

The Pompidou Center and the square that fronts it are lively, with lots of people, street theater, and activity inside and out—a perpetual street fair. Kids of any age enjoy the fun, colorful fountain (called *Homage to Stravinsky*) next to the Pompidou Center. Ride the escalator for a great city view from the top (ticket or Museum Pass required), and consider the good mezzanine-level café.

Cost, Hours, Location: €7, free first Sun of month, covered by Museum Pass, Wed-Mon 11:00-21:00, closed Tue, Mo: Rambuteau, tel. 01 44 78 12 33, www.centrepompidou.fr.

✪ See Pompidou Center Tour on page 202.

▲▲**Jewish Art and History Museum (Musée d'Art et Histoire du Judaïsme)**—This fascinating museum is located in a beautifully restored Marais mansion and tells the story of Judaism throughout Europe, from the Roman destruction of Jerusalem to the theft of famous artworks during World War II.

The museum illustrates the cultural unity maintained by this continually dispersed population. You'll learn about the history of Jewish traditions from bar mitzvahs to menorahs, and see the exquisite traditional costumes and objects around which daily life revolved. Don't miss the explanation of "the Dreyfus affair," a major event in early 1900s French politics. You'll also see photographs of and paintings by famous Jewish artists, including Chagall, Modigliani, and Soutine. A small but moving section is devoted to the deportation of Jews from Paris during World War II.

Helpful audioguides and many English explanations make

Northeast Paris: Marais Neighborhood and More

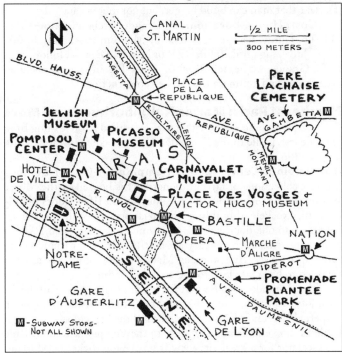

this an enjoyable history lesson (red numbers on small signs indicate the number you should press on your audioguide). Move along at your own speed.

Cost, Hours, Location: €7, includes audioguide, not covered by Museum Pass, Mon-Fri 11:00-18:00, Sun 10:00-18:00, closed Sat, 71 rue du Temple, Mo: Rambuteau or Hôtel de Ville a few blocks farther away, tel. 01 53 01 86 60, www.mahj.org.

▲▲**Picasso Museum (Musée Picasso)**—Tucked into a corner of the Marais and worth ▲▲▲ if you're a Picasso fan, this museum contains the world's largest collection of Picasso's paintings, sculptures, sketches, and ceramics, and includes his small collection of Impressionist art. The art is well-displayed in a fine old mansion with a peaceful garden café. The room-by-room English introductions help make sense of Picasso's work—from the Toulouse-Lautrec-like portraits at the beginning of his career to his gray-brown Cubist period to his return-to-childhood, Salvador Dalí–like finish. The well-done €3 English guidebook helps Picassophiles appreciate the context of his art and learn more about his interesting life. Most will be happy reading the posted

English explanations while moving at a steady pace through the museum—the ground and first floors satisfied my curiosity.

Cost, Hours, Location: €5.50, free first Sun of month, covered by Museum Pass, April–Sept Wed–Mon 9:30–18:00, Oct–March Wed–Mon 9:30–17:30, last entry 45 min before closing, closed Tue, 5 rue de Thorigny, Mo: St. Paul or Chemin Vert, tel. 01 42 71 25 21, www.musee-picasso.fr.

✪ See Picasso Museum Tour on page 231.

▲▲**Carnavalet Museum (Musée Carnavalet)**—The tumultuous history of Paris—starring the Revolutionary years—is well-portrayed in this converted Marais mansion. Explanations are in French only, but many displays are fairly self-explanatory. You'll see paintings of Parisian scenes, French Revolution paraphernalia, old Parisian store signs, a small guillotine, a model of 16th-century Ile de la Cité (notice the bridge houses), and rooms full of 17th-century Parisian furniture.

Cost, Hours, Location: Free, Tue–Sun 10:00–18:00, closed Mon; avoid lunchtime (12:00–14:00), when many rooms close; 23 rue de Sévigné, Mo: St. Paul, tel. 01 44 59 58 58.

✪ See Carnavalet Museum Tour on page 216.

Victor Hugo's House—France's literary giant lived in this house on place des Vosges from 1832 to 1848. Inside are posters advertising theater productions of his works, paintings of some of his most famous character creations, and a few furnished rooms.

Cost, Hours, Location: Free, Tue–Sun 10:00–18:00, last entry 17:40, closed Mon, 6 place des Vosges, tel. 01 42 72 10 16.

▲**Promenade Plantée Park**—This two-mile-long, narrow garden walk on a viaduct was once used for train tracks and is now a joy. Part of the park is elevated. At times, you'll walk along the street until you pick up the next segment. The shops below the viaduct's arches (a creative use of once-wasted urban space) make for entertaining window-shopping.

Cost, Hours, Location: Free, opens Mon–Fri at 8:00, Sat–Sun at 9:00, closes at sunset. It runs from place de la Bastille (Mo: Bastille) along avenue Daumesnil to Saint-Mandé (Mo: Michel Bizot). From place de la Bastille (follow "Sortie Opéra" or "Sortie rue de Lyon" from Bastille Métro station), walk down rue de Lyon with the Opera immediately on your left. Find the steps up the red brick wall a block after the Opera.

▲**Père Lachaise Cemetery (Cimetière du Père Lachaise)**—Littered with the tombstones of many of the city's most illustrious dead, this is your best one-stop look at Paris' fascinating, romantic past residents. More like a small city, the cemetery is confusing, but maps will direct you to the graves of Frédéric Chopin, Molière, Edith Piaf, Oscar Wilde, Gertrude Stein, Jim Morrison, Héloïse and Abélard, and many more. Buy the

helpful €2 map at the flower stores located near either entry.

Cost, Hours, Location: Free, Mon–Sat 8:00–18:00, Sun 9:00–18:00, actually closes at dusk. It's down rue Père Lachaise from Mo: Gambetta, or across the street from the Père Lachaise Métro stop (also reachable via bus #69).

🡺 See Père Lachaise Cemetery Tour on page 284.

North Paris: Montmartre

🡺 Connect these sights with the Montmartre Walk on page 123.

▲▲Sacré-Cœur and Montmartre—This Byzantine-looking basilica, while only 130 years old, is impressive (church free, open daily 7:00–23:00; €5 to climb dome, June–Sept daily 9:00–19:00, Oct–May daily 10:00–18:00).

The neighborhood's main square (place du Tertre), one block from the church, was once the haunt of Henri de Toulouse-Lautrec and the original bohemians. Today, it's mobbed with tourists and unoriginal bohemians, but it's still fun (to beat the crowds, go early in the morning).

Take the Métro to the Anvers stop (one more Métro ticket buys your way up the funicular and avoids the stairs) or the closer but less scenic Abbesses stop. A taxi to the top of the hill saves time and avoids sweat.

Dalí Museum (L'Espace Dalí)—The museum offers an entertaining look at some of Dalí's creations (€8, not covered by Museum Pass, Sept–June daily 10:00–18:30, July–Aug daily 10:00–21:30, 11 rue Poulbot).

Montmartre Museum (Musée de Montmartre)—This 17th-century home re-creates the traditional cancan and cabaret Montmartre scene with paintings, posters, photos, music, and memorabilia (€5.50, not covered by Museum Pass, Tue–Sun 10:00–12:30 & 14:00–18:00, closed Mon, 12 rue Cortot).

Pigalle—Paris' red-light district, the infamous "Pig Alley," is at the foot of butte Montmartre. *Ooh la la.* It's more shocking than dangerous. Walk from place Pigalle to place Blanche, teasing desperate barkers and fast-talking temptresses. In bars, a €150 bottle of cheap champagne comes with a friend. Stick to the bigger streets, hang onto your wallet, and exercise good judgment. Cancan can cost a fortune, as can con artists in topless bars. After dark, countless tour buses line the streets, reminding us that tour guides make big bucks by bringing their groups to touristy nightclubs like the famous Moulin Rouge (Mo: Pigalle or Abbesses).

Museum of Erotic Art (Musée de l'Erotisme)—Paris' sexy museum has five floors of risqué displays—mostly paintings and drawings—ranging from artistic to erotic to disgusting, with a few circa-1920 porn videos and a fascinating history of local brothels tossed in. It's in the center of the Pigalle red light

district (€7, no...it's not covered by Museum Pass, daily 10:00–2:00 in the morning, 72 boulevard de Clichy, Mo: Blanche).

Near Paris: Versailles

▲▲▲**Versailles**—Every king's dream, Versailles was the residence of French kings and the cultural heartbeat of Europe for about 100 years—until the Revolution of 1789 ended the notion that God deputized some people to rule for him on earth. Louis XIV spent half a year's income of Europe's richest country turning his dad's hunting lodge into a palace fit for a divine monarch. Louis XV and Louis XVI spent much of the 18th century gilding Louis XIV's lily. In 1837, about 50 years after the royal family was evicted, King Louis-Philippe opened the palace as a museum. Today you can visit parts of the huge palace and wander through acres of manicured gardens sprinkled with fountains and studded with statues. Europe's next-best palaces are Versailles wannabes.

Cost and Hours: €7.50 (main palace and both Trianon palaces covered by Museum Pass), €5.50 after 15:30, under 18 free. The gardens are free (except for weekends April–Sept, when it's €6), but there are extra charges for tours and the Grand and Petit Trianon châteaux. On summer weekends, the fountains perform in the garden. The palace is open April–Oct Tue–Sun 9:00–18:30, Nov–March Tue–Sun 9:00–17:30, closed Mon (last entry 30 min before closing, www.chateauversailles.fr). The gardens open early (7:00, 8:00 in winter) and smaller palaces open late (12:00).

○ See Versailles Day Trip on page 421.

Disappointments de Paris

Here are a few negatives to help you manage your limited time:

La Madeleine is a big, neoclassical church with a postcard facade and a postbox interior.

The Bastille is Paris' most famous non-sight. The square is there, but confused tourists look everywhere and can't find the prison of Revolution fame. The building's gone, and the square is good only for its nightlife as a jumping-off point for the Marais Walk (see page 106) or Promenade Plantée Park (see page 67).

The Latin Quarter is mostly a frail shadow of its once bohemian self. The blocks nearest the river (across from Notre-Dame) are more Tunisian, Greek, and Woolworth's than old-time Paris. The neighborhood merits a wander (kids love it), but you're better off focusing on the area around boulevard St. Germain and rue de Buci, and on the streets around the Maubert-Mutualité Métro stop. ○ See Left Bank Walk on page 135, and Historic Paris Walk on page 70.

HISTORIC PARIS WALK

Ile de la Cité and the Latin Quarter

Paris has been the cultural capital of Europe for centuries. We'll start where it did, on Ile de la Cité, with a foray onto the Left Bank, on a walk that laces together 80 generations of history: from Celtic fishing village to Roman city, bustling medieval capital, birthplace of the Revolution, bohemian haunt of the 1920s café scene, and the working world of modern Paris. Allow four hours to do justice to this three-mile walk.

ORIENTATION

Many sights that charge admission are covered by the Museum Pass, which for many travelers is a great time- and money-saver (1 day-€18, 3 consecutive days-€36, 5 consecutive days-€54, sold at participating sights). The Archaeological Crypt is a convenient, uncrowded place to buy your pass.

Notre-Dame: Free, church open daily 7:45–19:00; treasury-€2.50 (not covered by Museum Pass), daily 9:30–17:30; Sunday Mass at 8:30, 10:00 (Gregorian), 11:30 (international), and 12:45. Organ performances are usually on Sun at 16:30. Audioguides cost €5. Ask about free English tours, normally Wed and Thu at 12:00 and Sat at 14:30.

The tower climb (entrance along left side of church) is 400 steps and costs €7, but it's worth it for the gargoyle's-eye view of the cathedral, Seine, and city (July–Aug Mon–Fri 9:00–19:30, Sat–Sun 9:00–23:00; April–June and Sept daily 9:30–19:30, Oct–March daily 10:00–17:30, last entry 45 min before closing, covered by Museum Pass but no bypass line for passholders; to avoid crowds in peak season, arrive before 10:00 or after 18:00).

Historic Paris Walk

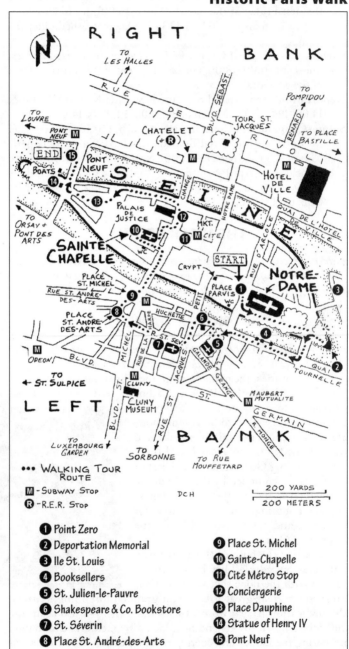

••• WALKING TOUR ROUTE
M – SUBWAY STOP
R – R.E.R. STOP

DCH

200 YARDS
200 METERS

1. Point Zero
2. Deportation Memorial
3. Ile St. Louis
4. Booksellers
5. St. Julien-le-Pauvre
6. Shakespeare & Co. Bookstore
7. St. Séverin
8. Place St. André-des-Arts
9. Place St. Michel
10. Sainte-Chapelle
11. Cité Métro Stop
12. Conciergerie
13. Place Dauphine
14. Statue of Henry IV
15. Pont Neuf

For those lucky enough to be here either on Easter or the first Friday of the month (15:00–16:00), Jesus' Crown of Thorns is on display. Tel. 01 42 34 56 10, www.cathedraldeparis .com.

Paris Archaeological Crypt: €3.50, covered by Museum Pass, Tue–Sun 10:00–18:00, closed Mon, entry 100 yards in front of the cathedral.

Deportation Memorial: Free, April–Sept daily 10:00–12:00 & 14:00–19:00, Oct–March daily 10:00–12:00 & 14:00–17:00.

Sainte-Chapelle and Conciergerie: €7 each, €10.50 combo-ticket for both, both covered by Museum Pass; Sainte-Chapelle March–Oct daily 9:30–18:00, Nov–Feb daily 9:00–17:00; Conciergerie April–Sept daily 9:30–18:00, Oct–March daily 10:00–17:00; last entry 30 min before closing for both, Mo: Cité, tel. 01 44 07 12 38.

THE WALK BEGINS

• *Start at Notre-Dame Cathedral on the island in the River Seine, the physical and historic bull's-eye of your Paris map. The closest Métro stops are Cité, Hôtel de Ville, and St. Michel, each requiring a short walk.*

NOTRE-DAME

• *On the square in front of the cathedral, stand far enough back to take in the whole façade. Find the circular window in the center.*

For centuries, the main figure in the Christian "pantheon" has been Mary, the mother of Jesus. Catholics petition her in times of trouble to gain comfort, and to ask her to convince God to be compassionate with them. The church is dedicated to "Our Lady" *(Notre Dame),* and there she is, cradling God, right in the heart of the facade, surrounded by the halo of the rose window. Though the church is massive and imposing, it has always stood for the grace and compassion of Mary, the "mother of God."

Imagine the faith of the people who built this cathedral. They broke ground in 1163 with the hope that someday their great-great-great-great-great-great grandchildren might attend the dedication Mass two centuries later, in 1345. Look up the 200-foot-tall bell towers and imagine a tiny medieval community mustering the money and energy for construction. Master masons supervised, but the people did much of the grunt work themselves

Paris Through History

250 B.C.	Small fishing village of the Parisii, a Celtic tribe.
52 B.C.	Julius Caesar conquers the Parisii capital of Lutetia (near Paris), and the Romans replace it with a new capital on the Left Bank.
A.D. 497	Rome falls to the Germanic Franks. King Clovis (482–511) converts to Christianity and makes Paris his capital.
885-886	Paris gets wasted in siege by Viking Norsemen = Normans.
1163	Notre-Dame cornerstone laid.
c. 1250	Paris is a bustling commercial city with a university and new construction, such as Sainte-Chapelle and Notre-Dame.
c. 1600	King Henry IV beautifies Paris with buildings, roads, bridges, and squares.
c. 1700	Louis XIV makes Versailles his capital, while Parisians grumble.
1789	Paris is the heart of France's Revolution, which condemns thousands to the guillotine.
1804	Napoleon Bonaparte crowns himself emperor in a ceremony at Notre-Dame.
1830 & 1848	Parisians take to the streets again in revolutions, fighting the return of royalty.
c. 1860	Napoleon's nephew, Napoleon III, builds Paris' wide boulevards.
1889	The centennial of the Revolution is celebrated with the Eiffel Tower. Paris enjoys wealth and middle-class prosperity in the belle époque (beautiful age).
1920s	After the draining Great War, Paris is a cheap place to live, attracting expatriates like Ernest Hemingway.
1940–1944	Occupied Paris spends the war years under gray skies and gray Nazi uniforms.
2005	Lance Armstrong wins his seventh Tour de France

for free—hauling the huge stones from distant quarries, digging a 30-foot-deep trench to lay the foundation, and treading like rats on a wheel designed to lift the stones up, one by one. This kind of backbreaking, arduous manual labor created the real hunchbacks of Notre-Dame.

• *"Walk this way" toward the cathedral, and view it from the bronze plaque on the ground (30 yards from the central doorway) marked...*

Point Zero

You're standing at the center of France, the point from which all distances are measured. It was also the center of Paris 2,300 years ago, when the Parisii tribe fished where the east-west river crossed a north-south road. The Romans conquered the Parisii and built their Temple of Jupiter where Notre-Dame stands today (52 B.C.). When Rome fell, the Germanic Franks sealed their victory by replacing the temple with the Christian church of St. Etienne in the sixth century. See the outlines of the former church in the pavement (in smaller gray stones), showing former walls and columns, angling out from Notre-Dame to Point Zero.

The grand equestrian statue (to your right, as you face the church) is of Charlemagne ("Charles the Great," 742–814), King of the Franks, whose reign marked the birth of modern France. He briefly united Europe and was crowned the first Holy Roman Emperor in 800, but after his death, the kingdom was divided into what would become modern France and Germany. (Maybe even greater than Charles are the nearby pay toilets—the cleanest you'll find in downtown Paris.)

Before its renovation 150 years ago, this square was much smaller, a characteristic medieval shambles facing a rundown church, surrounded by winding streets and higgledy-piggledy buildings. (Yellowed bricks in the pavement show the medieval street plan and even identify some of the buildings.) The church's huge bell towers rose above this tangle of smaller buildings,  inspiring Victor Hugo's story of a deformed bell-ringer who could look down on all of Paris.

Looking two-thirds of the way up Notre-Dame's left tower, those with binoculars or good eyes can find Paris' most photographed gargoyle. Propped on his elbows on the balcony rail, he watches all the tourists in line.

• *Much of Paris' history is right under your feet. Some may consider visiting it in the...*

Archaeological Crypt

Two thousand years of dirt and debris have raised the city's altitude. In the crypt (entrance 100 yards in front of Notre-Dame's entrance), you can see cellars and foundations from many layers of Paris: a Roman building with central heating; a wall that didn't keep the Franks out; the main medieval road that once led grandly up the square to Notre-Dame; and even (wow) a 19th-century sewer. (For more info, see page 47.)

• *Now turn your attention to the church facade. Look at the left doorway and, to the left of the door, find the statue with his head in his hands.*

Notre-Dame Facade

St. Denis

When Christianity began making converts in Roman Paris, the bishop of Paris (St. Denis) was beheaded as a warning to those for-

saking the Roman gods. But those early Christians were hard to keep down. St. Denis got up, tucked his head under his arm, headed north, paused at a fountain to wash it off, and continued until he found just the right place to meet his maker. The Parisians were convinced by this miracle, Christianity gained

ground, and a church soon replaced the pagan temple.

• *Above the central doorway, you'll find scenes from the Last Judgment.*

Central Portal

It's the end of the world, and Christ sits on the throne of judgment (just under the arches, holding both hands up). Below him, an

angel and a demon weigh souls in the balance; the demon cheats by pressing down. The good people stand to the left, gazing up to heaven. The naughty ones to the right are chained up and led off to a six-hour tour of the Louvre on a hot day. Notice the crazy, sculpted demons to the right, at the base of the arch. Find the flaming cauldron with the sinner diving into it headfirst. The lower panel shows Judgment Day, as angels with trumpets remind

worshippers that all social classes will be judged—clergy, nobility, army, and peasants. Below that, Jesus stands between the 12 apostles—each barefoot and with his ID symbol (such as Peter with his keys).

Notre-Dame Facade

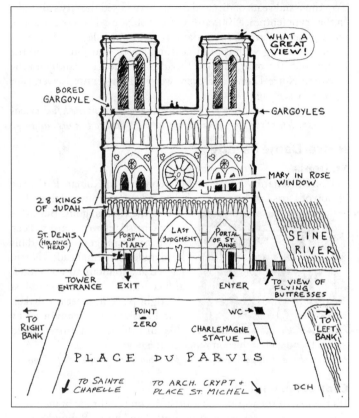

• *Take 10 paces back. Above the arches is a row of 28 statues, known as...*

The Kings of Judah

In the days of the French Revolution (1789–1799), these Biblical kings were mistaken for the hated French kings, and Notre-Dame represented the oppressive Catholic hierarchy. The citizens stormed the church, crying, "Off with their heads!" Plop, they lopped off the crowned heads of these kings with glee, creating a row of St. Denises that wasn't repaired for decades.

But the story doesn't end there. A schoolteacher who lived nearby collected the heads and buried them in his backyard for safekeeping. There they slept until 1977, when they were accidentally unearthed. Today, you can stare into the eyes of the original kings in the Cluny Museum, a few blocks away.

• *Enter the church and find a spot where you can view the long, high central aisle. (Be careful: Pickpockets attend church here religiously.)*

Notre-Dame Interior
Nave
Remove your metaphorical hat and become a simple bareheaded peasant, entering the dim medieval light of the church. Take a minute to let your pupils dilate, then take in the subtle, mysterious light show that God beams through the stained-glass windows. Follow the slender columns up 10 stories to the praying-hands arches of the ceiling, and contemplate the heavens. Let's say it's dedication day for this great stone wonder. The priest intones the words of the Mass that echo through the hall: *"Terribilis est locus iste"*—"This place is *terribilis*," meaning awe-inspiring or even terrifying. It's a huge, dark, earthly cavern lit with an unearthly light.

This is Gothic. Taller and filled with light, this was a major improvement over the earlier Romanesque style. Gothic architects needed only a few structural columns, topped by crisscrossing pointed arches to support the weight of the roof. This let them build higher than ever, freeing up the walls for windows.

Notre-Dame is designed in the shape of a cross, with the altar placed where the crossbeam intersects. The church can hold up to 10,000 faithful. And it's probably buzzing with visitors now, just as it was 800 years ago. The quiet, deserted churches we see elsewhere are in stark contrast to the busy, center-of-life places they were in the Middle Ages.

• *Walk up to the main altar.*

Altar
This marks the place where Mass is said and the bread and wine of Communion are blessed and distributed. In olden days, there were no chairs. This was the holy spot for Romans, Christians...and even atheists. When the Revolutionaries stormed the church, they gutted it and turned it into a "Temple of Reason." A woman dressed like the Statue of Liberty held court at the altar as a symbol of the divinity of Man. France today, while nominally Catholic, remains aloof from Vatican dogmatism. Instead of traditional wooden confessional booths, notice the open, glass-walled room (right aisle) where modern sinners seek counseling as much as forgiveness.

Right Transept (and Beyond)
A statue of Joan of Arc (Jeanne d'Arc, 1412–1431), dressed in armor and praying, honors the French teenager who rallied French soldiers to try to drive English invaders from Paris, before being burned at the stake for claiming to hear heavenly voices. Almost immediately, Parisians rallied to condemn Joan's execution, and finally, in 1909, here in Notre-Dame, the former "witch" was beatified.

Join the statue in gazing up to the blue-and-purple, rose-shaped window—with teeny green Mary and baby Jesus in the center—the only one of the three windows still with its original medieval glass.

A large painting back down to your right shows portly Thomas Aquinas (1225–1274) teaching, while his students drink from the fountain of knowledge. This Italian monk did undergrad and master's work at the multicultural University of Paris, then taught there for several years while writing his theological works. His "scholasticism" used Aristotle's logic to examine the Christian universe, aiming to fuse faith and reason.

Just past the altar are the walls of the choir, where more intimate services can be held in this spacious building. Peeking inside, behind the altar, you'll see a fine 17th-century *pietà* flanked by two kneeling kings: Louis XIII and Louis XIV. The south walls of the choir have Gothic carvings (restored in the 19th century) showing scenes from the life of Christ after his Resurrection. Notice the niches below these carvings—they mark the tombs of centuries of archbishops. Surrounding the choir are chapels, each dedicated to a particular saint and funded by a particular guild. The faithful can pause at their favorite, light a candle as an offering, and meditate in the cool light of the stained glass. (The nearby treasury, containing lavish robes and golden reliquaries, lacks English explanations and probably isn't worth the €2.50 entry fee.)

• *Amble around the ambulatory, spill back outside, and make a slow U-turn left. Enter the park through the iron gates along the riverside.*

Notre-Dame Side View

Along the side of the church, you'll notice the flying buttresses. These 50-foot stone "beams" that stick out of the church were the key to the complex Gothic architecture. The pointed arches we saw inside caused the weight of the roof to push outward rather than downward. The "flying" buttresses support the roof by pushing back inward. Gothic

architects were masters at playing architectural forces against each other to build loftier and loftier churches, with walls opened up for stained-glass windows.

Picture Quasimodo limping around along the railed balcony at the base of the roof among the gargoyles. These grotesque beasts sticking out from pillars and

buttresses represent souls caught between heaven and earth. They also function as rainspouts (from the same French root as "gargle") when there are no evil spirits to battle.

The neo-Gothic 300-foot spire is a product of the 1860 reconstruction of the dilapidated old church. Victor Hugo's book *The Hunchback of Notre-Dame* (1831) inspired a young architecture student named Eugène-Emmanuel Viollet-le-Duc to dedicate his career to a major renovation in Gothic style. Find Viollet-le-Duc himself at the base of the spire among the green apostles and evangelists (visible as you approach the back end of the church). The apostles look outward, blessing the city, while the architect (at top) looks up the spire, marveling at his fine work.

• *Behind Notre-Dame, cross the street and enter the iron gate into the park at the tip of the island.*

Deportation Memorial (Mémorial de la Déportation)

This memorial to the 200,000 French victims of the Nazi concentration camps (1940–1945) draws you into their experience. France was quickly overrun by Nazi Germany, and Paris spent the war years under Nazi occupation. Jews and dissidents were rounded up and deported—many never returned.

As you descend the steps, the city around you disappears. Surrounded by walls, you have become a prisoner. Your only freedom is your view of the sky and the tiny glimpse of the river below. Enter the dark, single-file chamber up ahead. Inside, the circular plaque in the floor reads, "They went to the end of the earth and did not return."

The hallway stretching in front of you is lined with 200,000 lighted crystals, one for each French citizen who died. Flickering at the far end is the eternal flame of hope. The tomb of the unknown deportee lies at your feet. Above, the inscription reads, "Dedicated to the living memory of the 200,000 French deportees sleeping in the night and the fog, exterminated in the Nazi concentration camps." The side rooms are filled with triangles—reminiscent of the identification patches inmates  were forced to wear—each bearing the name of a concentration camp. Above the exit as you leave is the message you'll find at all Nazi sites: "Forgive, but never forget."

Ile St. Louis

Back on street level, look across the river to the Ile St. Louis. If the Ile de la Cité is a tug laden with the history of Paris, it's

Ile St. Louis

1. Hôtel Jeu de Paume
2. Hôtel de Lutèce
3. Hôtel des Deux Iles
4. Hôtel Saint Louis
5. La Tastevin Rest.
6. Café Med
7. La Brasserie de l'Ile St. Louis
8. Rests. Nos Ancêtres les Gaulois & La Taverne du Sergeant Recruteur
9. Berthillon Ice Cream
10. Amorino Gelati
11. Le Cave du Franc Pinot (Jazz Club)
12. Good Picnic Spot
13. Rest. La Tour d'Argent

towing this classy little residential dinghy laden only with high-rent apartments, boutiques, characteristic restaurants, and famous sorbet shops.

This island wasn't developed until much later than the Ile de la Cité (17th century). What was a swampy mess is now harmonious Parisian architecture and one of Paris' most exclusive neighborhoods. Its uppity residents complain that the local ice cream shop—Berthillon—draws crowds until late into the night (31 rue St. Louis-en-l'Ile).

On the Left Bank (on your right), at the foot of the bridge across from Ile St. Louis, you'll find one of Paris' most exclusive restaurants, La Tour d'Argent. Because the top floor has floor-to-ceiling windows, your evening meal comes with glittering views—and a golden price (allow €200 minimum, though you get a free photo of yourself dining elegantly with Notre-Dame floodlit in the background).

• *From the tip of Ile de la Cité, cross the bridge to the Left Bank and turn right. Walk along the river, toward the front end of Notre-Dame. Stairs detour down to the riverbank if you need a place to picnic. This side view of the church from across the river is one of Europe's great sights and best from river level.*

LEFT BANK

The Rive Gauche, or the Left Bank of the Seine—"left" if you were floating downstream—still has many of the twisting lanes and narrow buildings of medieval times. The Right Bank is more modern and business-oriented, with wide boulevards and stressed Parisians in suits. Here along the riverbank, the "big business" is secondhand books, displayed in the green metal stalls on the parapet. These literary entrepreneurs pride themselves on their easygoing business style. With flexible hours and virtually no

overhead, they run their businesses as they have since medieval times. For more information, see "*Les Bouquinistes* (Riverside Vendors)" sidebar on page 376.

• *When you reach the bridge (pont au Double) that crosses over in front of Notre-Dame, veer to the left across the street to a small park (place Viviani, fill your water bottle from fountain on left). You'll find the small rough-stone church of St. Julien-le-Pauvre just after the square and pass Paris' oldest inhabitant—an acacia tree nicknamed Robinier, after the guy who planted it in 1602—that may once have shaded the Sun King.*

Medieval Paris (1000–1400)

Picture Paris in 1250, when the church of St. Julien-le-Pauvre was still new. Notre-Dame was nearly done (so they thought), Sainte-Chapelle had just opened, the University was expanding human knowledge, and Paris was fast becoming a prosperous industrial and commercial center. The area around the church gives you some of the medieval feel. Looking along nearby rue Galande, you'll see a few old houses leaning every which way. (La Guillotine Pub at #52 sports an authentic guillotine from 1792 on its wall.) In medieval days, people were piled on top of each other, building at all angles, as they scrambled for this prime real estate near the main commercial artery of the day—the Seine. The smell of fish competed with the smell of neighbors in this knot of humanity.

Narrow dirt (or mud) streets sloped from here down into the mucky Seine, until modern quays and embankments cleaned that up.

• *Return to the river and turn left on rue de la Bûcherie. At #37, drop into the...*

Shakespeare and Company Bookstore

In addition to hosting butchers and fishmongers, the Left Bank has been home to scholars, philosophers, and poets since medieval times. This funky bookstore—a reincarnation of the original shop  from the 1920s—has picked up the literary torch. Sylvia Beach, an American with a passion for free thinking, opened Shakespeare and Company for the post-WWI Lost Generation who came to Paris to find themselves. American writers flocked here for the cheap rents, fleeing the uptight, Prohibition-era United States. Beach's bookstore was famous as a meeting place of Paris' literary expatriate elite. Ernest Hemingway borrowed books from here regularly. James Joyce struggled to find a publisher for his now classic novel *Ulysses*—until Sylvia Beach published it. George Bernard Shaw, Gertrude Stein, and Ezra Pound also got their English fix here.

Today, the bookstore carries on that literary tradition. Struggling writers are given free accommodations upstairs in tiny rooms with views of Notre-Dame. Downstairs, travelers enjoy a great selection of used English books. Pick up the *Paris Voice* newspaper and say hi to owner George (thriving at 90 years old) and his daughter...Sylvia.

Notice the green water fountain (1900) in front of the bookstore, one of the many in Paris donated by the English philanthropist Sir Richard Wallace. The hooks below the caryatids once held metal mugs for drinking the water.

• *Continue to the rue du Petit-Pont (which becomes rue St. Jacques). This bustling north–south boulevard was the Romans' busiest boulevard 2,000 years ago, with chariots racing in and out of the city. (Roman-iacs can view remains from the 3rd-century baths, along with a fine medieval collection, at the nearby Cluny Museum, near the corner of boulevards St. Michel and St. Germain; see page 277.)*

Walking away from the river for one block, turn right at the Gothic church of St. Séverin and walk into the Latin Quarter.

St. Séverin

Don't ask me why, but it took a century longer to build this church than Notre-Dame. This is Flamboyant, or "flame-like," Gothic, and

you can see the short, prickly spires meant to make this building flicker in the eyes of the faithful. The church gives us a close-up look at gargoyles. This weird, winged species of flying mammal, now extinct, used to swoop down on unwary peasants, occasionally carrying off small children in their beaks. Today, they're most impressive in thunderstorms, when they vomit rain.

• *At #22 rue St. Séverin, you'll find the skinniest house in Paris, two windows wide. Rue St. Séverin leads right through...*

The Latin Quarter

While it may look more like the Greek Quarter today (cheap gyros abound), this area is the Latin Quarter, named for the language you'd have heard on these streets if you walked them in the Middle Ages. The University of Paris (founded 1215), one of the leading educational institutions of medieval Europe, was (and still is) nearby.

A thousand years ago, the "crude" or vernacular local languages were sophisticated enough to communicate basic human needs, but if you wanted to get philosophical, the language of choice was Latin. The class of educated elite of medieval Europe transcended nations and borders. From Sicily to Sweden, they spoke and corresponded in Latin. Now the most Latin thing about this area is the beat you may hear coming from some of the subterranean jazz clubs.

Along rue St. Séverin, you can still see the shadow of the medieval sewer system. The street slopes into a central channel of bricks. In the days before plumbing and toilets, when people still went to the river or neighborhood wells for their water, flushing meant throwing it out the window. At certain times of day, maids on the fourth floor would holler, *"Garde de l'eau!"* ("Watch out for the water!") and heave it into the streets, where it would eventually wash down into the Seine.

As you wander, remember that before Napoleon III commissioned Baron Haussmann to modernize the city with grand boulevards (19th century), Paris was just like this—a medieval tangle. The ethnic feel of this area is nothing new—it's been a melting pot and university district for almost 800 years.

• *Keep wandering straight and you'll come to...*

Boulevard St. Michel

Busy boulevard St. Michel (or "boul' Miche") is famous as the main artery for Paris' café and artsy scene, culminating a block away

(to the left), where it intersects boulevard St. Germain. Although nowadays you're more likely to find pantyhose at 30 percent off, there are still many cafés, boutiques, and bohemian haunts nearby.

The Sorbonne—the University of Paris' humanities department—is also close, if you want to make a detour, though entry is not allowed for visitors. (Turn left on boulevard St. Michel and walk two blocks south. Gaze at the dome from the place de la Sorbonne courtyard). Originally founded as a theological school, the Sorbonne began attracting more students and famous professors—such as St. Thomas Aquinas and Peter Abélard—as its prestige grew. By the time the school expanded to include other subjects, it had a reputation for bold, new ideas. Nonconformity is a tradition here, and Paris remains a world center for new intellectual trends.

• *Cross boulevard St. Michel. Just ahead is...*

Place St. André-des-Arts

This tree-filled square is lined with cafés. In Paris, most serious thinking goes on in cafés. For centuries, these have been social watering holes, where you can get a warm place to sit and stimulating conversation for the price of a cup of coffee. Every great French writer—from Voltaire and Jean-Jacques Rousseau to Jean-Paul Sartre and Jacques Derrida—had a favorite haunt.

Paris honors its writers. If you visit the Panthéon (described on page 57)—a few blocks up boulevard St. Michel and to the left—you will find French writers (Voltaire, Victor Hugo, Emile Zola, and Rousseau), inventors (Louis Braille), and scientists (including Marie and Pierre Curie) buried in a setting usually reserved for warriors and politicians.

• *Adjoining this square toward the river is the triangular place St. Michel, with a Métro stop and a statue of St. Michael killing a devil. Note: If you were to continue west along rue St. André-des-Arts, you'd find more Left Bank action.*

Place St. Michel

You're standing at the traditional core of the Left Bank's artsy, liberal, hippie, bohemian district of poets, philosophers, and winos. Nearby, you'll find international eateries, far-out bookshops, street singers, pale girls in black berets, jazz clubs, and—these days—tourists. Small cinemas show avant-garde films, almost always in the *version originale* (v.o.). For colorful wandering and café-sitting, afternoons and evenings are best. In the morning, it feels

sleepy. The Latin Quarter stays up late and sleeps in.

In less commercial times, place St. Michel was a gathering point for the city's malcontents and misfits. In 1830, 1848, and again in 1871, the citizens took the streets from the government troops, set up barricades *Les Miz*–style, and fought against royalist oppression. In World War II, the locals rose up against their Nazi oppressors (read the plaques under the dragons at the foot of the St. Michel fountain).

And in the spring of 1968, a time of social upheaval all over the world, young students battled riot batons and tear gas, took over the square, and declared it an independent state. Factory workers followed their call to arms and went on strike, toppling the de Gaulle government and forcing change. Eventually, the students were pacified, the university was reformed, and the Latin Quarter's original cobblestones were replaced with pavement, so future scholars could never again use the streets as weapons.

• *From place St. Michel, look across the river and find the spire of the Sainte-Chapelle church, with its weathervane angel nearby. Cross the river on pont St. Michel and continue north along the boulevard du Palais. On your left, you'll see the doorway to the Sainte-Chapelle. You'll need to pass through a metal detector to get into the Sainte-Chapelle complex. This is more than a tourist attraction—you're entering the courtyard of France's Supreme Court (to the right of Sainte-Chapelle). Once past security, you'll find restrooms ahead on the left. The line into the church may be long (but with a Museum Pass, you can bypass this line).*

Enter the humble ground floor (pick up an English info flier and check the concert schedule if you're interested).

SAINTE-CHAPELLE

Sainte-Chapelle, the triumph of Gothic church architecture, is a cathedral of glass like no other. It was built in 1248 for King Louis IX (the only French king who is now a saint) to house the supposed Crown of Thorns. Its architectural harmony is due to the fact that it was completed under the direction of one architect and in only five years—unheard of in Gothic times. Recall that Notre-Dame took over 200 years.

While the inside is beautiful, the exterior is basically functional. The muscular buttresses hold up the stone roof, so the walls are essentially there to display stained glass. The lacy spire is

Sainte-Chapelle

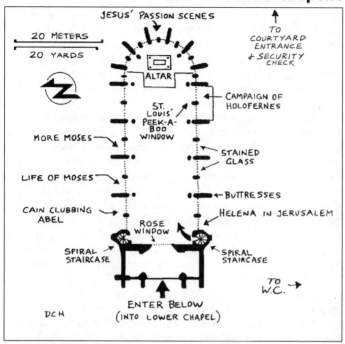

neo-Gothic—added in the 19th century. Inside, the layout clearly shows an *ancien régime* approach to worship. The low-ceilinged basement was for staff and more common folks—worshipping under a sky filled with painted fleurs-de-lis, a symbol of the king. Royal Christians worshipped upstairs. The paint job, a 19th-century restoration, helps you imagine how grand this small, painted, jeweled chapel was. (Imagine Notre-Dame painted like this....) Each capital is playfully carved with a different plant's leaves.

• *Climb the spiral staircase to the Haute Chapelle. Leave the rough stone of the earth and step into the light.*

It takes 13 tourists to build a Gothic church: six columns, six buttresses, and one steeple.

The Stained Glass

Fiat lux. "Let there be light." From the first page of the Bible, it's clear—light is divine. Light shines through stained glass like God's grace shining down to earth, and Gothic architects used

their new technology to turn dark stone buildings into lanterns of light. For me, the glory of Gothic shines brighter here than in any other church.

There are 15 separate panels of stained glass, with more than 1,100 different scenes, mostly from the Bible. These cover the entire Christian history of the world, from the Creation in Genesis (1st window on the left, as you face the altar), to the coming of Christ (over the altar), to the end of the world (the round, "rose"-shaped window at the rear of the church).

Each individual scene is interesting, and the whole effect is overwhelming. Allow yourself a few minutes to bask in the glow of the colored light before tackling the window descriptions below, then remember to keep referring to the map to find the windows.

• *Working clockwise from the entrance, here are some scenes worth a look. (Note: The sun lights up different windows at different times of day. Overcast days give the most even light. On bright, sunny days, some sections are glorious, while others look like a sheet of lead.)*

Genesis—Cain Clubbing Abel (1st window on the left—always dark because of a building butted up against it): On the bottom level in the third circle from left, we see God create the round earth and hold it up. On the next level up, we catch glimpses of naked Adam and Eve. On the third level (far right circle), Cain, in red, clubs his brother Abel, creating murder.

Life of Moses (2nd window, the bottom row of diamond panels): The first panel shows baby Moses in a basket, placed by his sister in the squiggly brown river. Next, he's found by the pharaoh's daughter. Then, he grows up. And finally, he's a man, a prince of Egypt on his royal throne.

More Moses (3rd window, in middle and upper sections): You'll see various scenes of Moses, the guy with the bright yellow horns—the result of a medieval mistranslation of the Hebrew word for "rays of light," or halo.

Jesus' Passion Scenes (over the altar): These scenes from Jesus' arrest and crucifixion were the backdrop for the Crown of Thorns, which originally was displayed on the altar. Stand a few steps back from the altar to look through the canopy to find Jesus in yellow shorts, carrying his cross (5th frame up from right bottom). A little below that, see Jesus being whipped (left) and—the key scene in this relic chapel—Jesus in purple, being fitted with the painful Crown of Thorns (right). Finally (as high as you can see), Jesus on the cross is speared by a soldier (trust me).

Campaign of Holofernes: On the bottom row are four scenes of colorful knights (refer to map to get reoriented). The second

Stained Glass Supreme

Craftsmen made glass—which is, essentially, melted sand—using this recipe:

- Melt one part sand with two parts wood ash.
- Mix in rusty metals to get different colors—iron makes red, cobalt makes blue, copper green, manganese purple, cadmium yellow.
- Blow glass into a cylinder shape, cut lengthwise, and lay flat.
- Cut into pieces with an iron tool, or by heating and cooling a select spot to make it crack.
- Fit pieces together to form a figure, using strips of lead to hold in place.
- Place masterpiece so high on a wall that no one can read it.

circle from the left is a battle scene (the campaign of Holofernes), showing three soldiers with swords slaughtering three men. The background is blue. The men have different-colored clothes—red, blue, green, mauve, and white. Notice some of the details. You can see the folds in the robes, the hair, and facial features. Look at the victim in the center—his head is splotched with blood. Details like the folds in the robes (see the victim in white, lower left) came either by scratching on the glass or by baking on paint. It was a painstaking process of finding just the right colors, fitting them together to make a scene...and then multiplying by 1,100.

Helena in Jerusalem (1st window on the right wall by entrance): This window tells the story of how Christ's Crown of Thorns found its way from Jerusalem to Constantinople to this chapel. Start in the lower left corner, where the Roman emperor Constantine (in blue, on his throne) waves goodbye to his Christian mom, Helena. She arrives at the gate of Jerusalem (next panel to the right). Her men (in the two-part medallion above Jerusalem) dig through ruins and find Christ's (tiny) cross and other relics. She returns to Constantinople with a stash of holy relics, including the Crown of Thorns. Nine hundred years later, French Crusader knights (the next double medallion above) invade the Holy Land and visit Constantinople. Finally, King Louis IX, dressed in blue (in the panel up one and to the right of

the last one) returns to France with the sacred relic.

Rose Window (above entrance): It's Judgment Day, with a tiny Christ in the center of the chaos and miracles. This window is 200 years newer then the rest, from the Flamboyant period. Facing west and the sunset, it's best late in the day.

If you can't read much into the individual windows, you're not alone. (For some tutoring, a little book with color photos is on sale downstairs with the postcards.)

Altar

The altar was raised up high to better display the relic around which this chapel was built—the Crown of Thorns. This was the crown

put on Jesus when the Romans were torturing and humiliating him before his execution. Notice the staircase: Access was limited to the priest and the king, who wore the keys to the shrine around his neck. Also see that there is no high profile image of Jesus anywhere—this chapel was all about the Crown.

King Louis IX, convinced he'd found the real McCoy, paid £135,000 for the Crown, £100,000 for the gem-studded shrine to display it in (destroyed in the French Revolution), and a mere £40,000 to build Sainte-Chapelle to house it. Today, the supposed Crown of

Thorns is kept in the Notre-Dame Treasury (and shown only on the 1st Friday of the month and during Easter).

Lay your camera on the ground and shoot the ceiling. Those pure and simple ribs growing out of the slender columns are the essence of Gothic structure.

• *Exit Sainte-Chapelle. Back outside, as you walk around the church exterior, look down to see the foundation and notice how much Paris has risen in the 750 years since Sainte-Chapelle was built. Next door to Sainte-Chapelle is the...*

Palais de Justice

Sainte-Chapelle sits within a huge complex of buildings that has housed the local government since ancient Roman times. It was the site of the original Gothic palace of the early kings of France. The only surviving medieval parts are Sainte-Chapelle and the Conciergerie prison.

Most of the site is now covered by the giant Palais de Justice,

Sainte-Chapelle Area

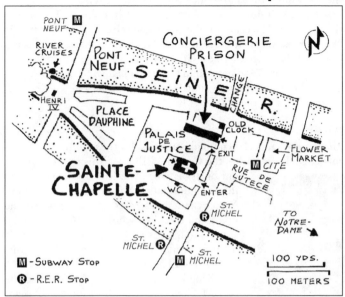

built in 1776, home of the French Supreme Court. The motto *Liberté, Egalité, Fraternité* (Liberty, Equality, Brotherhood) over the doors is a reminder that this was also the headquarters of the Revolutionary government. Here, they doled out justice, condemning many to imprison-  ment in the Conciergerie downstairs or to the guillotine.

• *Now pass through the big iron gate to the noisy boulevard du Palais. Cross the street to the wide pedestrian-only rue de Lutèce and walk about halfway down.*

Cité "Metropolitain" Stop

Of the 141 original, early-20th-century subway entrances, this is one of only a few survivors—now preserved as a national art treasure. (New York's Museum of Modern Art even exhibits one.) It marks Paris at its peak in 1900—on the cutting edge of modernism, but with an eye to beauty. The curvy, plantlike ironwork is a textbook example of Art Nouveau, the style that rebelled against the erector-set squareness of the Industrial Age. In Paris, only the stations at Abbesses and Porte Dauphine survive with their canopies.

The flower and plant market on place Louis Lépine is a pleasant detour. On Sundays, this square is all aflutter with a busy bird market. And across the way is the Prefecture de Police, where Inspector Clouseau of Pink Panther fame used to work, and where the local resistance fighters took the first building from the Nazis in August of 1944, leading to the Allied liberation of Paris a week later.

• *Pause here to admire the view. Sainte-Chapelle is a pearl in an ugly architectural oyster. Double back to the Palais de Justice, turn right and enter the Conciergerie (entrance on boulevard du Palais). Though pretty barren inside, the Conciergerie echoes with history and is free with the Museum Pass.*

Conciergerie

Positioned next to the courthouse, the Conciergerie was the gloomy prison famous as the last stop for 2,780 victims of the guillotine, including France's last Old Regime queen, Marie-Antoinette. Before then, kings had used the building to torture and execute failed assassins. (One of its towers along the river was called "the babbler," named for the pain-induced sounds that leaked from it.) When the Revolution (1789) toppled the king, the building kept its same function, but without torture. The progressive Revolutionaries proudly unveiled a modern and more humane way to execute people—the guillotine.

Inside, pick up a free map and breeze through. See the spacious, low-ceilinged Hall of Men-at-Arms (Room 2), with four large fireplaces, used as a guard room. This big room gives a feel for the grandeur of the Great Hall (upstairs, not open to visitors) where the Revolutionary tribunals grilled scared prisoners on their political correctness. The raised area at the far end of the room (Room 4, today's bookstore) was notorious as the walkway of the executioner, who was known affectionately as "Monsieur de Paris."

Upstairs is the Prisoners' Gallery, a hall where the condemned milled about, waiting for the open-air cart (tumbrel) to pull up outside to carry them to the guillotine on place de la Concorde. Some reconstructed cells show how the poor slept on straw, while the wealthy got a cot.

Up a few more steps is a memorial room with the names of the 2,780 citizens condemned to death by the guillotine. In alphabetical order, find: Anne-Elizabeth Capet (whose crime was being "sister of the tyrant"), Charlotte Corday (a noblewoman who snuck into the bathroom of the revolutionary writer, Jean-Paul Marat,

and stabbed him while he bathed), Georges Danton (prominent revolutionary who was later condemned for being insufficiently liberal, a nasty crime), Louis XVI ("called Capet: last king of France"), Marie-Antoinette, and—oh, the irony—Maximilien de Robespierre, the head of the Revolution, the man who sent so many to the guillotine, and who was eventually toppled, humiliated, imprisoned here, and beheaded.

Back downstairs, arrows lead through a small museum (with a guillotine blade) to a chapel that was the actual cell of Marie-Antoinette. The chapel was made by Louis XVIII, the brother of beheaded Louis XVI and the first king back on the throne after the restoration (in 1815, once Napoleon was booted). The paintings show Marie-Antoinette in her cell and receiving the Last Sacrament on the night before her beheading. The walls drip with silver embroidered tears.

The tour continues outside in the courtyard, where women prisoners were allowed a little fresh air (notice the original spikes still guarding from above). In the corner a door leads to a re-creation of Marie-Antoinette's cell (Room 12). Imagine the queen spending her last days—separated from her 10-year-old son, and now widowed because the king had already been executed. Mannequins, period furniture, and the real cell wallpaper set the scene. The guard stands modestly behind a screen while the queen psyches herself up with a crucifix. In the glass display case, see her actual crucifix, napkin, and small water pitcher. On October 16, 1793, the queen walked the corridor, stepped onto the cart, and was slowly carried to place de la Concorde, where she had a date with "Monsieur de Paris." A video in the next room gives a taste of prison life during the Reign of Terror.

• *Back outside, turn left on boulevard du Palais and head toward the river (north). On the corner is the city's oldest public clock. The mechanism of the present clock is from 1334, and even though the case is Baroque, it keeps on ticking.*

Turn left onto quai de l'Horloge and walk west along the river, past the round medieval tower called "the babbler." The bridge up ahead is the pont Neuf, where we'll end this walk. At the first corner, veer left into a sleepy triangular square called place Dauphine.

Place Dauphine

It's amazing to find such coziness in the heart of Paris. This city of two million is still a city of neighborhoods, a collection of villages. The French Supreme Court building looms behind like a

giant marble gavel. Enjoy the village-Paris feeling in the park. The
Caveau du Palais restaurant is well-placed on this tranquil park
for a drink or reasonable meal (day or night, 19 place Dauphine,
tel. 01 43 26 04 48). **La Rose de France** (opposite) is less expensive
and more casual. You may see lawyers on their lunch break playing
boules (see sidebar on page 312).
• *Continue through place Dauphine. As you pop out the other end, you're
face to face with a...*

Statue of Henry IV

Henry IV (1553–1610) is not as famous as his grandson, Louis
XIV, but Henry helped make Paris what it is today—a European
capital of elegant buildings and quiet squares. He built the place
Dauphine (behind you), the pont Neuf (to the right), residences
(to the left, down rue Dauphine), the Louvre's long Grand Gallery
(downriver on the right), and the tree-filled square Vert-Galant
(directly behind the statue, on the tip of the island). The square
is one of Paris' makeout spots; its name comes from Henry's own
nickname, the Green Knight, as Henry was a notorious ladies'
man. The park is a great place to relax, dangling your legs over the
concrete prow of this boat-shaped island.
• *From the statue, turn right onto the old bridge. Pause at the little nook
halfway across.*

Pont Neuf

The pont Neuf, or "new bridge," is Paris' oldest standing bridge
(built 1578–1607). Its 12 arches span the widest part of the river.
Unlike other bridges, this one never had houses or buildings growing on it. The turrets were originally for vendors and street entertainers. In the days of Henry IV, who promised his peasants "a
chicken in every pot every Sunday," this would have been a lively
scene. From the bridge, look downstream (west) to see the next
bridge, the pedestrian-only pont des Arts. Ahead on the Right
Bank is the long Louvre Museum. Beyond that, on the Left Bank
is the Orsay. And what's that tall black tower in the distance?

The Seine

Our walk ends where Paris began—on the Seine River. From
Dijon to the English Channel, the Seine meanders 500 miles,
cutting through the center of Paris. The river is shallow and slow
within the city, but still dangerous enough to require steep stone
embankments (built 1910) to prevent occasional floods.

In summer, the roads that run along the river are replaced
with acres of sand, as well as beach chairs and tanned locals, creating Paris *Plage* (see page 49). The success of the Paris *Plage* event
has motivated some city officials to propose the permanent removal

of vehicles from those fast lanes—turning this into riverside parks instead.

Any time of year, you'll see tourist boats and the commercial barges that carry 20 percent of Paris' transported goods. And on the banks, sportsmen today cast into the waters once fished by Paris' original Celtic inhabitants.

• *We're done. You can take a boat tour that leaves from near the base of pont Neuf on the island side (Vedettes du Pont Neuf, €10, tip requested, departs hourly on the hour, 2/hr after dark, has live guide with explanations in French and English). Or you could take my Left Bank Walk, which begins one bridge downriver (see page 135). Or catch the Métro to anywhere in Paris (the nearest Métro stop is Pont Neuf, across the bridge on the Right Bank).*

CHAMPS-ELYSEES WALK

*From the Arc de Triomphe
to the Tuileries Gardens*

Don't leave Paris without strolling the avenue des Champs-Elysées. This is Paris at its most Parisian: monumental sidewalks, stylish shops, grand cafés, and glimmering showrooms. This walk covers about three miles and takes three hours if done completely. It's a great stroll day or night. Métro stops are located about every three blocks along the Champs-Elysées (shahnz ay-lee-zay).

ORIENTATION

Arc de Triomphe: €8, covered by Museum Pass, daily April–Sept 10:00–23:00, Oct–March 10:00–22:30, last entry 30 min before closing, Mo: Charles de Gaulle-Etoile, tel. 01 43 80 31 31. The elevator, which runs to the museum level but not to the top (requires a 40-step climb), is only for the disabled.

Cuisine Art: Comptoir de L'Arc, a block from the Arc de Triomphe, is a bustling place dishing out good €11 salads and *plats du jour* (specials of the day) to local workers in refined surroundings just beyond the tourist flow (Mon–Fri 7:00–24:00, closed Sat–Sun, 73 avenue Marceau).

      Hôtel Crillon, on place de la Concorde, serves high tea daily 15:30–18:00 (tel. 01 44 71 15 00).

THE WALK BEGINS

Start at the Arc de Triomphe (take the Métro to Charles de Gaulle-Etoile, then follow *Sortie #1, Champs-Elysées/Arc de Triomphe* signs). At the top of the Champs-Elysées, face the arch. Underground WCs are on the other (south) side of Champs-Elysées, and an underground walkway leading to the arch is in front of you. Get to that arch. It's worthwhile even if you don't climb it; there's no

Champs-Elysées Walk

M – SUBWAY STOP

1 Arc de Triomphe
2 Comptoir de l'Arc Rest.
3 Dresdner Bank Building
4 McDonald's & Peugeot
5 Mercedes-Benz & Lido
6 Fouquet's Café-Rest.
7 Ladurée Tea Salon
8 Thomas Jefferson Plaque & Club Med
9 Arcades des Champs-Elysées, Sephora & English Pharmacy
10 Renault
11 Virgin Music, Disney, Gap & Quiksilver
12 De Gaulle Statue
13 Obelisk of Luxor
14 Hôtel Crillon
15 Pont de la Concorde
16 U. S. Embassy
17 U. S. Consulate
18 W. H. Smith Books

charge to wander around the base. Cross through the tunnel, take the first left up a few steps and buy your ticket (skip the ticket line if you have a Museum Pass or aren't ascending), then walk up to the arch. Stroll around left toward the Champs-Elysées, turn around, and face the arch.

The Arc de Triomphe
Exterior
The construction of the 165-foot-high arch was begun in 1809 to honor Napoleon's soldiers, who, in spite of being vastly outnumbered by the Austrians, scored a remarkable victory at the Battle of Austerlitz. Patterned after the ceremonial arches of ancient Roman conquerors (but more than twice the size), it celebrates Napoleon as emperor of a "New Rome." On the arch's massive left pillar, a relief sculpture shows a toga-clad Napoleon posing confidently, while an awestruck Paris—crowned by her city walls—kneels at his imperial feet. Napoleon died prior to the Arc's completion, but it was finished in time for his 1840 funeral procession to pass underneath, carrying his remains (19 years dead) from exile in St. Helena to Paris.

On the right pillar is the Arc's most famous relief, *La Marseillaise* (*Le Départ des Volontaires de 1792*, by François Rude). Lady Liberty—looking like an ugly reincarnation of Joan of Arc—screams, "Freedom is this way!" and points the direction with a sword. The soldiers below her are tired, naked, and stumbling, but she rallies them to carry on the fight against oppression.

Today, the Arc de Triomphe is dedicated to the glory of all French armies. Walk to its center and stand directly beneath (on

the faded eagle), surrounded by the lists of French victories since the Revolution—19th century on the arch, 20th century in the pavement. On the columns, you'll see lists of generals (with a line under the names of those who died in battle). Nearby, stand on the bronze plaque at the foot of the Tomb of the Unknown Soldier (from World War I). Every day at 18:30 since just after World War I, the flame has been rekindled and new flowers set in place.

Like its Roman ancestors, this arch has served as a parade gateway for triumphal armies (French or foe) and important ceremonies. From 1940 to 1944, a large swastika flew from here as Nazis goose-stepped down the Champs-Elysées. In August 1944, Charles de Gaulle led allied troops under this arch as they

celebrated liberation. Today, national parades start and end here with one minute of silence.

Interior and View from the Top

Ascend the Arc de Triomphe via the 284 steps—the staircase is inside the north pillar (the one closest to the ticket office). A wall mural by the ticket booth gives a sneak preview for the lazy (or those wondering if it's worth the climb).

Two-thirds of the way up, catch your breath in the small museum of the arch's history. You'll see photographs of the post-WWI victory parade under the arch *(Le Défilé de la Victoire)*, led by Allied commander-in-chief Marshal Ferdinand Foch. Stand next to screaming Lady Liberty's huge head. Find the black, framed picture of an enormous coffin placed under the arch to see how France mourned the death of the famous writer Victor Hugo. A display is devoted to various designs of the arch *(L'Achèvement de l'Arc de Triomphe)*. Ponder what other grand structure might have been placed on this spot if Napoleon hadn't come up with an arch. (The giant elephant was an actual proposal.)

From the top, you have an eye-popping view of *toute Paris*. You're gazing at the home of 11 million people, all crammed into an area the size of an average city in the States (the city center has 2,150,000 residents and covers 40 square miles). Paris has the highest density of any city in Europe, about 20 times greater than that of New York City.

Look down the Champs-Elysées east to the Tuileries Garden and the Louvre. Scan the cityscape of downtown Paris. Notice the symmetry. Each corner building surrounding the arch is part of an elegant grand scheme. The beauty of Paris—basically a flat basin with a river running through it—is man-made, with a harmonious relationship between the width of its grand boulevards and the uniformity in the height and design of the buildings. That lonely hill to the left is Montmartre, topped by the white dome of Sacré-Cœur; until 1860, this hill town was a separate city. Panning slowly to the right, see the blue top of the Pompidou Center, then the distant twin towers of Notre-Dame, the "state-capitol-dome" of the Panthéon, a block of small skyscrapers on a hill (the Quartier d'Italie), the golden

dome of Les Invalides, and the lonely-looking Montparnasse Tower, standing like the box the Eiffel Tower came in. It served as a wakeup call in the early 1970s to preserve the building height restrictions and strengthen urban design standards.

Cross the arch and look to the west. In the distance, the huge, white, rectangular Grande Arche de la Défense, standing amid skyscrapers, is the final piece of a grand city axis—from the Louvre, up the Champs-Elysées to the Arc de Triomphe, continuing as the avenue de la Grande Armée, and ending in a forest of skyscrapers at La Défense, three miles away. Former French President François Mitterrand had the Grande Arche built as a centerpiece of this mini-Manhattan (see page 64). Notice the contrast between the skyscrapers of La Défense and the uniform heights of the buildings closer to the Arc de Triomphe. Below you, the wide boulevard lined with grass and trees angling to your left is avenue Foch (named after the WWI hero), the best address to have in Paris (the Shah of Iran and Aristotle Onassis had homes here). The huge park at the end of avenue Foch is the Bois de Boulogne.

Gaze down at what appears to be a chaotic traffic mess. The 12 boulevards that radiate from the Arc de Triomphe (forming an *étoile*, or star) were part of Baron Haussmann's master plan for Paris: the creation of a series of major boulevards, intersecting at diagonals with monuments (such as the Arc de Triomphe) as centerpieces of those intersections.

His plan did not anticipate the automobile—obvious when you watch the traffic scene below. But see how smoothly it really functions. Cars entering the circle have the right of way (the only roundabout in France with this rule); those in the circle must yield. Still, there are plenty of accidents, often caused by tourists oblivious to the rules. Tired of disputes, insurance companies split the fault and damages of any Arc de Triomphe accident 50/50. The trick is to make a parabola—get to the center ASAP, and then begin working your way out two avenues before you want to exit.

• *We'll start our stroll down the Champs-Elysées at the Charles de Gaulle-Etoile Métro stop, on the north (sunnier) side of the street where the tunnel redeposits you. Look straight down the Champs-Elysées to the Tuileries Garden at the far end.*

The Champs-Elysées

You're at the top of one of the world's grandest and most celebrated streets, home to big business, celebrity cafés, glitzy nightclubs, high-fashion shopping, and international people-watching.

In 1667, Louis XIV opened the first section of the street as a short extension of the Tuileries Garden. This date is a considered the birth of Paris as a grand city. The Champs-Elysées soon became *the* place to cruise in your carriage. (It still is today—traffic can be jammed up even at midnight.) One hundred years later, the café scene arrived.

From the 1920s until the 1960s, this boulevard was pure elegance. Parisians actually dressed up to come here. It was mainly

residences, rich hotels, and cafés. Then, in 1963, the government pumped up the neighborhood's commercial metabolism by bringing in the RER (commuter train). Suburbanites had easy access, and pfft—there went the neighborhood.

• *Start your descent, pausing at the first tiny street you cross, rue de Tilsitt. This street is part of a shadow ring road—an option for drivers who'd like to avoid the chaos of the arch, complete with stoplights.*

A half block down rue de Tilsitt is the Dresdner Bank building's entry. It's one of the few survivors of a dozen uniformly U-shaped buildings in Haussman's original 1853 grand design. Peek into the foyer for a glimpse of 19th-century Champs-Elysées classiness.

Back on the main drag, look across to the other side of the Champs-Elysées at the big, gray, concrete-and-glass "Publicis" building. Ugh. In the 1960s, venerable old buildings (similar to the Dresdner Bank building) were leveled to make way for new commercial operations like Publicis. Then, in 1985, a law prohibited the demolition of the old building fronts that gave the boulevard a uniform grace. Today, many modern businesses hide behind preserved facades. Consider dashing to the center of the Champs for a great Arc view, then come back.

The coming of McDonald's—farther down on the left at #140—was a shock to the boulevard. At first, it was allowed to have only white arches painted on the window. Today, it spills out legally onto the sidewalk—provided it offers café-quality chairs and flower boxes—and dining *chez MacDo* has become typically Parisian. A €3 Big Mac here buys an hour of people-watching. (There's a WC inside.)

The *nouveau* Champs-Elysées, revitalized in 1994, has new benches and lamps, broader sidewalks, and a fleet of green-suited workers armed with high-tech pooper-scoopers. Blink away the modern elements, and it's not hard to imagine the boulevard pre-1963, with only the finest structures lining both sides all the way to the palace gardens.

Glitz

Fancy car dealerships include Peugeot, at #136 (showing off its futuristic concept cars next to the classic models), and Mercedes-Benz, a block down at #118. In the 19th century, this was an area for horse stables; today, it's the district of garages, limo companies, and car dealerships. If you're serious about selling cars in France, you must have a showroom on the Champs-Elysées.

Next to Mercedes is the famous Lido, Paris' largest cabaret (and a multiplex cinema). Walk way in. Check out the perky photos, R-rated videos, and shocking prices. Paris still offers the kind of burlesque-type spectacles combining music, comedy, and scantily

clad women performed here since the 19th century. Moviegoing on the Champs-Elysées is also popular, with theaters showing the very latest releases. Check to see if there are films you recognize, then look for the showings *(séances)*. A "v.o." *(version originale)* next to the time indicates the film will be in its original language.

• *Now cross the boulevard. Look up at the Arc de Triomphe, its rooftop bristling with tourists. Notice the architecture—old and elegant, new, and new-behind-old facades.*

Café Culture

Fouquet's café-restaurant (#99), under the red awning, is a popular spot among French celebrities, serving the most expensive shot of espresso I've found in downtown Paris (€4.80). Opened in 1899 as a coachman's bistro, Fouquet's gained fame as the hangout of France's WWI biplane fighter pilots—those who weren't shot down by Germany's infamous "Red Baron." It also served as James Joyce's dining room. Since the early 1900s, Fouquet's has been a favorite of French actors and actresses. The golden plaques by the entrance honor winners of France's Oscar-like film awards, the Césars—see plaques for Gérard Depardieu, Catherine Deneuve, Roman Polanski, Juliette Binoche, and many famous Americans (but not Jerry Lewis). Recent winners are shown inside. While the hushed interior is at once classy and intimidating, it's a grand experience if you dare (the outdoor setting is also great, and more relaxed). Fouquet's was recently saved from foreign purchase and eventual destruction when the government declared it a historic monument.

Ladurée (2 blocks downhill at #75, with green and purple awning) is a classic 19th-century tea salon/restaurant/*pâtisserie*. Its interior is right out of the 1860s. Wander in...even peeking into the cozy rooms upstairs. A coffee here is *très élégant* (only €3.30). The bakery sells traditional macaroons, cute little cakes, and gift-wrapped finger sandwiches to go (your choice of 4 mini-macaroons for €6).

• *Cross back to the lively (north) side of the street.*

At #92 (opposite Ladurée), a wall plaque marks the place Thomas Jefferson lived (with his 14-year-old slave, Sally Hemings) while serving as minister to France (1785–1789). He replaced the popular Benjamin Franklin, but quickly made his own mark, extolling the virtues of America's Revolution to a country approaching its own.

Club Med (#88), with its travel ads to sunny destinations, is a reminder of the French commitment to the vacation. Since 1936, the French, by law, have enjoyed five weeks of paid vacation (and every Catholic holiday invented). In the swinging '60s, Club Med made hedonism accessible to the middle-class French masses.

French Shopping

Stroll into the Arcades des Champs-Elysées mall at #76 (not the unappealing Galerie des Champs-Elysées, next door to Club Med). With its fancy lamps, mosaic floors, glass skylight, and classical columns, it captures faint echoes of the *années folles*—the "crazy years," as the roaring '20s were called in France. Architecture buffs can observe how flowery Art Nouveau became simpler, more geometrical Art Deco. Down the street, Galerie du Claridge (at #74) is a fine example of an old facade—with an ironwork awning, balconies, *putti*, and sculpted fantasy faces—fronting a new building.

Take your nose sightseeing at #72; glide down Sephora's ramp into a vast hall of cosmetics and perfumes (Mon–Sat 10:00–24:00, Sun 11:00–24:00). Grab a disposable white strip from a lovely clerk, spritz it with a sample, and sniff. The store is thoughtfully laid out: The entry hall (on the right) is lined with the new products—all open and ready (with sniff strips) to sample. In the main showroom, women's perfumes line the right wall and men's line the left wall—organized alphabetically by company, from Armani to Versace. The mesmerizing music, carefully chosen just for Sephora, actually made me crave cosmetics. At the rear of the store, you can have your face made over and your nails fixed like new. You can also get the advice of a "skin consultant."

At the corner of rue la Boétie, the English pharmacy is open until midnight, and map-lovers can detour one block down this street to shop at Espace IGN (Institut Géographique National), France's version of the National Geographic Society.

Car buffs and *Star Trek* fans should detour across the Champs and park themselves at the space-age bar in the Renault store (open until midnight, €2.50 espresso). The car exhibits change regularly, but the high-backed leather chairs looking down onto the Champs-Elysées are permanent.

International Shopping

Back on earth, a block farther down, the Virgin Megastore (#54) sells a world of music. Nearby, the Disney, Gap, and Quiksilver stores are reminders of global economics—the French seem to love these places as much as Americans do.

Rond-Point and Beyond

At the Rond-Point des Champs-Elysées, the shopping ends and the park begins. This round, leafy traffic circle is always colorful, lined with flowers or seasonal decorations (thousands of pumpkins at Halloween, hundreds of decorated trees at Christmas).

A long block past the Rond-Point, at avenue de Marigny, look to the other side of the Champs-Elysées to find a new statue of Charles de Gaulle—ramrod straight and striding out as he did

the day Paris was liberated in 1944. Charles stands in front of the glass-and-steel-domed Grand and Petit Palais exhibition halls, built for the 1900 World's Fair. Today, these examples of the "can-do" spirit of the early 20th century are museums. Impressive temporary exhibits fill the huge Grand Palais (on right, €10.50, €9 after 13:00, not covered by Museum Pass; get details on current exhibitions from TIs or in *Pariscope*). The Petit Palais (left side)—scheduled to reopen in the spring of 2006—houses a permanent collection of lesser paintings by Eugène Delacroix, Paul Cézanne, Claude Monet, Camille Pissarro, and other 18th-century masters.

Beyond the two palaces, pont Alexandre III leads over the Seine to the golden dome of Les Invalides. For the best view, walk to the center of the road. This exquisite bridge, spiked with golden statues and ironwork lamps, was built to celebrate a turn-of-the-20th-century treaty between France and Russia. Like the Grand and Petit Palais, it's a fine example of belle époque exuberance.

Les Invalides was built by Louis XIV as a veterans' hospital for his battle-weary troops (see Napoleon's Tomb and Army Museums Tour on page 259). The esplanade leading up to Les Invalides—possibly the largest patch of accessible grass in Paris—gives soccer balls and Frisbees a rare-in-Paris welcome.

From here, it's a straight shot down the last stretch of the Champs-Elysées. The plane trees (a kind of sycamore with peeling bark that does well in big-city pollution) are reminiscent of the big push Napoleon III made, planting 600,000 trees to green up the city.

• *View the 21-acre place de la Concorde from the obelisk in the center.*

Place de la Concorde

During the Revolution, this was the place de la Révolution. Many of the 2,780 beheaded during the Revolution lost their bodies here during the Reign of Terror. The guillotine sat on this square. A bronze plaque in the ground in front of the obelisk memorializes the place where Louis XVI, Marie-Antoinette, Georges Danton, Charlotte Corday, and Maximilien de Robespierre, among many others, were made "a foot shorter on top." Three people worked the guillotine: One managed the blade, one held the blood bucket, and one caught the head, raising it high to the roaring crowd.

The 3,300-year-old, 72-foot, 220-ton, red granite, hieroglyph-inscribed obelisk of Luxor now forms the centerpiece of place de la Concorde. Here—on the spot where Louis XVI was beheaded—his brother (Charles X) honored the executed with this obelisk. (Charles became king when the monarchy was restored after Napoleon.) It was carted here from Egypt in the 1830s. The gold pictures on the pedestal tell the story of its incredible two-year journey: Pulled down from the entrance to Ramses II's Temple of

Amon in Luxor; encased in wood; loaded onto a boat built to navigate both shallow rivers and open seas; floated down the Nile, across the Mediterranean, along the Atlantic coast, and up the Seine; and unloaded here, where it was re-erected in 1836. Its glittering gold-leaf cap is a recent addition  (1998), replacing the original stolen 2,500 years ago.

The obelisk also forms a center point along a line locals call the "royal perspective." You can hang a lot of history along this straight line (Louvre–obelisk–Arc de Triomphe–Grande Arche de la Défense). The Louvre symbolizes the old regime (divine right rule by kings and queens). The obelisk and place de la Concorde symbolize the people's revolution (cutting off the king's head). The Arc de Triomphe calls to mind the triumph of nationalism (victorious armies carrying national flags under the arch). And the huge modern arch in the distance, surrounded by the headquarters of multinational corporations, heralds a future in which business entities are more powerful than nations.

Across the river (south) stands the building where the French National Assembly meets (similar to our Congress). On the north side of place de la Concorde is Hôtel Crillon, Paris' most exclusive hotel. Of the twin buildings that guard the entrance to rue Royale (which leads to the Greek-style Church of the Madeleine), it's the one on the left. This hotel is so fancy that one of its belle époque rooms is displayed in New York's Metropolitan Museum of Art. Eleven years before the king lost his head on this square, Louis XVI met with Benjamin Franklin in this hotel to sign a treaty recognizing the United States as an independent country. (Today's low-profile, heavily fortified American Embassy is located next door.) For a memorable splurge, consider high tea at the Crillon (see "Les Grands Cafés de Paris," page 364).

And from the base of the Champs-Elysées, the beautiful Tuileries Garden leads through the iron gates to the Louvre (with a public WC just inside on the right). Pull up a chair next to the pond, or find one of the cafés in the gardens.

Nearby

Your guided walk is over. From here, you can go to the closest Métro stop (Concorde), north to a fancy shopping area (near place de la Madeleine—see page 380), into the park toward the Louvre, or across the river toward the Orsay Museum (read on).

If you walk to the river, you'll cross a freeway underpass similar to the one at the pont de l'Alma, three bridges downstream,

where Princess Diana lost her life in a 1997 car accident. The pont de la Concorde, built of stones from the Bastille prison (which was demolished by the Revolution in 1789), symbolizes that, with good government, *concorde* (harmony) can come from chaos. Stand mid-bridge and gaze upriver (east). If you use an imaginary clock as a compass, the Impressionist art museum L'Orangerie hides behind the trees at 10:00, and the tall building with the skinny chimneys at 11:00 is the architectural caboose of the sprawling Louvre palace. The thin spire of Sainte-Chapelle is dead center at 12:00, with the twin towers of Notre-Dame to its right. The Orsay Museum is closer on the right, connected with the Tuileries Garden by a sleek pedestrian bridge (the next bridge upriver).

MARAIS WALK

From Place Bastille to the Pompidou Center

This walk takes you through one of Paris' most characteristic quarters, the Marais, and finishes in the artsy Beaubourg district. When in Paris, you naturally want to see the big sights, but to experience the city you also need to visit a vital neighborhood.

The Marais, containing more pre-Revolutionary lanes and buildings than anywhere else in town, is more atmospheric than touristy. It's medieval Paris and the haunt of the old nobility. After the aristocrats left, the Marais became a dumpy bohemian quarter so sordid, it was nearly slated for destruction. But today, this thriving, trendy, real community is a joy to explore. It looks the way much of the city did until the mid-1800s, when Napoleon III had Baron Georges-Eugene Haussmann blast out the narrow streets to construct broad boulevards (wide enough for the guns and ranks of the army, too wide for revolutionary barricades), thus creating modern Paris. A big Haussmann-type boulevard was planned to slice efficiently through the Marais, but World War I got in the way.

ORIENTATION

Victor Hugo's House: Free, Tue–Sun 10:00–18:00, last entry 17:40, closed Mon, 6 place des Vosges.

Carnavalet Museum: Free, Tue–Sun 10:00–18:00, closed Mon, 23 rue de Sévigné.

Picasso Museum: €5.50, covered by Museum Pass, free first Sun of month, April–Sept Wed–Mon 9:30–18:00, Oct–March Wed–Mon 9:30–17:30, closed Tue, 5 rue de Thorigny.

Jewish Art and History Museum: €7, not covered by Museum Pass, Mon–Fri 11:00–18:00, Sun 10:00–18:00, closed Sat, 71 rue du Temple.

Marais Walk

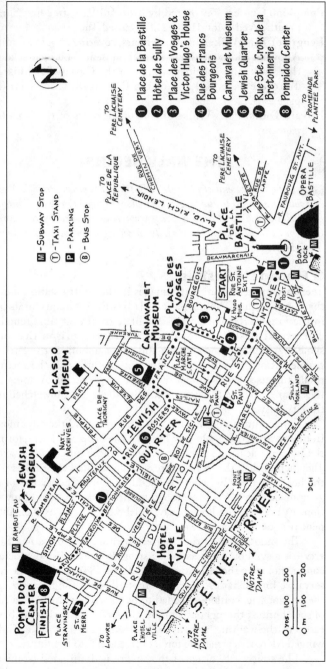

1 Place de la Bastille
2 Hôtel de Sully
3 Place des Vosges &
   Victor Hugo's House
4 Rue des Francs
   Bourgeois
5 Carnavalet Museum
6 Jewish Quarter
7 Rue Ste. Croix de la
   Bretonnerie
8 Pompidou Center

Ⓜ - Subway Stop
Ⓣ - Taxi Stand
Ⓟ - Parking
Ⓑ - Bus Stop

Pompidou Center: €7, covered by Museum Pass, free first Sun of month, Wed–Mon 11:00–21:00, closed Tue.

Length of This Walk: About two hours, covering about two miles. Allow an additional hour for each museum you include along this walk, and consider adding in the Carnavalet Museum Tour (see page 216) and/or the Picasso Museum Tour (see page 231).

Private Tours: Paris Walks offers guided tours of this area (see page 36).

THE WALK BEGINS

• *Start at the west end of place de la Bastille. From the Bastille Métro, exit following signs to rue St. Antoine (not the signs to rue du Faubourg St. Antoine). Ascend onto a noisy square dominated by the bronze Colonne de Juillet (July Column). The bronze god on the top is, like you, headed west.*

❶ Place de la Bastille

There are more revolutionary images in the Métro station murals than on the square. While place de la Bastille is famous for its part in the French Revolution of 1789, little from that time remains. The actual Bastille, a royal-fortress-turned-prison that once symbolized old-regime tyranny and now symbolizes the Parisian emancipation, is long gone. Only a brick outline of the fortress' round turrets survives (under the traffic where rue St. Antoine hits the square), though the story of the Bastille is indelibly etched into the city's psyche.

For centuries, the Bastille was used to defend the city (mostly from its own people). On July 14, 1789, the people of Paris stormed the prison, releasing its seven prisoners and hoping to find arms. They demolished the stone fortress and decorated their pikes with the heads of a few bigwigs. By shedding blood, the leaders of the gang made sure it would be tough to turn back the tides of revolution. Ever since, the French have celebrated July 14 as their independence day—Bastille Day.

The monument on the square—with its gilded statue of liberty—is a symbol of France's long struggle to establish democracy, commemorating the revolutions of 1830 and 1848. In 1830, the conservative king Charles X—who forgot all about the Revolution of the previous generation—needed to be tossed out. In 1848, a time of social unrest throughout Europe, the streets of Paris were barricaded by the working class, as dramatized in *Les Misérables*. Today, winged Mercury carries the torch of freedom into the future.

The southeast corner of the square is dominated (some say overwhelmed) by the flashy, curved, glassy-gray facade of the

controversial **Opéra Bastille**. In a symbolic attempt to bring high culture to the masses, former French President François Mitterrand

chose this square for the building that would become Paris' main opera venue, edging out Paris' earlier "palace of the rich," the Garnier-designed opera house (see page 60). Designed by the Uruguayan architect Carlos Ott, this grand Parisian project was opened with fanfare by Mitterrand on the 200th Bastille Day, July 14, 1989. While tickets are heavily subsidized to encourage the unwashed masses to attend, how much high culture they have actually enjoyed here is a subject of debate. (For opera ticket information, see page 390.)

You'll now turn your back on this Haussmann-style grandeur and walk down what was—before the Revolution—one of the grandest streets in Paris, rue St. Antoine. In 1350, there was a gate to the city here, Porte St. Antoine, defended by a drawbridge and fortress—a *bastille*.

• *Passing the Banque de France on your right (opposite a fine map of the area on the curb), head west down rue St. Antoine about four blocks into the Marais. At the intersection with rue de Birague, old hippies may wish to make a 100-yard detour to the left, down rue Beautrellis to #17, the nondescript apartment where Jim Morrison died. (For more on Jim, see page 290.) Otherwise, continue down rue St. Antoine, and at 62 rue St. Antoine, enter the grand courtyard of Hôtel de Sully (open until 19:00, fine bookstore inside). If the hotel is closed, you'll need to backtrack one block to rue de Birague to reach the next stop, place des Vosges.*

❷ Hôtel de Sully

During the reign of Henry IV, this area—originally a swamp *(marais)*—became the hometown of the French aristocracy. In the 17th century, big shots built their private mansions *(hôtels)*, like this one, close to Henry's ritzy place des Vosges. *Hôtels* that survived the Revolution now house museums, libraries, and national institutions.

The first (of 2) courtyards is carriage-friendly and elegant, separating the mansion from the noisy and very public street. Walking through the passageway to the back courtyard, notice the skillfully carved and painted ceilings in the bookshop and stairway.

Bastille Day in France

Bastille Day—July 14, the symbolic kickoff date of the French Revolution—became the French national holiday in 1880. Traditionally, Parisians celebrate at place de la Bastille starting at 20:00 on July 13, but the best parties are on the numerous smaller squares, where firefighter units sponsor dances. At 10:00 on the morning of the 14th, a grand military parade fills the Champs-Elysées. Then, at 22:30, there's a fireworks display at the Eiffel Tower (arrive by 20:30 to get a seat on the grass). *Vive la France!*

The peaceful back courtyard, as was common, has an *orangerie,* or greenhouse, for homegrown fruits and veggies through the winter; it's straight ahead, behind the French doors at the far end, now warming office workers. The bit of Gothic window tracery (on the right) is fun for a framed photo of your travel partner as a Madonna.

• *Continue through the small door at the far right corner of the second courtyard and pop out into one of Paris' finest squares.*

❸ Place des Vosges

Walk to the center, where Louis XIII on horseback gestures, "Look at this wonderful square my dad built." He's surrounded by locals enjoying their community park. Children frolic in the sandbox, lovers warm benches, and pigeons guard their fountains while trees shade this retreat from the glare of the big city. (Or is it raining?)

Study the architecture: nine pavilions (houses) per side. The two highest—at the front and back—were for the king and queen (but were never used). Warm red brickwork—some real, some fake—is topped with sloped slate roofs, chimneys, and another quaint relic of a bygone era, TV antennas. Beneath the arcades are cafés, art galleries, and restaurants—it's a romantic place for dinner (see page 353).

Henry IV (r. 1589–1610) built this centerpiece of the Marais in 1605 and called it "place Royal." As he hoped, it turned the Marais into Paris' most exclusive neighborhood. Just like Versailles 80 years later, this was a magnet for the rich and powerful of France. With the Revolution, the aristocratic splendor of this quarter passed. To encourage the country to

pay its taxes, Napoleon promised naming rights to the district that paid first—the Vosges region (near Germany).

In the 19th century, the Marais became a working-class quarter, filled with gritty shops, artisans, immigrants, and Jews. The insightful writer **Victor Hugo** lived at #6—at the southeast corner of the square—from 1832 to 1848. This was when he wrote much of his most important work, including his biggest hit, *Les Misérables.* You'll wander through eight plush rooms and enjoy a fine view of the square (marked by the French flag in the corner closest to the Bastille; see page 67).

• *Exit the square at the northwest corner. (Walk behind Louis XIII's horse, cross the street, and turn left in the arcade, sampling some upscale art galleries.) Exiting the square, head west on...*

❹ Rue des Francs Bourgeois

From the Marais of yesteryear, immediately enter the lively neighborhood of today. Stroll down a block of cafes and latest-fashion clothing stores. The courtyard at #13 leads to the "2 Mille et 1 Nuits" shop, with exotic lamps, glassware, and home furnishings in a nouveau Art Nouveau style (daily 11:00–19:30).

• *Follow rue des Francs Bourgeois west one block, and turn right on rue Sévigné to the...*

❺ Carnavalet Museum

Housed inside a Marais mansion, this museum focuses on the history of Paris, particularly the Revolution years (Tue–Sun 10:00–18:00, closed Mon, 23 rue de Sévigné). Since this is the best possible look at the elegance of the neighborhood back when place des Vosges was place Royal—and the museum is free—it's worthwhile to interrupt this walk and splice in the Carnavalet Museum Tour (page 216).

• *From the Carnavalet, continue west down rue des Francs Bourgeois. Turn left at the post office onto rue Pavée. A funky bookstore at 17 bis rue Pavée has more inside than meets the eye.*

Picasso fans will want to detour to the Picasso Museum (page 231), located two blocks north of here (closed Tue, 5 rue de Thorigny).

From rue Pavée, turn right onto rue des Rosiers (named for the roses that once lined the city wall), which runs straight for three blocks through Paris' Jewish Quarter, lively every day except Saturday.

❻ Jewish Quarter

Once considered the largest in Western Europe, Paris' Jewish Quarter grew in three waves. First, it expanded in the 19th century when Jews arrived from Eastern Europe, escaping pogroms (surprise attacks on villages). Next, Jews fled Nazi Germany (before 75 percent of them were taken to concentration camps). And,

most recently, Algerian exiles, both Jewish and Muslim, settled in—living together peacefully here in Paris. (Nevertheless, much of the street has granite blocks on the sidewalk—an attempt to keep out any terrorists' cars.)

Today, while rue des Rosiers is lined with colorful Jewish shops and kosher eateries, the district is being squeezed by the trendy boutiques of modern Paris. Notice the old bath, or *hamam*, at #4—while the sign above it says *Hamam*, it's now a furniture showroom. Next door, at #4-bis, the Ecole de Travail (trade school) has a plaque on the wall remembering the headmaster, staff, and students arrested and killed in Auschwitz in 1943 and 1944.

Jo Goldenberg's delicatessen/restaurant (first corner on left, 7 rue des Rosiers) serves typical—but not kosher—Eastern European Jewish cuisine. A plaque on the wall reminds locals of the 1982 terrorist bombing here that left six people dead. The nearby rue des Ecouffes (named for a bird of prey) is a derogatory reminder of the moneychangers' shops that once lined this lane.

Lunch: This is a fine place for a lunch break. You'll be tempted by kosher pizza and plenty of €4-falafel-to-go joints (*emporter* means "to go"). The best falafel is at **L'As du Falafel,** with a bustling New York deli atmosphere (at #34, sit-down or to go). The Sacha Finkelsztajn Yiddish bakery (at #27) is also good. **Chez Marianne** cooks up traditional Jewish meals (at corner of rue des Rosiers and rue des Hospitalieres St. Gervais; see page 357). Vegetarians appreciate the excellent cuisine at the popular Piccolo Teatro (closed Mon, near rue des Rosiers, 6 rue des Ecouffes, tel. 01 42 72 17 79).

• *Rue des Rosiers dead-ends into rue Vieille du Temple. Turn left, then take your first right on...*

❼ Rue Ste. Croix de la Bretonnerie

Gay Paree's main drag is lined with cafés, lively shops, and crowded bars at night. Check the posters at #7, Le Point Virgule theater, to see what form of edgy musical comedy is showing tonight (most productions are in French). At #38, peruse real estate prices in the area—€300,000 for a one-bedroom flat?!

• *Continue along rue Ste. Croix. At rue du Temple, some may wish to detour to the right. A half block to the right is* **The Studio,** *a café wonderfully located in the 17th-century courtyard of a dance school. You can sip a café crème—or have a Tex-Mex meal—surrounded by ballet, tap-dance, and tango (open daily, tasty salads, €12 plats du jour,*

41 rue de Temple, tel. 01 42 74 10 38). A block beyond that is the Jewish Art and History Museum (Mon–Fri 11:00–18:00, Sun 10:00–18:00, closed Sat, 71 rue du Temple, see page 65).

Continue west on rue Ste. Croix (which changes names to rue St. Merri). Up ahead, you'll see the colorful pipes of the...

❽ Pompidou Center

Survey this popular spot from the top of the sloping square. Tubular

escalators lead up to a great view and the modern art museum. ❍ See Pompidou Center Tour on page 202.

The Pompidou Center subscribes with gusto to the 20th-century architectural axiom, "form follows function." To get a more spacious and functional interior, the guts of this exoskel-etal building are draped on the outside and color-coded: vibrant red for people lifts, cool blue for air ducts, eco-green for plumbing, don't-touch-it yellow for electrical stuff, and white for bones. (Compare the Pompidou Center to another exoskeletal building, Notre-Dame.)

Enjoy the adjacent *Homage to Stravinsky* fountains. Jean Tinguely and Niki de Saint-Phalle designed these as a tribute to the composer: Every fountain represents one of his hard-to-hum scores. For low-stress meals, try the lighthearted Dame Tartine, which overlooks

the *Homage to Stravinsky* fountains and serves good, inexpensive meals, or walk up to the lively rue Montorgueil market street (see below).

Beyond the Marais

From the Pompidou, continue west along the cobbled pedestrian mall, crossing the busy boulevard de Sébastopol to the ivy-covered pavilions of Les Halles. Paris' down-and-dirty central produce market of 800 years was replaced by a glitzy but soul-less shopping center in the late 1970s. The mall's most endearing layer is its grassy rooftop park. (The Gothic St. Eustache Church overlooking this contemporary scene has a famous 8,000-pipe organ.)

For a more soulful shopping experience (similar to rue Cler), find your way behind St. Eustache Church and cross rue Montmartre onto the delightfully traffic-free rue Montorgueil (mohn-tor-go-ee). This street is the site of a flourishing market (open daily except Sun afternoon, Mon, and lunchtime—13:00–15:00—throughout the week). If you've walked here all the way from place Bastille, you deserve a break at one of the street's lively cafés.

RUE CLER WALK

The Art of Parisian Living

Paris is changing quickly, but a stroll down this street introduces you to a thriving, traditional Parisian neighborhood and offers helpful insights into the local culture.

Shopping for groceries is an integral part of daily life here. Parisians shop almost daily for three good reasons: Refrigerators are small (tiny kitchens), produce must be fresh, and it's an important social event. Shopping is a chance to hear about the butcher's vacation plans, see photos of the florist's new grandchild, relax over *un café*, and kiss the cheeks of friends (the French standard is twice for regular acquaintances, three times for friends you haven't seen in a while).

Rue Cler—traffic-free since 1984—offers plenty of space for tiny stores and their patrons to spill into the street. It's an ideal environment for this ritual to survive and for you to explore. The street is lined with all the necessary shops—wine, cheese, chocolate, bread—as well as a bank and a post office. And the shops of this community are run by people who've found their niche: boys who grew up on quiche, girls who know a good wine. The people in uniform you might see are likely from the Ecole Militaire (military school, Napoleon's alma mater, 2 blocks away).

If you wish to learn the fine art of living Parisian-style, rue Cler provides an excellent classroom. And if you want to assemble the ultimate French picnic, there's no better place. The Rue Cler Walk is the only tour in this guidebook you should start while hungry.

ORIENTATION

When to Go: Visit rue Cler when its market is open and lively (Tue–Sat 8:30–13:00 or 17:00–19:00, Sun 8:30–12:00, dead on Mon). Remember that these shops are busy serving regular

Rue Cler Walk

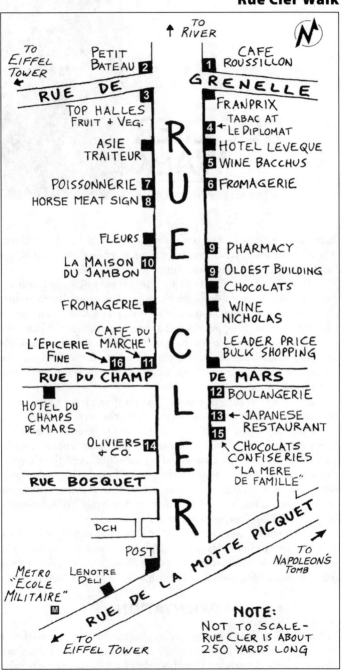

customers. Be polite (say *"Bonjour, Madame/Monsieur"* as you enter and *"Au revoir, Madame/Monsieur"* when you leave) and be careful not to get in the way.

Getting There: Start your walk where the pedestrian section of rue Cler does, at rue de Grenelle (Mo: Ecole Militaire or bus #69 stop).

THE WALK BEGINS

❶ Café Roussillon

This place, a neighborhood fixture, recently dumped its old-fashioned, characteristic look for the latest café style—warm, natural wood tones, easy lighting, and music. The various *chèque déjeuner* decals on the door advertise that this café accepts lunch "checks." In France, an employee lunch subsidy program is an expected perk. Employers—responding to strong tax incentives designed to keep the café culture vital—issue a voucher check (worth about €5) for each day an employee works in a month. Sack lunches are rare, since a good lunch is sacred.

Inside, drinks at the always active bar *(comptoir)* are about half the price of drinks at the tables. The blackboard lists wines sold by the little (7-centiliter) glass.

• *If you're shopping for designer baby clothes, you'll find them across the street at...*

❷ Petit Bateau

The French spend at least as much on their babies as they do on their dogs—dolling them up with designer jammies. This store is from a popular chain. Babies-in-the-know just aren't comfortable unless they're making a fashion statement (e.g., underwear with sailor stripes). In the last generation, an aging and actually shrinking population has been a serious problem for Europe's wealthier nations. But France, thanks to huge tax incentives, now has one of Europe's biggest baby populations. Babies are trendy today. While the average European family has about 1.6 children, the fertile French are now at about 2 kids per family. Tax deductions are big for your first two children, and then actually double after that.

• *Across the street, find...*

❸ Top Halles Fruits and Vegetables

Each morning, fresh produce is trucked in from farmers' fields to Paris' huge Rungis market—Europe's largest, near Orly Airport—and then dispatched to merchants with FedEx speed and precision.

Locals generally shop with a trolley, rather than use bags need-lessly. Good luck finding a shopping bag—locals bring their own. Notice how the French resist excessive packaging.

Parisians—who know they eat best by being tuned into the sea-sons—shop with their noses. Try it. Smell the cheap foreign strawberries. In June, one sniff of the torpedo-shaped French ones *(garriguettes)* and you know which is better. Find the herbs in the back. Is today's delivery in? Look at the price of those melons. What's the country of origin? It must be posted. If they're out of season, they come from Guadeloupe. Many people buy only local products.

The Franprix across the street is a small Safeway-type store. Opposite Grand Hôtel Lévêque is Asie Traiteur. Fast Asian food to go is popular in Paris. These shops—about as common as baker-ies now—are making an impact on Parisian eating habits.

• *Across the street, the giant Métro ticket high on the wall marks a...*

❹ Tabac

Just as the U.S. has liquor stores licensed to sell booze, the only place for people (over 16) to buy tobacco legally in France is at a tabac counter. Tobacco counters like this one are a much appreci-ated fixture of each neighborhood, offering lots of services and an interesting insight into the local culture.

Even non-smokers enjoy perusing the wares at a tabac (tah-bah). Notice how European laws require a bold warning sign on cigarettes—about half the size of the package—that says, bluntly, *fumer tue* (smoking kills). Even so, you may not be able to resist the temptation to pick up a *petit Corona*—your chance to buy a fine Cuban cigar for €1 without breaking the law.

Tabacs also serve their neighborhoods as a kind of govern-ment cash desk. They sell stamps and public-transit tickets (for the same price you'd pay at Métro stations—but they pocket a 5 percent profit). Locals pay for parking meters in tabacs by buying a card (see page 28)...or pay fines if they don't. Like back home, the LOTO is a big deal—and a lucrative way for the government to tax poor and less educated people.

• *Just past Grand Hôtel Lévêque is...*

❺ Wine Bacchus

Shoppers often visit the neighborhood wine shop last, once they've assembled their meal and are able to pick the appropriate wine. The wine is classified by region. Most "Parisians" have an affinity

to their home region that affects their choice of wine. Check out the great prices. Wines of the month—in the center—sell for about €5. You can get a fine bottle for €10. The clerk is a counselor who works with your needs and budget, and he can put a bottle of white in the fridge for you to pick up later (open until 20:00 except Sun). Notice the beer (rear left). Since this is a quality shop, there's nothing French—only Belgian specialty beers.

• *Next door, smell the...*

❻ Fromagerie

A long, narrow, canopied cheese table brings the *fromagerie* into the street. Wedges, cylinders, balls, and miniature hockey pucks are all powdered white, gray, and burnt marshmallow—it's a festival of mold. Much of the street cart and front window display is devoted only to the goat cheeses. Locals know the shape indicates the region of origin (e.g., a pyramid shape indicates a cheese from the Loire). And this is important. Regions create the *terroir* (physical and magical union of sun, soil, and generations of farmer love) which give the production—whether wine or cheese—its personality. *Ooh la la* means you're impressed. If you like cheese, show greater excitement with more *la*s. *Ooh la la la la.* My local friend once held the stinkiest glob close to her nose, took an orgasmic breath, and exhaled, "Yes, it smells like zee feet of angels." Go ahead...inhale.

Step inside and browse through some of more than 400 types of French cheese. A cheese shop—lab-jacket-serious but friendly,

and known as a "BOF" for *beurre, oeuf,* and *fromage*—is where people shop for butter, eggs, and cheese. In the back room are *les meules,* the big, 170-pound wheels of cheese (250 gallons of milk go into each wheel). The "hard" cheeses are cut from these. Don't eat the skin of these big ones...they're rolled on the floor. But the skin on most smaller cheeses—the Brie, the Camembert—is part of the taste. "It completes the package," says my local friend.

At dinner tonight, you can take the cheese course just before or instead of dessert. On a good cheese plate, you have a hard cheese (like Emmentaler—a.k.a. "Swiss cheese"), a flowery cheese (maybe Brie or Camembert), a bleu cheese, and a goat cheese—ideally from different regions. Because it's strongest, the goat cheese is usually eaten last.

• *Across the street, find the fish shop, known as the...*

❼ Poissonnerie

Fresh fish is brought into Paris daily from ports on the English Channel, 110 miles away. In fact, fish here is likely fresher than in many towns closer to the sea, because Paris is a commerce hub (from here, it's shipped to outlying towns). Anything wiggling? This *poissonnerie*, like all such shops, has been recently upgraded to meet the new Europe-wide hygiene standards.

• *Next door (under the awning) is a particularly tempting rue Cler storefront.*

❽ No More Horse Meat

While you'll eat souvlaki and crêpes in this shop today, the classy old storefront is a work of art that survives from the previous occupant. The inset stones and glass advertise horse meat: *Boucherie Chevaline*. The decorated front, from the 1930s and signed by the artist, would fit in a museum. But it belongs right here. Notice again, the door decorated with lunch coupon decals for local workers.

• *Across the street is the...*

❾ Pharmacy and Oldest Building

Wander on past the flower shop and pharmacy. (In France, the pharmacist makes the first diagnosis—if it's out of his league, he'll recommend a doctor.)

Next to the pharmacy, notice rue Cler's oldest and shortest building. It's from the early 1800s, when this street was part of a village near Paris and lined with buildings like this. Of course, over the years Paris engulfed these surrounding villages—and the street is a mishmash of architectural styles.

• *Across the street from this oldest house is...*

❿ La Maison du Jambon

A *charcuterie* sells mouthwatering deli food to go. Because Parisian kitchens are so small, these gourmet delis are handy, allowing hosts to concentrate on the main course and buy beautifully prepared side dishes to complete a fine dinner. Each day, the *charcuteries* cook up specials advertised on the *plat du jour* (special of the day) board outside. Note the system: Order, take your ticket to the cashier to pay, and return with the receipt to pick up your food.

• *A few doors down is...*

⓫ Café du Marché and More

Café du Marché, on the corner, is *the* place to sit and enjoy the action. It's rue Cler's living room, where locals gather before heading home, many staying for a relaxed and affordable dinner. The

owner priced his menu so that locals could afford to dine out on a regular basis, and it worked—many clients eat here five days a week. For a reasonable meal, grab a chair and check the chalk menu listing the *plat du jour.* For details on this restaurant, see page 349 in the Eating chapter.

The shiny, sterile Leader Price grocery store (across the street) is a Parisian Costco, selling bulk items. Because storage space is so limited in most Parisian apartments, bulk purchases are unlikely to become a big deal here. The latest trend is to stock up on non-perishables by shopping online, pick up produce three times a week, and buy fresh bread daily. The awful exterior of this store suggests a sneaky bending of the rules. Normally any proposed building modification on rue Cler must undergo a rigorous design review in order for the owner to obtain the required permit.

Notice how sidewalk "garbage cans" are actually green plastic bags. In the 1990s, Paris suffered a rash of bombings (bad guys improvised little bombs by hiding campstove cannisters in metal cans which provided the deadly "shrapnel" when they exploded). Local authorities solved this by replacing cans with these see-through bags.

• *From Café du Marché, cross rue du Champ de Mars to the store on the corner.*

⓬ *Boulangerie*

Since the French Revolution, the government has regulated the cost of a basic baguette. The *Prix du Pain* sign in the window tells you the going rate. Locals debate the merits of Paris' many *boulangeries.* It's said that a baker cannot be both good at bread and good at pastry. At cooking school, they major in one or the other, and locals say that when you do good bread, you have no time to do good pastry. Here, the baker does good bread. Another baker does the tasty little pastries for him.

• *Next door is a strangely out-of-place...*

⓭ **Japanese Restaurant**

Sushi is mysteriously for sale everywhere in Paris these days. Locals explain that the phenomenon is the same as when Chinese restaurants were spreading like gastronomic weeds. Real French restaurants were unable to compete, as the cheap Chinese places were actually just crime "fronts," whose real profits came from laundering "black money." In many districts, local authorities actually forbid business permits to Chinese restaurants. Some figure today's countless Japanese restaurants are mostly Chinese-owned and thriving for similar reasons.

• *A bit farther along and across the street is...*

⓮ Oliviers & Co. Olive Oils

This shop, typical of an upscale neighborhood like this, sells fine gourmet goodies from the south of France and olive oil from around the Mediterranean. They are happy to give visitors a taste test—with tiny spoons—of three distinct oils.

• *Across the street, you'll find...*

⓯ La Mère de Famille Gourmand Chocolats Confiseries

This shop has been in the neighborhood for 30 years. The wholesalers wanted the owner to take the new products, but she kept the old traditional candies, too. "The old ladies, they want the same sweets that made them so happy 80 years ago," she says. You can buy "naked bonbons" right out of the jar and chocolate by the piece. One hundred grams (about 10 pieces) costs €6.40.

Until a few years ago, chocolate was dipped and decorated in the back, where the merchants used to live. As was the tradition in rue Cler shops, the merchants resided and produced in the back and sold in the front.

• *For the perfect finale to this walk, backtrack a half block to Café du Marché, turn left on rue du Champ de Mars, and within a few steps, you'll reach...*

⓰ L'Epicerie Fine

This fine-foods boutique stands out from the rest because of its gentle owner, Pascal. His mission in life is to explain to travelers, in fluent English, what the French fuss over food is all about. Say *bonjour* to Pascal and let him tempt you with fine gourmet treats and generous tastes (balsamic vinegar, French and Italian olive oil, and caramel). Ask about his gourmet picnic basket—maybe tonight by the Eiffel Tower?

• *Rue Cler ends at the post office. The Ecole Militaire Métro stop is just around the corner. If you bought a picnic along this walk, you'll find benches and gardens nearby: From the post office, avenue de la Motte-Picquet leads to two fine parks—turn left for Napoleon's Tomb or right for the Eiffel Tower.*

MONTMARTRE WALK

*From Sacré-Cœur
to the Moulin Rouge*

Stroll along the hilltop of butte Montmartre amid traces of the people who've lived here—monks stomping grapes (1200s), farmers grinding grain in windmills (1600s), dust-coated gypsum miners (1700s), Parisian liberals (1800s), Modernist painters (1900s), and all the struggling artists, poets, dreamers, and drunkards who came here for cheap rent, untaxed booze, rustic landscapes, and cabaret nightlife.

While many tourists make the almost obligatory trek to the top of Paris' butte Montmartre, eat an overpriced crêpe, and marvel at the view, most miss out on the neighborhood's charm and history—both uncovered in this stroll. Allow about two hours for this two-mile, uphill/downhill walk.

We'll start at the radiant Sacré-Cœur church, wander through the hilltop village, browse affordable art, ogle the Moulin Rouge nightclub, and catch echoes of those who once partied to a bohemian rhapsody during the belle époque.

ORIENTATION

Sacré-Cœur: Free, basilica open daily 7:00–23:00. Dome–€5, ticket machine requires coins or Visa card, not covered by Museum Pass, daily June–Sept 9:00–19:00, Oct–May 10:00–18:00.

Dalí Museum (L'Espace Dalí): €8, not covered by Museum Pass, daily July–Aug 10:00–21:30, Sept–June 10:00–18:30, 11 rue Poulbot.

Montmartre Museum: €5.50, not covered by Museum Pass, Tue–Sun 10:00–12:30 & 14:00–18:00, closed Mon, 12 rue Cortot.

Museum of Erotic Art (Musée de l'Erotisme): €7, not covered by Museum Pass, daily 10:00–2:00, 72 boulevard de Clichy, Mo: Blanche.

When to Go: To minimize the crowds at Sacré-Cœur (worst on sunny weekends), arrive by 9:30. If crowds don't get you down, come for the sunset and stay for dinner (see Eating chapter, page 363). This walk is best under clear skies, when views are sensational. Regardless of when you go, prepare for more seediness than you're accustomed to in Paris.

Getting There: Take the Métro to Anvers (other nearby Métro stops are Abbesses and Pigalle). There are a couple of ways to avoid climbing the hill to Sacré-Cœur. The simplest approach is to take the Métro to Anvers, then take the funicular (mentioned in walk, below). Or, from place Pigalle, you can take the Montmartrobus, which drops you right by place du Tertre, near Sacré-Cœur (costs 1 Métro ticket, 4/hr).

A taxi from the Seine or the Bastille to Sacré-Cœur costs about €10.

Starring: Cityscape views, Sacré-Cœur, postcard scenes brought to life, and boring buildings where interesting people once lived.

THE WALK BEGINS

To reach Sacré-Cœur by Métro, get off at Anvers. The peeling and neglected Elysées Montmartre theater across the street is the oldest cancan dance hall in Paris, and the famous Chat Noir (Black Cat) Cabaret was at #84. Today, the Elysées Montmartre is a rowdy dance club and concert hall, signaling this area's transition. Historically, people have moved to this neighborhood for cheap rent. While it still feels neglected, urban gentrification is underway as young professionals restore dilapidated apartments, hotels renovate for a more upscale clientele, and rents increase.

Walk two blocks up rue de Steinkerque (the street to the right of Elysées Montmartre), through a bizarre, low-rent urban bazaar, past cheap clothing and souvenir shops (pick up inexpensive postcards and €2 blue jeans) to the grassy park way below the white Sacré-Cœur church. The terraced hillside was once dotted with openings to gypsum mines, the source of the white "plaster of Paris" that plastered Paris' buildings for centuries.

• Hike up to the church or ride the funicular (costs 1 Métro ticket, to the left, past the merry-go-round). The best view is just below the top flight of stairs.

❶ Sacré-Cœur Basilica and View

From Paris' highest point (420 feet), the City of Light fans out at your feet. Pan from left to right. The big triangular roof on your left is the Gare du Nord train station. The blue-and-red Pompidou Center is straight ahead, and the skyscrapers in the distance define

Montmartre Walk

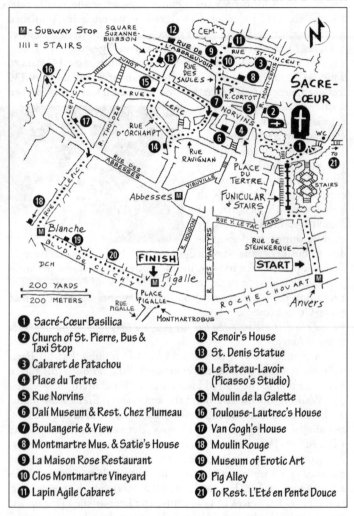

M — SUBWAY STOP
‖‖ = STAIRS

1. Sacré-Cœur Basilica
2. Church of St. Pierre, Bus & Taxi Stop
3. Cabaret de Patachou
4. Place du Tertre
5. Rue Norvins
6. Dalí Museum & Rest. Chez Plumeau
7. Boulangerie & View
8. Montmartre Mus. & Satie's House
9. La Maison Rose Restaurant
10. Clos Montmartre Vineyard
11. Lapin Agile Cabaret
12. Renoir's House
13. St. Denis Statue
14. Le Bateau-Lavoir (Picasso's Studio)
15. Moulin de la Galette
16. Toulouse-Lautrec's House
17. Van Gogh's House
18. Moulin Rouge
19. Museum of Erotic Art
20. Pig Alley
21. To Rest. L'Eté en Pente Douce

the southern limit of central Paris. Next is the domed Panthéon, atop Paris' other (and far smaller) butte. Then comes the modern Montparnasse Tower, and finally (if you're in position to see this far to the right), the golden dome of Les Invalides. Now face the church.

The Sacré-Cœur (Sacred Heart) basilica's exterior, with its onion domes and bleached-bone pallor, looks ancient, but was built only a century ago by Parisians humiliated by German invaders. Otto von Bismarck's Prussian army laid siege to Paris for more

than four months in 1870. Things got so bad for residents that urban hunting for dinner (to cook up dogs, cats, and finally rats) became accepted behavior. Convinced they were being punished for the country's liberal sins, France's Catholics raised money to build the church as a "praise the Lord anyway" gesture.

The five-domed, Roman-Byzantine basilica took 44 years to build (1875–1919). It stands on a foundation of 83 pillars sunk 130 feet deep, necessary because the ground beneath was honeycombed with gypsum mines. The exterior is laced with gypsum, which whitens with age.

Interior: In the impressive mosaic high above the altar, Christ exposes his sacred heart, burning with love and compassion for humanity. He's adored by angels, popes, and gentlemen in business suits who pledge they will build a church (seen in the background). Right now, in this church, at least one person is praying for Christ to be understanding of the world's sins—part of a tradition that's been carried out here, day and night, 24/7, since Sacré-Cœur's completion.

• *Find the first pillar to the left (as you face the altar), across from the statue of Mary.*

A plaque shows where the 13 WWII bombs that hit Paris fell—all in a line, all near the church—killing no one. This fueled local devotion to the Sacred Heart and to this church.

Walking clockwise around the ambulatory, find a scale model of the church. Continuing behind the altar, notice the colorful mosaics of the Stations of the Cross. Between stations VII and VIII, rub St. Peter's bronze foot and look up to the heavens.

Continue your circuit around the church. As you approach the entrance you'll walk straight towards stained glass windows dedicated to Joan of Arc (Jeanne d'Arc, 1412–1431). See the teenage girl as she hears the voices of two saints, and later as she takes up the sword of the Archangel Michael. Next, she kneels to take communion, then kneels before the bishop to tell him she's been sent by God to rally France's soldiers and save Orleans from English invaders. However, French forces allied with England arrest her, and she's burned at the stake as a heretic, dying with her eyes fixed on a crucifix and chanting, "Jesus, Jesus, Jesus...."

• *Exit the church. Once outside, a public WC is to your left, down 50 steps. To your right is the entrance to the church's...*

Dome and Crypt: For an unobstructed panoramic view of Paris, climb 260 feet up the tight and claustrophobic spiral stairs

to the top of the **dome** (especially worthwhile if you have kids with excess energy). The crypt is just a big empty basement.

• *Leaving the church, turn right and walk west along the ridge, following tree-lined rue Azaïs. At rue St. Eleuthère, turn right and walk uphill a block to the Church of St. Pierre-de-Montmartre (at top on right).*

The small square in front of the church is a convenient taxi stand and bus stop for the Montmartrobus to and from place Pigalle (costs 1 Métro ticket).

❷ Church of St. Pierre-de-Montmartre

This church was the center of Montmartre's first claim to fame, a sprawling abbey of Benedictine monks and nuns. The church is one of Paris' oldest (1147)—some say Dante prayed here—founded by King Louis VI and his wife, Adelaide. Find Adelaide's tombstone *(pierre tombale)* midway down on the left wall. Older still are the four gray columns inside that may have stood in a temple of Mercury or Mars in Roman times (two flank the entrance and two are behind the altar). The name "Montmartre" comes from the Roman "Mount of Mars," though later generations, thinking of their beheaded patron St. Denis, preferred a less pagan version, "Mount of Martyrs."

Along the right wall, rub St. Peter's toe (again), look up, and ask for *déliverance* from the tourist mobs outside. Now step back outside, where a sign for the Café and Cabaret la Bohème reminds visitors that in the late 19th and early 20th centuries, this was the world capital of bohemian life. The artist-filled place du Tertre awaits.

• *Before entering the square, a short detour to the right leads to 13 rue du Mont-Cenis, the former...*

❸ Cabaret de Patachou

This building, now a pleasant art gallery, is where singer Edith Piaf (1915–1963) once trilled "La Vie en Rose." Piaf—a destitute teenager who sang for pocket change in the streets of pre-WWII Paris—was discovered by a nightclub owner and became a star. Her singing inspired the people of Nazi-occupied Paris. In the heady days after the war, she sang about the joyous, rosy life in the city. For more on this warbling-voiced singer, see page 288.

• *Head back to the always lively square, and stand on its cusp for the best perspective of...*

❹ Place du Tertre—Bohemian Montmartre

Lined with cafés, shaded by acacia trees, and filled with artists, hucksters, and tourists, the scene mixes charm and kitsch in ever-changing proportions. The place du Tertre has been the town

Maurice Utrillo (1883–1955)

Born to a free-spirited single mom and raised by his grandmother, Utrillo had his first detox treatment at age 18. Encouraged by his mother and doctors, he started painting as occupational therapy. That, plus guidance from his mother (and later, from his wife), allowed him to live productively into his seventies, becoming wealthy and famous, despite occasional relapses into drink and mental problems.

Utrillo grew up in Montmartre's streets. He fought, broke street lamps, and haunted the cafés and bars, buying drinks with masterpieces. A very free spirit, he's said to have exposed himself to strangers on the street, yelling, "I paint with this!"

His simple scenes of streets, squares, and cafés in a vaguely Impressionist style became popular with commoners and scholars alike. He honed his style during his "white period" (c. 1909–1914), painting a thick paste of predominantly white tints—perfect for capturing Sacré-Cœur. In later years, after he moved out of Montmartre, he still painted the world he knew in his youth, using postcards and photographs as models.

Utrillo's mom, Suzanne Valadon, was a former trapeze performer and artist's model who posed for Toulouse-Lautrec, slept with Renoir, studied under Degas, and went on to become a notable painter in her own right. Her partner, a Spanish artist named André Utter, gave Maurice his family name (Utrillo = little Utter).

square of the small village of Montmartre since medieval times. (*Tertre* means "stepped lanes" in French.)

In 1800, a wall separated Paris from this hilltop village. To enter Paris, you had to pass tollbooths that taxed anything for sale. Montmartre was a mining community where the wine flowed cheap (tax-free) and easy. Life here was a working-class festival of cafés, bistros, and dance halls. Painters came here for the ruddy charm, the light, and the low rents. In 1860, Montmartre was annexed into the growing city of Paris. The "bohemian" ambience survived, and it attracted sophisticated Parisians ready to get down and dirty in the belle époque of cancan. The Restaurant Mer Catherine is often called the first bistro, since this is where Russian soldiers first coined the word by saying, "I'm thirsty, bring my drink *bistro*!" (meaning "right away").

The square's artists, who at times outnumber the tourists, are the great-great-grandkids of the Renoirs, van Goghs, and Picassos who once roamed here—poor, carefree, seeking inspiration, and occasionally cursing a world too selfish to bankroll their dreams.

• *Plunge headfirst into the square. The tourist office (Syndicat d'Initiative, daily 10:00–19:00) across the square sells good maps and a so-so audioguide tour. Just south of the square is the quiet, tiny place du Calvaire, with the rec-ommended café Chez Plumeau. But for now, continue west along the main drag, called...*

❺ Rue Norvins

Montmartre's oldest and main street is still the primary commer-cial artery, serving the current trade—tourism.

• *If you're a devotee of Dalí, take a detour left on rue Poulbot, leading to the...*

❻ Dalí Museum (L'Espace Dalí)

This beautifully lit black gallery (well-described in English) offers a walk through statues, etchings, and paintings by the master of surrealism. Don't miss the printed interview on the exit stairs.

• *Return to rue Norvins and continue west a dozen steps to the intersec-tion with rue des Saules, where you'll find a...*

❼ *Boulangerie* with a View

The venerable *boulangerie* (bakery) on the left, dating from 1900, is one of the last surviving bits of the old-time community, made

famous in a painting by the artist Maurice Utrillo (see sidebar on facing page).

From the *boulangerie*, look back up rue Norvins, then backpedal a few steps to catch the classic view of the dome of Sacré-Cœur rising above the roof-tops. The doorway of the nearby Auberge de la Bonne Franquette offers another famous dome view.

• *Let's leave the tourists. Follow rue des Saules downhill (north) onto the backside of Montmartre. A block downhill, turn right on rue Cortot to the...*

❽ Montmartre Museum and Satie's House

In what is now the museum (at 12 rue Cortot), Pierre-Auguste Renoir once lived while painting his best-known work, *Bal du*

Moulin de la Galette (pictured on page 132). Every day, he'd lug the 4' x 6' canvas from here to the other side of the butte to paint *(en plein aire)* the famous windmill ballroom, which we'll see later.

A few years later, Utrillo lived and painted here with his mom, Suzanne Valadon. In 1893, she carried on a torrid six-month relationship with the lonely, eccentric man who lived two doors up at #6—composer Erik Satie *(Trois Gymnopedies)*, who was eking out a living playing piano in Montmartre nightclubs.

The Montmartre Museum fills several floors in this creaky 17th-century manor house with paintings, posters, old photos, music, and memorabilia to recreate the traditional cancan and cabaret Montmartre scene. Highlights include several original Toulouse-Lautrec posters for the Moulin Rouge, a few paintings by Valadon and Utrillo, the original Lapin Agile sign, and displays (mostly in French, some English descriptions) on Montmartre's history, from gypsum mining to the Paris Commune to the Chat Noir Cabaret.

• *Return to the rue des Saules and walk downhill to...*

❾ La Maison Rose Restaurant

The restaurant, made famous by an Utrillo painting, was once frequented by Utrillo, Pablo Picasso, and Gertrude Stein. Today, it serves lousy food to nostalgic tourists.

• *Just downhill from the restaurant is Paris' last remaining vineyard.*

❿ Clos Montmartre Vineyard

What originally drew artists to Montmartre was country charm like this. Ever since the 12th century, the monks and nuns of the large abbey produced wine here. With vineyards, wheat fields, windmills, animals, and a village tempo of life, it was the perfect escape from grimy Paris. In 1576, puritanical laws taxed wine in Paris, bringing budget-minded drinkers to Montmartre. Today's vineyard is off-limits to tourists except during the annual grape-harvest fest (1st Sat in Oct), when a thousand costumed locals bring back the boisterous old days. The vineyard's annual production of 300 liters is auctioned off at the fest to support local charities.

• *Continue downhill to the intersection with rue St. Vincent.*

⓫ Lapin Agile Cabaret

The poster above the door gives the place its name. A rabbit *(lapin)* makes an agile leap out of the pot while balancing the bottle of wine that he can now drink—rather than be cooked in. This was the village's hot spot. Picasso and other artists and writers (Renoir, Utrillo, Paul Verlaine, Aristide Bruant, Amedeo Modigliani, etc.) would gather for "performances" that ranged from serious poetry, dirty limericks, sing-alongs, and parodies of the famous to

anarchist manifestos. Once, to play a practical joke on the avant-garde art community, patrons tied a paintbrush to the tail of the owner's donkey and entered the "abstract painting" that resulted in the Salon. Called *Sunset over the Adriatic,* it won critical acclaim and sold for a nice price.

The old Parisian personality of this cabaret survives. Each night, a series of performers take a small, French-speaking audience on a wistful musical journey back to the good old days (for details, see Nightlife chapter, page 390).

• *Before heading back uphill on rue des Saules to the boulangerie (at the intersection with rue Norvins), some may wish to make a detour (an extra 15 min) to a more residential part of Montmartre. If you're pooped, we'll meet you back at the boulangerie.*

⑫ Detour to Renoir's House and ⑬ St. Denis Statue

• *Walk up rue des Saules and turn right at La Maison Rose, heading west one block on rue de l'Abreuvoir. At the busty bust of the comic singer Dalida (1933–1987, who popularized disco in France), continue straight (west) along the small walkway called allée des Brouillards. You'll pass another of Renoir's homes (at #6). Walk down the steps at the walkway's end, then stroll up through the small, fenced, multilevel park called place Suzanne Buisson.*

In the park, find the stone statue of headless St. Denis. The early Christian bishop was sentenced to death by the Romans for spreading Christianity. As they marched him up to the top of Montmartre to be executed, the Roman soldiers got tired, and just beheaded him near here. But Denis popped right up, picked up his head, and carried on another three miles north before he finally died. The statue of Denis cradles his head in his hands, looks over a regulation-size *boules* court...and gets ready to play ball.

• *At the top of the park, turn left onto avenue Junot, which turns into rue Norvins. (Don't you wish you could just walk right through these darn hills? You'll pass a statue that looks like it could do it.) The boulangerie is at the top of rue Norvins.*

Once reunited at the boulangerie, we all go downhill (south)—not on car-filled rue Lepic, but down the pedestrian-only place J.B. Clement, hugging the buildings on our left. Turn right on rue Ravignan and follow it down to the "TIM Hôtel." Next door, at 13 place Emile Goudeau, is...

⑭ Le Bateau-Lavoir (Picasso's Studio)

A humble facade marks the place where modern art was born. Here, in a lowly artists' abode (destroyed by fire in 1970, rebuilt a few years later), as many as 10 artists lived and worked. This former piano factory, converted to cheap housing, was nicknamed

the "Laundry Boat" for its sprawling layout and crude facilities (sharing one water tap). It was "a weird, squalid place," wrote one resident, "filled with every kind of noise: arguing, singing, bedpans clattering, slamming doors, and suggestive moans coming from studio doors."

In 1904, a poor, unknown Spanish émigré named Pablo Picasso (1881–1973) moved in. He met dark-haired Fernande Olivier, his first real girlfriend, in the square outside. She soon moved in, lifting him out of his melancholy Blue Period into the rosy Rose Period. *La belle Fernande* posed nude for him, inspiring a freer treatment of the female form.

In 1907, Picasso started on a major canvas. For nine months, he produced hundreds of preparatory sketches, working long into the night. When he unveiled the work, even his friends were shocked. *Les Demoiselles d'Avignon* showed five nude women in a brothel (Fernande claimed they were all her), with primitive masklike faces and fragmented bodies. Picasso had invented Cubism.

For the next two years, he and his neighbors Georges Braque and Juan Gris revolutionized the art world. Sharing paints, ideas, and girlfriends, they made Montmartre "The Cubist Acropolis," attracting free-thinking "Moderns" from all over the world to visit their studios—the artists Modigliani and Henri Rousseau, the poet Guillaume Apollinaire, and American expatriate writer Gertrude Stein. By the time Picasso moved to better quarters (and dumped Fernande), he was famous. Still, Picasso would later say, "I know one day we'll return to Bateau-Lavoir. It was there that we were really happy—where they thought of us as painters, not strange animals."

• *Backtrack half a block uphill and turn left on rue d'Orchampt. Squirt out the other end at the intersection with rue Lepic, where you're face-to-face with a wooden windmill.*

⓯ Moulin de la Galette

Only two windmills *(moulins)* remain on a hill that was once dotted with 30 of them. Originally, they pressed monks' grapes and farmers' grain, and crushed gypsum rocks into powdery plaster of Paris. When the gypsum mines closed (c. 1850) and the vineyards sprouted apartments, this windmill turned into the ceremonial centerpiece of a popular outdoor dance hall. Renoir's *Bal du Moulin de la Galette* (in the Orsay) shows it in its heyday—a sunny Sunday afternoon in the acacia-shaded gardens with working-class people

dancing, laughing, drinking, and eating the house crêpes, called *galettes*. Some call Renoir's version the quintessential Impressionist work and the painting that best captures—on a large canvas in bright colors—the joy of the Montmartre lifestyle.

• *Follow rue Lepic as it winds down the hill. The green-latticed building on the right side was also part of the Moulin de la Galette. Rounding the bend, look to the right down rue Tourlaque. The building one block down rue Tourlaque was...*

⓰ Henri de Toulouse-Lautrec's House

Find the building on the southwest corner with the tall, brick-framed art studio windows under the heavy mansard roof. Every night, Toulouse-Lautrec (1864–1901)—a nobleman turned painter, whose legs were deformed in a horse-riding accident during his teenage years—would dress up here and then journey down rue Lepic to the Moulin Rouge. One of Henri's occasional drinking buddies and fellow artists lived nearby.

• *Continue down rue Lepic and, at #54, find...*

⓱ Vincent van Gogh's House

Vincent van Gogh lived here with his brother, enjoying a grand city view from his top-floor window from 1886 to 1888. In those two short years, van Gogh transformed from a gloomy Dutch painter of brown and gray peasant scenes into an inspired visionary with wild ideas and Impressionist colors.

• *Follow the rue Lepic downhill as it makes a hard right at #36, and continue to place Blanche. On busy place Blanche is the...*

⓲ Moulin Rouge

Ooh la la. The new Eiffel Tower at the 1889 World's Fair was nothing compared to the sight of pretty cancan girls kicking their legs at

the newly opened "Red Windmill." The nightclub seemed to sum up the belle époque—the age of elegance, opulence, sophistication, and worldliness. The big draw was amateur night, when working-class girls in risqué dresses danced "Le Quadrille" (dubbed "cancan" by a Brit). Wealthy Parisians slummed it by going there.

On most nights, you'd see a small man in a sleek black coat, checked pants, a green scarf, and a bowler hat peering through his pince-nez glasses at the dancers and making sketches of them—Henri de Toulouse-Lautrec. Perhaps he'd order an absinthe, the dense green liqueur (evil ancestor of today's pastis) that was the

toxic muse for so many great (and so many forgotten) artists. Toulouse-Lautrec's sketches of dancer Jane Avril and comic La Goulue hang in the Orsay.

After its initial splash, the Moulin Rouge survived as a venue for all kinds of entertainment. In 1906, the novelist Colette kissed her female lover onstage, and the authorities closed the "Dream of Egypt" down. Yves Montand opened for Edith Piaf (1944), and the two fell in love offstage. It's hosted such diverse acts as Ginger Rogers, Dalida, and the Village People—together on one bill (1979). Mikhail Baryshnikov strode across its stage (1986). And the club celebrated its centennial (1989) with Ray Charles, Tony Curtis, Ella Fitzgerald, and...Jerry Lewis.

Tonight they're showing...well, walk into the open-air entryway or step into the lobby to mull over the photos, show options, and prices.

• *Turn left out of the Moulin Rouge. The Blanche Métro stop is here in place Blanche, a good place to end. (Plaster of Paris from the gypsum found on this mount was loaded sloppily at place Blanche...the white square.) Others may want to sully themselves by continuing east to the...*

⓳ Museum of Erotic Art

Basically a sexy art gallery, this museum has five floors of displays—mostly paintings and drawings—ranging from artistic to erotic to disgusting. They also toss in a few circa-1920 porn videos and a fascinating history of local brothels (see page 68).

• *Outside, farther down the boulevard, you'll find...*

⓴ Pig Alley

The stretch of the boulevard de Clichy from place Blanche eastward (toward Sacré-Cœur) to place Pigalle is the den mother of all iniquities. Today, sex shops, peep shows, live sex shows, and hot dog stands line the busy boulevard de Clichy. Dildos abound.

It's raunchy now, but the area has always been the place where bistros had tax-free status, wine was cheap, and prostitutes roamed freely. In World War II, GIs nicknamed Pigalle "Pig Alley."

Bars lining the streets downhill from place Pigalle (especially rue Pigalle) are lively with working girls eager to share a drink with anyone passing by. Escape home from the fine Art Nouveau Métro stop, Pigalle.

LEFT BANK WALK

From the Seine to Luxembourg Garden

The Left Bank is as much an attitude as it is an actual neighborhood. But this two-hour walk, which is a little over a mile—from the Seine to St. Germain-des-Prés to Luxembourg Garden—captures some of the artistic, intellectual, and counterculture spirit long associated with the south side of the river. We'll pass through an upscale area of art galleries, home-furnishing boutiques, antique dealers, bookstores, small restaurants, classic cafés, evening hotspots, and the former homes of writers, painters, and composers.

Though trendy now, the area still has the offbeat funkiness that has always defined the Rive Gauche. (*Gauche,* or left-handed, has come to imply social incorrectness, like giving a handshake with the wrong—left—hand.)

This walk dovetails perfectly with the shopping stroll (see "Sèvres-Babylone to St. Sulpice" in Shopping, page 379). It also works well after a visit to the Louvre or after the Historic Paris Walk (see page 70). It's ideal for connoisseurs of contemporary art galleries.

ORIENTATION

Delacroix Museum: €5, covered by Museum Pass, Thu–Mon 9:30–17:00, closed Tue, free first Sun of month. Tel. 01 44 41 86 50, www.musee-delacroix.fr.

St. Germain-des-Prés: Free, daily 8:00–20:00.

Left Bank Walk

1. Pont des Arts
2. Statue of Voltaire
3. Roger-Viollet Shop
4. Oscar Wilde's Hotel
5. George Sand's House
6. La Palette Café
7. Le Petit Prince Shop
8. Richard Wagner's House
9. Delacroix Museum
10. Abbey Mansion
11. Heart of the Left Bank
12. Café le Procope
13. Odéon Cinemas
14. St. Germain-des-Prés
15. Les Deux Magots Café & Le Café de Flore
16. Rue des Canettes
17. Marché St. Germain Mall
18. St. Sulpice
19. Luxembourg Garden
20. To Bon Marché Dept. Store

St. Sulpice: Free, daily 7:30–19:30, Sun morning organ concerts (see page 55).
Luxembourg Garden: Free, daily dawn until dusk.

THE WALK BEGINS

• *Start on the pedestrian-only bridge across the Seine, the pont des Arts (next to Louvre, Mo: Pont Neuf or Louvre-Rivoli).*

Pont des Arts

Before dozens of bridges crossed the Seine, the two riverbanks were like different cities—royalty on the right, commoners on the

left. This bridge has always been a pedestrian bridge...long a popular meeting point for lovers.

Under the dome of the Institut de France (the building the pont des Arts leads to), 40 linguists meet periodically to decide whether it's acceptable to call computer software *"le software"* (as the French commonly do), or whether it should be the French word *logiciel* (which the linguists prefer). The Académie Française, dedicated to halting the erosion of French culture, is wary of new French words with strangely foreign sounds—like *le week-end*, *le marketing*, and *le fast-food*.

Besides the Académie Française, the Institut houses several other Académies, such as the Académie des Beaux-Arts, which is dedicated to subjects like music and painting, appropriate for the Left Bank.

• *Circle around the right side of the Institut de France building to the head of rue de Seine. You're immediately met by a statue in a street-corner garden.*

Statue of Voltaire

"Jesus committed suicide." The mischievous philosopher Voltaire could scandalize a party with a wicked comment like that, delivered with an enigmatic smile and a twinkle in the eye (meaning if Christ is truly God, he could have prevented his crucifixion). Voltaire—a commoner more sophisticated than the royalty who lived across the river—introduces us to the Left Bank.

Born François-Marie Arouet (1694–1778), he took up Voltaire as his one-word pen name. Although Voltaire mingled with aristocrats, he was constantly in trouble for questioning the ruling class and fueling ideas that would soon spark a revolution. He did

11 months in the Bastille prison, then spent 40 years in virtual exile from his beloved Paris. Returning as an old man, he got a hero's welcome so surprising it killed him.

The rue de Seine and adjoining streets are lined with art galleries and upscale shops selling lamps, sconces, vases, bowls, and statues for people who turn their living rooms into art.

• *From here, we'll head south down rue de Seine to boulevard St. Germain, making a few detours along the way. First stop is at 6 rue de Seine...*

Roger-Viollet

Look in the windows at black-and-white photos from Paris' history—a half-built Eiffel Tower, Hitler in Paris, and so on (the display changes often). This humble shop is the funky origin of a worldwide press agency dealing in historic photographs. The family of photographer Henri Roger expanded his photographs into an archive of millions of photos, chronicling Paris' changes through the years.

• *At the first intersection, a half-block detour to the right leads to 13 rue des Beaux-Arts and...*

Oscar Wilde's Hotel

Oscar Wilde (1854–1900), the Irish playwright with the flamboyant clothes and outrageous wit, died in this hotel on November 30, 1900 (don't blame the current owners).

Just five years before, he'd been at his peak. He had several plays running simultaneously in London's West End, and had returned to London triumphant from a lecture tour through America. Then, news of his love affair with a lord leaked out, causing a scandal, and he was sentenced to two years in prison for "gross indecency." Wilde's wife abandoned him, refusing to let him see their children again.

After his prison term, a poor and broken Wilde was exiled to Paris, where he succumbed to an ear infection and died here in a (then) shabby hotel room. Among his last words in the rundown place were: "Either this wallpaper goes, or I do."

Wilde is buried in Paris (see Père Lachaise Cemetery Tour, page 286).

• *Return to rue de Seine and continue south. A plaque at 31 rue de Seine marks...*

George Sand's House

George Sand (1804–1876) divorced her abusive husband, left her children behind, and moved into this apartment, determined to become a writer. In the year she lived here (1831), she wrote articles for *Le Figaro* while turning her real-life experiences with men into

a sensational novel, *Indiana*. It made her a celebrity and allowed her to afford a better apartment.

George Sand is known for her novels, her cross-dressing (men's suits, slicked-down hair, and cigars), and for her complex love affair with a sensitive pianist from Poland, Frédéric Chopin.

• *At 43 rue de Seine is...*

La Palette Café

Though less famous than more historic cafés, this is a "real" one, where a *café crème*, beer, or glass of wine at an outdoor table costs less than €5. Inside, the 100-year-old, tobacco-stained wood paneling and faded Art Nouveau decor exude Left Bank chic. Toulouse-Lautrec would have liked it here. Have something to drink at the bar, and examine your surroundings; notice the artist palettes above the bar. Nothing seems to have changed since it was built in 1903, except the modern espresso machine (open daily, tel. 01 43 26 68 15).

• *You could follow rue de Seine straight down to boulevard St. Germain. But we'll branch off, veering right down small rue de l'Echaudé. Four doors up, at 6 rue de l'Echaudé, is...*

Le Petit Prince Shop

Books, dolls, cards, and bibs mass-market the quirky children's tale written by Antoine de Saint-Exupéry (1900–1944). In *The Little Prince* (1943), a pilot crashes in the Sahara, where a mysterious little prince takes him to various planets, teaching him about life from a child's wise perspective.

"Saint-Ex" was himself a daring aviator who had survived wrecks in the Sahara. When the Nazis invaded, he fled to America, where he wrote and published *The Little Prince*. A year later, he enlisted, then disappeared while flying a spy mission for the Allies. Lost for six decades, his plane was recently found off the coast of Marseilles. The cause of the crash remains a mystery, part of a legend as enduring in France as Amelia Earhart's in the States.

• *A half-block detour to the right down rue Jacob (to #14) leads to...*

Richard Wagner's House

Having survived a storm at sea on the way here, the young German composer (1813–1883) spent the gray winter of 1841–1842 in Paris in this building writing *The Flying Dutchman*, an opera about a ghost ship. It was the restless young man's lowest point of poverty. Six months later, a German company staged his first opera *(Rienzi)*, plucking him from obscurity and leading to a production of *The Flying Dutchman* that launched his career.

Now the premises are occupied by a hip-looking bar.

• *Backtrack along rue Jacob, then turn right and continue south on rue Furstemberg to #6, the...*

Delacroix Museum (Musée National Eugène Delacroix)

The painter Eugène Delacroix (1798–1863) lived here on this tiny, quiet square. Today, his home is a museum with paintings and memorabilia, delightful for his fans, but skippable for most (€5, covered by Museum Pass, Wed–Mon 9:30–17:00, closed Tue). While there are no English descriptions, you'll find a helpful English flier at the top of the stairs.

You start in an **anteroom** with a chronology of his life. An ambassador's son, Delacroix moved to Paris and studied at the Beaux-Arts. By his early 20s, he had exhibited at the Salon. His *Liberty Leading the People* (1831, see page 165) was an instant classic, a symbol of French democracy. Trips to North Africa added exotic, Muslim elements to his palette. He hobnobbed with aristocrats and bohemians like George Sand and Frédéric Chopin (whom he painted). He painted large-scale murals for the Louvre, Hôtel de Ville, and Luxembourg Palace.

In 1857, his health failing, Delacroix moved here, seeking a quiet home/studio where he could concentrate on his final great works for the Church of St. Sulpice (which we'll see later).

Next comes the **living room**, decorated with his mahogany writing desk and a haunting painting of Mary Magdalene. To the left is the **bedroom** (with fireplace) where he died in 1863, nursed by his long-time servant, Jenny Le Guillou (see her portrait). Backtracking, you pass through the **library**, then go outside and down some stairs to his **studio** *(atelier)* in the pleasant backyard.

Delacroix built the studio to his own specifications, with high ceilings, big windows, and a skylight, ideal for an artist working prior to electric lights. See his easel and painting table, plus more paintings, including a small-scale study for *The Death of Sardanapalus,* which hangs in the Louvre. Some of Delacroix's most popular works were book illustrations (lithographs for Goethe's *Faust,* Revolutionary history, and Shakespeare). Admire Delacroix's artistic range—from messy, colorful oils to meticulously detailed lithographs. This room has frequent exhibits from various artists.

Finally, in the peaceful **backyard**, soak up the meditative atmosphere that inspired Delacroix's religious paintings in St. Sulpice.

• *Rue Furstemberg runs directly into the Abbey Mansion. This mansion (1586) was the administrative center for the vast complex of monks gathered around the nearby church of St. Germain-des-Prés.*

Facing the mansion, turn left on rue de l'Abbaye and work your way two blocks east to the intersection of rue de Seine and rue de Buci. This intersection is, arguably, the...

Heart of the Left Bank

Explore. The rue de Buci hosts *pâtisseries* and a produce market by day, and bars by night. Mixing earthiness and elegance, your Left

Bank is here. A right on rue de Buci leads to boulevard St. Germain. A left on rue de Buci leads to place St. Michel and the Latin Quarter.

• Wherever you wander, we'll meet up a block south of here on boulevard St. Germain. But first, I'm making a several-block detour to find Voltaire's favorite café. Head east (left) on rue de Buci, which in a few blocks becomes rue St. André-des-Arts, and cross rue de l'Ancienne Comédie. At #61, turn right into the pedestrian-only passageway called Cour du Commerce St. André, where you'll find the back door to...

Café le Procope

Le Procope (with its front door entrance at 13 rue de l'Ancienne Comédie) is just one of many eating options in this pleasant restaurant mall.

Founded in 1686, Le Procope is one of the world's oldest continuously operating restaurants, and was one of Europe's first places to sample an exotic new stimulant—coffee—recently imported from the Muslim culture.

In the 1700s, Le Procope caffeinated the Revolution. Voltaire reportedly drank 30 cups a day, fueling his intellectual passion (his favorite table bears his carved initials). Benjamin Franklin recounted old war stories about America's Revolution. Robespierre, Danton, and Marat plotted coups over cups of double-short-two-percent-frappuccinos. And a young lieutenant named Napoleon Bonaparte ran up a tab he never paid.

Located midway between university students, royalty, and the counterculture Comédie Française, Le Procope attracted literary types who loved the free newspapers, writing paper, and quill pens. Today, the coffeehouse is an appealing restaurant (affordable if mediocre *menus*, open daily). If you're discreet, you can wander the ground floor, with its memorabilia-plastered walls.

• The Cour du Commerce spills out onto boulevard St. Germain at an intersection (and Métro stop) called...

Odéon

Paris' many lovers of film converge here for the latest releases at several multiplexes in the area. Looking south up rue de l'Odéon, you can see the classical columns of the front of Théâtre de l'Odéon, the descendant of the original Comédie Française (now housed in Palais Royale).

• *Walk to the right (west) along busy boulevard St. Germain for six blocks, passing Café Vagenande (famous for its plush Art Nouveau interior) and other fashionable, noisy cafés with outdoor terraces. You'll reach the large stone church and square of...*

St. Germain-des-Prés

Paris' oldest church, dating from the 11th century (the square bell tower is original), stands on a site where a Christian church has stood since the fall of Rome. (The first church was destroyed by Vikings in the 885–886 siege.)

The restored interior is still painted in the medieval manner, as were Notre-Dame and others. The church is in Romanesque style, with round—not pointed—arches over the aisles of the nave.

The square outside is one of Paris' great gathering spots on warm evenings. Musicians, mimes, and fire-eaters entertain café patrons. The church is often lit up and open late. This is where the rich come to see and be seen, and the poor come for a night of free spectacle.

• *Note that Métro stop St. Germain-des-Prés is here, and the Mabillon stop is just a couple of blocks east. On place St. Germain-des-Prés, you'll find...*

Les Deux Magots Café and Le Café de Flore

Since opening in 1885, "The Two Chinamen Café" (wooden statues inside) has taken over Le Procope as the café of ideas. From Oscar Wilde's Aestheticism (1900) to Picasso's Cubism (1910s) to Hemingway's spare prose ('20s) to Sartre's Existentialism (with his girlfriend Simone de Beauvoir and Albert Camus, 1930s and '40s) to rock singer Jim Morrison ('60s), worldwide movements have been born in the simple atmosphere of these two cafés. Le Café de Flore, once frequented by Picasso, is more hip, but Deux Magots, right next door, is more inviting for just coffee (€4.50 espresso). Across the street is Brasserie Lipp, a classic brasserie where Hemingway wrote much of *A Farewell to Arms*. (See also "Les Grands Cafés de Paris," page 364.)

• *From place St. Germain-des-Prés, cross boulevard St. Germain and head south toward the Montparnasse Tower (in the distance) on rue Bonaparte. Turn left on busy rue du Four, then right on...*

Rue des Canettes

Small, midpriced restaurants, boutique shops, and comfortable brewpubs make this a pleasant nightspot. It's easy to find a *plat du jour* or a two-course *formule* for under €20. Chez Georges (at #11) is the last outpost of funkiness (and how!) in an increasingly gentrified neighborhood (see Eating, page 362).

• *A one-block detour left down rue Guisarde leads to more restaurants, shops, and pubs, and the Marché St. Germain shopping mall, a former farmers' market where fish and produce have been replaced by the Gap and other chain stores.*

    Continue south on rue des Canettes to the church of...

St. Sulpice

The impressive neoclassical arcaded facade, with two round, half-finished towers, is modeled on St. Paul's in London. It has

a remarkable organ and offers Sunday morning concerts (see page 55). The lone café on the square in front (Café de la Mairie) is always lively and perfectly located for a break.

    Inside, circle the church counterclockwise, making a few stops. In the first chapel on the right, find Delacroix's three murals (on the chapel's ceiling and walls) of fighting angels, completed during his final years fighting illness. They sum up his long career, from Renaissance/Baroque roots to furious Romanticism to proto-Impressionism.

    The most famous is the agitated *Jacob Wrestling the Angel.* The two grapple in a leafy wood that echoes the wrestlers' rippling energy. Jacob fights the angel to a standstill, bringing him a well-earned blessing for his ordeal. The shepherd Laban and

his daughter Rachel (Jacob's future wife) hover in the background, hinting at the next chapter in Jacob's story. Get close and notice the thick brushwork that influenced the next generation of Impressionists—each leaf is a single brushstroke, often smudging two different colors in a single stroke. The "black" pile of clothes in the foreground is built from rough strokes of purple, green, and white. (Too much glare? Take a couple of steps to the right to view it. Also, there are three light buttons nearby.)

The Da Vinci Code in St. Sulpice

In Dan Brown's novel (see page 56), this church is supposedly where the secret society, the Priory of Sion, was said to have held mysterious rituals. (In fact, there's a stained glass window in the church with the letters P and S, but the church has actually posted a bilingual sign refuting the claims of "a recently written novel.") In the novel, Silas the murderous monk seeks the "keystone" under a pavement stone in St. Sulpice's astrological clock (which Brown embellishes into a mysterious "rose line"). Sister Sandrine watches from the church's interior balcony, and later has a nasty encounter here with Silas.

On the opposite wall, *Heliodorus Chased from the Temple* has the smooth, seamless brushwork of Delacroix's prime. The Syrian Heliodorus has killed the king, launched a coup, and now enters the Jewish Temple in Jerusalem trying to steal the treasure. Angry angels launch themselves at him, sending him sprawling. The vibrant, clashing colors, swirling composition, and over-the-top subject are trademark Delacroix Romanticism. On the ceiling, *The Archangel Michael* drives demons from heaven.

Notice the unmarked door at the foot of the three steps leading to Delacroix's chapel. On Sundays just after noon, this door opens, and you can go upstairs to the organ loft to hear music played for the Mass.

Walking up the right side of the church, pause at the fourth chapel, with a statue of Joan of Arc and wall plaques listing hundreds upon hundreds of names. These are France's WWI dead—from this congregation alone. In the chapel at the far end of the church, ponder the cryptic symbolism of Mary and Child lit by a sunburst, standing on an orb, and trampling a snake, while a stone cloud tumbles down to a sacrificial lamb.

Continue clockwise around the church. On the wall of the left (north) transept is an Egyptian-style obelisk used as a gnomon, or part of a sundial. At Christmas Mass, the sun shines into the church through a tiny hole—it's opposite the obelisk, high up on the south wall (in the upper-right window pane). The sunbeam strikes a mark on the obelisk indicating the winter solstice. Then, week by week, the sunbeam moves down the obelisk and across the bronze rod in the floor, until, at midsummer, the sun lights up the area near the altar.

In the final chapel before the exit, you may see a display on the

Luxembourg Garden

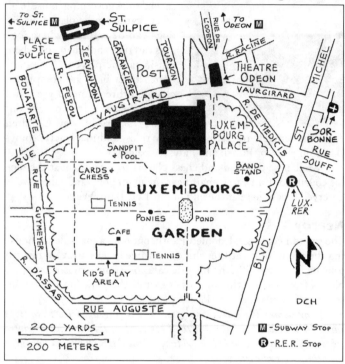

Shroud of Turin. This burial cloth (which is in Turin) is purported to have wrapped Christ, who left it with a mysterious, holy stain in his image.

• *Turning left out of the church, continue south on rue Férou, which leads directly to the fenced-in Luxembourg Garden. Enter the garden by turning right on busy rue de Vaugirard, then left on rue Guynemer, where you'll find an entrance gate.*

Luxembourg Garden

Paris' most beautiful, interesting, and enjoyable garden/park/recreational area is a great place to watch Parisians at rest and play. These 60-acre private gardens, dotted with fountains and statues, are the property of the French Senate, which meets here in the Luxembourg Palace.

The palace was begun in 1615 by Marie de Médicis. Recently widowed (by Henry IV) and homesick for Florence, she built the palace as a re-creation of her girlhood home, the Pitti Palace. When her son grew to be Louis XIII, he drove his mother from the palace, exiling her to Germany.

Luxembourg Garden has special rules governing its use (e.g., where cards can be played, where dogs can be walked, where joggers can run, and when and where music can be played). The brilliant flower-beds are completely changed three times a year, and the boxed trees are brought out of the *orangerie* in May. Children enjoy the rentable toy sailboats, pony rides, and marionette shows (Les Guignols, or Punch and Judy; see page 57).

Challenge the card and chess players to a game (near the tennis courts), or find a free chair near the main pond and take a well-deserved break, here at the end of our Left Bank Walk.

Nearby

The grand neoclassical-domed Panthéon, now a mausoleum housing the tombs of great Frenchmen, is three blocks away and worth touring (see page 57). The historic cafés of Montparnasse are a few blocks from the southwest-corner exit of the park (on rue Vavin, see "Les Grands Cafés de Paris," page 364).

• *Getting home: The Luxembourg Garden is ringed with Métro stops (all a 10-min walk away). North of the garden, the two closest Métro stops are St. Sulpice and Odéon. A convenient RER stop (Luxembourg) is at the park's east entry.*

LOUVRE TOUR

(Musée du Louvre)

Paris walks you through world history in three world-class museums—the Louvre (ancient world to 1850), the Orsay (1850–1914, including Impressionism), and the Pompidou (20th century to today). Start your "art-yssey" at the Louvre. With more than 30,000 works of art, the Louvre is a full inventory of Western civilization. To cover it all in one visit is impossible. Let's focus on the Louvre's specialties—Greek sculpture, Italian painting, and French painting.

We'll see "Venuses" through history, from scrawny Stone Age fertility goddesses to the curvy *Venus de Milo*, from the wind-blown *Winged Victory of Samothrace* to placid medieval Madonnas, from *Mona Lisa* to the symbol of modern democracy. We'll see how each generation defines beauty differently, and gain insight into long-ago civilizations by admiring the things they found beautiful.

In addition—for those with a little more time—we can visit some impressive chunks of stone from the "Cradle of Civilization," modern-day Iraq.

ORIENTATION

Cost: €8.50, €6 after 18:00 on Wed and Fri, free on first Sun of month, covered by Museum Pass. Tickets good all day; reentry allowed. Optional additional charges apply for temporary exhibits.

Hours: Wed–Mon 9:00–18:00, closed Tue. Most wings open Wed and Fri until 21:45. Evening visits are peaceful, and the pyramid glows after dark. Galleries start shutting down 30 minutes early. The last entry is 45 minutes before closing. Crowds are worst on Sun, Mon, Wed, and mornings.

Getting There: You have a variety of options.

By Subway: The Métro stop Palais Royal-Musée du Louvre is closer to the entrance than the stop called Louvre-Rivoli. From the Palais Royal-Musée du Louvre stop, you can stay underground to enter the Louvre, or exit above ground if you want to enter the Louvre through the pyramid (more details below).

By Bus: Handy bus #69 runs every 10 minutes from the Marais and rue Cler neighborhoods to the Louvre, dropping off passengers next to the Palais Royal-Musée du Louvre Métro stop on rue de Rivoli. Note that bus #69 stops running after 21:00.

By Taxi: A taxi stand is on rue de Rivoli next to the Palais Royal-Musée du Louvre Métro station.

Getting In: There is no grander entry than through the main entrance at the pyramid in the central courtyard, but metal detectors (not ticket-buying lines) create a long line at times. There are several ways to avoid the line:

If you have a Museum Pass, you can use the group entrance in the pedestrian passageway between the pyramid and rue de Rivoli (under the arches, a few steps north of the pyramid, find the uniformed guard at the entrance, with the escalator down).

Otherwise, you can enter the Louvre from its (usually less crowded) underground entrance, accessed through the "Carrousel du Louvre" shopping mall. Enter the mall at 99 rue de Rivoli (the door with the red awning, daily 8:30–23:00) or directly from the Métro stop Palais Royal-Musée du Louvre (stepping off the train, exit to the left, following signs to Carrousel du Louvre-Musée du Louvre).

Information: Pick up the free *Louvre Plan/Information* in English at the information desk under the pyramid as you enter. Tel. 01 40 20 53 17, recorded info: 01 40 20 51 51, www.louvre.fr.

Buying Tickets: Inside the pyramid, self-serve ticket machines are faster than the ticket windows (they accept euro notes, coins, and Visa cards, but not MasterCard).

Louvre Tours: The 90-minute English-language tours leave three times daily except Sun (normally at 11:00, 14:00, and 15:45, €5 plus your entry ticket, tour tel. 01 40 20 52 63). Sign up for tours at the *Acceuil des Groupes* area. Digital audioguides (available for €5 at entries to the 3 wings, at top of escalators) give you a directory of about 130 masterpieces, allowing you to dial a commentary on included works as you stumble upon them. While I prefer the free, self-guided tour described below, the audioguide provides some interesting complementary information. Eager

Louvre Overview

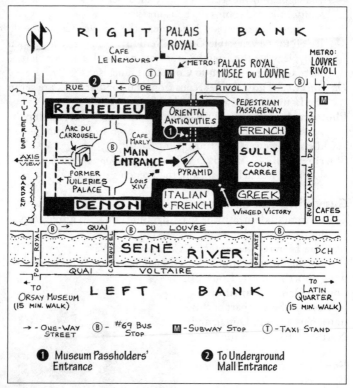

students should consider renting one as a supplement.

Length of This Tour: Allow two hours.

Checkrooms and WCs: Located under the escalators to the Denon and Richelieu wings. The coat check *(Vestiaire)*—which can have a torturously slow line (worst early in the morning and late afternoon)—does not take bags. The baggage check, *Bagagerie* (which doesn't take coats—unless they're stuffed into bags—cameras, or other valuables) is separate from the coat check and generally has almost no line.

Cuisine Art and More: The Louvre has several cafés, including Café Mollien, located near the end of our tour (€10 for sandwich, chips, and drink on terrace overlooking pyramid; see page 166). The underground shopping mall (the Carrousel du Louvre, west of the pyramid) has a dizzying assortment of decent-value, smoke-free eateries (up the escalator near the inverted pyramid). The mall also has glittering boutiques, a post office (after passing security), and the Palais Royal-Musée du Louvre Métro entrance. Stairs at the far end take

you right into the Tuileries Garden, a perfect antidote to the stuffy, crowded rooms of the Louvre.

For a fine, elegant lunch near the Louvre, cross rue de Rivoli to the venerable **Café le Nemours** (€10–12 salads, open daily; leaving the Louvre, cross rue de Rivoli and veer left, 2 place Colette, adjacent to Comédie Française).

Da Vinci Code **Fans:** Some scenes from the popular book are set in the Louvre and nearby (see sidebar on page 56).

Photography: Photography without a flash is allowed. (Flash photography is tolerated, but frowned upon, in some rooms—it distracts viewers and ruins paintings.)

Starring: *Venus de Milo*, *Winged Victory of Samothrace*, *Mona Lisa*, Raphael, Michelangelo, and the French painters.

Surviving the Louvre

Orient from underneath the glass pyramid. Pick up a free map at the information desk.

The Louvre, the largest museum in the Western world, fills three wings of this immense, U-shaped palace. The Richelieu wing (north side of Louvre) houses Oriental antiquities (covered in the 2nd part of this tour), plus French, Dutch, and Northern art. The Sully wing (east side) has the extensive French painting and ancient Egypt collections.

For this part of the tour, we'll concentrate on the Louvre's Denon wing (south side), which houses many of the superstars: ancient Greek sculpture, Italian Renaissance painting, and French neoclassical and Romantic painting.

Expect changes—the sprawling Louvre is constantly in flux. If you can't find a particular work, ask a guard where it is. Point to the photo in your book and ask, *"Où est, s'il vous plaît?"* (it rhymes). And move quickly.

You'll find English hand-held explanations throughout the museum that you can add to my descriptions along this tour. Try to finish the tour with enough energy left to browse.

THE TOUR BEGINS

• *From inside the big glass pyramid, you'll see signs to the three wings. Head for the Denon wing.*

Escalate up one floor. After showing your ticket, take the first left you can, follow signs to Antiquités Grecques, *and climb a set of stairs*

The Louvre—Pre-Classical Greece

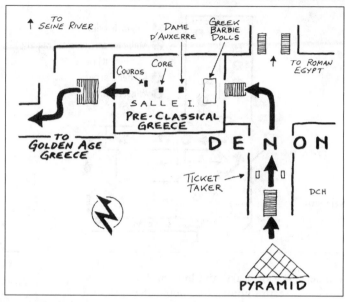

to the brick–ceilinged Salle 1: Grèce préclassique (Salle = Room). Enter prehistory.

DENON WING—GREECE (3,000 B.C.–A.D. 1)

Pre-Classical Greek Statues

These statues are noble but crude. The Greek Barbie dolls (3000 B.C.) are older than the pyramids, as old as writing itself. These pre-rational voodoo dolls whittle women down to their life-giving traits. A woman *(Dame d'Auxerre)* pledges allegiance to stability. Another *(Core)* is essentially a column with breasts. A young, naked man *(Couros)* seems to have a gun to his back—his

hands at his sides, facing front, with sketchy muscles and a mask-like face. "Don't move."

The early Greeks, who admired such statues, found stability more attractive than movement. Like their legendary hero, Odysseus, the Greek people had spent generations

The Louvre—Greek Statues

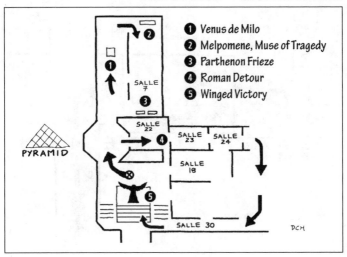

❶ Venus de Milo
❷ Melpomene, Muse of Tragedy
❸ Parthenon Frieze
❹ Roman Detour
❺ Winged Victory

PYRAMID

SALLE 7

SALLE 22

SALLE 23   SALLE 24

SALLE 18

SALLE 30

DCH

wandering, war-weary, and longing for the comforts of a secure home. The noble strength and sturdiness of these works looked beautiful.

• *Exit Salle 1 at the far end, and climb the stairs one flight. At the top, veer 10 o'clock left, where you'll soon see* Venus de Milo, *floating above a sea of worshipping tourists. It's been said that, among the warlike Greeks, this was the first statue to unilaterally disarm.*

Venus de Milo (Aphrodite, c. 100 B.C.)

The *Venus de Milo* (or goddess of love, from the Greek island of Melos) created a sensation when it was discovered in 1820. Europe was already in the grip of a

classical fad, and this statue seemed to sum up all that ancient Greece stood for. The Greeks pictured their gods in human form (meaning humans are godlike), telling us they had an optimistic view of the human race. *Venus'* well-proportioned body embodies the balance and orderliness of the Greek universe.

Split *Venus* down the middle from nose to toes and see how the two halves balance each other. *Venus* rests on her right foot (called *contrapposto,* or "counterpoise"), then lifts her left leg, setting her whole body in motion. As the left leg rises, her right shoulder droops down. And as her knee points one way, her head turns

Golden Age Greece

The great Greek cultural explosion that changed the course of history unfolded over 50 years (starting around 450 B.C.) in Athens, a Greek town smaller than Muncie, Indiana. Having united the Greeks to repel a Persian invasion, Athens rebuilt, with the Parthenon as the centerpiece of the city. The Greeks dominated the ancient world through brain, not brawn, and their art shows their love of rationality, order, and balance. The ideal Greek was well-rounded—an athlete and a bookworm, a lover and a philosopher, a carpenter who played the piano, a warrior and a poet. In art, the balance between timeless stability and fleeting movement made beauty.

In a sense, we're all Greek. Democracy, mathematics, theater, philosophy, literature, and science were practically invented in ancient Greece. Most of the art that we'll see in the Louvre either came from Greece or was inspired by it.

the other. *Venus* is a harmonious balance of opposites, orbiting slowly around a vertical axis. The twisting pose gives a balanced S-curve to her body (especially noticeable from the back view) that the Greeks and succeeding generations found beautiful.

Other opposites balance as well, like the smooth skin of her upper half that sets off the rough-cut texture of her dress (size 14). She's actually made from two different pieces of stone plugged together at the hips (the seam is visible). The face is realistic and anatomically accurate, but it's also idealized, a goddess, too generic and too perfect. This isn't any particular woman, but Everywoman—all the idealized features that appealed to the Greeks.

Most "Greek" statues are actually later Roman copies. This is a rare Greek original. This "epitome of the Golden Age" was actually sculpted three centuries after the Golden Age, though in a retro style.

What were her missing arms doing? Some say her right arm held her dress, while her left arm was raised. Others say she was hugging a man statue or leaning on a column. I say she was picking her navel.

• *Orbit* Venus. *This statue is interesting and different from every angle. Remember the view from the back—we'll see it again later. Make your reentry to Earth behind* Venus. *With your back to hers,* make *a U-turn to the right, doubling back down a room lined with Greek statues. Try to find even one that's not* contrapposto. *The large statue of Melpomene, holding the frowning mask of Tragedy, dominates the room. At the far end (in Salle 7, the Salle du Parthénon), you'll bump into two carved panels on the wall.*

Parthenon Frieze (Fragment de la Frise des Panathénées, c. 440 B.C.)

These stone fragments once decorated the exterior of the greatest Athenian temple, the Parthenon, built at the peak of the Greek Golden Age. The right panel shows a centaur sexually harassing a woman. It tells the story of how these rude creatures crashed a party of humans. But the Greeks fought back and threw the brutes out, just as Athens (metaphorically) conquered its barbarian neighbors and became civilized.

The other relief shows the sacred procession of young girls who marched up the hill every four years with an embroidered veil for the 40-foot-high statue of Athena, the goddess of wisdom. Though headless, the maidens speak volumes about Greek craftsmanship. Carved in only a couple inches of stone, they're amazingly realistic—more so than anything we saw in the

pre-Classical period. They glide along horizontally (their belts and shoulders all in a line), while the folds of their dresses drape down vertically. The man in the center is relaxed, realistic, and *contrapposto*. Notice the veins in his arm. The maidens' pleated dresses make them look as stable as fluted columns, but their arms and legs step out naturally—the human form is emerging from the stone.

• *Make a lo-o-o-ng (50-step) loop behind the Parthenon Frieze panels, turning left into Salle 22, the Antiquités Romaines, for a...*

Roman Detour (Salles 22–30)

Stroll among the Caesars and try to see the person behind the public persona. Besides the many faces of the ubiquitous Emperor *Inconnu* ("unknown"), you might spot Augustus (Auguste), the first emperor, and his wily wife, Livia (Livie). Their son Tiberius (Tibere) was the Caesar that Jesus Christ "rendered unto." Caligula was notoriously corrupt, curly-haired Domitia murdered her hus-

band, Hadrian popularized the beard, Trajan ruled the Empire at its peak, and Marcus Aurelius (Marc Aurele) presided stoically over Rome's slow fall.

The pragmatic Romans (500 B.C.–A.D. 500) were great conquerors, but bad artists. One area in which the Romans excelled was realistic portrait busts, especially of their emperors, who were

worshipped as gods on earth. Fortunately for us, the Romans also had a huge appetite for Greek statues and made countless copies. They took the Greek style and wrote it in capital letters, adding a veneer of sophistication to their homes, temples, baths, and government buildings.

The Roman rooms take you past several sarcophagi, an impressive mosaic floor that fills a massive courtyard, and beautiful wall-mounted mosaics from the ancient city of Antioch. Weary? Kick back and relax with the statues in the Etruscan Lounge (in Salle 18).

• *Continue through Room 30, noticing the fine palace ceilings as well as the impressive museum exhibits, and eventually spilling out at the base of stairs leading up to the First Floor and the dramatic...*

Winged Victory of Samothrace
(*Victoire de Samothrace,* c. 190 B.C.)

This woman with wings, poised on the prow of a ship, once stood on a hilltop to commemorate a naval victory. Her clothes are wind-

blown and sea-sprayed, clinging to her body close enough to win a wet T-shirt contest. (Notice the detail in the folds of her dress around the navel, curving down to her hips.) Originally, her right arm was stretched high, celebrating the victory like a Super Bowl champion, waving a "we're-number-one" finger.

This is the *Venus de Milo* gone Hellenistic, from the time after the culture of Athens was spread around the Mediterranean by Alexander the Great (c. 325 B.C.). As *Victory* strides forward, the wind blows her and her wings back. Her feet are firmly on the ground, but her wings (and missing arms) stretch upward. She is a pillar of vertical strength, while the clothes curve and whip around her. These opposing forces create a feeling of great energy, making her the lightest two-ton piece of rock in captivity.

The earlier Golden Age Greeks might have considered this statue ugly. Her rippling excitement is a far cry from the dainty Parthenon maidens and the soft-focus beauty of *Venus.* And the statue's off-balance pose, like an unfinished melody, leaves you hanging. But Hellenistic Greeks loved these cliff-hanging scenes of real-life humans struggling to make their mark.

In the glass case nearby is *Victory's* open right hand with an outstretched finger, discovered in 1950, a century after the statue itself was unearthed. When the French discovered this was in Turkey, they negotiated with the Turkish government for the rights

to it. Considering all the other ancient treasures the French had looted from Turkey in the past, the Turks thought it only appropriate to give France the finger.

• *Enter the octagonal room to the left as you face the* Winged Victory, *with Icarus bungee-jumping from the ceiling. Find a friendly window and look out toward the pyramid.*

View from the Octagonal Room: The Louvre as a Palace

The Louvre, the former royal palace, was built in stages over eight centuries. On your right (the eastern Sully wing) was the original medieval fortress. Next, another palace, the Tuileries, was built 500 yards to the west—in the now open area past the pyramid and the triumphal arch. Succeeding kings tried to connect these two palaces, each one adding another section onto the long, skinny north and south wings. Finally, in 1852, after three centuries of building, the two palaces were connected, creating a rectangular Louvre. Nineteen years later, the Tuileries Palace burned down during a riot, leaving the U-shaped Louvre we see today.

The glass pyramid was designed by the American architect I. M. Pei (1989). Many Parisians hated the pyramid, just like they used to hate another new and controversial structure 100 years ago—the Eiffel Tower.

In the octagonal room, a plaque at the base of the dome explains that France's Revolutionary National Assembly (the same people who brought you the guillotine) founded this museum in 1793. What could be more logical? You behead the king, inherit his palace and art collection, open the doors to the masses, and, *voilà!* You have Europe's first public museum.

• *From the octagonal room, enter the Apollo Gallery (Galerie d'Apollon).*

Apollo Gallery

The Gallery gives us a feel for the Louvre as the glorious home of the French kings (before Versailles). Imagine a chandelier-lit party in this room, drenched in stucco and gold leaf, with tapestries of leading Frenchmen and paintings with mythological and symbolic themes. The inlaid tables made from marble and semi-precious stones and many other art objects show the wealth of France, Europe's number one power for two centuries.

Stroll past glass cases of royal dinnerware to the far end of the room. In a glass case are the crown jewels, including the jewel-studded crown of Louis XV and the 140-carat Regent Diamond, which once graced crowns worn by Louis XV, Louis XVI, and Napoleon.

• *The Italian collection (Peintures Italiennes) is on the other side of Winged Victory. Cross in front of Winged Victory to the other side and pause (in Salle 1) at the two Botticelli fresco paintings on the wall to the left. These pure maidens, like colorized versions of the Parthenon frieze, give us a preview of how ancient Greece would be "reborn" in the Renaissance. But first, continue into the large Salle 3.*

THE MEDIEVAL WORLD (1200–1500)

Cimabue—*The Madonna of the Angels* (1280)

During the Age of Faith (1200s), most every church in Europe had a painting like this one. Mary was a cult figure—bigger than even the 20th-century Madonna—adored and prayed to by the faith-ful for bringing baby Jesus into the world.

After the collapse of the Roman Empire (c. A.D. 500), medieval Europe was a poorer and more violent place, with the Christian Church being the only constant in troubled times.

Altarpieces like this followed the same formula: Somber iconic faces, stiff poses, elegant folds in the robes, and generic angels. Violating 3-D space, the angels at the "back" of Mary's throne are the same size as those holding the front. These holy figures are laid flat on a gold background like cardboard cutouts, existing in a golden never-never land, as though the faithful couldn't imagine them as flesh-and-blood humans inhabiting our dark and sinful earth.

Giotto—*St. Francis of Assisi Receiving the Stigmata* (c. 1290–1295)

Francis of Assisi (c. 1181–1226), a wandering Italian monk of renowned goodness, kneels on a rocky Italian hillside, pondering the pain of Christ's torture and execution. Suddenly, he looks up, startled, to see Christ him-self, with six wings, hovering above. Christ shoots lasers from his wounds to burn marks on the hands, feet, and side of the empathetic monk. Francis went on to breathe the spirit of the Renaissance into medieval Europe. His humble love of man and nature inspired artists like Giotto to portray real human beings with real emotions and living in a physi-cal world of beauty.

Like a good filmmaker, Giotto (c. 1266–1337; JOT-toh) doesn't just *tell* us what happened, he *shows* us in present tense, freezing the scene at the most dramatic moment. Though the perspective is crude—Francis' hut is smaller than he is, and Christ is somehow shooting at Francis while facing us—Giotto creates the illusion of 3-D, with a foreground (Francis), middle ground (his hut), and background (the hillside). Painting a 3-D world on a 2-D surface is tough, and after a millennium of Dark Ages, artists were rusty.

In the *predella* (the panel of paintings below the altarpiece), birds gather at Francis' feet to hear him talk about God. Giotto catches the late arrivals in midflight, an astonishing technical feat for an artist more than a century before the Renaissance.

The simple gesture of Francis' companion speaks volumes about his amazement. Breaking the stiff, iconic mold for saints, Francis bends forward at the waist to talk to his fellow creatures. The diversity of the birds—"red and yellow, black and white"—symbolizes how all human-kind is equally precious in God's sight. Meanwhile, while the tree bends down symmetrically to catch a few words from the beloved hippie of Assisi.

• *The long Grand Gallery displays Italian Renaissance painting, some masterpieces, some not.*

ITALIAN RENAISSANCE

The Grand Gallery

Built in the late 1500s to connect the old palace with the Tuileries Palace, The Grand Gallery displays much of the Louvre's Italian Renaissance art. From the doorway, look to the far end and consider this challenge: I hold the world's record for the Grand Gallery Heel-Toe-Fun-Walk-Tourist-Slalom, going end to end in one minute, 58 seconds, two injured. Time yourself. Along the way, notice some of the...

Features of Italian Renaissance Painting

• **Religious:** Lots of Madonnas, children, martyrs, and saints.
• **Symmetrical:** The Madonnas are flanked by saints, two to the left, two to the right, and so on.
• **Realistic:** Real-life human features are especially obvious in the occasional portrait.

- **Three-Dimensional:** Every scene gets a spacious setting with a distant horizon.
- **Classical:** You'll see some Greek gods and classical nudes, but even Christian saints pose like Greek statues, and Mary is a *Venus* whose face and gestures embody all that was good in the Christian world.

Andrea Mantegna—*St. Sebastian* (c. 1480)

This isn't the patron saint of acupuncture. St. Sebastian was a Christian martyr, although here he looks more like a classical Greek statue. Notice the *contrapposto* stance (all of his weight resting on one leg) and the Greek ruins scattered around him. His executioners look like ignorant medieval brutes bewildered by this enlightened Renaissance man. Italian artists were beginning to learn how to create human realism and earthly beauty on the canvas. Let the Renaissance begin.

• *Look for the following masterpieces by Leonardo and Raphael in the Grand Gallery.*

Leonardo da Vinci—*Virgin, Child, and St. Anne (La Vierge a l'Enfant Jésus avec Sainte-Anne,* c. 1510)

Three generations—grandmother, mother, and child—are arranged in a pyramid, with Anne's face as the peak and the lamb as the

lower right corner. Within this balanced structure, Leonardo sets the figures in motion. Anne's legs are pointed to our left. (Is Anne *Mona?* Hmm.) Her daughter Mary, sitting on her lap, reaches to the right. Jesus looks at her playfully while turning away. The lamb pulls away from him. But even with all the twisting and turning, this is still a placid scene. It's as orderly as the geometrically perfect universe created by the Renaissance god.

There's a psychological kidney punch in this happy painting. Jesus, the picture of childish joy, is innocently playing with a lamb—the symbol of his inevitable sacrificial death.

The Louvre has the greatest collection of Leonardos in the world—five of them. Look for the neighboring *Virgin of the Rocks* and *John the Baptist.* Leonardo was the consummate Renaissance man. Musician, sculptor, engineer, scientist, and sometimes painter, he combined knowledge from all areas to create beauty. If he were alive today, he'd create a Unified Field Theory in physics—and set it to music.

The Louvre—Grand Gallery

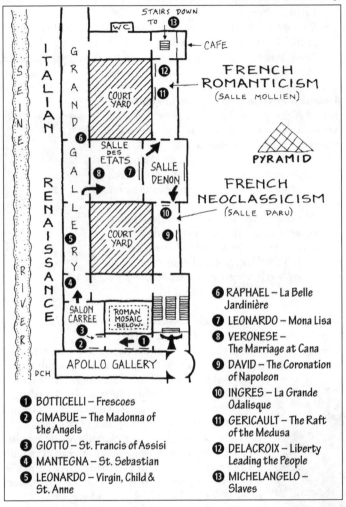

1 BOTTICELLI – Frescoes
2 CIMABUE – The Madonna of the Angels
3 GIOTTO – St. Francis of Assisi
4 MANTEGNA – St. Sebastian
5 LEONARDO – Virgin, Child & St. Anne
6 RAPHAEL – La Belle Jardinière
7 LEONARDO – Mona Lisa
8 VERONESE – The Marriage at Cana
9 DAVID – The Coronation of Napoleon
10 INGRES – La Grande Odalisque
11 GERICAULT – The Raft of the Medusa
12 DELACROIX – Liberty Leading the People
13 MICHELANGELO – Slaves

Raphael—*La Belle Jardinière* (1507)

Raphael (roff-eye-ELL) perfected the style Leonardo pioneered. This configuration of Madonna, Child, and John the Baptist is also a balanced pyramid with hazy grace and beauty. Mary is a mountain of maternal tenderness (the title translates as "The Beautiful Gardener"), as she eyes her son with a knowing look and holds his hand in a gesture of union. Jesus looks up innocently, standing *contrapposto* like a chubby Greek statue. Baby John the Baptist kneels lovingly at Jesus' feet, holding a cross hinting at his playmate's sacrificial death. The interplay of the gestures and gazes

Italian Renaissance (1400–1600)

A thousand years after Rome fell, plunging Europe into the Dark Ages, the Greek ideal of beauty was reborn in 15th-century Italy. The Renaissance—or "rebirth" of the culture of

ancient Greece and Rome—was a cultural boom that changed people's thinking about every aspect of life. In politics, it meant democracy. In religion, it meant a move away from Church dominance and toward the assertion of man (humanism) and a more personal faith. Science and secular learning were revived after centuries of superstition and ignorance. In architecture, it was a return to the balanced columns and domes of Greece and Rome.

In painting, the Renaissance meant realism, and for the Italians, realism was spelled "3-D." Artists rediscovered the beauty of nature and the human body. With pictures of beautiful people in harmonious, 3-D surroundings, they expressed the optimism and confidence of this new age.

gives the masterpiece both intimacy and cohesiveness while Raphael's blended brush strokes varnish the work with an iridescent smoothness.

With Raphael, the Greek ideal of beauty reborn in the Renaissance reached its peak. His work spawned so many imitators who cranked out sickly sweet, generic Madonnas that we often take him for granted. Don't. This is the real thing.

• *The* Mona Lisa (La Joconde) *is in the Salle des Etats, midway down the Grand Gallery, on the right. After several years and a €5 million renovation,* Mona *has returned to the Salle des Etats, standing alone behind glass on her own false wall. Six million heavy-breathing people crowd in each year to glimpse the most ogled painting in the world. (You can't miss her. Just follow the signs...the crowds...it's the only painting you can hear...with all the groveling crowds, you can even smell it.)*

Leonardo da Vinci—*Mona Lisa* (1503–1506)

Leonardo was already an old man when François I invited him to France. Determined to pack light, he took only a few paintings with him. One was a portrait of a Lisa del Giocondo, the wife of a wealthy Florentine merchant. When Leonardo arrived, François

immediately fell in love with the painting, making it the center-piece of the small collection of Italian masterpieces that would, in three centuries, become the Louvre museum. He called it *La Gioconda*. We know it as a contraction of the Italian for "my lady Lisa"—*Mona Lisa*.

Mona may disappoint you. She's smaller than you'd expect, darker, engulfed in a huge room, and hidden behind a glaring pane of glass. So, you ask, "Why all the hubbub?" Let's take a closer look. Like any lover, you've got to take her for what she is, not what you'd like her to be.

The famous smile attracts you first. Leonardo used a hazy technique called *sfumato*, blurring the edges of *Mona*'s mysterious smile. Try as you might, you can never quite see the corners of her mouth. Is she happy? Sad? Tender? Or is it a cynical supermodel's smirk? Every viewer reads it differently, projecting his own mood onto *Mona*'s enigmatic face. *Mona* is a Rorschach inkblot...so, how are you feeling?

Now look past the smile and the eyes that really do follow you (most eyes in portraits do) to some of the subtle Renaissance elements that make this work work. The body is surprisingly massive and statue-like, a perfectly balanced pyramid turned at an angle, so that we can see its mass. Her arm is resting lightly on the chair's armrest, almost on the level of the frame itself, like she's sitting in a window looking out at us. The folds of her sleeves and her gently folded hands are remarkably realistic and relaxed. The typical Leonardo landscape shows distance by getting hazier and hazier.

The overall mood is one of balance and serenity, but there's also an element of mystery. Her smile and long-distance beauty are subtle and elusive, tempting but always just out of reach, like strands of a street singer's melody drifting through the Métro tunnel. *Mona* doesn't knock your socks off, but she winks at the patient viewer.

• *Before leaving* Mona, *stand back and just observe the paparazzi scene. The huge canvas opposite* Mona *is...*

Paolo Veronese—*The Marriage at Cana* (1562–1563)

Stand 10 steps away from this enormous canvas to where it just fills your field of vision, and suddenly...you're in a party! Help yourself to a glass of wine. This is the Renaissance love of beautiful things gone hog-wild. Venetian artists like Veronese painted the good life of rich, happy-go-lucky Venetian merchants.

In a spacious setting of Renaissance architecture, colorful

lords and ladies decked out in their fanciest duds feast on a great spread of food and drink, while the musicians fuel the fires of good fun. Servants prepare and serve the food, jesters play, and animals roam. In the upper left, a dog and his master look on. A sturdy line-backer in yellow pours wine out of a jug (right foreground). The man in white samples some wine and thinks, "Hmm, not bad," while nearby a ferocious cat battles a lion. The wedding couple at the far left is almost forgotten.

Believe it or not, this is a religious work showing the wedding celebration where Jesus turned water into wine. And there's Jesus in the dead center of 130 frolicking figures, wondering if maybe wine coolers might not have been a better choice. With true Renaissance optimism, Venetians pictured Christ as a party animal, someone who loved the created world as much as they did.

Now, let's hear it for the band! On bass—the bad cat with the funny hat—Titian the Venetian! And joining him on viola—Crazy Veronese!

• *Exit behind* Mona *into the Salle Denon. The dramatic Romantic room is to your left, and the grand neoclassical room is to your right (see the map on page 160). The two rooms feature the most exciting French canvases in the Louvre. In the neoclassical room, kneel before the largest canvas in the Louvre.*

FRENCH NEOCLASSICISM (1780–1850)

Jacques-Louis David—*The Coronation of Napoleon* (1806–1807)

Napoleon holds aloft an imperial crown. This common-born son of immigrants is about to be crowned emperor of a "New Rome." He has just made his wife, Josephine, the empress, and she kneels at his feet. Seated behind Napoleon is the pope, who journeyed from Rome to place the imperial crown on his head. But Napoleon felt that no one was worthy of the task. At the last moment, he shrugged the pope aside, grabbed the crown, held it up for all to see...and crowned himself. The pope looks p.o.'d.

After the French people decapitated their king during the Revolution (1793), their fledgling democracy floundered in chaos. France was united by a charismatic, brilliant, temperamental, upstart general who kept his feet on the ground, his eyes on the horizon, and his hand in his coat—Napoleon Bonaparte. Napoleon quickly conquered most of Europe and insisted on being made emperor (not merely king). The painter David (dah-veed) recorded

the coronation for posterity.

The radiant woman in the gallery in the background center wasn't actually there. Napoleon's mother couldn't make it to see her boy become the most powerful man in Europe, but he had David paint her in anyway. (There's a key on the frame telling who's who in the picture.)

The traditional place of French coronations was the ultra-Gothic Notre-Dame cathedral. But Napoleon wanted a setting that would reflect the glories of Greece and the grandeur of Rome. So interior decorators erected stage sets of Greek columns and Roman arches to give the cathedral the architectural political correctness you see in this painting. (The *Pietà* statue on the right edge of the painting is still in Notre-Dame today.)

David was the new emperor's official painter and propagandist, in charge of color-coordinating the costumes and flags for public ceremonies and spectacles. (Find his self-portrait with curly gray hair in the *Coronation*, way up in the second balcony, peeking around the tassel directly above Napoleon's crown.) His "neoclassical" style influenced French fashion. Take a look at his *Madame Juliet Récamier* portrait on the opposite wall, showing a modern Parisian woman in ancient garb and Pompeii hairstyle reclining on a Roman couch. Nearby paintings, such as *The Death of Socrates* and *The Oath of the Horatii (Le Serment des Horaces)*, are fine examples of neoclassicism, with Greek subjects, patriotic sentiment, and a clean, simple style.

• *As you double back toward the Romantic room, stop at...*

Jean-Auguste-Dominique Ingres— *La Grande Odalisque* (1819)

Take *Venus de Milo*, turn her around, lay her down, and stick a hash pipe next to her, and you have the *Grande Odalisque*. OK, maybe you'd have to add a vertebra or two.

Using clean, polished, sculptural lines, Ingres (ang-gruh, with a soft "gruh") exaggerates the S-curve of a standing Greek nude. As in the *Venus de Milo*, rough folds of cloth set off her smooth

skin. The face, too, has a touch of *Venus'* idealized features (or like Raphael's kindergarten teacher), taking nature and improving on it. Contrast the cool colors of this statue-like nude with Titian's golden girls.

Ingres preserves *Venus'* backside for posterior—I mean, posterity.
• *Cross back through the Salle Denon (where you might spot a painting high up entitled* The Death of Walter Mondale) *and into a room gushing with...*

FRENCH ROMANTICISM (1800–1850)

Théodore Géricault—*The Raft of the Medusa*
(*Le Radeau de la Méduse,* 1819)

In the artistic war between hearts and minds, the heart style was known as Romanticism. Stressing motion and emotion, it was the flip side of cool, balanced neoclassicism, though they both flourished in the early 1800s.

What better setting for an emotional work than a shipwreck? Clinging to a raft is a tangle of bodies and lunatics sprawled over each other. The scene writhes with agitated, ominous motion—the ripple of muscles, churning clouds, and choppy seas. On the right is a deathly green corpse dangling overboard. The face of the man at left, cradling a dead body, says it all—the despair of spending weeks stranded in the middle of nowhere.

This painting was based on the actual sinking of the ship *Medusa* off the coast of Africa in 1816. About 150 packed onto the raft. After floating in the open seas for 12 days—suffering hardship and hunger, even resorting to cannibalism—only 15 survived. The story was made to order for a painter determined to shock the public and arouse its emotions. That painter was young Géricault (zhair-ee-ko). He interviewed survivors and honed his craft sketching dead bodies in the morgue and the twisted faces of lunatics in asylums, capturing the moment when all hope is lost.

But wait. There's a stir in the crowd. Someone has spotted something. The bodies rise up in a pyramid of hope, culminating in a waving flag. They wave frantically, trying to catch the attention of the tiny ship on the horizon, their last desperate hope... which did finally save them. Géricault uses rippling movement and powerful colors to catch us up in the excitement. If art controls your heartbeat, this is a masterpiece.

Eugène Delacroix—*Liberty Leading the People*
(*La Liberté Guidant le Peuple,* 1830)

The year is 1830. King Charles had issued the 19th-century equivalent of a "Patriot Act" and his subjects were angry. The Parisians have taken to the streets once again, *Les Miz*–style, to fight royalist

oppressors. The people triumphed—replacing the king with Louis-Philippe who was happy to rule within the constraints of a modern constitution. There's a hard-bitten proletarian with a sword (far left), an intellectual with a top hat and a sawed-off shotgun, and even a little boy brandishing pistols.

Leading them on through the smoke and over the dead and dying is the figure of Liberty, a strong woman waving the French flag. Does this symbol of victory look familiar? It's the *Winged Victory*, wingless and topless.

To stir our emotions, Delacroix (del-ah-kwah) uses only three major colors—the red, white, and blue of the French flag. France is the symbol of modern democracy and this painting has long stirred its citizens' passion for liberty. The French weren't the first to adopt democracy (Americans were), nor are they the best working example of it, but they've had to work harder to achieve it than any other country. No sooner would they throw one king or dictator out than they'd get another. They're now working on their fifth republic.

This symbol of freedom is a fitting tribute to the Louvre, the first museum ever opened to the common rabble of humanity. The good things in life don't belong only to a small wealthy part of society, but to everyone. The motto of France is *Liberté, Egalité, Fraternité*—liberty, equality, and the brotherhood of all.

• *Exit the room at the far end (past a café) and go downstairs, where you'll bump into the bum of a large, twisting male nude looking like he's just waking up after a thousand-year nap.*

MORE ITALIAN RENAISSANCE

Michelangelo—*Slaves* (1513–1515)
These two statues by earth's greatest sculptor are a fitting end to this museum—works that bridge the ancient and modern worlds. Michelangelo, like his fellow Renaissance artists, learned from the Greeks. The perfect anatomy, twisting poses, and idealized faces look like they could have been done 2,000 years earlier.

The so-called *Dying Slave* (also called the *Sleeping Slave*, looking like he should be stretched out on a sofa) twists listlessly against his T-shirt-like bonds, revealing his smooth skin. Compare the polished detail of the rippling, bulging left arm with the sketchy details of the face and neck. With Michelangelo, the body does the talking. This is probably the most sensual nude ever done by the master of the male body.

The *Rebellious Slave* fights against his bondage. His shoulders turn one way while his head and leg turn the other. He looks

upward, straining to get free. He even seems to be trying to free himself from the rock he's made of. Michelangelo said that his purpose was to carve away the marble to reveal the figures God put inside. This slave shows the agony of that process and the ecstasy of the result.

• *Tour over! These two may be slaves of the museum, but you are free to go. You've seen the essential Louvre. But, of course, there's so much more. After a break (or on a 2nd visit), consider a stroll through a few rooms containing some of the Louvre's oldest and biggest pieces. Bible students, amateur archaeologists, and Iraq War vets may find the collection especially interesting. It's in the Richelieu Wing.*

RICHELIEU WING

Oriental Antiquities (Antiquités Orientales)

Saddam Hussein is only the latest iron-fisted, palace-building conqueror to fall in Iraq's long history, which stretches back to the dawn of civilization. Civilization began 6,000 years ago in Iraq, between the Tigris and Euphrates Rivers, in the area called the Fertile Crescent.

In the Louvre's Richelieu wing, you can sweep quickly through 2,000 years of Iraq's ancient history, enjoying some of the Louvre's biggest and oldest artifacts. See how each new civilization toppled the previous one—pulling down its statues, destroying its palaces, looting its cultural heritage, and replacing it with victory monuments of its own...only to be toppled again by the next wave of history.

• *From under the pyramid, enter the Richelieu wing. Show your ticket, then take the first right. Go up one flight of stairs and one escalator to the ground floor* (rez-de-chaussée). *Walk straight off the escalator and*

enter Salle 1-a (Mesopotamie Archaïque) and come face to face with fragments of the broken...

Stela of the Vultures (Stele de victoire d'Eannatum, roi de Lagash, c. 2450 B.C.)

As old as the pyramids, this stela (ceremonial stone pillar) may be the oldest depiction of a historical event—the battle between the city of Lagash (100 miles north of modern Basra) and its archrival, Umma.

The Louvre—Oriental Antiquities

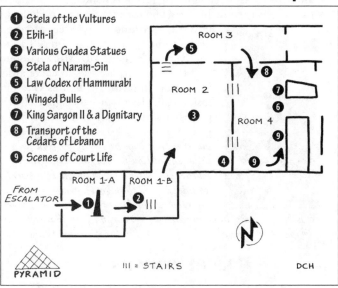

1 Stela of the Vultures
2 Ebih-il
3 Various Gudea Statues
4 Stela of Naram-Sin
5 Law Codex of Hammurabi
6 Winged Bulls
7 King Sargon II & a Dignitary
8 Transport of the Cedars of Lebanon
9 Scenes of Court Life

ROOM 3
ROOM 2
ROOM 4
ROOM 1-A
ROOM 1-B
FROM ESCALATOR

III = STAIRS

PYRAMID

DCH

Bearded King Eannatum waves the eagle flag of Lagash with one hand, while with the other, he clubs a puny enemy soldier trapped in a battle net, making his enemies pledge allegiance to Lagash's gods.

Circle around to the flip side of the stela for the rest of the story, "reading" from top to bottom. Top level: Behind a wall of shields, a phalanx of helmeted soldiers advances, trampling the enemy underfoot. They pile the corpses (right), while vultures swoop down from above to pluck the remains. Middle level: The king waves to the crowd from

his chariot in the victory parade. Bottom level: They dig a mass grave—one of 20 for the 36,000 enemy dead—while a priest (top of the fragment) gives thanks to the gods. A tethered ox (see his head) is about to become a burnt sacrifice.

The inscription on the stela is in cuneiform, the world's first written language, invented by the Sumerians.

• *Continue into Salle 1-b, with the blissful statue of...*

Just Enough Geography and History for This Tour

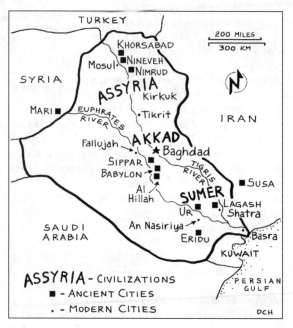

The northern half of Iraq is mountainous, and the southern half is the delta of the Tigris and Euphrates Rivers. Baghdad sits roughly in between north and south, along the Tigris. The Sumerians inhabited the south, the Assyrians the north, and the Akkadians and Babylonians the center, around Baghdad.

Here's a brief timeline:

3500–2400 B.C. Sumerian city-states flourish between the Tigris and Euphrates Rivers. Sumerians invent writing.

2300 B.C. Akkadians invade Sumer.

1750 B.C. Hammurabi establishes first Babylonian empire.

710 B.C. Sargon II rules over a vast Assyrian-controlled empire, encompassing modern Iraq, Israel, Syria, and Egypt.

612 B.C. Babylonians revolt against the Assyrians and destroy the Assyrian capital of Nineveh (300 miles north of Baghdad), then build their own near Baghdad.

Ebih-il, The Superintendent of Mari (c. 2400 B.C.)

Bald, bearded, blue-eyed Ebih-il (his name is inscribed on his shoulder) sits in his fleece skirt, folds his hands reverently across his chest and gazes rapturously into space, dreaming of...Ishtar. Ebih-il was a priest in the goddess Ishtar's temple, and the statue is dedicated to her.

Ishtar was the chief goddess of many Middle Eastern peoples. As goddess of both love and war, she was a favorite of horny soldiers. She was a giver of life (this statue is dedicated "to Ishtar the virile"), yet also miraculously a virgin. She was also a great hunter with bow and arrow, and a great lover ("Her lips are sweet...her figure is beautiful, her eyes are brilliant...women and men adore her," sang the *Hymn to Ishtar*, c. 1600 B.C.).

Ebih-il adores her eternally with his eyes made of seashells and lapis lazuli. The smile on his face reflects the pleasure the goddess has just given him, perhaps through one of the sacred prostitutes who resided in Ishtar's Temple.

• *Go up the five steps behind* Ebih-il, and *turn left into Salle 2, containing a dozen statues all of the same man, named...*

Gudea, Prince of Lagash (c. 2125–2110 B.C.)

Gudea (r. 2141–2122 B.C.), in his wool stocking cap, folds his hands and prays to the gods to save his people from invading barbarians. One of Sumeria's last great rulers, the peaceful and pious Gudea (his name means "the destined") rebuilt temples (where these statues once stood) to thank the gods for their help.

• *Behind you, find the rosy-colored...*

Stela of Naram-Sin (Stele de victoire de Naram-Sin, roi d'Akkad, c. 2230 B.C.)

After a millennium of prosperity, Sumeria was plundered (c. 2250 B.C.), and Akkadia became the new king of the mountain. Here, King Naram-Sin climbs up to the sunny heavens, crowned with the horned helmet of a god. His soldiers look up to admire him as he tramples his enemies. Next to him, a victim tries to remove a spear from his neck, while another pleads to the conqueror for mercy.

Ancient Places in the News Today

Lagash, the ancient city of Prince Gudea (see page 170), is near modern **Shatra**, in southeast Iraq. In March 2003, American invasion forces met some of their stiffest resistance in Shartra (before the fall of Baghdad). "Chemical Ali"—Saddam's cousin and the Ace of Spades in America's deck of most-wanted Iraqis—was thought to be holed up in the city; he eluded capture for a few more months. After shelling Shatra with planes, helicopters, and tanks, U.S. Marines took the town and were met by Iraqis with signs saying *Welcome to Iraq.*

The Stela of the Vultures (on page 167) depicts battles between Lagash and Umma, near modern **An Nasiriyah**. It was there that, in March of 2003, a U.S. convoy took a wrong turn, was ambushed by Iraqis, and Pfc. Jessica Lynch was captured. Nine days later, a U.S. helicopter full of soldiers stormed the An Nasiriyah hospital, and Lynch was airlifted away to a hero's welcome. Later reports revealed that she'd suffered wounds from the crash of her truck during the attack and that she was being tended in the Iraqi hospital.

Sargon II built his palace outside **Mosul**, now a Kurdish center in northern Iraq. After U.S. soldiers drove insurgents from Fallujah (in the fall of 2004), many resettled in Mosul. On December 29, 2004, insurgents launched a daring attack in the city center. They set off a truck bomb, then when U.S. soldiers arrived on the scene, they attacked. The firefight left one U.S. soldier and 25 Iraqis dead.

Hammurabi's Code, though discovered in Iran, may once have stood in ancient Babylon, 50 miles south of Baghdad in **Al Hillah**. On February 28, 2005, a suicide car bomb detonated in a crowd of Iraqi police officers, killing 125, the deadliest such blast yet. On May 30, 2005, two more suicide bombers let loose in a crowd of police officers, killing 20—examples of the new tactic of warfare that emerged in the Iraq War.

• *Exit Salle 2 at the far end, entering Salle 3, with the large black stela of Hammurabi.*

Law Codex of Hammurabi, King of Babylon (c. 1760 B.C.)

Hammurabi (r. c. 1792–1750 B.C.) established the next great civilization, ruling as King of Babylon (50 miles south of modern Baghdad). He proclaimed 282 laws, all inscribed on this eight-foot black basalt stela—one of the first formal legal documents—four centuries before the Ten Commandments. Stelas such as this likely dotted Hammurabi's empire, and this one may have stood in Babylon before being moved to Susa, Iran.

At the top of the stela, Hammurabi (standing and wearing Gudea's hat of kingship) receives the scepter of judgment from the god of justice and the sun, who radiates flames from his shoulders. The inscription begins, "When Anu the Sublime...called me, Hammurabi, by name...I did right, and brought about the well-being of the oppressed."

Next come the laws, scratched in cuneiform down the length of the stela, some 3,500 lines reading right-to-left. The laws cover very specific situations, everything from lying, theft, and trade to marriage and medical malpractice. The legal innovation was the immediate retribution for wrongdoing, often with poetic justice. Here's a sample:

#1: If any man ensnare another falsely, he shall be put to death.

#57: If your sheep graze another man's land, you must repay 20 gur of grain.

#129: If a couple is caught in adultery, they shall both be tied up and thrown in the water.

#137: If you divorce your wife, you must pay alimony and child support.

#218: A surgeon who bungles an operation shall have his hands cut off.

#282: If a slave shall say, "You are not my master," the master can cut off the slave's ear.

The most quoted laws—summing up the spirit of ancient Middle Eastern justice—are #196 ("If a man put out the eye of another man, his eye shall be put out") and #200 (a tooth for a tooth).

• *Enter the large Salle 4, dominated by colossal winged bulls with human heads. These sculptures—including five winged bulls and many relief panels along the walls—are from the...*

Palace of Sargon II

Sargon II, the Assyrian king (r. 721–705 B.C.) spared no expense on his palace (see various reconstructions of the palace on plaques in Salle 4). In Assyrian society, the palace of the king—not the temple of the gods—was the focus of life, and each ruler demonstrated his authority with large residences.

Sargon II actually built a whole new city for his palace, just north of the traditional capital of Nineveh (modern-day Mosul). He called it Dur Sharrukin ("Sargonburg"), and the city's vast dimensions were 4,000 cubits by—oh, excuse me—it covered

The Assyrians

This Semitic people from the agriculturally-challenged hills of northern Iraq became traders and conquerors, not farmers. They conquered their southern neighbors and dominated the Middle East for 300 years (c. 900–600 B.C.).

Their strength came from a superb army (chariots, mounted cavalry, and seige engines), a policy of terrorism against enemies ("I tied their heads to tree trunks all around the city," reads a royal inscription), ethnic cleansing and mass deportations of the vanquished, and efficient administration (roads and express postal service). They have been called "The Romans of the East."

about 150 football fields pieced together. The whole city was built on a raised, artificial mound, and the palace itself (25 acres) sat even higher, surrounded by walls, with courtyards, temples, the king's residence, and a wedding-cake-shaped temple (called a ziggurat) dedicated to the god Sin.

• *Start with the two biggest bulls, which support a (reconstructed) arch, get close.*

Winged Bulls (c. 710 B.C.)

These 30-ton, 14-foot alabaster bulls with human faces once guarded the entrance to the throne room of the Assyrian King Sargon II. A visitor to the palace back then could have looked over the bulls' heads and seen a 15-story ziggurat (a stepped-pyramid temple) towering overhead. The winged bulls were guardian spirits to keep out demons and intimidate liberals.

Between their legs are cuneiform inscriptions such as: "I, Sargon, King of the Universe, built palaces for my royal residence.... I had winged bulls with human heads carved from great blocks of mountain stone, and I placed them at the doors facing the four winds as powerful divine guardians.... My creation amazed all who gazed upon it ."

• *We'll see a few relief panels from the palace, working counterclockwise around the room. Start with the panel just to the left of the two big bulls (as you face them). Find the bearded, earringed man in whose image the bulls were made.*

King Sargon II and a Dignitary
(*Le roi Sargon II et un haut dignitaire,* c. 710 B.C.)

Sargon II, wearing a fez-like crown with a cone on the top and straps down the back, cradles his scepter and raises his staff to

receive a foreign ambassador who's come to pay tribute. Sargon II controlled a vast empire, consisting of modern-day Iraq and extending westward to the Mediterranean and Egypt.

Before becoming emperor, Sargon II was a conquering general who invaded Israel (2 Kings 17:1-6). After a three-year seige, he took Jerusalem

and deported much of the population, inspiring the legends of the "Lost" Ten Tribes. The prophet Isaiah saw him as God's tool to punish the sinful Israelites, "to seize loot and snatch plunder, and to trample them down like mud in the streets" (Isaiah 10:6).

• *On the wall to the left of Sargon are four panels depicting the...*

Transport of the Cedars of Lebanon
(Transport du bois de cèdre du Liban)

Boats carry the finest quality logs for Sargon II's palace, crossing

a wavy sea populated with fish, turtles, crabs, and mermen. The transport process is described in the Bible (1 Kings 5:9): "My men will haul them down from Lebanon to the sea, and I will float them in rafts to the place you specify."

• *Continue counterclockwise around the room—past more big winged animals, past the huge hero Gilgamesh crushing a lion—until you reach more relief panels. These depict...*

Scenes of Court Life

The brown, eroded gypsum panels we see were originally painted and varnished. Placed side by side, they would have stretched over a mile. The panels read like a comic strip, showing the king's men parading in to serve him.

First, soldiers *(Guerrier en armée)* sheath their swords and fold their hands reverently. A winged spirit prepares them to enter the king's presence

by shaking a pine cone to anoint them with holy perfume. Next, servants (see photo on previous page) hurry to the throne room with the king's dinner, carrying his table, chair, and bowl. Other servants ready the king's horses and chariots.

From Sargon to Saddam

Sargon II's palace remained unfinished, and was later burned and buried. Sargon's great Assyrian empire dissolved over the next few generations. When the Babylonians revolted and conquered their northern neighbors (612 B.C.), the whole Middle East applauded. As the Bible put it: "Nineveh is in ruins—who will mourn for her?.... Everyone who hears the news claps his hands at your fall, for who has not felt your endless cruelty?" (Nahum 3:7, 19).

The new capital was Babylon (50 miles south of modern Baghdad), ruled by King Nebuchadnezzar, who conquered Judea (586 B.C., the Bible's "Babylonian Captivity") and built a palace with the Hanging Gardens, one of the Seven Wonders of the World.

Over the succeeding centuries, Babylon/Baghdad fell to Persians (539 B.C.), Greeks (Alexander the Great, 331 B.C.), Persians again (2nd century B.C.), Arab Muslims (A.D. 634), Mongol hordes (Genghis Khan's grandson, 1258), Iranians (1502), Ottoman Turks (1535), British-controlled kings (1921), and military regimes (1958), the most recent headed by Saddam Hussein (1979).

In A.D. 2003, five thousand years of invasions, violence, and regime change finally came to an end when peace, prosperity, and democracy were established for all time in Iraq by the United States of America under the benevolent guidance of George W. Bush.

ORSAY MUSEUM TOUR

(Musée d'Orsay)

The Musée d'Orsay (mew-zay dor-say) houses French art of the 1800s (specifically, 1848–1914), picking up where the Louvre leaves off. For us, that means Impressionism, the art of sun-dappled fields, bright colors, and crowded Parisian cafés. The Orsay houses the best general collection of Manet, Monet, Renoir, Degas, van Gogh, Cézanne, and Gauguin anywhere. If you like Impressionism, visit this museum. If you don't like Impressionism, visit this museum. I personally find it a more enjoyable and rewarding place than the Louvre. Sure, ya gotta see the *Mona Lisa* and *Venus de Milo*, but after you get your gottas out of the way, enjoy the Orsay.

ORIENTATION

Cost: €7.50; €5.50 after 16:15 and on Sun, free first Sun of month, covered by Museum Pass. Tickets are good all day. Museum Pass-holders can enter quickly on the right side of the building, ticket-buyers enter along the left (river) side.

Free Entry near Closing: Right when the ticket booth stops selling tickets (17:00 on Tue–Wed and Fri–Sun, 20:45 on Thu), you're welcome to scoot in free of charge. (They won't let you in much after that, however.) For one hour, you'll have the art mostly to yourself before the museum closes. The Impressionism galleries upstairs start shutting down first, so go there right away.

Hours: June 20–Sept 20 Tue–Sun 9:00–18:00, Sept 21–June 19 Tue–Sat 10:00–18:00, Sun 9:00–18:00, Thu until 21:45 year-round, always closed Mon. Last entry one hour before closing. The Impressionist galleries begin closing at 17:15, frustrating unwary visitors. Note that the Orsay is crowded on Tuesday, when the Louvre is closed.

Getting There: It sits above the RER-C stop called Musée d'Orsay. The nearest Métro stop is Solférino, three blocks south of the Orsay. Bus #69 from the Marais neighborhood stops at the museum on the river side (quai Anatole France); from the rue Cler area, it stops behind the museum on the rue du Bac. From the Louvre, catch bus #69 along rue de Rivoli; otherwise, it's a lovely 15-minute walk through the Tuileries and across the river on the pedestrian bridge to the Orsay. A taxi stand is in front of the museum on quai Anatole France.

Getting In: As you face the front of the museum from rue de la Légion d'Honneur (with the river on your left), passholders enter on the right side of the museum (Entrance C) and ticket purchasers enter along the river side (Entrance A).

Information: The booth inside the entrance provides free floor plans in English. Tel. 01 40 49 48 41, www.musee-orsay.fr.

Orsay Tours: Audioguides are €5. English-language guided tours usually run daily (except Sun) at 11:30 (90-min tours-€6). Tours in English focusing on the Impressionists are offered Tuesdays at 14:30 (€6, sometimes also on other days). I recommend the free, self-guided tour described below.

Length of This Tour: Allow two hours.

Cloakroom *(Vestiaire):* It's the usual—no big bags allowed in the museum, no valuables allowed in checked bags.

Cuisine Art: There's a pricey but *très* elegant restaurant on the second floor, with affordable tea and coffee served 15:00–17:30. A simple fifth-floor café is sandwiched between the Impressionists; above it is an easy self-service place with sandwiches and drinks.

Photography: Photography without a flash is allowed.

Starring: Manet, Monet, Renoir, Degas, van Gogh, Cézanne, and Gauguin.

THE TOUR BEGINS

Gare d'Orsay: The Old Train Station

• *Pick up a free English map upon entering, buy your ticket, and check your bag. Belly up to the stone balustrade overlooking the main floor, and orient yourself.*

Trains used to run right under our feet down the center of the gallery. This former train station, or *gare*, barely escaped the wrecking ball in the 1970s, when the French realized it'd be a great place to house the enormous collections of 19th-century art scattered throughout the city.

The Orsay's "19th Century"
(1848–1914)

Einstein and Geronimo. Abraham Lincoln and Karl Marx. The train, the bicycle, the horse and buggy, the automobile, and the balloon. Freud and Dickens. Darwin's *Origin of Species* and the Church's Immaculate Conception. Louis Pasteur and Billy the Kid. V. I. Lenin and Ty Cobb.

The 19th century was a mix of old and new, side by side. Europe was entering the modern Industrial Age, with cities, factories, rapid transit, instant communication, and global networks. At the same time, it clung to the past with traditional, rural—almost medieval—attitudes and morals.

According to the Orsay, the "19th century" began in 1848 with the socialist and democratic revolutions (Marx's *Communist Manifesto*). It ended in 1914 with the pull of an assassin's trigger, which ignited World War I and ushered in the modern world. The museum shows art that is also both old and new, conservative and revolutionary.

The main floor has early 19th-century art—as usual, Conservative on the right, Realism on the left. Upstairs (not visible from here) is the core of the collection—the Impressionist rooms. If you're pressed for time, go directly there (see directions following "Opéra Exhibit" on page 185). We'll start with the Conservatives and early rebels on the ground floor, then head upstairs to see how a few visionary young artists bucked the system and revolutionized the art world, paving the way for the 20th century. Finally, we'll end the tour with "the other Orsay" on the mezzanine level. Clear as Seine water? *Bien.*

• *Walk down the steps to the main floor, a gallery filled with statues.*

CONSERVATIVE ART

Main Gallery Statues

No, this isn't ancient Greece. These statues are from the same era as the Theory of Relativity. It's the Conservative art of the French schools that was so popular throughout the 19th century. It was well-liked because it's beautiful. The balanced poses, perfect anatomy, sweet faces, curving lines, and gleaming white stone—all of this is very appealing. (I'll bad-mouth it later, but for now appreciate the exquisite craftsmanship of this "perfect" art.)

• *Take your first right into the small Room 1, marked "Ingres et l'Ingrisme." Look for a nude woman with a pitcher of water.*

Orsay Ground Floor—Overview

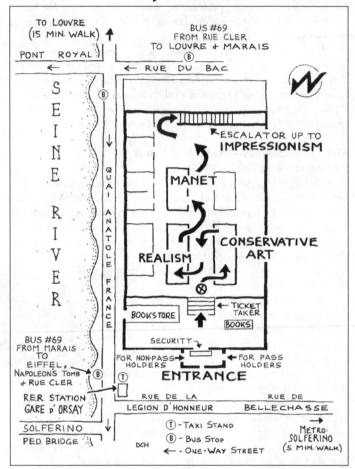

```
TO LOUVRE
(15 MIN. WALK)                    BUS #69
                              FROM RUE CLER
PONT  ROYAL                   TO LOUVRE + MARAIS
                                    Ⓑ
            ← RUE DU BAC
S
E
I                         ESCALATOR UP TO
N                         IMPRESSIONISM
E
                          MANET
R
I
V                                    CONSERVATIVE
E          REALISM                   ART
R

QUAI ANATOLE FRANCE
                          ⊗
                                    ← TICKET
                                       TAKER
            BOOKSTORE              BOOKS

            SECURITY
BUS #69
FROM MARAIS          FOR NON-PASS →   ← FOR PASS
TO                   HOLDERS             HOLDERS
EIFFEL,
NAPOLEON'S TOMB      ENTRANCE
+ RUE CLER  Ⓑ
            Ⓣ
R.E.R. STATION       RUE DE LA          RUE DE
GARE D'ORSAY         LEGION D'HONNEUR   BELLECHASSE

SOLFERINO            Ⓣ - TAXI STAND
PED. BRIDGE          Ⓑ - BUS STOP       METRO:
                     ← - ONE-WAY STREET SOLFERINO
              DCH                       (5 MIN. WALK)
```

Jean-Auguste-Dominique Ingres— *The Source (La Source,* 1856)

Let's start where the Louvre left off. Ingres (ang-gruh, with a soft "gruh"), who helped cap the Louvre collection, championed a neoclassical style. *The Source* is virtually a Greek statue on canvas. Like *Venus de Milo*, she's a balance of opposite motions—her hips tilt one way, her breasts the other; one arm goes up, the other down; the water falling from the pitcher matches the fluid curve of her body. Her skin is porcelain-smooth, painted with seamless brush strokes.

Ingres worked on this over the course of 35 years and considered it his "image of perfection." Famous in its day, *The Source* influenced many artists whose classical statues and paintings are in this museum.

In this and the next few rooms, you'll see more of these visions of idealized beauty—nude women in languid poses, Greek myths, and so on. The "Romantics," like Eugène Delacroix, added bright colors, movement, and emotion to the classical coolness of Ingres.
• *Walk uphill (quickly, this is background stuff) to the last room (Room 3), and find a pastel blue-green painting.*

Alexandre Cabanel—*The Birth of Venus* (*La Naissance de Vénus,* 1863)

Cabanel lays Ingres' *The Source* on her back. This goddess is a perfect fantasy, an orgasm of beauty. The Love Goddess stretches back seductively, recently birthed from the ephemeral foam of the wave. This is art of a pre-Freudian society, when sex was dirty and mysterious and had to be exalted into a more pure and divine form. The sex drive was channeled into an acute sense of beauty. French folk would literally swoon in ecstasy before these works of art.

The art world of Cabanel's day was dominated by two conservative institutions: The Academy (the state-funded art school) and the Salon, where works were exhibited to the buying public. The public loved Cabanel's *Venus* (and Napoleon III purchased it).

Get a feel for the ideal beauty and refined emotion of these Greek-style works. (Out in the gallery, you'll find a statue of another swooning Venus.) Go ahead, swoon. If it feels good, enjoy it. Now, take a mental cold shower, and let's cross over to the "wrong side of the tracks," to the art of the early rebels.
• *Exit Room 3 into the main gallery, turn left, and head back toward the entrance, turning right into Room 4, marked* Daumier *(opposite the Ingres room).*

REALISM—EARLY REBELS

Honoré Daumier—*Celebrities of the Happy Medium* (*Célébrités du juste milieu,* 1832–1835)

This is a liberal's look at the stuffy bourgeois establishment that controlled the Academy and the Salon. In these 36 bustlets, Daumier, trained as a political cartoonist, exaggerates each subject's most distinct characteristic to capture with vicious precision the pomposity and self-righteousness of these self-appointed

Orsay—Conservative Art and Realism

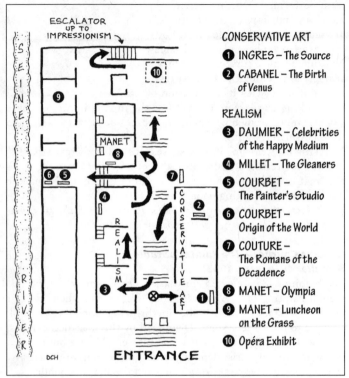

ESCALATOR
UP TO
IMPRESSIONISM

SEINE RIVER

MANET

REALISM

CONSERVATIVE ART

ENTRANCE

DCH

CONSERVATIVE ART
1. INGRES – The Source
2. CABANEL – The Birth of Venus

REALISM
3. DAUMIER – Celebrities of the Happy Medium
4. MILLET – The Gleaners
5. COURBET – The Painter's Studio
6. COURBET – Origin of the World
7. COUTURE – The Romans of the Decadence
8. MANET – Olympia
9. MANET – Luncheon on the Grass
10. Opéra Exhibit

arbiters of taste. The labels next to the busts give the name of the person being caricatured, his title or job (most were members of the French parliament), and an insulting nickname (like "gross, fat, and satisfied" and Monsieur "Platehead"). Give a few nicknames yourself. Can you find Reagan, Clinton, Yeltsin, Thatcher, and Rumsfeld?

These people hated the art you're about to see. Their prudish faces tightened as their fantasy world was shattered by the Realists.

• *Go uphill four steps and through a leafy room to the final room, #6.*

Jean-François Millet—*The Gleaners* (*Les Glaneuses,* 1867)

Millet (mee-yay) shows us three gleaners, the poor women who pick up the meager leavings after a field has already been harvested

by the wealthy. Millet grew up on a humble farm. He didn't attend the Academy and despised the uppity Paris art scene. Instead of idealized gods, goddesses, nymphs, and winged babies, he painted simple rural scenes. He was strongly affected by the socialist revolution of 1848, with its affirmation of  the working class. Here he captures the innate dignity of these stocky, tanned women who bend their backs quietly in a large field for their small reward.

This is "Realism" in two senses. It's painted "realistically," unlike the prettified pastels of Cabanel's *Birth of Venus*. And it's the "real" world—not the fantasy world of Greek myth, but the harsh life of the working poor.

• *Exit Room 6 into the main gallery, and make a U-turn to the left, climbing the steps to a large alcove with two huge canvases. On the left is...*

Gustave Courbet—*The Painter's Studio* (*L'Atelier du Peintre*, 1855)

The Salon of 1855 rejected this dark-colored, sprawling, monumental painting of..."What's it about?" In an age when "Realist painter" was equated with "bomb-throwing Socialist," it took courage to buck the system. Dismissed by the so-called experts, Courbet (coor-bay) held his own one-man exhibit. He built a shed in the middle of Paris, defiantly hung his art out, and basically

 mooned the shocked public.

Courbet's painting takes us backstage, showing the gritty reality behind the creation of pretty pictures. We see Courbet himself in his studio, working diligently on a Realistic landscape, oblivious to the confusion around him. Milling around are ordinary citizens, not Greek heroes. The woman who looks on is not a nude Venus but a naked artist's model. And the little boy with an adoring look on his face? Perhaps it's Courbet's inner child, admiring the artist who sticks to his guns, whether it's popular or not.

• *Just to the right hangs a small painting that had a big impact in its day...*

Gustave Courbet—*Origin of the World* (*L'Origine du Monde*, 1866)

Courbet must have loved scandal. Imagine the commotion that this painting stirred: It's an almost photo-realistic portrait of

exactly what's *not* supposed to be in a portrait. (Originally, this uninhibited crotch, belly, and breast shot was hidden behind a sliding panel.) Looking back, Courbet's piece seems to mark the arrival of a new, more exuberant age.

• *Return to the main gallery. Back across "the tracks," the huge canvas you see is...*

Thomas Couture—*The Romans of the Decadence* (*Les Romains de la Décadence,* 1847)

We see a fin de siècle (end-of-century) society that looks like it's

packed in a big hot tub. It's stuffed with too much luxury, too much classical beauty, too much pleasure; it's wasted, burned out, and in decay. The old, backward-looking order was about to be slapped in the face.

• *Continue up the gallery, then left into Room 14 ("Manet"). Find the reclining nude.*

Edouard Manet—*Olympia* (1863)

"This brunette is thoroughly ugly. Her face is stupid, her skin cadaverous. All this clash of colors is stupefying." So wrote a critic when Edouard Manet's nude hung in the Salon. The public hated it, attacking Manet (man-ay) in print, and literally attacking the canvas.

Think back on Cabanel's painting, *The Birth of Venus:* an idealized, pastel, Vaseline-on-the-lens beauty—soft-core pornography, the kind you see selling lingerie and perfume.

Manet's nude doesn't gloss over anything. The pose is classic, used by Titian, Goya, and countless others. But this is a Realist's take on the classics. The sharp outlines and harsh, contrasting colors are new and shocking. Her hand is a clamp, and her stare is shockingly defiant, with not a hint of the seductive, hey-sailor look of most nudes. This prostitute, ignoring the

flowers sent by her last customer, looks out as if to say, "Next." Manet replaced soft-core porn with hard-core art.

Edouard Manet (1832–1883) had an upper-class upbringing and some formal art training, and he had been accepted by the Salon. He could have cranked out pretty nudes and been a successful painter. Instead, he surrounded himself with a group of young

artists experimenting with new techniques. With his reputation and strong personality, he was their master, though he learned equally from them.

• *Climb the small set of stairs in Room 14. Across the hall (and slightly to the right) is Room 19, where you'll find...*

Edouard Manet—*Luncheon on the Grass* (*Le Déjeuner sur l'Herbe,* 1863)

A shocked public looked at this and wondered: What are these scantily clad women doing with these men? Or rather, what will they be doing after the last baguette is eaten? It wasn't the nudity, but the presence of the men in ordinary clothes, that suddenly made the nudes look naked. Once again, the public judged the painting on moral rather than artistic terms.

A new revolutionary movement is budding—Impressionism. Notice the background: the messy brushwork of trees and leaves, the play of light on the pond, and the light that filters through the trees onto the woman who stoops in the haze. Also note the strong contrast of colors (white skin, black clothes, green grass). This is a true out-of-doors painting, not a studio production. Let the Impressionist revolution begin.

• *Upstairs that revolution is in full bloom. But first, continue to the far end of the gallery, where you'll walk on a glass floor over a model of Paris.*

Opéra Exhibit

Expand to 100 times your size and hover over this scale-model section of the city. In the center sits the 19th-century Opéra Garnier, with its green-domed roof.

Nearby, you'll also see a cross-section model of the Opéra. You'd enter from the right end, buy your ticket in the foyer, then move into the entrance hall with its grand staircase, where you could see and be seen by *toute* Paris. At curtain time, you'd find

your seat in the red and gold auditorium, topped by a glorious painted ceiling. (The current ceiling, done by Marc Chagall, is even more wonderful than the one in the model). Notice that the stage, with elaborate riggings to raise and lower scenery, is as big as the seating area. Nearby, there

Orsay—Impressionism

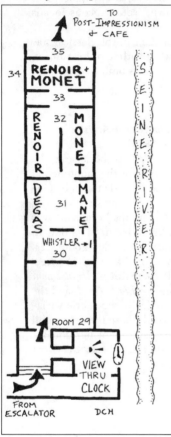

are models of set designs from some famous productions. These days, Parisians enjoy their Verdi and Gounod at the modern opera house at place de la Bastille.

• *Behind the Opéra model (go left around model), a covered escalator leads to the often crowded Impressionist rooms. To read ahead, consider wandering to the quiet far-left corner of the ground floor, where you'll find a huge painting of a hot-air-balloonist's-eye view of pre–Eiffel Tower Paris (c. 1855).*

Ride the escalator to the top floor. Take your first left for a commanding view of the Orsay. The second left takes you past a bookshop and a giant "backwards" clock (with great city views) to the art, starting in Room 29. The Impressionist collection is scattered somewhat randomly through the next few rooms. Shadows dance and the displays mingle. You'll find nearly all of the following paintings, but exactly where they're hung is a lot like their brushwork... delightfully sloppy. (If you don't see a described painting, ask a guard or just move on. It's either hanging farther down or it's on vacation.)

IMPRESSIONISM

Rooms 29–34: Manet, Degas, Monet, Renoir, and More

Light! Color! Vibrations! You don't hang an Impressionist canvas—you tether it. Impressionism features bright colors, easygoing open-air scenes, spontaneity, broad brushstrokes, and the play of light.

The Impressionists made their canvases shimmer by using a simple but revolutionary technique. Let's say you mix red, yellow, and green together—you'll get brown, right? But Impressionists didn't bother to mix them. They'd slap a thick brushstroke of yellow down, then a stroke of green next to it, then red next to that. Up close, all you see are the three messy strokes, but as you back

up...*voilà!* Brown! The colors blend in the eye, at a distance. But while your eye is saying "bland old brown," your subconscious is shouting, "Red! Yellow! Green! Yes!"

There are no lines in nature. Yet someone in the classical tradition (Ingres, for example) would draw an outline of his subject, then fill it in with color. But the Impressionists built a figure with dabs of paint...a snowman of color.

• *In Room 30, find...*

James Abbott McNeill Whistler—*Portrait of the Artist's Mother (Portrait de la Mère de l'Auteur, 1871)*

Why's it so famous? I don't know either. Perhaps because it's by an American, and we see in his mother some of the monumental solidity of our own ancestral moms, who were made tough by pioneering the American wilderness.

Or perhaps because it was so starkly different in its day. In a roomful of golden goddesses, it'd stand out like a fish in a tree. The alternate title is *Arrangement in Gray and Black, No. 1,* and the whole point is the subtle variations of dark shades softened by the rosy tint of her cheeks. Nevertheless, the critics kept waiting for it to come out in Colorization.

• *In Room 31, left side of the room, is work by...*

Edgar Degas—*The Dance Class (La Classe de Danse, c. 1873–1875)*

Clearly, Degas loved dance and the theater. (Catch his statue, *Tiny Dancer, 14 Years Old,* in the glass case.) The play of stage lights off his dancers, especially the halos of ballet skirts, is made to order for an Impressionist. In *The Dance Class,* bored, tired dancers scratch their backs restlessly at the end of a long rehearsal. And look at the bright green bow on the girl with her back to us. In the Impressionist style, Degas slopped green paint onto her dress and didn't even say, *"Excusez-moi."*

Edgar Degas (1834–1917, day-gah) was a rich kid from a family of bankers who got the best classical-style art training. Adoring Ingres' pure lines and cool colors, he painted in the Academic style. His work was exhibited in the Salon. He gained success and a good reputation, and

Impressionism

The camera threatened to make artists obsolete. Now a machine could capture a better likeness faster than you could say Etch-a-Sketch.

But true art is more than just painting reality. It gives us reality from the artist's point of view, with the artist's personal impressions of the scene. Impressions are often fleeting, so you have to work quickly.

The "Impressionist" painters rejected camera-like detail for a quick style more suited to capturing the passing moment. Feeling stifled by the rigid rules and stuffy atmosphere of the Academy, the Impressionists took as their motto, "Out of the studio, into the open air." They grabbed their berets and scarves and went on excursions to the country, where they set up their easels (and newly invented tubes of premixed paint) on riverbanks and hillsides, or they sketched in cafés and dance halls. Gods, goddesses, nymphs, and fantasy scenes were out; common people and rural landscapes were in.

The quick style and everyday subjects were ridiculed and called childish by the "experts." Rejected by the Salon, the Impressionists staged their own exhibition in 1874. They brashly took their name from an insult thrown at them by a critic who laughed at one of Monet's "impressions" of a sunrise. During the next decade, they exhibited their own work independently. The public, opposed at first, was slowly won over by the simplicity, the color, and the vibrancy of Impressionist art.

then...he met the Impressionists.

Degas blends classical lines with Impressionist color, spontaneity, and everyday subjects from urban Paris. Degas loved the unposed "snapshot" effect, catching his models off guard. Dance students, women at work, and café scenes are seen from an odd angle that's not always ideal, but makes the scene seem more real.

Edgar Degas—*In a Café, or The Glass of Absinthe* (*Au Café, dit L'Absinthe,* 1876)

Degas hung out with low-life Impressionists, discussing art, love, and life in the cheap cafés and bars in Montmartre. Here, a weary lady of the evening meets morning with a last lonely, coffin-nail drink in the glaring light of a four-in-the-morning café. The pale green drink forming the center of the composition is the toxic substance, absinthe, that fueled many artists and burned out many more.

• *The next rooms (32–34) feature works by two Impressionist masters at their peak, Monet and Renoir. You're looking at the quintessence of Impressionism. (If you don't find a particular painting by Monet or Renoir, it may be hanging farther along, in Room 39.)*

Pierre-Auguste Renoir—*Dance at the Moulin de la Galette* (*Bal du Moulin de la Galette*, 1876)

On Sunday afternoons, working-class folk would dress up and head for the fields on butte Montmartre (near Sacré-Cœur basilica) to dance, drink, and eat little crêpes *(galettes)* till dark. Pierre-Auguste Renoir (1841–1919, ren-wah) liked to go there to paint the common Parisians living and loving in the afternoon sun. The sunlight filtering through the trees creates a kaleidoscope of colors, like the 19th-century equivalent of a mirror ball throwing darts of light onto the dancers.

He captures the dappled light with quick blobs of yellow, staining the ground, the men's jackets, and the sun-dappled straw hat (right of center). Smell the powder on the ladies' faces. The painting glows with bright colors. Even the shadows on the ground, which should be gray or black, are colored a warm blue. Like a photographer who uses a slow shutter speed to show motion, Renoir paints a waltzing blur.

Renoir's work is lighthearted, with light colors, almost pastels. He seems to be searching for an ideal, the pure beauty we saw on the ground floor. In later years, he used more and more red tones, as if trying for even more warmth.

Claude Monet—*The Cathedral of Rouen* (*La Cathédrale de Rouen*, 1893)

Claude Monet (1840–1926, mo-nay) is the father of Impressionism. He fully explored the possibilities of open-air painting and tried to faithfully reproduce nature's colors with bright blobs of paint.

Monet went to Rouen, rented a room across from the cathedral, set up his easel...and waited. He wanted to catch "a series of differing impressions" of the cathedral facade at various times of day and year. He often had several canvases going at once. In all, he did 30 paintings of the cathedral, and each is unique. The time-lapse

series shows the sun passing slowly across the sky, creating different-colored light and shadows. The labels next to the art describe the conditions: in gray weather, in the morning, morning sun, full sunlight, etc.

As Monet zeroes in on the play of colors and light, the physical subject—the cathedral—is dissolving. It's only a rack upon which to hang the light and color. Later artists would boldly throw away the rack, leaving purely abstract modern art in its place.

Claude Monet—Paintings from Monet's Garden at Giverny

One of Monet's favorite places to paint was the garden he landscaped at his home in Giverny, west of Paris (and worth a visit if you like Monet more than you hate crowds). The Japanese bridge and the water lilies floating in the pond were his two favorite subjects. As Monet aged and his eyesight failed, he made bigger canvases of smaller subjects. The final water lilies are monumental smudges of thick paint surrounded by  paint-splotched clouds reflected on the surface of the pond.

You can see more Monet at the Marmottan Museum (see Marmottan Museum Tour, page 251). His most famous water lilies are at the L'Orangerie Museum (scheduled to reopen sometime in 2006), across the river in the Tuileries Garden.

Camille Pissarro, Alfred Sisley, and Others

We've neglected many of the founders of the Impressionist style. Browse around and discover your own favorites. Pissarro is one of mine. His grainy landscapes are more subtle and subdued than the flashy Monet and Renoir, but, as someone said, "He did for the earth what Monet did for the water."

• *Notice the skylight above you: These Impressionist rooms are appropriately lit by ever-changing natural light. Then carry on to Room 35.*

POST-IMPRESSIONISM

Vincent van Gogh

Impressionists have been accused of being "light"-weights. The colorful style lends itself to bright country scenes, gardens, sunlight on the water, and happy crowds of simple people. It took a remarkable genius to add profound emotion to the Impressionist style.

Vincent van Gogh (1853–1890, van-go; or van-HOCK by the Dutch and the snooty)—like Michelangelo, Beethoven, Rembrandt, Wayne Newton, and a select handful of others—put

so much of himself into his work that art and life became one. In this room, you'll see both van Gogh's painting style and his life unfold.

Vincent van Gogh—*Peasant Woman Near the Hearth* (*Paysanne près de l'atre,* 1885)

Vincent was the son of a Dutch minister. He too felt a religious calling, and he spread the gospel among the poorest of the poor—peasants and miners in overcast Holland and Belgium. He painted these hardworking, dignified folks in a crude, dark style reflecting the oppressiveness of their lives...and the loneliness of his own as he roamed northern Europe in search of a calling.

Vincent Van Gogh—*Self-Portrait, Paris* (*Portrait de l'Artiste,* 1887)

Encouraged by his art-dealer brother, van Gogh moves to Paris, and *voilà!* The color! He meets Monet, drinks with Paul Gauguin

and Henri de Toulouse-Lautrec, and soaks up the Impressionist style. (See how he builds a bristling brown beard using thick strokes of red, yellow, and green side by side.)

At first, he paints like the others, but soon he develops his own style. By using thick, swirling brush strokes, he infuses life into even inanimate objects. Van Gogh's brush strokes curve and thrash like a garden hose pumped with wine.

Vincent van Gogh—*Midday* (*La Méridienne,* 1890, based on a painting by Millet)

The social life of Paris becomes too much for the solitary van Gogh. He moves to the South of France. At first, in the glow of the bright spring sunshine, he has a period of incredible creativity and happiness, as he is overwhelmed by the bright colors, landscape vistas, and common people—an Impressionist's dream.

Vincent van Gogh—*Van Gogh's Room at Arles* (*La Chambre de Van Gogh à Arles,* 1889)

But being alone in a strange country begins to wear on him. An ugly man, he finds it hard to get a date. The close-up perspective of this painting

Orsay—Post-Impressionism

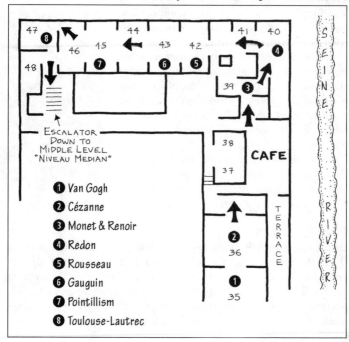

- **1** Van Gogh
- **2** Cézanne
- **3** Monet & Renoir
- **4** Redon
- **5** Rousseau
- **6** Gauguin
- **7** Pointillism
- **8** Toulouse-Lautrec

makes his tiny rented room look even more cramped. He invites his friend Gauguin to join him, but after two months together arguing passionately about art, nerves get raw. Van Gogh threatens Gauguin with a knife, which drives his friend back to Paris. In crazed despair, van Gogh mutilates his own ear.

The people of Arles realize they have a madman on their hands and convince van Gogh to seek help. He enters a mental hospital.

Vincent van Gogh—*The Church at Auvers-sur-Oise* (*L'Eglise d'Auvers-sur-Oise,* 1890)

Van Gogh's paintings done in the peace of the mental hospital are more meditative—fewer bright landscapes, more closed-in scenes with deeper and almost surreal colors. The sky is cobalt blue and the church's windows are also blue, as if we're looking right through the building to an infinite sky. There's a road that leads from us to the church, then splits to go behind. A choice must be made. Which way?

Van Gogh, the preacher's son, saw paint-
ing as a calling, and he approached it with a spiritual intensity.

Vincent van Gogh—*Self-Portrait, St. Rémy* (1889)

Van Gogh wavered between happiness and madness. He despaired of ever being sane enough to continue painting.

This self-portrait shows a man engulfed in a confused background of brush strokes that swirl and rave, setting in motion the waves of the jacket. But in the midst of this rippling sea of mystery floats a still, detached island of a face with probing, questioning, yet wise eyes.

Do his troubled eyes know that only a few months on, he will take a pistol and put a bullet through his chest?

• *Vincent van Gone. Continue to room 36.*

Paul Cézanne

Paul Cézanne (1839–1906, say-zahn) brought Impressionism into the 20th century. After the color of Monet, the warmth of Renoir, and van Gogh's passion, Cézanne's rather impersonal canvases can be difficult to appreciate. Bowls of fruit, landscapes, and a few portraits were Cézanne's passion. Because of his style (not the content), he is often called the first Modern painter.

Paul Cézanne—*Self-Portrait* (*Portrait de l'Artiste* c. 1873–1876)

Cézanne was virtually unknown and unappreciated in his lifetime. He worked alone, lived alone, and died alone, ignored by all but

a few revolutionary young artists who understood his efforts. Cézanne's brush was a blunt instrument. With it, he'd bludgeon reality into submission, drag it across a canvas, and leave it there to dry. But Cézanne, the mediocre painter, was a great innovator. His work spoke for itself—which is good because, as you can see here, he had no mouth.

Paul Cézanne—*Landscape* (*Rochers près des Grottes au dessus de Château-Noir,* 1904)

Cézanne used chunks of green, tan, and blue paint as building blocks to construct this rocky brown cliff. Where the Impressionists built a figure out of a mosaic of individual brushstrokes, Cézanne used blocks of paint to give it a more solid, geometrical shape. A

block of paint forming part of a rock in the foreground is the same size as one in the background, flattening the scene into a wall of brushstrokes.

These chunks are like little "cubes." It's no coincidence that his experiments in reducing forms to their geometric basics influenced the...Cubists.

Paul Cézanne—*The Card Players*
(*Les Joueurs de Cartes*, c. 1890–1895)

These aren't people. They're studies in color and pattern. The subject matter—two guys playing cards—is less important than the pleasingly balanced pattern they make on the canvas, two sloping forms framing a cylinder (a bottle) in the center. Later, abstract artists would focus solely on the shapes and colors.

The jacket of the player to the right is a patchwork of tans, greens, and browns. Even the "empty" space between the men—painted with fragmented chunks of color—is almost as tangible as they are. As one art scholar put it: "Cézanne confused intermingled forms and colors, achieving an extraordinarily luminous density in which lyricism is controlled by a rigorously constructed rhythm." Just what I said—chunks of color.

• *Exit to the café and consider a well-deserved break. From the café, continue ahead, walking under the large green beam, following signs reading* Impressionisme/Post-Impressionisme, 39–48. *A hallway leads past WCs to Room 39, which often displays work by Monet and Renoir (and may include paintings covered earlier in this tour). Then continue into dark Room 40 in the right corner...*

Odilon Redon

Flip out the lights and step into Odilon Redon's mysterious fin de siècle world. If the Orsay's a zoo, this is the nocturnal house. Prowl around. This is wild, wild stuff. It's intense—imagine Richard Nixon on mushrooms playing sax.

If the Impressionists painted by sunlight, Odilon Redon (1840–1916) painted by moonlight. His pastels (protected by dim lighting) portray dream imagery and mythological archetypes. Classed as Symbolism, Redon's weird work later inspired the Surrealists.

• *Coming out of the darkness, pass into the gallery lined with metal columns, containing the primitive art of Rousseau and Gauguin. Start in the first alcove to the left.*

PRIMITIVES

Henri Rousseau—*War*
(*La Guerre,* or *La Chevauchée de la Discorde,* 1894)

War, in the form of a woman with a sword, flies on horseback across the battlefield leaving destruction in her wake: broken bare trees, burning clouds in the background, and heaps of corpses picked at by the birds. Some artists, rejecting the harried, scientific, and rational world, remembered a time before "isms," when works of art weren't scholarly "studies in form and color," but voodoo dolls full of mystery and magic power. They learned from the art of primitive tribes in Africa and the South Seas, trying to recreate a primal Garden of Eden of peace and wholeness. In doing so, they created another "ism": Primitivism.

Henri Rousseau (1844–1910), a man who painted like a child, was an amateur artist who palled around with all the great painters, but they never took his naive style of art seriously. Like a child's drawing of a nightmare, the images are primitive—flat and simple, with unreal colors—but the effect is both beautiful and terrifying.

• *Farther along this columned gallery, you'll find work by...*

Paul Gauguin—*Arearea,* or *Joyousness* (*Joyeusetés,* 1892)

Paul Gauguin (1848–1903, go-gan) got the travel bug early in childhood and grew up wanting to be a sailor. Instead, he became a stockbroker. In his spare time, he painted, and was introduced to the Impressionist circle. He learned their bright clashing colors, but diverged from this path about the time van Gogh waved a knife in his face. At the age of 35, he got fed up with it all, quit his

job, abandoned his wife (her stern portrait bust may be nearby) and family, and took refuge in his art. He traveled to the South Seas in search of the exotic, finally settling on Tahiti.

In Tahiti, Gauguin found his Garden of Eden. He simplified his life into a routine of eating, sleeping, and painting. He simplified his painting still more, to flat images with heavy black outlines filled in with bright, pure colors. He painted the native girls in their naked innocence (so different from Cabanel's

seductive *Venus*). But this simple style had a deep undercurrent of symbolic meaning.

Arearea shows native women and a dog. In the "distance" (there's no attempt at traditional 3-D here), a procession goes by with a large pagan idol. What's the connection between the idol and the foreground figures, who are apparently unaware of it? In primitive societies, religion permeates life. Idols, dogs, and women are holy.

• *Farther along, find...*

Pointillist Paintings (Lots of Dots)

Pointillism, as illustrated by many paintings in the next rooms, brings Impressionism to its logical conclusion—little dabs of different colors placed side by side to blend in the viewer's eye. In works such as *The Circus* (*Le Cirque*, 1891), Georges Seurat (1859–1891) uses only red, yellow, blue, and  green points of paint to create a mosaic of colors that shimmers at a distance, capturing the wonder of the dawn of electric lights.

• *In darkened Room 47 are pastels by...*

Henri de Toulouse-Lautrec—*The Clownesse Cha-U-Kao* (1895)

Henri de Toulouse-Lautrec (1864–1901) was the black sheep of a noble family. At age 15, he broke both legs, which left him disabled. Shunned by his family, a freak to society, he felt more at home

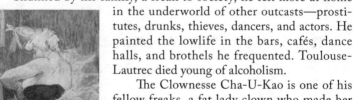 in the underworld of other outcasts—prostitutes, drunks, thieves, dancers, and actors. He painted the lowlife in the bars, cafés, dance halls, and brothels he frequented. Toulouse-Lautrec died young of alcoholism.

The Clownesse Cha-U-Kao is one of his fellow freaks, a fat lady clown who made her living by being laughed at. She slumps wearily after a performance, indifferent to the applause, and adjusts her dress to prepare for the curtain call.

Toulouse-Lautrec was a true *impressionist*, catching his models in candid poses. He worked spontaneously, never correcting his mistakes, as you can see from the blotches on her dark skirt and the unintentional yellow sash that hangs down. Can you see a bit of Degas here, in the subject matter, snapshot pose, and colors?

Henri de Toulouse-Lautrec—*Jane Avril Dancing (Jane Avril dansant, 1891)*

Toulouse-Lautrec hung out at the Moulin Rouge dance hall in Montmartre. One of the most popular dancers was this slim, graceful, elegant, and melancholy woman, who stood out above the rabble of the Moulin Rouge. Her legs keep dancing while her mind is far away. Toulouse-Lautrec, the artist-ocrat, might have identified with her noble face—sad and weary of the nightlife, but immersed in it.

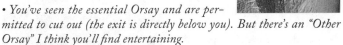

• *You've seen the essential Orsay and are permitted to cut out (the exit is directly below you). But there's an "Other Orsay" I think you'll find entertaining.*

To reach the middle level ("niveau 2"), go down three flights (escalator nearby), turn left and cross to the other side of the gallery.

Along the way, on the middle level, peek into Le Restaurant du Musée. This was part of the original hotel that adjoined the station—built in 1900, abandoned after 1939, condemned, and restored to the elegance you see today. The restaurant is pricey, but there's affordable coffee and tea 15:00–17:30 daily except Thursday.

Now find the palatial Room 51, with mirrors and chandeliers, marked Salle des Fêtes.

THE "OTHER" ORSAY—MIDDLE LEVEL

The beauty of the Orsay is that it combines all the art of the 1800s (1848–1914), both modern and classical, in one building. The classical art, so popular in its own day, has been maligned and was forgotten in the 20th century. It's time for a reassessment. Is it as gaudy and gawd-awful as we've been led to believe? From our 21st-century perspective, let's take a look at the opulent fin de siècle French high society and its luxurious art.

The Grand Ballroom (Salle des Fêtes)

When the Orsay hotel was here, this was one of France's poshest nightspots. You can easily imagine gowned debutantes and white-gloved dandies waltzing the night away to the music of a chamber orchestra. Notice:

• The interior decorating: raspberry marble-ripple ice-cream

The "Other" Orsay—Middle Level

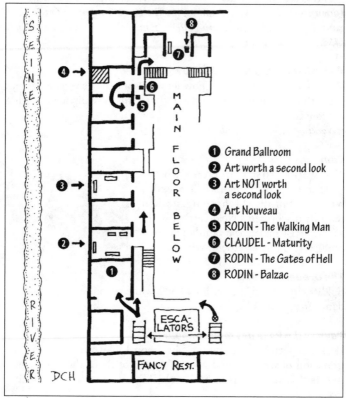

1. Grand Ballroom
2. Art worth a second look
3. Art NOT worth a second look
4. Art Nouveau
5. RODIN - The Walking Man
6. CLAUDEL - Maturity
7. RODIN - The Gates of Hell
8. RODIN - Balzac

DCH

columns, pastel-colored ceiling painting, gold work, mirrors, and leafy garlands of chandeliers.

- The statue *Bacchante Couchée* sprawled in the middle of the room. Familiar pose? If not, you flunk this tour.
- *La Nature,* a statue of a woman dressed in multicolored marble.
- The statue *Aurore,* with her canopy of hair, hide-and-seek face, and silver-dollar nipples, looking like a shampoo ad.
- The large painting *The Birth of Venus (La Naissance de Vénus)* by William Bouguereau. Van Gogh once said: "If I painted like Bouguereau, I could make money. But the public will never change—they only love sweet things."

Is this stuff beautiful or merely gaudy? Divine or decadent?
• *Exit the Salles des Fêtes and turn left, then left again onto the mez-zanine overlooking the main gallery. Enter the first room on the left (#55).*

Art Worth a Second Look

We've seen some great art; now let's see some not-so-great art—at least, that's what modern critics tell us. This is realistic art with a subconscious kick.
• *Working clockwise, you'll see...*

Cain

The world's first murderer, with the murder weapon still in his belt, is exiled with his family. Archaeologists had recently discovered a Neanderthal skull, so the artist makes the family part of a prehistoric hunter/gatherer tribe.

The Dream (Le Rêve)

Soldiers lie still, asleep without beds, while visions of Gatling guns dance in their heads.

Payday (La Paye des Moissonneurs)

Peasants getting paid, painted by Leon L'Hermitte, called "the grandson of Courbet and Millet." The subtitle of the work could be, "Is this all there is to life?" (Or, "The Paycheck...after deductions.")

The Excommunication of Robert le Pieux

The bishops exit after performing the rite. The king and queen are stunned, the scepter dropped. The ritual candle has been snuffed out; it falls, fuming, echoing through the huge hall.... Is this art, or only cheap theatrics?
• *Continue down the mezzanine. Skip the next room, then go left into Room 59.*

Art Not Worth a Second Look

The Orsay's director once said: "Certainly, we have bad paintings. But we have only the greatest bad paintings." And here they are.

Serenity

An idyll in the woods. Three nymphs with harps waft off to the right. These people are stoned on something.

The School of Plato
(L'Ecole de Platon)

Subtitled "The Athens YMCA." A Christ-like Plato surrounded by adoring, half-naked nubile youths gives new meaning to the term "Platonic relationship."

Will the pendulum shift so that one day art like *The School of Plato* becomes the new, radical avant-garde style?

• *Return to the mezzanine and continue to the far end. Enter the last room on the left (#65) and head for the far corner, Room 66.*

ART NOUVEAU

Alexandre Charpentier—Dining Room of Adrien Benard
(Boiserie de la Salle à Mangé de la Propriété Benard)

The Industrial Age brought factories, row houses, machines, train stations, geometrical precision—and ugliness. At the turn of the 20th century, some artists reacted against the unrelieved geometry of harsh, pragmatic, iron-and-steel Eiffel Tower art with a "new

art"—Art Nouveau. (Hmm. I think I had a driver's ed teacher by that name.) This wood-paneled dining room, with its carved vines, leafy garlands, and tree-branch arches, is one of the finest examples of Art Nouveau.

Like nature, which also abhors a straight line, Art Nouveau artists used the curves of flowers and vines as their pattern. They were convinced that "practical" didn't have to mean "ugly" as well. They turned everyday household objects into art. (Another well-known example of Art Nouveau is the curvy, wrought-ironwork of some of Paris' early Métro entrances, commissioned by the same man who ordered this dining room for his home.)

• *Browse through the Art Nouveau rooms to the left. You'll spill out back onto the mezzanine. Grab a seat in front of the Rodin statue of a man missing everything but his legs.*

Auguste Rodin—The Walking Man
(L'Homme Qui Marche, c. 1900)

Like this statue, Auguste Rodin (1840–1917) had one foot in the past and one stepping into the future. Rodin combined classical solidity with Impressionist surfaces to become the greatest sculptor since Michelangelo.

This muscular, forcefully striding man could be a symbol of

the Renaissance Man with his classical power. With no mouth or hands, he speaks with his body. Get close and look at the statue's surface. This rough, "unfinished" look reflects light like the rough Impressionist brushwork, making the statue come alive, never quite at rest in the viewer's eye.

• *Near the far end of the mezzanine, you'll see a small bronze couple* (L'Age Mur) *by Camille Claudel, a student of Rodin's.*

Camille Claudel—*Maturity (L'Age Mûr, 1899–1903)*

Camille Claudel, Rodin's student and mistress, may have portrayed their doomed love affair here. A young girl desperately reaches out to an older man, who is led away reluctantly by an older woman. The center of the composition is the empty space left when their hands separate. In real life, Rodin refused to

leave his wife, and Camille (see her head sticking up from a block of marble nearby) ended up in an insane asylum.

Auguste Rodin—*The Gates of Hell*
(*Porte de l'Enfer, 1880–1917*)

Rodin worked for decades on these doors depicting Dante's hell, and they contain some of his greatest hits, small statues that he later executed in full size. Find *The Thinker* squatting above the doorway, contemplating Man's fate. And in the lower left is the same kneeling man eating his children *(Ugolin)* that you'll see in full size nearby. Rodin paid models to run, squat, leap, and spin around his studio however they wanted. When he saw an interesting pose, he'd yell, "freeze" (or "statue maker") and get out his sketch pad. (For more on *The Gates of Hell* and Rodin, see the Rodin Museum Tour, page 248.)

Auguste Rodin—*Honoré de Balzac* (1897)

The great French novelist is given a heroic, monumental ugliness. Wrapped in a long cloak, he thrusts his head out at a defiant angle, showing the strong individualism and egoism of the 19th-century Romantic movement. Balzac is proud and snooty—but his body forms a question mark, and underneath the twisted features we can see a touch of personal pain and self-doubt. This is hardly camera-eye realism—

Balzac wasn't that grotesque—but it captures a personality that strikes us even if we don't know the man.

From this perch, look over the main floor at all the classical statues between you and the big clock and realize how far we've come—not in years, but in style changes. Many of the statues below—beautiful, smooth, balanced, and idealized—were done at the same time as Rodin's powerful, haunting works. Rodin is a good place to end this tour. With a stable base of 19th-century stone, he launched art into the 20th century.

POMPIDOU CENTER TOUR

(Centre Pompidou)

Some people hate modern art. But the Pompidou Center contains possibly Europe's best museum of 20th-century art. After the super-serious Louvre and Orsay, finish things off with this artistic kick in the pants. You won't find classical beauty here, no dreamy Madonnas-and-Children—just a stimulating, offbeat, and, if you like, instructive walk through nearly every art style of the wild and crazy last century.

The Pompidou's "permanent" collection...isn't. It changes so often that a painting-by-painting tour is impossible. So this chapter is more a general overview of the major trends of 20th-century art, with emphasis on artists you'll find in the Pompidou. Read this chapter ahead of time for background, or take it with you to the museum to look up specific painters as you stumble across their work.

In 2006, expect the collection to be in greater flux than usual. The two-floor collection will be condensed to one as they do building maintenance.

ORIENTATION

Cost: There are separate tickets sold for several different exhibits in the building. You want the *Musée National d'Art Moderne* (€7, free on 1st Sun of month, covered by Museum Pass). Buy tickets on the ground floor. If lines are long, use the red ticket machines (which take only credit cards; follow English instructions). Other temporary exhibits require separate admission (or an all-day pass).

Hours: Wed–Mon 11:00–21:00, closed Tue.

Getting There: Métro stop Rambuteau or, a few blocks farther away, Hôtel de Ville. Bus #69 from the Marais and rue Cler

also stops a few blocks away at Hôtel de Ville. The wild, color-coded exterior makes it about as hard to locate as the Eiffel Tower. To use the escalator to reach the museum (4th floor), you need to show a ticket for the museum or a Museum Pass.

Information: Tel. 01 44 78 12 33, www.centrepompidou.fr. Parisians call the complex the "Centre Beaubourg" (sahn-truh boh-boor), but official publications call it the "Centre Pompidou."

Length of This "Tour": Allow one hour.

Coat Check: Ground floor.

Cuisine Art: You'll find the cool Café La Mezzanine on Level 1 and the snobby Chez Georges view restaurant on Level 6. Across from the entrance/exit, on rue Rambuteau, is the efficient and cheap Flunch self-service cafeteria. My favorite places line the playful fountain, *l'Homage à Stravinsky*: Dame Tartine and Crêperie Beaubourg (to the right as you face the museum entrance; both have reasonable prices).

Shopping: There's a terrific museum store with fun gift ideas just before the ticket taker and tubed esclators.

Starring: Matisse, Picasso, Chagall, Dalí, Warhol, and contemporary art.

Overview

The *Musée National d'Art Moderne: Collection Permanente* (what we'll see) is on the fourth and fifth floors, reached by the escalator to the left as you enter. (During the 2006 renovation, you'll find a condensed collection on either the 4th or 5th floor.) But there's plenty more art scattered all over the building, some free, some requiring a separate ticket. Ask at the ground floor information booth, or just wander.

THE TOUR BEGINS

Exterior

That slight tremor you may feel comes from Italy, where Michelangelo has been spinning in his grave ever since 1977, when the Pompidou Center first revolted Paris. Still, it's an appropriate modern temple for the controversial art it houses.

The building is "exoskeletal" (like Notre-Dame or a crab), with its functional parts—the pipes, heating ducts, and escalator—on the outside, and the meaty art inside. It's the epitome of modern architecture, where "form follows function."

• *Buy your ticket on the ground floor, then ride up the escalator (or run up the down escalator to get in the proper mood) to the entrance (on either the fourth or fifth floor in 2006). When you see the view, your opinion of the Pompidou's exterior should improve a good 15 percent.*

Enter, show your ticket, and ask for the floor plan (plan du musée) *to locate the artists described below, and don't hesitate to ask, "Où est Kandinsky?" Some rooms have informative, handheld English explanations available in wall slots.*

MODERN ART 1905–1960

A.D. 1900: A new century dawns. War is a thing of the past. Science will wipe out poverty and disease. Rational Man is poised at a new era of peace and prosperity....

Right. This cozy Victorian dream was soon shattered by two world wars and rapid technological change. Nietzsche murdered God. Freud washed ashore on the beach of a vast new continent inside each of us. Einstein made everything merely "relative." Even the fundamental building blocks of the universe, atoms, were behaving erratically.

The 20th century—accelerated by technology and fragmented by war—was exciting and chaotic, and the art reflects the turbulence of that century of change.

• *Twentieth-century art resents being put in chronological order. I've described major modern art trends in a linear way, even though you'll find the rooms less orderly. Read and wander. If you don't see what you're looking for, it'll pop up later.*

Cubism: Reality Shattered (1907–1912)

I throw a rock at a glass statue, shatter it, pick up the pieces, and glue them onto a canvas. I'm a Cubist.

Pablo Picasso (1881–1973) and Georges Braque (1882–1963)

Born in Spain, Picasso moved to Paris as a young man, settling into a studio (the Bateau-Lavoir) in Montmartre. He worked with next-door neighbor Georges Braque in poverty so dire they often

didn't know where their next bottle of wine was coming from. They corrected each other's paintings (it's hard to tell whose is whose without the titles), and they shared ideas, meals, and girlfriends while inventing a whole new way to look at the world.

They show the world through a kaleidoscope of brown and gray. The subjects are somewhat recognizable (with the help of the titles), but they are broken into geometric shards (let's call them "cubes," though there are many different shapes), then pieced back together.

Cubism gives us several different angles of the subject at once—say, a woman seen from the front and side angles simultaneously, resulting in two eyes on the same side of the nose. This involves showing three dimensions, plus Einstein's new fourth dimension, the time it takes to walk around the subject to see other angles. Newfangled motion pictures could capture this moving, 4-D world, but how to do it on a 2-D canvas? The Cubist "solution" is a kind of Mercator projection, where the round world is sliced up like an orange peel and then laid as flat as possible.

Notice how the "cubes" often overlap. A single cube might contain both an arm (in the foreground) and the window behind (in the background), both painted the same color. The foreground and the background are woven together, so that the subject dissolves into a pattern.

Picasso: Synthetic Cubism (1912–1915) and Beyond

If the Cubists were as smart as Einstein, why couldn't they draw a picture to save their lives? Picasso was one modern artist who could draw exceptionally well (see his partly finished *Harlequin*). But he constantly explored and adapted his style to new trends, and so became the most famous painter of the century. Scattered throughout the museum are works from the many periods of Picasso's life.

Picasso soon began to use more colorful "cubes" (1912–1915). Eventually, he used curved shapes to build the subject, rather than the straight-line shards of early Cubism.

Picasso married and had children. Works from this period (the 1920s) are more realistic, with full-bodied (and big-nosed) women and children. He tries to capture the solidity, serenity, and volume of classical statues.

As his relationships with women deteriorated, he vented his sexual demons by twisting the female body into grotesque balloon-animal shapes (1925–1931).

All through his life, Picasso explored new materials. He made collages, tried his hand at making "statues" out of wood, wire, or whatever, and even made statues out of everyday household objects. These "multimedia" works, so revolutionary at the time, have become stock-in-trade today.

Marc Chagall (1887–1985)

Marc Chagall, at age 22, arrived in Paris with the wide-eyed wonder of a country boy. Lovers are weightless with bliss. Animals smile and wink at us. Musicians, poets, peasants, and dreamers ignore gravity, tumbling in slow-motion circles high above the rooftops. The colors are deep, dark, and earthy—a pool of mystery

with figures bleeding through below the surface. (Chagall claimed his early poverty forced him to paint over used canvases, inspiring the overlapping images.)

Chagall's very personal style fuses many influences. He was raised in a small Russian village, which explains his "naive" outlook and fiddler-on-the-roof motifs. His simple figures are like Russian Orthodox icons, and his Jewish roots produced Old Testament themes. Stylistically, he's thoroughly modern—Cubist shards, bright Fauve colors, and Primitive simplification. This otherworldly style was a natural for religious works, and so his murals and stained glass, which feature both Jewish and Christian motifs, decorate buildings around the world—including the ceiling of Paris' Opéra Garnier (Mo: Opéra).

Georges Rouault (1871–1958)

Young Georges Rouault was apprenticed to a stained-glass-window-maker. Enough said?

The paintings have the same thick, glowing colors, heavy black outlines, simple subjects, and (mostly) religious themes. The style is modern, but the mood is medieval, solemn, and melancholy. Rouault captures the tragic spirit of those people—clowns, prostitutes, and sons of God—who have been made outcasts by society.

Henri Matisse (1869–1954)

Matisse's colorful "wallpaper" works are not realistic. A man is a few black lines and blocks of paint. The colors are unnaturally bright. There's no illusion of the distance and 3-D that were so

important to Renaissance Italians. The "distant" landscape is as bright as things close up, and the slanted lines meant to suggest depth are crudely done.

Traditionally, the canvas was like a window that you looked "through" to see a slice of the real world stretching off into the distance. Now, a camera could do that better. With Matisse, you look "at" the canvas, like wallpaper. *Voilà!* What was a crudely drawn scene now becomes a sophisticated and decorative pattern of colors and shapes.

Though fully "modern," Matisse built on 19th-century art—the bright colors of Vincent van Gogh, the primitive figures of Paul Gauguin, the colorful designs of Japanese prints, and the Impressionist patches of paint that only blend together at a distance.

Primitive Masks and Statues
Matisse was one of the Fauves ("wild beasts") who, inspired by African and Oceanic masks and voodoo dolls, tried to inject a bit of the jungle into bored French society. The result? Modern art that looked primitive: long, mask-like faces with almond eyes; bright, clashing colors; simple figures; and "flat," two-dimensional scenes.

Abstract Art
Abstract art simplifies. A man becomes a stick figure. A squiggle is a wave. A streak of red expresses anger. Arches make you want a cheeseburger. These are universal symbols that everyone from a caveman to a banker understands. Abstract artists capture the essence of reality in a few lines and colors, and they capture things even a camera can't—emotions, abstract concepts, musical rhythms, and spiritual states of mind. With abstract art, you don't look "through" the canvas to see the visual world, but "at" it to read the symbolism of lines, shapes, and colors.

Wassily Kandinsky (1866–1944)
The bright colors, bent lines, and lack of symmetry tell us that

Kandinsky's world was passionate and intense.

Notice titles like *Improvisation* and *Composition*. Kandinsky was inspired by music, an art form that's also "abstract," though it still packs a punch. Like a jazz musician improvising a new pattern of notes from a set scale, Kandinsky plays with new patterns of related colors, as he looks for just the right combination. Using lines and color, Kandinsky translates the unseen reality into a new medium...like lightning crackling over the radio. Go, man, go.

Piet Mondrian (1872–1944)
Like blueprints for modernism, Mondrian's T-square style boils painting down to its basic building blocks (black lines, white canvas) and the three primary colors (red, yellow, and blue), all arranged in orderly patterns.

(When you come right down to it, that's all painting ever has been. A schematic drawing of, say, the *Mona Lisa,* shows that it's less about a woman than about the triangles and rectangles of which she's composed.)

Mondrian started out painting realistic landscapes of the orderly fields in his native Netherlands. Increasingly, he simplified them into horizontal and vertical patterns. For Mondrian, who was heavy into Eastern mysticism, "up vs. down" and "left vs. right" were the perfect metaphors for life's dualities: "good vs. evil," "body vs. spirit," "man vs. woman." The canvas is a bird's-eye view of Mondrian's personal landscape.

Constantin Brancusi (1876–1957)

Brancusi's curved, shiny statues reduce things to their essence. A bird is a single stylized wing, the one feature that sets it apart from other animals. He rounds off to the closest geometrical form, so a woman's head becomes a perfect oval on a cubic pedestal.

Humans love symmetry (maybe because our own bodies are roughly symmetrical) and find geometric shapes restful, even worthy of meditation. Brancusi follows the instinct for order that has driven art from earliest times, from circular Stonehenge and Egyptian pyramids, to Greek columns and Roman arches, to Renaissance symmetry and the Native American "medicine wheel."

Paul Klee (1879–1940)

Paul Klee's small and playful canvases are deceptively simple, containing shapes so basic they can be read as universal symbols. Klee thought a wavy line, for example, would always suggest motion, while a stick figure would always mean a human—like the psychiatrist Carl Jung's universal dream symbols, part of our "collective unconscious."

Klee saw these universals in the art of children, who express themselves without censoring or cluttering things up with learning. His art has a childlike playfulness and features simple figures, painted in an uninhibited frame of mind.

Klee also turned to nature. The same forces that cause the wave to draw a line of foam on the beach can cause a meditative artist to draw a squiggly line of paint on a canvas. The result is a universal shape. The true artist doesn't just paint nature, he becomes Nature.

Design: Chairs by Gerrit Rietveld and Alvar Aalto

Hey, if you can't handle modern art, sit on it! (Actually, don't.) The applied arts—chairs, tables, lamps, and vases—are as much a part of the art world as the fine arts. (Some say the first art object was the pot.) As machines became as talented as humans, artists embraced new technology and mass production to bring beauty to the masses.

Fernand Léger (1881–1955)

Fernand Léger's style has been called "Tubism"—breaking the world down into cylinders, rather than cubes. (He supposedly got his inspiration during World War I from the gleaming barrel of a cannon.) Léger captures the feel of the encroaching Age of Machines, with all the world looking like an internal-combustion engine.

Robert Delaunay (1885–1941) and Sonia Delaunay (1885–1979)

This husband and wife both painted colorful, fragmented canvases (including a psychedelic Eiffel Tower) that prove the modern style doesn't have to be ugly or puzzling.

World War I: The Death of Values

Ankle-deep in mud, a soldier shivers in a trench, waiting to be ordered "over the top." He'll have to run through barbed wire, over fallen comrades, and into a hail of machine-gun fire, only to capture a few hundred yards of meaningless territory that will be lost the next day. This soldier was not thinking about art.

World War I left nine million dead. (During the war, France often lost more men in a single day than America lost in all of Vietnam.) The war also killed the optimism and faith in mankind that had guided Europe since the Renaissance. Now, rationality just meant schemes, technology meant machines of death, and morality meant giving your life for an empty cause.

Expressionism: Ernst Ludwig Kirchner, Max Beckmann, George Grosz, Chaim Soutine, Otto Dix, and Oskar Kokoschka

Cynicism and decadence settled over postwar Europe. Artists "expressed" their disgust by showing a distorted reality that emphasized the ugly. Using the lurid colors and simplified figures

of the Fauves, they slapped paint on in thick brushstrokes and depicted a hypocritical, hard-edged, dog-eat-dog world that had lost its bearings. The people have a haunted look in their eyes, the fixed stare of corpses and those who have to bury them.

Dada: Marcel Duchamp's Urinal (1917)

When people could grieve no longer, they turned to grief's giddy twin: laughter. The war made all old values a joke, including artistic ones. The Dada movement, choosing a purposely childish name, made art that was intentionally outrageous: a moustache on the *Mona Lisa,* a shovel hung on a wall, or a modern version of a Renaissance "fountain"—a urinal (by either Marcel Duchamp or I. P. Freeley, 1917). It was a dig at all the pompous prewar artistic theories based on the noble intellect of Rational Women and Men. While the experts ranted on, Dadaists sat in the back of the class and made cultural fart noises.

Hey, I love this stuff. My mind says it's sophomoric, but my heart belongs to Dada.

Surrealism: Salvador Dalí, Max Ernst, and René Magritte (1920–1940)

Greek statues with sunglasses, a man as a spinning top, shoes becoming feet, and black ants as musical notes...Surrealism. The world was moving fast, and Surrealists caught the jumble of images. The artist scatters seemingly unrelated things on the canvas, which leaves us to trace the links in a kind of connect-the-dots without numbers. If it comes together, the synergy of unrelated things can be pretty startling. But even if the juxtaposed images don't ultimately connect, the artist has made you think, rerouting

your thoughts through new neural paths. If you don't "get" it...you got it.

Complicating the modern world was Freud's discovery of the "unconscious" mind that thinks dirty thoughts while we sleep. Many a Surrealist canvas is

an uncensored, stream-of-consciousness "landscape" of these deep urges, revealed in the bizarre images of dreams.

In dreams, sometimes one object can be two things at once: "I dreamt that you walked in with a cat...no, wait, maybe you were the cat...no...." Surrealists paint opposites like these and let them speak for themselves.

Salvador Dalí (1904–1989)

Salvador Dalí could draw exceptionally well. He painted "unreal" scenes with photographic realism, thus making us believe they could really happen. Seeing familiar objects in an unfamiliar setting—like a grand piano adorned with disembodied heads of Lenin—creates an air of mystery, the feeling that anything can happen. That's both exciting and unsettling. Dalí's images—crucifixes, political and religious figures, naked bodies—pack an emotional punch. Take one mixed bag of reality, jumble in a blender, and serve on a canvas...Surrealism.

Abstract Surrealists: Joan Miró, Alexander Calder, and Jean Arp

Abstract artists described their subconscious urges using color and shapes alone, like Rorschach inkblots in reverse.

The thin-line scrawl of Joan Miró's work is like the doodling of a three-year-old. You'll recognize crudely drawn birds, stars, animals, and strange cell-like creatures with whiskers ("Biological Cubism"). Miró was trying to express the most basic of human emotions using the most basic of techniques.

Alexander Calder's mobiles hang like Mirós in the sky, waiting for a gust of wind to bring them to life.

And talk about a primal image! Jean Arp builds human beings out of amoeba-like shapes.

Decorative Art: Pierre Bonnard, Balthus, and Later Picasso and Braque

Most 20th-century paintings are a mix of the real world ("representation") and the colorful patterns of "abstract" art. Artists purposely distort camera-eye reality to make the resulting canvas more decorative. So, Picasso flattens a woman into a pattern of colored shapes, Bonnard makes a man from a shimmer of golden paint, and Balthus turns a boudoir scene into colorful wallpaper.

Patterns and Textures: Jean Dubuffet, Lucio Fontana, and Karel Appel

Increasingly, you'll have to focus your eyes to look "at" the canvases, not "through" them.

Enjoy the lines and colors, but also a new element: texture.

Some works have very thick paint piled on, and so you can see the brush stroke clearly. Some have substances besides paint applied to the canvas, such as Dubuffet's brown, earthy rectangles of real dirt and organic waste. Fontana punctures the canvas so that the fabric itself (and the hole) becomes the subject. Artists show their skill by mastering new materials. The canvas is a tray, serving up a delightful array of different substances with interesting colors, patterns, shapes, and textures.

Alberto Giacometti (1901–1966)

Giacometti's skinny statues have the emaciated, haunted, and faceless look of concentration camp survivors. The simplicity of the figures may be "primitive," but these aren't stately, sturdy, Easter Island heads. Here, man is weak in the face of technology and the winds of history.

• *At the end of the floor, circle across the main aisle and work your way back to where you started.*

Abstract Expressionism

America emerged from World War II as the globe's superpower. With Europe in ruins, New York replaced Paris as the art capital of the world. The trend was toward bigger canvases, abstract designs, and experimentation with new materials and techniques. It was called "Abstract Expressionism"—expressing emotions and ideas using color and form alone.

Jackson Pollock (1912–1956)

"Jack the Dripper" attacks convention with a can of paint, dripping and splashing a dense web onto the canvas. Picture Pollock in his studio, as he jives to the hi-fi, bounces off the walls, and throws paint in a moment of enlightenment. Of course, the artist loses some control this way—control over the paint flying in mid-air and over himself, now in an ecstatic trance. Painting becomes a whole-body activity, a "dance" between the artist and his materials.

The act of creating is what's important, not the final product. The canvas is only a record of that moment of ecstasy.

Big, Empty Canvases: Barnett Newman and Robert Rauschenberg

All those big, empty canvases with just a few lines or colors—what reality are they trying to show?

In the modern world, we find ourselves insignificant specks in a vast and indifferent universe. Every morning, each of us must confront that big, blank, existentialist canvas and decide how we're going to make our mark on it. Like, wow.

Another influence was the simplicity of Japanese landscape painting. A Zen master studies and meditates for years to achieve the state of mind in which he can draw one pure line. These canvases, again, are only a record of that state of enlightenment. (What is the sound of one brush painting?)

On more familiar ground, postwar painters were following in the footsteps of artists such as Mondrian, Klee, and Kandinsky (whose work they must have considered "busy"). The geometrical forms here reflect the same search for order, but these artists painted to the 5/4 asymmetry of Dave Brubeck's "Take Five."

THE CONTEMPORARY COLLECTION 1960–PRESENT

Pop Art: Andy Warhol (1928–1987)

America's postwar wealth made the consumer king. Pop art is created from the "pop"-ular objects of that throwaway society—a soup can, a car fender, mannequins, tacky plastic statues, movie icons, advertising posters. Take something out of Sears and hang it in a museum, and you have to think about it in a wholly different way.

Is this art? Are all these mass-produced objects beautiful? Or crap? If they're not art, why do we work so hard to acquire them? Pop art, like Dada, questions our society's values.

Andy Warhol (who coined the expression "15 minutes of fame" and became a pop star) concentrated on another mass-produced phenomenon: celebrities. He took publicity photos of famous people and repeated them. The repetition—like the constant bombardment we get from repeated images on television—cheapens even the most beautiful things.

Contemporary Art: New Media for a New Century

The "modern" world is history. Picasso and his ilk are now gathering dust and boring art students everywhere. Minimalist painting and abstract sculpture are old-school. Enter the "postmodern" world, as seen through the eyes of current artists.

You'll see fewer traditional canvases or sculptures. Artists have traded paintbrushes for blowtorches (Miró said he was out to "murder" painting), and blowtorches for computer mouses. Mixed media work is the norm, combining painting, sculpture, photography, welding, film/slides/video, computer programming,

new resins, plastics, industrial techniques, and lighting and sound systems.

Here are some of the trends:

Installations: An entire room is given to an artist to prepare. Like entering an art funhouse, you walk in without quite knowing what to expect (I'm always thinking, "Is this safe?"). Using the latest technology, the artist engages all your senses, by controlling the lights, sounds, and sometimes even smells.

Assemblages: Artists raid Dumpsters, recycling junk into the building blocks for larger "assemblages." Each piece is intended to be interesting and tell its own story, and so is the whole sculpture. Weird, useless, Rube Goldberg machines make fun of technology.

Natural Objects: A rock in an urban setting is inherently interesting.

The Occasional Canvas: This comes as a familiar relief. Artists of the New Realism labor over painstaking, hyper-realistic canvases to recreate the glossy look of a photo or video image.

Interaction: Some exhibits require your participation, whether you push a button to get the contraption going, touch something, or just walk around the room. In some cases, the viewer "does" art rather than just stares at it. If art is really meant to change, it has to move you, literally.

Deconstruction: Late-20th-century artists critiqued (or "deconstructed") society by examining our underlying assumptions. One way to do it is to take a familiar object (say, a crucifix) out of its normal context (a church), and place it in a new setting (a jar of urine). Video and film can deconstruct something by playing it over and over, ad nauseum. Ad copy painted on canvas deconstructs itself.

Conceptual Art: The *concept* of which object to pair with another to produce maximum effect is the key. (Urine + crucifix = million-dollar masterpiece.)

Performance Art: This is a kind of mixed media of live performance. Many artists—who in another day would have painted canvases—have turned to music, dance, theater, and performance art. This art form is often interactive, by dropping the illusion of a performance and encouraging audience participation. When you finish with the Pompidou Center, go outside for some of the street theater.

Playful Art: Children love the art being produced today. If it doesn't put a smile on your face, well, then you must be a jaded grump like me, who's seen the same repetitious s#%t passed off as "daring" since Warhol stole it from Duchamp. I mean, it's *so* 20th-century.

VIEW ART

Before leaving, escalate up to the sixth floor. Near the *très* snooty Chez Georges view restaurant (where just looking is not OK), take a walk along the tube that runs the length of the building for great Paris cityscapes.

CARNAVALET MUSEUM TOUR

(Musée Carnavalet)

At the Carnavalet Museum, French history unfolds in a series of stills—like a Ken Burns documentary, except you have to walk. The Revolution is the highlight, but you get a good overview of everything, from Louis XIV-period rooms, to Napoleon, to the belle époque.

ORIENTATION

Cost: Free.

Hours: Tue–Sun 10:00–18:00, closed Mon. Avoid lunchtime (12:00–14:00), since many rooms close.

Getting There: It's in the heart of the Marais district at 23 rue de Sévigné (Mo: St. Paul), and on the Marais Walk (page 106).

Information: Get the free (necessary) map. Tel. 01 44 59 58 58, www.v1.paris.fr/musees/musee_carnavalet.

Length of This Tour: Allow 90 minutes.

Starring: François I, Louis XIV, Louis XV, Louis XVI, the Bastille, Robespierre, the guillotine, Napoleon, Napoleon III, the Paris Commune, and the belle époque.

Overview

The museum, which opened in 1880, is housed in two Marais mansions connected by a corridor. The first half of the museum (pre-Revolution) is difficult to follow—rooms numbered out of order, no English descriptions, and sections closed due to understaffing. See this part quickly, so that you can concentrate your energy on the Revolution and beyond. If you get lost or frustrated, we'll meet up again in Room 45 (on the 1st floor), where the Revolution begins.

THE TOUR BEGINS
MAIN BUILDING—1500-1789

• *Begin outside in the...*

Courtyard

You're surrounded by the in-your-face richness of the *ancien régime*—back when people generally accepted the notion that some were born to rule, and most were born to be ruled. And the embodiment of that age stands atop the statue in the center: Louis XIV, the ultimate divine monarch.

Notice the date: July 14, 1689, exactly 100 years before the French Revolution ended all that. This statue is a rare surviving pre-Revolutionary bronze. In 1792, nearly all of them were melted down to make weapons, as Revolutionary France took on the rest of Europe in an all-out war. Notice the relief below—a great piece of counter-Reformation propaganda. France (the angel with the royal shield) and heaven (portrayed by the angel protecting the Communion Host) are literally stomping the snakes and reformers of Protestantism (Hus, Calvin, Wycliffe, and Luther).

• *Now find Room 7 on the ground floor. It's not obvious where it is—grab a free map and ask a guard ("Où est salle sept?"; oo ay sahl set). Once again, if you get lost or rooms are closed, we'll meet up again in Room 45, on the first floor (page 217).*

1500s—Renaissance and Reformation

Room 7

A **model of Ile de la Cité** (made by a monk around 1900) shows the medieval city before France became a world power—crowded, narrow-laned, and steeple-dotted, with houses piled even on top of bridges. There's Notre-Dame on the east end, and Sainte-Chapelle, with its royal palace and gardens, on the west. The only straight road in town was the old Roman road that splits the island north–south and is still used today.

King François I (1494–1547, r. 1515–1547) brought Paris into the modern world. Handsome, athletic François—a writer of poems, leader of knights, and lover of women—embodied the optimism of the Italian Renaissance. *"Le grand roi François"* (it rhymes) centralized the government around his charismatic self and made a rebuilt Louvre his home. He affirmed his absolute right to rule every time he ordered something done: "For such is our pleasure!"

Room 8 & Room 9

Renaissance open-mindedness brought religious debate, leading to open warfare between Catholics and Protestants (called Huguenots in France). You'll find paintings here of the Catholic **King Charles IX** (1550–1574, r. 1560–1574) and his mother, **Catherine de Médicis,** who plotted to assassinate several prominent Protestants. Their plan quickly snowballed into the slaughter of thousands of Parisian Huguenots on St. Bartholomew's Day in 1572. Paintings in both of these rooms show events organized by the **Catholic League:** parades, Bible studies, and the occasional Protestant barbecue to keep the faithful in good spirits.

Room 10

King Henry IV (1553–1610, r. 1589–1610, Louis XIV's grandfather) was perhaps France's most popular king. His **bust** depicts him with a faint smile and smile lines around the eyes, capturing his reputation as a witty conversationalist and friend of commoners. Henry helped reconcile Catholics and Protestants and rebuilt Paris. Still, that didn't stop a Revolutionary mob from tearing his equestrian statue to pieces *(Fragment du monument)*. See **engravings** of Henry's second wife, Marie de Médicis, and of some of Henry's building projects (including place Dauphine and place des Vosges). The grotesque **stone faces** are four of the 300 that adorn Henry's greatest creation, the pont Neuf.

• *Head upstairs to the first floor.*

FIRST FLOOR

The Luxury of Louis XIV, XV, and XVI

• *Browse around the furnished rooms, getting a feel for the luxurious life of France's kings and nobles before the Revolution. In fact, several rooms are straight out of the mansions lining the nearby place des Vosges. Use the following material as background. See you in Room 45.*

Louis XIV (1638–1715, r. 1643–1715)

The flowery walls, Greek-myth ceiling paintings, and powdered-wig portraits give a tiny glimpse of the opulence of Louis XIV and his greatest monument, the palace at Versailles. You'll see luxurious wallpaper, tables, chairs, parquet floors, clocks, gaming tables, statues, paintings, and even a doghouse that costs more than a peasant hut. Versailles was the physical symbol of Louis' absolute power over the largest, most populous, and richest nation in Europe.

    Louis XIV Style: Baroque. In rooms from this period, ceilings are decorated with curved ornamental frames (cartouches) that hold paintings of Greek myths, and furnishings are gilded.

The heavy tables and chairs have thick, curved legs, animal feet, and bronze corner-protectors.

Louis XV (1710–1774, r. 1715–1774)

Louis XV ascended the throne of Europe's most powerful nation when his great-grandfather, the Sun King, died after reigning for 72 years. Only five years old at the time, he was for many years a figurehead, while the government was run by his mentors: a regent during his childhood, his teacher during his youth, one of his many mistresses (Madame de Pompadour) during his middle age, and bureaucrats by the end. Louis was intelligent and educated, and he personally embraced the budding democratic ideals of the Enlightenment, but he spent his time at Versailles, where he gamed and consorted with Europe's most cultured and beautiful people. Meanwhile, France's money was spent on costly wars with Austria and England (including the American "French and Indian War"). Louis, basking in the lap of luxury and the glow of the Enlightenment, looked to the horizon and uttered his prophetic phrase: *"Après moi—le déluge!"* ("After me—the flood!")

Louis XV Style: Rococo. The rooms are decorated in pastel colors, with lighter decoration and exotic landscapes. The chairs are made of highly polished, rare woods, with delicate curved legs and padded seats and backs. Note the Chinese decor and objects such as the Ming vase.

Louis XVI (1754–1793, r. 1774–1792)

With a flood watch in effect, the next Louis stubbornly clung to the rules of the *ancien régime* (the traditional chessboard society with king on top, pawns on bottom, and bishops that walk diagonally).

While peasants groaned in the fields, the rich enjoyed their mansions: parties lit by chandeliers glimmering off mirrors, the sound of a string quartet, exotic foods from newly colonized lands, billiards in one room and high-stakes card games in another, a Molière comedy downstairs, dangerous talk by radicals like Voltaire and Jean-Jacques Rousseau, and dangerous liaisons among social butterflies—male and female—dressed in high heels, makeup, wigs, and perfume.

Louis XVI Style: Neoclassical. Influenced by recently excavated Pompeii, the rooms are simpler—with classical motifs—and the furniture is straighter. The chairs' straight legs taper to a point.

• *From Room 45, follow signs to* Revolution, 19th and 20th Centuries. *A long corridor leads to the next building. Hike up the hardwood stairs to the second floor and* La Révolution Française.

SECOND FLOOR

The Revolution: 1789–1799

No period of history is as charged with the full range of human emotions and actions as the French Revolution: bloodshed, martyrdom, daring speeches, murdered priests, emancipated women, back-stabbing former friends—all done in the name of government "by, for, and of the people." Common people with their everyday concerns were driving the engine of history. Or perhaps they were only foam bubbles swept along in the shifting tides of vast socio-economic trends.

Room 101: The Estates-General

It's 1789, France is bankrupt from wars and corruption, and the people want change. The large **allegorical painting** *L'espoir du bonheur* shows King Louis XVI in the boat of France, navigating stormy seas. Lady Truth is trying to light the way, but the winged demon of tyranny keeps nagging at the king. Above shines the fleur-de-lis, whose petals are labeled with the three social groups that held all power in France: clergy, king, and nobles. Now they are laced together by the new power...the people.

In May, the king called each sector of society together at Versailles to solve the financial crisis. But in a bold and unheard-of move, the Third Estate (the people), tired of being outvoted by the clergy and nobility, split and formed their own National Assembly (see *The Oath of the Jeu-de-Paume* on the opposite wall, a preparatory sketch by Jacques-Louis David for a huge canvas that was never painted). Amid the chaos of speeches, debate, and deal-making, they raised their hands, bravely pledging to stick together until a new constitution was written. Vacillating between democratic change and royalist repression, **Louis XVI** (see his pink-faced portrait to the left) ordered the Assembly to dissolve (they refused), sent 25,000 Swiss mercenary soldiers to Paris, and fired his most popular, liberal minister.

Room 102: The Bastille (July 14, 1789)

The Bastille (see the **model**) was a medieval fortress turned prison. With its eight towers and 100-foot-high walls, it dominated the Parisian skyline, a symbol of oppression. (See the series of **paintings** that illustrate some of the following events.)

On the hot, muggy morning of July 14, Paris' citizens waited

on edge, listening to reports of attacks on the populace by the king's Swiss guards. A crowd formed, marched on the Invalides armory, and seized 30,000 rifles...but no gunpowder. Word spread  that it was stored across town at the Bastille. The mob grew bigger and angrier as it went. By noon, they stood at the foot of the walls of the Bastille and demanded gunpowder. They captured the fort's governor, then two citizens managed to scale the wall and cut the chains. The drawbridge crashed down and the mob poured through. Terrified guards opened fire, killing dozens and wounding hundreds. At the battle's peak, French soldiers in red and blue appeared on the horizon...but whose side were they on? A loud cheer went up as they pointed their cannons at the Bastille and the fort surrendered. The mob trashed the Bastille, opened the dark dungeons, and brought seven prisoners into the light of day. They then stormed City Hall (Hôtel de Ville) and arrested the mayor, who was literally torn apart by the hysterical crowd. His head was stuck on a stick and carried through the city. The Revolution had begun.

Today, the events of July 14 are celebrated every Bastille Day, with equally colorful festivities. The Bastille itself was soon dismantled, stone by stone—nothing remains but the open space of place de la Bastille—but the memory became a rallying cry throughout the Revolution: *"Vive le quatorze juillet!"* ("Long live July 14th!").

Room 103: The Celebration
(*La Fête de la Fédération,* 1789)
Imagine the jubilation! To finally be able to shout out things formerly whispered in fear.

The large painting of *La Fête de la Fédération* shows the joy and exuberance of the newly freed people, as they celebrate the first Bastille Day (July 14, 1790). Liberty! Equality! Fraternity! Members of every social class (even including, it appears, 3 women) hugged, kissed, and mingled on the Champ de Mars, where the Eiffel Tower stands today. The crowd built an artificial mound for heroes of the Revolution to ascend while a choir sang. Women, dressed to symbolize Truth, Freedom, Justice, and other capital-letter virtues,

were worshipped in a new kind of secular religion. Public demonstrations like these must have infuriated the king, queen, bishops, and nobles, who were now quarantined in their palaces, fuming impotently.

The ***Declaration of the Rights of Man and the Citizen*** (see 2 different versions) made freedom the law. The preamble makes it clear that "*Le Peuple Français*" (the French people)—not the king—were the ultimate authority. "Men are born free and equal," it states, possessing "freedom of the individual, freedom of conscience, freedom of speech."

Room 104: Louis XVI Quietly Responds (De la Monarchie à la République, 1789–1792)

Louis XVI (see the bust)—studious, shy, aloof, and easily dominated—was stunned by the ferocious summer of 1789. The Bastille's violence spread to the countryside, where uppity peasants tenderized their masters with pitchforks. The Assembly was changing France with lightning speed: abolishing Church privileges, nationalizing nobles' land, and declaring the king irrelevant. Louis accepted his role as a rubber-stamp monarch, hoping the furor would pass and trying to appear idealistic and optimistic.

But looming on the horizon was...***Le docteur Joseph-Ignace Guillotin*** (see portrait, opposite the window). The progressive Assembly abolished brutal, medieval-style torture and executions. In their place, Dr. Guillotin proposed a kinder, gentler execution device that would make France a model of compassion. The guillotine—also known as "the national razor" or simply "The Machine"—could instantly make someone "a head shorter at the top." (In 1977, it claimed its last victim; now capital punishment is abolished.)

Room 105: The Royalty Loses Its Head (La Famille Royale, 1793)

Louis' wife, **Queen Marie-Antoinette** (several portraits), became the focus of the citizens' disgust. Reports flew that she spent extravagantly and plunged France into debt. More decisive than her husband, she steered him toward repressive measures to snuff out the Revolution. Worst of all, she was foreign-born, known simply as "The Austrian," and soon Austria was trying to preserve the monarchy by making war on the French. A rumor spread—one that had been common among the poor in France for over a decade—that when Marie was informed that the Parisians

had no bread to eat, she had sneered, "Let them eat cake!" ("Cake" was the term for the burnt crusts peeled off the oven and generally fed only to the cattle.) Historians today find no evidence Marie ever said it.

Enraged and hungry, 6,000 Parisian women (backed by armed men) marched through the rain to Versailles to demand lower bread prices. On the night of October 5, 1789, a small band infiltrated the palace, burst into the Queen's room, killed her bodyguards, and chased her down the hall. The royal family was kidnapped and taken to Paris, where—though still monarchs—they were under house arrest in the Tuileries Palace (which once stood where the Louvre today meets the Tuileries Garden).

Three years later, the royal family became actual prisoners (see the reconstructed and rather cushy **Prison du Temple** in Room 106) after trying to escape to Austria to begin a counter-revolution. One of their servants pretended to be a German baroness, while Louis dressed up as her servant (the irony must have been killing him). When a citizen recognized Louis from his portrait on a franc note, the family was captured, thrown into prison, and soon put on trial as traitors to France. The National Convention (the Assembly's successor) declared the monarchy abolished.

The royal family—Louis, Marie-Antoinette, and their eight-year-old son—was tearfully split up (see the painting **Les adieux de Louis XVI à sa famille** in Room 105), and Marie-Antoinette was imprisoned in the Conciergerie.

On January 21, 1793 (see **execution painting**), King Louis XVI (excuse me, "Citizen Capet") was led to the place de la Concorde and laid face down on a slab, and then—shoop!—a thousand years of monarchy that dated back before Charlemagne was decapitated.

On October 16, 1793 (see **painting**), Marie-Antoinette also met her fate on place de la Concorde. Genteel to the end, she apologized to the executioner for stepping on his foot. The blade fell, the blood gushed, and her head was shown to the crowd on a stick—an exclamation point
for the new rallying cry: *Vive la nation!*

Little Louis XVII died in prison at age 10. (Notice his cute **portrait**—*Le Dauphin*—in the corner next to his mother portrayed as a widow in prison.) Rumors spread that the boy-king had escaped, fueled by Elvis-type sightings and impersonators. But recent DNA evidence confirms that the *dauphin* (heir to the throne) did indeed die in prison in 1795.

Room 108: The Reign of Terror
(*La Convention—La Terreur,* 1793–1794)

Here are **portraits** of key players in the Revolutionary spectacle. Some were moderate reformers, some radical priest-killers. With Europe ganging up on the Revolution, they all lived in fear that any backward step could tip the delicate balance of power back to the *ancien régime.* Enemies of the Revolution were everywhere—even in their own ranks.

By the summer of 1793, the left-of-center Jacobin party took control of France's fledgling democracy. Pug-faced but silver-tongued **Georges Danton** (see portrait of a Newt Gingrich look-alike) drove the Revolution with his personal charisma and bold speeches: "To conquer the enemies of the fatherland, we need daring, more daring, daring now, always daring." He led the "Committee of Public Safety" to root out and execute those enemies, even moderates opposed to the Jacobins.

More radical still, **Jean-Paul Marat** (the "Friend of the People," portrait next to Danton) dressed and burped like a man of the street, but he wrote eloquently against all forms of authority. Wildly popular with the commoners, he was seen by others as a loose cannon. A beautiful 25-year-old noblewoman named **Charlotte Corday** decided it was her mission in life to save France by silencing him. On July 11, 1793, she entered his home under the pretext of giving him names of counter-revolutionaries. Marat, seated in a bathtub to nurse a skin condition, wrote the names down and said, "Good. I'll have them all guillotined." Corday stood up, whipped a knife out from under her dress, and stabbed him through the heart. Corday was guillotined, and Marat was hailed as a martyr to the cause.

Marat's death was further "proof" that counter-revolutionaries were everywhere. For the next year (summer of 1793 to summer of 1794, see **paintings of guillotine scenes**), the Jacobin government arrested, briefly tried, and then guillotined everyone suspected of being "enemies of the Revolution": nobles, priests, the rich, and many true Revolutionaries who simply belonged to the wrong political party. More than 2,500 Parisians were beheaded, 18,000 were executed by other means, and tens of thousands died in similar violence throughout the country. The violence begun at the **Bastille** in July 1789 would climax in July 1794.

Master of the Reign of Terror was **Maximilien de Robespierre** (the portrait opposite Danton's), a 35-year-old lawyer who promoted the Revolution with a religious fervor. By July 1794, the guillotine was slicing 30 necks a day. In Paris' main squares, grim executions alternated with politically correct public spectacles that honored "Liberty," "Truth," and the heroes of France. As the death toll rose, so did public cynicism. Finally, Robespierre even

sentenced to death his old friend Danton, who had spoken out against the bloodshed. As Danton knelt under the blade, he joked, "My turn." The people had had enough.

Room 109: Terror Ends
(*Thermidor—Le Directoire*, July 1794)

Engravings show the chaos—riots, assassinations, food shortages, inflation—that fueled Robespierre's meteoric fall from power. Robespierre's own self-righteousness made him an easy target. On July 27, 1794, as Robespierre prepared to name the daily list of victims, his fellow committee members started yelling "Tyrant!" and shouted him down. Stunned by the sudden fall from grace, Robespierre unsuccessfully attempted suicide by shooting himself in the mouth.

The next day, he walked the walk he'd ordered thousands to take. Hands tied behind his back, he was carried through the streets on a two-wheeled cart, while citizens jeered and spat on him. At the guillotine, the broken-down demagogue had no last words, thanks to his wounded jaw. When the executioner yanked off the bandage, Robespierre let out a horrible cry, the blade fell, and the Reign of Terror came to an end.

From 1795 to 1799, France caught its breath, ruled by the Directory, a government so intentionally weak and decentralized (two houses of parliament, five executives, and no funding) that it could never create another Robespierre.

Room 110: France vs. Europe (La Guerre)

The blade that dropped on Louis XVI rattled royal teacups throughout Europe. Even as early as 1792, France had to defend its young democracy against Austria and Prussia. France's new army was composed of ordinary citizens from a universal draft and led by daring young citizen-officers, who sang a stirring, bloodthirsty new song, "La Marseillaise." Surprisingly, they quickly defeated the apathetic mercenaries they faced. France vowed to liberate all

Europe from tyranny. Europe feared that, by "exporting Revolution," France would export democracy...plus senseless violence and chaos.

A young Corsican named **Napoleon Bonaparte** (see the bust) rose quickly through the ranks and proved himself by fighting royalists in Italy, Egypt, and on the streets of Paris. In 1799, the 29-year-old general returned to Paris as a conquering hero. Backed by an adoring public, he dissolved the Directory, established order, and gave himself the Roman-style title of "first consul."

French National Anthem: "La Marseillaise"

The genteel French have a gory past.

Allons enfants de la Patrie,	Let's go, children of the motherland,
Le jour de gloire est arrivé.	The day of glory has arrived.
Contre nous de la tyrannie	The blood-covered flag of tyranny
L'étendard sanglant est levé.	Is raised against us.
L'étendard sanglant est levé.	Is raised against us.
Entendez-vous dans les campagnes	Do you hear these ferocious soldiers
Mugir ces féroces soldats?	Howling in the countryside?
Qui viennent jusque dans nos bras	They're coming nearly into our grasp
Egorger vos fils et vos compagnes.	To slit the throats of your sons and your women.
Aux armes, citoyens,	Grab your weapons, citizens,
Formez vos bataillons,	Form your battalions,
Marchons, marchons,	We march, we march,
Qu'un sang impur	So that their impure blood
Abreuve nos sillons.	Will fill our furrows (trenches).

Room 111: The Revolution vs. Religion (*Vandalisme et Conservation*)

Three-fourths of France's churches were destroyed or vandalized during the Revolution, a backlash against the wealthy and politically repressive Catholic Church. In Notre-Dame, Christ was mothballed, and a woman dressed as "Dame Reason" was worshipped on the altar.

Room 113: Souvenirs of Revolution

After the Reign of Terror, *Liberté, Egalité, Fraternité* was just a slogan, remembered fondly on commemorative **plates and knick-knacks**. The Revolution was history.

• *The visit continues down four flights of stairs—or down the elevator—on the ground floor.*

Room 115: Napoleon Conquers Europe
(*Le Premier Empire,* 1799–1815)

Here's **Napoleon I** (1769–1821, r. as emperor 1804–1815) at the peak of power, master of Western Europe (see **portrait**, **breastplate**, **pistols**, and **death mask** in glass case). Dressed in his general's uniform, he's checking the maps to see who's left to conquer. Behind him is a throne with his imperial seal. This Corsican-born commoner, educated in Paris' military schools, became a young Revolutionary and a daring general, rising to prominence as a champion of democracy. Once in power, he preached revolution, but in fact became a dictator and crowned himself emperor (1804).

During the Empire, all things classical became popular. Wealthy socialites such as **Juliette Récamier** (see painting) donned robes and lounged on couches, while Paris was rebuilt with neoclassical monuments, such as the Arc de Triomphe, to make it the "New Rome."

In 1812, Napoleon foolishly invaded Russia, thus starting a downward spiral that ended in defeat by allied Europe at the Battle of Waterloo in Belgium (1815). Napoleon was exiled. He died in 1821 on the island of St. Helena, off the coast of Africa.

Room 118: The Monarchy Restored
(*La Restauration,* 1815–1830)

After almost 25 years in exile, royalty returned. **Louis XVIII** (1755–1824, r. 1815–1824) was the younger brother of headless Louis XVI. He returned to Paris with the backing of Europe's royalty and reclaimed the crown as a constitutional monarch (see the crowd scene of *Entrée du Louis XVIII à Paris, le 3 mai 1814*).

The next king, retro-looking **Charles X** (1757-1836, r. 1824-1830, youngest brother of Louis XVI), in glorious coronation robes, revived the fashion and oppression of the *ancien régime* as he plotted to dissolve the people's Assembly. But the French people were not about to turn the clock back.

Room 119: Revolution of 1830 *(Juillet 1830)*

Parisians again blocked off the narrow streets with barricades to fight the king's red-coated soldiers (see various **street battle paintings**). The people stormed the Louvre (biggest painting) and the king's palace, slaughtering the mercenary Swiss Guards. After "Three Glorious Days" of fighting, order was restored by Louis-Philippe (see **model**), an unassuming nobleman who appeared on the balcony of the Hôtel de Ville and was cheered by royalists, the middle class, and peasants alike. They made him king.

Room 120: Constitutional Monarchy
(*La Monarchie de Juillet,* 1830–1848)

King Louis-Philippe (1773–1850, r. 1830–1848, see black bust)—a

former lieutenant turned banker, with a few drops of royal blood—was a true constitutional monarch, harmlessly presiding over an era of middle-class progress fueled by the Industrial Revolution. Still, liberal reforms came too slowly. New factories brought division between wealthy employers and poor workers, and only 200,000 out of 30 million French citizens (1:150) could vote.

Room 121: Revolution of 1848
(La Deuxième République)

In February 1848—a time of Europe-wide depression and socialist strikes—Parisians took to the streets again **(battle scenes).** They battled at the Bastille, Palais-Royal, Panthéon, and place de la Concorde, and they toppled the king. Even prosperous accountants and shoe salesmen caught the spirit of revolution. After five decades of dictators (including Napoleon), retread Bourbons (the Restoration), and self-proclaimed monarchs (Louis-Philippe), France was back in the hands of the people—the Second Republic.

Room 122: Romanticism (Le Romantisme)

Freedom of expression, the uniqueness of each person, the glories of the human spirit and the natural world—these values from the 1789 Revolution were extolled by artists of the 1800s known as Romantics.

Working clockwise, you'll see **caricature busts** of many famous Frenchmen and visitors to the center of European culture, Paris. There's Victor Hugo (author of *Les Misérables* and *The Hunchback of Notre-Dame*), Frédéric Chopin (Polish pianist who charmed Parisian society), Giuseppe Verdi (composer of stirring operas, such as *Aida*), and Gioacchino Rossini (*Lone Ranger* theme).

There are also **paintings** of Romantic painter Eugène Delacroix and glamorous pianist Franz Liszt and his mistress, Marie d'Agoult—the ultimate Romantic. She left her husband and children to follow the dynamic Liszt on a journey of self-discovery in Italy and Switzerland—"the years of pilgrimage."

• *Journey upstairs and to the left toward* "Paris: Du Second Empire à nos jours"—*From the Second Empire to Today.*

Room 128: Napoleon III and the Second Empire
(Le Deuxième Empire, 1852–1870)

Louis-Napoleon Bonaparte (1808–1873, r. as emperor 1852–1871; in the big painting, with red pants and sash, waxed moustache, and goatee) was the nephew of the famous Emperor Napoleon I. He used his well-known name to get elected president by a landslide in 1848, and then combined democracy with monarchy to be voted

"Emperor Napoleon III." He suppressed opposition while promoting liberal reforms as well as economic and colonial expansion.

Here he hands an order to **Baron Georges Haussmann** (mutton-chop sideburns) to modernize Paris. Haussmann cut the wide, straight boulevards of today to move goods, open up the crowded city...and prevent barricades for future revolutions. Parks, railroad stations, and the Opéra Garnier made Paris the model for world capitals. (Room 129 shows building projects.)

The **boat-like cradle** (Room 128) is a copy of the famous cradle of Napoleon II (1811–1832, known to history as the King of Rome), the only son of Napoleon I, who died at 21 of tuberculosis before ever ruling anything.

Napoleon III pursued popular wars (the **model** in Room 129 celebrates Crimean War vets, 1855) and unpopular ones (backing Austrian Emperor Maximilian in Mexico). In the summer of 1870, he personally led a jubilant French Army to crush upstart Prussia—"On to Berlin!" Uh-oh.

Room 130: The Franco-Prussian War
(*Le Siège de Paris*, 1870–1871)

Within weeks, the overconfident French were surrounded, Napoleon III himself was captured, and he surrendered. Paris was stunned. (See the big **painting of a crowd** hearing the news on the legislature steps.) The Germans quickly put a stranglehold on Paris, and a long, especially cold winter settled in.

Some would not give up. Without an emperor, they proclaimed yet another democratic republic (France's 3rd in a century) and sent minister Léon Gambetta in a newfangled balloon **(painting)** over the Germans' heads to rally the countryside to come save Paris. The Parisians themselves held out bravely **(painting of Tuileries** as army camp), but German efficiency and modern technology simply overwhelmed the French.

Room 131: The Paris Commune
(*La Commune*, Spring 1871)

The Republic finally agreed to a humiliating surrender. Paris' liberals—enraged at the capitulation after such a brave winter and fearing a return of monarchy—rejected the surrender and proclaimed their own government, the Paris Commune. **Portraits** honor the proud idealists, who barricaded themselves inside Paris' neighborhoods, refusing to bow to the German emperor.

Then, in one "bloody week" in May **(battle scenes),** French

troops backing the Republic stormed through Paris, leaving 15,000 dead, 5,000 jailed, and 8,000 deported. The Commune was snuffed out, but the memory was treasured by generations of liberals in popular **souvenirs:** a jar of bread from the hungry winter, a carrier pigeon's feather, a box reading *"Vive la Commune!"*

The church of Sacré-Cœur (see **painting** way up high) was built after the war as a form of national penance for the sins of liberalism.

Rooms 132–142: The Beautiful Age (*La Belle Epoque, 1871–1914*)

The Third Republic restored peace to a prosperous middle-class society. The **Eiffel Tower** (Room 132) marked the 1889 centennial of the Revolution, and the **Statue of Liberty** (Room 133) honored America's revolution.

Paris was a capital of world culture, a city of **Impressionist painters** (Room 135); of writers and actors, including the actress **Sarah Bernhardt** (Room 136), called the world's first international star ("a force of nature, a fiery soul, a marvelous intelligence, a magnificent creature of the highest order," raved one of the smitten); of **Georges Bizet** (Room 136), composer of *Carmen;* of balls, carriages, cafés, and parks (**paintings,** Rooms 137–140).

And it was the city of Art Nouveau. Two delightful turn-of-the-20th-century Parisian shops—spliced into this old-regime mansion—illustrate the curvy, decorative Art Nouveau style: the *très chic* **Café de Paris** (Room 141) and the **Boutique Fouquet** (Room 142). Imagine browsing through jewelry in the spindly splendor of this world. Peacocks peer through stained glass as nubile nymphs sit atop fountains.

Room 145: World War I (1914–1918)

Three costly wars with Germany—the Franco-Prussian War, World War I, and World War II—drained France's resources. Although **Marshal Foch** (big painting above the elevator) is hailed as the man who coordinated the Allied armies to defeat Germany in World War I, France was hardly a winner. More than 1.5 million Frenchmen died, a generation was lost, and the country would be a pushover when Hitler invaded in 1940. France's long history as a global superpower was over.

Room 147: *Remembrance of Things Past* (*La Vie Littéraire du XXe Siècle*)

The last room is filled with portraits of Paris' 20th-century literary greats. By producing such figures as the writer **Marcel Proust** (see his reconstructed bedroom) and the dreamy writer/filmmaker **Jean Cocteau,** France has remained a cultural superpower.

PICASSO
MUSEUM
TOUR

(Musée Picasso)

The 20th century's greatest artist was the master of many styles (Cubism, Surrealism, Expressionism, etc.) and of many media (painting, sculpture, prints, ceramics, and assemblages). Still, he could make anything he touched look unmistakably like "a Picasso."

The Picasso Museum walks you through the evolution of the artist's long life and many styles. The women he loved and the global events he lived through appear in his canvases, filtered through his own emotional response. You don't have to admire Picasso's lifestyle or like his modern painting style. But a visit here might make you appreciate the sheer vitality and creativity of this hardworking and unique man.

ORIENTATION

Cost: €5.50, free first Sun of month, covered by Museum Pass. (Notice the clever computer screen showing in pink and blue who's in and who's out.)

Hours: April–Sept Wed–Mon 9:30–18:00, Oct–March Wed–Mon 9:30–17:30, last entry 45 min before closing, closed Tue.

Information: Tel. 01 42 71 25 21, www.musee-picasso.fr.

Getting There: 5 rue de Thorigny, Mo: St. Paul or Chemin Vert.

Length of This Tour: Allow one hour.

Overview

Start upstairs on the first floor. A thoughtfully laid out series of rooms leads you chronologically through Picasso's life. This chapter follows the museum's logic and is intended as a supplement to their excellent English information. It's also shorter, for those who want to see the whole museum quickly, then browse. While the

order of the rooms is fairly permanent, the museum rotates its large collection of paintings often, so don't be dismayed if you don't find a particular work. The top floor shows a revolving collection of exhibits relating to the life and work of Picasso.

THE TOUR BEGINS

Pablo Picasso (1881–1973)
Born in Spain, the son of an art teacher, the teenaged Picasso quickly advanced beyond his teachers. He mastered camera-eye realism, but also showed an empathy for the people he painted that was insightful beyond his years. (Unfortunately, the museum has very few early works. Many doubters of Picasso's genius warm to him somewhat after seeing his excellent draftsmanship and facility with oils from his youth.) As a teenager in Barcelona, he fell in with a bohemian crowd that mixed wine, women, and art.

In 1900, Picasso set out to make his mark in Paris, the undisputed world capital of culture. He rejected the surname his father had given him (Ruíz) and chose his mother's instead, making it his distinctive one-word brand: Picasso.

Room 1: Early Years and Blue Period (1895–1903)
The brash Spaniard quickly became a poor, homesick foreigner, absorbing the styles of many painters (especially Henri de Toulouse-Lautrec) while searching for his own artist's voice. He found companionship among fellow freaks and outcasts on butte Montmartre (see paintings of jesters, circus performers, and garish cabarets). When his best friend committed suicide (*Death of Casagemas*, 1901), Picasso plunged into a "Blue Period," painting emaciated beggars, hard-eyed pimps, and himself, bundled up against the cold, with eyes all cried out (*Autoportrait*, 1901; see photo on page 231). Photos in the glass case show slices of Paris' cutting-edge art scene in 1901.

Room 2: Rose Period (1904–1907)
In 1904, Picasso moved into his Bateau-Lavoir home/studio on Montmartre (see Montmartre Walk, page 132), got a steady girlfriend, and suddenly saw the world through rose-colored glasses (the Rose Period, though the museum has very few of these).

Rooms 2 and 3: Masks, *Les Demoiselles d'Avignon* (1904–1906) and Cubist Experiments (1907–1909)
Only 25 years old, Picasso reinvented painting. Fascinated by the primitive power of African and Iberian tribal masks, he sketched human faces with simple outlines and almond eyes (*Autoportrait*,

1906). Intrigued by the body of his girlfriend, Fernande Olivier, he sketched it from every angle, then experimented with showing several different views on the same canvas (see various nude studies).

A hundred paintings and nine months later, Picasso gave birth to a monstrous canvas of five nude, fragmented prostitutes with mask-like faces—*Les Demoiselles d'Avignon* (1907). The paint-

ing hangs in New York's Museum of Modern Art, but you'll see a similar-looking painting in Room 3 (*Three Figures Under a Tree*, 1907–1908). His friends were speechless, his enemies reviled it, and almost overnight, Picasso was famous.

Picasso went to the Louvre for a special exhibit on Cézanne, then returned to the Bateau-Lavoir to expand on Cézanne's chunky style and geometric simplicity—oval-shaped heads, circular breasts, and diamond thighs (see landscapes). Picasso rejected traditional 3-D. Instead of painting, say, a distant hillside in dimmer tones than the trees in the bright foreground, Picasso did it all bright, making the foreground blend into the background, and turning a scene into an abstract design. Modern art was being born.

Room 4: Cubism (1910–1917)

With his next-door neighbor, Georges Braque, Picasso invented Cubism, a fragmented, "cube"-shaped style. He'd fracture a musician (*Man with a Violin*, 1911) into a barely recognizable jumble of facets, and facets within facets. Even empty space is composed of these "cubes," all of them the same basic color, that weave together the background and foreground. Picasso sketches reality from every angle, then pastes it all together, a composite of different views. The monochrome color (mostly gray or brown) is less important than the experiments with putting the 3-D world on a 2-D canvas in a modern way. (For more on Cubism, see the Pompidou Center Tour, page 202.)

In a few short years, Picasso had turned painting in the direction it would go for the next 50 years.

Room 4b: Synthetic Cubism

Analytic Cubism (1907–1913) broke the world down into small facets, to "analyze" the subject from every angle. Now it was time to "synthesize" it back together with the real world.

These "constructions" are still-life paintings (a 2-D illusion)

augmented with glued-on, real-life materials—wood, paper, rope, or chair caning (the real 3-D world). The contrast between real objects and painted objects makes it clear that while traditional painting is a mere illusion, art can be more substantial.

Personally, Picasso's life had fragmented into a series of relationships with women. He finally met (1917) and married a graceful Russian dancer with the Ballet Russes, Olga Kokhlova (*Portrait of Olga in an Armchair*, 1917, in Room 4).

Room 5: Picasso's Personal Collection

Picasso had an encyclopedic knowledge of art history and a caricaturist's ability to easily "quote" another artist's style, which he would adapt to his own uses. In this room, see Picasso's sources, from Pierre-Auguste Renoir's plump women to Cézanne's chunky surfaces to the simple outlines and bright colors of Henri Matisse, his friend and rival in the contest to be Century's Greatest Painter. He and Matisse, who met in Paris and later lived near each other in the south of France, would occasionally trade masterpieces, letting the other pick out his favorite.

Room 6: Classicism, Family Life at the Beach (1918–1924)

Now he was a financially secure husband and father (see the portrait of his 3-year-old son, *Paul en Harlequin*, 1924), and with the disastrous Great War over, Picasso took his family for summer vacations on the Riviera. There, he painted peaceful scenes of women and children at the beach.

A trip to Rome inspired him to emulate the bulky mass of ancient statues, transforming them into plump but graceful women, with Olga's round features. Picasso could create the illusion of a face or body bulging out from the canvas, like a cameo or classical bas-relief. Watching kids drawing in the sand with a stick, he tried drawing a figure without lifting the brush from the canvas.

Room 7: Surrealism and Women (1925–1929)

In 1927, a middle-aged Picasso stopped a 17-year-old girl outside the Galeries Lafayette department store (by the Opéra Garnier) and said, "Mademoiselle, you have an interesting face. Can I paint it? I am Picasso." She said, "Who?"

The two had little in common, but the unsophisticated Marie-

Thérèse Walter and the short, balding artist developed a strange attraction for each other. Soon, Marie-Thérèse moved into the house next door to Picasso and his wife, and they began an awkward three-wheeled relationship. Worldly Olga was jealous, young Marie-Thérèse was insecure and clingy, and Picasso the workaholic artist faithfully chronicled the erotic/neurotic experience.

Using a Surrealist style, he lets the id speak. These women—a jumble of clashing colors and twisted limbs—open their toothy mouths and scream their frustration (*Large Nude on a Red Armchair*, 1929). The artist and his model were becoming hopelessly entangled. Picasso needed a big ego to keep his big id out of trouble.

• *From Room 7, consider a detour up to the second floor, which hosts temporary exhibits on Picasso and selections from his 2,000 prints. Our tour continues downstairs in...*

Room 8: The Bathers Room 9: Boisgeloup (1930–1935)

Picasso twists women into balloon-animal shapes lounging on the beach. With his increasing fame, even Picasso's sandcastles were worth hanging in a museum.

See the photo (Room 8 info plaque) of young, athletic Marie-Thérèse with her classic profile—big chin and long nose with a straight bridge. Picasso would never tire of portraying her (see several versions of *Head of a Woman*, 1931, in Room 9). In 1935, Marie-Thérèse gave birth to their daughter, Maya.

Room 10: Spain—Bullfights, Minotaurs, *Guernica*

Picasso, an unrepentantly macho Spaniard, loved bullfights, seeing them as a metaphor for the timeless human interaction between the genders. Me bull, you horse, I gore you.

The minotaur (a bull-headed man) symbolized man's war- ring halves: half rational human (Freud's superego) and half rag- ing beast (the id). Picasso could be both tender and violent with women, thus playing out both sides of this love/war duality.

Take the Spanish imagery in this room—of bulls, scream- ing horses, a woman with a can- dle—put it all on one monumental canvas (bigger even than the big

Picasso's Women

Women were Picasso's main subject. As an artist, he used women both as models and as muses. Having sex with his model allowed him to paint not just the woman's physical features, but also the emotional associations of their relationship. At least that's what he told his wife.

In today's psychobabble, Picasso was an egotistical and abusive male, a sex addict fueled by his own insecurities and inability to connect intimately with women.

In the lingo of Picasso's crowd—steeped in the psycho-analysis of Freud and Jung—relations with women allowed him to express primal urges, recover repressed memories, confront his relationship with his mother, discover hidden truths, connect with his anima (female side), and recreate the archetypal experiences lived since the beginning of time.

After about 1910, Picasso almost never painted (only sketched) from a posed model. His "portraits" of women were often composites of several different women from his large catalog of memories, filtered through emotional associations.

Here are some of Picasso's models/mistresses/muses:

María Picasso y López—his mom—wrote him a letter almost every day until her death. In childhood, Picasso was raised as a lone boy among the many women of his extended family.

Dark-haired **Fernande Olivier**, an artist's model who'd lived a wild life, was Picasso's first real love. They lived together (1904–1909) in Montmartre (with a dog and a 10-year-old street urchin they'd taken in) when Picasso was inventing Cubism, and her features are seen in *Les Demoiselles d'Avignon*. Fernande claimed that Picasso locked her in or hid her shoes so she couldn't go out while he was gone.

collage in Room 11), and you get *Guernica* (1937, on display in Madrid), Picasso's most famous work, which summed up the pain of Spain's brutal Civil War (1936–1939).

• *Down on basement level...*

Room 12: Sculpture Garden
Picture Picasso with goggles and a blow-torch, creating 3-D Cubist statues out of scrap metal. He was the master of many media (as we'll see), and often turned 20th-century industrial junk into art. In the figure just down the ramp en route to Room 13, a ladle becomes a head, sticks are legs, and garden claws are hands. A true scavenger, Picasso took what he found, played with it, and transformed it into something interesting.

In May of 1913, Fernande left him for good, his father died, and **Eva Gouel** moved in. Picasso launched into Synthetic Cubism. Eva died two years later of tuberculosis.

Elegant **Olga Kokhlova** (1896–1955) gave Picasso a son (Pablo, Jr.) and 10 years of stability. They lived high class, hobnobbing with the international set surrounding the Ballet Russes.

Athletic **Marie-Thérèse Walter** (1910–1977) knew nothing of art and never mixed with Picasso's sophisticated crowd. But even as she put on weight, Picasso found her figure worthy to paint. They had a daughter together named Maya (b. 1935).

Sparkly-eyed **Dora Maar** (1909–1998) was the anti-Marie-Thérèse—a woman who could converse with Picasso about his art.

Françoise Gilot (b. 1921), a painter herself, is often depicted with a flower, perhaps symbolizing the new life (and two children) she gave to an aging Picasso. She stubbornly forced Picasso to sever ties with Dora Maar before she'd settle in. When Picasso dumped her for his next conquest (1954), she went on to write a scathing tell-all book. Their children, Claude and Paloma, grew up amid lawsuits over whether they could use their father's famous last name.

Jacqueline Roque (1927–1986) married the god of painting when he was 80 and she was 33. She outlived him, but later took her own life.

So, I guess Picasso's ideal model would be a composite—a brainy but tubercular dancer with a curvaceous figure, as well as a youthful flower-child who could pose like a slut but remind him of his mother.

Room 13: The Muses

Picasso met the artsy, sophisticated photographer Dora Maar over

coffee at Les Deux Magots in 1936. She photographed him in his studio working on *Guernica*, and they became involved. Picasso still kept ties with Marie-Thérèse while also working out a complicated divorce from Olga.

Compare portraits of his two mistress-muses. Blonde Marie-Thérèse, with her big, straight nose and round chin, is full-figured and curvy (The Body). Dark-haired Dora Maar is slender, with long red nails and sparkling, intelligent eyes (The Mind).

Picasso's Residences

The Spaniard lived almost all of his adult life in France, mostly in Paris and the south of France. Over the years, Picasso had 13 different studios in Paris, mainly in the Montmartre and Montparnasse neighborhoods. Picasso liked both France and Spain, but after 1936, he vowed never again to set foot in Fascist-controlled Spain, and he never did.

Dora is often pictured crying. Go figure. She's attached to a physically abusive married man who refuses to leave his other mistress.

Room 14: Ceramics
The minute Picasso discovered ceramics (1947), the passion consumed him. Working in a small, family-owned ceramics factory in the south of France, he shaped wet clay, painted it, and fired up a dozen or more pieces a day—2,000 in a single year. He created plates with faces, bird-shaped vases, woman-shaped bottles, bull-shaped statues, and colorful tiles. Working in this timeless medium, he gives a modernist's take on classic motifs: red-and-black Greek vases, fauns, primitive goddesses, Roman amphorae, and so on.

Room 15: Multimedia
A bicycle seat with handlebar horns becomes the *Head of a Bull* (1942). This is quintessential Picasso—a timeless motif (minotaurs) made of 20th-century materials and done with a twinkle in his eye.

Room 16: World War II (1940–1945)
In 1940, Nazi tanks rolled into Paris. Picasso decided to stay for the duration and live under gray skies and gray uniforms. Not only did he suffer from wartime shortages, condescending Nazis, and the grief of having comrades killed or deported, he had girl trouble. "The worst time of my life," he said. His beloved mother had died, and he endured the endless, bitter divorce from Olga, all the while juggling his two longtime, feuding mistresses—as well as the occasional fling.

Still, he continued working, and his canvases from this period are only slightly more gray and gloomy.

Room 18: The South of France (1948–1954)
Sun! Color! Water! Spacious skies! Freedom!

At war's end, he left Paris and all that emotional baggage

behind, finding fun in the sun in the South of France. Sixty-five-year-old Pablo Picasso was reborn, enjoying worldwide fame and the love of a beautiful 23-year-old painter named Françoise Gilot. She soon offered him a fresh start at fatherhood, giving birth to son Claude and daughter Paloma.

Picasso spent mornings swimming in the Mediterranean, days painting, evenings partying with friends, and late nights painting again, like a madman. Dressed in rolled-up white pants and a striped sailor's shirt, bursting with pent-up creativity, he often cranked out more than a painting a day. Ever-restless Picasso had finally found his Garden of Eden and rediscovered his joie de vivre.

These works set the tone for the rest of Picasso's life—sunny, light-hearted, childlike, experimenting in new media, and using motifs of the sea, of Greek mythology (fauns, centaurs), and animals (birds, goats, and pregnant baboons). His childlike doves became an international symbol of peace. These joyous themes announce Picasso's newfound freedom in a newly liberated France.

• *Head upstairs to...*

Room 19: The Studio/Luncheon on the Grass (1955–1961)

With no living peers in the world of art, the great Picasso dialogued with dead masters, reworking paintings by Edouard Manet, Diego de Velázquez, and others. Oh yes, also in this period he met mistress number...um, whatever—27-year-old Jacqueline Roque, whom he married.

Room 20: The Last Period (1961–1973)

He was fertile to the end, still painting with bright thick colors at age 91. Throughout his long life, Picasso was intrigued by portraying people—always people, ignoring the background—conveying their features with a single curved line and their moods with colors. These last works have the humor and playfulness of someone much younger. As it is said of Picasso, "When he was a child, he painted like a man. When he was old, he painted like a child."

RODIN MUSEUM TOUR

(Musée Rodin)

Auguste Rodin (1840–1917) was a modern Michelangelo, sculpting human figures on an epic scale, revealing through the body their deepest thoughts and feelings. Like many of Michelangelo's unfinished works, Rodin's statues rise from the raw stone around them, driven by the life force. With missing limbs and scarred skin, these are prefab classics, making ugliness noble. Rodin's people are always moving restlessly. Even the famous *Thinker* is moving. While he's plopped down solidly, his mind is a million miles away. The museum presents a full range of Rodin's work, housed in a historic mansion where he once lived and worked. The gardens are picnic-perfect (BYO), or try the café.

ORIENTATION

The entire museum is being gradually renovated over the next few years; expect some changes to this tour. (For now, the main change is where you enter—a half-block east of the normal entry.)

Cost: €5, €3 on Sun, free on the first Sun of month, €1 for garden only, all covered by Museum Pass.

Hours: April–Sept Tue–Sun 9:30–17:45, gardens close at 18:45. Oct–March Tue–Sun 9:30–16:45, gardens close at 17:00. Closed Mon. Last entrance 30 minutes before closing.

Getting There: It's at 77 rue de Varenne, near Napoleon's Tomb (Mo: Varenne). Bus #69 stops at Grenelle-Bellechasse.

Information: Tel. 01 44 18 61 10, www.musee-rodin.fr.

Tours: Audioguides covering the museum and gardens cost €4.

Length of This Tour: Allow one hour.

Cuisine Art: There is a peaceful if pricey café in the gardens behind the museum. For better options, leave the museum, cross the

Rodin Museum

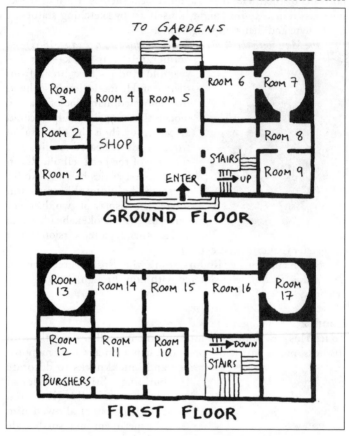

TO GARDENS

ROOM 3
ROOM 4
ROOM 5
ROOM 6
ROOM 7
ROOM 2
SHOP
ROOM 8
ROOM 1
STAIRS
ENTER
UP
ROOM 9

GROUND FLOOR

ROOM 13
ROOM 14
ROOM 15
ROOM 16
ROOM 17
ROOM 12
ROOM 11
ROOM 10
DOWN
STAIRS
BURGHERS

FIRST FLOOR

Esplanade des Invalides, and find many recommended cafés and restaurants in the rue Cler area (see page 347).

THE TOUR BEGINS

• *As you enter the mansion, pick up a museum plan with room numbers (this tour is keyed to that plan), turn left, and walk through the shop to start a circular tour of the ground floor.*

Room 1

Rodin's early works match the belle époque style of the time—noble busts of bourgeois citizens, pretty

portraits of their daughters, and classical themes. Born of work-ing-class roots, Rodin taught himself art by sketching statues at the Louvre and then sculpting copies.

The Man with the Broken Nose (*L'Homme au nez cassé*, 1865)—a deliberately ugly work—was 23-year-old Rodin's first break from the norm. He meticulously sculpted this deformed man (one of the few models the struggling sculptor could afford), but then the clay statue froze in his unheated studio, and the back of the head fell off. Rodin loved it! Art critics hated it. Rodin persevered. (Note: The museum rotates the display of two different versions—the broken-headed one and another, repaired version Rodin made later that critics accepted.)

See the painting of Rodin's future wife, Rose Beuret *(Portrait de Madame Rodin),* who suffered with him through obscurity and celebrity.

Room 2

To feed his new family, Rodin cranked out small-scale works with his boss' name on them—portraits, ornamental vases, nymphs,

and knickknacks to decorate buildings. Still, the series of mother-and-childs (Rose and baby Auguste?) allowed him to experiment on a small scale with the intertwined twosomes he'd do later.

His job gave him enough money to visit Italy, where he was inspired by Michelangelo's boldness, monumental scale, restless figures, and "unfinished" look. Rapidly approaching middle age, Rodin was ready to rock.

Room 3

Rodin moved to Brussels, where his first major work, *The Bronze Age* (*L'âge d'airain*, 1877), brought controversy and the fame that surrounds it. This nude youth (see photo, facing page), perhaps inspired by Michelangelo's *Dying Slave* in the Louvre, awakens to a new world. It was so lifelike that Rodin was accused of not sculpting it himself but simply casting it directly from a live body.

The boy's left hand looks like he should be leaning on a spear, but it's just that missing element that makes the pose more tenuous and interesting.

The art establishment still snubbed Rodin as an outsider, and no wonder. Look at his ultra-intense take on the winged symbol of France *(La Défense)*—this Marseillaise screams, "Off with their heads!" at the top of her lungs. Rodin was a slave to his muses, and some of them inspired monsters.

Room 4

Like the hand of a sculptor, *The Hand of God (La main de Dieu,* 1896) shapes Adam and Eve from the mud of the earth to which they will return. Rodin himself worked in "mud," using his hands to model clay figures, which were then reproduced in marble or bronze, usually by his assistants. Spin this masterpiece on its turntable (I'm serious, give it a turn). Rodin wants you to see it from every angle. He first worked from the front view, then checked the back and side profiles, then filled in the in-between.

In *The Kiss* (1888–1889), a passionate woman twines around a solid man for their first, spontaneous kiss. In their bodies, we can almost read the thoughts, words, and movements that led up to this meeting of lips. *The Kiss* was the first Rodin work the public loved. Rodin despised it, thinking it simple and sentimental.

Other works in this room show embracing couples who seem to emerge from the stone just long enough to love. Rodin left many works "unfinished," reminding us that all creation is a difficult process of dragging a form out of chaos.

Room 5

The two hands that form the arch of *The Cathedral (La Cathédrale,* 1908) are actually two right hands (a man's and a woman's?).

In the room's center, a bronze man strides forward, as bold as the

often-controversial Rodin. The armless and head-less *Walking Man* (*L'Homme Qui Marche*, 1900–1907) plants his back foot forcefully, as though he's about to step, while his front foot already has stepped. Rodin, who himself had one foot in the past, one in the future, captures two poses at once.

Rodin worked with many materials—he chiseled marble (though not often), modeled clay, cast bronze, worked plaster, painted, and sketched. He often created different versions of the same subject in different media.

Room 6

This room displays works by Camille Claudel, mostly in the style of her master. The 44-year-old Rodin took 18-year-old Camille as his pupil, muse, colleague, and lover. We can follow the arc of their relationship:

Rodin was inspired by young Camille's beauty and spirit, and he often used her as a model. (See several versions of her head.)

As his student, "Mademoiselle C" learned from Rodin, doing portrait busts in his lumpy style. Her bronze bust of Rodin (by the door) shows the steely-eyed sculptor with strong front and side profiles, barely emerging from the materials they both worked with.

Soon they were lovers. *The Waltz* (*La Valse*, 1892) captures the spinning exuberance the two must have felt as they embarked together on a new life. The couple twirls—hands so close but not touching—in a delicate balance.

But Rodin was devoted as well to his lifelong companion, Rose (see her face emerging from a block of marble). Claudel's *Maturity*

(*L'Âge Mûr*, 1895–1907) shows the breakup. A young woman on her knees begs the man not to leave her, as he's led away reluctantly by an older woman. The center of the composition is the hole left where their hands drift apart.

Rodin did leave Camille. Overwhelmed by grief and jealousy, she went crazy and had to be institutionalized until she died. *The Wave* (*La Vague*, 1900), carved in green onyx in a very un-Rodin style, shows tiny, helpless women huddled under a wave about to engulf them.

Room 7 & Room 8

What did Rodin think of women? Here are many different images from which you can draw conclusions.

Eve (1881) buries her head in shame, hiding her nakedness. But she can't hide the consequences—she's pregnant.

Rodin became famous, wealthy, and respected, and society ladies all wanted him to do their portraits. In Room 8, you'll also see his last mistress *(La Duchesse de Choiseul),* who lived with him here in this mansion.

Room 9

This dimly lit room is filled with Rodin's sketches (temporary exhibits may occupy this space). The first flash of inspiration for a huge statue might be a single line sketched on notepaper. Rodin wanted nude models in his studio at all times—walking, dancing, and squatting—in case they struck some new and interesting pose. Rodin thought of sculpture as simply "drawing in all dimensions."

• *Upstairs, you'll find a glass display case that tries hard to explain...*

The Bronze Casting Process

Rodin made his bronze statues not by hammering sheets of metal, but by using the classic "lost wax" technique. He'd start by shaping the figure out of wet plaster. This figure becomes a model that's covered with a form-fitting mold. Pour molten bronze into the narrow space between the model and the mold around it, let it cool, remove the mold, and—*voilà!*—you have a hollow bronze statue ready to be polished and varnished. With a mold, you could produce other copies, which is why there are many authorized bronze versions of Rodin's masterpieces all over the world.

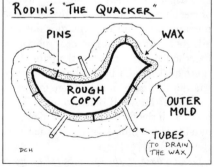

As the display case teaches, there are actually a number of additional steps involving two models and two molds. Rodin used the original plaster model to make a first mold, which was used to make a heat-resistant clay copy of the original plaster model. He sanded down the clay copy, coated it with a wax skin, and then touched up the wax to add surface details. He used this touched-up copy to make the more detailed, final mold. He fitted the mold with ventilation tubes and started pouring in the molten bronze. The wax melted away—the "lost wax" technique—and the bronze

cooled and hardened in its place, thus forming the final bronze statue.

Room 10 & Room 11

The Thinker was to have been the centerpiece of a massive project that Rodin wrestled with for decades—a doorway encrusted with characters from Dante's *Inferno*. These *Gates of Hell* were never completed (we'll later see the unfinished piece in the garden), but the studies for it (in this room) are some of Rodin's masterpieces.

These figures struggle to come into existence. Rodin was fascinated by the theory of evolution—not Darwin's version of the survival of the fittest, but the Frenchman Jean-Baptiste Lamarck's. His figures survive not by the good fortune of random mutation (Darwin), but by their own striving (Lamarck). They are driven by the life force, a restless energy that animates and shapes dead matter (Lamarck and Henri-Louis Bergson). Rodin must have felt that force even as a child, when he first squeezed soft clay and saw a worm emerge.

In Room 11, you'll see studies of the human body in all its aspects—open, closed, wrinkled, intertwined.

Room 12

A virtual unknown until his mid-30s, Rodin slowly began receiving major commissions for public monuments. *The Burghers of Calais* (*Bourgeois de Calais*, in the center of the room, described below in garden section) depicts the actual event in 1347, when, in order to save their people, the city fathers surrendered the keys of the city—and their own lives—to the king of England. Rodin portrays them not in some glorious pose drenched in pomp and allegory, but as a simple example of men sacrificing their lives together. As they head to the gallows, with ropes already around their necks, each body shows a distinct emotion, ranging from courage to despair. Compare the small plaster model in this room with the final, life-size bronze group outside the window in the garden (near the street).

• *Double back to the wing overlooking the gardens.*

Room 15

Rodin's feverish attempts to capture a portrait of the novelist Balzac ranged from a pot-bellied Bacchus to a headless nude cradling an erection. In a moment of inspiration, Rodin threw a plaster-soaked

robe over the nude and watched it dry into what would become the proud, final, definitive version.

Room 17
Legendary lovers kiss, embrace, and intertwine in yin-yang bliss.

Room 14
See Rodin's portrait busts of celebrities and some paintings by (yawn, are we through yet?) Vincent van Gogh, Claude Monet, and Pierre-Auguste Renoir. Rodin enjoyed discussions with Monet and other artists and incorporated their ideas in his work. Rodin is often considered an Impressionist because he captured spontaneous "impressions" of figures and created rough surfaces that catch reflected light.

Room 13
By the end of his life, Rodin was more famous than his works. (Newsreel footage of him is often on display nearby.) Get a sense of Rodin's working process by comparing the small plaster "sketches" (in the glass case) with the final, large-scale marble versions that line the walls.

THE GARDENS

Rodin lived and worked in this mansion, renting rooms alongside Henri Matisse, the poet Rainer Maria Rilke (Rodin's secretary), and the dancer Isadora Duncan. He loved placing his creations in the overgrown gardens. These are his greatest works, Rodin at his most expansive. The epic human figures are enhanced, not dwarfed, by nature.

• *Leaving the house, there are five more stops: Two on the left and three on the right. Beyond these stops is a big, breezy garden ornamented with statues, a cafeteria, and a WC.*

The Thinker (Le Penseur, 1906)
Leaning slightly forward, tense and compact, every muscle work-ing toward producing that one great thought, Man contemplates his fate. No constipation jokes, please.

This is not an intel-lectual, but a linebacker who's realizing there's more to life than frat parties. It's the first man

evolving beyond his animal nature to think the first thought. It's anyone who's ever worked hard to reinvent himself or to make something new or better. Said Rodin: "It is a statue of myself."

There are 29 other authorized copies of this statue, one of the most famous in the world.

• *To the left of* The Thinker, *you'll find...*

Balzac (1898)

The iconoclastic novelist turns his nose up at the notion he should be honored with a statue. This final version also stands in the Musée d'Orsay and on a street median in Montparnasse. When the statue was unveiled, the crowd booed, a fitting tribute to both the defiant novelist and the bold man who sculpted him.

• *Along the street near the ticket booth are...*

The Burghers of Calais (1889)

The six city fathers trudge to their execution, and we can read in their faces and poses what their last thoughts are. They mill about, dazed, as each one deals with the decision he's made to sacrifice himself for his city.

• *Circling counterclockwise...*

The man carrying the key to the city tightens his lips in determination. The bearded man is weighed down with grief. Another buries his head in his hands. One turns, seeking reassurance from

his friend, who turns away and gestures helplessly. The final key-bearer (in back) raises his hand to his head.

Each is alone in his thoughts, but they're united by their mutual sacrifice, by the base they stand on, and by their weighty robes— gravity is already dragging them down to their graves.

Pity the poor souls, view the statue from various angles (you can't ever see all the faces at once); then thank King Edward III, who, at the last second, pardoned them.

• *Follow* The Thinker's *gaze across the gardens. Standing before a tall white backdrop is a big dark door*—The Gates of Hell.

The Gates of Hell (La Porte de l'Enfer, 1880–1917)

These doors (never meant to actually open) were never finished for a museum that was never built. But the vision of Dante's trip into hell gave Rodin a chance to explore the dark side of human experience. "Abandon hope all ye who enter in," was hell's motto.

Rodin Museum Gardens

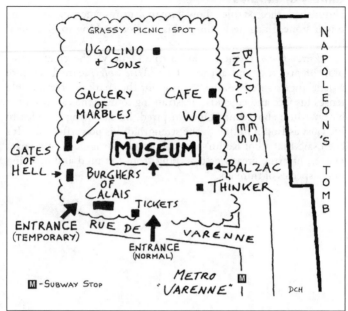

The three Shades at the top of the door point down—that's where we're going. Beneath the Shades, pondering the whole scene from above, is Dante as the Thinker. Below him, the figures emerge from the darkness just long enough to tell their sad tale of depravity. There's Paolo and Francesca (in the center of the right door), who were driven into an illicit love affair that brought them here. Ugolino (left door, just below center) crouches in prison over his kids. This poor soul was so driven by hunger that he ate the corpses of his own children. On all fours like an animal, he is the dark side of natural selection. Finally, find what some say is Rodin himself (at the very bottom, inside the right doorjamb, where it just starts to jut out), crouching humbly.

You'll find some of these figures writ large in the garden. *The Thinker* is behind you, *The Shades* (c. 1889) are 30 yards to the right, and *Ugolino* (1901–1904) dines in the fountain at the far end.

It's appropriate that the *Gates*—Rodin's "cathedral"—remained unfinished. He was always a restless artist for whom the process of discovery was as important as the finished product.

• *To the right of* The Gates of Hell *is a glassed-in building, the...*

Gallery of Marbles

Unfinished, these statues show human features emerging from the rough stone. Imagine Rodin in his studio, working to give them life.

Victor Hugo (at the far end of the Gallery), the great champion of progress and author of *Les Misérables*, leans back like Michelangelo's nude *Adam*, waiting for the spark of creation. He tenses his face and cups his ear, straining to hear the call from the blurry Muse above him. Once inspired, he can bring the idea to life (just as Rodin did) with the strength of his powerful arms. It's been said that all of Rodin's work shows the struggle of mind over matter, of brute creatures emerging from the mud and evolving into a species of thinkers.

MARMOTTAN MUSEUM TOUR

(Musée Marmottan Monet)

The Marmottan has the best collection of works by the master Impressionist, Claude Monet. In this mansion on the fringe of urban Paris, you can walk through Monet's life, from black-and-white sketches to colorful open-air paintings to the canvas that gave Impressionism its name. The museum's highlights are scenes of his garden at Giverny, including larger-than-life water lilies.

ORIENTATION

Cost: €7. The Marmottan is not covered by the Museum Pass.

Hours: Tue–Sun 10:00–18:00 (last entry at 17:30), closed Mon.

Getting There: It's in southwest Paris at 2 rue Louis Boilly. The Métro, RER, and buses all work: Take the Métro to La Muette, then walk six blocks in 10 minutes, following brown signs down chaussée de la Muette through the delightful, kid-filled park to the museum. (Take a few minutes in the park to enjoy the action at the old time, kid-powered carousel.) Or take the RER-C from the rue Cler area (Invalides or Pont de l'Alma), get off at Boulainvilliers stop, follow *sortie* Singer, turn left on rue Singer, turn right up rue Boulainvilliers, and then turn left down chaussée de la Muette to get to the museum. Bus #63 is handy from the rue Cler and St. Sulpice (buses #32, #22, and #52 also serve the museum). For a post-museum stroll, see page 54.

Information: Tel. 01 44 96 50 33, www.marmottan.com.

Length of This Tour: Allow one hour.

Photography: Not allowed. Cameras must be checked.

Starring: Claude Monet, including: *Impression: Sunrise* (shown above); portraits of Rouen Cathedral, Gare St. Lazare, and Houses of Parliament; scenes from Giverny; and water lilies.

Overview

The museum traces Monet's life chronologically, but in a way that's as rough and fragmented as a Monet canvas. The collection is reorganized periodically and some paintings go on road shows, so have patience and keep the big picture.

Basement: Entirely devoted to Monet, with works from throughout his life—mostly from his gardens at Giverny (including water lilies).

Ground Floor: Bookstore, a timeline of Monet's life, and some Monet memorabilia. The rest is an eclectic collection of non-Monet objects—period furnishings, a beautifully displayed series of illuminated manuscript drawings, and non-Monet paintings done in the seamless-brushstroke style that Monet rebelled against.

First Floor (upstairs): Often devoted to special exhibits. Otherwise, paintings by Impressionist colleagues Pierre-Auguste Renoir, Camille Pissarro, Berthe Morisot, and more.

THE TOUR BEGINS

GROUND FLOOR

• *Turn left after entering and walk to the end of the hall to the timeline on the wall.*

Claude Monet (1840–1926)

Claude Monet was the leading light of the Impressionist movement that revolutionized painting in the 1870s. Fiercely independent and dedicated to his craft, Monet gave courage to Renoir and others in the face of harsh criticism.

Timeline, Memorabilia, and Portraits of Monet and His Family

Though it's in French, you can follow the **pictures** to survey Monet's long life:

Born in Paris in 1840, Monet began his art career sketching **caricatures** of local townspeople. Baby **Jean** was born to Monet and his partner **Camille** in 1867, the year his work was rejected by the Salon. They moved to the countryside of **Argenteuil,** where he developed his open-air, Impressionist style. *Impression: Sunrise* was his landmark work at the breakthrough 1874 Impressionist Exhibition. He went on to paint several series of scenes such as *Gare Saint-Lazare* at different times of day.

After the birth of **Michel,** Camille's health declined and she later died. Monet traveled a lot, painting landscapes **(Bordighera),** people **(Portrait de Poly),** and more series including the famous

Cathedral of Rouen. In 1890, he settled down at his farmhouse in **Giverny** and married **Alice Hoschede.** He traveled less, but did visit London to paint the **Halls of Parliament.** Mostly, he painted his own **water lilies** and **flowers** in an increasingly messy style. He died in 1926 a famous man.

One of Monet's actual palettes is displayed nearby, alongside portraits of his wife and children.

BASEMENT LEVEL

• *Drop downstairs and trace the stages of Monet's life in (very) condensed form. The basement is one big room divided into three "rooms." Start with Monet's black-and-white drawings in a glass case, then work clockwise around the room.*

ROOM 1: FROM LE HAVRE TO LONDON (1857–1900)

Growing Up in Le Havre (1840–1860): Caricature Drawings (c. 1858)

Teenage Monet's first works—black-and-white, meticulously drawn, humorous sketches of small-town celebrities—are as different as can be from the colorful, messy oils that would make him famous. Still, they show his gift for quickly capturing an overall impression with a few simple strokes.

The son of a grocer, Monet defied his family, insisted he was an artist, and sketched the world around him—beaches, boats, and small-town life. A fellow artist, Eugène Boudin, encouraged him to don a scarf, set up his easel outdoors, and paint the scene exactly as he saw it. Today, we say: "Well, duh!" But "open-air" painting was unorthodox for artists trained to study their subjects thoroughly in the perfect lighting of a controlled studio setting.

At 19, Monet went to Paris but refused to enroll in the official art schools. The letters (in the glass case) from Monet asking for survival money from his friends show the price he paid for his early bohemian lifestyle.

The 1870s: Pure Impressionism

Monet·teamed up with Renoir and Alfred Sisley, leading them on open-air painting safaris to the countryside. Inspired by the

realism of Edouard Manet, they painted everyday things—landscapes, seascapes, street scenes, ladies with parasols, family picnics—in bright, basic colors.

In 1870, Monet married his girlfriend, Camille (the dark-haired woman in many of his paintings), and moved just outside Paris to the resort town of Argenteuil. Playing host to Renoir, Manet, and others, he perfected the Impressionist style—painting nature as a mosaic of short brushstrokes of different colors placed side by side, suggesting shimmering light.

First, he simplified. In *On the Beach at Trouville* (*Sur la Plage à Trouville*, 1870–1871), a lady's dress is a few thick strokes of paint. With paintings like *Stroll Near Argenteuil* (*Promenade près*

d'Argenteuil, 1873), Monet gradually broke things down into smaller dots of different shades. If you back up from a Monet canvas, the pigments blend into one (for example, red plus green plus yellow equals a brown boat). Still, they never fully resolve, creating the effect of shimmering light. Monet limited his palette to a few bright basics—cobalt blue, white, yellow, two shades of red, and emerald green abound. But no black—even shadows are a combination of bright colors.

Monet's constant quest was to faithfully reproduce nature in blobs of paint. His eye was a camera lens set at a very slow shutter speed to admit maximum light. Then he "developed" the impression made on his retina with an oil-based solution. Even as the heartbroken Monet watched Camille die of tuberculosis in 1879, he was (he admitted later) intrigued by the changing colors in her dying face.

Impression: Sunrise (*Impression Soleil Levant,* 1873)

Here's the painting that started the revolution—a simple, serene view of boats bobbing under an orange sun (see photo on page 251). At the first public showing by Monet, Renoir, Degas, and others in Paris in 1874, critics howled at this work and ridiculed the title. "Wallpaper," one called it. The sloppy brushstrokes and ordinary subject looked like a study, not a finished work. The style was dubbed "Impressionist"—an accurate name.

The misty harbor scene obviously made an "impression" on Monet, who faithfully rendered the fleeting moment in quick strokes of paint. The waves are simple horizontal brushstrokes. The sun's reflection on the water is a few thick, bold strokes of orange

Monet's Family

You'll likely see portraits of Monet's wife and children. Monet's first wife, Camille, died in 1879, leaving Monet to raise 12-year-old Jean and babe-in-arms Michel. (Michel would grow up to inherit the family home and many of the paintings that ended up here.) But Monet was also involved with Alice Hoschede, who had recently been abandoned by her husband. Alice moved in with her six kids and took care of the dying Camille, and the two families made a Brady Bunch merger. Baby Michel became bosom buddies with Alice's baby, Jean-Pierre, while teenage Jean Monet and stepsister Blanche fell in love and later married.

tipped with white. They zigzag down the canvas, the way a reflection shifts on moving water.

Monet the Traveler

In search of new light and new scenes, Monet traveled throughout France and Europe. As you enjoy canvases painted in all kinds of weather, picture Monet at work—hiking to a remote spot; carrying an easel, several canvases, brushes (large-size), a palette, tubes of paint (an invention that made open-air painting practical), food and drink, a folding chair, and an umbrella; and wearing his trademark hat, with a cigarette on his lip. He weathered the elements, occasionally putting himself in danger by clambering on cliffs to get the shot.

The key was to work fast, before the weather changed and the light shifted, completely changing the colors. Monet worked "wet-in-wet," applying new paint before the first layer dried, mixing colors on the canvas, and piling them up into a thick paste.

The 1890s: Series

Monet often painted the same subject several times under different light (such as one of Paris' train stations, the *Gare St. Lazare*, 1870s). In the 1890s, he conceived of a series of paintings to be shown as a group, giving a time-lapse view of a single subject.

He rented several rooms offering different angles overlooking the *Rouen Cathedral* and worked on up to 14 different canvases at a time, shuffling the right one onto the easel as the sun moved across the sky. The cathedral is made of brown stone, but at sunset it becomes gold and pink with blue shadows, softened by thick smudges of paint. The true subject is not the cathedral, but the full spectrum of light that bounces off it.

These series—of the cathedral, of haystacks, poplars, and

mornings on the Seine—were very popular. Monet, poverty-stricken until his mid-40s, was slowly becoming famous, first in America, then London, and finally in France.
• *Just before leaving the first room, you'll see...*

The 1900s: London

Turning a hotel room into a studio, Monet—working on nearly a hundred different canvases simultaneously—painted the changing light on the River Thames. The *London Houses of Parliament, Reflected in the Thames* (*Londres, Le Parlement, Reflets sur la Tamise*, 1905) stretch and bend with the tide. *Charing Cross Bridge* is only a few smudgy lines enveloped in fog.

London's fog epitomized Monet's favorite subject—the atmosphere that distorts distant objects. That filtering haze gives even different-colored objects a similar tone, resulting in a more harmonious picture. When the light was just right and the atmosphere glowed, the moment of "instantaneity" had arrived, and Monet worked like a madman.

In truth, many of Monet's canvases were begun quickly in the open air, and then painstakingly perfected later in the studio. He composed his scenes with great care—clear horizon lines give a strong horizontal axis, while diagonal lines (of trees or shorelines) create solid triangles. And he wasn't above airbrushing out details that might spoil the composition—such as Cleopatra's Needle near Charing Cross.

• *Continue into the next room.*

ROOM 2 & ROOM 3: PAINTINGS OF GIVERNY (1883–1926)

Rose Trellises and the Japanese Bridge (several versions)

In 1883, Monet's brood settled into a farmhouse in Giverny (50 miles west of Paris). Financially stable and domestically blissful, he turned Giverny into a garden paradise and painted nature without the long commute.

These canvases immerse you in Monet's garden at Giverny. Each canvas is fully saturated with color, the distant objects as bright as the close ones. Monet's mosaic of brushstrokes forms a colorful design that's beautiful even if you just look "at" the canvas like wallpaper. He wanted his paintings to be realistic and three-dimensional, but with a pleasant, two-dimensional pattern.

In the last half of his life, Monet's world shrank—from the broad vistas of the world traveler to the tranquility of his home, family, and garden. But his artistic vision expanded as he painted smaller details on bigger canvases and helped invent modern abstract art.

In 1890, Monet started work on his Japanese garden, inspired by tranquil scenes from the Japanese prints he collected. He  diverted a river to form a pond, planted willows and bamboo on the shores, filled the pond with water lilies, then crossed it with this wooden footbridge. As years passed, the bridge became overgrown with wisteria. Compare several different versions. He painted it at different times of day and year, exploring different color schemes.

Monet uses the bridge as the symmetrical center of simple, pleasing designs. The water is drawn with horizontal brushstrokes that get shorter as you move up the canvas (farther away), creating the illusion of distance. The horizontal water contrasts with the vertical willows, while the bridge "bridges" the sides of the square canvas and laces the scene together.

In 1912, Monet began to go blind. Cataracts distorted his perception of depth and color, and sent him into a tailspin of despair. The (angry?) red paintings date from this period.

Early Water Lilies (Nymphéas, several versions)

As his vision slowly failed, Monet concentrated on painting close-ups of the surface of the pond and its water lilies by using red, white, yellow, lavender, and various combos. Some lilies are just a few broad strokes on a bare canvas (a study), while others are piles of paint formed with overlapping colors.

But more than the lilies, the paintings focus on the changing reflections on the surface of the pond. Pan slowly around the room and watch the pond go from predawn to bright sunlight to twilight.

Early lily paintings (c. 1900) show the shoreline as a reference point. But increasingly, Monet cropped the scene ever closer, until there was no shoreline, no horizon, no sense of what's up or down. Lilies float among clouds. Stepping back from the canvas, you see the lilies just hang there on the museum wall, suspended in space. The surface of the pond and the surface of the canvas are one. Modern abstract art—a colored design on a flat surface—is just around the corner.

• *Enter the final, round room and find the big tree trunk.*

Big Weeping Willow (*Le Saule Pleureur,* 1918–1919)

Get close—Monet did—and analyze the trunk. Rough "brown" bark is made of thick strokes (an inch wide and 4 inches long) of pink, purple, orange, and green. Impressionism lives. But to get these colors to resolve in your eye, you'd have to back up all the way to Giverny.

Later Water Lilies (*Nymphéas,* 1915–1926)

Like Beethoven going deaf, blind Monet wrote his final symphonies on a monumental scale. He planned a series of huge, six-foot-tall canvases of water lilies to hang in special rooms at L'Orangerie (scheduled to reopen in the spring of 2006). He built a special studio with skylights and wheeled easels, and he worked on these paintings obsessively. A successful eye operation in 1923 gave him new energy. Here at the Marmottan are smaller-scale studies for that series.

Some lilies are patches of thick paint circled by a squiggly "caricature" of a lily pad. Monet simplifies in a way that Henri Matisse and Pablo Picasso would envy. But getting close, you see that the lily is made of many brushstrokes, and also that each brushstroke is itself a mixture of different colored paints.

Monet is thought of as a lightweight, but he deals with the fundamentals of life, especially in his later work, featuring green lilies floating among lavender clouds reflected in the blue water. Staring into Monet's pond, we see the intermingling of the four classical elements, earth (foliage), air (the sky), fire (sunlight), and water—the primordial soup where life begins.

When Monet died in 1926, he was famous. Starting with meticulous line drawings, he had evolved into an open-air realist, then Impressionist color analyst, then serial painter, and finally master of reflections. As the subjects of his work became fuzzier, the colors and patterns predominated. Monet builds a bridge between Impressionism and modern abstract art.

NAPOLEON'S TOMB AND ARMY MUSEUMS TOUR

If you've ever considered being absolute dictator of a united Europe, come here first. Hitler did, but still went out and made the same mistakes as his role model. (Hint: Don't invade Russia.)

Napoleon's tomb rests beneath the golden dome of Les Invalides church. Around the church, in a former veterans' hospital built by Louis XIV, are various military museums. You can see Napoleon's horse stuffed and mounted, Louis XIV-era uniforms and weapons, and much more. The best part is the World War II wing in the Army Museum (Musée de l'Armee; see page 264).

In 2006, the Army Museum's West Wing is scheduled to reopen after extensive renovation, while the East Wing is likely to be closed for renovation.

ORIENTATION

Cost: €7, covered by Museum Pass.

Hours: April–Sept daily 10:00–18:00, summer Sun until 19:00, Oct–March daily 10:00–17:00. Closed the first Mon of every month except July–Sept.

Getting There: The tomb is at the Hôtel des Invalides at 129 rue de Grenelle (near Rodin Museum, Mo: La Tour Maubourg, Varenne, or Invalides). Bus #69 from the Marais and rue Cler area is also handy. The museum is a 10-minute walk from rue Cler. There are two entries, one from the grand Esplanade des Invalides (river side) and the other from behind the gold dome on avenue de Tourville.

Information: English handouts at the ticket office (tel. 01 44 42 37 72, www.invalides.org).

Length of This Tour: Women—two hours, men—three hours.

Cuisine Art: A reasonable cafeteria is next to the ticket office,

Overview: Napoleon's Tomb and Army Museums

The Invalides complex has several sights, each with a different entrance. All are included in your ticket price. For their locations, see the map in this chapter and the free English map/guide available in the ticket hall.

▲▲▲**Napoleon's Tomb**—The emperor lies under the golden dome of the Invalides church (at the back of the complex, farthest from the river).

▲▲▲**World War II Wing**—Interesting coverage of this critical war (entrance at southwest corner of courtyard).

▲▲**Army Museum: East Wing**—French military history, with focus on Napoleon (entrance on east side of courtyard; likely closed for renovation in late 2005).

▲**Army Museum: West Wing**—Weapons through the ages, with a good WWI section (entrance on west side of courtyard; scheduled to reopen in 2006).

Pick your favorite war. With limited time, visit only Napoleon's Tomb and the excellent World War II wing. Most other displays consist of dummies in uniforms and endless glass cases full of muskets without historical context.

the rear gardens are picnic-perfect and the rue Cler is a five-minute walk (see page 348).

Nearby: You'll likely see the French playing *boules* on the esplanade (as you face Les Invalides, look for the dirt area to the upper right; for the rules of *boules,* see page 312).

THE TOUR BEGINS

• *Start at Napoleon's tomb, underneath the golden dome. The entrance is from the back end (farthest from the Seine) of this vast complex of churches and museums.*

NAPOLEON'S TOMB

Enter the church, gaze up at the dome, then lean over the railing and bow to the emperor lying inside the red, porphyry-scrolled tomb. If the lid were opened, you'd find an oak coffin inside, holding another ebony coffin, housing two lead ones, then mahogany, then tinplate... until finally, you'd find Napoleon himself, staring up, with his head

closest to the door. When his body was exhumed from the original grave and transported here (1840), it was still perfectly preserved, even after 19 years in the ground.

Born of humble Italian heritage on the French-owned isle of Corsica, Napoleon Bonaparte (1769–1821) went to school at Paris' Ecole Militaire (Military School), quickly rising through the ranks amid the chaos of the Revolution. The charismatic "Little Corporal" won fans by fighting for democracy at home and abroad. In 1799, he assumed power and, within five short years, conquered most of Europe. The great champion of the Revolution had become a dictator, declaring himself emperor of a new Rome.

Napoleon's red tomb on its green base stands 15 feet high in the center of a marble floor. It's exalted by the dome above, where dead Frenchmen cavort with saints and angels, forming a golden halo over Napoleon.

Napoleon is surrounded by family. After conquering Europe, he installed his big brother, Joseph, as king of Spain (turn around to see Joseph's black-and-white marble tomb in the alcove to the left of the door); his little brother, Jerome, became king of Westphalia (tucked into the chapel to the right of the door); and his baby boy, Napoleon II (downstairs), sat in diapers on the throne of Rome.

In other alcoves, you'll find more dead war heroes, including Marshal Ferdinand Foch, the Commander in Chief of the multinational Allied forces in World War I, his tomb lit with otherworldly blue light. These heroes, plus many painted saints, make this the French Valhalla in the Versailles of churches.

The Crypt

• *The stairs behind the altar (with the corkscrew columns) take you down to crypt level for a closer look at the tomb.*

Wandering clockwise, read the names of Napoleon's battles on the floor around the base of the tomb. Rivoli marks the battle where the rookie 26-year-old general took a ragtag band of "citizens" and thrashed the professional Austrian troops in Italy, returning to Paris a celebrity. In Egypt *(Pyramides)*, he fought Turks and tribesmen to a standstill. The exotic expedition caught the public eye and he returned home a legend.

Napoleon's huge victory over Austria at Austerlitz on the first anniversary of his coronation made him Europe's top dog. At the head of the million-man Great Army *(La Grande Armée)*, he made a three-month blitz attack through Germany and Austria. As a general, he was daring, relying on top-notch generals and on a

Napoleon Bonaparte
(1769–1821)

Born to Italian parents on the French-ruled isle of Corsica, he attended French schools, though he'd speak the language with an Italian accent to the end of his days. After graduating from Paris' Ecole Militaire (trained in the latest high-tech artillery), his military career took an unexpected turn when the Revolution erupted (1789), and he chose to return to Corsica to fight royalist oppression.

In 1793, as commander of artillery, he besieged Toulon, forcing the royalists to surrender, and earning his first great victory. He later defended the Revolutionary government from royalist mobs in Paris by firing a "whiff of grapeshot" into the crowd (1795). Such daring military exploits and personal charisma earned him promotions and the nickname "The Little Corporal"—not for his height (he was an average 5'6") but as a term of endearment from the rank-and-file. When he married the classy socialite Josephine Beauharnais, Napoleon became a true celebrity. In 1798, having conquered Italy, Austria, and Egypt, Napoleon returned to Paris, where the weak government declared him First Consul—ostensibly as the champion of democracy, but in fact, a virtual dictator of much of Europe. He was 29 years old.

Over the next years, he solidified his reign with military victories over Europe's kings—now allied against France. Under his rule, France sold the Louisiana Purchase to America, and legal scholars drew up the Code of Napoleon, a system of laws still used by many European governments today. In 1804, his power peaked when he crowned himself emperor in a ceremony in Notre-Dame blessed by the pope. The Revolutionary general was now, paradoxically, part of Europe's royalty. Needing an heir to the throne, he divorced barren Josephine and married an Austrian duchess, Marie Louise, who bore him the boy known to historians as "The King of Rome."

In 1812, Napoleon decided to invade Russia, and the horrendous losses from that failed venture drained his power. It was pigpile on France, and Europe's nations toppled Napoleon, sending him to exile on the isle of Elba (1814). Napoleon escaped long enough to raise an army for a final hundred-days campaign before finally being defeated by British and Polish forces at the Battle of Waterloo (1815). Guilty of war crimes, he was sentenced to exile on the remote South Atlantic island of St. Helena, where he talked to his dog, studied a little English, penned his memoirs, spoke his final word—"Josephine"—and died.

mobile force of independent armies. His personal charisma on the battlefield was said to be worth 10,000 additional men.

Pause in the battles to gaze at the grand statue of Napoleon the emperor in the alcove at the head of the tomb—royal scepter and orb of Earth in his hands. By 1804, all of Europe was at his feet. He held an elaborate ceremony in Notre-Dame, where he proclaimed his wife, Josephine, an empress, and himself—the 35-year-old son of humble immigrants—as emperor. The laurel wreath, the robes, and the Roman eagles proclaim him the equal of the Caesars. The floor at the statue's feet marks the grave of his son, Napoleon II (*Roi de Rome*, 1811–1832).

Around the crypt are relief panels showing Napoleon's constructive side. Dressed in toga and laurel leaves, he dispenses justice, charity, and pork-barrel projects to an awed populace.

• *In the first panel to the right of the statue...*

He establishes an Imperial University to educate naked boys throughout "*tout l'empire.*" The roll of great scholars links modern France with those of the past: Plutarch, Homer, Plato, and Aristotle. Three panels later, his various building projects (canals, roads, and so on) are celebrated with a list and his quotation, "Everywhere I passed, I left durable benefit." *("Partout ou mon regne à passé....")*

Hail Napoleon. Then, at his peak, came his fatal mistake.

• *Turn around and look down to Moscowa (the Battle of Moscow)...*

Napoleon invaded Russia with 600,000 men, and returned to Paris with 60,000 frostbitten survivors. Two years later, the Russians marched into Paris, and Napoleon's days were numbered. After a brief exile on the isle of Elba, he skipped parole, sailed to France, bared his breast, and said, "Strike me down or follow me!" For 100 days, they followed him, finally into Belgium, where the British hammered the French at the Battle of Waterloo (conspicuously absent on the floor's decor). Exiled again by a war tribunal, he spent his last years in a crude shack on the small South Atlantic island of St. Helena.

• *To get to the Courtyard of Honor and the various military museums, exit the same way you entered, make a U-turn right, and march past the cafeteria and ticket hall. Pause halfway down the long hallway. On the right through the glass, you'll see...*

Napoleon's Tombstone (Pierre Tombal)

This bare stone slab beside weeping willows once rested atop Napoleon's grave on the island of St. Helena. The epitaph was never finished, since the French and British wrangled over what to call the hero/tyrant. The stone simply reads, "Here lies..."

• *Continuing to the end of the hallway, you'll find the entrance to the World War II museum (in the southwest corner of the main courtyard).*

Go upstairs, following signs to General de Gaulle: Deuxième Guerre Mondiale, 39/45.

ARMY MUSEUM: WORLD WAR II WING

World War II was the most destructive of Earth's struggles. In this exhibit, the war unfolds in photos, displays, and newsreels, with special emphasis on the French contribution. You may never have realized that it was Charles de Gaulle who won the war for us.

The free museum map is helpful for locating the displays we'll see. Climb to the top floor and work back down, from Germany's quick domination (third floor), to the Allies turning the tide (second floor), to the final surrender (first floor).

There are fine English descriptions throughout. Be ready—rooms come in rapid succession—and treat the following text as just an overview.

Third Floor—Axis Aggression

Room 1: Treaty of Versailles to 1939 (Du Traité de Versailles à 1939)

In 1918, the "war to end all wars" ground to a halt, leaving 10 million dead, Germany defeated, and France devastated (if victorious). For the next two decades, Adolf Hitler would feed off German resentment over the Treaty of Versailles, which humiliated and ruined Germany.

Room 2: The Defeat of 1940 (La Défaite de 1940)

On September 1, 1939, Hitler invaded Poland, starting World War II. France and Britain mobilized, but Germany did nothing for six months. Then, in the spring of 1940 came the Blitzkrieg ("lightning war"), and Germany's better-trained and better-equipped soldiers and tanks (see turret) swept west through Belgium. France was immediately overwhelmed, and British troops barely escaped across the English Channel from Dunkirk. Within a month, Nazis were goose-stepping down the Champs-Elysées, and Hitler was on his way to Napoleon's tomb.

Room 3: The Appeal of June 18, 1940

Just like that, virtually all of Europe was dominated by Fascists. During those darkest days, as France fell and Nazism spread across the Continent, one Frenchman—an obscure military man named Charles de Gaulle—refused to admit defeat. He escaped

Napoleon's Tomb and Army Museums

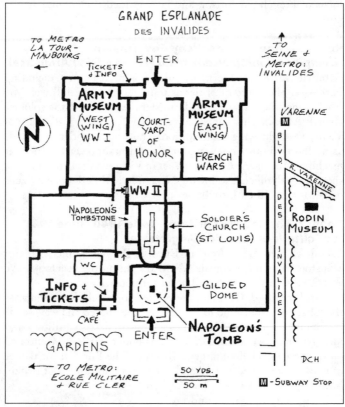

to London, made inspiring speeches over the radio, and slowly convinced a small audience of French expatriates that victory was still possible.

• *Through the small door to your right is...*

Room 4: Charles de Gaulle (1890–1970)

This 20th-century John of Arc had an unshakable belief in his

mission to save France. He was born into a literate, upper-class family, raised in military academies, and became a WWI hero and POW. After the war, he helped administer the occupied Rhineland. When World War II broke out, he was only a minor officer (the title of "Brigadier General" was hastily acquired during the invasion). He had limited political experience and was virtually

unknown to the French public. But he rallied France, became the focus of French patriotism, and later guided the country in the postwar years.

Room 5 & Room 6: The Vichy Government
(L'Empire colonial: un enjeu; La France après l'Armistice)

After the surrender, Germany ruled northern France, including Paris—see the photo of Hitler as tourist at the Eiffel Tower. The Nazis allowed the French to administer the south and the colonies (North Africa). This puppet government, centered in the city of Vichy, was right-wing and traditional, bowing to Hitler's demands as he looted France's raw materials and manpower for the war machine. (The movie *Casablanca*, set in Vichy-controlled Morocco, shows French officials following Nazi orders while French citizens defiantly sing "The Marseillaise.")

Room 7: The Battle of Britain—June 1940–June 1941
(La Solitude et Bataille d'Angleterre)

Facing a "New Dark Age" in Europe, British Prime Minister Winston Churchill pledged, "We will fight on the beaches.... We will fight in the hills. We will never surrender."

In June 1940, Germany mobilized to invade Britain across the Channel. From June to September, they paved the way, sending bombers—up to 1,500 planes a day—to destroy military and industrial sites. When Britain wouldn't budge, Hitler concentrated on London and civilian targets. This was "The Blitz" of the winter of 1940, which killed 30,000 and left London in ruins. But Britain hung on, armed with newfangled radar, speedy Spitfires, and an iron will.

They also had the Germans' secret "Enigma" code. The "Enigma machine" (in display case), with its set of revolving drums, allowed German commanders to scramble orders in a complex code that could safely be broadcast to their troops. The British (with crucial help from Poland) captured a machine, broke the code (a project called "Ultra"), and then monitored German airwaves. For the rest of the war, they had advance knowledge of many top-secret plans. (Occasionally, Britain even let Germany's plans succeed—sacrificing their own people—to avoid suspicion.)

By spring of 1941, Hitler had given up any hope of invading the Isle of Britain. Churchill said of his people: "This was their finest hour."

Room 10: Germany Invades the Soviet Union—
June 1941 *(L'Allemagne Envahit l'Union Soviétique)*

Perhaps hoping to one-up Napoleon, Hitler sent his state-of-the-art tanks speeding toward Moscow (betraying his former ally,

Joseph Stalin). By winter, the advance had stalled at the gates of Moscow and was bogged down by bad weather and Soviet stubbornness. The Third Reich had reached its peak. From now on, Hitler would have to fight a two-front war. The French Renault tank (displayed) was downright puny compared to the big, fast, high-caliber German Panzers. This war was often a battle of factories, to see who could produce the latest technology fastest and in the greatest numbers. And what nation might that be...?

Room 12: The United States Enters the War
(Les Etats-Unis dans la Guerre)

"On December 7, 1941, a date which will live in infamy" (as F.D.R. put it), Japanese planes made a sneak attack on the U.S. base at Pearl Harbor, Hawaii, and destroyed the pride of the Pacific fleet in two hours.

The U.S. quickly declared war on Japan and her ally, Germany. In two short years, America had gone from isolationist observer to supplier of Britain's arms to full-blown war ally against fascism. The U.S. now faced a two-front war—in Europe against Hitler, and in Asia against Japan's imperialist conquest of China, Southeast Asia, and the South Pacific.

America's first victory came when Japan tried a sneak attack on the U.S. base at Midway Island (June 3, 1942). This time—thanks to the Allies who cracked the "Enigma" code—America had the aircraft carrier U.S.S. *Enterprise* (see model) and two of her buddies lying in wait. In five minutes, three of Japan's carriers (with valuable planes) were fatally wounded, their major attack force was sunk, and Japan and the U.S. were dead even, settling in for a long war of attrition.

Though slow to start, America eventually had an army of 16 million strong, 80,000 planes, the latest technology, $250 million a day, unlimited raw materials, and a population of Rosie the Riveters fighting for freedom to a boogie-woogie beat.

• *Continue downstairs to the second floor.*

Second Floor, 1942–1944—The Tide Turns

In 1942, the Continent was black with fascism and Japan was secure on a distant island. The Allies had to chip away on the fringes.

Room 13: Battle of the Atlantic
(La Bataille de l'Atlantique)

German U-boats (short for *Unterseeboot*, see model) and battleships such as the *Bismarck* patrolled Europe's perimeter, where they laid spiky mines and kept America from aiding Britain. (Until long-range transport planes were invented near war's end, virtually all military transport was by ship.) The Allies traveled in convoys with air cover, used sonar and radar, and dropped depth charges, but for years, they endured the loss of up to 60 ships per month.

• *Don't bypass Room 14, tucked in the corner.*

Room 14: The War Turns—
El-Alamein, Stalingrad, and Guadalcanal

Three crucial battles in autumn of 1942 put the first chink in the Fascist armor. Off the east coast of Australia, 10,000 U.S. Marines (see kneeling soldier in glass case 14D) took an airstrip on Guadalcanal, while 30,000 Japanese held the rest of the tiny, isolated island. For the next six months, the two armies were marooned together, duking it out in thick jungles and malaria-infested swamps while their countries struggled to reinforce or rescue them. By February 1943, America had won and gained a crucial launch pad for bombing raids.

A world away, German tanks under General Erwin Rommel rolled across the vast deserts of North Africa. In October 1942, a well-equipped, well-planned offensive by British General Bernard Montgomery attacked at El-Alamein, Egypt, with 300 tanks. (See British tank soldier in 14F.) "Monty" drove "the Desert Fox" east into Tunisia for the first real Allied victory against the Nazi *Wehrmacht* war machine.

Then came Stalingrad. (See kneeling Soviet soldier in 14E.) In August 1942, Germany attacked the Soviet city, an industrial center and gateway to the Caucasus oil fields. By October, the Germans had battled their way into the city center and were fighting house-to-house, but their supplies were running low, the Soviets wouldn't give up, and winter was coming. The snow fell, their tanks had no fuel, and relief efforts failed. Hitler ordered them to fight on through the bitter cold. On the worst days, 50,000 men died. (America lost a total of 58,000 in Vietnam.) Finally, on January 31, 1943, the Germans surrendered, against Hitler's orders. The six-month totals? Eight hundred thousand German and other Axis soldiers dead, 1.1 million Soviets dead. The Russian campaign put hard miles on the German war machine.

Also in 1942, the Allies began long-range bombing of German-held territory, including saturation bombing of civilians. It was global war and total war.

Room 15: The Allies Land in North Africa (Le Débarquement en Afrique du Nord, La Campagne de Tunisie)

Winston Churchill and U.S. President Franklin D. Roosevelt (see photo with de Gaulle), two of the century's most dynamic and

strong-willed statesmen, decided to attack Hitler indirectly by invading Vichy-controlled Morocco and Algeria. On November 8, 1942, 100,000 Americans and British—under the joint command of an unknown, low-key problem-solver named General Dwight ("Ike") Eisenhower—landed on three separate beaches (including Casablanca). More than 120,000 Vichy French soldiers, ordered by their superiors to defend the Fascist cause, confronted the Allies and...gave up. (See display of some standard-issue guns: Springfield rifle, Colt 45, Thompson machine gun, hand grenade.)

The Allies moved east, but bad weather, their own inexperience, and the powerful Afrika Korps under Rommel stopped them in Tunisia. But with flamboyant General George S. ("Old Blood-and-Guts") Patton punching from the west and Monty pushing from the south, they captured the port town of Tunis on May 7, 1943. The Allies now had a base from which to retake Europe.

Room 17: The French Resistance (L'Unification de la Résistance, also see displays in Room 20)

Inside occupied France, other ordinary heroes fought the Nazis— the "underground," or Resistance. Within loaves of bread, bakers hid radios to secretly contact London. Barmaids passed along tips from tipsy Nazis. Communists in black berets cut telephone lines. Farmers hid downed airmen in haystacks. Housewives spread news from the front with their gossip. Printers countered Nazi propaganda with pamphlets.

Jean Moulin (see photo in museum), de Gaulle's assistant, secretly parachuted into France and organized these scattered heroes into a unified effort. In May 1943, Moulin was elected chairman of the National Council of the Resistance. A month later, he was arrested by the Gestapo (Nazi secret police), imprisoned, tortured, and sent to Germany, where he died in transit. Still, Free France now had a (secret) government again, rallied around de Gaulle, and was ready to take over when liberation came.

Room 18: The Red Army
(L'Armée Rouge Reprend l'Initiative)
Monty, Patton, and Ike were certainly heroes, but the war was won on the Eastern Front by Soviet grunts, who slowly bled Germany dry. Maps show the shifting border of the Eastern front.

Room 21: The Allies Land in Italy
(Premiers Débarquements Alliés en Europe)
On July 10, 1943, the assault on Hitler's European fortress began. More than 150,000 Americans and British sailed from Tunis and landed on the south shore of Sicily. (See maps and video clips of the campaigns.) Speedy Patton and methodical Monty began a "horse race" to take the city of Messina (the U.S. won the friendly competition by a few hours). They met little resistance from 300,000 Italian soldiers and were actually cheered as liberators by the Sicilian people. Their real enemies were the 50,000 German troops sent by Hitler to bolster his ally, Benito Mussolini. By September, the island was captured. On the mainland, Mussolini was arrested by his own people and Italy surrendered to the Allies. Hitler quickly poured troops into Italy (and reinstalled Mussolini) to hold off the Allied onslaught.

In early September, the Allies launched a two-pronged landing onto the beaches of southern Italy. Finally, after four long years of war, free men set foot on the European continent.

Room 22: The Italian Campaign (La Campagne d'Italie)
Lieutenant General Mark Clark, leading the slow, bloody push north to liberate Rome, must have been reminded of the French trenches he'd fought in during World War I. As in that bloody war, the fighting in Italy was a war of attrition, fought on the ground by foot soldiers and costing many lives for just a few miles.

In January 1944, the Germans dug in between Rome and Naples at Monte Cassino, a rocky hill topped by the monastery of St. Benedict. Thousands died as the Allies tried inching up the hillside. In frustration, the Allies air-bombed the historic monastery to smithereens (see photo), killing hundreds of monks...but no Germans, who dug in deeper. Finally, after four months of vicious, sometimes hand-to-hand combat, the Allies (Americans, Brits, Free French, Poles, Italian partisans, Indians, etc.) stormed the monastery, and the German back was broken.

Meanwhile, 50,000 Allies had landed on Anzio (a beach near Rome) and held the narrow beachhead for months against massive German attacks. When reinforcements arrived, Allied troops broke out and joined the two-pronged assault on the capital. Without a single bomb threatening its historic treasures, Rome fell on June 4, 1944.

• *Room 23 shows a film (with chairs) on...*

Room 23: D-Day—June 6, 1944, "Operation Overlord"

Three million Allies and six million tons of materiel were massed in England in preparation for the biggest fleet-led invasion in history—across the Channel to France, then eastward to Berlin. The Germans, hunkered down in northern France, knew an invasion was imminent, but the Allies kept the details top secret. On the night of June 5, 150,000 soldiers boarded ships and planes without knowing where they were headed until they were underway. Each one carried a note from General Eisenhower: "The tide has turned. The free men of the world are marching together to victory."

At 6:30 in the morning on June 6, 1944, Americans spilled out of troop transports into the cold waters off a beach in Normandy, code-named Omaha. The weather was bad, seas were rough, and the prep bombing had failed. The soldiers, many seeing their first action, were dazed and confused. Nazi machine guns pinned them against the sea. Slowly, they crawled up the beach on their stomachs. A thousand died. They held on until the next wave of transports arrived.

All day long, Allied confusion did battle with German indecision; the Nazis never really counterattacked, thinking D-Day was just a ruse instead of the main invasion. By day's end, the Allies had taken several beaches along the Normandy coast and began building artificial harbors, providing a tiny port-of-entry for the reconquest of Europe. The stage was set for a quick and easy end to the war. Right.

• *Go downstairs to the...*

First Floor—The War Ends...Very Slowly (June 1944–August 1945)

Room 24: Battle of Normandy
(La Bataille de Normandie)

For a month, the Allies (mostly Americans) secured Normandy by taking bigger ports (Cherbourg and Caen) and amassing troops and supplies for the assault on Germany. In July, they broke out and sped eastward across France, with Patton's tanks covering up to 40 miles a day. They had "Jerry" on the run.

Room 25: Landing in Provence, August 1944
(Le Débarquement de Provence)

On France's Mediterranean coast, American troops under General Alexander Patch landed near Cannes (see parachute photo), took Marseilles, and headed north to meet up with Patton.

Room 26: "Les Maquis"

French Resistance guerrilla fighters helped reconquer France from behind the lines. (Don't miss the folding motorcycle in its parachute case.) The liberation of Paris was started by a Resistance attack on a German garrison.

Room 27: Liberation of Paris

As the Allies marched on Paris, Hitler ordered his officers to torch the city—but they sanely disobeyed and prepared to surrender. On August 26, 1944, General Charles de Gaulle walked ramrod-straight down the Champs-Elysées, followed by Free French troops and U.S. GIs passing out chocolate and Camels. Two million Parisians went ape.

Room 28: On to Berlin—Offensive from the West
(Vers Berlin—Offensives de l'Ouest)

The quick advance through France, Belgium, and Luxembourg bogged down at the German border in autumn of 1944. Patton outstripped supply lines, a parachute invasion of Holland (Battle of Arnhem) was disastrous, and bad weather grounded planes and slowed tanks.

On December 16, the Allies met a deadly surprise. An enormous, well-equipped, energetic German army appeared from nowhere, punched a "bulge" deep into Allied lines, and demanded surrender. General Anthony McAuliffe sent a one-word response—"Nuts!"—and the momentum shifted. The Battle of the Bulge was Germany's last great offensive.

The Germans retreated across the Rhine River, blowing up bridges behind them. The last bridge, at Remagen, was captured by the Allies just long enough to cross and establish themselves on German soil. Soon, U.S. tanks were speeding down the autobahns and Patton could wire the good news back to Ike: "General, I have just pissed in the Rhine."

Soviet soldiers did the dirty work of taking fortified Berlin by launching a final offensive in January 1945 and surrounding the city in April. German citizens fled west to surrender to the more-benevolent Americans and Brits. Hitler, defiant to the end, hunkered in his underground bunker. (See photo of ruined Berlin.)

On April 28, 1945, Mussolini and his girlfriend were killed and hung by their heels in Milan. Two days later, Adolf Hitler and his new bride, Eva Braun, avoided similar humiliation by committing suicide (pistol in mouth) and having their bodies burned beyond recognition. Germany formally surrendered on May 8, 1945.

In Corridor to the Left of Room 28: Concentration Camps

Lest anyone mourn Hitler or doubt this war's purpose, gaze at photos from Germany's concentration camps. Some camps held political enemies and prisoners of war, including two million French. Others were expressly built to exterminate peoples considered "genetically inferior" to the "Aryan master race"—particularly Jews, Gypsies, homosexuals, and the mentally ill.

Room 29: War of the Pacific (*Les batailles du Pacifique*)

Often treated as an afterthought, the final campaign against Japan was a massive American effort, costing many lives but saving millions from Japanese domination.

Japan was an island bunker surrounded by a vast ring of fortified Pacific islands. America's strategy was to take one island at a time, "island-hopping" until close enough for B-29 Superfortress bombers to attack Japan itself. The war spread across thousands of miles. In a new form of warfare, ships carrying planes led the attack and prepared tiny islands for troops to land and build an airbase. While General Douglas MacArthur island-hopped south to retake the Philippines ("I have returned!"), others pushed north toward Japan.

In February 1945, marines landed on Iwo Jima, a city-size island-volcano close enough to Japan (800 miles) to launch air raids. Twenty thousand Japanese had dug in on the volcano's top and were picking off the advancing Americans. On February 23, several U.S. soldiers raised the Stars and Stripes on the mountain (that famous photo), which inspired their mates to victory at a cost of nearly 7,000 men.

Japan Surrenders (*Capitulation du Japon*)

On March 9, Tokyo was firebombed, and 90,000 were killed. Japan was losing, but a land invasion would cost hundreds of thousands of lives. The Japanese had a reputation for choosing death over the shame of surrender—they even sent bomb-laden "kamikaze" planes on suicide missions.

America unleashed its secret weapon, an atomic bomb (origi-

nally suggested by German-turned-American Albert Einstein). On August 6, a B-29 dropped one (named "Little Boy," see the replica dangling overhead) on the city of Hiroshima and instantly vaporized 100,000 people and four square miles.

Three days later, a second bomb fell on Nagasaki. The next day, Emperor Hirohito unofficially surrendered. The long war was over, and U.S. sailors returned home to kiss their girlfriends in public places.

War Totals *(Les actes de conclusion)*

The death toll for World War II (September 1939–August 1945) totaled 80 million soldiers and civilians. The Soviet Union lost 26 million, China 13 million, France 580,000, and the U.S. 340,000.

World War II changed the world, with America emerging as the dominant political, military, and economic superpower. Europe was split in two. The western half recovered, with American aid. The eastern half remained under Soviet occupation. For 45 years, the U.S. and the Soviet Union would compete—without ever actually doing battle—in a "Cold War" of espionage, propaganda, and weapons production that stretched from Korea to Cuba, from Vietnam to the moon.

• *Return to the large Courtyard of Honor, where Napoleon honored his troops and de Gaulle once kissed Churchill. The Army Museum flanks both sides of the courtyard. The West Wing is World War I (scheduled to reopen in 2006), East Wing is French Military (Louis XIV, Revolution, Napoleon; scheduled to be closed through much of 2006).*

Cross the courtyard, enter the east wing under the golden letters, and go up to the second floor (which Americans would consider the 3rd floor) to reach the east wing exhibits (elevator available, WC downstairs). Skip the first room and enter Salle Louis XIV.

ARMY MUSEUM—EAST WING

This museum traces uniforms and weapons through French history, from Louis XIV to World War I, with emphasis on Napoleon. As you circle the second floor, you'll follow the history and art of French warfare from about 1700 to 1850: Pre-Revolution, Revolution, Napoleon, and Restoration. Most rooms have some English info posted. Notice how many of the room names have been given to Métro stops.

Salle Louis XIV

Louis XIV unified the army as he unified the country, creating the first modern nation-state with a military force. In these first dozen room, you'll see how gunpowder was quickly turning swords, pikes, and lances to pistols, muskets, and bayonets. Uniforms became more uniform, and everyone got a standard-issue flintlock.

• *Browse the first dozen or so rooms, turn the corner and pass beneath a lighted sign:* Première République. *Enter the...*

Salle Guerres de la République

With the Revolution, the king's Royal Army became the people's National Guard, protecting their fledgling democracy from Europe's monarchies, while spreading revolutionary ideas by conquest. At the Battle of Lodi (1796, see the model with tiny toy soldiers), the French and Austrians faced off on opposites sides of a northern Italian river, trying to capture the crucial bridge and using cannons to clear the way for a cavalry charge. Young, relatively obscure Bonaparte personally sighted the French cannons on the enemy—normally the job of a lesser officer—which turned the tide of battle and earned himself a reputation and nickname, "The Little Corporal."

• *A couple of rooms farther along is the...*

Salle Boulogne

See General Bonaparte's hat, sword, and medals. The tent (behind screen) shows his bivouac equipment: a bed with mosquito netting, a director's chair, and a table that you can imagine his generals hunched over as they made battle plans.

• *Continue, turning the corner to the...*

Salle Austerlitz

Now at the peak of his power, Emperor Napoleon (in the famous portrait by Jean-Auguste-Dominique Ingres) stretches his right arm to supernatural lengths.

Salle Eylau

Behold Napoleon's beloved Arabian horse, Le Vizir, who weathered many a campaign and grew old with him in exile (stuffed, in a glass case).

Salle Montmirail

A portrait catches a dejected Napoleon after his first abdication in 1814. A glass case is dedicated to Napoleon's son, the "Roi de Rome." His little soldier boots are there, and an engraving shows the child king in a royal carriage. When he grew up (miniature portrait in the center), he looked a lot like his dad—a fact that kept French Royalists wary until his death. Junior's mother (engraving to the left) was Marie-Louise, whom Napoleon married after divorcing barren Josephine.

• *Turn the corner into a long, faded blue corridor, the...*

Corridor de Tarascon

Napoleon's big white dog (in a glass case to left), his companion in exile on Elba, suffered the same fate as the horse. On the wall to the left of the dog hang proclamations of thanks and good-byes (announcing the surrender at Waterloo) that Napoleon sent to his soldiers and the French people. Directly behind the dog (other side of the wall), a shining breastplate shows the effectiveness of British artillery in the battle of Waterloo. A dozen steps further along  you'll find Napoleon's death mask. It's opposite the blue drapes that hide a reconstruction of a room in his final home on St. Helena (step inside the drapes). Picture a lonely man suffering from ulcers sitting here in his nightcap and slippers, playing chess, not war.

Exit the long blue corridor, and you'll see an American flag (in a glass case) along with the French tricolor flag, honoring the Marquis de Lafayette of France, the general who helped George Washington take Yorktown.

• *Turn right before the American flag to exit.*

The Musée des Plans Reliefs (top floor of east wing) has 17th- and 18th-century models (1:1,600 scale) of France's cities, used by the French to devise strategies to thwart enemy attacks (see English flier at the door). Survey a city and ponder which hillside you'd use to launch an attack. Big models of Mont St. Michel and Antibes lie at either end. Other floors of this wing are filled with temporary exhibits.

ARMY MUSEUM—WEST WING

Across the courtyard is a twin museum in the west wing. The ground floor covers military implements, from stone axes to Axis powers. One of its highlights is an exhibit on "The Great War," World War I. This wing has been closed for a major renovation and is scheduled to reopen in 2006.

When reopened, the World War I wing will include displays on the strategies and weapons used for the first time during this war—trenches, machine guns, flamethrowers, poison gas, airplanes, tanks, and more. Travelers will leave with a better understanding of the events, inventions, and personalities that collided in this war to end all wars.

CLUNY MUSEUM TOUR

(Musée National du Moyen Age)

The "National Museum of the Middle Ages" doesn't sound quite so boring as I sink deeper into middle age myself. Aside from the solemn religious art, there is some lively stuff here.

Paris emerged on the world stage in the "Middle Ages," the time between ancient Rome and the Renaissance. Europe was awakening from a thousand-year slumber. Trade was booming, people actually owned chairs, and the Renaissance was moving in like a warm front from Italy.

ORIENTATION

Cost and Hours: €5.50, €4 on Sun, free on first Sun of the month, covered by Museum Pass, Wed–Mon 9:15–17:45, closed Tue.

Getting There: The museum, a five-minute walk from the Ile de la Cité, is a block above the intersection of boulevards St. Germain and St. Michel at 6 place Paul Painlevé (Mo: Cluny-La Sorbonne, St. Michel, or Odéon; bus #63 from rue Cler or #86 from the Marais).

Information: Pick up the free and handy museum map guide. Tel. 01 53 73 78 16, www.musee-moyenage.fr.

Length of This Tour: Allow one hour, though you could spend much more time here. While this self-guided tour covers the museum's greatest hits, there's much more to the underrated Cluny (such as medieval weaponry, 8th-century Visigothic crowns, a wonderful chapel with an elaborate stone ceiling, and a medieval garden). For details, see the museum's free map.

Photography: OK without flash.

Baggage Check: Required and free.

Cuisine Art: Just a few blocks away, the charming place de la Sorbonne has several good cafés (see page 360; walk up boulevard St. Michel towards the Panthéon).

THE TOUR BEGINS

• *The museum hosts occasional special exhibits that can affect the permanent collection described below.*

Start in the first room after the bookshop...

Room 2: Tapestries

The first art you see is not some grim, gray crucifixion, but six colorful wool-and-silk tapestries that celebrate the secular pleasures of life on a country estate. The humans mingle harmoniously with the trees, flowers, and animals of the glorious physical world. (Note that it's not unusual for a tapestry to be missing from the six described here.)

Reading clockwise: 1) A lady with a puppy spins wool, while her husband relaxes with the morning paper. 2) A naked woman takes a chilly bath and enjoys fruits, jewels, and music—the good things of a material world becoming increasingly less sinful. 3) The family picks fruit from their plentiful orchards. 4) Out in the garden, the sexes mingle unchaperoned by the Church. A lady takes a breath mint while a troubadour puts the moves on her servant. 5) A lord goes hunting with his falcon, dog, and servant. 6) A lady embroiders a pillow.

Having survived their Y1K crisis, these people realize the world won't end, and they turn their attention to the beauty of their surroundings.

Room 3: Fabrics Brought Back by Crusaders

Colorful woven fabrics were brought back to France by crusaders, who went off to conquer barbarian infidels, but returned with tales of enlightened peoples on the fringes of Europe.

Room 6: Stained Glass

Enter the Dark Ages, when life was harsh and violent, angels and demons made regular appearances, and the Church was your only refuge. This room offers a rare close-up look at stained glass, which gave poor people a glimpse of the glories of heaven. These panels (many from the basilica of light, Sainte-Chapelle) give us a window into the magical, supernatural,

Cluny—Ground Floor

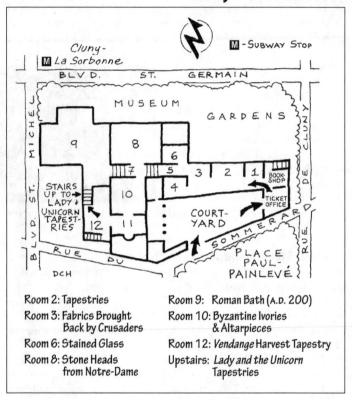

Room 2: Tapestries
Room 3: Fabrics Brought
        Back by Crusaders
Room 6: Stained Glass
Room 8: Stone Heads
        from Notre-Dame

Room 9: Roman Bath (A.D. 200)
Room 10: Byzantine Ivories
        & Altarpieces
Room 12: *Vendange* Harvest Tapestry
Upstairs: *Lady and the Unicorn*
        Tapestries

miraculous—and often violent—medieval mind.

Read clockwise around the room, all at eye level (the bottom): 1) The angel Gabriel blasts his horn on Resurrection morning, which rousts the grateful dead from their coffins. Notice that Gabriel's royal robe is made up of several different pieces of glass—purples, whites, blues—held together with lead. 2) Naked Christ is baptized in the squiggly River Jordan. 3) A red-faced, horned, horny demon, accompanied by an equally lascivious wolf and henchman, carries off a frightened girl in red to do unspeakable acts. 4) Blond, pious Joseph is sold into slavery to camel merchants by his plotting brothers.

Next wall: 5) Samson is about to pull down the temple... 6) Then he has his eyes gouged out by Philistines. 7) Slaughter on the battlefield. Men with bloodstained hands and faces hack at each other with golden swords. 8) Aaron, disobeying God and Moses, worships a golden calf. 9) A king on a throne closes his eyes to all this wickedness.

Next wall (with some panels from the first Gothic church, St. Denis): 10) Two monks with prayer books gaze up, as one of their brothers disappears into heaven. The Latin inscription, *"hec est via,"* means "This is the way." 11) Seated Jesus, in a royal purple robe, is consoled by two angels. 12) Theophilus ("Lover of God")

has struck a Faustian deal—shaking hands with the red-faced devil, yet feeling buyer's remorse. 13) Sleeping St. Martin is visited by a heavenly vision. 14) Angels in Rock-and-Roll Heaven.

Last wall: Four apostles— John (Ioannes), James (with his scallop shell), Paul, and Peter (Petrus, with key).

Before leaving, turn around and take in all the narrative medieval glass.

Room 8: Stone Heads from Notre-Dame

This room has occasional exhibits as well as the permanent displays, so prepare to search for the objects described.

The 21 stone heads (sculpted 1220–1230) of the Biblical kings of Judah once decorated the front of Notre-Dame. In 1793, an angry mob of Revolutionaries mistook the kings of Judah for the kings of France and abused and decapitated the statues. (Today's heads on the Notre-Dame statues are reconstructions.) Someone gathered up the heads and buried them in his backyard near the present-day Opéra Garnier. There they slept for two centuries, unknown and noseless, until 1977, when some diggers accidentally unearthed them and brought them to an astounded world. Their stoic expressions accept what fate, time, and liberals have done to them.

The statue of Adam (nearby) is also from Notre-Dame. He's scrawny and flaccid by Renaissance standards. And it will be another 200 years before naked Adam can step out from behind that bush.

Room 9: Roman Bath

This echoing cavern was a Roman *frigidarium*. Pretty cool. The museum is located on the site of a Roman bathhouse, which was in the center of town during the Roman years. After hot baths and exercise in adjoining rooms, ordinary Romans would take a cold dip in the sunken pool (in the alcove), then relax cheek to cheek with notables such as Emperor Julian the Apostate (see his statue), who lived right next door. As the empire decayed in the 4th century, Julian avoided the corrupt city of Rome and made Paris a northern power base.

The 40-foot-high ceiling is the largest Roman vault in France, and it took the French another 1,000 years to improve on that crisscross-arch technology. The sheer size of this room—constructed in A.D. 200, when Rome was at its peak—gives an idea of the epic scale in which the Romans built, and it inspired Europeans to greatness during the less-civilized Middle Ages.

The four square column fragments *(Pilier des Nautes)* are the oldest man-made objects you'll see from Paris. Using the small model (in glass case) you can see how these pillars once fit together to support a 20-foot-high altar to the king of the gods in the Temple of Jupiter, where Notre-Dame now stands. The carving on one ("TIB. CAESARE") says it was built in the time of the Emperor Tiberius, A.D. 14–37, and was paid for by the Parisian boatmen's union (see them holding their shields). On another column, find the horned Celtic god Cernunnos, the Stag Lord and god of the hunt. The eclectic Romans allowed this local "druid" god to support the shrine of Jupiter, in league with their own Vulcan, who hammers, and Castor and Pollux, who pet their horses.

Room 10: Byzantine Ivories and Altarpieces

Rome lived on after the fall of the empire. The finely carved

Byzantine ivories (first glass case) show how pagan gods, emperors, and griffins became Christian saints, gargoyles, and icons. Constantinople—the eastern half of the empire that survived the fall—preserved Roman tastes and imagery. In painting, Byzantine gold-background icons inspired medieval altarpieces, like some in this room. Study the exquisite detail, especially in the Crucifix in the righthand corner. (Adam and Eve, in the tiny panel below, are not really "sword fighting.")

Rome also lived on in the "Roman"-esque grandeur of Christian churches like St. Germain-des-Prés (see the 12 column capitals). In the central capital, Christ sits in robes on a throne, ruling the world like a Roman emperor. These capitals were originally painted, much like the painted wooden statues across the room.

Don't leave this room before eyeing the tusk of a narwhal (on the wall), which must have convinced superstitious folk to believe in unicorns.

Room 12: *Vendange* Harvest Tapestry

The large tapestry shows grape-stomping peasants during the

vendange, the annual autumn harvest and wine celebration. A peasant man treads grapes in a vat, while his wife collects the juice. A wealthy man gives orders. Above that, a peasant with a big wart turns a newfangled mechanical press. On the right, you'll see the joy of picking—pawns, knights, and queens all working side by side.

• *Go upstairs to...*

Room 13 (upstairs): *The Lady and the Unicorn* Tapestries

As Europeans emerged from the Dark Ages, they rediscovered the beauty of the world around them.

These six mysterious tapestries were designed by an unknown (but probably French) artist before A.D. 1500 and were woven in Belgium out of wool and silk. Loaded with symbols—some serious, some playful—they have been interpreted many ways, but, in short, the series deals with each of the five senses (handheld English explanations that you can pick up from slots hanging on the wall add more detail).

• *Moving clockwise around the room...*

Taste: A blond lady takes candy from a servant's dish to feed it to her parakeet. A unicorn and a lion look on. At the lady's feet, a monkey also tastes something, while the little white dog behind her wishes he had some. This was the Age of Discovery, when Columbus and Vasco da Gama spiced up Europe's bland gruel with new fruits, herbs, and spices.

The lion (symbol of knighthood?) and unicorn (symbol of "bourgeois nobility," purity, or fertility?) wave flags with the coat of arms of the family that commissioned the tapestries—three silver crescents in a band of blue.

Hearing: Wearing a stunning dress, the lady plays sweet music on an organ, which soothes the savage beasts around her. The pattern and folds of the tablecloth are lovely. Humans and their fellow creatures live in harmony in an enchanted blue garden filled with flowers, all set in a red background.

Sight: The unicorn cuddles up and looks at himself in the lady's mirror, pleased with what he sees. The lion turns away and snickers. As the Renaissance dawns, vanity is a less than deadly sin.

Admire the great artistic skill in some of the detail work, such as the necklace and the patterns in her dress. This tapestry had quality control in all its stages: the drawing of the scene, its enlargement and transfer to a cartoon, and the weaving. Still, the

design itself is crude by Renaissance 3-D standards. The fox and rabbits, supposedly in the distance, simply float overhead, as big as the animals at the lady's feet.

Smell: The lady picks flowers and weaves them into a sweet smelling wreath. On a bench behind, the monkey apes her. The flowers, trees, and animals are exotic and varied. Each detail is exquisite alone, but step back, and they blend together into pleasing patterns.

Touch: This is the most basic and dangerous of the senses.

The lady "strokes the unicorn's horn," if you know what I mean, and the lion gets the double entendre. Unicorns, a species extinct since the Age of Reason, were so wild that only the purest virgins could entice and tame them. Medieval Europeans were exploring the wonders of love and the pleasures of sex. The Renaissance is coming.

Tapestry #6: The most talked-about tapestry gets its name from the words on our lady's tent: *A Mon Seul Désir* (To My Sole Desire). What *is* her only desire? Is it jewelry, as she grabs a necklace from the jewel box? Or is she putting the necklace away and renouncing material things in order to follow her only desire?

Our lady has tried all things sensual and is now prepared to follow the one true impulse. Is it God? Or love? Her friends the unicorn and lion open the tent doors. Flickering flames cover the tent. Perhaps she's stepping out from the tent. Or is she going in to meet the object of her desire? Human sensuality is awakening, an old dark age is ending, and the Renaissance is emerging.

PERE LACHAISE CEMETERY TOUR

(Cimetière du Père Lachaise)

Enclosed by a massive wall and lined with 5,000 trees, the peaceful, car-free lanes and dirt paths of Père Lachaise cemetery encourage park-like meandering. Named for Father *(Père)* La Chaise, whose job was listening to Louis XIV's sins, the cemetery is relatively new, having opened in 1804 to accommodate Paris' expansion. Today, this city of the dead (pop. 70,000) still accepts new residents, but real estate prices are very high.

The 100-acre cemetery is big and confusing, with thousands of graves and tombs crammed every which way, and only a few streets to navigate by. The maps available from any of the nearby florists help guide your way. But better still, take my tour and save lots of time as you play grave-hunt with the cemetery's other visitors. This walk takes you on a one-way tour between two convenient Métro/bus stops (Gambetta and Père Lachaise), connecting a handful of graves from some of this necropolis' best-known residents.

ORIENTATION

Cost: Free.

Hours: Mon–Sat 8:00–18:00, Sun 9:00–18:00. If it gets dark before 18:00, the cemetery closes at dusk.

Getting There: Catch bus #69 to the end of the line (see tour, page 304) or take the Métro to the Gambetta stop. If you're arriving on bus #69, it will stop at place Gambetta on avenue du Père Lachaise, two blocks from the cemetery. If you're taking the Métro, exit at Gambetta Métro (not the Père Lachaise Métro stop), take *sortie* #3 (Père Lachaise exit), turn left, and follow signs to Père Lachaise. Either way, it's two short blocks up avenue du Père Lachaise, which ends at the cemetery. Along the route, you'll pass flower shops

selling €2 maps (not necessary for this tour, but helpful for finding additional graves) and a WC just inside the Porte Gambetta entrance to Père Lachaise.

Information: Tel. 01 55 25 82 10.

Length of this Tour: Allow 90 minutes to do this walk, and another 30 minutes for your own detours. Bring good walking shoes to help on the rough, cobbled streets.

Cuisine Art: As you approach the cemetery, there are several cafés near Métro stop Gambetta and along avenue Père Lachaise.

Starring: Oscar Wilde, Edith Piaf, Gertrude Stein, Molière, Jim Morrison, Frédéric Chopin, Héloïse and Abélard, Colette, and Rossini.

Overview

From the Porte Gambetta entrance, we'll walk roughly south-

west (mostly downhill) through the cemetery. At the end of the tour, we'll exit Porte Principale onto boulevard Ménilmontant, near the Père Lachaise Métro entrance and another bus #69 stop. (You can follow the tour heading the other direction, but it's not recommended, since it's confusing—and almost completely uphill.)

Remember to keep referring to the map on page 287 (note that north is not up on the map), and follow street signs posted at intersections.

THE TOUR BEGINS

• *Entering the cemetery at the Porte Gambetta entrance, walk straight up avenue des Combattants past World War memorials, cross avenue Transversale No. 3, pass the first building, and look left to the...*

❶ Columbarium/Crematorium

Marked by a dome with a gilded flame and working chimneys on top, the Columbarium sits in a courtyard surrounded by about 1,300 niches, small cubicles for the cremated remains, often decorated with real or artificial flowers.

Beneath the courtyard (steps leading underground) are about 12,000 smaller niches, including one for Maria Callas (1923–1977), an American-born opera diva known for her versatility, flair for drama, and affair with Aristotle Onassis (niche #16258, down aisle J).

• *Backtrack to avenue Transversale No. 3 and turn right, heading southeast on avenue Transversale No. 3. Turn left on avenue Carette*

and walk half a block to the block-of-stone tomb (on the left) with heavy-winged angels trying to fly.

❷ Oscar Wilde (1854–1900)

The writer and martyr to homosexuality is mourned by "outcast men" (as the inscription says), and by wearers of heavy lipstick, who cover the tomb and the angels' emasculated privates with kisses. Despite Wilde's notoriety, an inscription says "He died fortified by the Sacraments of the Church." There's a short résumé scratched into the tomb. For more on Wilde and his death in Paris, see page 138.

> *"Alas, I am dying beyond my means."*
>
> —Oscar Wilde

• *Continue along avenue Carette and turn right (southeast) down avenue Circulaire. A block and a half down, you'll reach Gertrude Stein's unadorned, easy-to-miss grave (on the right just before a yellow stone structure).*

❸ Gertrude Stein (1874–1946)

While traveling through Europe, the twenty-something American dropped out of med school and moved to Paris, her home for the rest of her life. She shared an apartment at 27 rue de Fleurus (a couple blocks west of Luxembourg Garden) with her brother Leo and, later, with her female life partner, Alice B. Toklas (who's also buried here, see gravestone's flipside). Every Saturday night, Paris' brightest artistic lights converged *chez vingt-sept* for dinner and intellectual stimulation. Picasso painted her portrait, Hemingway sought her approval, and Virgil Thompson set her words to music.

America discovered "Gerty" in 1933 when her memoirs, the slyly titled *Autobiography of Alice B. Toklas*, hit the bestseller list. After 30 years away, she returned to America for a triumphant lecture tour. Her writing is less well-known than her persona, except for the oft-quoted "A rose is a rose is a rose."

Stein's last words: When asked, "What is the answer?," she said, "What is the question?"

• *Ponder Stein's tomb again and again and again, and continue southeast on avenue Circulaire to where it curves to the right. Emaciated statues remember victims of the concentration camps. At the corner of the cemetery, veer left off the road a few steps, to the wall marked* Aux Morts de la Commune.

Père Lachaise Cemetery Tour

TOUR

1. Columbarium/Crematorium
2. Oscar Wilde
3. Gertrude Stein
4. Mur des Fédérés
5. Edith Piaf
6. Molière
7. Jim Morrison
8. Frédéric Chopin
9. Héloïse & Abélard
10. Colette
11. Gioacchino Rossini
12. Baron Haussmann

OTHER NOTABLE TOMBS

A. Jacques-Louis David
B. Théodore Géricault
C. Eugène Delacroix
D. J. A. D. Ingres
E. Georges Seurat
F. Amadeo Modigliani
G. Marcel Proust
H. Sarah Bernhardt
J. Yves Montand & Simone Signoret

❹ Mur des Fédérés

The "Communards' Wall" marks the place where the quixotic Paris Commune came to a violent end.

In 1870, Prussia invaded France, and the country quickly collapsed and surrendered—all except the city of Paris. For six months, through a bitter winter, the Prussians laid siege to the city. Defiant Paris held out, even opposing the French government, which had fled to Versailles and was collaborating with the Germans. Parisians formed an opposition government that was revolutionary and socialist, called the Paris Commune.

The Versailles government sent French soldiers to retake Paris. In May 1871, they breached the west walls and swept eastward. French soldiers fought French citizens, and tens of thousands died during a bloody week of street fighting (La Semaine Sanglante). The last resisters holed up inside the walls of Père Lachaise and made an Alamo-type last stand before they were finally overcome.

At dawn on May 28, 1871, the 147 Communards were lined up against this wall and shot by French soldiers. They were buried in a mass grave where they fell. With them, the Paris Commune died, and the city entered five years of martial law.

• *Return to the road, continue to the next (unmarked) street, avenue Transversale No. 3, and turn right. A half block uphill, Edith Piaf's grave is on the right. It's not directly on the street, but one grave in, behind a grave with a small grey cross. "Edith Gassion-Piaf" rests among many graves. Hers is often adorned with photos, fresh flowers, and love notes.*

❺ Edith Piaf (1915–1963)

A child of the Parisian streets, she was raised in her grandma's bordello and her father's traveling circus troupe. The teenager sang in Paris' streets for spare change, where a nightclub owner discovered her. Waif-like and dressed in black, she sang in a warbling voice under the name "Le Mome Piaf" (The Little Sparrow). She became the toast of pre-WWII Paris society.

Her offstage love life was busy and often messy, including a teenage pregnancy (her daughter "Marcelle Dupont, 1933–1935" is buried along with her), a murdered husband, and a heartbreaking affair with co-star Yves Montand.

With her strong but trembling voice, she buoyed French spirits under the German occupation, and her most famous song, "La Vie en Rose" (The Rosy Life) captured the joy of postwar Paris.

Her personal life declined into ill health, alcohol, and painkillers, while onstage she sang, *"Non, je ne regrette rien"* ("No, I don't regret anything").

• *From Edith Piaf's grave, continue up along avenue Transversale No. 3 , and turn left on avenue Greffulhe. Follow Greffulhe straight (even when it narrows), until it dead-ends at avenue Transversale des Marronières No. 1. Continue ahead on a dirt path, stepping through the graves, where you reach "chemin Molière et La Fontaine." Turn right. Molière lies 30 yards down, on the right side of the street, just below the highest point of this lane.*

❻ Molière (1622–1675)

In 1804, the great comic playwright was the first to be reburied in Père Lachaise, a publicity stunt that gave instant prestige to the new cemetery.

Born in Paris, Molière was not of noble blood, but as the son of the king's furniture supervisor, he had connections. The 21-year-old Molière joined a troupe of strolling players, who ranked very low on the social scale, touring the provinces. Twelve long years later, they returned to Paris to perform before Louis XIV. Molière, by now an accomplished comic actor, cracked the king up. He was instantly famous—writing, directing, and often starring in his own works. He satirized rich nobles, hypocritical priests, and quack doctors, creating enemies in high places.

On February 17, 1675, an aging Molière went on stage in the title role of his latest comedy, *The Imaginary Invalid.* Though ill, he insisted he had to go on, concerned for all the little people. His role was of a hypochondriac who coughs to get sympathy. The deathly ill Molière effectively faked coughing fits...which soon turned to real convulsions. The unaware crowd roared with laughter while his fellow players fretted in the wings.

In the final scene, Molière's character becomes a doctor himself in a mock swearing-in ceremony. The ultimate trouper, Molière finished his final line—*"Juro"* ("I accept")—and collapsed while coughing blood. The audience laughed hysterically. He died shortly after.

Irony upon irony for the master of satire: Molière—a sick man whose doctors thought he was a hypochondriac—dies playing a well man who is a hypochondriac, succumbing onstage while the audience cheers.

Molière lies next to his friend and fellow writer, La Fontaine (1621–1695), who wrote a popular version of Aesop's Fables.

"We die only once, and for such a long time."

—Molière

• *Continue downhill on chemin Molière (which becomes the paved chemin du Bassin), and turn left on avenue de la Chapelle. It leads to the Rond Point roundabout intersection. Here (left side), you'll find the Egyptian-style obelisk of **Champollion**, who broke the code of hieroglyphics on the Rosetta Stone.*

Cross Carrefour Rond Point and continue straight (on unmarked chemin de la Bédoyère). Just a few steps along, veer to the right onto chemin Lauriston. Keep to the left on chemin de Lesseps, and look (immediately) for the temple on the right with three wreaths. Jim lies just behind, often with a personal security guard. You can't miss the commotion.

❼ Jim Morrison (1943–1971)

An American rock star has perhaps the most visited tomb in the cemetery. An iconic, funky bust of the rocker, which was stolen by fans, was replaced with a more toned-down headstone. Even

so, his faithful still gather here at all hours. The headstone's Greek inscription reads: "To the spirit (or demon) within." Graffiti-ing nearby tombs, fans write: "You still Light My Fire" (referring to Jim's biggest hit), "Ring my bell at the Dead Rock Star Hotel," and "Mister Mojo Risin'" (referring to the legend that Jim faked his death and still lives today, age 68).

Jim Morrison—singer for the popular rock band The Doors (named for the "Doors of Perception" they aimed to open)—arrived in Paris in the winter of 1971. He was famous; notorious for his erotic onstage antics; alcoholic; and burned out. Paris was to be his chance to leave celebrity behind, get healthy, and get serious as a writer.

Living under an assumed name in a nondescript sublet apartment near place Bastille (head west down rue St. Antoine, and turn left to 17 rue Beautrellis), he spent his days as a carefree artist. He scribbled in notebooks at Café de Flore and Les Deux Magots (❂ see Left Bank Walk, page 142), watched the sun set from the steps of Sacré-Cœur, visited Baudelaire's house, and jammed with street musicians. He drank a lot,

took other drugs, gained weight, and his health declined.

In the wee hours of July 3, he died in his bathtub at age 27, officially of a heart attack, but likely from an overdose. (Any police investigation was thwarted by Morrison's social circle of heroin users, leading to wild rumors surrounding his death.)

Jim's friends approached Père Lachaise Cemetery about burying the famous rock star there, in accordance with his wishes. The director refused to admit him, until they mentioned that Jim was a writer. "A writer?" he said, and found a spot.

> *"This is the end, my only friend, the end."*
> —Jim Morrison

• *Return to Rond Point, cross it, and retrace your steps—sorry, but there are no straight lines connecting these dead geniuses. Retrace your steps up avenue de la Chapelle. At the intersection with the small park and chapels, turn left onto avenue Laterale du Sud. Walk down two sets of stairs and turn left onto narrow chemin Denon. "Fred" Chopin's grave—usually with flowers and burning candles—is halfway down on the left.*

❽ Frédéric Chopin (1810–1849)

Fresh-cut flowers and geraniums on the gravestone speak of the emotional staying power of Chopin's music, which still connects souls across the centuries. A muse sorrows atop the tomb and a carved relief of Chopin in profile captures the delicate features of this sensitive artist.

The 21-year-old Polish pianist arrived in Paris, fell in love with the city, and never returned to his homeland (which was occupied by an increasingly oppressive Russia). In Paris, he could finally shake off the "child prodigy" label and performance schedule he'd lived with since age seven. Cursed with stage fright ("I don't like concerts. The crowds scare me, their breath chokes me, I'm paralyzed by their stares..."), and with too light a touch for big venues, Chopin preferred playing at private parties for Paris' elite. They were wowed by his technique, his ability to make a piano sing, and his melodic, soul-stirring compositions. Soon he was recognized as a pianist, composer, and teacher, and even idolized as a brooding genius. He ran in aristocratic circles with fellow artists, such as pianist Franz Liszt, painter Delacroix, novelists Victor Hugo and Balzac, and composer Rossini. (All but Liszt lie in Père Lachaise.)

Chopin composed nearly 200 pieces, almost all for piano, in

Other Notable Tombs

Though not along our walking tour, the following folks can be found on our map, as well as the €2 map you get from the florists.

❶ Jacques-Louis David (1748–1825)—Section 56
The classic neoclassical painter, David, chronicled the heroic Revolution and the Napoleonic Era. See his *Coronation of Napoleon* in the Louvre (page 163).

❷ Théodore Géricault (1791–1824)—Section 12
Géricault was the master of painting extreme situations (ship-wrecks, battles) and extreme emotions (noble sacrifice, courage, agony, insanity) with Romantic realism. See his *Raft of the Medusa* in the Louvre (page 165).

❸ Eugène Delacroix (1798–1863)—Section 49
For more on this Romantic painter, see his *Liberty Leading the People* in the Louvre (page 165), or visit the Delacroix Museum (see Left Bank Walk, page 140).

❹ Jean-August-Dominique Ingres (1780–1867)—Section 23
Often considered the anti-Delacroix, Ingres was a painter of placid portraits and bathing nudes, using curved outlines and smooth-surfaced paint. Despite his deliberate distortions (see his beautifully deformed *La Grande Odalisque* in the Louvre, page 164), he was hailed as the champion of traditional neoclassical balance against the furious Romantic style (see his *The Source* in the Orsay, page 179).

❺ Georges Seurat (1859–1891)—Section 66
Georges spent Sunday afternoons in the park with his easel, capturing shimmering light using tiny dots of different-colored paint. See his Pointillist canvas *The Circus* in the Orsay (page 195).

❻ Amadeo Modigliani (1884–1920)—Section 96, not far from Edith Piaf
Poor, tubercular, and strung out on drugs and alcohol in Paris, this young Italian painter forged a personal style. His portraits and nudes have African-mask-like faces, and elongated necks and arms.

many different styles—from lively Polish dances, to the Bach-like counterpoint of his *Preludes,* to the moody, romantic *Nocturnes.*

In 1837, the quiet, refined, dreamy-eyed genius met the scandalous, assertive, stormy novelist George Sand (see page 138 in the Left Bank Walk). Sand was swept away by Chopin's music and artistic nature. She pursued him, and sparks flew. Though the romance faded quickly, they continued living together for nearly a decade in an increasingly bitter love-hate relationship. When

❼ Marcel Proust (1871–1922)—Section 85

Some who make it through the seven volumes and 3,000 pages of Proust's autobiographical novel, *Remembrance of Things Past*, close the book and cry, "Brilliant!" Others get lost in the meandering, stream-of-consciousness style and forget that the whole "Remembrance" began with the taste of a *madeleine* (cookie) that triggered a flashback to Proust's childhood, as relived over the last 10 years of his life, during which he labored alone in his apartment on boulevard Haussmann—midway between the Arc de Triomphe and Gare de l'Est—penning his life story with reflections on Time (as we experience it, not clock time) and Memory, in long sentences.

❽ Sarah Bernhardt (1844–1923)—Section 44

The greatest female actress of her generation, she conquered Paris and the world. Charismatic Sarah made a triumphant tour of America and Europe (1880–1881) starring in *La Dame aux Camelias*. No one could die onstage like Sarah, and in the final scene—when her character succumbs to tuberculosis—she had cowboys and railroad workers sniffling in the audience. Of her hundred-plus stage roles and many silent films, perhaps her most memorable role may have been playing...Hamlet (1899). Offstage, her numerous affairs and passionate, capricious personality set a standard for future divas to aspire to.

❾ Yves Montand (1921–1991) and
**   Simone Signoret (1921–1985)—Section 44**

Yves Montand was a film actor and nightclub singer with blue-collar roots, left-wing politics, and a social conscience. Montand's career was boosted by his lover, Edith Piaf, when they appeared together at the Moulin Rouge during World War II. Yves went on to stardom throughout the world (except in America, thanks partly to a 1960 flop film with Marilyn Monroe, *Let's Make Love*). In 1951, he married actress Simone Signoret, whose on-screen persona was the long-suffering lover. They remain together still, despite rumors of Yves' womanizing. After their deaths, their eternal love was tested in 1998, when Yves' body was exhumed to take a DNA sample for a paternity suit (it wasn't him).

Chopin developed tuberculosis, Sand nursed him for years (Chopin complained she was killing him). Sand finally left, Chopin was devastated, and he died two years later at age 39. At the funeral, they played perhaps Chopin's most famous piece, the *Funeral March*. (It's that 11-note dirge that everyone knows.) The grave contains Chopin's body, but his heart lies in Warsaw, embedded in a church column.

"The earth is suffocating. Swear to make them cut me open, so that I won't be buried alive."

—Chopin, on his deathbed

• *Continue walking down chemin Denon, as it curves down and to the right. Stay left at the* chemin du Coq *sign and step onto avenue Casimir Perier. Turn right and walk downhill 30 yards, looking to the left, over the tops of the graves, looking for a tall monument that looks like a church with a cross perched on top. Under this stone canopy lie...*

❾ Héloïse (c. 1101–1164) and Abélard (1079–1142)

Born nearly a millennium ago, these are the oldest residents in Père Lachaise, and their story is timeless.

In an age of faith and Church domination, the independent scholar Peter Abélard dared to say, "By questioning, we learn truth." Brash, combative, and charismatic, Abélard shocked and titillated Paris with his secular knowledge and reasoned critique of Church doctrine. He set up a school on the Left Bank (near today's Sorbonne) that would become the University of Paris. Bright minds from all over Europe converged on Paris, including Héloïse, the brainy niece of the powerful canon of Notre-Dame.

Abélard was hired (c. 1118) to give private instruction to Héloïse. Their intense intellectual intercourse quickly flared into physical passion and a spiritual bond. They fled Paris and married in secret, fearing the damage to Abélard's career. After a year, Héloïse gave birth to a son (named Astrolabe), and the news was out, soon reaching Héloïse's uncle. The canon exploded, sending a volley of thugs to Abélard's bedroom in the middle of the night, where they castrated him.

Disgraced, Abélard retired to a monastery, and Héloïse to a convent, never again to live as man and wife. But for the next two decades, the two remained intimately connected by the postal service, exchanging letters of love, devotion, and intellectual discourse that survive today. (The dog at Abelard's feet symbolizes their fidelity to each other.) Héloïse went on to become an influential abbess, and Abélard bounced back with some of his most critical writings. (He was forced to burn his *Theologia* in 1121, and was on trial for heresy when he died.) Abélard used logic to analyze Church pronouncements—a practice that would flower into the "scholasticism" accepted by the Church a century later.

When they died, the two were buried together in Héloïse's

convent. The canopy tomb we see today (1817) is made from stones from Héloïse's convent and Abélard's monastery.

> *"Thou, O Lord, brought us together, and when it pleased Thee, Thou hast parted us."*
>   —From a prayer of Héloïse and Abélard

• *Continue walking downhill along avenue Casimir Perier, until it crosses avenue Principale, the street at the cemetery's main entrance. Cross Principale to find Colette's grave (3rd grave from corner on right side).*

⑩ Colette (1873–1954)

France's most honored female writer led an unconventional life—thrice-married and linked romantically with other women—and wrote about it in semi-autobiographical novels. Her first fame came from a series of novels about naughty teenage Claudine's misadventures. In her thirties, she went on to a career as a music hall performer, scandalizing Paris by pulling a Janet Jackson onstage. Her late novel, *Gigi* (1945)—about a teenage girl groomed to be a professional mistress who blossoms into independence—became a musical film starring Leslie Caron and Maurice Chevalier (1958). Thank heaven for little girls!

> *"The only misplaced curiosity is trying to find out here, on this side, what lies beyond the grave."*
>   —Colette

• *Retrace your steps to avenue Principale and go uphill a half block. On the left, find Rossini, with Haussman a few graves up.*

⑪ Gioacchino Rossini (1792–1868)

Dut. Dutta-dut. Dutta dut dut dut dut dut dut dut, dut dut dut dut dut dut dut....

The composer of the *William Tell Overture* (a.k.a. the *Lone Ranger* theme) was Italian, but he moved to Paris (1823) to bring his popular comic operas to France. Extremely prolific, he could crank out a three-hour opera in literally weeks, including the highly successful *Barber of Seville* (based on a play by Pierre Beaumarchais, who is also buried in Père Lachaise). When *Guillaume Tell* debuted (1829), Rossini, age 37, was at the peak of his career as an opera composer.

Then he stopped. For the next four decades, he never again wrote an opera, and scarcely wrote anything else. He moved to Italy, went through a stretch of bad health, and then returned to Paris, where his health and spirits revived. He even wrote a little

music in his old age. Rossini's impressive sepulchre is empty, as his remains were moved to Florence.

⑫ Baron Georges-Eugene Haussmann (1809–1891)

Love him or hate him, Baron Haussmann made the Paris we see today. In the 1860s, Paris was a construction zone, with civil servant Haussmann overseeing the city's modernization. Narrow medieval lanes were widened and straightened into broad, traffic-carrying boulevards. Historic buildings were torn down. Sewers, bridges, and water systems were repaired. Haussmann blew the boulevard St. Michel through the formerly quaint Latin Quarter (as part of Emperor Napoleon III's plan to prevent revolutionaries from barricading narrow streets). The Opéra Garnier, Bois de Boulogne park, and avenues radiating from the Arc de Triomphe were all part of Haussmann's grand scheme, which touched 60 percent of the city. How did he finance it all? That's what the next government wanted to know when they canned him.

Thank God You Can Leave

• *Have you seen enough dead people? To leave the cemetery, return downhill on avenue Principale and exit onto boulevard de Ménilmontant. The Père Lachaise Métro stop is one long block to the right. To find the bus #69 stop heading west to downtown, cross boulevard de Ménilmontant and walk down the right side of rue de la Roquette; the stop is four blocks down, on the right-hand side.*

BUS #69 SIGHTSEEING TOUR

From the Eiffel Tower to Père Lachaise Cemetery

Why pay €25 for a tour company to give you an overview of Paris when city bus #69 can do it for €1.40? Get on the bus and settle in for a ride through some of the city's most interesting neighborhoods. Or hop on and off using this tour as a fun way to lace together many of Paris' most important sightseeing districts. On this ride from the Eiffel Tower to Père Lachaise Cemetery, you'll learn how great the city's bus system is—and you'll wonder why you've been tunneling by Métro under this gorgeous city. And if you're staying in the Marais or rue Cler neighborhoods, line #69 is a useful route for just getting around town (except on Sun, when it does not run).

ORIENTATION

Cost: €1.40 per ride.

Getting There: Eastbound line #69 leaves from the Eiffel Tower on avenue Joseph Bouvard (the street that becomes rue St. Dominique as it crosses the Champ de Mars). The first stop is at the southwestern end of the avenue, across from the Eiffel Tower (with the tower at your back, walk through the grassy park; avenue Joseph Bouvard is the 2nd street you'll cross). You may want to start on the eastern end of avenue Joseph Bouvard (2nd stop, just before avenue de la Bourdonnais). Stops are located about every three blocks along the route shown on the map in this chapter. At whatever stop you plan to catch the bus, check if "#69" is posted at the stop to make sure you're on the right route.

Bus Tips: Métro tickets work on buses, but you can't use the same ticket to transfer between the systems, or use them for more than one bus ride. You can also buy a ticket from the bus

driver. All tickets must be validated in the machine behind the driver. Board through the front door and exit through the rear door. Push a red button to signal that you want to get off at the next stop. Buses run every 10 to 20 minutes (6:30–21:30). If you're hopping on and off, you'll need to stamp a new ticket for each segment of the trip.

When to Go: Not on Sunday, when there's no service. Avoid weekday rush hours (8:00–9:30 & 17:30–19:30), and skip it if it's hot (buses are not air-conditioned). On an evening bus ride, you'll enjoy floodlit monuments and a magical ambience on the streets (last trip at 21:15).

Length of This Tour: Allow one hour.

Overview

Handy line #69 crosses the city east–west, running between the Eiffel Tower and Père Lachaise, and passing these great monuments and neighborhoods: Eiffel Tower, Ecole Militaire, rue Cler, Les Invalides, Louvre Museum, Ile de la Cité, Ile St. Louis, Hôtel de Ville, Pompidou Center, Marais, Bastille, and Père Lachaise. You don't have to do the whole enchilada; get on and off wherever you like.

This tour is best done in the direction it's written (east from the Eiffel Tower to Père Lachaise Cemetery), since one-way streets change the route in the other direction. Grab a window seat—right side is best. If you get on at one of the first stops, you're most likely to secure a good seat.

Many find the Bastille a good ending point (where you can hop out and begin our walking tour of the Marais, page 106). This ride also ties in well after a visit to the Eiffel Tower. Think of this as an overview. The sights you'll survey are written up in more depth elsewhere in the book. OK—let's roll.

THE TOUR BEGINS

Champ de Mars and Eiffel Tower

Your tour begins below this 1,000-foot, reddish-brown hood ornament. While you're waiting for the bus, you could read up on the Eiffel Tower (page 49). The park surrounding you is called Champ de Mars (named for the god of war). It served as a parade ground for the military school, Ecole Militaire, that seals the park at the right end. Napoleon Bonaparte is the school's most famous graduate.

In 1889, the Champ de Mars was covered with a massive temporary structure to house exhibitions of all sorts; it was a celebration of the Centennial World's Fair, the same event for which the Eiffel Tower was built. The apartments surrounding the park are

Bus #69 Tour

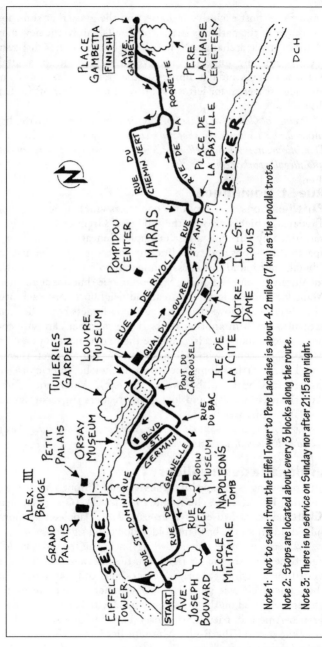

Note 1: Not to scale; from the Eiffel Tower to Pere Lachaise is about 4.2 miles (7 km) as the poodle trots.

Note 2: Stops are located about every 3 blocks along the route.

Note 3: There is no service on Sunday nor after 21:15 any night.

among the most exclusive in Paris, and the grass that runs down the center of the park was strictly off-limits—until the new mayor changed made a change. Now the neighborhood has discovered the joys of picnic dinners. Warm evenings are grand social affairs, as friends share candlelit dinners on the grass. Soccer balls fly past and dogs scavenge for leftovers, all within the glow of the Eiffel Tower.

• *Leaving the Champ de Mars, the bus slices through the 7th arrondissement along its primary shopping street. As you head onto rue St. Dominique, notice how well your driver navigates past delivery trucks and illegally parked cars.*

Rue St. Dominique

Paris functions as a city of a countless small neighborhoods. This area, which was once the village of Grenelle (before it was subsumed by Paris), is a fine example. Beneath several floors of apartments, shops and cafés line the streets, giving the district a vibrancy not found in lifeless commercial districts. You can shop for anything you need on rue St. Dominique (but not at any hour). Many locals never leave the area, and neighbors trust each other. The dry cleaner knows that if his customer forgets her wallet, she'll return to pay him another time. If the plumber can only come during work hours, locals can leave their apartment keys with the nearest shop owner, who will make sure the plumber gets them.

This area has long been popular with Americans—the American Church (2 blocks to the left), American Library, American University, and lots of my readers (in recommended hotels) call this area home.

• *After crossing boulevard de la Tour Maubourg, you'll enter the open world of Esplanade des Invalides.*

Esplanade des Invalides

This sprawling esplanade links the river and Europe's first veteran's hospital, Les Invalides, built under Louis XIV (✪ see Napoleon's Tomb and Army Museums Tour, page 259). Napoleon lies powerfully dead under the brilliant golden dome (on right).

Afternoon *boules* (lawn bowling), near the Invalides building under the trees on the far right, is a fun spectator sport. I spend more time watching the player's expressions and mannerisms than the game itself (see page 312). In summer, American football games are played on the grassy esplanade with teams composed of Franco-American friends. They even have a league and drink beer after the games. The Rodin Museum lies just beyond the esplanade, left of Les Invalides.

Look left and see the pont d'Alexandre III (Alexander III Bridge) crossing the Seine. Spiked with golden statues and

ironwork lamps, the bridge was built to celebrate a turn-of-the-20th-century treaty between France and Russia. Just across the bridge are the glass-and-steel-domed Grand and Petit Palais exhibition halls, built for the 1900 World's Fair. Like the bridge, they are fine examples of belle époque architecture. Impressive temporary exhibits fill the huge Grand Palais, while the smaller Petit Palais houses a permanent collection of 19th-century paintings by Eugène Delacroix, Paul Cézanne, Claude Monet, Pablo Picasso, and other masters. The Air France building (just this side of the river) is a stop for the airport shuttle (4/hr).

• *Leaving Les Invalides, you'll reenter narrow streets lined with government buildings. Many of France's most important ministries occupy this staid side of Les Invalides (look for police guarding doorways and for people in suits speaking in hushed tones). Opposite the frilly Gothic church (on right) sprawls the Ministry of Defense, originally the mansion of Napoleon's mother.*

Boulevard St. Germain and Rue du Bac

You'll emerge from the street flanked by government buildings onto the stylish and leafy boulevard St. Germain, where colorful furniture stores tempt this neighborhood's upper-crust residents. Several blocks farther down lies the boulevard St. Germain, with its famous cafés frequented by existentialists Albert Camus and Jean-Paul Sartre. But we turn left onto rue du Bac and cross streets (to the right) filled with antiques, art galleries, and smart hotels. The Orsay Museum is a few blocks to the left (if you need an art break, the best stop for this museum is Pont Royal on rue du Bac, just before the river; ✪ see Orsay Museum Tour on page 176).

• *Next, you'll cross the river and enter the Right Bank.*

Jardin des Tuileries and Louvre Museum

The Tuileries Garden lies straight ahead as you cross the Seine. This was the royal garden of the Louvre palace—come here after touring the Louvre to clear your mind (✪ see Louvre Tour, page 147). There are several cafés scattered among these pretty gardens, and ponds with toy boats for rent. After turning right along the river, you'll follow the immense Grand Gallery of the Louvre, dominating the left side of the street, and café-boats on the right. (There are about 2,000 barges docked on the Seine in Paris.)

The U-shaped Louvre, once the biggest building in the world, now houses 12 miles of galleries wallpapered with thousands of the world's greatest paintings. Various kings added new wings, identifying their contribution with their initials and medallions carved into the decor.

At the end of the Grand Gallery on the right is the view-perfect pedestrian bridge, pont des Arts (✪ the beginning of the

Left Bank Walk, page 135). That curved building with a dome on the other side is where the Académie Française has met since the 1600s to defend the French language from corrupting influences (like English), and to compose the official French dictionary.

• *Next on the right is the island where Paris was founded. Get ready for quick right–left–right head movements.*

Ile de la Cité

The river splits around this island where Paris began over 2,000 years ago. The first bridge you see dates from about 1600. While it's called pont Neuf, meaning "new bridge," it's Paris' oldest. Pont Neuf leads to an equestrian statue of King Henry IV, who doesn't face a tiny and romantic tip-of-the-island park from which Seine tour boats depart (see listing for Vedettes du Pont-Neuf on page 93).

On your left is Paris' primary department-store shopping district. Next along this street are sidewalk pet stalls—a hit with local children, who dream of taking home a turtle, canary, or rabbit. Back across the river, find the squat and round medieval towers of the Conciergerie, named for the *concierge* (or caretaker) who ran these offices when the king moved to the Louvre. The towers guard the Ile de la Cité's law courts, the Palais de Justice, the prison famous as the last stop for those about to be guillotined. That intricate needle—the spire of Sainte-Chapelle—marks the most beautiful Gothic interior in Paris. You'll see the substantial twin towers of Notre-Dame Cathedral soon after the Conciergerie. Back to the left, the grand Hôtel de Ville (Paris' city hall) stands proudly behind playful fountains. Each of the 20 *arrondissements* (governmental areas) in Paris has its own city hall, and this one is the big daddy of them all. In the summer, the square in front of Hôtel de Ville hosts sand volleyball courts, and at Christmas time, a big ice-skating rink. A quick look back across the river finds the modern pedestrian bridge that connects Paris' two islands.

• *Our bus leaves the river after city hall, and angles left around a church and into the Marais, turning right on rue St. Antoine.*

Le Marais

This is jumbled, medieval Paris at its finest. It's been a swamp, an aristocratic district, and a bohemian hangout. Today, classy stone mansions sit alongside trendy bars, keeping the antique shops and fashion-conscious boutiques company. The Picasso Museum, Carnavalet Museum, Victor Hugo's House, Jewish Art and History Museum, and Pompidou Center all have Marais addresses. On your left, a couple of blocks past city hall, you'll see

the oldest houses in Paris, right around #13. Rue St. Antoine, the main street through the Marais, was the main street of Paris in medieval times. The small-but-grand Church of St. Paul and St. Louis (on the right) is the only Jesuit church in Paris. It was the neighborhood church of Victor Hugo. Rue St. Antoine leads to Bastille Square.

• *A giant pillar marks the center of the huge place de la Bastille. If your trip ends here, get off before entering place de la Bastille. Options if you get off: Marais Walk (page 106), canal boat tour (page 35), Promenade Plantée Park (page 67), and Marais eateries (page 353).*

Place de la Bastille

The namesake of this square, a fortress-turned-prison that symbolized royal tyranny, is long gone. But for centuries, the fortress that stood here was used to defend the city, mostly from its own people. On July 14, 1789, angry Parisians swarmed the Bastille, released its prisoners, and kicked off the French Revolution. Since then, the French celebrate their Independence Day on July 14 (a.k.a. Bastille Day) as enthusiastically as we commemorate July 4.

• *You'll cross over the canal St. Martin in the middle of place de la Bastille (look to the right). The canal runs from the Seine under the tree-lined boulevard Richard Lenoir (on the left) to northern Paris. You'll curve in front of Opéra Bastille. Leaving place de la Bastille, you'll angle left up rue de la Roquette all the way to Père Lachaise.*

Rue de la Roquette

This street begins at the Bastille in a young, hip, and less-touristed neighborhood. Here you'll find a fun mix of galleries, seedy bars, and trendy, cheap eateries. The first street to the right is rue de Lappe (described on page 392). One of the wildest nightspots in Paris, rue de Lappe is filled with a dizzying array of wacky bistros, bars, and dance halls.

• *The bus eventually turns left onto boulevard de Ménilmontant (which locals happily associate with a famous Maurice Chevalier tune) and rumbles past the Père Lachaise Cemetery. While the bus stops at the front gate of the vast cemetery, I'd recommend staying on to place Gambetta, where bus #69 ends its trip through the heart of Paris. Place Gambetta's centerpiece is another grandiose City Hall (this one for the 20th arrondisement). You'll also see some inviting cafés and avenue du Père Lachaise (opposite City Hall). Follow this street 100 yards, past flower shops selling cyclamen, heather, and chrysanthemums—the standard flowers for funerals and memorials—to the gate of the cemetery. Take a short stroll through the evocative home of so many permanent Parisians (Mo: Gambetta or Père Lachaise).*

Père Lachaise Cemetery

Navigating the labyrinthine rows is a challenge, but maps and my walking tour (✪ see Père Lachaise Cemetery Tour, page 284) will help you find the graves of greats such as Frédéric Chopin, Oscar Wilde, Gertrude Stein, and Jim Morrison. The tour is over. What better place for your final stop?

SLEEPING

I've focused most of my recommendations on four safe, handy, and colorful neighborhoods: the village-like rue Cler (near the Eiffel Tower), the artsy and trendy Marais (near place de la Bastille), the lively and Latin yet classy Luxembourg (on the Left Bank), and a more remote but homey feeling neighborhood near Canal St. Martin (just north of the Marais).

For each neighborhood, I list good hotels, helpful hints, and a selection of restaurants (see Eating chapter). Before choosing a hotel, read the descriptions of the four neighborhoods closely. Each offers different pros and cons, and your neighborhood is as important as your hotel for the success of your trip. Less expensive and less central accommodations are also listed in various chapters: Versailles Day Trip, Chartres Day Trip, More Day Trips (Fontainebleau, Giverny, Auvers-sur-Oise, and Disneyland Paris), and Shopping (place de Bercy). For accommodations near the two major airports, see the Transportation Connections chapter.

Reserve ahead for Paris—the sooner, the better. Conventions clog Paris in September (worst), October, May, and June (very tough). Holidays are busy. In 2006, be ready for unusually big crowds during these holiday periods, and book your accommodations well in advance: Easter Sunday (April 16; the week before and after—April 9–23—is also crowded), Labor Day weekend (April 29–May 1), Ascension weekend (May 25–28), Pentecost weekend (June 3–5—less crowded, but still popular for weekends away), Bastille Day (July 14; the week around it—July 9–16—is also very busy), Assumption weekend (Aug 12–15), All Saints' Day (Nov 1), Armistice Day weekend (Nov 10–12), and the winter holidays (Dec 16–Jan 3).

A comfortable hotel in Paris costs less than a comparable hotel in London, Amsterdam, Rome, or most major U.S. cities.

It's a good hotel city. I like places that are clean, small, central, traditional, friendly, and a good value. Most places I list have at least four of these six virtues.

In this book, the price for a double room will normally range from €31 (very simple, toilet and shower down the hall) to €320 (grand lobbies, maximum plumbing, and the works), with most clustering around €85–125.

TYPES OF ACCOMMODATIONS

Hotels

The French have a simple hotel rating system depending on amenities (zero through four stars, indicated in this book by * through ****). One star is simple, two has most of the comforts, and three is generally just a two-star with a fancier lobby and more elaborately designed rooms. Four stars offer more luxury than you have time to appreciate. Two- and three-star hotels are required to have an English-speaking staff, though virtually all hotels I recommend have someone who speaks English (unless I note otherwise in the listing).

Generally, the number of stars does not reflect room size or guarantee quality. Some two-star hotels are better than many three-star hotels. One- and two-star hotels are inexpensive, but some three-star (and even a few four-star hotels) offer good value, justifying the extra cost. Unclassified hotels (no stars) can be bargains or depressing dumps. Look before you leap, and lay before you pay (upon departure).

Old, characteristic budget Parisian hotels have always been cramped. Retrofitted with toilets, private showers, and elevators (as most are today), they are even more cramped. Recommended hotels have an elevator unless otherwise noted.

Most hotels have lots of doubles and a few singles, triples, and quads. Traveling alone can be expensive, as singles (except for the rare closet-type rooms that fit only one twin bed) are simply doubles used by one person—so they cost about the same as a double. Room prices vary within each hotel depending on size, and whether the room has a bath or shower and twin beds or a double bed (tubs and twins cost more than showers and double beds). A triple and a double are often the same room, with a double bed and a sliver-sized single, and quad rooms usually have two double beds. Hotels cannot legally allow more in the room than what's shown on their price list. Modern hotels generally have a few family-friendly rooms that open to each other *(chambres communiquantes)*.

You can save as much as €20–25 by finding the rare room without a private shower or toilet. A room with a bathtub costs €10–15 more than a room with a shower, and is generally larger.

Types of Rooms

Study the price list on the hotel's Web site or posted at the desk, so you know your options. Receptionists often don't mention the cheaper rooms (they assume you want a private bathroom or a bigger room). Here are the types of rooms and beds:

une chambre sans douche et WC	room without a private shower or toilet (rare these days)
une chambre avec cabinet de toilette	room with a toilet but no shower (some hotels charge for down-the-hall showers)
une chambre avec bain et WC	room with private bathtub and toilet
une chambre avec douche et WC	room with private shower and toilet
chambres communiquantes	connecting rooms (ideal for families)
un grand lit	double bed (55 inches wide)
deux petits lits	twin beds (30–36 inches wide)
deux lits séparés	two beds separated
un lit de cent-soixante	queen-size bed (literally, 160 centimeters, or 63 inches, wide)
un lit dépliant	folding bed
un bérceau	baby crib
un lit d'enfant	children's bed

Hotels often have more rooms with tubs than showers and are inclined to give you a room with a tub (which the French prefer).

A double bed is €10–15 cheaper than twins, though rooms with twin beds tend to be larger, and French double beds are smaller than American double beds. Some hotels have queen-size beds (a bed that's 63 inches wide—most doubles are 55). To see if a hotel has queen-size beds, ask, *"Avez-vous un lit de cent-soixante?,"* (ah-vay-voo uh lee duh sahn-swah-sahnt). Some hotels push two twins together under king-size sheets and blankets.

If you prefer a double bed (instead of twins) and a shower (instead of a tub), you need to ask for it—and you'll save up to €30 at more expensive hotels. If you'll take either twins or a double, ask generically for *une chambre pour deux* (room for two) to avoid being needlessly turned away.

You'll almost always have the option of breakfast at your hotel, which is pleasant and convenient, but it's more than the

price of breakfast at the corner café, with less ambience (though you get more coffee at your hotel). Some hotels offer only the classic continental breakfast for about €8–10, while others offer buffet breakfasts for about €10–14 (cereal, yogurt, fruit, cheese, croissants, juice, and hard-boiled eggs)—which I usually spring for. While hotels hope you'll buy their breakfast, it's optional unless otherwise noted.

French hotels must charge a daily room tax *(taxe du séjour)* of about €1 per person per day. While some hotels include it in the price list, most add it to your bill.

Rooms are safe. Still, keep cameras and money out of sight. Towels aren't routinely replaced every day; drip-dry and conserve. If that French Lincoln-log pillow isn't your idea of comfort, American-style pillows (and extra blankets) are sometimes in the closet or available on request. To get a pillow, ask for *"Un oreiller, s'il vous plaît"* (un oh-ray-yay, see voo play).

If you're planning to visit Paris in the summer, the extra expense of an air-conditioned room can be money well spent. Most hotel rooms with air conditioners come with a control stick (like a TV remote) that generally has the same symbols and features: fan icon (click to toggle through wind power, from light to gale); louver icon (choose steady airflow or waves); snowflake and sunshine icons (cold air or heat, depending on season); clock ("O" setting: run x hours before turning off; "I" setting: wait x hours to start); and the temperature control (20 or 21 degrees Celsius is comfortable; also see thermometer diagram in the appendix).

Get advice from your hotel for safe parking. Consider long-term parking at either airport—Orly is closer, and much easier for drivers to navigate than Charles de Gaulle. Garages are plentiful (€20–25/day, with special rates through some hotels). Curb parking is free at night (19:00–9:00), all day Sunday, and throughout the month of August. (For more information, see "Parking in Paris," page 416.)

Your hotelier can direct you to the nearest Internet café *(café internet,* kah-fay an-ter-net) and self-service launderette *(laverie automatique,* lah-vay-ree oh-to-mah-teek).

Hostels

Parisian hostels charge about €20–25 per bed. Travelers of any age are welcome if they don't mind dorm-style accommodations and meeting other travelers. Cheap meals are sometimes available, and kitchen facilities are usually provided for do-it-yourselfers. Hostelling International hostels (also known as "official" hostels) require a hostel membership and charge a few extra euros for non-members. If you'll be staying for several days in an official hostel,

Sleep Code

(€1 = about $1.20, country code: 33)

To help you sort easily through these listings, I've divided the rooms into three categories based on the price for a standard double room with bath:

$$$ **Higher Priced:** Most rooms €150 or more.
  $$ **Moderately Priced:** Most rooms between €100–150.
   $ **Lower Priced:** Most rooms €100 or less.

To give maximum information in a minimum of space, I use the following code to describe the accommodations. Prices listed are per room, not per person. Unless otherwise noted, English is spoken and breakfast is not included (if not included, it's usually optional). You can assume a hotel takes credit cards unless you see "cash only" in the listing.

    S = Single room (or price for one person in a double).
    D = Double or Twin room. "Double beds" are often two twins sheeted together and are usually big enough for nonromantic couples.
    T = Triple (generally a double bed with a single).
    Q = Quad (usually two double beds).
    b = Private bathroom with toilet and shower or tub.
    s = Private shower or tub only (the toilet is down the hall).

According to this code, a couple staying at a "Db-€140" hotel would pay a total of €140 (about $170) for a double room with a private bathroom.

consider buying a membership card before you go (www.hihostels .com). Other "independent" hostels have no such requirements.

Apartments

It's easy, though not necessarily cheaper, to rent a furnished apartment in Paris. Consider this option if you're either traveling with a family or staying two weeks or longer. For listings, see "For Longer Stays" at the end of this chapter.

PRACTICALITIES

Country Code

To phone France, you'll need to know its country code: 33. To call France from the U.S. or Canada, dial 011 - 33 - local number (without the initial 0). If calling France from another European country, dial 00 - 33 - local number (without the initial 0).

Making Reservations

Remember, it's important to reserve ahead for Paris. To make a reservation from home, e-mail, fax, or call the hotel. E-mail is preferred and simple English is fine. Phone and fax costs are reasonable. To fax, use the form in the Appendix, or print a copy from www.ricksteves.com/reservation.

If you're not sure how long you'll stay, guess long (it's hard to add days at the last minute), but then cancel once you know the real length of your stay—some hotels require seven days' notice.

A two-night stay in August would be "2 nights, 16/8/06 to 18/8/06." Europeans write the date day/month/year, and European hotel jargon uses your day of departure.

If you e-mail or fax a reservation request and receive a response with rates stating that rooms are available, this is not a confirmation. You must confirm that the rates are fine and that you indeed want the room. One night's deposit is generally required. A credit-card number will usually be accepted as a deposit, though you may need to send a signed traveler's check or a bank draft in the local currency. If sending your card number, do it by fax or phone (rather than e-mail) to keep it private, safer, and out of cyberspace. Don't give your credit-card number as a deposit unless you're absolutely sure you want to stay at the hotel on the dates you requested and are clear that they have a room available. If you don't show up, you'll be billed for one night, and even if you cancel, you may not receive your entire deposit back.

Reconfirm your reservation a few days in advance for safety. Be sure to honor (or cancel) your reservation.

IN THE RUE CLER NEIGHBORHOOD

(7th *arrondissement*, Mo: Ecole Militaire, La Tour-Maubourg, or Invalides)
Rue Cler, lined with open-air produce stands six days a week, is a safe, tidy, village-like pedestrian street. It's so French that when I step out of my hotel in the morning, I feel like I must have been a poodle in a previous life. How such coziness lodged itself between the high-powered government district and the wealthy Eiffel Tower and Invalides areas, I'll never know. This is a neighborhood of wide, tree-lined boulevards, stately apartment buildings, and lots of Americans. The American Church, American Library, American University, and many of my readers call this area home. Hotels here are relatively spacious and a good value, considering the elegance of the neighborhood and the higher prices of the more cramped hotels in other central areas. And for sightseeing, you're within walking distance of the Eiffel Tower, Napoleon's Tomb, the

Seine River, and the Orsay and Rodin Museums.

Become a local at a rue Cler café for breakfast, or join the afternoon crowd for *une bière pression* (a draft beer). On rue Cler, you can eat and browse your way through a street full of pastry shops, delis, cheese shops, and colorful outdoor produce stalls. Afternoon *boules* (outdoor bowling) on the Esplanade des Invalides is a relaxing spectator sport (look for the dirt area to the upper right as you face Les Invalides; see sidebar on page 312). The manicured gardens behind the golden dome of Napoleon's Tomb are free, peaceful, and filled with flowers (at southwest corner of grounds, closes at about 19:00).

While hardly a happening nightlife spot, rue Cler offers many low-impact after-dark activities. Take an evening stroll above the river through the parkway between pont de l'Alma and pont des Invalides. For an after-dinner cruise on the Seine, it's a 15-minute walk to the river and the Bateaux-Mouches (see page 35). For a post-dinner cruise on foot, saunter into Champ de Mars park to admire the glowing Eiffel Tower. For more ideas on Paris after hours, see the Nightlife chapter.

Tourist Information: Your neighborhood TI is at the Eiffel Tower (May–Sept daily 11:00–18:42, closed Oct–April, all-Paris TI tel. 08 92 68 30 00).

American Church: The American Church and Franco-American Center is the community center for Americans living in Paris, and it should be one of your first stops if you're planning to stay awhile. They offer interdenominational worship services (every Sun at 11:00) and occasional concerts (most Sun at 17:00 or 18:00 Sept–May—but not every week), and distribute the useful *Paris Voice* and *France-U.S.A. Contacts* (reception open Mon–Sat 9:30–13:00 & 14:00–22:30, Sun 9:00–14:00 & 15:00–19:00, 65 quai d'Orsay, Mo: Invalides, tel. 01 40 62 05 00, www.acparis .org). For more details, see page 24 in the Orientation chapter.

Services: There's a **post office** at the end of rue Cler on avenue de la Motte-Picquet, and a handy **SNCF train office** at 78 rue St. Dominique (Mon–Sat 8:30–19:30, closed Sun).

Markets: Cross Champ de Mars park to mix it up with bargain-hunters at the twice-weekly open-air market, **Marché Boulevard de Grenelle,** under the Métro a few blocks southwest of Champ de Mars park (Wed and Sun until 12:30, between Mo: Dupleix and Mo: La Motte-Picquet-Grenelle). The Epicerie de la Tour **grocery** is open until midnight (197 rue de Grenelle). **Rue St. Dominique** is the area's boutique-browsing street.

Internet Access: Two Internet cafés compete in this neighborhood: **Com Avenue** is best (€5/hr, shareable and multi-use accounts, Mon–Sat 10:00–20:00, closed Sun, 24 rue du Champ

The Rules of *Boules*

Throughout Paris—and particularly on Les Invalides' big "front lawn" near the rue Cler neighborhood—you'll see citizens playing *boules*.

Each player starts with three iron balls, with the object of getting them close to the target, a small wooden ball called a *cochonnet*. The first player tosses the *cochonnet* about 30 feet, then throws the first of his iron balls near the target. The next player takes a turn. As soon as a player's ball is closest, it's the other guy's turn. Once all balls have been thrown, the score is tallied—the player with the closest ball gets one point for each ball closer to the target than his opponent's. The loser gets zero. Games are generally to 15 points.

A regulation *boules* field is 10 feet by 43 feet, but the game is played everywhere—just scratch a throwing circle in the sand, toss the *cochonnet,* and you're off. Strategists can try to knock the opponent's balls out of position, knock the *cochonnet* itself out of position, or guard their best ball with the other two.

de Mars); **Cyber World Café** is more expensive, but open later (Mon–Sat 12:00–22:00, Sun 12:00–20:00, 20 rue de l'Exposition, tel. 01 53 59 96 54).

Métro Connections: Key Métro stops are Ecole Militaire, La Tour-Maubourg, and Invalides. The RER-C line runs from the pont de l'Alma and Invalides stations, serving Versailles to the west; Auvers-sur-Oise to the north; and the Orsay Museum, Latin Quarter (St. Michel stop), and Austerlitz train station to the east.

Bus Routes: Smart travelers take advantage of these helpful bus routes (see map on page 314 for stop locations): Line **#69** runs east-west along rue St. Dominique and serves Les Invalides, Orsay, Louvre, Marais, and Père Lachaise Cemetery (Mon–Sat only—no Sun service; see Bus #69 Sightseeing Tour, page 297). Line **#63** runs along the river (the quai d'Orsay), serving the Latin Quarter along boulevard St. Germain to the east (ending at Gare de Lyon), and Trocadéro and the Marmottan Museum to the west. Line **#92** runs along avenue Bosquet, north to the Champs-Elysées and Arc de Triomphe (far better than the Métro) and south to the Montparnasse Tower. Line **#87** runs on avenue de la Bourdonnais and serves St. Sulpice, Luxembourg Garden, the Sèvres-Babylone shopping area, and Gare de Lyon (also more convenient than Métro for these destinations). Line **#28** runs on boulevard de la Tour-Maubourg and serves Gare St. Lazare.

In the Heart of Rue Cler

Many of my readers stay in the rue Cler neighborhood. If you want to disappear into Paris, choose a hotel elsewhere. The first five hotels listed below are within Camembert-smelling distance of rue Cler; the others are within a five- to 10-minute stroll.

$$$ Hôtel Relais Bosquet* ** is modern, spacious, and a bit upscale, with snazzy, air-conditioned rooms, electric darkness blinds, and big beds. Gerard and his friendly staff are politely formal and offer free breakfasts to anyone booking direct with this book in 2006 (standard Db-€150, spacious Db-€170, ask about occasional promotional rates and off-season discounts, claim free Rick Steves breakfast at time of booking, extra bed-€20, family suites, free Internet in lobby, parking-€14, 19 rue du Champ de Mars, tel. 01 47 05 25 45, fax 01 45 55 08 24, www.relaisbosquet .com, hotel@relaisbosquet.com).

$$ Hôtel la Motte Picquet* **, at the end of rue Cler, is elaborately decorated and feminine-feeling. Most of its 18 adorable and spendy rooms face a busy street, but the twins are on the quieter side (Sb-€115–125, standard Db-€145, bigger Db with air-con-€180, 30 avenue de la Motte-Picquet, tel. 01 47 05 09 57, fax 01 47 05 74 36, www.hotelmottepicquetparis.com, book@hotelmottepicquetparis .com).

$$ Hôtel Beaugency* **, a particularly good value on a quieter street a short block off rue Cler, has 30 small cookie-cutter rooms, a helpful staff, and a lobby you can stretch out in (Db-€105–110, these special rates promised in 2006 with this book, air-con, 21 rue Duvivier, tel. 01 47 05 01 63, fax 01 45 51 04 96, www.hotel-beaugency .com, infos@hotel-beaugency.com, Christelle).

Warning: The next two hotels are super values, but very busy with my readers (reserve long in advance).

$ Grand Hôtel Lévêque ** is ideally located, with a helpful staff (Christophe and Pascale), a singing maid, and a slow-dance elevator. The simple but well-designed rooms have all the comforts, including air-conditioning and ceiling fans (S-€57, Db-€87–110 depending on views and beds, Tb-€125 for 2 adults and 1 child only, 1st breakfast free for readers of this book in 2006, additional breakfasts aren't worth the €8 price, 29 rue Cler, tel. 01 47 05 49 15, fax 01 45 50 49 36, www.hotel-leveque.com, info@hotel-leveque.com).

$ Hôtel du Champ de Mars ** , with charming pastel rooms and helpful owners Françoise and Stephane, is a homier rue Cler option. This plush little hotel has a Provence-style, small-town feel from top to bottom. Rooms are small but comfortable, and an excellent value. Single rooms can work as tiny doubles (Sb-€73, Db-€79–83, Tb-€100, 30 yards off rue Cler at 7 rue du Champ de Mars, tel. 01 45 51 52 30, fax 01 45 51 64 36, www.hotelduchampdemars .com, reservation@hotelduchampdemars.com).

Rue Cler Hotels

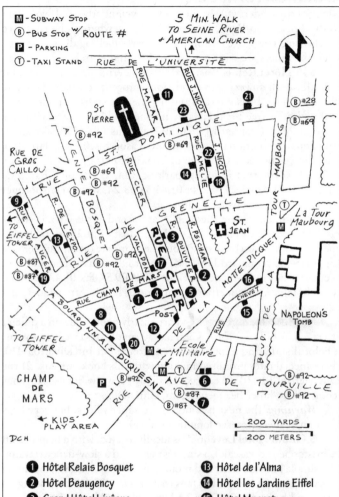

M – Subway Stop
B – Bus Stop w/ Route #
P – Parking
T – Taxi Stand

5 Min. Walk to Seine River & American Church

RUE DE L'UNIVERSITÉ

1 Hôtel Relais Bosquet
2 Hôtel Beaugency
3 Grand Hôtel Lévêque
4 Hôtel du Champ de Mars
5 Hôtel la Motte Picquet
6 Hôtels le Tourville & de Turenne
7 Hôtel Splendid
8 Hôtel de la Bourdonnais
9 Hôtel Londres Eiffel
10 Eber-Mars Hôtel
11 Hôtel de la Tulipe
12 Hôtel Royal Phare

13 Hôtel de l'Alma
14 Hôtel les Jardins Eiffel
15 Hôtel Muguet
16 Hôtel de l'Empereur
17 Hôtel du Cadran
18 Best Western Eiffel Park
19 Hôtel Kensington
20 Hôtel Prince
21 Hôtel le Pavillon
22 Hôtel Amélie
23 SNCF Office

Rue Cler Musts for Temporary Residents

- Watch *boules* action in the afternoon on the Esplanade des Invalides (see sidebar on page 312).
- Relax in the flowery park at the southwest corner of Les Invalides, where avenue de Tourville meets boulevard de la Tour-Maubourg.
- See the Eiffel Tower at night (dinner picnics are best).
- Linger at a rue Cler café and observe daily life.
- Take a Bateaux-Mouches cruise after dark (see page 35).

Near Rue Cler, Close to Ecole Militaire Métro Stop

The following listings are a five-minute walk from rue Cler, near Métro stop Ecole Militaire or RER: Pont de l'Alma.

$$$ Hôtel le Tourville**** is the classiest and most expensive of my rue Cler listings. It's surprisingly intimate for its four stars—from its designer lobby and vaulted breakfast area to its pretty but small pastel rooms (small standard Db-€170, superior Db-€220, Db with private terrace-€240, junior suite for 3–4 people-€310–330, air-con, 16 avenue de Tourville, tel. 01 47 05 62 62, fax 01 47 05 43 90, www.hoteltourville.com, hotel@tourville.com).

$$$ Hôtel de la Bourdonnais*** is a *très* Parisian place, mixing Old World elegance with professional service, comfortable and generous public spaces, and mostly spacious, traditionally decorated rooms (Sb-€125, Db-€155, Tb-€175, Qb-€195, Sophie promises a 10 percent discount with this book in 2006, air-con, Internet in lobby, 111 avenue de la Bourdonnais, tel. 01 47 05 45 42, fax 01 45 55 75 54, www.hotellabourdonnais.fr, hlb@hotellabourdonnais.fr).

$$ Hôtel Prince**, across avenue Bosquet from the Ecole Militaire Métro stop, has a spartan lobby and good rooms at very reasonable rates, considering they're air-conditioned (Sb-€70, Db with shower-€89, Db with tub-€107, Tb-€115, 66 avenue Bosquet, tel. 01 47 05 40 90, fax 01 47 53 06 62, www.hotel-paris-prince.com).

$$ Eber-Mars Hôtel**, on a busy street, is a good midrange value. Its larger-than-average rooms have weathered furnishings. The hotel also features oak-paneled public spaces and a beam-me-up-Jacques, coffin-sized elevator (Db-€100–120, Tb-€150, Qb-€160, 20 percent cheaper Nov–March and July–Aug, breakfast is free for readers of this book in 2006, 117 avenue de la Bourdonnais, tel. 01 47 05 42 30, fax 01 47 05 45 91, www.hotelebermars.com, reservation@hotelebermars.com, manager Jean-Marc is a wealth of information for travelers).

$ Hôtel Royal Phare** is a simple yet solid value—ideal for backpackers—facing the busy Ecole Militaire Métro stop. The 34

basic rooms are unimaginative, but pink-pastel comfortable; those on the courtyard are quietest (Sb-€65, Db with shower-€70, Db with tub-€85, Tb-€105, claustrophobic hallways, 40 avenue de la Motte-Picquet, tel. 01 47 05 57 30, fax 01 45 51 64 41, www.hotel-royalphare-paris.com, royalphare-hotel@wanadoo.fr).

$ Hôtel de Turenne** is simple and well-located, with the cheapest air-conditioned rooms I found. Even though the halls are depressing, the lobby is smoky, and the rooms could use some work, the price is right. There are five truly single rooms and several connecting rooms good for families (Sb-€64, Db-€74-86, Tb-€104, extra bed-€10, 20 avenue de Tourville, tel. 01 47 05 99 92, fax 01 45 56 06 04, hotel.turenne.paris7@wanadoo.fr).

Near Rue Cler, Closer to Rue St. Dominique (and the Seine)

$$ Hôtel Londres Eiffel*** is my closest listing to the Eiffel Tower and Champ de Mars park. A particularly good value, it offers immaculate, warmly decorated rooms, cozy public spaces, Internet access, and air-conditioning. The helpful staff takes good care of their guests. It's less convenient to the Métro (10-min walk); handy bus #69 and RER: Pont de l'Alma are better options (Sb-€99–105, Db-€110–150, deluxe Db-€155–175, extra bed-€20, 1 rue Augerau, tel. 01 45 51 63 02, fax 01 47 05 28 96, www.londres-eiffel.com, info@londres-eiffel.com). Show them this book in 2006 for a free Seine cruise.

$$ Hôtel de la Tulipe***, three blocks from rue Cler toward the river, is unique. The 20 smallish but artistically decorated rooms—each one different—come with little, stylish bathrooms and surround a seductive wood-beamed lounge and a peaceful, leafy courtyard (Db-€140, Tb-€160, 2-room suite for up to 5 people-€250, no elevator or air-con, 33 rue Malar, tel. 01 45 51 67 21, fax 01 47 53 96 37, www.paris-hotel-tulipe.com, friendly Bernhard behind the desk).

$ Hôtel de l'Alma** is in need of attention and new beds, but it's well-located on "restaurant row." It has sleepable rooms, small bathrooms, a *petite* courtyard, and reasonable rates (Sb-€85, Db-€95 with this book in 2006, includes breakfast, 32 rue de l'Exposition, tel. 01 47 05 45 70, fax 01 45 51 84 47, www.alma-paris-hotel.com, Carine).

$ Hôtel Kensington** has tight and worn rooms and less personality, but it's a fair value (Sb-€55, Db-€70, big Db on back side-€85, extra bed-€12, Eiffel Tower views for those who ask, 79 avenue de la Bourdonnais, tel. 01 47 05 74 00, fax 01 47 05 25 81, www.hotel-kensington.com, hk@hotel-kensington.com, Daniele).

Near La Tour-Maubourg Métro Stop

The next three listings are within two blocks of the intersection of avenue de la Motte-Picquet and boulevard de la Tour-Maubourg.

$$$ Hôtel les Jardins Eiffel***, on a quiet street, feels like a modern motel, but earns its three stars with professional service, its own parking garage (€21/day), and a spacious lobby. The 80 rooms—some with private balconies (ask for a room *avec petit balcon*)—are comfortable, if unimaginative (Sb-€136, Db-€157, extra bed-€30 or free for a child up to 10, claim a 15 percent Rick Steves discount when you book direct in 2006, check online for occasional even better deals, air-con, Internet in lobby, 8 rue Amélie, tel. 01 47 05 46 21, fax 01 45 55 28 08, www.hoteljardinseiffel.com, paris@hoteljardinseiffel.com).

$$ Hôtel Muguet**, a peaceful, stylish, and immaculate refuge, gives you three-star comfort for a two-star price. This delightful place offers 43 tasteful, air-conditioned rooms, a greenhouse lounge, and a small garden courtyard. The hands-on owner, Catherine, gives her guests a restful and secure home in Paris (Sb in a double room-€95, Db with one big bed-€110, twin Db-€125, big Db with view and balcony-€165, Tb-€160, 11 rue Chevert, tel. 01 47 05 05 93, fax 01 45 50 25 37, www.hotelmuguet.com, muguet@wanadoo.fr).

$ Hôtel de l'Empereur** lacks intimacy, but it's roomy and a fair value. Its 38 pleasant rooms come with real wood furniture and all the comforts except air-conditioning. Streetside rooms have views, but some noise; fifth-floor rooms have small balconies and Napoleonic views (Db-€90, Tb-€120, Qb-€140, 2 rue Chevert, tel. 01 45 55 88 02, fax 01 45 51 88 54, www.hotelempereur.com, contact@hotelempereur.com).

Lesser Values in the Rue Cler Area

Given how fine this area is, these are acceptable last choices.

$$$ Hôtel du Cadran***, while perfectly located and with a nice lobby, lacks charm in its tight, narrow, and way overpriced rooms (Db-€170–180, air-con, 10 rue du Champ de Mars, tel. 01 40 62 67 00, fax 01 40 62 67 13, www.hotelducadran.com).

$$$ Hôtel Splendid*** is Art Deco modern, professional, and worth your while if you land one of its three suites with great Eiffel Tower views. Sixth-floor rooms have small terraces and sideways tower views. All of the rooms seem a bit pricey, as they are not air-conditioned. Ask about their occasional promotional rates (Db-€170, Db with balcony and view-€180, Db suite-€230, 29 avenue de Tourville, tel. 01 45 51 24 77, fax 01 44 18 94 60, splendid@club-internet.fr).

$$$ Best Western Eiffel Park*** is a dead quiet, concrete business hotel with all the comforts, a friendly staff, 36 pleasant if

unexceptional rooms, and a rooftop terrace (Db-€170–185, check online for promotional rates, 17 bis rue Amélie, tel. 01 45 55 10 01, fax 01 47 05 28, 68, www.eiffelpark.com, reservation@eiffelpark .com).

$ Hôtel Amélie**, in a skinny building, is a midrange possibility with no lobby, no elevator, and shabby halls but decent rooms (Db-€85–105, 5 rue Amélie, tel. 01 45 51 74 75, fax 01 45 56 93 55, www.hotelamelie.fr, hotelamelie@wanadoo.fr).

$ Hôtel le Pavillon** is quiet, with no-frills rooms, no elevator, and cramped halls in a charming location (Sb-€80, Db-€85, Tb, Qb, or Quint/b-€135, 54 rue St. Dominique, tel. 01 45 51 42 87, fax 01 45 51 32 79, patrickpavillon@aol.com).

IN THE MARAIS NEIGHBORHOOD

(4th *arrondissement*, Mo: Bastille, St. Paul, and Hôtel de Ville)
Those interested in a more Soho/Greenwich Village locale should make the Marais their Parisian home. Not long ago, it was a forgotten Parisian backwater, but now the Marais is one of Paris' most popular residential, tourist, and shopping areas. This is jumbled, medieval Paris at its finest, where classy stone mansions sit alongside trendy bars, antique shops, and fashion-conscious boutiques. The streets are a fascinating parade of artists, students, tourists, immigrants, and babies in strollers munching baguettes. The Marais is also known as a hub of the Parisian gay and lesbian scene. This area is *sans doute* livelier (and louder) than the rue Cler area.

In the Marais, you have these sights close at hand: Picasso Museum, Carnavalet Museum, Victor Hugo's House, the Jewish Art and History Museum, and the Pompidou Center. You're also a manageable walk from Paris' two islands (Ile St. Louis and Ile de la Cité), home to Notre-Dame and the Sainte-Chapelle. The Opéra Bastille, Promenade Plantée park, place des Vosges (Paris' oldest square), Jewish Quarter (rue des Rosiers), and nightlife-packed rue de Lappe are also walkable. (For sight descriptions, see "Northeast Paris," page 65; for the Opéra, see page 108.)

Most of my recommended hotels are located a few blocks north of the Marais' main east–west drag, the rue St. Antoine/rue de Rivoli.

Tourist Information: The nearest TI is in Gare de Lyon (Mon–Sat 8:00–18:00, closed Sun, all-Paris TI tel. 08 92 68 30 00).

Services: Most banks and other services are on the main drag, rue de Rivoli, which becomes rue St. Antoine. Marais **post offices** are on rue Castex and on the corner of rue Pavée and rue des Francs Bourgeois. There's an **SNCF Boutique** where you can take care of all train needs on rue St. Antoine at rue de Turenne (Mon–Sat 8:30–20:00, closed Sun). A quieter SNCF Boutique

Marais Musts for Temporary Residents

- Have dinner or a drink on place du Marché Ste. Catherine.
- Dine or enjoy a drink on place des Vosges.
- Take a late-night art gallery stroll around place des Vosges.
- Stroll the Promenade Plantée elevated park (see page 67).
- Mix it up with local shoppers one morning at the Marché de la place d'Aligre.
- Walk the Ile St. Louis after dark and enjoy the floodlit view of Notre-Dame (see page 392).
- Check out the late-night action in rue de Lappe (if you dare).

lies nearer Gare de Lyon at 5 rue de Lyon (Mon–Sat 8:30–18:00, closed Sun).

Markets: The Marais has two good open-air markets: the sprawling **Marché de la Bastille,** around place de la Bastille (Thu and Sun until 12:30); and the more intimate, untouristy **Marché de la place d'Aligre** (daily 9:00–12:00, cross place de la Bastille and walk about 10 blocks down rue du Faubourg St. Antoine, turn right at rue de Cotte to place d'Aligre; or, easier, take Métro line 8 from Bastille toward Créteil-Préfecture to the Ledru-Rollin stop and walk a few blocks southeast from there). Two little **grocery shops** are open until 23:00 on rue St. Antoine (near intersection with rue Castex). For your Parisian Sears, find the **BHV** next to Hôtel de Ville.

Bookstore: The Marais is home to the friendliest English-language bookstore in Paris, **Red Wheelbarrow** (daily 10:00–19:00, 22 rue St. Paul, Mo: St. Paul, tel. 01 42 77 42 17). Abigail and Penelope sell most of my guidebooks and carry a great collection of other books about Paris and France.

Internet Access: Try **@aron** (3 rue des Ecouffes, Mo: St. Paul, tel. 01 42 71 05 07), **Paris CY** (8 rue de Jouy, Mo: St. Paul, tel. 01 42 71 37 37), or **Cyber Cube** (12 rue Daval, Mo: Bastille, tel. 01 49 29 67 67).

Métro Connections: Key Métro stops in the Marais are, from east to west: Bastille, St. Paul, and Hôtel de Ville (Sully-Morland, Pont Marie, and Rambuteau stops are also handy). Métro service to the Marais neighborhood is excellent, with direct service to the Louvre, Champs-Elysées, Arc de Triomphe, and La Défense (all on line 1); the rue Cler area and Opéra Garnier (line 8 from Bastille stop); and four major train stations: Gare de Lyon, Gare du Nord, Gare de l'Est, and Gare d'Austerlitz.

Bus Routes: Line **#69** on rue St. Antoine takes you eastbound to Père Lachaise Cemetery (see tour on page 284) and westbound to the Louvre, Orsay, and Rodin Museums, plus Napoleon's Tomb, ending at the Eiffel Tower (Mon–Sat only—no Sun service; see Bus #69 Sightseeing Tour, page 297). Line **#86** runs down boulevard Henri IV, crossing Ile St. Louis and serving the Latin Quarter along boulevard St. Germain. Line **#87** follows a similar route, but also serves Gare de Lyon to the east and the Eiffel Tower and rue Cler neighborhood to the west. Line **#96** runs on rues Turenne and François Miron and serves the Louvre and boulevard St. Germain (near Luxembourg Garden), ending at the Gare Montparnasse. Line **#65** runs from Gare de Lyon up rue de Lyon, around place de la Bastille, and then up boulevard Beaumarchais to the Gare de l'Est and Gare du Nord.

Taxis: You'll find taxi stands on place de la Bastille (where boulevard Richard Lenoir meets the square), on the north side of rue St. Antoine (where it meets rue Castex), and on the south side of rue St. Antoine (in front of St. Paul Church).

Near Place des Vosges

$$$ Hôtel des Chevaliers***, a pretty little boutique hotel with a handsome lobby one block northwest of place des Vosges, offers small, delicate rooms with air-conditioning. Eight of its 24 rooms are off the street and quiet—worth requesting (Db-€150, 30 rue de Turenne, Mo: St. Paul, tel. 01 42 72 73 47, fax 01 42 72 54 10, www.chevaliers-paris-hotel.com, info@hoteldeschevaliers.com).

$$ Hôtel Castex***, well-situated on a quiet street near place de la Bastille, feels Spanish, from the formal entry to the red-tiled floors and dark wood accents. A clever system of connecting rooms allows families total privacy between two rooms, each with its own bathroom. Rooms are narrow but tasteful and air-conditioned, and the elevator is big by Parisian standards. Your fourth night is free in August and from November through February, except around New Year's (Sb-€95–115, Db-€120–140, Tb-€190–220, good €10 buffet breakfast is free through 2006 for readers of this book, just off place de la Bastille and rue St. Antoine, 5 rue Castex, Mo: Bastille, tel. 01 42 72 31 52, fax 01 42 72 57 91, www.castexhotel.com, info@castexhotel.com).

$$ Hôtel Bastille Spéria***, a short block off place de la Bastille, offers business-type service. The 42 well-configured rooms are modern and comfortable, with big beds and air-conditioning. Walls are thin, and the elevator operates at glacial speed, but it's English-language-friendly, from the *International Herald Tribune*s in the lobby to the history of the Bastille posted in the elevator (Sb-€100, Db-€125–150, child's bed-€20, excellent buffet breakfast-€13, 1 rue de la Bastille, Mo: Bastille, tel. 01 42 72 04 01,

Marais Hotels

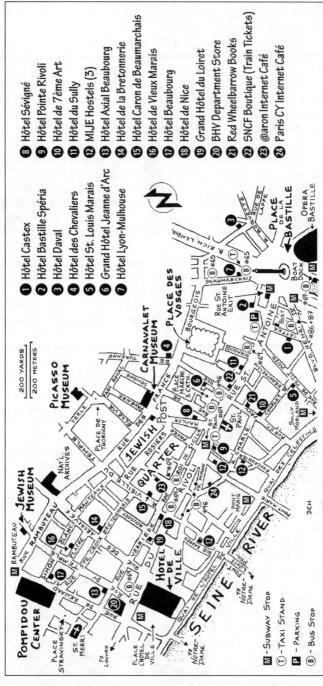

1. Hôtel Castex
2. Hôtel Bastille Spéria
3. Hôtel Daval
4. Hôtel des Chevaliers
5. Hôtel St. Louis Marais
6. Grand Hôtel Jeanne d'Arc
7. Hôtel Lyon-Mulhouse
8. Hôtel Sévigné
9. Hôtel Pointe Rivoli
10. Hôtel de 7ème Art
11. Hôtel du Sully
12. MIJE Hostels (3)
13. Hôtel Axial Beaubourg
14. Hôtel de la Bretonnerie
15. Hôtel Caron de Beaumarchais
16. Hôtel de Vieux Marais
17. Hôtel Beaubourg
18. Hôtel de Nice
19. Grand Hôtel du Loiret
20. BHV Department Store
21. Red Wheelbarrow Books
22. SNCF Boutique (Train Tickets)
23. @aron Internet Café
24. Paris CY Internet Café

M – Subway Stop
T – Taxi Stand
P – Parking
B – Bus Stop

fax 01 42 72 56 38, www.hotel-bastille-speria.com, info@hotel
-bastille-speria.com).

$$ Hôtel St. Louis Marais**, tiny and welcoming, is lost on
a quiet residential street between the river and rue St. Antoine.
The lobby is inviting, and the 20 rooms are cozy, but not air-
conditioned (small Sb-€59, standard Sb-€91, small Db-€107, stan-
dard Db-€125, Tb-€140, no elevator but only 3 floors, ask about
newer street-level annex rooms, bargain-priced parking-€12, 1 rue
Charles V, Mo: Sully Morland, tel. 01 48 87 87 04, fax 01 48 87 33
26, www.saintlouismarais.com, slmarais@noos.fr).

$ Hôtel de 7ème Art**, two blocks south of rue St. Antoine
toward the river, is a relaxed, Hollywood-nostalgia place. It has
a full-service café-bar and Charlie Chaplin murals, but no eleva-
tor. Its 23 good-value rooms lack imagination, but are comfortable
enough (with air-conditioning). The large rooms are American-
spacious (small Db-€80, standard Db-€100, large Db-€115–140,
extra bed-€20, 20 rue St. Paul, Mo: St. Paul, tel. 01 44 54 85 00,
fax 01 42 77 69 10, hotel7art@wanadoo.fr).

$ Grand Hôtel Jeanne d'Arc**, a lovely and well-tended hotel
with thoughtfully appointed rooms, is ideally located for (and
very popular with) connoisseurs of the Marais. It's a fine value
and worth booking way ahead. Sixth-floor rooms have views, and
corner rooms are wonderfully bright in the City of Light, though
no rooms are air-conditioned. Rooms on the street can be noisy
until the bars close (Sb-€60–86, Db-€86, larger twin Db-€100,
Tb-€120, good Qb-€150, 3 rue de Jarente, Mo: St. Paul, tel. 01 48
87 62 11, fax 01 48 87 37 31, information@hoteljeannedarc.com).

$ Hôtel Lyon-Mulhouse** is less intimate but a good deal,
with half of its 40 pleasant rooms on a busy street off place de la
Bastille. Its bigger, quieter rooms at the back are worth the extra
euros (Sb-€65, Db-€75, twin Db-€90, Tb-€100, Qb-€125, no air-
con, 8 boulevard Beaumarchais, Mo: Bastille, tel. 01 47 00 91 50,
fax 01 47 00 06 31, hotelyonmulhouse@wanadoo.fr).

$ Hôtel Daval**, an unassuming place with good rates on the
lively side of place de la Bastille, is ideal for night owls (Db-€72,
Tb-€85, Qb-€92, 21 rue Daval, Mo: Bastille, tel. 01 47 00 51 23,
fax 01 40 21 80 26, hoteldaval@wanadoo.fr).

$ Hôtel Sévigné** is a sharp little air-conditioned hotel with
lavender halls, tidy and comfortable rooms at excellent prices, and
an owner (M. Mercier) of few words (Sb-€64, Db-€74–86, Tb-
€100, Qb-€120, 2 rue Malher, Mo: St. Paul, tel. 01 42 72 76 17, fax
01 42 78 68 26, www.le-sevigne.com, contact@le-sevigne.com).

$ Hôtel Pointe Rivoli*, across from the St. Paul Métro stop,
is a jumbled treehouse of rooms in the thick of the Marais, with
Paris' steepest stairs (no elevator), dark halls, and modest, air-
conditioned rooms at reasonable rates (Sb-€65, Db-€78, Tb-€115,

125 rue St. Antoine, Mo: St. Paul, tel. 01 42 72 14 23, fax 01 42 72 51 11, pointerivoli@libertysurf.fr).

$ Hôtel du Sully, sitting right on rue St. Antoine, is nothing fancy. The entry is long and narrow; the rooms are dimly lit but sleepable; and friendly M. Zeroual is in charge (Db-€55, Tb-€72, 48 rue St. Antoine, Mo: St. Paul, tel. 01 42 78 49 32, fax 01 44 61 76 50).

$ MIJE Youth Hostels: The Maison Internationale de la Jeunesse et des Etudiants (MIJE) runs three classy old residences clustered a few blocks south of rue St. Antoine. Each is well-maintained, with simple, clean, single-sex, one- to four-bed rooms for travelers of any age. None has an elevator or double beds, each has Internet access, and all rooms have showers. You can stay seven days maximum, and the rates favor single travelers (2 people can find a double in a very simple hotel for a similar price). You can pay more to have your own room, or pay less and room with as many as three others (all prices per person: Sb-€43, Db-€33, Tb-€30, Qb-€28, cash only, includes breakfast but not towels; required membership card-€2.50 extra/person; rooms locked 12:00–15:00, curfew at 1:00 in the morning). The hostels are **MIJE Fourcy** (€11 dinners available to anyone with a membership card, 6 rue de Fourcy, just south of rue de Rivoli), **MIJE Fauconnier** (11 rue du Fauconnier), and the best, **MIJE Maubisson** (12 rue des Barres). They all share the same contact information (tel. 01 42 74 23 45, fax 01 40 27 81 64, www.mije.com, accueil@mije.com) and Métro stop (St. Paul). Reservations are accepted (2 months ahead by e-mail, 1 month ahead by phone), though you must show up by noon or call the morning of arrival to confirm a later arrival time.

Near the Pompidou Center

These hotels are farther west, closer to the Pompidou Center than to place de la Bastille. The Hôtel de Ville Métro stop works well for all of these hotels, unless a closer stop is noted.

$$$ Hôtel Axial Beaubourg*,** in the thick of things a block from Hôtel de Ville toward the Pompidou Center, has a minimalist lobby and 28 overpriced but plush rooms, many with wood beams. If you cancel with less than seven days' notice, you'll lose your one-night deposit (standard Db-€175, big Db-€210, air-con, 11 rue du Temple, tel. 01 42 72 72 22, fax 02 42 72 03 53, www .axialbeaubourg.com, infos@axialbeaubourg.com).

$$$ Hôtel Caron de Beaumarchais*** feels like a folk museum, with its 20 sweet little rooms and a lobby cluttered with bits from an elegant 18th-century Marais house. Short antique collectors love this place (small back-side Db-€145, larger Db facing the front-€160, air-con, Wi-Fi in all rooms, 12 rue Vieille du Temple, tel. 01 42 72 34 12, fax 01 42 72 34 63, www.carondebeaumarchais .com, hotel@carondebeaumarchais.com).

$$ Hôtel de la Bretonnerie*,** three blocks from the Hôtel de Ville, makes a fine Marais home. It has a big, welcoming lobby, classy decor, and tastefully appointed rooms with an antique, open-beam warmth (perfectly good standard "classic" Db-€110, bigger "charming" Db-€145, Db suite-€180, Tb-€170, Tb suite-€205, Qb suite-€235, no air-con, between rue Vieille du Temple and rue des Archives at 22 rue Ste. Croix de la Bretonnerie, tel. 01 48 87 77 63, fax 01 42 77 26 78, www.bretonnerie.com, hotel@bretonnerie.com).

$$ Hôtel de Vieux Marais,** with a quirky owner, is tucked away on a quiet street two blocks east of the Pompidou Center. Rooms are a fair value here except in high season (Db-€115, but increases to €145 March–mid-July, extra bed-€24, air-con, just off rue des Archives at 8 rue du Plâtre, Mo: Rambuteau or Hôtel de Ville, tel. 01 42 78 47 22, fax 01 42 78 34 32, www.vieuxmarais .com, hotel@vieuxmarais.com).

$$ Hôtel Beaubourg*** is a fine three-star value on a quiet street in the shadow of the Pompidou Center. Its 28 rooms are wood-beam comfy and air-conditioned, and the inviting lounge is warm and pleasant (standard Db-€105, bigger twin Db-€120, 11 rue Simon Le Franc, Mo: Rambuteau, tel. 01 42 74 34 24, fax 01 42 78 68 11, www.hotelbeaubourg.com, htlbeaubourg@hotellerie.net).

$$ Hôtel de Nice,** on the Marais' busy main drag, is a turquoise-and-rose, "Marie-Antoinette does tie-dye" place. Its narrow halls are littered with paintings and covered with carpets, and its 23 non-air-conditioned rooms are filled with thoughtful touches and include tight bathrooms. Twin rooms, which cost the same as doubles, are larger and on the street side—but have effective double-paned windows (Sb-€74, Db-€105, Tb-€128, Qb-€140, extra bed-€20, 42 bis rue de Rivoli, tel. 01 42 78 55 29, fax 01 42 78 36 07, www.hoteldenice.com, contact@hoteldenice.com).

$ Grand Hôtel du Loiret** is a centrally located backpacker hotel, though the rooms are better than you might think (S-€48, Db-€64-84, Tb-€95, 8 rue des Mauvais Garçons, tel. 01 48 87 77 00, fax 01 48 04 96 56, www.hotel-loiret.fr, hotelduloiret@hotmail .com).

Near the Marais, on Ile St. Louis

The peaceful, residential character of this river-wrapped island, its brilliant location, and homemade ice cream have drawn Americans for decades, allowing hotels to charge dearly for their rooms. There are no budget values here, but the island's coziness and proximity to the Marais, Notre-Dame, and the Latin Quarter help compensate for higher rates. The hotels listed below are shown on the map on page 80. All are on the island's main drag, the rue St. Louis-en-l'Ile, where I list several restaurants (see page 358). Use Mo: Pont Marie or Sully-Morland.

$$$ Hôtel du Jeu de Paume********, located in a 17th-century tennis center, is the most expensive hotel I list in Paris. When you enter its magnificent lobby, you'll understand why. Greet Scoop, the hotel dog, then ride the glass elevator for a half-timbered-tree-house experience, and marvel at the cozy lounges. The 30 quite comfortable rooms are carefully designed and *très* tasteful, though small for the price (you're paying for the location and public spaces). Most rooms face a small garden, and all are pin-drop peaceful (Sb-€165, standard Db-€230, larger Db-€280, deluxe Db-€310, 54 rue St. Louis-en-l'Ile, tel. 01 43 26 14 18, fax 01 40 46 02 76, www.jeudepaumehotel.com).

The following two hotels are owned by the same person. For both, if you must cancel, do so a week in advance or pay fees:

$$$ Hôtel de Lutèce*** is the better, cozier value on the island, with a sit-a-while, wood-paneled lobby, a fireplace, warmly designed rooms, and friendly Nathalie at the reception. Twin rooms are larger and the same price as double rooms (Db-€166, Tb-€182, air-con, 65 rue St. Louis-en-l'Ile, tel. 01 43 26 23 52, fax 01 43 29 60 25, www.hotel-ile-saintlouis.com, lutece@hotel-ile-saintlouis.com).

$$$ Hôtel des Deux Iles*** is brighter and more colorful, with marginally smaller rooms (Db-€166, 59 rue St. Louis-en-l'Ile, tel. 01 43 26 13 35, fax 01 43 29 60 25, www.hotel-ile-saintlouis.com, 2isles@hotel-ile-saintlouis.com).

$$$ Hôtel Saint Louis*** has less personality but good rooms with parquet floors, air-conditioning, and comparatively good rates (Db-€142–158, 75 rue St. Louis-en-l'Ile, tel. 01 46 34 04 80, fax 01 46 34 02 13, slouis@noos.fr).

LUXEMBOURG GARDEN AREA (ST. SULPICE TO PANTHÉON)

(5th and 6th *arrondissements*, Mo: St. Sulpice, Mabillon, Odéon, and Cluny La Sorbonne; RER: Luxembourg)
This neighborhood revolves around Paris' loveliest park and offers quick access to the city's best shopping streets and grandest café-hopping. Sleeping in the Luxembourg area offers a true Left Bank experience without a hint of the low-end commotion of the nearby Latin Quarter tourist ghetto. The Luxembourg Garden, boulevard St. Germain, Cluny Museum, and Latin Quarter are all at your doorstep. Here you get the best of both worlds: youthful Left Bank energy and the classy trappings that surround the monumental Panthéon and St. Sulpice Church. Hotels in this central area are generally more expensive than in other areas I list.

Having the Luxembourg Garden at your back door allows strolls through meticulously cared-for flowers, a great kids' play

area (see Paris with Children, page 371), and a purifying escape from city traffic. Place St. Sulpice offers an elegant, pedestrian-friendly square and some of Paris' best boutiques (see Shopping, page 379). Sleeping in the Luxembourg area also puts several movie theaters at your fingertips (at Métro stop: Odéon), as well as lively cafés on the boulevard St. Germain, rue de Buci, rue des Canettes, place de la Sorbonne, and place de la Contrescarpe, all of which buzz with action until late.

While it takes only 15 minutes to walk from one end of this neighborhood to the other, I've located the hotels by the key monument they are close to (St. Sulpice Church, the Odéon Theater, and the Panthéon). No hotel is further than a five-minute walk from the Luxembourg Garden.

Tourist Information: The nearest TI is across the river in Gare de Lyon (Mon–Sat 8:00–18:00, closed Sun, all-Paris TI tel. 08 92 68 30 00).

Markets: The colorful **street market** at the south end of rue Mouffetard is a worthwhile 10- to 15-minute walk down from these hotels (Tue–Sat 8:00–12:00 & 15:30–19:00, Sun 8:00–12:00, closed Mon, 5 blocks south of place de la Contrescarpe, Mo: Place Monge).

Bookstore: The **Village Voice** bookstore carries a full selection of English-language books (including mine) and is near St. Sulpice (6 rue Princesse, tel. 01 46 33 36 47).

Internet Access: You'll find it at **XS Arena** (always open, between the Luxembourg Garden and Panthéon at 17 rue Soufflot) and at **Cyber Cube** (daily 10:00–22:00, 5 rue Mignon, near the Odéon Métro stop, tel. 01 53 10 30 50).

Métro Connections: Métro lines #10 and #4 serve this area (#10 connects to the Austerlitz train station, and #4 goes to the Montparnasse, Est, and Nord train stations). Neighborhood stops are Cluny La Sorbonne, Mabillon, Odéon, and St. Sulpice. RER-B (Luxembourg station is handiest) provides direct service to Charles de Gaulle airport and Gare du Nord trains, and access to Orly airport via the Orlybus (transfer at Denfert-Rochereau).

Bus Routes: Buses **#63**, **#86**, and **#87** run eastbound through this area on boulevard St. Germain, and westbound along rue des Ecoles, stopping on place St. Sulpice. Lines #63 and #87 provide direct connections to the rue Cler area. Line #63 also serves the Orsay, Invalides, Rodin, and Marmottan Museums and Gare de Lyon. Lines #86 and #87 run to the Marais, and #87 continues east to Gare de Lyon.

Hotels Near St. Sulpice Church
(6th *arrondissement*)

These hotels are all within a block of St. Sulpice Church, and two

blocks from the famous boulevard St. Germain. This is nirvana for boutique-minded shoppers—and you'll pay extra for the location. Métro stops St. Sulpice and Mabillon are equally close.

$$$ Hôtel Relais St. Sulpice*,** on the small street just behind St. Sulpice Church, feels like a cozy bar, with a melt-in-your-chair lounge and 26 carefully designed, air-conditioned rooms, most of which surround a leafy glass atrium (Db-€170–205 depending on size, most Db-€170–180, sauna free for guests, 3 rue Garancière, tel. 01 46 33 99 00, fax 01 46 33 00 10, www.relais -saint-sulpice.com, relaisstsulpice@wanadoo.fr).

$$$ Hôtel la Perle*** is a pricey pearl in the thick of the lively rue des Canettes, a block off place St. Sulpice. At this snappy, modern, business-class hotel, sliding glass doors open onto the traffic-free street and a fun lobby built around a central bar and atrium greets you (standard Db-€173, bigger Db-€195, luxury Db-€235, air-con, 14 rue des Canettes, tel. 01 43 29 10 10, fax 01 43 34 51 04, www.hotellaperle.com, booking@hotellaperle.com).

$$$ Hôtel de l'Abbaye*** feels lost on a quiet street just west of Luxembourg Garden. It's a find for well-heeled connoisseurs of this appealing area. This luxury refuge, set back from the street, offers refined lounges inside and out, and quite comfortable rooms with every amenity (Db-€214, bigger Db-€320, 10 rue Cassette, tel. 01 45 44 38 11, fax 01 45 48 07 86, www.hotel-abbaye.com, hotel.abbaye@wanadoo.fr).

$$ Hôtel Bonaparte** sits between boutiques, a few steps from place St. Sulpice on the smart rue Bonaparte. While the 29 air-conditioned rooms don't live up to the handsome entry, they're homey, comfortable, and generally spacious, with big bathrooms, molded ceilings, and clashing bedspreads (Sb-€87, Db-€108, big Db-€131, Tb-€134, required €8 breakfast, 61 rue Bonaparte, tel. 01 43 26 97 37, fax 01 46 33 57 67, www.hotelbonaparte.fr).

$$ Hôtel le Récamier,** tucked in the corner of place St. Sulpice, feels like grandma's house. Flowery wallpaper, dark halls, and spotless, just-what-you-need rooms (no TVs)—some with views of the square—make this a good, if high-priced for the comfort, Paris refuge (S-€90, Sb-€110, D-€90, Db-€110, bigger Db-€130, Tb-€176, Qb-€218, 3 bis place St. Sulpice, tel. 01 43 26 04 89, fax 01 46 33 27 73, e-mail address?—what's that?).

Near the Odéon Theater

These hotels are between the Odéon Métro stop and Luxembourg Garden (5 blocks east of St. Sulpice), and may have rooms when others don't. Rooms in this area—both handy and elegant—are a particularly good value. In addition to the Odéon Métro stop, the RER-B Luxembourg stop is a short walk away.

Hotels and Restaurants near St. Sulpice and the Odéon Theater

1 Hôtel Relais St. Sulpice
2 Hôtel la Perle
3 Hôtel Bonaparte
4 Hôtel le Récamier
5 Hôtel Michelet Odéon
6 Grand Hôtel des Balcons & Hôtel Delavigne
7 Hôtel de l'Abbaye
8 Hôtel le Relais Médicis
9 Hôtel Stella
10 La Crêpe Rit du Clown
11 Chez Georges
12 Le Café de Flore & Les Deux Magots
13 Café Bonaparte
14 Café le Procope
15 Cyber Cube Internet Café
16 Village Voice Books

Luxembourg Musts for Temporary Residents

- Waste oodles of time at Luxembourg Garden, sitting in a green chair, with your feet propped up on the pond's edge.
- Observe Daniel Roth's Sunday organ mastery up close at St. Sulpice Church (see page 55).
- Join the locals at the only café on place St. Sulpice for a morning coffee or afternoon drink.
- Stroll the rue Mouffetard day or night, and stop for a drink on place Contrescarpe.
- Spend too much for a coffee at a grand café and watch the world go by (see "Les Grands Cafés de Paris," page 364).
- Wander the rue de Buci and find Voltaire's favorite café (see Left Bank Walk, page 141).
- Ponder the history of France in the Panthéon (see page 57).

$$$ Hôtel le Relais Médicis* is perfect in every way—if you would like to live in a Monet painting and can afford it. Its 16 rooms surround a fragrant little garden courtyard and fountain, giving you a countryside break fit for a Medici in the heart of Paris. This delightful place—tastefully decorated with a floral Old World charm, hues of Provence, and permeated with thoughtfulness and quality—gives four-star comfort at three-star prices (Sb-€158, Db-€178–€225, about €50 cheaper mid-July–Aug, sumptuous €10 Continental breakfast required, faces the Odéon Theater at 23 Rue Racine, tel. 01 43 26 00 60, fax 01 40 46 83 39, www.relaismedicis.com, reservation@relaism edicis.com). Don't confuse this with the similarly named but far less swanky Hôtel des Médicis, described below.

$$ Grand Hôtel des Balcons has an inviting lobby and 50 spick-and-span rooms with interesting colors and generous space. Some rooms have narrow balconies (Db-€110–120, big corner Db-€140, big Tb-€180, look for summer discounts online, fans in rooms, a block below the Odéon Theater, 3 Casimir-Delavigne, tel. 01 46 34 78 50, fax 01 46 34 06 27, www.balcons.com, resa @balcons.com).

$$ Hôtel Delavigne* has a warm lobby and 34 traditionally decorated rooms. The beds may be a bit soft for some (Db-€115, bigger twin Db-€130, Tb-€130-145, €15 cheaper mid-July–Aug, 1 rue Casimir-Delavigne, tel. 01 43 29 31 50, fax 01 43 29 78 56, www.hoteldelavigne.com, resa@hoteldelavigne.com).

$$ Hôtel Michelet Odéon sits shyly in a corner of place de l'Odéon, a block from the Luxembourg Garden. Most of the 24

spacious, simple rooms have views (Db-€95–115, Tb-€135, Qb-€150, 6 place de l'Odéon, tel. 01 53 10 05 60, fax 01 46 34 55 35, www.hotelmicheletodeon.com, hotel@micheletodeon.com).

$ **Hôtel Stella*** has been in the family for 100 years, and this time-warp place has just about run out of steam. Its well-worn wooden staircase, honky-tonk pianos, cartoon fuse boxes, ramshackle rooms, and rough, exposed timbers make it too basic for most—but a delight for cheapskate backpackers with a poem to write (Sb-€45, Db-€55, Tb-€75, Qb-€85, cash only, no breakfast, no public spaces, no complaining, some of its 24 rooms are huge, great location next to Polidor Restaurant at 41 rue Mr. le Prince, tel. 01 40 51 00 25, hotelstella@hotmail.com).

Near the Panthéon and Rue Mouffetard

The last three listings are cheap dives, but in a great area.

$$ **Hôtel des Grandes Ecoles*** is idyllic. A short cobbled lane leads to three buildings protecting a flower-filled garden courtyard, preserving a sense of tranquility rare in downtown Paris. Its 51 rooms are reasonably spacious and comfortable, many with large beds. This romantic spot is deservedly popular, so call well in advance (Db-€105–130 depending on size, extra bed-€20, parking-€30, 75 rue du Cardinal Lemoine, Mo: Cardinal Lemoine, tel. 01 43 26 79 23, fax 01 43 25 28 15, www.hotel-grandes-ecoles .com, hotel.grandes.ecoles@wanadoo.fr, mellow Marie speaks English, Mama does not).

$ **Hôtel des 3 Collèges**** is bright and well-run, with generous public spaces, claustrophobic hallways, and tight yet comfy rooms (Db-€91–99, Tb-€150, 16 rue Cujas, tel. 01 43 54 67 30, fax 01 46 34 02 99, www.3colleges.com, hotel@3colleges.com).

$ **Hôtel Cluny Sorbonne**** is smartly managed, a good deal, and conveniently located across from the famous university, just below the Panthéon. Rooms are clean and comfortable, with wood furnishings. Its public spaces are spacious, plain, and bright (standard Db-€85, big Db-€100, really big Db-€140, 8 rue Victor Cousin, tel. 01 43 54 66 66, fax 01 43 29 68 07, www.hotel-cluny.fr, cluny@club-internet.fr). They plan to add air-conditioning in 2006.

$ **Hôtel des Médicis** is a cheap, stripped-down, soiled-linoleum dive flanked by Chinese takeouts. Request Jim Morrison's old room, if you dare (dirt—and I mean dirt—cheap: S-€16–20, D-€31–35, 214 rue St. Jacques, Mo: Cluny La Sorbonne or RER-B Luxembourg, tel. 01 43 54 14 66, hotelmedicis@aol.com, Denis).

$ **Hôtel Central*,** wedged between two cafés, has a smoky, dingy reception, a steep, slippery stairway, so-so beds, and somewhat mildewed rooms. Bottom line: It's youth-hostel cheap, but with a charm romantic hobos can appreciate. All rooms have showers, but toilets are down the hall (Ss-€32–37, Ds-€45–50, cash

Hotels and Restaurants near the Panthéon

M – Subway Stop
R – R.E.R. Stop

1. Hôtel Cluny Sorbonne
2. Hôtel des 3 Collèges
3. Hôtel des Grandes Ecoles
4. Port-Royal-Hôtel
5. Hôtel de l'Espérance
6. Hôtel de France
7. Hôtel des Médicis
8. Hôtel Central
9. Y&H Hostel
10. Rest. les Vignes du Panthéon & Terra Nera
11. Restaurant Perraudin
12. Café le Soufflot
13. Place de la Sorbonne Eateries
14. Restaurant Polidor
15. Brasserie Bouillon Racine
16. Café Delmas
17. Cave de la Bourgogne
18. XS Arena Internet Café

only, no elevator, 6 rue Descartes, Mo: Cardinal Lemoine, tel. 01 46 33 57 93). Do your best to get a smile out of Madame Pilar, who doesn't speak English.

$ Y&H Hostel is easygoing, well-run, and English-speaking, with Internet access, kitchen facilities, and acceptable hostel conditions. It sits in the center of all the rue Mouffetard bar, café, and people action...which can be good or bad (beds in 4–6-bed rooms-€23, beds in double rooms-€26, includes breakfast, sheets-€2.50, no lockers, rooms closed 11:00–16:00 but reception stays open, curfew at 2:00 in the morning, reservations secured with credit card number but pay in cash, 80 rue Mouffetard, Mo: Place Monge, tel. 01 47 07 47 07, fax 01 47 07 22 24, www.youngandhappy.fr, smile@youngandhappy.fr). They have 14 doubles and are open to "anyone with an open mind."

Farther Away from the Seine, at the Bottom of Rue Mouffetard

These hotels, away from the Seine and other tourists in an appealing work-a-day area, offer more room for your euro. They require a longer walk or Métro ride to sights, but often have rooms when other accommodations are booked up. Rue Mouffetard is the bohemian soul of this area, running south from its heart, place de la Contrescarpe, to rue de Bazeilles. Two thousand years ago, it was the principal Roman road south to Italy. Today, this small, meandering street has a split personality. The lower half thrives in the daytime as a pedestrian shopping street. The upper half sleeps during the day but comes alive after dark, teeming with bars, restaurants, and nightlife. Use Métro stops Censier-Daubenton or Les Gobelins.

$ Port-Royal-Hôtel* has only one star, but don't let that fool you. This 46-room place is polished bottom to top and has been well-run by the same proud family for 67 years. You could eat off the floors of its spotless, comfy rooms. Ask for a room away from the street (S-€39–51, D-€51, big hall showers-€2.50, Db-€77–87 depending on size, Tb-€89, cash only, requires cash deposit, on busy boulevard de Port-Royal at #8, Mo: Les Gobelins, tel. 01 43 31 70 06, fax 01 43 31 33 67, portroyalhotel@wanadoo.fr).

$ Hôtel de l'Espérance** is a solid two-star value. It's quiet, pink, fluffy, and comfortable, with thoughtfully appointed rooms, complete with canopy beds and flamboyant and friendly owners Helen and André Aymard (Sb-€70, Db-€78–86, 15 rue Pascal, Mo: Censier-Daubenton, tel. 01 47 07 10 99, fax 01 43 37 56 19, hotel.esperance@wanadoo.fr).

$ Hôtel de France** is set on a busy street, with adequately comfortable rooms, fair prices, and a charming owner, Madame Margo. The best and quietest rooms are *sur la cour* (on the

courtyard), though streetside rooms are okay (Sb-€70, Db-€85–92, 108 rue Monge, Mo: Censier Daubenton, tel. 01 47 07 19 04, fax 01 43 36 62 34, hotel.de.fce@wanadoo.fr).

NEAR CANAL ST. MARTIN

(10th and 11th *arrondissements*, Mo: République, Oberkampf)
This up-and-coming neighborhood is just north of the Marais, between place de la République and Canal St. Martin. It feels real and reminds me of how many other neighborhoods looked 20 years ago. This area is the least touristy of those I list, and its hotels and restaurants tend to be great values (for restaurant suggestions, see page 363; for nighttime fun, head over to rue Oberkampf and join the crowd). This neighborhood is less polished and more remote—but if you can put up with some rough edges and don't mind using the Métro and buses for all of your sightseeing, you'll save plenty (hotels are €20–40 less for comparable rooms than in other areas I list).

The murky canal is the central feature of this unpretentious area, with pleasing walkways, arching footbridges, and occasional boats plying its water. A flowery parkway covers the canal where it goes underground toward place de la Bastille. When the weather agrees, the entire neighborhood seems to descend on the canal in late afternoon, filling the cafés, parkway, and benches. This neighborhood is convenient to the Nord and Est train stations (about 15 min by foot to either) and is also a 15-minute walk from the Pompidou Center and the place des Vosges in the Marais.

Market: The parkway plays host to an open-air market on Tuesdays and Fridays until 14:00.

Métro Connections: The important République Métro station is near all hotels listed, and is served by five different lines that provide direct service to much of Paris, including the Marais (Mo: Bastille and Hôtel de Ville), rue Cler (Mo: Ecole Militaire), Pompidou Center, the Opéra Garnier, the Champs-Elysées (Mo: F. Roosevelt), the Eiffel Tower (Mo: Trocadéro), Père Lachaise Cemetery, and the Austerlitz, Est, and Nord train stations.

Bus Routes: Bus #65 connects place de la République with the Marais and Gare de Lyon via the rue du Temple, and the Nord and Est train stations along boulevard de Magenta.

Near Oberkampf Métro Station

These hotels cluster near each other. The best budget values line rue Malte between avenue de la République and boulevard Voltaire. The Oberkampf Métro station is a bit closer than the République one.

Hotels and Restaurants near Canal St. Martin

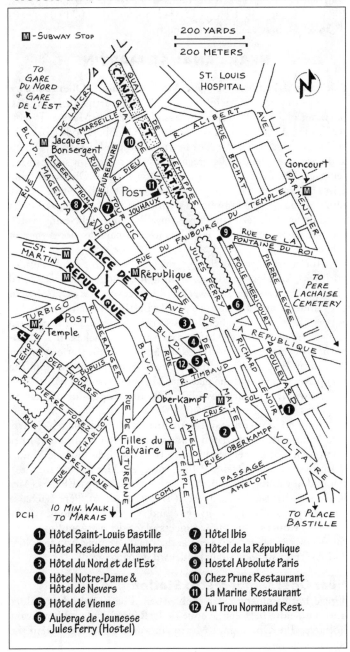

❶ Hôtel Saint-Louis Bastille
❷ Hôtel Residence Alhambra
❸ Hôtel du Nord et de l'Est
❹ Hôtel Notre-Dame & Hôtel de Nevers
❺ Hôtel de Vienne
❻ Auberge de Jeunesse Jules Ferry (Hostel)
❼ Hôtel Ibis
❽ Hôtel de la République
❾ Hostel Absolute Paris
❿ Chez Prune Restaurant
⓫ La Marine Restaurant
⓬ Au Trou Normand Rest.

$$ Hôtel Saint-Louis Bastille*** is a very sharp boutique hotel with a welcoming, wood-beamed lobby, light stone floors throughout, and carefully selected furnishings. It's situated across from the canal parkway (Sb-€80, Db-€100–120, Tb-€135, 114 boulevard Richard Lenoir, Mo: Oberkampf, tel. 01 43 38 29 29, fax 01 43 38 03 18, www.saintlouisbastille.com, slbastille@noos.fr).

$ Hôtel Residence Alhambra** is well-run and a good value, with a big (by Paris standards) leafy courtyard with tables. The room decor is plain and the lobby is spacious (Sb-€64, Db-€71–76, Tb-€87–107, Qb-€122, no air-con, 13 rue de Malte, tel. 01 47 00 35 52, fax 01 43 57 98 75, www.hotelalhambra.fr, info@hotelalhambra.fr).

$ Hôtel du Nord et de l'Est** makes me feel good when I enter (thanks to its spacious, warm lobby)—and even better when I see the rates. About half of its 46 rooms are sharp, with plush carpet, firm beds, and air-conditioning. The other rooms—€10 cheaper—are more basic, with no air-conditioning (Db-€75–85, extra bed-€20, 49 rue de Malte, tel. 01 47 00 71 00, fax 01 43 57 51 16, www.hotel-nord-est.com, info@hotel-nord-est.com).

$ Hôtel Notre-Dame** is modern and a fair value (Ss-€45–53, Sb-€61, Db-€73, Tb-€86) 51 rue Malte, tel. 01 47 00 78 76, fax 01 43 55 32 31, www.hotel-notredame.com, notredame@hotel-notredame.com).

$ Hôtel de Nevers* might be the best budget deal in Paris, and reminds me of how all hotels used to be. It's a vintage, Old World, one-star place with smiling Sophie and her cats, Misty and Lea, ready to greet you (S-€32, Sb-€40, D-€35–45, Db-€50–55, Tb-€78, 53 rue de Malte, tel. 01 47 00 56 18, fax 01 43 57 77 39, www.hoteldenevers.com, reservation@hoteldenevers.com).

$ Hôtel de Vienne*, a throwback to the bathroom-down-the-hall days, is ideal for backpackers (S-€28, D-€33, Ds-€42, Db-€47, tel. 01 48 05 44 42, fax 01 48 05 44 26, www.hoteldevienne.com, hoteldevienne@aol.com).

$ Auberge de Jeunesse Jules Ferry is a fun youth hostel that accepts no reservations—arrive before 10:00 to be assured a room (€20 per bunk in a sink-equipped rooms of 2, 4, or 6 people; more for non-members, rooms closed 10:00–14:00, 8 boulevard Jules Ferry, tel. 01 43 57 55 60, fax 01 40 14 82 09, www.fuaj.fr).

Near the Canal and Place de la République

To find these hotels from place de la République, walk toward boulevard de Magenta and turn right on rue Léon Jouhaux. Use the République Métro stop.

$ Hôtel Ibis**, barely off the place de la République toward the canal, is a cheery if less personal value, with air-conditioning and white rooms in need of new paint (Db-€84, €74 Fri–Sun, extra

bed-€10, 9 rue Léon Jouhaux, tel. 01 42 40 40 50, fax 01 42 40 11 12, h0751@accor.com).

$ Hôtel de la République**, a block toward the canal from the place de la République, is well-run. Rooms are sufficiently comfortable, with good natural light, showers instead of baths, and small balconies on the fifth floor (Sb-€50–61, Db-€60–71, Tb-€70–81, includes buffet breakfast with this book in 2006, 31 rue Albert Thomas, Mo: République, tel. 01 42 39 19 03, fax 01 42 39 22 66, www.republiquehotel.com).

$ Hostel Absolute Paris is part two-star hotel, part four-beds-per-room hostel. It's in the thick of this lively area, facing the canal and filled with backpackers. The rooms are industrial-strength clean and adequately comfortable—only worth considering for dorm-style accommodations (€23 each in 4-bed room with private bathroom, Db-€85, Tb-€100, includes breakfast, 1 rue de la Fontaine du Roi, tel. 01 47 00 47 00, fax 01 47 00 47 02, www.absolute-paris.com).

FOR LONGER STAYS

Staying a week or longer? Consider the advantages that come with renting a furnished apartment. Complete with a small, equipped kitchen and living room, this option is also great for families on shorter visits. Among the many English-speaking organizations ready to help, the following have proven most reliable. Their Web sites are generally excellent and essential to understanding your options. Read the conditions of rental carefully.

The agencies listed below are middlemen, offering an ever-changing selection of private apartments for rent on a weekly basis (or longer). If staying a month or longer, save money by renting directly from the apartment owners. Check out the housing section in the ad paper *France-U.S.A. Contacts* (available at the American Church and elsewhere in Paris) or check out www.fusac.fr.

Paris Appartements Services rents studios (€92–152/night) and one-bedroom apartments (€134–214/night) in central neighborhoods (2 rue d'Argout, tel. 01 40 28 01 28, fax 01 40 28 92 01, www.paris-apts.fr).

Home Rental Service has been in business for 14 years and offers a big selection of apartments throughout Paris with no agency fees (120 Champs-Elysées, tel. 01 42 25 65 40, www.homerental.fr).

Locaflat offers accommodations ranging from studios to five-room apartments (63 avenue de la Motte-Picquet, tel. 01 43 06 78 79, fax 01 40 56 99 69, www.locaflat.com).

Immo Marais has over 100 apartments in all sizes in the Marais (60 rue Roi de Sicile, tel. 01 42 74 06 17, www.immomarais.fr).

Paris Perfect is a French-owned, London-based business that seeks the "perfect apartment" for its clients and is selective about what they offer. All apartments are named for wines, and their service gets good reviews (to reach their British tel. & fax from the U.S., dial tel. 011 44 20 79 38 29 39, fax 011 44 20 79 37 21 15, www.parisperfect.com).

EATING

The Parisian eating scene is kept at a rolling boil. Entire books (and lives) are dedicated to the subject. Paris is France's wine and cuisine melting pot. While it lacks a style of its own (only French onion soup is truly Parisian), it draws from the best of France. Paris could hold a gourmets' Olympics and import nothing.

Parisians eat long and well. Relaxed lunches, three-hour dinners, and endless hours of sitting in outdoor cafés are the norm. Local cafés, cuisine, and wines become a highlight of any Parisian adventure—sightseeing for your palate. Even if the rest of you is sleeping in a cheap hotel, let your taste buds travel first-class in Paris. (They can go coach in London.)

You can eat well without going broke, but choose carefully—you're just as likely to blow a small fortune on a mediocre meal as you are to dine wonderfully for €20. Follow the suggestions offered below, and you'll have a better dining experience.

Breakfast

Petit déjeuner (puh-tee day-zhuh-nay) is typically *café au lait,* hot chocolate, or tea; a roll with butter and marmalade; and a croissant—though more hotels are starting to provide breakfast buffets with juice, fruit, cereal, yogurt, and cheese (usually for a few extra euros, and well worth it). While breakfasts are available at your hotel (about €8–14), they're cheaper at corner cafés (but no coffee refills; see also "Café Culture," below). It's fine to buy a croissant or roll at a bakery and eat it with your cup of coffee at a café. Better still, some bakeries offer worthwhile breakfast deals with juice, croissant, and coffee or tea for about €3 (consider the chain of bakeries called La Brioche Dorée). If the urge for an egg in the morning gets the best of you, drop into a café and order *une omelette* or

oeufs sur le plat (fried eggs). You could also buy or bring from home plastic bowls and spoons, buy a box of cereal and a small box of milk, and eat in your room before heading out for coffee.

Picnics and Snacks

Great for lunch or dinner, Parisian picnics can be first-class affairs and adventures in high cuisine. Be daring. Try the smelly cheeses, ugly pâtés, sissy quiches, and minuscule (usually drink-able) yogurts. Local shopkeepers are accustomed to selling small quantities of produce. Try the tasty salads to go and ask for *une fourchette en plastique* (a plastic fork).

Gather supplies early for a picnic lunch; you'll probably visit several small stores to assemble a complete meal, and many close at noon. Look for a *boulangerie* (bakery), a *crémerie* or *fromagerie* (cheeses), a *charcuterie* (deli items, meats, and pâtés), an *épicerie* or *magasin d'alimentation* (small grocery store with veggies, drinks, and so on), and a *pâtisserie* (delicious pastries). For fine picnic shopping, check out the street market recommendations in the Shopping chapter. While wine is taboo in public places in the U.S., it's *pas de problème* in France.

Supermarchés offer less color and cost, more efficiency, and adequate quality. Department stores often have supermarkets in the basement, along with top-floor cafeterias offering not-really-cheap but low-risk, low-stress, what-you-see-is-what-you-get meals. For a quick meal to go, look for food stands and bakeries selling takeout sandwiches and drinks. For an affordable sit-down meal, try a *crêperie* or café.

In stores, unrefrigerated soft drinks and beer are half the price of cold drinks. Milk and boxed fruit juice are the most inexpensive drinks. Avoid buying drinks to go at streetside stands; you'll find them far cheaper in a shop. Try to keep a water bottle with you. Water quenches your thirst better and cheaper than anything you'll find in a store or café. I drink tap water in Paris and use that to refill my bottle. You'll pass many fountains on Paris streets with good water (but if it says *non potable*, it's not drinkable).

For good lunch picnic sites, consider these suggestions. The Palais Royal (across place du Palais Royal from the Louvre) is a good spot for a peaceful, royal picnic, as is the little triangular Henry IV park on the west tip of Ile de la Cité. The pedestrian pont des Arts bridge, across from the Louvre, has great views and plen-tiful benches, as does the Champ de Mars park below the Eiffel Tower. For great people-watching, try the Pompidou Center (by the *Homage to Stravinsky* fountains), the elegant place des Vosges (closes at dusk), the gardens behind Les Invalides and surrounding the Rodin Museum, and the Tuileries and Luxembourg Gardens.

Café Culture

French cafés (or brasseries) provide budget-friendly meals and a relief from museum and church overload. Feel free to order only a bowl of soup and a salad or *plat* (main course) for lunch or dinner at a café.

Cafés generally open by 7:00, but closing hours vary. Unlike restaurants, which open only for lunch and dinner, meals are served throughout the day at most cafés—making them the best option for a late lunch or an early dinner.

It's easier for the novice to sit and feel comfortable when you know the system. Check the price list first, which by law must be posted prominently. You'll see two sets of prices; you'll pay more for the same drink if you're seated at a table *(salle)* than if you're seated at the bar or counter *(comptoir)*. At large cafés, outside tables are most expensive, and prices can rise after 22:00.

Your waiter probably won't overwhelm you with friendliness. Notice how hard they work. They almost never stop. Cozying up to clients (French or foreign) is probably the last thing on their minds.

Standard Menu Items: *Croque monsieur* (grilled ham and cheese sandwich) and *croque madame* (*monsieur* with a fried egg on top) are generally served day and night. Sandwiches are least expensive, but plain—and much better—at the *boulangerie* (bakery). To get more than a piece of ham *(jambon)* on a baguette, order a sandwich *jambon crudité*, which means garnished with veggies. Omelettes come lonely on a plate with a basket of bread. The daily special—*plat du jour* (plah dew zhoor), or just *plat*—is your fast, hearty hot plate for €10–16. Regardless of what you order, bread is free; to get more, just hold up your bread basket and ask, *"Encore, s'il vous plaît."*

Salads: I order salads for lunch and for lighter dinners. They're typically large—one is perfect for lunch or a light dinner, or split between two people as a first course. Among the classics are *salade niçoise* (nee-swaz), a specialty from Nice that typically includes green salad topped with green beans, boiled potatoes (sometimes rice), tomatoes (sometimes corn), anchovies, olives, hard-boiled eggs, and lots of tuna; *salade au chèvre chaud,* a mixed green salad topped with warm goat cheese and toasted bread croutons; and *salade composée,* "composed" of any number of ingredients, such as *lardons* (bacon), *comte* (a Swiss-style cheese), *roquefort* (blue cheese), *œuf* (egg), *noix* (walnuts), *jambon* (ham, generally thinly sliced), *saumon fumé* (smoked salmon), and the highly suspect *gesiers* (chicken livers). To get salad dressing on the side, order *la sauce à part* (lah sohs ah par).

Wine and Beer: House wine at the bar is cheap (about €3 per glass, cheapest by the pitcher—*pichet*, pee-shay), and the local

Coffee and Tea Lingo

By law, the waiter must give you a glass of tap water with your coffee or tea if you request it; ask for *"un verre d'eau, s'il vous plaît"* (uhn vayr doh, see voo play).

Coffee

French	Pronounced	English
un express	uh nex-press	shot of espresso
une noisette	oon nwah-zeht	espresso with a shot of milk
café au lait	kah-fay oh lay	coffee with lots of steamed milk (closest to an American latte)
un grand crème	uhn grahn krehm	big café au lait
un petit crème	uhn puh-tee	small café au lait
un grand café noir	uhn grahn kah-fay nwahr	cup of black coffee, closest to American-style
un décaffiné	uhn day-kah-fee-nay	decaf—available in any of the above drinks

Tea

French	Pronounced	English
un thé nature	uhn tay nah-tour	plain tea
un thé au lait	uhn tay oh lay	tea with milk
un thé citron	uhn tay see-trohn	tea with lemon
une infusion	oon an-few-see-yohn	herbal tea

beer is cheaper on tap (*une pression;* oon pres-yohn) than in the bottle (*bouteille;* boo-teh-ee). France's best beer is Alsatian; try Kronenbourg or the heavier Pelfort (even heavier is the Belgian beer Leffe). *Une panaché* (oon pan-a-shay) is a refreshing French shandy (7-Up and beer). For a fun, bright, nonalcoholic drink of 7-Up with mint syrup, order *un diablo menthe* (uhn dee-ah-bloh mahnt). Kids love the local lemonade (*citron pressé;* see-trohn preh-say, you'll need to add sugar) and the flavored syrups mixed with bottled water (*sirops à l'eau;* see-roh ah loh). The ice cubes melted after the last Yankee tour group left.

Tipping

Virtually all cafés and restaurants include a service charge in the bill (usually 15 percent, referred to as *service compris* or *prix net*),

but it's polite to round up for a drink or meal well-served. This bonus tip is usually about 5 percent of the bill (e.g., if your bill is €19, leave €20). In the rare instance that service is not included (the menu states *service non compris*), tip 15 percent. When you hand your payment plus a tip to your waiter, you can say, "*C'est bon*" (say bohn), meaning, "It's good." If you order your food at a counter, don't tip.

Restaurants

Choose restaurants filled with locals, not places with big neon signs boasting *We Speak English*. Consider your hotelier's opinion. If a restaurant doesn't post its prices outside, move along.

Restaurants open for dinner around 19:00, and small local favorites get crowded after 21:00. To minimize smoke and crowds, go early (around 19:30). Many restaurants close Sunday and Monday.

If a restaurant serves lunch, it generally begins at 11:30 and goes until 14:00, with last orders taken at about 13:30. If you're hungry when restaurants are closed (late afternoon), go to a café; most serve all day.

If you ask for the *menu* (muh-noo) at a restaurant, you won't get a list of dishes; you'll get a fixed-price meal. *Menus* (also called *formules*), which include three or four courses, are generally a good value if you're hungry: You get your choice of soup, appetizer, or salad; your choice of three or four main courses with vegetables; plus a cheese course and/or a choice of desserts. Service is included (*service compris* or *prix net*), but wine and other drinks are generally extra. Restaurants that offer a *menu* for lunch often charge about €5 more for the same *menu* at dinner.

Ask for *la carte* if you want to see a menu and order à la carte, like the locals do. Request the waiter's help in deciphering the French. Go with his or her recommendations and anything *de la maison* (of the house), as long as it's not an organ meat *(tripes, rognons, andouillette)*. Galloping gourmets should bring a menu translator; the *Marling Menu-Master* is good. The *Rick Steves' French Phrase Book,* with a Menu Decoder, works well for most travelers. The wines are often listed in a separate *carte des vins*.

In France, an *entrée* is the appetizer. *Le plat* or *le plat du jour* (plate of the day) is the main course with vegetables (usually €10–16). If all you want is a salad or soup find a café instead.

Parisians are willing to pay for bottled water with their meal (*eau minérale;* oh mee-nay-rahl) because they prefer the taste over tap water. If you prefer a free pitcher of tap water, ask for *une carafe d'eau* (oon kah-rahf doh). Otherwise, you may unwittingly buy bottled water. To get inexpensive wine at a restaurant, order table wine in a pitcher (*un pichet;* uhn pee-shay), rather than a bottle

Why French Women Don't Get Fat

Americans are recognized by their large rear ends. And French women just don't get fat. At least those are the popular images. If it's true that French women aren't fat, the reason is lifestyle and what is—to them—common sense: They eat small quantities. Rather than snack, they smoke. They avoid processed food and fast food. They drink lots of water. Their lifestyle—less time in cars and in front of TVs—just naturally includes lots of exercise. And they fall in love with abandon.

But recently the French have measured a 20 percent increase in obesity, especially among children. The government has begun a propaganda campaign to promote eating fruit and vegetables. And, in a bold move, they're taking vending machines out of schools.

(though finer restaurants usually offer only bottles of wine). If all you want is a glass of wine, ask for *un verre de vin* (uhn vehr duh van). A half carafe of wine is *un demi-pichet* (uhn duh-mee pee-shay), a quarter carafe (ideal for one) is *un quart* (uhn kar).

To get a waiter's attention, simply say, *"S'il vous plaît"* (see voo play)—please.

PARISIAN CUISINE

There is no "Parisian cuisine" to speak of. The principal advantage of dining in Paris is that you can sample fine cuisine from throughout France. Many restaurants specialize in a particular region's cuisine (I list restaurants specializing in food from Provence, Burgundy, Alsace, Normandy, Dordogne, Languedoc, and the Basque region). So be a galloping gourmet and try a few of these regional restaurants (see "French Specialties by Region," page 344).

The French eat dinner in courses, rather than all on one plate. For general, classic, anywhere-in-France dishes, consider these suggestions:

First Course *(Entrée)*
Soupe à l'oignon: Hot, salty, and filling, French onion soup is a beef broth served with cheesy bread croutons floating on top.
Salade au chèvre chaud: A mixed green salad topped with warmed goat cheese and croutons.
Salade niçoise: While famous as a specialty from Nice, in southern France, this classic salad is served throughout the country. There are many versions, though most include a base of green salad topped with green beans, boiled potatoes (sometimes rice),

French Specialties by Region

Alsace
The German influence is obvious: sausages, potatoes, onions, and sauerkraut. Look for *choucroute garnie* (sauerkraut and sausage—although it seems a shame to eat it in a fancy restaurant), the more traditionally Alsatian *baeckeoffe* (potato, meat, and onion stew), *rösti* (an oven-baked potato-and-cheese dish), fresh trout, and *foie gras*.

Burgundy
Considered by many to be France's best, Burgundian cuisine is peasant cooking elevated to an art. This wine region excels in *coq au vin* (chicken with wine sauce), *bœuf bourguinonne* (beef stew cooked with wine, bacon, onions, and mushrooms), *œufs en meurette* (eggs poached in red wine), *escargots* (snails), and *jambon persillé* (ham with garlic and parsley).

Basque
Mixing influences from the mountains, sea, Spain, and France, it's dominated by seafood, tomatoes, and red peppers. Look for anything *basquaise* (cooked with tomatoes, eggplant, red peppers, and garlic), such as *thon* (tuna) or *poulet* (chicken). Try *piperade,* a dish combining peppers, tomatoes, garlic, and eggs (ham optional), and *ttoro,* a seafood stew that is the Basque answer to bouillabaisse.

Languedoc and Périgord
The cuisine of these regions is referred to in Paris as "Southwest cuisine" *(cuisine du sudouest).* This hearty peasant cooking uses full-bodied red wines and lots of duck. Try the hearty *cassoulet* (white bean, duck, and sausage stew), *canard* (duck), *pâté de foie*

tomatoes, anchovies, lots of tuna, and hard-boiled eggs.

Crudités: A mix of raw and lightly cooked, fresh vegetables, usually including grated carrots, celery root, tomatoes, and beets, often with a hefty dose of vinaigrette dressing. If you want the dressing on the side, say, *"La sauce à côté, s'il vous plaît"* (lah sohs ah koh-tay see voo play).

Escargots: Snails cooked in parsley-garlic butter. You don't even have to like the snail itself. Just dipping your bread in garlic butter is more than satisfying. Prepared a variety of ways, the classic is *à la bourguignonne* (served in their shells).

Huîtres: Oysters served raw any month and delivered fresh from nearby Brittany. This food is particularly popular at Christmas and New Year's, when every café seems to have overflowing baskets lining the storefront.

gras (goose liver pâté), *pommes sarladaise* (potatoes fried in duck fat), *truffes* (truffles, earthy mushrooms), and anything with *noix* (walnuts).

Normandy and Brittany
Normandy specializes in cream sauces, organ meats (sweetbreads, tripe, and kidneys—the "gizzard salads" are great), and seafood *(fruits de mer)*. Dairy products are big here. Munch some *moules* (mussels) and *escalope normande* (veal in cream sauce). Brittany is famous for its oysters and crêpes. Both regions use lots of *cidre* (hard apple cider) in their cuisine.

Provence
The almost extravagant use of garlic, olive oil, herbs, and tomatoes makes Provence cuisine France's liveliest. To sample it, order anything *à la provençale*. Among the area's spicy specialties are *ratatouille* (a thick mixture of vegetables in an herb-flavored tomato sauce), *brandade* (a salt cod, garlic, and cream mousse), *aioli* (a garlicky mayonnaise often served atop fresh vegetables), *tapenade* (a paste of puréed olives, capers, anchovies, herbs, and sometimes tuna), *soupe au pistou* (vegetable soup with basil, garlic, and cheese), and *soupe à l'ail* (garlic soup).

Riviera
The Côte d'Azur gives Provence's cuisine a Mediterranean flair. Local specialties are bouillabaisse (the spicy seafood stew/soup that seems worth the cost only for those with a seafood fetish), *bourride* (a creamy fish soup thickened with aioli garlic sauce), and *salade niçoise* (nee-swaz; a tasty tomato, potato, olive, anchovy, and tuna salad).

Pâtés and *Terrines:* Slowly cooked ground meat (usually pork, though chicken and rabbit are also common) that is highly seasoned and served in slices with mustard and *cornichons* (little pickles). Pâtés are smoother than the similarly prepared but more chunky *terrines*.

Foie gras: Rich and buttery in consistency, this pâté is made from the swollen livers of force-fed geese (or ducks, in *foie de canard*). Spread it on bread with your knife, and do not add mustard to this pâté dish.

Main Course *(Plat Principal)*
Coq au vin: This Burgundian dish is chicken marinated ever so slowly in red wine, then cooked until it melts in your mouth. It's served (often family-style) with vegetables.

Bœuf bourguinonne: Another Burgundian specialty, this classy beef stew is cooked slowly in red wine, then served with onions, potatoes, and mushrooms.

Steak: Referred to as *pavé, bavette,* or *entrecôte,* French steak is usually thinner than American steak and is always served with sauces (*au poivre* is a pepper sauce, *une sauce roquefort* is a cheese sauce). By American standards, the French undercook meats: rare, or *saignant* (seh-nyahn) is close to raw; medium, or *à point* (ah pwan) is rare; and well-done, or *bien cuit* (bee-yehn kwee) is medium.

Steak tartare: This wonderfully French dish is for adventurous types only. It's very lean, raw hamburger served with spices (usually Tabasco, onions, salt, and pepper on the side) and topped with a raw egg.

Gigot d'agneau: Leg of lamb served in many styles, often with white beans. The best lamb is *pré salé,* which means the lamb has been raised in salt-marsh lands (like at Mont St. Michel).

Confit de canard: This Southwest favorite is duck that has been preserved in its own fat, then cooked in its fat, and often served with potatoes cooked in the same fat. Not for dieters.

Saumon: You'll see salmon dishes served in various styles. The salmon usually comes from the North Sea and is always served with sauce, most commonly a sorrel *(oseille)* sauce.

Cheese Course *(Le Fromage)*

In France, the cheese course is served just before (or instead of) dessert. It not only helps with digestion, it gives you a great opportunity to sample the tasty regional cheeses. There are more than 400 different French cheeses to try. Many restaurants will offer a cheese platter, from which you select a few different cheeses. A good cheese plate has four types: hard cheese (like Emmentaler—a.k.a. Swiss cheese), a flowery cheese (like Brie or Camembert), a bleu or Roquefort cheese, and a goat cheese.

Cheeses most commonly served in Paris are *brie de Meaux* (mild and creamy, from just outside Paris), Camembert (semi-creamy and pungent, from Normandy), *chèvre* (goat cheese with a sharp taste, usually from the Loire), and Roquefort (strong and blue-veined, from south-central France).

If you'd like a little of several types of cheese from the cheese plate, say, *"Un assortiment, s'il vous plaît"* (uhn ah-sor-tee-mahn, see voo play). If you serve yourself from the cheese plate, observe French etiquette and keep the shape of the cheese. To avoid being gauche, politely shave off a slice from the side or cut small wedges.

Dessert *(Le Dessert)*

If you order espresso, it will always come after dessert. To have coffee with dessert, ask for *"café avec le dessert"* (kah-fay ah-vehk

---

Restaurant Price Code

To help you choose among these listings, I've divided the restaurants into three categories, based on the price for a typical meal without wine.

$$$ **Higher Priced**—Most meals €35 or more.
 $$ **Moderately Priced**—Most meals between €20–35.
  $ **Lower Priced**—Most meals under €20.

---

luh day-sayr). See the list of coffee terms on page 341.

Crème brulée: A rich, creamy, dense, caramelized custard.

Tarte tatin: This is apple pie like grandma never made, with caramelized apples cooked upside down, but served upright.

Mousse au chocolat: Chocolate mousse.

Ile flottante: This lighter dessert consists of islands of meringue floating on a pond of custard sauce.

Profiteroles: Cream puffs filled with vanilla ice cream, smothered in warm chocolate sauce.

Tartes: Narrow strips of fresh fruit, baked in a crust and served in thin slices (without ice cream).

Sorbets: Known to us as sherbets, these light, flavorful, and fruity ices are sometimes laced with brandy.

RESTAURANTS

My recommendations are centered around the same great neighborhoods listed in the Sleeping chapter; you can come home exhausted after a busy day of sightseeing and find a good selection of restaurants right around the corner. And evening is a fine time to explore any of these delightful neighborhoods, even if you're sleeping elsewhere.

To save piles of euros, review the budget eating tips above and restaurant recommendations below. Remember that service is almost always included (so little or no tipping is required), and consider dinner picnics (great take-out dishes available at *charcuteries*).

Rue Cler Neighborhood

The rue Cler neighborhood caters to its residents. Its eateries, while not destination places, have an intimate charm. My favorites are small mom-and-pop eateries that love to serve traditional French food at good prices to a local clientele. You'll generally find great dinner *menus* for €20–30 and *plats du jour* for around €12–16. Eat early with tourists or late with locals. For all restaurants listed in

this area, use the Ecole Militaire Métro stop (unless another station is listed).

Close to Ecole Militaire, Between Rue de la Motte Picquet and Rue de Grenelle

$$$ Café de l'Esplanade is your opportunity to be surrounded by chic, yet older and sophisticated Parisians enjoying top-notch traditional cuisine as foreplay. There's not a tourist in sight. It has a sprawling floor plan: Half its tables (with well-stuffed chairs) fill a plush, living-room-like interior, and the other half are lined up outside under its elegant awning facing the grand Esplanade des Invalides in front of Napoleon's Tomb. Dress competitively, as this is *the* place to be seen in the 7th *arrondissement* (€20 *plats du jour*, €45 plus wine for dinner, open daily, reserve ahead—especially if you want a curbside table, non-smoking room in the back, 52 rue Fabert, Mo: La Tour-Maubourg, tel. 01 47 05 38 80). This is the only actual business on the entire esplanade that stretches all the way to the Champs-Elysées.

✓ $$$ Léo le Lion—small, softly lit, and traditional, with velvet booths—is well respected by locals for both fish and meat. The plush interior feels like a marionette theater (€20 *plats*, closed Sun, 23 rue Duvivier, tel. 01 45 51 41 77).

✓ $$$ Restaurant Pasco is perched elegantly overlooking Les Invalides. While chic and sophisticated, it feels accessible to the tourist. Pasco Vignes is popular with locals for his modern Mediterranean cuisine, generously endowed with olive oil (€12–20 *plats*, closed Mon, 74 boulevard de la Tour-Maubourg, Mo: La Tour-Maubourg, tel. 01 44 18 33 26).

$$ Le Florimond is ideal for a special occasion. The ambience, while spacious and quiet, is also intimate and welcoming. Locals come for classic French cuisine with elegant indoor or breezy streetside seating. Friendly English-speaking Laurent—with his playful ties changing daily—will take good care of you (€32 *menu*, closed Sun, good and reasonable wine selection and explosively tasty stuffed cabbage, reservations smart, non-smoking, 19 avenue de la Motte Picquet, tel. 01 45 55 40 38).

$$ Thoumieux, the neighborhood's classy, traditional Parisian brasserie, is a popular local institution. It's big and white-tablecloth dressy, with formal, no-nonsense waiters. As the owner is from southwest France, much of the menu is as well (€15 lunch *menu*, 3-course €33 dinner *menu* includes wine, open daily, 79 rue St. Dominique, Mo: La Tour-Maubourg, tel. 01 47 05 49 75). They open at 18:30, and head waiter Pascal advises making a reservation if arriving after 20:00.

$$ La Terrasse du 7ème is a sprawling, happening café with classic outdoor seating and a living-room-like interior with comfy

love seats. Located on a corner, it overlooks a grand and busy intersection with a constant parade of people marching by. A meal here is like dinner theater—and the show is slice-of-life Paris (no fixed-price *menu*, great *salade niçoise*, open daily until 2:00 in the morning, at Ecole Militaire Métro stop, tel. 01 45 55 00 02).

$$ Le Petit Niçois (literally, "The Little Nice") feels *très* Mediterranean, from its warm colors to its menu selections. This is where rue Cler natives go for their southern seafood fix (€24 *menu*, open daily, 10 rue Amélie, tel. 01 45 51 83 65).

$ Café du Marché boasts the best seats, coffee, and prices on rue Cler. The owner's philosophy: Brasserie on speed—crank out great food at great prices to trendy locals and savvy tourists. It's high-energy, with waiters who barely have time to smile...*très* Parisian. This place is ideal if you want a light lunch or dinner (good, hearty €10 salads) or a more substantial but simple meal (filling €11 *plats du jour*, listed on chalkboard; open Mon–Sat 11:00–23:00, Sun 11:00–17:00, arrive before 19:30 for dinner—it's packed at 21:00, can be smoky, at the corner of rue Cler and rue du Champ de Mars, at 38 rue Cler, tel. 01 47 05 51 27). Their new **Tribeca Restaurant**, next door, offers similar value but more space, a calmer ambience, more patient service, and a menu focusing on pizza and Italian cuisine.

$ Ulysée en Gaule, in a prime location right on rue Cler, offers good, cheap, front-row seats for the people-watching fun. The Ulysée family—Stephanos, Chrysa, and their English-speaking son, Vassilis—seem to make friends with all who drop by for a bite. The family loves to serve Greek dishes, and their excellent crêpes (to go or sit down for €2 extra) are your cheapest rue Cler hot meal (daily 8:00 arrive before 19:3022:30, 28 rue Cler, tel. 01 47 05 61 82).

$ Petite Brasserie PTT is a classic time warp, popular with postal workers and offering traditional café fare at reasonable prices next to the PTT (post office) on rue Cler. They offer a great *deux pour douze* breakfast deal for Rick Steves readers: two American breakfasts (normally €8 each) for €12 total (closed Sun, opposite 53 rue Cler).

$ Café le Bosquet is a vintage Parisian brasserie with dressy waiters and a classic interior or sidewalk tables on a busy street. Come here for a bowl of French onion soup, a salad, or a three-course *menu* (€18), and mix it up with waiters Daniel, Nina, and Antoine (closed Sun, many choices—including vegetarian options—from a fun menu, the house red wine is plenty good, reservations smart on weekends, corner of rue du Champ de Mars and avenue Bosquet, at 46 avenue Bosquet, tel. 01 45 51 38 13).

Rue Cler Restaurants

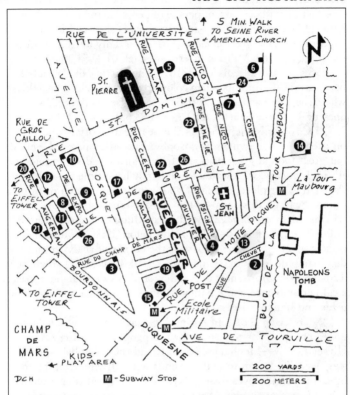

RUE DE L'UNIVERSITE
5 MIN. WALK
TO SEINE RIVER
+ AMERICAN CHURCH
N

ST. PIERRE
RUE MALAR
RUE NICOT
DOMINIQUE
COMTE
TOUR MAUBOURG
AVENUE
ST.
RUE CLER
RUE AMELIE
RUE NICOT
RUE DE GROS CAILLOU
RUE
DE BOSQUET
RUE DE L'EXPO
GRENELLE
ST. JEAN
La Tour-Maubourg
TO EIFFEL TOWER
RUE AUGEREAU
RUE VALADON
RUE CLER
R. DUVIVIER
R. PSICHARI
LA MOTTE PICQUET
RUE
A. BOURDONNAIS
RUE DU CHAMP
DE MARS
CHEVET
RUE DE LA
BLVD. DE
NAPOLEON'S TOMB
TO EIFFEL TOWER
POST
Ecole Militaire
CHAMP DE MARS
KIDS' PLAY AREA
DUQUESNE
AVE DE TOURVILLE

DCH   M – SUBWAY STOP

200 YARDS
200 METERS

1. Café du Marché & Tribeca Rest.
2. Restaurant Pasco
3. Café le Bosquet
4. Léo le Lion
5. L'Affriolé & L'Ami Jean
6. Au Petit Tonneau
7. Brasserie Thoumieux
8. Le P'tit Troquet
9. Restaurant la Serre
10. La Fontaine de Mars
11. La Varangue
12. Chez Agnès
13. Le Florimond
14. Café de l'Esplanade
15. La Terrasse du 7ème
16. Ulysée en Gaule
17. Real McCoy
18. Pourjauran Bakery
19. Petite Brasserie PTT
20. Café Constant
21. La Gourmandise Pizzeria
22. Café la Roussillon
23. Le Petit Niçois
24. O'Brien's Pub
25. Lenôtre Deli
26. Late-Night Groceries (2)

Between Rue de Grenelle and the River

$$$ Altitude 95 is in the Eiffel Tower, 95 meters (about 300 feet) above the ground (€21–31 lunches, €50 dinners, dinner seatings nightly at 19:00 and 21:00, reserve well ahead for a view table; before you ascend to dine, drop by the booth between the north/ *nord* and east/*est* pillars to buy your Eiffel Tower ticket and pick up a pass that enables you to skip the line; Mo: Bir-Hakeim or Trocadéro, RER: Champ de Mars-Tour Eiffel, tel. 01 45 55 20 04, fax 01 47 05 94 40).

$$$ L'Affriolé is a small, trendy eatery where you'll compete with young professionals to get a table. Stepping into this elegant but rollicking dining hall, you immediately feel you're eating at a restaurant well-deserving of its rave reviews. Menu selections change daily, and the wine list is extensive, with some good bargains (€35 *menu*, closed Sun–Mon, 17 rue Malar, Mo: La Tour-Maubourg, tel. 01 44 18 31 33).

$$$ Au Petit Tonneau is a souvenir of old Paris. Fun-loving owner-chef Madame Boyer prepares everything herself, wearing her tall chef's hat like a crown as she rules from her family-style kitchen. The small, plain dining room doesn't look like it's changed in the 25 years she's been in charge. Her steaks and lamb are excellent (€28 for 2 courses, €35 3-course *menu*, open daily, can get smoky—come early, 20 rue Surcouf, Mo: La Tour-Maubourg, tel. 01 47 05 09 01).

$$$ La Fontaine de Mars is a longtime favorite for locals, charmingly situated on a classic, tiny Parisian street and jumbled square. It's a happening scene, with tables jammed together for the serious business of good eating. Reserve a table on the ground floor in advance, or risk eating in the non-smoking room upstairs without the fun street-level ambience (€25 *plats*, open nightly, where rue de l'Exposition and rue St. Dominique meet, at 129 rue St. Dominique, tel. 01 47 05 46 44).

$$ Le P'tit Troquet, a petite eatery taking you back to the Paris of the 1920s, is gracefully and earnestly run by Dominique. She's particularly proud of her foie gras and lamb. The delicious, three-course €29.50 *menu* comes with fun, traditional choices. Its delicate charm and gourmet flair make this a favorite of connoisseurs (closed Sun, reservations smart, 28 rue de l'Exposition, tel. 01 47 05 80 39).

$$ Chez Agnès, the smallest of my recommended Paris restaurants, is not for everyone. It's tiny, flowery, family-style, and filled with kisses on the cheek. Eccentric but sincere Agnès (a French-Tahitian Roseanne Barr) does it all—cooking in her minuscule kitchen and serving, too. Agnès, who cooks "French with an exotic twist" and clearly loves her work, makes children feel right at home. Don't come for a quick dinner (€23 *menu*, closed Mon, 1 rue Augereau, tel. 01 45 51 06 04).

$$ L'Ami Jean offers excellent Basque specialties at fair prices. The chef has made his reputation on the quality of his cuisine, not on the dark, simple decor. Arrive by 19:30 or call ahead—by 20:00, there's a line out the door of people waiting to join the shared tables and lively commotion of happy eaters (€15 for a plate of mixed Basque tapas, €28 *menu*, closed Sun–Mon, 27 rue Malar, Mo: La Tour-Maubourg, tel. 01 47 05 86 89).

$ Café Constant is a tiny, mod, two-level place that feels more like a small bistro–wine bar than a café. They serve delicious and reasonably priced dishes (€12 *plats*) in a fun setting to a well-established clientele (closed Sun-Mon, corner of rue Augereau and rue St. Dominique, next to recommended Hotel Londres Eiffel).

$ La Varangue is an entertaining one-man show featuring English-speaking Phillipe, who ran a French catering shop in Pennsylvania for three years. He lives upstairs, and clearly has found his niche serving a mostly American clientele, who are all on a first-name basis. The food is cheap and basic (don't come here for high cuisine), the tables are few, and he opens early (at 17:30). Norman Rockwell would dig his tiny dining room. Try his snails and chocolate cake...but not together (€10 *plats*, €15.20 *menu*, always a vegetarian option, closed Sun, 27 rue Augereau, tel. 01 47 05 51 22).

$ La Gourmandise is a tiny, friendly pizzeria across the street from La Varangue. Its good, cheap pizza is ideal for kids (closed Sun, 28 rue Augereau, tel. 01 45 55 45 16).

$ Restaurant la Serre is reasonably priced and worth considering (€11–15 *plats*, good onion soup and duck specialties, closed Sun–Mon, 29 rue de l'Exposition, tel. 01 45 55 20 96, Margot).

Picnicking

Rue Cler is a moveable feast that gives "fast food" a good name. The entire street is clogged with connoisseurs of good eating. Only the health-food store goes unnoticed. A festival of food, the street is lined with people whose lives seem to be devoted to their specialty: polished produce, rotisserie chicken, crêpes, or cheese.

✪ For a self-guided tour of all the temptations, see the Rue Cler Walk on page 115.

For a magical picnic dinner at the Eiffel Tower, assemble it in no fewer than five shops on rue Cler. Then lounge on the best grass in Paris, with the dogs, Frisbees, a floodlit tower, and a cool breeze in the parc du Champ de Mars.

Asian delis (generically called *Traiteur Asie*) provide tasty, low-stress, low-price takeout treats (€6 dinner plates, the one on rue Cler near rue du Champ de Mars has tables). **Ulysée en Gaule,** the Greek restaurant on rue Cler across from Grand Hôtel Lévêque, sells take-away crêpes (described above). The elegant **Lenotre** *charcuterie* offers mouthwatering meals to go (open daily

until 23:00, at Ecole Militaire Métro stop). **Real McCoy** is a little shop selling American food and sandwiches (closed Sun, 194 rue de Grenelle). There are small **late-night groceries** at 186 and 197 rue de Grenelle (open nightly until midnight).

Breakfast

Hotel breakfasts, while convenient, are generally not a good value. For a great rue Cler start to your day, drop by the **Petite Brasserie PTT** (a 2-min walk from most area hotels, described above), where managers Jerome and Eric promise Rick Steves readers a *deux pour douze* breakfast special (2 "American" breakfasts—juice, coffee, croissant, ham, and eggs—for €12). **Café la Roussillon** serves a good American-style breakfast for €9 (open daily, at corner of rue de Grenelle and rue Cler, tel. 01 45 51 47 53). To eat breakfast while watching Paris go to work, stop by **La Terrasse du 7ème** (described above). The **Pourjauran** bakery, offering great baguettes, hasn't changed in 70 years (20 rue Jean Nicot).

Nightlife

This sleepy neighborhood is not ideal for night owls, but there are a few notable exceptions. **Café du Marché** and **La Terrasse du 7ème** (both listed above) are busy with a Franco-American crowd until at least midnight, as is the flashier **Café la Roussillon** (nightly, corner of rue de Grenelle and rue Cler). **O'Brien's Pub** is a relaxed Parisian rendition of an Irish pub (77 avenue St. Dominique, Mo: La Tour-Maubourg).

Marais Neighborhood

The trendy Marais is filled with locals enjoying good food in colorful and atmospheric eateries. The scene is competitive and changes all the time. I've listed an assortment of eateries—all handy to recommended hotels—that offer good food at reasonable prices, plus a memorable experience. For maximum ambience, go to place des Vosges or place du Marché Ste. Catherine (several restaurants listed below on each of these squares).

On Romantic Place des Vosges

On this square, which offers Old World Marais elegance, you'll find four very different eateries. Enjoy a square stroll around the entire arcade—fun art galleries alternate with enticing restaurants. Choose the restaurant that best fits your mood and budget; each one has perfect arcade seating and provides big space-heaters to make outdoor dining during colder months an option. Also consider a drink or desert on the square at Café Hugo or Nectarine after eating elsewhere. To reach place des Vosges, use the St. Paul or Bastille Métro stations.

$$$ Restaurant Coconnas is the dressiest option, with classic French cuisine, refined ambience, black-suited waiters, and artfully presented gourmet dishes (€30 *plats*, €15 *entrées* and deserts, closed Mon, on the river side of the square at #2, tel. 01 42 78 58 16).

$$$ Ma Bourgogne is a classic old eatery where you'll sit under arcades in a whirlpool of Frenchness, as bowtied and black-aproned waiters serve you traditional Burgundian specialties: steak, *coq au vin*, lots of French fries, escargot, and great red wine. Service at this institution comes with food but few smiles (€32 *menu*, open daily, dinner reservations smart, cash only, at north-west corner at #19, tel. 01 42 78 44 64).

$ Nectarine is small and demure—with a wicker, pastel, and feminine ambience. This peaceful teahouse serves healthy €10 salads, quiches, and €12 *plats du jour* both day and night. Its fun menu lets you mix and match omelets and crêpes. Its huge deserts are split-table, and dropping by here late for sweets and a drink is a peaceful way to end your day (open daily, at #16, tel. 01 42 77 23 78).

$ Café Hugo, named for the square's most famous resident, is best for drinks only, as the cuisine does not live up to its setting (open daily, at #22).

Near the Bastille

To reach these restaurants, use the Bastille Métro stop.

$$ Brasserie Bofinger, an institution for over a century, is famous for fish and traditional cuisine with Alsatian flair. You're surrounded by brisk, black-and-white-attired waiters. The sprawling interior features elaborately decorated rooms reminiscent of the Roaring Twenties. Eating under the grand 1919 *coupole* is a memorable treat (as is using the "historic" 1919 WC downstairs). Check out the boys shucking and stacking seafood platters out front before you enter. Their €33 three-course *menu,* while not top cuisine, includes wine and is a good value. The kids' menu makes this restaurant family-friendly (open daily and nightly, reservations smart, mostly non-smoking, 5 rue de la Bastille, don't be confused by the lesser "Petite" Bofinger across the street, tel. 01 42 72 87 82).

$$ Chez Janou, a Provençal bistro, tumbles out of its corner building and fills its broad sidewalk with happy eaters. At first glance, you know this is a find. Don't let the trendy and youthful crowd intimidate you—it's relaxed and charming, with helpful and patient service. While the curbside tables are inviting, I'd sit inside to immerse myself in the happy commotion. The style is French Mediterranean, with an emphasis on vegetables (€15 *plats du jour* that change with the season, open daily, 2 blocks beyond place des Vosges at 2 rue Roger Verlomme, tel. 01 42 72 28 41). They're proud of their 81 different varieties of *pastis* (licorice-flavored liqueur; €3.50 each, browse the list).

$$ L'Impasse, a relaxed bistro on a quiet alley, serves an enthusiastically French three-course *menu* for €28. Françoise, a former dancer and artist, runs the place *con brio* (closed Sun, 4 impasse de Guémenée, tel. 01 42 72 08 45). Françoise promises anyone with this book a free glass of *byrrh*—it's pronounced "beer," but it's a French port-like drink. The restaurant is next to a self-serve launderette (open nightly until 21:30—clean your clothes while you dine).

$$ Bistrot les Sans Culottes, a zinc-bar classic on lively rue de Lappe, serves traditional French cuisine with a proper respect for fine wine (€24 3-course *menu*, closed Mon, 27 rue de Lappe, tel. 01 48 05 42 92). Stay out past your bedtime. Eat here. Then join the rue de Lappe party.

$ Au Temps des Cerises is a *très* local wine bar. While they serve lunch plates, it's better for an early dinner or a pre-dinner glass of wine. "Dinner" will be limited to bread, dry sausage, cheese, and wine served by goateed Yves and his wife, Michele. A mixed plate of cheese (€3.50), meat (€3.50), and a carafe of good wine (€3–6) surrounded by the intimate and woody, Old World ambience can be a good light meal (Mon–Fri until 20:00, closed Sat–Sun, at rue du Petit-Musc and rue de la Cerisaie).

$ Vins des Pyrénées is younger and livelier, with fun ambience, inexpensive meals, some smoke, and a reasonable wine list (open daily, 25 rue Beautreillis, tel. 01 42 72 64 94).

Closer to Hôtel de Ville

These eateries, near the Pompidou Center, appear on the map on page 356. To reach them, use the Hôtel de Ville Métro stop.

$$$ Au Bourguignon du Marais is a small wine bar–bistro south of rue de Rivoli. Wine-lovers won't want to miss it. Gentle, English-speaking Jacques offers excellent Burgundy wines that blend well with his fine, though limited, selection of *plats du jour*. The escargots are the best I've had, and the dessert was...*délicieux* (allow €35–45 with wine, closed Sat–Sun, call by 19:00 to reserve, 52 rue Francois Miron, tel. 01 48 87 15 40).

Trendy Marais Square: **The street called rue de Bourg-Tibourg** (just off rue de Rivoli), busy with a fun assortment of popular eateries under its bushy trees, is worth surveying. **$$ Le Fou d'En Face** specializes in wine and *pot-au-feu* (beef stew-€19). The lively and cheap **$ Restaurante Sant Antonio** serves up pizza, salads, and Italian. **$$ Feria Café** offers a traditional French menu.

$ BHV Department Store's fifth-floor cafeteria provides nice views, an escape from the busy streets below, and no-brainer, point-and-shoot cafeteria cuisine (Mon–Sat 11:30–18:00, closed Sun, at intersection of rue du Temple and rue de la Verrerie, 1 block from Hôtel de Ville).

Marais Restaurants

1 Place du Marché Ste.
  Catherine Eateries
2 Vins des Pyrénées
3 Nectarine & Café Hugo
4 Ma Bourgogne
5 L'Impasse
6 To Chez Janou
7 Brasserie Bofinger
8 Restaurant Coconnas
9 L'Enoteca
10 L'As du Falafel
11 Au Bourguignon du
   Marais
12 Bistrot les Sans Culottes
13 Rue de Bourg-Tibourg
   Eateries
14 Camille Brasserie
15 Le Pick-Clops Bar Rest.
16 Chez Marianne
17 Au Temps des Cerises
18 Le Vieux Comptoir Bar
19 La Perla Bar
20 The Quiet Man Irish Pub
21 BHV Cafeteria

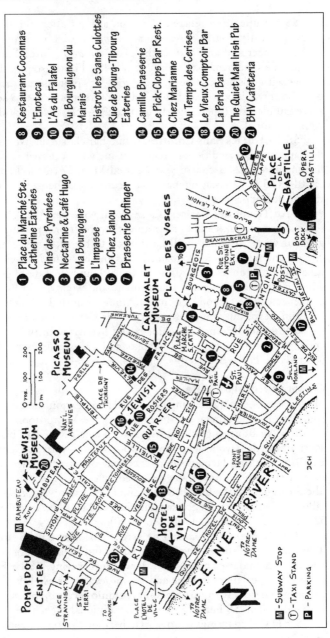

M - SUBWAY STOP
T - TAXI STAND
P - PARKING

In the Heart of the Marais

These are closest to the St. Paul Métro stop.

$$ *On place du Marché Ste. Catherine:* ** This small, romantic square, just off rue St. Antoine, is an international food festival cloaked in extremely Parisian, leafy-square ambience. On a balmy evening, this is clearly a neighborhood favorite, with five popular restaurants offering €20–30 meals. Survey the square, and you'll find a popular French bistro (Le Marché**) and inviting eateries serving Italian, Korean, Russian, and Greek. You'll eat under the trees, surrounded by a futuristic-in-1800 planned residential quarter.

$$ L'Enoteca is a high-spirited, half-timbered wine bar-restaurant serving reasonably priced Italian cuisine (no pizza) with a tempting *antipasti* bar. It's a relaxed, open setting with busy, blue-aproned waiters serving two floors of local eaters (€10 pastas, €15 *plats*, open daily, across from L'Excuse at rue St. Paul and rue Charles V, 25 rue Charles V, tel. 01 42 78 91 44).

$ Camille, a traditional corner brasserie, is a neighborhood favorite with great indoor and sidewalk seating. White-aproned waiters serve €10 salads and very French *plats du jour* (from €16) to a down-to-earth but sophisticated clientele (open daily, 24 rue des Francs Bourgeois at corner of rue Elzévir, tel. 01 42 72 20 50).

$ Le Pick-Clops Bar Restaurant is a happy peanuts-and-lots-of-cocktails diner with bright neon, loud colors, and a garish local crowd. It's perfect for immersing yourself in today's Marais world—a little boisterous, a little edgy, a little gay, fun-loving, easygoing...and no tourists. Sit inside, on old-fashioned diner stools, or streetside to watch the constant Marais parade. The name means "Steal the Cigarettes"—but you'll pay €10 for your big salad (daily 7:00–24:00, 16 rue Vieille du Temple, tel. 01 40 29 02 18).

$ Several hardworking **Chinese fast-food eateries**, great for a €6 meal, line rue St. Antoine.

On Rue des Rosiers in the Jewish Quarter

To reach the Jewish Quarter, use the St. Paul Métro stop.

$ Chez Marianne, a neighborhood fixture, offers classic Jewish meals and Parisian ambience. Choose from several indoor zones with a cluttered wine shop/deli ambience, or sit outside. You'll select from two dozen "Zakouski" elements to assemble your €15 plate (great vegetarian options, eat cheap with a €6 falafel plate, or even cheaper with take-away, long hours daily, corner of rue des Rosiers and rue des Hospitalieres St. Gervais, tel. 01 42 72 18 86).

$ L'As du Falafel seems to dominate the falafel scene in the Jewish quarter. Monsieur Isaac, the "Ace of Falafel" here since 1979, brags he's got "the biggest pita on the street...and he fills it up." Your inexpensive Jewish cuisine comes on plastic plates and

a bustling ambience that seems to prove he's earned his success. While the €6 "special falafel" is the big hit, many Americans enjoy his lighter chicken version *(medaillon de poulet grillé)*. Their takeout service draws a constant crowd (day and night until late, 34 rue des Rosiers).

Picnicking

Picnic at peaceful place des Vosges (closes at dusk) or on the Ile St. Louis *quais* (see below). Stretch your euros at the basement super-market of the **Monoprix** department store (closed Sun, near place des Vosges on rue St. Antoine). Two small **grocery shops** are open until 23:00 on rue St. Antoine (near intersection with rue Castex).

Breakfast

For an incredibly cheap breakfast, try **Hilaire boulangerie-pâtisserie,** where the hotels buy their croissants (coffee machine—€0.70, cheap baby quiches, 1 block off place de la Bastille, corner of rue St. Antoine and rue de Lesdiguières).

Nightlife

The best scene is the dizzying array of wacky eateries, bars, and dance halls on **rue de Lappe**. This street is what the Latin Quarter wants to be. Just east of the stately place de la Bastille, it's one of the wildest nightspots in Paris. Sitting amid the chaos like a van Gogh painting is the popular, old-time **Bistrot les Sans Culottes** (see above).

Trendy cafés and bars—popular with gay men—also cluster on rue Vieille du Temple, rue des Archives, and rue Ste. Croix de la Bretonnerie (close at about 2:00 in the morning). You'll find a line of bars and cafés providing front-row seats for the buff parade on rue Vieille du Temple, a block north of rue de Rivoli. Nearby, rue des Rosiers bustles with youthful energy, but there are no cafés to observe from. **Le Vieux Comptoir** is a tiny, lively, and just-hip-enough bar (off place des Vosges at 8 rue de Birague). **Vins des Pyrénées** is young and fun—find the small bar in the back (see above). **La Perla** is full of Parisian yuppies in search of the perfect margarita (26 rue François Miron). **The Quiet Man** is a traditional Irish pub with happy hour from 16:00 to 20:00 (5 rue des Haudriettes).

The most enjoyable peaceful evening may be simply donning your floppy "three musketeers" hat and slowly strolling around the place des Vosges, window-shopping the art galleries.

Ile St. Louis

The Ile St. Louis is a romantic and peaceful neighborhood to window-shop for plenty of promising dinner possibilities. Cruise

the island's main street for a variety of options, from cozy *crêper-ies* to Italian eateries (intimate pizzerias and upscale) to typical brasseries (a few with fine outdoor seating facing the bridge to Ile de la Cité). After dinner, sample Paris' best sorbet and stroll across to the Ile de la Cité to see an illuminated Notre-Dame, or enjoy a scenic drink on the deck of a floating café moored under the Notre-Dame's right transept. All of these listings line the island's main drag, the rue St. Louis-en-l'Ile (see map on page 80; to get here, use the Pont Marie Métro stop). Consider skipping dessert to enjoy a stroll licking the best ice cream in Paris (described under "Ice-Cream Dessert," on page 360).

$$$ Le Tastevin is an eight-table, mother-and-son-run restaurant serving top-notch traditional French cuisine with white-tablecloth, candlelit, gourmet elegance under heavy wooden beams. The *menus* start with three courses at about €30 and offer plenty of classic choices that change with the season to ensure freshness (open daily, good wine list, reserve for late-evening eating, 46 rue St. Louis-en-l'Ile, tel. 01 43 54 17 31; owner Madame Puisieux speaks just enough English, while her son, Jean-Philippe, tends the kitchen).

$$ *Medieval Theme Restaurants:* Nos Ancêtres les Gaulois on rue St. Louis-en-l'Ile is famous for its rowdy, medieval-cellar atmosphere. Ideal for barbarians—as the name ("Our Ancestors the Gauls") implies—they serve all-you-can-eat buffets with straw baskets of raw veggies (cut whatever you like with your dagger), massive plates of pâté, a meat course, and all the wine you can stomach for €35. The food is just food; burping is encouraged. If you want to eat a lot, drink a lot of wine, be surrounded with tourists, and holler at your friends while receiving smart-aleck buccaneer service, this food fest can be fun (open daily from 19:00, at #39, tel. 01 46 33 66 07). **La Taverne du Sergeant Recruteur,** next door, serves up the same formula with a different historic twist: The "Sergeant Recruiter" used to get young Parisians drunk and stuffed here, then sign them into the army. You might swing by both and choose the…"ambience" is not quite the right word…that fits your mood.

$$ La Brasserie de l'Ile St. Louis is situated at the prow of the island's ship as it faces Ile de la Cité, offering purely Alsatian cuisine (try the *choucroute garni* for €17), served in Franco-Germanic ambience with no-nonsense brasserie service. This is your perfect balmy-evening perch for watching the Ile St. Louis promenade—or, if it's chilly, the interior is plenty characteristic for a memorable night out (closed Wed, no reservations, 55 quai de Bourbon, tel. 01 43 54 02 59).

$ Café Med, near Notre-Dame at #77, is best for inexpensive salads, crêpes, and light €12 *menus* in a tight but cheery setting

(limited wine list, open daily, tel. 01 43 29 73 17, charming Eva). There's a similar *crêperie* just across the street.

Riverside Picnic
On sunny lunchtimes and balmy evenings, the *quai* on the Left Bank side of Ile St. Louis is lined with locals who have more class than money, spreading out tablecloths and even lighting candles for elegant picnics. Otherwise, it's a great walk for people-watching.

Ice-Cream Dessert
Half the people strolling Ile St. Louis are licking an ice-cream cone, because this is the home of *les glaces Berthillon*. The original **Berthillon** shop, at 31 rue St. Louis-en-l'Ile, is marked by the line of salivating customers (closed Mon–Tue). It's so popular that the wealthy people who can afford to live on this fancy island complain about the congestion it causes. For a less famous but at-least-as-tasty treat, the homemade Italian gelato a block away at **Amorino Gelati** is giving Berthillon competition (no line, bigger portions, easier to see what you want, and they offer little tastes—Berthillon doesn't need to, 47 rue St. Louis-en-l'Ile, tel. 01 44 07 48 08). Having some of each is not a bad thing.

Luxembourg Neighborhood
Sleeping in the Luxembourg neighborhood puts you near many appealing dining and after-hours options. Because my hotels in this area cluster around the Panthéon and St. Sulpice Church (see Sleeping chapter), I've organized restaurant listings the same way. Restaurants near the Panthéon tend to be calm, those around St. Sulpice more boisterous; it's a short walk from one area to the other. Anyone sleeping in this area is close to the inexpensive eateries that line the always-bustling rue Mouffetard. You're also within a 15-minute walk of the *grands cafés* of St. Germain and Montparnasse (with Paris' first café and famous artist haunts; see "Les Grands Cafés de Paris," page 364).

Near the Panthéon
For locations, see the map on page 331.

These eateries are served by the Cluny-La Sorbonne Métro stop and the RER-B Luxembourg station.

$$ Les Vignes du Panthéon, on a quiet street a block from the Panthéon, is homey, formal, and traditional. It features a zinc bar, original flooring, white tablecloths, and whispering ambience. The mostly local clientele will make you feel you're truly in Paris (€17–20 *plats*, closed Sat–Sun, English menu posted outside, 4 rue des Fossés St. Jacques, tel. 01 43 54 80 81).

$$ Terra Nera is a small Italian restaurant with a privileged position on a broad sidewalk overlooking a peaceful square just a block from the Panthéon. Its noisy red facade gives it a fun and casual feel. Two can easily split the big *antipasti* (ask for mozzarella with it) and each get a pasta main course for a total of about €22 per person (closed Sun, limited and pricey wine list, 18 rue des Fossés St. Jacques, tel. 01 43 54 83 09). That *other* Italian restaurant across the street serves more basic, cheaper pizzas and pastas.

$$ Restaurant Perraudin is a welcoming, family-run, red-checkered-tablecloth eatery understandably popular with tourists. Gentle M. Rameau serves classic *cuisine bourgeoise* with an emphasis on Burgundian dishes. The decor is classic turn-of-the-20th-century, with big mirrors and old wood paneling, and the volume is rollicking (*bœuf bourguignon* is a specialty here, €28 *menus*, closed Sat-Sun, between the Panthéon and Luxembourg Garden at 157 rue St. Jacques, tel. 01 46 33 15 75).

$ Le Soufflot is my favorite café between the Panthéon and Luxembourg Garden, with a nifty, library-like interior and outdoor tables on a wide sidewalk with point-blank views of the Panthéon. The cuisine is café-classic: great €10 salads, omelets, and *plats du jour* (open daily, a block below the Panthéon on the right side of rue Soufflot as you walk toward Luxembourg Garden, tel. 01 43 26 57 56).

$ *Place de la Sorbonne:* This cobbled and leafy square, with a small fountain facing the Sorbonne University just a block from the Cluny Museum, offers several decent opportunities for a quick outdoor lunch or light dinner. At the tiny **Baker's Dozen,** you'll pay take-away prices for salads and sandwiches you can sit down to eat (daily €5 salad and quiche special, open daily until 19:00). **Café de l'Ecritoire** is a typical, lively brasserie with happy diners enjoying €9 salads, €12 *plats,* and fine square seating (daily, 3 place de la Sorbonne, tel. 01 43 54 60 02).

Near the Odéon Theater

To reach these, use the Odéon Métro stop. In this same neighborhood is Café le Procope, listed under "Les Grands Cafes de Paris," below.

$$ Brasserie Bouillon Racine takes you back to 1906 with an Art Nouveau carnival of carved wood, stained glass, and old-time lights reflected in beveled mirrors. The over-the-top décor, energetic waiters, and affordable menu combines to give it an inviting conviviality. Check upstairs before choosing a table (€18 *plats,* traditional French with lots of fish and meat, daily 12:00–23:00, 3 rue Racine, tel. 01 44 32 15 60).

$ Restaurant Polidor, a neighborhood fixture since the 19th

century, is much-loved for its unpretentious quality cooking, fun old Paris ambience, and good value. Their menu features *plats* from every corner of France, and their *menu fraicheur* is designed for lighter summer eating (€19 3-course *menu*, daily 12:00–14:30 & 19:00–23:00, cash only, no reservations, 41 rue Monsieur-Le-Prince, tel. 01 43 26 95 34, Amelia).

On Rue Mouffetard

Lying several blocks behind the Panthéon, rue Mouffetard is a conveyer belt of comparison-shopping eaters with wall-to-wall budget options (fondue, crêpes, Italian, falafel, and Greek). Come here to join the fun parade of diners and eat a less-expensive meal (you get what you pay for). This street stays up late and likes to party (particularly place de la Contrescarpe). The gauntlet starts and finishes with fun squares, each with a fine café (recommended below) to eat, drink, and watch the action. The top square is pedestrian and touristic. The bottom square is more real and Parisian. And anywhere between is no-man's land for consistent quality. Still, strolling with so many fun-seekers is enjoyable, whether you eat here or not. To get here, use the Censier-Daubenton Métro stop.

$ **Café Delmas**, at the top of rue Mouffetard on picturesque place de la Contrescarpe, is *the* place to see and be seen. Come here for a before- or after-dinner drink on the broad outdoor terrace, or for typical café cuisine (€12 salads, €15 *plats*, great chocolate ice cream, open daily).

$ **Cave de la Bourgogne** serves reasonably priced café fare at the bottom of rue Mouffetard, with picture-perfect tables on a raised terrace, and a warm interior (specials listed on chalkboards, open daily, 144 rue Mouffetard).

Near St. Sulpice Church

Rue des Canettes and Rue Guisarde: For an entirely different experience, roam the streets between the St. Sulpice Church and boulevard St. Germain, abounding with restaurants, *crêperies*, wine bars, and jazz haunts (use Mo: St. Sulpice). Find rue des Canettes and rue Guisarde, and window-shop the many French and Italian eateries—most with similar prices, but each with a slightly different feel. For excellent crêpes, try **La Crêpe Rit du Clown** (Mon–Sat 12:00–23:00, closed Sun, 6 rue des Canettes, tel. 01 46 34 01 02). And for a bohemian pub with a cigarette-rolling gang surrounded by black-and-white photos of the artsy and revolutionary French Sixties, have a drink at **Chez Georges.** Sit in a cool little streetside table nook, or venture downstairs to find a smoky, drippy-candle, traditionally French world in the Edith Piaf–style dance cellar

(cheap drinks from old-fashioned menu, Tue–Sat 14:00–2:00 in the morning, closed Sun–Mon and in Aug, 11 rue des Canettes).

Elsewhere in Paris

Along Canal St. Martin

Escape the crowded tourist areas and enjoy a cool canalside experience. Take the Métro to place de la République and walk down rue Beaurepaire to Canal St. Martin. There you'll find two worthwhile cafés. They're both lively, with similarly reasonable prices; you decide: **$ Chez Prune** (canal ambience inside and out, well-prepared food, €10 salads, €15 *plats*, open daily, 71 quai de Valmy, tel. 01 42 41 30 47) or **$ La Marine** (closed Sun, 2 blocks to the right as you leave Chez Prune, 55 bis quai de Valmy, tel. 01 42 39 69 81).

$ Au Trou Normand, away from the canal and near the recommended hotels on rue Malte, is a small, red-checkered-tablecloth eatery with cheap meals (€12 *plats,* open daily, just off boulevard Voltaire at 9 rue J.P. Timbaud, tel. 01 48 05 80 23).

Near the Louvre

$ Café le Nemours, a staunchly Parisian fixture serving pricey but good light lunches, is tucked into the corner of the Palais Royal adjacent to the Comédie Française (leaving the Louvre, cross rue de Rivoli and veer left). Elegant with brass and Art Deco, and with outdoor tables under an arcade two minutes from the pyramid, this spot makes a great post-Louvre retreat (fun and filling €11 salads, open daily, 2 place Colette, Mo: Palais Royal, tel. 01 42 61 34 14).

Near Opéra Garnier

$ Bouillon Chartier is a noisy, old, classic eatery. It's named for the bouillon it served the neighborhood's poor workers back in 1896, when its calling was to provide an affordable warm meal for those folks. Workers used to eat *à la gamelle* (from a tin lunch box). That same spirit—complete with surly waiters and a cheap menu—survives today. With over 300 simple seats and 15 frantic waiters, you can still see the napkin drawers for its early regulars (€15 *menus*, open daily 11:30–15:00 & 18:00–22:00, west of the Opéra Garnier near boulevard Poissonniere, 7 rue de Faubourg-Montmartre, Mo: Bonne-Nouvelle, tel. 01 47 70 86 29).

Montmartre

Montmartre is extremely touristy, with many mindless mobs following guides to cancan shows. But the ambience is undeniably fun, and an evening up here overlooking Paris is a quintessential experience in the City of Light. The steps in front of Sacré-Cœur

are perfect for a picnic with a view. Along the touristy main drag (near place du Tertre and just off it), several fun piano bars serve reasonable crêpes with great people-watching. To reach this area, use the Anvers Métro stop. More eateries are mentioned in the Montmartre Walk chapter on page 123.

$$ Restaurant Chez Plumeau, just off the jam-packed place du Tertre, is touristy yet moderately priced, with indifferent service and great seating on a tiny, characteristic square (€28 *menu*, elaborate €15 salads, closed Wed, place du Calvaire, tel. 01 46 06 26 29).

$ L'Eté en Pente Douce hides under generous branches below the crowds on a classic neighborhood corner. It features fine indoor and outdoor seating, €10 *plats du jour* and salads, vegetarian options, and good wines (open daily, 23 rue Muller, many steps below Sacré-Cœur to the left as you leave, down the stairs below the WC, tel. 01 42 64 02 67).

Dinner Cruises

Several companies offer dinner cruises on the Seine. While touristy, they offer a unique chance to dine as illuminated Paris floats by. Prices vary from €35 to €125, depending on the "elegance" and drinks you require. Your hotel will have brochures and can reserve, though you might save by contacting the cruise companies directly.

$$$ Bateaux Parisiens Tour Eiffel has €92 cruises, including a three-course meal with champagne, red and white wine, music, and dancing (nightly, port de la Bourdonnais, Mo: Trocadéro, tel. 01 44 11 33 44, www.bateauxparisiens.com).

$$ At "Quai 55," the boat **Capitaine Fracasse** offers a basic €39 dinner cruise (open daily in summer, closed Mon, boats depart from middle of pont Bir-Hakeim—1 bridge downriver from Eiffel Tower, Mo: Bir-Hakeim, tel. 01 46 21 48 15, www.quai55.com).

LES GRANDS CAFES DE PARIS

Here's a short list of grand Parisian cafés, worth the detour only if you're not in a hurry or on a tight budget (some ask outrageous prices for a shot of espresso). Think of these cafés as museums. Try to understand why they matter just as much today as they did yesterday (see sidebar). For tips on Parisian cafés, see "Café Culture" on page 340.

St. Germain-des-Prés

For locations, see the map on page 328. Use the St. Germain-des-Prés Métro stop.

Where the boulevard St. Germain meets rue Bonaparte,

History of Cafés in Paris

The first café in the Western world was in Paris—established in 1686 at Le Procope (still a restaurant today; see below). The French had just discovered coffee, and their robust economy was growing a population of pleasure-seekers and thinkers looking for places to be seen, to exchange ideas, and to plot revolutions—both political and philosophical. And with the advent of theaters like the Comédie Française, the necessary artsy, coffee-sipping crowds were birthed. By 1700, more than 300 cafés had opened their doors; at the time of the Revolution (1789), there were over 1,800 cafés in Paris. Revolutionaries from Jean-Paul Marat and Napoleon to Salvador Dalí enjoyed the spirit of free-thinking that the cafés engendered.

Café society took off in the early 1900s. Life was changing rapidly, with new technology and wars on a global scale. Many retreated to Parisian cafés to try to make sense of the confusion. Vladimir Lenin, Leon Trotsky, Igor Stravinsky, Ernest Hemingway, F. Scott Fitzgerald, James Joyce, Albert Einstein, Jean-Paul Sartre, Gene Openshaw, and Albert Camus were among the devoted café society. Some virtually lived at their favorite café, where they kept their business calendars, entertained friends, and ate every meal. Parisian apartments were small, walls were thin (still often the case), and heating (particularly during war times) was minimal, making the warmth of cafés all the harder to leave.

There are more than 12,000 cafés in Paris today, though their numbers are shrinking. They're still used for business meetings, encounter sessions, political discussions, and romantic interludes. Most Parisians are loyal to their favorites and know their waiter's children's names.

you'll find two famous cafés (both open daily). **Les Deux Magots** offers great outdoor seating and a warm interior. Once a favorite of Ernest Hemingway (in *The Sun Also Rises*, Jake met Brett here) and of Jean-Paul Sartre (he and Simone de Beauvoir met here), the café is today filled with international tourists. **Le Café de Flore**, right next door, feels much more local, hip, and literary—wear your black turtleneck. Pablo Picasso was a regular at the time he painted *Guernica*. The smoky interior is popular with Europeans.

For scenic outdoor seating and the same delightful view for less, skip these cafés and set up for coffee or a light lunch at **Café Bonaparte** (big salads, from Les Deux Magots go 1 block up rue Bonaparte toward river). You're farther from the large boulevards, but still in the thick of this pleasant café-sitting area.

Paris' first and most famous, **$ Café le Procope**, lies an enchanting five-minute stroll away. This was a *café célèbre*, drawing

notables such as Voltaire, Rousseau, Honoré de Balzac, Emile Zola, Maximilien de Robespierre, Victor Hugo, and two Americans, Benjamin Franklin and Thomas Jefferson (beautiful restaurant and café but average cuisine, open daily 10:00–24:00, 13 rue de l'Ancienne Comédie, tel. 01 40 46 79 00). To reach this café from Café Bonaparte, walk down rue de l'Abbaye, then continue onto rue de Bourbon-le-Château. Veer left on the picturesque rue de Buci (more cafés), and turn right just after crossing rue de l'Ancienne Comédie. Go up the passageway at 59–61 to find Le Procope.

Boulevard du Montparnasse

An eclectic assortment of historic cafés gathers along the busy boulevard du Montparnasse near its intersection with boulevard Raspail (Mo: Vavin). Combine these historic cafés with a visit to the Luxembourg Garden, which lies just a few blocks away, down rue Vavin (next to Le Select).

$$$ Le Dome, right at the intersection of boulevard Raspail and boulevard du Montparnasse, offers a dramatic contrast to the party atmosphere of La Coupole (below). Small, elegant, and refined in every way—with green leather booths and polished wood paneling—Le Dome makes me want to dress up and look better than I do. While La Coupole is not known for its cuisine, Le Dome is. Come here for a splurge dinner (figure €60 per person with wine, open daily, 108 boulevard du Montparnasse, tel. 01 43 35 25 81).

$$ La Coupole, built in the 1920s, was decorated by aspiring artists (Fernand Léger, Constantin Brancusi, and Marc Chagall, among others) in return for free meals. It still supports artists with regular showings on its vast walls. This cavernous café feels like a classy train station, with grand chandeliers, velvet booths, brass decor, and tuxedoed waiters by the dozen (an unappealing modern glass building towers above). Bring your friends and make noise. The food is fine, but that's not the reason you came (€34 *menu* includes a half bottle of wine, open daily, restaurant serves food from 12:00 until the wee hours, come early to get better service and less smoke, 102 boulevard du Montparnasse, tel. 01 43 20 14 20).

$$ Le Select, a more relaxed and traditional café, was popular with the more rebellious types...Leon Trotsky, Jean Cocteau, and Pablo Picasso loved it. It feels more conformist today, with good outdoor seating and pleasant tables just inside the door—though the locals hang out at the bar further inside (€10–12 salads, €16 *plats*, open daily, 99 boulevard du Montparnasse, across from La Coupole, tel. 01 45 48 38 24).

Avenue des Champs-Elysées

To reach these two cafés, use the George V Métro stop.

$$$ Fouquet's opened in 1899 as a coachman's bistro. It gained fame as the hangout of France's WWI biplane fighter pilots—those who weren't shot down by Germany's infamous "Red Baron." It also served as James Joyce's dining room. Today, it's pretty stuffy—unless you're a film star. The golden plaques at the entry are from winners of France's film awards (like the Oscars), the Césars. While the intimidating interior is impressive, the outdoor setting is Champs-Elysées great, with pay-for-view espresso (€4.80). Fouquet's was recently saved from foreign purchase and eventual destruction when the government declared it a historic monument (open daily, 99 avenue des Champs-Elysées).

$$ Ladurée, a block downhill, is the classic 19th-century tea salon/restaurant/*pâtisserie* on Paris' grandest boulevard (open daily, a block below avenue George V at #75). Its interior is right out of the 1860s. Wander around...you can even peek into the cozy rooms upstairs. A coffee here with a selection of four little macaroons is *très élégant.* The bakery makes traditional macaroons, cute little cakes, and gift-wrapped finger sandwiches.

On Place de la Concorde

$$$ Hôtel Crillon's four-star elegance can be yours for an afternoon. Considered the most exclusive (and expensive) hotel in Paris (and the last of the great hotels to be French-owned), this gives you a tantalizing taste of château life. Wear the best clothes you packed, arrive after 15:00, let the bellhop spin the door, and settle into the royal blue chairs in the *salon du thé* (€10 for a pot of tea or double *café au lait,* about €30 for high tea served daily 15:30–18:00 with a live harp serenade, 10 place de la Concorde, Mo: Concorde). You'll be surrounded by famous people you won't recognize.

At Gare de Lyon

$$$ Le Train Bleu is a grandiose restaurant with a low-slung, leather-couch café-bar area built right into the train station for the Paris Exhibition of 1900 (which also saw the construction of the pont Alexandre III and the Grand and Petit Palais). It's a simply grand-scale-everything experience, with over-the-top, belle époque decor that speaks of another age, when going to dinner was an event—a chance to see and be seen—and intimate dining was out. Forty-one massive paintings of scenes along the old rail lines tempt diners to consider a short getaway. Many films have featured this restaurant. Reserve ahead for dinner, or drop in for a drink before your train leaves (€43 *menu*, €7 beer, €4.60 espresso,

open daily, up the stairs opposite track L, tel. 01 43 43 09 06, www .le-train-bleu.com).

Honorable Mention

$ Café de la Mosque, behind the Jardins des Plantes and attached to Paris' largest mosque, beams you straight to Morocco, with North African tearoom decor and a full menu to match (daily 9:00–24:00, 39 rue Geoffroy St. Hilaire, Mo: Place Monge, tel. 01 43 31 38 20).

$ Café la Palette, on *le* Left Bank, is across the river and a few blocks from the Louvre. Over 100 years old, this café feels real and unaffected by the passage of time (reasonably priced drinks; see Left Bank Walk, page 135).

PARIS WITH CHILDREN

Paris works surprisingly well with children—smart adults enjoy the "fine art" of simply being in Paris' great neighborhoods, parks, and monuments while observing their kids uncover the City of Light. After enjoying so many kid-friendly sights, your children may want to return to Paris before you do. Consider these tips:

- Hotel selection is critical. Stay in a kid-friendly area near a park. The rue Cler and Luxembourg neighborhoods are both good. If you're staying a week or more, rent an apartment (see "For Longer Stays," page 336).
- Before you go, get your kids into the Parisian spirit by reading (see the book list, below). Bring along plenty of kids' books; they're harder to find and expensive in Paris. If you run out, visit Red Wheelbarrow Bookstore (daily 10:00–19:00, 22 rue St. Paul, Mo: St. Paul, tel. 01 42 77 42 17).
- If traveling with infants, pack a light stroller and a child backpack. Strollers are tough in the Métro and not allowed at many sights (use a backpack instead), but are ideal for neighborhood walks.
- Don't overdo it. Tackle one key sight each day (Louvre, Orsay, Versailles), and mix it with a healthy dose of fun activities. Try to match kid activities with areas where you'll be sightseeing to minimize unnecessary travel (e.g., the Louvre is near the kid-friendly Palais Royal's courtyards and Tuileries Garden). Kids prefer the Louvre after dark, when it's very quiet (Wed and Fri only).
- The double-decker bus tours (see page 34) are a great way to start your visit.
- Follow this book's crowd-beating tips to a T. Kids despise long lines more than you do.

- Eat dinner early before the sophisticated local crowd dines (19:00–19:30 at restaurants, earlier at cafés). Skip romantic places. Try relaxed cafés (or fast-food restaurants) where kids can move around without bothering others. Picnics work well.
- The cheapest toy selection is usually in the large department stores, such as Bon Marché (see Shopping chapter, page 377).
- French marionette shows, called *guignols,* are fun for everyone. They take place in several locations in Paris, mostly in big parks. See *Pariscope* or *L'Officiel des Spectacles* (sold at newsstands), under "Marionettes," for times and places. Even in French, the plots are easy to follow, and the price is right (€2–4). Arrive 20 minutes early for good seats.
- Involve your children in the trip. Let them help choose daily activities, lead you through the Métro, and so on.
- The best thing we did on a recent trip was buy a set of *boules* (a form of outdoor bowling—for the rules, see the sidebar on page 312). We'd play *boules* before dinner, side by side with real players at the neighborhood field. Buy your *boules de pétanque* at the BHV store in the Marais (next to Hôtel de Ville) or at any sporting-goods store. The *boules* make great if weighty souvenirs, and are fun to play back at home.
- Some Paris parks host temporary amusement parks. The summer Ferris wheel and rides in the Tuileries Garden are the best—my daughter preferred it to Disneyland Paris (for Disneyland Paris details, see page 475). Consider visiting an amusement park as an end-of-trip reward.
- Note that Wednesdays can be busy days at children's sights, since school lets out early.

Kid's Reading List

Pick up books at the library and rent videos. Watch or read the Madeline stories by Ludwig Bemelmans, *The Hunchback of Notre-Dame* by Victor Hugo, *The Three Musketeers* by Alexandre Dumas, or Dumas' *The Man in the Iron Mask. Anni's Diary of France,* by Anni Axworthy, is a fun, picture-filled book about a young girl's trip; it could inspire your children.

How Would You Survive in the Middle Ages?, by Fiona MacDonald, is an appealing "guide" for kids. Serious kid-historians will devour *The Kingfisher History Encyclopedia.* If your children are interested in art, get your hands on *The History of Art for Young People* by Anthony Janson and *Discovering Great Artists: Hands-On Art for Children in the Styles of the Great Masters* by MaryAnn Kohl. (Also see "Recommended Books and Movies," which has some good choices for teenagers, on page 7 in the Introduction.)

TOP TEN SIGHTS AND ACTIVITIES

Luxembourg Garden—This is my favorite place to mix kid business with pleasure. This perfectly Parisian park has it all—from tennis courts to cafés—as well as an extensive big-toys play area with imaginative slides, swings, jungle gyms, and chess games (see map on page 328). To find the big-toys play area, head to the southwest corner (small fee, entry good all day, open daily, many parents watch from chairs outside the play area). Kids also like the speedy merry-go-round, the small pony rides (by the tennis courts) and the toy rental sailboats in the main pond (activities open daily in summer, otherwise only Wed and Sat–Sun). Near the main building is a toddler wading pool and sand pit (free). Adults and kids enjoy the terrific puppet shows *(guignols)* held in the afternoons near the children's play area, also located in the southwest corner of the park (€2–5, times listed in *Pariscope* as "Marionnettes du Luxembourg" under "Enfants" section). The park has big, open areas perfect for kicking a ball. Kids can even play in the grass opposite the palace (Mo: St. Sulpice, Odéon, or Notre-Dame-des-Champs, tel. 01 43 26 46 47).

Eiffel Tower, Champ de Mars Park, and Trocadéro—You could fill an entire kid-fun day here. Come early and ride the elevator up the tower before crowds appear, or ride it above the lights at night (see page 49). The Champ de Mars park stretches out from the tower's base, with picnic-perfect benches, big toys, sand pits, pony rides, and pedal go-carts. Big toys are located at the non-river end of the park (with your back to the tower, it's to the right). The pony rides and go-carts are in the center in the park (after 11:00 Wed, Sat–Sun, and on all summer days; after 15:00 otherwise, Mo: Ecole Militaire; RER-C: Champ de Mars-Tour Eiffel stop; or bus #69).

All ages enjoy the view from Trocadéro across the river to the Eiffel Tower, especially after dark (Mo: Trocadéro). There's a terrific, kid-friendly **National Maritime Museum** (Musée National de la Marine) docked at Trocadéro, with all things nautical and many ship models (kids-€7, adults-€9, includes helpful audioguide, covered by Museum Pass, Wed–Mon 10:00–18:00, closed Tue, the museum is to your right as you face the tower from Trocadéro square). See page 52 for more information. The Musée de l'Homme, next door, is an anthropological museum, but has zero information in English.

Notre-Dame, Towers, and Crypt—Paris' famous Gothic cathedral doesn't have to be dry and dull. Replay Quasimodo's stunt and climb the tower (go early to avoid long lines). Kids love being on such a lofty perch with a face-to-face look at a gargoyle. The crypt on the square in front of Notre-Dame is quick and interesting. Kids

can push buttons to highlight remains of Roman Paris and leave with a better understanding of how different civilizations build on top of each other. In-line skaters perform amazing stunts just to the right of the cathedral as you face it. (What's more amazing is that the city permits such an activity at this location.) The small but beautiful park along the river outside Notre-Dame's right transept has sandboxes, picnic benches, and space to run (Mo: Cité). ✪ See Historic Paris Walk, page 70.

River Boat Rides—A variety of boats offer one-hour Seine cruises on huge glass-domed boats, with departures until 22:30 (best at sunset or after dark). Or hop on a Batobus, a river bus connecting eight stops along the river: Eiffel Tower, Champs-Elysées, Orsay/place de la Concorde, Louvre, Notre-Dame, St. Germain-des-Prés, Hôtel de Ville, and Jardin des Plantes. Longer boat trips ply the tranquil waters of the Canal St. Martin between the Bastille and Bassin de la Villette (See "Tours—By Boat," page 35).

Arc de Triomphe and Champs-Elysées—This area is popular with teenagers, day and night. Mine can't get enough of it. Watch the crazy traffic rush around the Arc de Triomphe for endless entertainment, then stroll the avenue des Champs-Elysées, with its car dealerships (particularly Renault's space-age café), Virgin Megastore (music), Disney store, and the river of humanity that flows along its broad sidewalks. Take your teenager to see a movie on the Champs-Elysées ("v.o." next to the showtime means it's shown in the original language). ✪ See Champs-Elysées Walk, page 101.

Versailles—This massive complex of palaces, gardens, fountains, and forest can be a good family getaway if well-planned. Do the gardens first and the interior late, when crowds subside. Rent a bike or (even better) a golf cart to explore the gardens. Driving around the grounds in a golf cart, while pricey (€20/hr), is great fun and extremely easy. (They'll want parents to do the driving for liability reasons, but once away from the palace, you're on your own.) Or you can row row row a boat on the canal. The Hamlet has barnyard animals. Be careful of crowds on weekends, when the fountains are flowing. ✪ See Versailles Day Trip, page 421.

Jardin des Plantes—These colorful gardens are a must for gardeners and good for kids. Located across the river from the Marais, the park is short on grass but tall on kid activities, including a small zoo *(ménagerie)* near the river, several play areas, and two kid-friendly natural science museums (closed Tue). Young kids enjoy the dinosaur exhibit at the Galerie d'Anatomie Comparée et de Paléontologie; there are no English explanations, but they're not really needed (kids-€4, adults-€6, Wed–Mon 10:00–17:00, closed Tue, entry includes Musée de Minéralogie for rock lovers, entrance faces river next to McDonald's). The Grande Galerie de

l'Evolution, at the non-river end of the park, is a dazzling museum describing the evolution of animals, with huge models and fun exhibits. While there are some English explanations in rooms, the €5 English *Discovery Guide-Gallerie de l'Evolution* helps (kids-€6, adults-€8, not covered by Museum Pass, Wed–Mon 10:00–18:00, closed Tue, tel. 01 40 79 30 00). From the park entrance on place Valhubert, the museums line the left side of the park (Mo: Gare d'Austerlitz or Jussieu). Outside the park, just behind Grande Galerie de l'Evolution, is the Moroccan-themed Café de la Mosque (see page 368 in the Eating chapter).

Pompidou Center—Teens like the Pompidou Center for its crazy outdoor entertainers, throngs of young people, happening cafés, and fun fountains next door. Inside, the temporary exhibits and gift shops on the main floor are visually impressive. The *Star Wars*-esque escalator to the top is fun for all ages, but you need to have a Museum Pass or a ticket for the Modern Art Museum to escalate (Mo: Rambuteau). ✪ See Pompidou Center Tour, page 202.

Jardin des Enfants aux Halles—This is a terrific place to drop your child for an hour (ages 7–11 only, no adults allowed inside, call at least an hour ahead to reserve, tel. 01 45 08 07 18). It's outdoors, in front of Les Halles shopping center near St. Eustache church. Kids get one supervised hour (that's it) to negotiate a great play area filled with clever activities, including a small toboggan ride, a maze, a volcano, and much more (the staff speaks enough English and is accustomed to non-French-speaking kids, €0.40, Tue and Thu–Fri 9:00–12:00 & 14:00–18:00, Wed and Sat 10:00–18:00, Sun 13:00–18:00, closed Mon, 105 rue Rambuteau, Mo: Les Halles).

Aquaboulevard—Paris' best pool/water slide/miniature golf complex is easy to reach and a timely escape from the museum scene. Indoor and outdoor pools with high-flying slides, waves, geysers, and whirlpool tubs draw kids of all ages. It's pricey (and steamy inside) but a fun opportunity to see soaked Parisians at play. Ride the Métro to the end of line 8 (Balard stop), walk two blocks under the elevated freeway, veer left across the traffic circle, and find Aquaboulevard in a complex of theaters and shops (kids under 12-€10/6 hrs, adults-€25/6 hrs, much cheaper rates for more than one visit, English-speaking staff, keep a €1 coin for lockers, boys and men need Speedo-style swimsuits—€6–10 at the Decathlon sporting-goods store right there, see map on page 378 for location, tel. 01 40 60 10 00).

SHOPPING

Shopping can provide a good break between Paris' heavyweight museums and monuments. And, if approached carefully, boutique browsing can be a culturally enlightening experience. In this chapter, you'll find information on shopping for souvenirs, clothing, food, and bargains.

Most travelers are interested in finding a few souvenirs and maybe an article of clothing. Here's a simplified approach that works for most:

- If you just need souvenirs, find a souvenir shop or consult your neighborhood supermarket for that Parisian box of tea, jam, or cookies—perfect for tucking into your suitcase at the last minute.
- For more elaborate purchasing plans, the city's large department stores offer relatively painless one-stop shopping in elegant surroundings.
- Neighborhood boutiques offer the greatest reward at the highest risk. While clerks and prices can be intimidating, the selection is more original and the experience is totally Parisian.

Tips

Before you enter a Parisian store, remember:

- In small stores, always say, *"Bonjour, Madame/Mademoiselle/Monsieur"* when entering and *"Au revoir, Madame/Mademoiselle/Monsieur"* when leaving.
- The customer is not always right. In fact, figure the clerk is doing you a favor by waiting on you.
- Except in department stores, it's not normal for the customer to handle clothing. Ask first before you pick up an item.
- Forget returns (and don't count on exchanges).
- Saturdays are busiest.

Key Phrases

English	French	Pronounced
Just looking.	*Je regard.*	zhuh ruh-gar
How much is it?	*Combien?*	kohm-bee-ehn
Too big/small/ expensive	*Trop grand/petit /cher*	troh grahn/ puh-tee/sher
May I try it on?	*Je peux l'essayer?*	zhuh puh luh-say-yay
Can I see more?	*Puis-je en voir d'autres?*	pweezh'en vwahr doh-truh
I'd like this.	*Je voudrais ça.*	zhuh voo-dray sah
On sale	*Solde*	sold
Discounted price	*Prix réduit*	pree ray-dwee
Big discounts	*Prix choc*	pree shock

- Observe French shoppers. Then imitate.
- Don't feel obliged to buy. The expression for "window-shopping" in French is *faire du lèche-vitrines* (literally, "window-licking").

Souvenir Shops

Avoid souvenir carts in front of famous monuments. Prices and selection are better in shops and department stores. Look around the Pompidou Center, on the streets of Montmartre, and in department stores (see below). The riverfront stalls near Notre-Dame sell a variety of used books, magazines, and tourist paraphernalia in the most romantic setting; see "*Les Bouquinistes* (Riverside Vendors)" sidebar. You'll find relatively good deals at the souvenir shops that line rue d'Arcole between Notre-Dame and Hôtel de Ville.

Rue de Rivoli, the grand street running alongside the Louvre, is filled with crass hawkers selling knickknacks to tourists. If you want to buy fun posters and postcards, patronize the boutiques by the river instead.

Department Stores (*Les Grands Magasins*)

Like cafés, department stores were invented here (surprisingly, not in America). While the stores seem overwhelming at first, they generally work like ours, and those listed here are accustomed to wide-eyed foreign shoppers and generally have English-speaking staff. These stores are not only beautiful monuments to a more relaxed, elegant era, but also a great lesson in how others live. It's instructive to see what's in style, check out Parisians' current taste

Les Bouquinistes (Riverside Vendors)

The used-book sellers *(bouquinistes)* you see along the Seine around Notre-Dame are a Parisian fixture. It seems they've been here forever—at least since the mid-1500s, when shops and stalls lined most of the bridges in Paris. In 1557, these merchants were labeled as thieves for selling forbidden Protestant pamphlets during the Wars of Religion (Parisians were staunchly Catholic).

The term *bouquinistes* (boo-keen-eest) probably comes from the Dutch word *boeckin*, meaning "small book." First using wheelbarrows to transport and sell their goods, these hardy entrepreneurs eventually fastened trays with thin leather straps to the parapets of the bridges. After the Revolution, business boomed when entire libraries were seized from nobles or clergymen and ended up for sale cheap on the banks of the Seine. In 1891, *bouquinistes* received permission to permanently attach their boxes to the quaysides. Today, the waiting list is eight years to become one of Paris' 250 *bouquinistes*.

Each *bouquiniste* is given four boxes (*boîtes*—each 6 feet long, 14 inches high, and 2.5 feet deep), and rent is paid only for the stone on which the boxes rest (less than €100 per year). The most coveted spots are awarded based on seniority. Maintenance costs, including the required *vert* wagon paint (the green color of old train cars), is paid by the *bouquinistes*. With little overhead, prices are usually cheaper than in most shops. While these days, tourists buy magnets and posters more than vintage books, officially the city allows no more than one box of souvenirs for every three boxes of books.

Bouquinistes must be open at least four days a week. Wednesdays are best (when school is out), and warm, dry days are golden (notice that every item is wrapped in protective plastic). And yes, they do leave everything inside when they lock up at night; metal bars and padlocks keep things safe.

in clothes and furniture, and compare the selection with stores back home.

Parisian department stores begin with their spectacular perfume sections, almost always on the ground floor, and worth a visit to see how much space is devoted to scented water. Helpful information desks are usually near the perfume section (pick up the handy floor plan in English). Most stores have a good selection of souvenirs and toys at fair prices, plus reasonable restaurants; some have view terraces. Stores are generally open Monday through Saturday from 10:00 to 19:00, and all are jammed on Saturdays.

Galeries Lafayette and Printemps: You'll find both **Galeries**

Lafayette and **Printemps** (pran-tom) department stores in several Parisian neighborhoods. The most convenient and best sit side by side behind the old Opéra, complementing that monument's similar, classy era (Mo: Chaussée d'Antin-La Fayette, Havre-Caumartin, or Opéra). Both stores sprawl over three buildings and consume entire city blocks. The selection is huge, but the crowds can be overwhelming (especially on summer Saturdays).

At the Galeries Lafayette near the Opéra Garnier, don't miss the belle époque dome or the rooftop view and café on the seventh floor (open daily May–Sept, reasonable prices, enter through cafeteria on 6th floor). Fashion shows for the public take place all year at Galeries Lafayette on Tuesdays at 10:00 (call 01 42 82 30 25 to confirm time and to reserve—they speak English, in auditorium on 7th floor). Continue your shopping by walking from this area to the place Vendôme (see "Boutique Strolls," below).

Bon Marché: Combine a visit to Paris' oldest department store with a great neighborhood shopping experience. Take the Métro (or bus #87) to Sèvres-Babylone and find the Bon Marché behind a small park. The Bon Marché opened in 1852, when interest in iron and steel construction led to larger structures (like train stations, exhibition halls, and Eiffel Towers). The Bon Marché was the first large-scale store to offer fixed prices (no bargaining) and a huge selection of items under one glass roof. This rocked the commercial world and forever changed the future of shopping. High-volume sales allowed low prices and created loyal customers—can you say "Costco"?

Start your tour at the perfume section in the center—check out the excellent scarf selection next to this area—then escalate up a few floors for a better perspective. Consider a new couch (furniture on top floor) and review the toy selection in the basement. Graze the gourmet groceries in the store's second building (next door, ideal for food souvenirs like mustards, teas, and chocolates). I buy a small picnic here for the park in front.

To find my favorite boutique-store streets, walk through the small park and down rue de Sèvres, passing the grand Hôtel Lutècia on your right (see "Sèvres-Babylone to St. Sulpice," below).

La Samaritaine: This leading Parisian department store, near the pont Neuf along the Seine, was closed in 2005 after inspections found it to be in violation of many safety codes. It has been closed for major renovation until at least 2011, and may not even reopen as a department store.

Boutique Strolls
I enjoy sifting through window displays, pausing at corner cafés, and feeling the rhythm of neighborhood life. It's like a vacation

Shopping in Paris

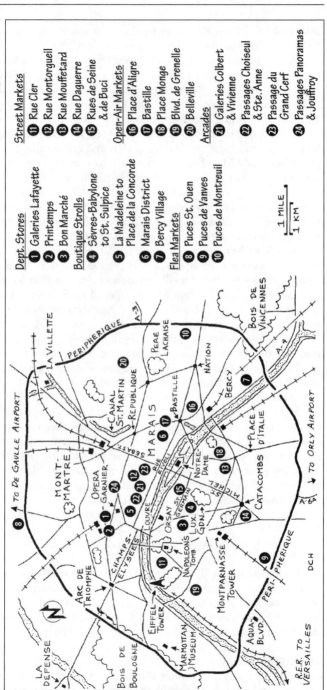

Dept. Stores
1. Galeries Lafayette
2. Printemps
3. Bon Marché

Boutique Strolls
4. Sèvres-Babylone to St. Sulpice
5. La Madeleine to Place de la Concorde
6. Marais District
7. Bercy Village

Flea Markets
8. Puces St. Ouen
9. Puces de Vanves
10. Puces de Montreuil

Street Markets
11. Rue Cler
12. Rue Montorgueil
13. Rue Mouffetard
14. Rue Daguerre
15. Rues de Seine & de Buci

Open-Air Markets
16. Place d'Aligre
17. Bastille
18. Place Monge
19. Blvd. de Grenelle
20. Belleville

Arcades
21. Galeries Colbert & Vivienne
22. Passages Choiseul & Ste. Anne
23. Passage du Grand Cerf
24. Passages Panoramas & Jouffroy

1 MILE
1 KM

from my sightseeing-focused vacation. While shops are more intimate, sales clerks are more formal—mind your manners. Here are four very different areas to lick some windows.

Sèvres-Babylone to St. Sulpice

This shopping stroll allows you to sample smart clothing boutiques and clever window displays while enjoying one of Paris' more handsome neighborhoods. This leisurely, one-hour saunter starts at the Bon Marché department store (described above) and ends at the church of St. Sulpice. It can also easily be extended to the nearby Luxembourg Garden or boulevard St. Germain, tying in well with this book's Left Bank Walk (see page 135).

After visiting the Bon Marché (Mo: Sèvres-Babylone), walk by the small park and cross boulevard Raspail, with Hôtel Lutècia to your right, and start down the rue de Sèvres. Some stores on this walk are open Sunday.

La Maison du Chocolat, next to Hôtel Lutècia (19 rue de Sèvres), makes a good first stop. The shop sells delicious ice-cream cones and handmade chocolates in exquisitely wrapped boxes. Then cross the street, walk down a block and find a seat at the atmospheric **Au Sauvignon Café** (10 rue de Sèvres), ideal for lunch or a drink and well-situated for watching the conveyor belt of shoppers glide by. Check out the zinc bar and picture-crazy interior. There's a **Mephisto** shoe store around the corner. A block farther down rue de Sèvres, a wicked half-man, half-horse statue stands guard.

From here, boutique-lined streets fan out like spokes on a wheel (from left to right): rue de Grenelle, rue du Dragon, rue du Cherche Midi, and rue du Vieux Colombier. Each street merits a detour if you're a serious shopper. Rue du Cherche Midi (follow the horse's fanny) offers an ever changing but always chic selection of shoe, purse, and clothing stores. Find Paris' best bread—beautiful round loaves with designer crust—at **Poilâne** at #8 (on the right). Next door at the small **Cuisine de Bar** café, open-faced *tartines* sandwiches and salads with bread are served (closed Sun–Mon). It's a *bar à pains.*

When back at the horse, turn right and continue down rue du Vieux Colombier. At **Longchamps** (#21), you can hunt for a stylish bag in any color. Cross busy rue de Rennes, gasping at the dreadful Montparnasse Tower (on the right), and continue down Vieux Colombier. Many stores in this area offer just one or two items, but in a variety of colors and patterns. Check out **Vilebrequin** if the man or *petit-garçon* in your life needs a swimsuit. St. Sulpice awaits a block farther down. The **Café de la Mairie** (to your left as you face the church) has a privileged location on this lovely square. From here, you can visit St. Sulpice (see page 143) and either cross the square to Luxembourg Garden (page 145) or backtrack to rue

Bonaparte, turning right to reach the boulevard St. Germain (and more shopping and several Grands Cafés, described on page 364).

For Paris's best pastries—according to local shopkeepers and my wife—continue along rue St Sulpice, with the church on your right, passing **Café Estrella** (#34, excellent teas and coffee with *real* French roast; ask the friendly owner, Jean-Claude). Just beyond, take the second left on rue de Seine (marked *rue du Tournon* to the right) and find **Gérard Mulot's Pâtisserie/Bakery**. Try his chocolate macaroons and savory quiches—oh, baby (76 rue de Seine, tel. 01 43 26 85 77).

From here, the closest Métro station is Odéon. To get there, continue on rue du Seine up to boulevard St. Germain and walk a couple of blocks to the right.

Place de la Madeleine, Rue Royale, Place Vendôme, and Place de la Concorde

The ritzy streets connecting these high-priced squares are a magnificent mile of gourmet food shops, jewelry stores, four-star hotels, perfumeries, and exclusive clothing boutiques. No area better shows the value Parisians place on outrageously priced products. If you include the place Vendôme detour (with brief stops to shop), this walk takes about two hours. For most, the one-hour walk *sans* detour, ending on place de la Concorde, offers a sufficient sample of conspicuous consumption.

Place de la Madeleine: Start at place de la Madeleine for a gourmet food fantasy (see map on page 378; Mo: Madeleine—follow *sortie* signs to #4 or #5 rue Tronchet, at the back of the Madeleine). Work your way counterclockwise around the square, starting at the black-and-white awnings of **Fauchon,** behind the basilica (26–30 place de la Madeleine, to your left as you exit the Métro). This bastion of over-the-top food products has faded from its glory days. Today, it caters to a largely tourist clientele—though it can still make your mouth water and your pocketbook ache. There used to be other Fauchon outposts all over Paris, until competitor Le Nôtre bought them all. Now the only Fauchon that remains is this granddaddy store—the place where it all began. Two separate shops are necessary to meet demand. The *Traiteur* (Mon–Sat 8:00–21:00, closed Sun, tel. 01 70 39 38 96) is like a delicatessen with prepared foods—meats, meals, *pâtisseries* (pastries), breads, and cookies (of course, there are always *Madeleines* on this square). Above the *Traiteur,* you can have a meal or a drink in the *Salon de Thé* (Mon–Sat 12:00–21:00, closed Sun, tel. 01 70 39 38 92). The *Confiserie et Epicerie* (candies and grocery) is the shop across the small street (Mon–Sat 9:00–20:00, closed Sun). The various sections are each worth a quick glance, even though you'll see better elsewhere. But the *Epicerie*—on the ground floor, with its

exotic spreads and jams—is a must. Stroll downstairs and find "the prestigious alcohols" (*les Alcools de Prestige*, in small glass case at the rear), containing €7,000 bottles of century-old Cognac—who buys this stuff? There's also a room devoted to Champagne, and, of course, carefully selected wine. Ride the padded pink elevator up to the aromatic tea shop and exotic spice room, and a surprise tea room with reclining couches and a few peaceful courtyard tables (Mon–Sat 12:00–18:00, closed Sun).

Turn right out of Fauchon's and find **Hédiard** across the square (at #21, Mon–Sat 8:30–21:00, closed Sun, tel. 01 43 12 88 85). This older, more appealing, and more accessible gourmet food shop was founded in 1854. It offers elegantly displayed produce and meats, a slick atrium wine shop, and a nifty café above (take the glass elevator up for a coffee or lunch). The small red containers make good souvenirs, with flavored mustards, jams, coffee, candies, and tea. Anyone can enter the glass doors of the wine cellar, marked *Le Chais*, and be greeted by the sommelier, but you need special permission to access *Les Vénérables* wines.

Next to Hédiard at #19 is **La Maison des Truffes,** the house of truffles (Mon–Sat 9:30–21:00, closed Sun, tel. 01 42 66 10 01). Check out the window display of black mushrooms that sell for about €180 a pound. Inside, you'll find several cozy little tables with a €60 tasting *menu* and a €20 daily *menu*. You'll also see every possible food that can be made with truffles—even Armagnac brandy—as well as white truffles from Italy that sell for €2,500 a pound. Small jars have black truffles for €40.

At #17, **Caviar Kaspia,** you can add Iranian caviar, eel, and vodka to your truffle collection. The restaurant upstairs serves what you see downstairs—at exorbitant prices (Mon–Sat 10:00–24:00, closed Sun).

Rue Royale: Passing the snazzy Baccarat crystal shop on your right and keeping straight, cross three crosswalks and trade expensive food for more expensive things. Strut one block down the rue Royale. At rue St. Honoré, cross rue Royale—pausing in the middle for a great view both ways—and find **Ladurée**, an out-of-this-world pastry break in an 1800s setting (look for the green awning, open daily until 21:00).

Place Vendôme: A detour left on rue St. Honoré leads several blocks past clothing boutiques and a great toy store (**Au Nain Bleu** at corner, #408) to place Vendôme (turn left on rue de Castiglione). The *très* elegant place Vendôme is home to the Ritz Hôtel on the left (Hemingway liberated the bar in World War II) and upper-crust jewelry stores—**Van Cleef & Arpels**, **Dior**, **Chanel**, **Cartier**, and others (if you have to ask how much...). Only jewelry stores are allowed on place Vendôme. The square was created by Louis XIV during the 17th century as a setting for a statue of himself. One hundred and

fifty years later, Louis XIV was replaced by a statue of Napoleon.

Leave place Vendôme by walking up rue de la Paix—strolling by still more jewelry, high-priced watches, and crystal—and enter place de l'Opéra, where you'll find the *Paris Story* film, a TI, the Opéra Garnier (see page 60), and Galleries Lafayette and Printemps—if you're not shopped out yet (see above). Or return to our walk on rue Royale.

Place de la Concorde: You can pass on the place Vendôme detour and continue two more blocks down rue Royale to its end at place de la Concorde. Browse the crystal shops (follow the lighted cobbles into the **Galerie Royale** at #11 for a royal selection of crystal), then cross rue Royale to pick up your new car at the **Audi Boutique**. At place de la Concorde, find **Hôtel Crillon** for the appropriate finish to this walk (see "Les Grands Cafés de Paris," page 364).

Marais

For more eclectic, avant-garde stores, peruse the artsy shops between the Pompidou Center and place des Vosges. Stick to the west-to-east axes formed by rue Ste. Croix de la Bretonnerie, rue des Rosiers, rue des Francs Bourgeois, and rue St. Antoine. (These streets are part of the Marais Walk; see map on page 107.) On Sunday afternoons, when the rest of Paris naps, this area buzzes with shoppers and café crowds.

Don't miss the luxurious tea extravaganza at **Mariage Frères,** just off rue Ste. Croix de la Bretonnerie at 30 rue du Bourg Tibourg.

If you need a *chocolat* fix (the movie and the candy), walk down rue Vieille du Temple toward rue du Rivoli and find **Cacao et Chocolat** at #36, with deliciously beautiful chocolates, served in a place that feels right out of the movie *Chocolat*.

Between place des Vosges and the Carnavalet Museum, **rue des Francs Bourgeois** is the epicenter of Marais chic, with hyper-trendy boutiques. At #47, check out *art du buro* with Parisian-cool office supplies, and at #40, find the beautiful yarn and patterns of Pelote at Laines, Anny Blatt, where owner Christine is likely to be knitting behind the counter when not helping clients.

Complete your walk with a tasty pastry at Paumier Pâtisserie et Confiserie (#52). This is a local favorite, with four small tables and delicious *pâtisseries*, cookies, coffee, and hot chocolate.

Bercy Village

For a contemporary, more casual, and less frenetic shopping experience—and a look at Paris' latest urban renewal project—come to Bercy Village (daily 11:00–21:00 year-round). This formerly run-down district of 18th- and 19th-century wine warehouses is now

a gleaming, trendy mix of old and new—one of Paris' hot spots for shopping and evening fun. This neighborhood swapped barrels for boutiques and has been transformed into an outdoor shopping mall. The Cour St. Emilion, named for one of Bordeaux's wine villages, is lined with cafés and appealing shops. Rail tracks are still embedded in the cobbles, and photos of its original purpose hang under the passages. **Club Med** greets you with its *zone de plaisir* complex of shops and restaurants that positively throb at night. Quiz nights, concerts, and "Friday Night Fever" keep a young clientele well-entertained. Don't miss the **French National Museum store** and the **Animalis** pet shop.

Getting There: Taking the Métro to Bercy Village is half the fun. You'll ride Paris' newest Métro line, nicknamed "the Meteor." This futuristic line #14 is totally automated, allowing passengers to walk the length of the train and sit at the very front to watch tunnels come and go (no more driver). In each station, tracks are enclosed in high walls, with sliding doors that match the parked train and make the platforms suicide-proof. After you get off at Cour St. Emilion, the escalator deposits you in the pedestrian-friendly heart of the district. You'll see typical French shops like Resonances, Sephora, and FNAC, as well as "Zeus" (a vast, glassy, banana-shaped exhibition center), Cinecite (a plush complex of 18 cinemas), and plenty of lively eateries.

Sleeping in Bercy Village: $ **Hotel Ibis**** is a chain hotel offering very cheap and small but clean, modern, and efficient rooms across from Cour St. Emilion (Db-€60–70, 2 place de l'Europe, tel. 01 49 77 11 97, fax 01 49 77 81 91, h2041@accor-hotels.com).

Flea Markets

Paris plays host to three sprawling flea markets (*marché aux puces;* mar-shay oh-poos; literally translated, since *puce* is French for flea). These oversized garage sales were started in the Middle Ages, when middlemen would sell old, flea-infested clothes and discarded possessions of the wealthy at bargain prices to eager peasants. Buyers were allowed to rummage through piles of aristocratic garbage.

No event better brings together the melting-pot population of Paris than these carnival-like markets. Some find them claustrophobic and crowded, others find French *diamants*-in-the-rough and return happy. All three of Paris' flea markets take place over weekends and two are open Mondays, the calmest day. Come early to avoid crowds. You can bargain a bit (best deals are made with cash at the end of the day), though don't expect swinging deals here. Wear your money belt; pickpockets enjoy these wall-to-wall-shopper events.

The **Puces St. Ouen** (poos sahn-wahn) is the mother of all

flea markets, with more than 2,000 vendors selling everything from flamingos to faucets, but mostly antiques (Sat 9:00–18:00, Sun 10:00–18:00, Mon 11:00–17:00, closed Tue–Fri, pretty dead the first 2 weeks of Aug, tel. 01 58 61 22 90, www.st-ouen-tourisme.com and www.parispuces.com). Near as I can tell, the term "antique" covers anything from funky art objects to Louis XVI chairs. Thirteen different "antique markets" and endless stalls fill this strange area just outside Paris. Space was created in the 1800s, when the city wall was demolished (now a freeway), which left large tracts of land open. The vacuum eventually was filled by street vendors, then antique dealers. The hodgepodge pattern of markets reflects their unplanned evolution. Strolling the markets can feel more like touring a souk in North Africa, a place of narrow alleys packed with people and too much to see.

Even if antiques, African objects, and T-shirts aren't your thing, many will find this market worth the Métro ride. Come for lunch in one of the many lively and reasonable cafés and receive a reality check, away from the beautiful people and glorious monuments of Paris. You'll get a dose of life in "the 'burbs."

To get to the Puces St. Ouen, take Métro line #4 to the end of the line at Porte de Clingancourt, then carefully follow *Sortie, Marché aux Puces* signs. Walk straight out of the Métro down avenue de la Porte de Clingancourt, passing by leather stores and through blocks of trinkets and cheap clothing stalls. Your destination is just beyond the elevated freeway (white bridge). Cross under the freeway, leaving Paris and entering the suburb of St. Ouen, veering left on the angled street. Turn left onto rue des Rosiers, the spine that links the many markets of St. Ouen. Most markets consist of a series of covered alleys, each specializing in a different angle on antiques, bric-a-brac, and junk. You'll see Marchés Vernaison, Dauphine, Biron, and Paul Bert by walking down rue des Rosiers, then turning left on rue Paul Bert, then left again on rue Jules Vallès and returning to the Métro.

Puces de Vanves is comparatively tiny and civilized, and preferred by many flea-market connoisseurs who find better deals at less famous markets (Sat–Sun 7:00–17:00, closed Mon–Fri, Mo: Porte de Vanves). The mega-**Puces de Montreuil** is the least organized and most traditional of them all, with chatty sellers and competitive buyers (Sat–Mon 8:00–18:00, closed Tue–Fri, Mo: Porte de Montreuil).

Open-Air Markets
Browse these markets for picnics, or find a corner café from which to appreciate the scene. I've listed Paris' most appealing markets below.

Street Markets

Several traffic-free street markets like rue Cler overflow with flow-ers, produce, fish vendors, and butchers, illustrating how most Parisians shopped before the invention of supermarkets and depart-ment stores. Markets are open daily except Sunday afternoons, Monday, and lunchtime throughout the week (13:00–15:00).

Rue Cler is a refined street market serving an upscale neigh-borhood near the Eiffel Tower (Mo: Ecole Militaire; for details, see Rue Cler Walk, page 115).

Rue Montorgueil is a thriving and less touristed mar-ket street. Ten blocks from the Louvre and five blocks from the Pompidou Center, rue Montorgueil (mohn-tor-go-ee) is famous as the last vestige of the once massive Les Halles market (just north of St. Eustache church, Mo: Etienne Marcel). Once the home of big warehouses and wholesale places to support the market, these have morphed into retail outlets to survive. Other traffic-free streets cross rue Montorgueil—don't miss the nearby covered arcade, passage du Grand Cerf (down rue Marie Stuart at the Les Halles end of rue Montorgueil).

Rue Daguerre, near the Catacombs and off avenue du Général Leclerc, is the least touristy of the four street mar-kets (Mo: Denfert-Rochereau; for Catacombs description, see page 59).

Rue de Seine and rue de Buci combine to make a central and colorful market within easy reach of many sights (Mo: Odéon; see also "Les Grands Cafés de Paris," page 364, and Left Bank Walk, page 135).

Larger, Morning-Only Markets

Offering cheaper prices and more selection, these markets take over selected boulevards and squares throughout Paris generally from 8:00 to 12:30. Expect a lively combination of flea- and street-market atmosphere and items.

Marché de la place d'Aligre, 10 blocks behind the Opéra Bastille down rue de Faubourg St. Antoine, is an intimate open-air market where you'll see few tourists (daily 9:00–12:00, place d'Aligre, Mo: Ledru-Rollin).

Marché de la Bastille is huge, with a vast selection of prod-ucts (Thu and Sun, Mo: Bastille); consider combining either of these two markets with a stroll through Promenade Plantée park (see page 67) and the Marais Walk (page 106).

Marché place Monge is comparatively minuscule, specializ-ing in high-quality foods (Wed, Fri, and Sun; near rue Mouffetard, Mo: Monge).

Marché boulevard de Grenelle, a few blocks southwest of Champ de Mars park and the rue Cler area, is packed with

produce, non-perishable goods, and Parisians in search of a good value (Wed and Sun, between Dupleix and La Motte Picquet-Grenelle Métro stops).

Marché Belleville is big and very untouristy (Tue and Fri, Mo: Belleville).

Arcaded Shopping Streets *(Passages)*

More than 200 of these covered shopping streets once crisscrossed Paris, providing much-needed shelter from the rain. The first were built during the American Revolution, though the ones you'll see date from the 1800s. Today, only a handful remain to remind us where shopping malls got their inspiration, although they now sell things you would be more likely to find in flea markets than at JC Penney. Here's a short list to weave into your sightseeing plan. (They're located on the color map of Paris at the beginning of this book.)

Galerie Vivienne, behind the Palais Royal off rue des Petits-Champs and a few blocks from the Louvre, are the most refined and accessible of the *passages* for most, though they don't reflect the typical, more funky *passages* (Mo: Pyramides or Palais Royal). Check out Le Grand Colbert, a surprisingly affordable yet elegant restaurant with decent cuisine.

Passage Choiseul and **Passage Ste. Anne,** four blocks west of Galerie Colbert and Galerie Vivienne, are classic examples of most Parisian *passages,* selling used books, paper products, trinkets, and snacks (down rue des Petits-Champs toward avenue de l'Opéra, same Métro stops).

Passage du Grand Cerf is a more elegant arcade, easily combined with a visit to the nearby rue Montorgueil street market described above (Mo: Etienne Marcel).

Passage Panoramas and **Passage Jouffroy** are long galleries that connect with several other smaller *passages* to give you the best sense of the elaborate network of arcades that once existed (on both sides of boulevard Montmartre, between Métro stops Grands Boulevards/rue Montmartre and Richelieu Drouot).

Getting a VAT Refund

Wrapped into the purchase price of your Parisian souvenirs is a Value Added Tax (VAT) that's generally about 19.6 percent. If you make a purchase in France of more than €175 at a store that participates in the VAT refund scheme, you're entitled to get most of that tax back. Personally, I've never felt that VAT refunds are worth the hassle, but if you do, here's the scoop.

You must be over 15 and if you're lucky, the merchant will subtract the tax when you make your purchase; this is more likely if the store ships the goods to your home. Otherwise, you'll need to:

Get the paperwork. Have the merchant completely fill out the necessary refund document (*Bordereay de Vente a l'Exportation*—also called a "cheque"). You'll have to present your passport at the store.

Get your stamp at the border. Process your cheque(s) at your last stop in the EU (e.g., at the airport) by the customs agent who deals with VAT refunds. It's best to keep your purchases in your carry-on for viewing, but if they're too large or considered too dangerous (such as knives) to carry on, then track down the proper customs agent to inspect them before you check your bag. You're not supposed to use your purchased goods before you leave. If you show up at customs wearing your chic new French ensemble, officials might look the other way—or deny you a refund.

Collect your refund. You'll need to return your stamped document to the retailer or its representative. Many merchants work with a service, such as Global Refund or Premier Tax Free, which have offices at major airports, ports, or border crossings. These services, which extract a 4 percent fee, can refund your money immediately in your currency of choice or credit your card (within 2 billing cycles). If you have to deal directly with the retailer, mail the store your stamped documents, and wait. It could take months.

Customs

You can take home $800 in souvenirs per person duty-free. The next $1,000 is taxed at a flat 3 percent. After that, you pay the individual item's duty rate. You can also bring in a liter of alcohol (slightly more than a standard-sized bottle of wine), a carton of cigarettes, and up to 100 cigars duty-free. Don't bring home absinthe or Cuban cigars, which are illegal here. As for food, anything in cans (such as foie gras or meat products) or sealed jars is acceptable. Skip cheeses, dried meats, fruits, and vegetables. To check customs rules and duty rates, visit www.customs.gov.

NIGHTLIFE

Paris is brilliant after dark. Save energy from your day's sightseeing and experience the City of Light lit. Whether it's a concert at the Sainte-Chapelle, a boat ride on the Seine, a walk in Montmartre, a hike up the Arc de Triomphe, or a late-night café, you'll see Paris come alive. Night walks in Paris are wonderful. Any of the self-guided walking tours in the book are terrific after dark.

The *Pariscope* magazine (€0.40 at any newsstand, in French) offers a complete weekly listing of music, cinema, theater, opera, and other special events—I decipher this useful periodical for you below. The *Paris Voice* newspaper, in English, has a monthly review of Paris entertainment (available at any English-language bookstore, French-American establishments, or the American Church, www.parisvoice.com).

Pariscope

The weekly *Pariscope* (€0.40) or *L'Officiel des Spectacles* (€0.35) is essential if you want to know what's going on in Paris. I prefer *Pariscope*. Pick one up at a newsstand and page through it.

The magazine, all in French, begins with culture news, then lists "Théâtre" and what's playing at all key theater venues. "Musique and Concerts Classiques" follow, listing each day's events (program, location, time, price), including both opera houses if performances are scheduled. Remember that some concerts are free *(entrée libre)*.

"Visites et Promenades" covers outdoor events, including outdoor theater, flea markets, sound-and-light shows *(son et lumières)*, key monuments like the Eiffel Tower and Arc de Triomphe, river cruises, parks, zoos, and aquariums.

The "Enfants" section covers a myriad of possible children's activities. "Spectacles" are shows (like magic shows); you'll also

see many "Marionettes" shows and "Cirques" (circuses)—both are fun, even for non-French-speakers.

A third of the magazine is devoted to *Cinéma*—a Parisian forte. The "Films en Exclusivité" pages list all the films playing in town. While a code marks films as "Comédie," "Documentaire," "Karaté," "Erotisme," and so on, the key mark for tourists is "v.o.," which means *version originale* (original-language version). "Dessin Animé" means cartoon. Films are listed alphabetically, by neighborhood ("Salles Paris"), and by genre. To find a showing near your hotel, simply match the arrondissement. "Salles Périphérie" are out in the suburbs.

The next section, "Arts," lists current hours for temporary expositions and all the museums (*tlj* = daily, *sf* = except, *Ent* = entry price, *TR* = reduced price—usually for students and children).

The "Sport et Bien-Etre" section lists public pools, hikes, steam baths, and sporting venues.

For cancan mischief, look under "Paris la Nuit."

Music

Jazz Clubs—With a lively mix of American, French, and international musicians, Paris has been an internationally acclaimed jazz capital since World War II. Unfortunately, many clubs are smoky, some wedge too many customers into too few tables, others are downright expensive, and some are guilty of all of the above. You'll pay €10–25 to enter a jazz club (one drink may be included; if not, expect to pay €5–10 per drink; beer is cheapest). See *Pariscope* magazine under "Musique" for listings, or, even better, the American Church's *Paris Voice* paper for a good monthly review, or drop by the clubs to check out the calendars posted on their front doors. Music starts after 21:00 in most clubs. Some offer dinner concerts from about 20:30 on. Here are several good bets:

Caveau de la Huchette, a characteristic old jazz club, fills an ancient Latin Quarter cellar with live jazz and frenzied dancing every night (about €10 admission on weekdays, €14 on weekends, €6 drinks, Tue–Sun 21:30–2:30 in the morning or later, closed Mon, 5 rue de la Huchette, Mo: St. Michel, recorded info tel. 01 43 26 65 05, www.caveaudelahuchette.fr).

For a hotbed of late-night activity and jazz, go to the two-block-long rue des Lombards, at boulevard Sébastopol, midway between the river and the Pompidou Center (Mo: Châtelet). **Au Duc des Lombards,** right at the corner, is one of the most popular and respected jazz clubs in Paris, with concerts generally at 21:00 (42 rue des Lombards, tel. 01 42 33 22 88). **Le Sunside** offers more traditional jazz—Dixieland and big band—and fewer crowds, with concerts generally at 21:00 (60 rue des Lombards, tel. 01 40 26 21 25).

At the more down-to-earth and mellow **La Cave du Franc Pinot,** you can enjoy a glass of chardonnay at the main-floor wine bar, then drop downstairs for a cool jazz scene. They have good dinner-and-jazz values as well—allow about €50 per person (closed Sun–Mon, located on Ile St. Louis where pont Marie meets the island, 1 quai de Bourbon, Mo: Pont Marie, tel. 01 46 33 60 64).

Old-Time Parisian Cabaret on Montmartre: Au Lapin Agile— This historic cabaret maintains the atmosphere of the heady days when bohemians would gather here to enjoy wine, song, and sexy jokes. For €24, you gather with about 25 French people in a dark room for a drink and as many as 10 different performers—mostly singers with a piano. Performers range from sweet and innocent Amélie types to naughty Maurice Chevalier types. While tourists are welcome, it's exclusively French, with no accommodation for English-speakers (and non-French-speakers will be lost). You sit at carved wooden tables in a dimly lit room, taste the traditional drink, and are immersed in a true Parisian ambience. The soirée covers traditional French standards, love ballads, sea chanteys, and more. The crowd sings along, as it has here for a century (Tue–Sun 21:00–2:00 in the morning, closed Mon, 22 rue des Saules, tel. 01 46 06 85 87, www.au-lapin-agile.com; also see page 130 of Montmartre Walk).

Classical Concerts—For classical music on any night, consult *Pariscope* magazine; the "Musique" section under "Concerts Classiques" lists concerts (both free and for a fee). Look for posters at tourist-oriented churches. From March through November, these churches regularly host concerts: St. Sulpice, St. Germain-des-Prés, Ste. Madeleine, St. Eustache, St. Julien-le-Pauvre, and Sainte-Chapelle. It's worth the €15-23 entry for the pleasure of hearing Mozart while surrounded by the stained glass of the tiny Sainte-Chapelle (it's unheated—bring a sweater). Look also for daytime concerts in parks, such as the Luxembourg Garden. Even the Galeries Lafayette department store offers concerts. Many concerts are free *(entrée libre)*, such as the Sunday atelier concert sponsored by the American Church (Sept–May at 17:00 or 18:00 but not every week, 65 quai d'Orsay, Mo: Invalides, RER: Pont de l'Alma, tel. 01 40 62 05 00).

Opera—Paris is home to two well-respected opera venues. The Opéra Bastille is the massive modern opera house that dominates place de la Bastille. Come here for state-of-the-art special effects and modern interpretations of classic ballets and operas. In the spirit of this everyman's opera, unsold seats are available at a big discount to seniors and students 15 minutes before the show (Mo: Bastille, tel. 01 43 43 96 96). The Opéra Garnier, Paris' first opera house, hosts opera and ballet performances. Come here for less expensive tickets and grand belle époque decor (Mo: Opéra, tel. 01

44 73 13 99). For tickets, call 01 44 73 13 00, go to the opera ticket offices (open 11:00–18:00), or—best—reserve on the Web at www .opera-de-paris.fr (for both opera houses).

Art in the Evening

Various **museums** are open late on different evenings, offering the opportunity for more relaxed, less-crowded visits: Louvre (Wed and Fri until 21:45), Orsay (Thu until 21:45), and Pompidou Center (Wed–Mon until 21:00).

Art gallery openings are a fun way to check out new work by contemporary artists. Opening night receptions *(vernissage)* are both classy and free. Check upcoming events listed in the *Paris Voice* newspaper (described above, www.parisvoice.com), or just follow my Left Bank Walk (on page 135) and see what's happening.

Seine River Cruises

Bateaux-Mouches offer one-hour cruises on huge glass-domed boats (or open-air decks in summer) with departures along the Seine, including from the Eiffel Tower (every 20–30 min, runs daily 10:00–22:30, see page 35).

Night Walks

Go for a walk to best appreciate the City of Light. Break for ice cream, pause at a café, and enjoy the sidewalk entertainers as you join the post-dinner Parisian parade. Use any of this book's self-guided walking tours as a blueprint, and remember to avoid poorly lit areas and stick to main thoroughfares. Consider the following suggestions; most are partial versions of this book's longer walking tours.

Champs-Elysées and the Arc de Triomphe—The avenue des Champs-Elysées glows after dark. Start at the Arc de Triomphe, then stroll down Paris' lively grand promenade. A right turn on avenue George V leads to the Bateaux-Mouches river cruises. A movie on the Champs-Elysées is a fun experience (weekly listings in *Pariscope* under "Cinéma"). ❂ See Champs-Elysées Walk, page 95.

Trocadéro and Eiffel Tower—This is one of Paris' most spectacular views at night. Take the Métro to the Trocadéro stop and join the party on place de la Trocadéro for a magnificent view of the glowing Eiffel Tower. It's a festival of gawkers, drummers, street acrobats, and entertainers. Pass the fountains and cross the river to the base of the tower, worth the effort even if you don't go up. See "Eiffel Tower," page 49.

From the Eiffel Tower, you can stroll through parc du Champ de Mars past Frisbees, soccer balls, and romantic couples, and take the Métro home (Ecole Militaire stop, across avenue de la Motte

Picquet from far southeast corner of park). Or there's a handy RER stop (Champ de Mars-Tour Eiffel) two blocks west of the Eiffel Tower.

Ile St. Louis and Notre-Dame—Take the beautiful Historic Paris Walk (❂ see page 70) after a dinner on Ile St. Louis (see page 79).

To get to Ile St. Louis, take the Métro (line #7) to the Pont Marie stop, then cross pont Marie to Ile St. Louis. Turn right up rue St. Louis-en-l'Ile, stopping for dinner—or at least a Berthillon ice cream at #31 or Amorino Gelati at #47. At the end of Ile St. Louis, cross pont St. Louis to Ile de la Cité, with a great view of Notre-Dame. Cross to the Left Bank on quai de l'Archevêché, and drop down to the river to the right for the best floodlit views. Consider a drink aboard one of the boats along the river, then end your walk on place du Parvis Notre-Dame in front of Notre-Dame, or continue across the river to the Latin Quarter.

Place de la Concorde, Place Vendôme, and Place de l'Opéra—These three squares tie together nicely for an elegant post-dinner walk (❂ see Shopping, page 374). Take the Métro to place de la Concorde and splurge for a pricey drink at the most expensive hotel in Paris (Hôtel Crillon, see "Les Grands Cafés de Paris," page 364). Get out to the obelisk for a terrific view of the Champs-Elysées and the beautifully lit, Greek-looking National Assembly building (to your left looking up the Champs-Elysées). Now, walk up rue Royale toward the Madeleine church, turn right on rue St. Honoré, then left after several blocks on rue Castiglione. The sumptuous place Vendôme makes me wish I were rich. Exit place Vendôme at the opposite end and walk up the rue de la Paix to find Opéra Garnier, stunning at night (see page 60; Mo: Opéra is right there to take you home).

Montmartre—Take the funicular to the area near Sacré-Cœur and join the party (❂ see Montmartre Walk, page 123). Follow our walking tour as far as you like, but keep to the top of the hill (avoid place Pigalle and boulevard de Rochechouart). Have a drink on place du Tertre and get your portrait sketched. Montmartre was a nighttime destination for Parisians in search of a lively evening even before the Impressionists arrived. For some old-time cabaret music, consider **Au Lapin Agile** (described above). Sit in front of the church (to leave the rabble, jump the fence for a spot on the grass) and marvel at the city stretching forever at your feet.

Rue de Lappe—Take a walk on Paris' wild side along the three-block stretch of rue de Lappe behind the Bastille, from boulevard Richard Lenoir to rue de Charonne (Mo: Bastille). Nightclubs, bouncer-staffed bars, and youthful, boy-meets-girl energy power this late-night scene.

Place St. Germain-des-Prés and Odéon—These areas are close to each other, worth combining for evening fun. **Place St. Germain-des-Prés,** along the Left Bank's main east–west route, hosts street theater and musicians that are better than ones you'll hear in the Métro. The St. Germain-des-Prés church is often lit up and open at night, and Parisians sip drinks at two famous nearby cafés: Les Deux Magots and Le Café de Flore—see page 142 (Mo: St. Germain-des-Prés). Nearby, night owls prowl along rues des Canettes and Guisarde (see "Near St. Sulpice Church" on page 362 of the Eating chapter). The Odéon, a few blocks away, is home to several movie theaters and still more lively cafés.

After-Dark Bus Tour

Several companies offer evening tours of Paris. I've described the company offering the most tours below. These trips are sold through your hotel (brochures in lobby) or directly at the offices listed below. You save no money by buying direct.

Paris Illumination Tours, run by Paris Vision, connect all the great illuminated sights of Paris with a 100-minute bus tour in 12 languages. The double-decker buses have huge windows, but the most desirable front seats are sometimes reserved for customers who've bought tickets for the overrated Moulin Rouge. Left-side seats are better. Visibility is fine in the rain.

You'll stampede on with a United Nations of tourists, get a set of headphones, dial up your language, and listen to a tape-recorded spiel (which is interesting, but includes an annoyingly bright TV screen and a pitch for the other, more-expensive excursions). Uninspired as it is, the ride provides an entertaining first-night overview of the city at its floodlit and scenic best. Bring your city map to stay oriented as you go. You're always on the bus, but the driver slows for photos at viewpoints (adults–€24, kids under 11 ride free, departures 19:00–22:00 depending on time of year, usually April–Oct only, reserve 1 day in advance, departs from Paris Vision office at 214 rue de Rivoli, across the street from Mo: Tuileries, tel. 01 42 60 30 01, fax 01 42 86 95 36, www.parisvision.com).

Floodlit Paris Taxi Tour

For an alterative, consider the self-guided taxi tour below. Seeing the City of Light floodlit is one of Europe's great travel experiences and, for most, a great finale to a day in Paris. It's worth ▲▲. For about the cost of two seats on a big bus tour, you can hire your own cab and have a glorious hour of illuminated Paris on your terms and schedule. The downside: You don't have the high vantage point and big windows. The upside: You go when and where you like.

Tour Overview: This is a circular, one-hour route—from Notre-Dame to the Eiffel Tower along the Left Bank, then back

along the Right Bank. Or tailor-make your own plan, starting and ending where you'd like, and making any stops along the way that traffic will allow.

Taxi Logistics: Taxis have a strict meter (€26/hr plus about €1 per kilometer), so if you do a 20-kilometer, one-hour tour, you'll pay €46. If your cabbie works well with you and is fun, you'd round things up to €50. (Some cabbies may work off the meter for you, but establish a firm hourly rate if you do this.) Traffic is light and lights are bright between 22:00 and 24:00. If you leave Notre-Dame at about half past the hour, you'll get to the Eiffel Tower as it twinkles (the first 10 min of each hour after dark). You can fit up to four in a cab, though this is tight for decent sightseeing (with 3, everyone gets a window). Photocopy the taxi instructions on page 396 and make sure the cabbie understands the plan (and enjoys the challenge). And you're on your way. Roll the windows down, learn your driver's name and use it, work with him to select a good radio station, and turn the cab light on to read if you like (this is no problem for the driver). Stop when you like (remembering the meter runs about at about €0.50 per minute when stopped). Learn and use the key words:

English	French	Pronounced
Stop, please.	*Arrêtez, s'il vous plaît.*	ah-ret-tay see voo play
Slower, please.	*Lentement, s'il vous plaît.*	lawn-tuh-mohn see voo play
I love Paris!	*J'aime Paris!*	zhem pah-ree

The Tour Begins: Start at **Notre-Dame** (taxi stand just in front, on left). Drive over pont d'Arcole to **Hôtel de Ville**, then turn right along the Seine (the white stripe of light is a modern bridge connecting the 2 islands).

Cross **Ile St. Louis** on pont Marie. Stop on the next bridge (pont de la Tournelle) just after the island, get out, and giggle with delight at the city and floodlit Notre-Dame. Then turn right along the Seine on quai de la Tournelle past Notre-Dame.

Drive west along the entire length of the long **Louvre** (once the world's biggest building—across the river), then under the **Orsay Museum** (above you, on left). The **National Assembly** (on left) faces **place de la Concorde** (on right, with plush Hôtel Crillon floodlit beyond the obelisk). The ornate **pont Alexandre** comes next (on right).

Turn left down Esplanade des Invalides to the gilded dome of **Les Invalides**, marking Napoleon's tomb. Circle left around Invalides for a close-up view of the brilliant dome. Get out at **place Vauban** (behind the dome) and marvel at the symmetry.

Take avenue de Tourville to avenue Bourdonnais, which runs alongside the **Champ de Mars** park (former military training grounds, now serving as the Eiffel Tower's backyard). Turn left onto avenue Joseph Bouvard, leading to a circle made to-order for viewing the **Eiffel Tower**. Get out and gasp.

Pont d'Iéna leads from right in front of the tower across the Seine to **place Trocadéro** for another grand Eiffel view (get out again for the best distant photo).

Avenue Kléber leads through one of Paris' ritziest neighborhoods to the **Arc de Triomphe**. Battle twice around the eternal flame marking the Tomb of the Unknown Soldier and Paris' craziest traffic circle. Notice the rules of the road: Get to the center ASAP, those entering have the right-of-way, and any accidents are no-fault (insurance companies just split the costs down the middle).

When ready to continue, say the rhyme, "**Champs-Elysées**, *s'il vous plaît*." Cruise down Europe's grandest boulevard to the bold white obelisk marking the former site of the guillotine, **place de la Concorde.**

Circle once (maybe twice) around place de la Concorde, picking out all the famous landmarks near and far. Then continue east along the Seine on quai Tuileries (the 2 train-station clocks across the river mark the **Orsay Museum**) and sneak (via a taxi/bus-only lane) into the courtyard of the **Louvre** for a close look at the magically floodlit **pyramid**. Stop here.

Return to the riverfront along the Right Bank and pass the oldest bridge in Paris, **pont Neuf,** and the impressive **Conciergerie** with its floodlit medieval turrets (this is where Marie-Antoinette was imprisoned during the Revolution). Turn right on pont de Notre-Dame and you complete the loop back where you (and Paris) started, at the **Notre-Dame** on the Ile de la Cité.

Montmartre Extra: For about €20 more (one-way), you can extend your night drive to Montmartre and end your taxi tour there. You'll pass many more floodlit sights and you'll experience the night scene on Paris' rollicking hill. The steps in front of Sacré-Cœur are filled with tourists and pickpockets. The café scene on and around place du Tertre is always lively. It's touristy and fun for those with the right mindset. (For more on Montmartre, see the self-guided walking tour on page 123.) If you choose to return to your hotel by subway, remember that the Métro closes down at 00:30 in the morning. Or you can stay in your taxi and return home for another €15–20.

Here's the route from the Louvre: Drive from the Louvre, through place Vendôme (with Hôtel Ritz on your left), to the Opéra Garnier, then go up rue de la Chaussée past the Trinity Church, then drive up rue Jean Baptiste to rue Pigalle. Drive up

Taxi Instructions

Good evening, Monsieur/Madame. We are tourists and would like a tour of Paris at night. Are you willing to take us on the following route? We expect to be with you an hour with a few short stops. We will pay the metered rate. How much do you expect this to cost?

Bonsoir, Monsieur/Madame. Nous sommes des touristes et nous voulons faire un circuit touristique de Paris illuminé. Est-ce que vous serriez d'accord pour suivre la route suivante? Nous restons avec vous une heure, avec quelques petits arrêts. Nous paierons le montant indiqué sur le compteur. Combien ca couter?

1. Notre-Dame
2. Hôtel de Ville
3. Pont Marie
4. Pont de la Tournelle (arrêt)
5. Quai de la Tournelle
6. Musée d'Orsay
7. Esplanade des Invalides
8. Invalides
9. Place Vauban/Eglise du Dome (arrêt)
10. Champ de Mars (place Jacques Rueff—arrêt)
11. Tour Eiffel
12. Pont d'Iena
13. Place du Trocadéro (arrêt)
14. Avenue Kléber
15. Arc de Triomphe (2 revolutions)
16. Champs-Elysées
17. Place Concorde (1 revolution)
18. Quai François Mitterand
19. Musée du Louvre/Place du Carrousel/Pyramide (arrêt)
20. Quai du Louvre
21. Notre-Dame

Merci!

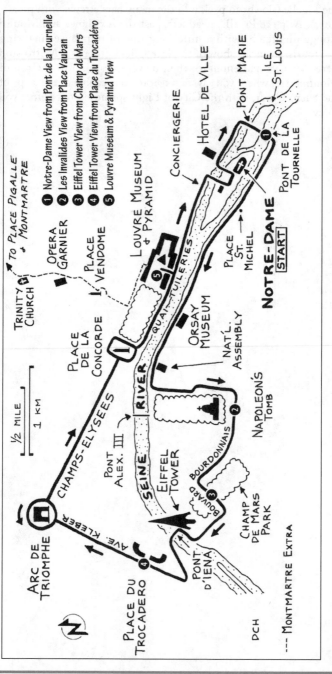

Floodlit Paris Taxi Tour

1 Notre-Dame View from Pont de la Tournelle
2 Les Invalides View from Place Vauban
3 Eiffel Tower View from Champ de Mars
4 Eiffel Tower View from Place du Trocadéro
5 Louvre Museum & Pyramid View

rue Pigalle (slowly, to peek into the many bars strewn with prosti-tutes). At place Pigalle, head left, past the sex shows and Moulin Rouge nightclub (with a mile-long line of tour buses marking the touristy cancan shows), to place Clichy (there's a Métro stop here if you've had enough), then drive up, up, up to the top of Montmartre, where you say *au revoir* to your cabbie at the steps of the Sacré-Cœur, with the City of Light spreading out before you forever.

TRANSPORTATION CONNECTIONS

This chapter covers Paris' two main airports, one nearby airport, six train stations, main bus station, and includes parking tips for drivers.

When leaving Paris, get to your departure point early to allow time for waiting in lines. Figure on three hours for an overseas flight; one to two hours for flights within Europe (particularly if flying a budget airline—they often have long check-in lines); and one hour for a train trip (including Eurostar) or a bus ride.

AIRPORTS

Charles de Gaulle Airport

Paris' primary airport has two main terminals, T-1 and T-2, and two lesser terminals, T-3 and T-9. Most flights from the U.S. serve T-1 or T-2. Due to construction at T-1, it's impossible to predict which airlines will serve this terminal in 2006—call ahead or check their Web site (tel. 01 48 62 22 80, www.adp.fr). In 2005, SAS, United, US Airways, and Lufthansa served T-1. Air France, British Airways, Continental, American, Alitalia, Northwest, and KLM served T-2. Smaller airlines use T-3 (though some major airlines are expected to use this terminal during T-1's construction), and charter flights usually leave from T-9. Terminals are connected every few minutes by a free *navette* (shuttle bus), though a new train should be completed by mid-2006 that will zip travelers between the terminals effortlessly. The RER (Paris suburban train, connecting to Métro) stops at T-2 and near T-1 and T-3, and the TGV (tay-zhay-vay, stands for *train à grande vitesse*—high-speed, long-distance train) station is at T-2. There is no baggage storage at the airport. Beware of pickpockets on *navettes* between terminals, and especially on RER trains. Do not take an unauthorized

taxi from the men greeting you on arrival. Official taxi stands are well-signed.

Terminal 1 (T-1)

This circular terminal has one main entry and covers three floors—arrival (*arrivées*, top floor), departure (*départs*, 1 floor down) and shops/boutiques (basement level). For information on getting to Paris, see "Transportation between Charles de Gaulle Airport and Paris," below.

Arrival Level: You'll find a variety of services at the gates listed below. Expect changes to this information as airport construction proceeds. Blue signs will verfiy the gates listed below.

- Gate 36: Called "Meeting Point" *(Point de Rencontre)*, this gate has an information counter with English-speaking staff, a cafe, and an ATM. Ask here for directions to Disneyland shuttle (€14, daily 7:30–21:00).
- Gate 2: Outside are Air France buses to Paris and Orly Airport (see below).
- Gate 10: Outside are Roissy-Buses to Paris (buy tickets from driver); upstairs is access to car rental.
- Gate 16: A bank with lousy rates for currency exchange.
- Gate 18: Taxis outside.
- Gate 20: Shuttle buses *(navettes)* for Terminal 2 and the RER trains to Paris. Take the elevator down to level *(niveau)* 2, then walk outside (line #1 serves T-2 including the TGV station; line #2 goes directly to the RER station). By mid 2006, a new intra-airport train will shuttle riders between the various terminals in a snap.

Departure Level *(niveau 3)*: This is limited to flight check-in, though you will find ADP information desks here. Those departing from T-1 will find restaurants, a PTT (post office), a pharmacy, boutiques, and a handy grocery store one floor below the ticketing desks *(niveau 2 on the elevator)*.

Terminal 2 (T-2)

This long, horseshoe-shaped terminal is dominated by Air France and is divided into several subterminals (or halls), each identified by a letter. You can walk from one hall to the other. Halls are connected to the RER, the TGV station, and T-1 every five minutes with free *navettes* (shuttle buses—line #5 runs to T-1).

The RER and TGV stations are below the Sheraton Hotel (access by *navette* or on foot). Stops for *navettes*, Air France buses, and Roissy Buses are all well-marked and near each hall (see "Transportation Between Charles de Gaulle Airport and Paris," below). ADP information desks are located near Gate 5 in each hall. Car-rental offices, post offices, pharmacies, and

ATMs *(point d'argent)* are also well-signed.

Transportation Between Charles de Gaulle Airport and Paris

Three efficient public-transportation routes, taxis, and airport shuttle vans link the airport's terminals with central Paris. All are well-marked, and stops are centrally located at all terminals. If you're carrying lots of baggage—or are just plain tired—airport shuttle vans or taxis (better) are well worth the extra cost. If you arrive in the afternoon, ask about current traffic conditions into Paris and consider the RER train.

To get to the rue Cler area, the Roissy bus and Métro combination is the most convenient public-transport route. To reach the Marais, your best public-transport option is the Air France bus to the Gare de Lyon, with a quick trip on Métro line #1 to your hotel neighborhood. Both routes are described below. For the Luxembourg Garden area, take RER-B to the Luxembourg stop. For the Canal St. Martin area, take RER-B to Gare du Nord, then transfer to Métro line 5 (direction place d'Italie), and get off at place de la Republique. All your options into Paris are well-marked, but if you have trouble, ask any airport employee.

RER trains stop near T-1 and at T-2, cost €9, and run every 15 minutes with stops in central Paris at Gare du Nord, Châtelet-Les Halles, St. Michel, and Luxembourg. Beware of pickpockets preying on jet-lagged tourists on these trains; wear your money belt. The other transportation options described below have far fewer theft problems.

Roissy-Buses run every 15–20 minutes to Paris' Opéra Garnier 6:30–21:00 (€8.50, 40–60 min). You'll arrive at a bus stop on rue Scribe at the American Express office, on the left side of the Opéra building. To get to the Métro entrance, turn left out of the bus, heading towards the front of the Opéra. For rue Cler hotels, take the #8 Métro line (direction: Balard) to La Tour Maubourg or Ecole Militaire. For hotels in the Marais neighborhood, take the same #8 line (direction: Créteil Préfecture) to the Bastille stop.

Air France buses serve central Paris and continue to Orly Airport about every 15–30 minutes from 5:45 to 23:00 on three different routes. Allow 45 minutes to the Arc de Triomphe and Porte Maillot; 45 minutes to the Gare de Lyon train station; 60 minutes to Montparnasse Tower/train station; and 80 minutes to Orly Airport. To reach Marais hotels from the Gare de Lyon, take Métro line #1 (direction: La Défense) to the Bastille, St. Paul, or Hôtel de Ville stops. The one-way ticket to Orly Airport costs €16; all other routes cost €12 one-way, €18 round-trip.

Taxis with luggage will run about €50 with bags, more if traffic is bad.

Airport shuttles offer transportation between either of Paris' airports and your hotel, and (since they have more space than cabs) are good for single travelers or families of four or more. Airport pickup must be booked ahead and can be slow given unpredictable arrival times of international flights (plan on a 30-minute wait at the airport; taxis are easier for getting into Paris). Airport shuttles cost about €20–30 for one person, €30–40 for two, and €40–52 for three. Some offer deals if you do a round trip, and most are more expensive at night (20:00–6:00 in the morning). Be clear on where and how you are to meet your driver.

Golden Air is the most reliable of the many shuttles (from Paris to Charles de Gaulle: €27 for one person, €17 per person for two; from Charles de Gaulle to Paris: €35 for one person, €20 per person for two; these special prices possible only for readers of this book in 2006, tel. 01 34 10 12 92, fax 01 34 10 93 89, www.paris -airport-shuttle-limousine.com, goldenair@goldenair.net).

From Paris to Charles de Gaulle

Airport shuttles work well for getting to the airport, since the timing doesn't depend on the unpredictable arrival of various flights (see above). If your hotel does not work with a shuttle service, reserve directly (book this trip at least a day in advance—most hoteliers will make the call for you).

Your hotel can call a **taxi.** Usually 20 minutes ahead is enough time, unless your flight is very early (always ask ahead at your hotel). Specify that you want a real taxi *(un taxi normal),* and not a limo service that costs €20 more. Remember, you pay a bit more on Sundays, before 7:00, and after 19:00.

If taking the **RER** to the airport, you want RER line B. Make sure the sign over the platform shows *Roissy-Charles de Gaulle* as a stop served, since the line splits and not every train on this line serves the airport. If you're not clear, ask another rider *(air-o-por sharl duh Gaul?).* T-1 is the first RER stop at Charles de Gaulle; T-2 is the second stop.

Sleeping at or near Charles de Gaulle Airport

Hôtel Ibis**, outside the RER Roissy Rail station near T-3 (the 1st RER stop coming from Paris), offers standard and predictable accommodations (Db-€80-90, near *navette* stop, free and fast shuttle bus to all terminals, tel. 01 49 19 19 19, fax 01 49 19 19 21, h1404@accor.com). **Novotel***** is next door and the next step up (weekend Db-€135, weekday Db-€160, tel. 01 49 19 27 27, fax 01 49 19 27 99, www.novotel.com).

The small village of **Roissy en France** (you'll see signs just before the airport as you come from Paris), which gave its name to the airport (Roissy Charles de Gaulle), has better-value chain

hotels with free shuttle service to the airport (6/hr, 15 min). There, you can shop for your last Parisian dinner or an early morning café breakfast. Choose between **Hotel Campanile** (Db-€65, tel. 01 34 29 80 40, fax 01 34 29 80 39, www.campanile.fr, roissy@campanile .fr) and the **Hotel Kyriad Prestige** (Db-€85, tel. 01 34 29 00 00, fax 01 34 29 00 11, www.kyriad.fr, roissy@kyriadprestige.fr).

To avoid rush-hour traffic, drivers can consider sleeping north of Paris in either **Auvers-sur-Oise** (30 min west of airport, see accommodations on page 474) or in the pleasant medieval town of **Senlis** (15 min north of airport) at the modest **Hostellerie de la Porte Bellon** (Db-€62-77, central at 51 rue Bellon, near rue de la République, tel. 03 44 53 03 05, fax 03 44 53 29 94). If you don't have a car, sleep elsewhere.

Orly Airport

This airport feels small. It's good for rental-car pickup and drop-off, as it's closer to Paris and far easier to navigate than Charles de Gaulle Airport.

Orly has two terminals: Sud (south) and Ouest (west). Air France flights arrive at Ouest, and all others use Sud. At the Sud terminal, you'll exit the baggage claim (near Gate H) and see signs directing you to city transportation, car rental, and so on. Turn left to enter the main terminal area, and you'll find exchange offices with bad rates, an American Express office, an ATM, the ADP (*Espace Tourisme*, a quasi-tourist office that offers free city maps and basic sightseeing information, open until 24:00), and an SNCF rail desk (next to ADP, daily 7:45–12:00 & 13:00–20:00, sells train tickets and even Eurailpasses). Downstairs is a sandwich bar, WCs, a bank (same bad rates), a newsstand (buy a phone card), and a post office. Car-rental offices are located in the parking lot in front of the terminal opposite Gate C. For flight info on any airline serving Orly, call 01 49 75 15 15. For information on either of Paris' airports, visit www.adp.fr.

Transportation between Orly Airport and Paris

Several efficient public-transportation routes, taxis, and a couple of airport shuttle services link Orly with central Paris. The gate locations listed below apply to Orly Sud, but the same transportation services are available from both terminals.

Air France buses (outside Gate K) run to Montparnasse train station (with many Métro lines) and to Invalides Métro stop (€8 one-way, €12 round-trip, 4/hr, 40 min to Invalides). These buses are handy for those staying in or near the rue Cler neighborhood (from Invalides bus stop, take the Métro to La Tour Maubourg or Ecole Militaire to reach recommended hotels; see also "RER trains," below). Air France buses also run to Charles de Gaulle

Airport (€16, 2/hr, 80 min). Remember that to continue on the Métro, you'll need to buy a separate ticket (for ticket types and prices, see "Getting Around Paris" in the Orientation chapter, page 28).

Jetbus (outside Gate H, €5.50, 4/hr) is the quickest way to the Paris subway and a good way to the Marais and Luxembourg Garden neighborhoods. Take Jetbus to the Villejuif Louis Aragon Métro stop. To reach the Marais neighborhood, take the Métro to the Sully Morland stop. For the Luxembourg area, take the same train to the Censier Daubenton or Place Monge stops.

The **Orlybus** (outside Gate H, €6, 3/hr) takes you to the Denfert-Rochereau RER-B line and the Métro, offering subway access to central Paris, including the Luxembourg Area and Notre-Dame Cathedral, as well as the Gare du Nord train station.

Shuttle Buses to Disneyland also depart from Gate H (€14, daily 8:30–19:30, confirm gate and schedule at ADP Espace Tourisme office—described above).

These two routes provide access to Paris via **RER trains:** an ADP shuttle **(Orly Rail bus)** takes you to RER-C (Pont d'Orly stop), with connections to Gare d'Austerlitz, St. Michel/Notre-Dame, Musée d'Orsay, Invalides, and Pont de l'Alma stations and is handy for some Rue Cler hotels (outside Gate G, 4/hr, €5.50). **Orlyval trains** take you to the Antony stop on RER-B (serving Luxembourg, Châtelet-Les Halles, St. Michel, and Gare du Nord stations in central Paris, €9, includes RER ticket).

Taxis are to the far right as you leave the terminal, at Gate M. Allow €25–35 with bags for a taxi into central Paris.

Airport shuttles are good for single travelers or families of four or more, but better from Paris to the airport (see page 402 for a company to contact; from Orly, figure about €23/1 person, €30/2 people, less for larger groups and kids).

From Paris to Orly

For information on airport shuttles and taxis, see page 402. If taking the **Jetbus** from the Marais to the airport, make sure before you board the Métro that your train is going to Villejuif Louis Aragon (not Mairie d'Ivry), as the route splits at the end of the line. **Orlyval** train riders need to make sure the RER-B line from central Paris serves the Antony stop, and Orly Rail bus users must ensure that the RER-C train serves the Pont d'Orly stop.

Sleeping near Orly Airport

Two chain hotels, owned by the same company, are your best option near Orly. **Hôtel Ibis**** is reasonable, basic, and close by (Db-€65, tel. 01 56 70 50 60, fax 01 56 70 50 70, h1413@accor .com). **Hôtel Mercure***** provides more comfort for a higher

price (Db-€130–160, tel. 01 49 75 15 50, fax 01 49 75 15 51, h1246@accor-hotels.com). Both have free shuttles to the terminal.

Beauvais Airport

Budget airlines such as Ryanair use Beauvais Airport, offering dirt-cheap airfares, but leaving you 50 miles north of Paris. Still, this small airport has direct buses to Paris (see below). It's ideal for drivers who want to rent a car here and head to Normandy or north to Belgium. The airport is basic (the terminal for departing passengers and baggage claim is under a tent, and waiting areas are crowded and have few services), but it's being improved as it deals with an increasing number of passengers (airport tel. 08 92 68 20 66, www.aeroportbeauvais .com; Ryanair tel. 08 92 68 20 73, www.ryanair.com).

Transportation between Beauvais Airport and Paris: Buses depart from the airport about 20 minutes after flights arrive, taking you to Porte Maillot, which has a Métro and RER stop on the west edge of Paris (bus costs €13, takes 90 min). Buses depart Paris for Beauvais Airport three hours before scheduled flight departures (catch bus at Porte Maillot in parking lot on boulevard Pershing next to Hôtel Concorde-Lafayette). Bus tickets must be booked 24 hours in advance; call Beauvais Airport for details or buy tickets on their Web site (see contact info above).

Taxis run from Beauvais Airport to Paris: €120 to central Paris, €130 to Orly Airport, and €110 to Charles de Gaulle Airport. Taxis to Beauvais' train station or city center cost €11. **Trains** connect Beauvais and Paris Gare du Nord (20/day, 80 min).

TRAINS

Station Overview

Paris is Europe's rail hub, with six major train stations, each serving different regions: Gare de l'Est (eastbound trains), Gare du Nord (northern France and Europe), Gare St. Lazare (northwestern France), Gare d'Austerlitz (southwestern France and Europe), Gare de Lyon (southeastern France and Italy), and Gare Montparnasse (northwestern France and TGV service to France's southwest). Any train station has schedule information, can make reservations, and sell tickets for any destination. Buying tickets is handier from an SNCF neighborhood office—including those at the Louvre, Invalides, Orsay, Versailles, and airports—or at your neighborhood travel agency. It's worth the small fee. Look for *SNCF* signs in their window that indicate they sell train tickets.

Schedules change by season, weekday, and weekend. Verify train schedules shown in this book (to study ahead on the Web, check Germany's excellent all-Europe Web site, http://bahn .hafas.de/english.html). The nationwide information line for train

Paris' Train Stations

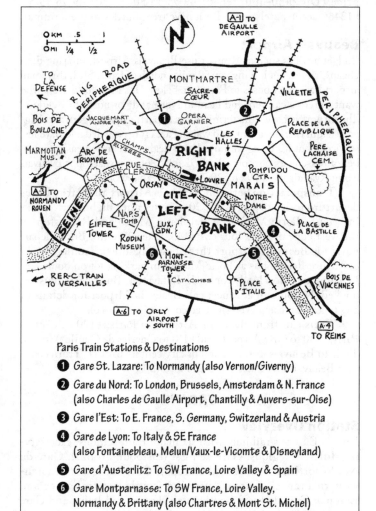

Paris Train Stations & Destinations

❶ Gare St. Lazare: To Normandy (also Vernon/Giverny)

❷ Gare du Nord: To London, Brussels, Amsterdam & N. France (also Charles de Gaulle Airport, Chantilly & Auvers-sur-Oise)

❸ Gare l'Est: To E. France, S. Germany, Switzerland & Austria

❹ Gare de Lyon: To Italy & SE France (also Fontainebleau, Melun/Vaux-le-Vicomte & Disneyland)

❺ Gare d'Austerlitz: To SW France, Loire Valley & Spain

❻ Gare Montparnasse: To SW France, Loire Valley, Normandy & Brittany (also Chartres & Mont St. Michel)

schedules and reservations is tel. 3635. Dial this four-digit number, then press 3 for reservations or ticket purchase when you get the message (you may get sent to a French-only phone tree as SNCF tries to automate its services; if so, hang up and ask your hotelier for help). Press 321 for Eurostar information, or 322 for Thalys. This incredibly helpful, time-saving service costs €0.34 per minute from anywhere in France (ask for an English-speaking agent and hope for the best, allow 5 min per call). The time and energy you save easily justifies the telephone torture, particularly when

France's Public Transportation

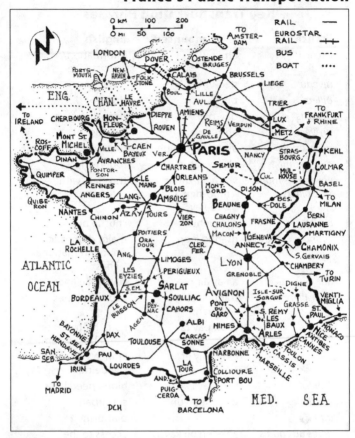

making seat reservations (note that phoned reservations must be picked up at least 30 min prior to departure).

All six train stations have banks or change offices, ATMs, information desks, telephones, cafés, newsstands, and clever pickpockets. Because of security concerns, not all have baggage check, though those with this service are identified below.

Métro and RER trains, as well as buses and taxis, are well-marked at every station. When arriving by Métro, follow signs for *Grandes Lignes–SNCF* to find the main tracks.

Each station offers two types of rail service: long distance to other cities, called *Grandes Lignes* (major lines); and suburban service to outlying areas, called *banlieue* or RER. Both *banlieue* and RER trains serve outlying areas and the airports; the only difference is that *banlieue* lines are operated by SNCF (France's train system, called Transilien) and RER lines are operated by RATP

Key Transportation Phrases

French	Pronounced	English
accueil	ah-koy	information/assistance
niveau	nee-voh	level
billets	bee-yay	tickets
départs	day-par	departures
arrivées	ah-ree-vay	arrivals
aller simple	ah-lay sam-pluh	one-way
aller-retour	ah-lay ruh-toor	round-trip
voyageurs munis de billets	voh-yah-zhoor moo-nee duh bee-yay	travelers with tickets
navette	nah-veht	shuttle bus
Grandes Lignes	grahnd leen	major domestic and international lines
RER	air ay air	suburban lines
Transilien	trahn-seel-ee-yehn	suburban lines
RATP	er ah pay tay	Paris' Métro and bus system
SNCF	es en say ef	France's country-wide train system
TGV	tay zhay vay	high-speed lines
banlieue	bahn-lee-yuh	suburban
quai	kay	platform
accès aux quais	ahk-seh oh kay	access to the platforms
voie	vwah	track
retard	ruh-tar	delay
salle d'attente	sahl dah-tahnt	waiting room
consigne	kohn-seen	baggage check
consigne automatique	kohn-seen oh-toh-mah-teek	storage lockers
première classe	pruhm-yair klahs	first class
deuxième classe	duhz-yehm klahs	second class
point d'argent	pwan dar-zhahn	ATM
PTT	pay tay tay	post office

(Paris' Métro and bus system). You may also see ticket windows identified as *Ile de France*. This is for Transilien (SNCF) trains serving destinations outside Paris in the Ile de France region (usually no longer than an hour from Paris).

Paris train stations can be intimidating, but if you slow down, avoid peak times, take a deep breath, and ask for help, you'll find them manageable and efficient. Bring a pad of paper for clear communication at ticket/info windows. All stations have helpful *accueil* (information) booths; the bigger stations have roving helpers, usually in red vests. They're capable of answering rail questions more quickly than the information or ticket windows.

Gare du Nord

This vast station serves cities in northern France and international destinations north of Paris, including Copenhagen, Amsterdam (see "To Brussels and Amsterdam by Thalys Train," below), and the Eurostar to London (see "To London by Eurostar Train," below), as well as two of the day trips described in this book (Chantilly and Auvers-sur-Oise).

Arrive early to allow time to navigate this station. From the Métro, follow *Grandes Lignes* signs (main lines) and keep going up until you reach the tracks at street level. *Grandes Lignes* depart from tracks 3–21, suburban *(banlieue)* lines from tracks 30–36, and RER trains depart from tracks 37–44 (tracks 41–44 are 1 floor below). Glass train information booths *(accueil)* are scattered throughout the station, and information-helpers circulate (all rail staff are required to speak English).

The tourist information kiosk opposite track 16 is a hotel reservation service for Accor chain hotels (they also have free Paris maps). Information booths for the **Thalys** (high-speed trains to Brussels and Amsterdam) are opposite track 8. All non-Eurostar ticket sales are opposite tracks 3–8. Passengers departing on **Eurostar** (London via Chunnel) must buy tickets and check in on the second level, opposite track 6. (Note: Britain's time zone is one hour earlier; times listed on Eurostar tickets are local times—Parisian time for departing Paris and the British time you'll arrive in London.) Monet-esque views over the trains and peaceful, air-conditioned cafés hide on the upper level, past the Eurostar ticket windows (find the cool view WCs down the steps in the café). Baggage check, taxis, and rental cars are at the far end, opposite track 3 and down the steps.

Key Destinations Served by Gare du Nord *Grandes Lignes:* **Brussels** (12/day, 1.5 hrs, see "To Brussels and Amsterdam by Thalys Train," page 413), **Bruges** (18/day, 2 hrs, change in Brussels, one direct), **Amsterdam** (10/day, 4 hrs, see "To Brussels and Amsterdam by Thalys Train," page 413), **Copenhagen** (1/day,

16 hrs, two night trains), **Koblenz** (6/day, 5 hrs, change in Köln), and **London** Eurostar via Chunnel (17/day, 3 hrs, tel. 08 36 35 35 39, see "To London by Eurostar Train," page 414).

By *Banlieue*/RER Lines: **Chantilly-Gouvieux** (hrly, fewer on weekends, 35 min), **Charles de Gaulle Airport** (2/hr, 30 min, runs 5:30–23:00, track 4), **Auvers-sur-Oise** (2/hr, 1 hr, transfer at Pontoise or St. Ouen).

Gare Montparnasse

This big and modern station covers three floors, serves lower Normandy and Brittany, and offers TGV service to the Loire Valley and southwestern France, as well as suburban service to Chartres. At street level, you'll find a bank, *banlieue* trains serving Chartres (you can also reach the *banlieue* trains from the second level), and ticket windows for Ile de France trains in the center, just past the escalators.

Most services are provided on the second (top) level, where the *Grandes Lignes* arrive and depart. Ticket windows and an information booth are to the far left (with your back to glass exterior). *Banlieue* trains depart from tracks 10–19. The main rail information office is opposite track 15. Taxis and car rentals are to the far left as you leave the tracks. Air France buses to Orly and Charles de Gaulle Airports stop in front of the station, down the escalators and outside.

Key Destinations Served by Gare Montparnasse: Chartres (20/day, 1 hr, *banlieue* lines), **Pontorson/Mont St. Michel** (5/day, 4.5 hrs, via Rennes, then take bus from Pontorson; or take train to Pontorson via Caen, then bus from Pontorson), **Dinan** (7/day, 4 hrs, change in Rennes and Dol), **Bordeaux** (14/day, 3.5 hrs), **Sarlat** (5/day, 6 hrs, change in Bordeaux, Libourne, or Souillac), **Toulouse** (11/day, 5 hrs, most require change, usually in Bordeaux), **Albi** (7/day, 6–7.5 hrs, change in Toulouse, also night train), **Carcassonne** (8/day, 6.5 hrs, most require changes in Toulouse and Bordeaux, direct trains take 10 hrs), and **Tours** (14/day, 1 hr).

Gare de Lyon

This huge and bewildering station offers TGV and regular service to southeastern France, Italy, and other international destinations (for more trains to Italy, see "Gare de Bercy," below). Frequent *banlieue* trains serve Melun (near Vaux-le-Vicomte) and Fontainebleau (some depart from the main *Grandes Lignes* level, more frequent departures are from one level down, follow RER-D signs, and ask at any *accueil* or ticket window where the next departure leaves from). Don't leave this station without relaxing in Le Train Bleu Restaurant lounge, up the stairs opposite track G (see page 367).

Train Tips

- Arrive at the station with plenty of time before your departure to find the right platform, confirm connections, and so on. In small towns, your train may depart before the station opens; if so, go directly to the tracks and find the overhead sign that confirms your train stops at that track.
- Check schedules in advance. Upon arrival at a station, find out your departure possibilities. Large stations have a separate information window or office; at small stations, the ticket office gives information.
- If you have a rail flexipass, write the date on your pass each day you travel.
- Validate tickets (not passes) and reservations in orange machines before boarding. If you're traveling with a pass and have a reservation for a certain trip, you must validate the reservation.
- Reservations for any TGV train as are required and often sell out. You can reserve any train at any station, or through SNCF Boutiques (small offices in city centers). There is a limited number of reservations allocated for railpass users during peak times—reserve as far ahead as you can for Friday and Sunday afternoons and Saturday mornings.
- Before getting on a train, confirm that it's going where you think it is. For example, ask the conductor or any local passenger, *"A Chartres?"* (ah shart-ruh; meaning, "To Chartres?").
- Some trains split cars en route. Make sure your train car is continuing to your destination by asking, *"Cette voiture va à Chartres?"* (seht vwah-toor vah ah Shart-ruh; meaning, "This car goes to Chartres?").
- If a seat is reserved, it will be labeled *réservé*, with the cities to and from which it is reserved.
- Verify with the conductor all transfers you must make (*"Correspondance à?"*; meaning, "Transfer to where?").
- To guard against theft, keep your bags right overhead; don't store them on the racks at the end of the car.
- Note your arrival time, so you'll be ready to get off.
- Use the train's free WCs before you get off.

Grande Ligne trains arrive and depart from one level, but are divided into two areas (tracks A–N and 5–23). They are connected by the long platform along tracks A and 5, and by the hallway adjacent to track A and opposite track 9. This hallway has all the services, including ticket windows, ticket information, banks, and shops (including Virgin Records/Books). *Banlieue* ticket windows are just inside the hall adjacent to track A *(billets Ile de France)*. *Grandes Lignes* and *banlieue* lines share the same tracks. A tourist office (Mon–Sat 8:00–18:00, closed Sun) and a train information office are both opposite track L. From the RER or Métro, follow signs for *Grandes Lignes Arrivées* and take the escalator up to reach the platforms. Train information booths *(accueil)* are opposite tracks A and 11 and downstairs. Baggage check (daily 6:45–22:45) is down the stairs opposite track 13 (keep straight off the escalator then turn left). Taxi stands are well-signed in front of, and under- neath, the station. If you need a quiet waiting area, here are two to choose from: the Train Bleu's pricey bar-lounge opposite track G, or opposite track 13, follow *consigne* (baggage check) signs down one floor and make a U-turn to the right.

Air France buses to Montparnasse (easy transfer to Orly Airport) and direct to Charles de Gaulle Airport stop outside the station's main entrance (opposite tracks A to L, walk across the parking lot—the stop is opposite the Café Europeen; €12, 2/hr, normally at :15 and :45 after the hour).

Key Destinations Served by Gare de Lyon: Vaux-le-Vicomte (train to Melun, hrly, 30 min), **Fontainebleau** (nearly hrly, 45 min), **Beaune** (12/day, 2.5 hrs, most require change in Dijon), **Dijon** (15/day, 1.5 hrs), **Chamonix** (9/day, 9 hrs, change in Lyon and St. Gervais; 1 night train), **Annecy** (14/day, 4–7 hrs), **Lyon** (16/day, 2.5 hrs), **Avignon** (9/day in 2.5 hrs, 6/day in 4 hrs with change), **Arles** (14/day, 5 hrs, most with change in Marseille, Avignon, or Nîmes), **Nice** (14/day, 5.5–7 hrs, many with change in Marseille), ***Venice** (3/day, 3/night, 11-15 hrs, most require changes), ***Rome** (2/day, 5/night, 15–18 hrs, most require changes), and **Bern** (9/day, 5–11 hrs, most require changes, night train).

*Gare de Bercy: This smaller station handles some night train service to Italy during renovation work at the Gare de Lyon (Mo: Bercy, one stop east of Gare de Lyon on line #14).

Gare de l'Est

This single-floor station (with underground Métro), which serves eastern France and international destinations east of Paris, will see major construction throughout 2006 to accommodate new TGV service to Reims and Strasbourg. Expect changes from this description: Train information booths are at tracks 1 and 26; the info booth at track 18 is for Transilien trains serving suburban

areas; ticket windows are in the big hall opposite track 8; luggage storage *(consigne)* is through the hall opposite track 12; and Métro access is opposite track 18.

Key Destinations Served by Gare de l'Est: Note that starting in 2007, many of these trip times will be much shorter, thanks to new TGV train service—**Colmar** (12/day, 5.5 hrs, change in Strasbourg, Dijon, or Mulhouse), **Strasbourg** (14/day, 4.5 hrs, many require changes), **Reims** (12/day, 1.5 hrs), **Verdun** (5/day, 3 hrs, change in Metz or Chalon), **Munich** (5/day, 9 hrs, some require changes, night train), **Vienna** (7/day, 13–18 hrs, most require changes, night train), **Zürich** (10/day, 7 hrs, most require changes, night train), and **Prague** (2/day, 14 hrs, night train).

Gare St. Lazare

This relatively small station serves upper Normandy, including Rouen and Giverny. All trains arrive and depart one floor above street level. Follow signs to *Grandes Lignes* from the Métro to reach the tracks. Ticket windows are in the first hall at departure level. *Grandes Lignes* (main lines) depart from tracks 17–27; *banlieue* (suburban) trains depart from 1–16. The train information office *(accueil)* is opposite track 15. There's a post office (PTT) along track 27, and WCs are opposite track 19. There is no baggage check. You'll find many shops and services one floor below the departure level.

Key Destinations Served by Gare St. Lazare: Giverny (train to Vernon, 5/day, 45 min—see schedule in Giverny Day Trip on page 472—then bus or taxi 10 min to Giverny), **Rouen** (15/day, 75 min), **Honfleur** (6/day, 3 hrs, via Lisieux, then bus), **Bayeux** (9/day, 2.5 hrs, some with change in Caen), and **Caen** (12/day, 2 hrs).

Gare d'Austerlitz

This small station provides non-TGV service to the Loire Valley, southwestern France, and Spain. All tracks are at street level. The information booth is opposite track 17, and all ticket sales are in the hall opposite track 10. Baggage check, WCs, and car rental are near track 27, along the side of the station, opposite track 21. To get to the Métro, you must walk outside and along either side of the station.

Key Destinations Served by Gare d'Austerlitz: Amboise (8/day in 2 hrs, 12/day in 1.5 hrs with change in St. Pierre-des-Corps), **Cahors** (7/day, 5–7 hrs, most with changes), **Barcelona** (1/day, 9 hrs, change in Montpellier, night trains), **Madrid** (2 night trains only, 13–16 hrs), and **Lisbon** (1/day, 24 hrs).

To Brussels and Amsterdam by Thalys Train

The pricey Thalys train has the monopoly on the rail route (for a cheaper option, try the Eurolines bus; see below). Without a

railpass, you'll pay about €80–100 second class for the Paris–Amsterdam train (compared to €45 by bus) or about €60–80 second class for the Paris–Brussels train (compared to €25 by bus). Even with a railpass, you need to pay for train reservations (second class-$13, first class-$26). Book at least a day ahead, as seats are limited. Or hop on the bus, Gus.

To London by Eurostar Train

The fastest and most convenient way to get from the Eiffel Tower to Big Ben is by rail. Eurostar, a joint service of the Belgian, British, and French railways, is the speedy passenger train that zips you (and up to 800 others in 18 sleek cars) from downtown Paris to downtown London (12–15/day, 3 hrs) faster and easier than flying. The actual tunnel crossing is a 20-minute, black, silent, 100-mile-per-hour non-event. Your ears won't even pop. Easy TGV connections in Lille can take you to Charles de Gaulle Airport, Disneyland Paris (1/day direct Eurostar, more often with transfer at Lille), or southern France without even stopping in Paris.

Eurostar Fares

Channel fares (essentially the same between London and Paris or Brussels) are reasonable but complicated. Prices vary depending on when you travel, whether you can live with restrictions, and whether you're eligible for any discounts (youth, seniors, and railpass holders all qualify). Rates are lower for round trips and off-peak travel (midday, midweek, low-season, and low-interest). For specifics, visit www.ricksteves.com/rail/eurostar.htm.

As with airfares, the most expensive and flexible option is a **full-fare ticket** with no restrictions on refundability (even refundable after the departure date; for a one-way trip, figure around $375 in first class, $255 second class). A first-class ticket comes with a meal (a dinner departure nets you more grub than breakfast), but it's not worth the extra expense.

Also like the airlines, **cheaper tickets** come with more restrictions and are limited in number (so they sell out more quickly; for second-class, one-way tickets, figure $90–200). Non-full-fare tickets have severe restrictions on refunds (best-case scenario: you'll get 25 percent back; but with the cheapest options, you'll get nothing). But several do allow you to change the specifics of your trip once before departure.

Those traveling with a railpass for Britain, France, or Belgium should look first at the **passholder** fare, an especially good value for one-way Eurostar trips (around $75).

Buying Eurostar Tickets

Refund and exchange restrictions are serious, so don't reserve until

Eurostar Routes

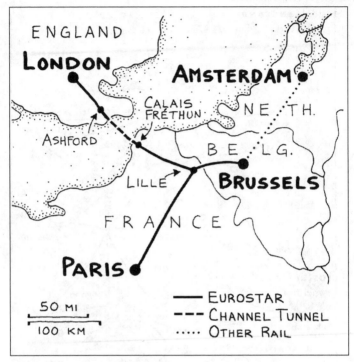

you're sure of your plans. If you're confident about the time and date of your crossing, order ahead from the U.S. Only the most expensive ticket (full fare) is fully refundable, so if you want to have more flexibility, hold off—keeping in mind that the longer you wait, the more likely the cheapest tickets will sell out (you might end up having to pay for first class).

You can check and book fares by phone or online in the U.S. (order online at www.ricksteves.com/rail/eurostar.htm, prices listed in dollars; order by phone at U.S. tel. 800-EUROSTAR) or in France (French tel. 08 92 35 35 39, www.eurostar.com, prices listed in euros). While tickets are usually cheaper if purchased in the U.S., fares offered in Europe follow different discount rules—so it can be worth it to check www.eurostar.com before buying. If you buy from a U.S. company, you'll pay for ticket delivery in the U.S.; if you book with the European company, you'll pick up your ticket at the train station. In Europe, you can buy your Eurostar ticket at any major train station in any country, at neighborhood SNCF offices, or at any travel agency that handles train tickets (expect a booking fee).

Driving in France: Distance and Time

Note that France's time zone is one hour later than Britain's. Times listed on tickets are local times.

BUSES

The main bus station is the Gare Routière du Paris-Gallieni (28 avenue du Général de Gaulle, in suburb of Bagnolet, Mo: Gallieni, tel. 01 49 72 51 51). Buses provide cheaper—if less comfortable and more time-consuming—transportation to major European cities. Eurolines' buses depart from here (tel. 08 36 69 52 52, www.eurolines .com). Look on their Web site for offices in central Paris.

DRIVING

Parking in Paris

Street parking is free 19:00–9:00 on Sunday, and in August. To pay for streetside parking, you must go to a tabac and buy a

parking card *(une carte parking)*. Insert the card into the meter and punch the desired amount of time (€10 buys 6 hours), then take the receipt and put it inside your windshield. For a longer stay, consider parking for less at an airport (about €10/day) and taking public transport or a taxi into the city. You'll pay more to park in a downtown lot (about €20/day, €44/3 days, and €10/day more after that). There are other underground lots at St. Sulpice, the Panthéon, and Bastille (www.vincipark.com). Otherwise, ask your hotelier for suggestions.

DAY TRIPS
FROM PARIS

VERSAILLES DAY TRIP

(Château de Versailles)

If you've ever wondered why your American passport has French writing in it, you'll find the answer at Versailles (vehr-"sigh"). The powerful court of Louis XIV at Versailles set the standard of culture for all of Europe, right up to modern times. Versailles was every king's dream palace. Today, if you're planning to visit just one palace in all of Europe, make it Versailles. And if you have a car, or simply prefer a smaller town base for sightseeing Paris, see my hotel recommendations on page 444.

ORIENTATION

Visiting Versailles, with all of its many options (and admission fees), can seem daunting—but it really shouldn't be. It's simple: Tour the State Apartments with the Hall of Mirrors, then enjoy the gardens and Trianon Palaces. Here are all the details:

Cost: There are several different parts of the palace, each with a separate admission. The **State Apartments,** which this chapter's self-guided tour takes you through, cost €7.50 (€5.50 after 15:30, under 18 free, covered by Paris Museum Pass, €4.50 for optional audioguide).

The **gardens** are free, except on weekends April–Sept, when the fountains blast and the price shoots up to €6 (see "Fountain Spectacles," below).

Entering the **Grand and Petit Trianon Palaces** costs €5 together (both covered by Paris Museum Pass).

There are several other, lesser sights: the **King's Private Apartments** (costs €4.50 for audioguide, or visit with guided tour, see "Tours," below), the sumptuous **Opera House** (only by guided tour, see below), and the **Mesdames Apartments** (exclusively covered by One-Day Pass, see below).

A **One-Day Pass** covers your entrance to just about everything, gives you cut-the-line privileges, and provides audioguides throughout your visit. If you're seeing everything (and don't have a Paris Museum Pass), this can be a money-saver. The pass gives you priority access to the State Apartments, the King's Private Apartments, Mesdames Apartments, both Trianon Palaces, the shuttle train around the gardens, and Les Grand Eaux Musicales (see "Fountain Spectacles," below; note that these run only on summer weekends). If you buy this pass in Paris, it covers your train ride to and from Paris (€21, sold at Paris train stations, RER stations that serve Versailles, and at FNAC department stores). The same pass (without transportation) is sold for €20 at the palace.

Guided Tours: There are scheduled guided tours of Versailles in English (€5/60 min, €7/90 min, €9/2 hrs; note that if you lack a Paris Museum Pass, you have to pay the €7.50 entry fee for the State Apartments separately from any tour). To take a guided tour, make reservations at Entrance D immediately upon arrival, as tours can sell out by 13:00 (1st tours generally begin at 10:00; last tours usually depart at 15:00, but as late as 16:00). The tours can be long, but those with an appetite for the palace history enjoy them. Even if you decide not to pay for the tour up front, keep your ticket as proof you've paid for the palace entry—in case you decide to take a guided tour after you've wandered through Versailles by yourself. For a basic visit, this chapter's self-guided tour (below) works great.

Audioguide Tours: Audioguides are available for two itineraries—the State Apartments (which this book covers) and the King's Private Apartments (each 60 min and €4.50, not including palace admission).

Hours: The **palace** is open April–Oct Tue–Sun 9:00–18:30, Nov–March Tue–Sun 9:00–17:30, closed Mon. Last entry is 30 minutes before closing. The **Grand and Petit Trianon Palaces** open at noon and close when the palace does. The **gardens** are open daily from 7:00 (8:00 in winter) to sunset (as late as 21:30 or as early as 17:30).

When to Go: In summer, Versailles is especially crowded between 10:00 and 13:00, and all day Tue and Sun. For fewer crowds, go early or late: Either arrive by 9:00 (when the palace opens, touring the palace first, then the gardens) or after 15:30 (you'll get a reduced entry ticket, but note that the last guided tours of the day generally depart at 15:00, though sometimes as late as 16:00). If you arrive midday, see the gardens first and the palace later, at 15:00. The gardens and palace are great late.

Getting There: Take the **RER-C train** (€6 round-trip, 30 min one-way) from any of these RER stops: Gare d'Austerlitz,

---

Versailles Renovation—2006 to 2010

The château will be undergoing a massive reorganization to better accommodate its hordes of visitors in the next few years. Rather than the various entries and tours, one grand and user-friendly entry will eventually allow all visitors to enter and flow freely through everything in the palace and grounds for one simple (but higher) price. The palace attic, currently unused, will become a vast 19th-century French history museum. A path across the giant cobbles will enable people who use wheelchairs more comfortable access. And there will be many more toilets. The first step in this vision: Starting in 2006, the gardens are free (except during the fountain spectacles on spring and summer weekends).

St. Michel, Musée d'Orsay, Invalides, Pont de l'Alma, and Champ de Mars. Any train whose name starts with a V (e.g., "Vick") goes to Versailles; don't board other trains. Get off at the last stop (Versailles R.G., or "Rive Gauche"—not Versailles C.H., which is farther from the palace), and exit through the turnstiles by inserting your ticket. To reach the château, turn right out of the train station, then left at the first boulevard. It's a 10-minute walk to the palace. (If you want to visit Versailles and Chartres on the same day using public transportation, see page 447.)

Your Eurailpass covers this inexpensive trip, but it uses up a valuable "flexi" day. To get free passage, show your railpass at an SCNF ticket window—for example, at the Invalides or Musée d'Orsay RER stop—and get a *contremarque de passage*. Keep this ticket to exit the system.

When returning to Paris from Versailles, look through the windows past the turnstiles for the departure board. Any train leaving Versailles serves all downtown Paris RER stops on the C line (they're marked on the schedule as stopping at *"toutes les gares jusqu'à Austerlitz,"* meaning "all stations up to Austerlitz").

Taxis for the 30-minute ride between Versailles and Paris cost about €30.

To reach Versailles from Paris by **car,** get on the *périphérique* freeway that circles Paris, and take the toll-free A13 autoroute toward Rouen. Follow signs into Versailles, then look for *château* signs and park in the huge pay lot in front of the palace. The drive takes about 30 minutes one-way.

Information: A helpful TI is just past the Sofitel Hôtel on your walk from the RER station to the palace (April–Sept daily

Touring Versailles from A to M

Note that all of this information is subject to change over the next several years (see "Versailles Renovation—2006 to 2010," page 423). But in 2006, the following is what you *should* find at Versailles:

• *Stand in the courtyard to orient yourself to Versailles' entrances.*

Entrance A to State Apartments (Without Pass): If you don't have a Paris Museum Pass or One-Day Pass, and you want to tour the palace on your own (by following my self-guided tour or using the €4.50 audio-guide), join the line at Entrance A. Enter the palace and take a one-way walk through the State Apartments from the King's Wing, through the Hall of Mirrors, and out via the Queen's and Nobles' Wing.

Entrance B-2 to State Apartments (for Passholders): This entrance is for people with a Paris Museum Pass or One-Day Pass who want to tour the palace on their own (following my self-guided tour or the €4.50 audioguide). Note that those having taken a guided tour can enter the State Apartments without a wait through this entrance.

Entrance C to King's Private Apartments (Without One-Day Pass): If you lack a One-Day Pass, enter here to tour Louis XIV's private bedroom, other rooms, and the Hall of Mirrors, with the help of a dry but informative audioguide (€4.50 admission includes audioguide, not covered by Paris Museum Pass). The Sun King's bedroom and Hall of Mirrors are part of the State Apartments tour, so the King's Private Apartments offer nothing really different to the casual visitor than what you'll see on the main State Apartments tour.

Entrance C-2 to King's Private Apartments (for One-Day Passholders): Same as C, but for visitors with a One-Day Pass.

Entrance D to King's Private Apartments and Opera (with a Guided Tour): This is the place to book a guided tour (see page 422), and where you enter when it's time for your tour to begin. You'll visit the King's Private Apartments (Louis XV, Louis XVI, and Marie-Antoinette), the chapel, and the Opera.

Entrance M to Mesdames Apartments (for One-Day Passholders): This exhibit gives a look at the private apartments

Versailles Entrances

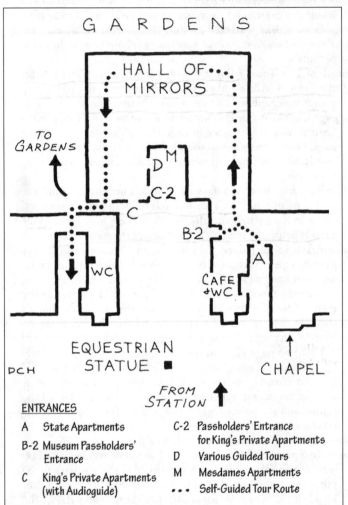

GARDENS

HALL OF MIRRORS

TO GARDENS

D M
C-2
C
B-2
A
WC
CAFE & WC

DCH

EQUESTRIAN STATUE ■

CHAPEL

FROM STATION

ENTRANCES

A   State Apartments

B-2 Museum Passholders' Entrance

C   King's Private Apartments (with Audioguide)

C-2 Passholders' Entrance for King's Private Apartments

D   Various Guided Tours

M   Mesdames Apartments

••• Self-Guided Tour Route

of the eight daughters of King Louis XV (exclusively for visitors with the One-Day Pass, includes 30-min audioguide). It's Versailles' least interesting sight, as the rooms are quite barren, there's little about their lives to actually see, and the commentary is mostly about the paintings hanging on the walls.

9:00–19:00, Oct–March daily 9:00–18:00, tel. 01 39 24 88 88, www.chateauversailles.fr). You'll also find information booths inside the château (at Entrances A and B-2) and, during peak season, kiosks scattered around the courtyard. The useful *Versailles Orientation Guide* brochure explains your sightseeing options.

Length of This Tour: Allow two hours for the palace and two for the gardens. Add another two hours to cover your round-trip transit time, and it's a six-hour day trip from Paris.

Baggage Check: A free checkroom is at Entrance A. This is not a "coat service," but a place to check forbidden items (food, big bags, baby carriages, and so on). If you qualify, it's free, easy, and leaves you unencumbered and better able to enjoy your time here.

WCs: Reminiscent of the days when dukes urinated behind the potted palm trees, WCs are few and far between at Versailles. Those in the palace generally come with very long lines. Make a point to use the public WC just before the palace gates.

Cuisine Art: In the **palace**, the cafeteria and WCs are next to the general entry (Entrance A). There's a sandwich kiosk and a decent restaurant at the canal in the gardens.

In the **town**, you'll find restaurants on the street to the right of the parking lot (as you face the château), though the best eateries line the pleasant market square, place du Marché, in the town center (for recommended restaurants, see the map on page 427 and the listings on page 445). A handy McDonald's is immediately across from the train station (WC without crowds, Internet café next door), and a fun assortment of appealing restaurants line rue de Satory between the station and the palace (below and to the left of the château as you face it; see map).

Photography: Allowed indoors without a flash.

Fountain Spectacles: On spring and summer weekends, classical music fills the king's backyard, and the garden's fountains are in full squirt (April–Sept Sat–Sun 10:30–12:00 & 15:00–16:30, finale 16:50–17:00). On these "spray days," the gardens cost €6 (not covered by Paris Museum Pass, ask for a map of fountains). Louis had his engineers literally reroute a river to fuel these fountains. Even by today's standards, they are impressive. Pick up the helpful *Les Grandes Eaux Musicales* brochure at any information booth. Also ask about the various impressive evening spectacles (Sat in July–Aug).

Equestrian Performances: The Equestrian Performance Academy (Academie du Spectacle Equestre) has brought the art of horseback riding back to Versailles. You can watch

Versailles

WALKING TIMES
Train Station to Château = 10 min.
Château to Grand Trianon = 30 min.
Grand Trianon to Hamlet = 20 min.
Le Hamlet to Château = 30 min.

🅿 –PARKING

GRAND TRIANON
SUMMER HOUSE
TEMPLE OF LOVE
GRAND CANAL
BIKE RENTAL
PETIT TRIANON
APOLLO BASIN
COLONNADE
HAMLET
GARDENS
LATONA BASIN
NEPTUNE BASIN
ORANGERIE
CHATEAU
KING'S VEG. GARDEN
SATORY
AVE DE GAULLE
L'EUROPE
PLACE DU VIEUX MARCHE
VERSAILLES R.G. R.E.R. TRAIN STN.
TO PARIS
TOWN
DCH

❶ Hôtel de France
❷ Hôtel le Cheval Rouge
❸ Hôtel Ibis Versailles
❹ Hôtel du Palais
❺ Hôtel d'Angleterre
❻ Rest. la Bœuf à la Mode
❼ Rest. A la Côte Bretonne
❽ Rest. le Limousin
❾ Equestrian Performances

its rigorous training sessions, including "equestrian fenc-
ing," performed to classical music inside the main area of
Versailles (€7, 60 min, shows at 10:00 and 11:00 on Thu–Sun
only). The stables (Grande Ecurie)—where you can buy
tickets—are across the square from the château, next
to the post office. Information: Tel. 01 39 02 07 14, www
.acadequestre.fr.
Starring: Louis XIV and the *ancien régime*.

Kings and Queens and Guillotines

• *You could read this on the train ride to Versailles. Relax...the palace is the last stop.*

Come the Revolution, when they line us up and make us stick out our hands, will you have enough calluses to keep them from shooting you? A grim thought, but Versailles raises these kinds of questions. It's the symbol of the *ancien régime*, a time when society was divided into rulers and the ruled, when you were born to be rich or to be poor. To some, it's the pinnacle of civilization; to others, the sign of a civilization in decay. Either way, it remains one of Europe's most impressive sights.

Versailles was the residence of the king and seat of France's government for a hundred years. Louis XIV (r. 1643–1715) moved out of the Louvre in Paris, the previous royal residence, and built an elaborate palace in the forests and swamps of Versailles, 10 miles west. The reasons for the move were partly personal—Louis XIV loved the outdoors and disliked the sniping environs of stuffy Paris—and partly political.

Louis XIV was creating the first modern, centralized state. At Versailles, he consolidated Paris' scattered ministries so that he could personally control policy. More importantly, he invited France's nobles to Versailles in order to control them. Living a life of almost enforced idleness, the "domesticated" aristocracy couldn't interfere with the way Louis ran things. With 18 million people united under one king (England had only 5.5 million), a booming economy, and a powerful military, France was Europe's number-one power.

Around 1700, Versailles was the cultural heartbeat of Europe, and French culture was at its zenith. Throughout Europe, when you said "the king," you were referring to the French king...Louis XIV. Every king wanted a palace like Versailles. Everyone learned French. French taste in clothes, hairstyles, table manners, theater, music, art, and kissing spread across the Continent. That cultural dominance continued, to some extent, right up to the 20th century.

Louis XIV

At the center of all this was Europe's greatest king. He was a true Renaissance man, a century after the Renaissance: athletic, good-looking, a musician, dancer, horseman, statesman,

art-lover, lover. For all his grandeur, he was one of history's most polite and approachable kings, a good listener who could put even commoners at ease in his presence.

Louis XIV called himself the Sun King because he gave life and warmth to all that he touched. He was also thought of as Apollo, the Greek god of the sun. Versailles became the personal temple of this god on earth, decorated with statues and symbols

of Apollo, the sun, and Louis XIV himself. The classical themes throughout underlined the divine right of France's kings and queens to rule without limit.

Louis XIV was a hands-on king who personally ran affairs of state. All decisions were made by him. Nobles, who in other countries were the center of power, became virtual slaves dependent on Louis XIV's generosity. For 70 years, he was the perfect embodiment of the absolute monarch. He summed it up best himself with his famous rhyme—*"L'état, c'est moi!"* (lay-tah say-mwah): "The state, that's me!"

Another Louis or Two to Remember

Three kings lived in Versailles during its century of glory. Louis XIV built it and established French dominance. Louis XV, his great-grandson (Louis XIV reigned for 72 years), carried on the tradition and policies, but without the Sun King's flair. During Louis XV's reign (1715–1774), France's power abroad was weakening, and there were rumblings of rebellion from within.

France's monarchy was crumbling, and the time was ripe for a strong leader to reestablish the old feudal order. They didn't get one. Instead, they got Louis XVI (r. 1774–1792), a shy, meek bookworm, the kind of guy who lost sleep over Revolutionary graffiti... because it was misspelled. Louis XVI married a sweet girl from the Austrian royal family, Marie-Antoinette, and together they retreated into the idyllic gardens of Versailles while Revolutionary fires smoldered.

THE TOUR BEGINS

• *Start outside the palace at the equestrian statue of Louis XIV.*

The Original Château and the Courtyard

The part of the palace directly behind the horse statue (the section with the clock) is the original château, once a small hunting lodge where little Louis XIV spent his happiest boyhood years. Naturally, the Sun King's private bedroom (the 3 arched windows beneath the clock) faced the rising sun. The palace and grounds are laid out on an east–west axis.

Once king, Louis XIV expanded the lodge by attaching wings, creating the present U-shape. Later, the long north and south wings were built. The total cost of the project has been estimated at half of France's entire GNP for one year.

Think how busy this courtyard must have been 300 years ago. There were as many as 5,000 nobles here at any one time, each with an entourage. They'd buzz from games to parties to amorous rendezvous in sedan-chair taxis. Servants ran about delivering secret messages and roast legs of lamb. Horse-drawn carriages arrived at the fancy gate with their finely dressed passengers, having driven up the broad boulevard that ran directly from Paris (the horse stables still line the boulevard). Incredible as it seems, both the grounds and most of the palace were public territory, where even the lowliest peasant could come to gawk (so long as they followed a dress code). Then, as now, there were hordes of tourists, pickpockets, palace workers, and men selling wind-up children's toys.

• *You'll see signs marking the various entrances (A, B, B-2, C, D, and M) into the U-shaped palace. For this tour of the State Apartments, which covers the ceremonial center of the palace, start at Entrance A (if you need to pay admission) or Entrance B-2 (if you have a Paris Museum Pass or One-Day Pass). You'll be directed first through the 21 rooms of the history museum, with paintings on the background of Versailles and its kings.*

The audioguide tour of the State Apartments (€4.50, or included with One-Day Pass) complements this chapter's self-guided tour. For those who want more information, it's a good value.

Our tour starts upstairs, in the room that overlooks the lavish Royal Chapel with its pipe organ. (Note: As you jostle through the crowded corridors of the palace, pickpockets will be working the tourist crowds.)

The State Apartments
Royal Chapel
Every morning at 10:00, the organist and musicians struck up the music, these big golden doors opened, and Louis XIV and his family walked through to attend Mass. While Louis XIV sat here on the upper level and looked down on the golden altar, the lowly nobles below knelt with their backs to the altar and looked up—worshipping Louis worshipping God. Important religious ceremonies took place here, including the marriage of young Louis XVI to Marie-Antoinette.

In the vast pagan "temple" that is Versailles—built to glorify one man, Louis XIV—this Royal Chapel is a paltry tip of the hat to that "other" god...the Christian one. It's virtually the first, last, and only hint of Christianity you'll see in the entire complex. Versailles celebrates Man, not God, by raising Louis XIV to almost godlike status, the personification of all good human qualities. In a way, Versailles is the last great flowering of Renaissance humanism and revival of the classical world.

• *Take a map flier and enter the next room, a large space with a fireplace and a colorful painting on the ceiling.*

Hercules Drawing Room
Pleasure ruled. The main suppers, balls, and receptions were held in this room. Picture elegant partygoers in fine silks, wigs, rouge, lipstick, and fake moles (and that's just the men), as they dance to the strains of a string quartet.

On the wall opposite the fireplace is an appropriate painting showing Christ in the middle of a Venetian party. The work—by Paolo Veronese, a gift from the Republic of Venice—was one of Louis XIV's favorites, so they decorated the room around it. (Stand by the fireplace for the full effect: The room's columns, arches, and frieze match the height and style of Veronese's painted architecture, which makes the painting an extension of the room.)

The ceiling painting of Hercules being crowned a god gives the room its name. Hercules (with his club) hurries up to heaven on a chariot, late for his wedding to the king of the god's daughter. Louis XIV built the room for his own daughter's wedding reception in the style of the day—pure Baroque. As you wander, the palace feels bare, but remember that entire industries were created to furnish and decorate the place with carpets, mirrors, furniture, and tapestries.

• *From here on, it's a one-way tour—getting lost is not allowed. Follow the crowds into the small green room with a goddess in pink on the ceiling. The names of the rooms generally come from the paintings on the ceilings.*

The King's Wing

Salon of Abundance

If the party in the Hercules Room got too intense, you could always step in here for some refreshments. Silver trays were loaded up with liqueurs, exotic stimulants (coffee), juice, chocolates, and, on really special occasions, three-bean salad.

The ceiling painting shows the cornucopia of riches poured down on invited guests. Around the edges of the ceiling are painted versions of the king's actual dinnerware and treasures. The two black chests of drawers are from Louis' furniture collection (most of it was lost in the Revolution). They rest on heavy bases and are heavily ornamented—the so-called Louis XIV style.

Louis himself might be here. He was a gracious host who enjoyed letting his hair down at night. If he took a liking to you, he might sneak you through those doors there (in the middle of the wall) and into his own private study, or "cabinet of curiosities," where he'd show off his collection of dishes, medals, jewels, or... the *Mona Lisa,* which hung on his wall. Louis' favorite show-and-tell items are now in the Louvre.

The paintings on the walls are of Louis XIV's heirs. He reigned more than 70 years and outlived three of them, finally leaving the crown to his pink-cheeked, five-year-old great-grand-son, Louis XV (on the right).

Venus Room

Love ruled at Versailles. In this room, couples would cavort beneath the Greek goddess of love (on the ceiling), who sends down a canopy of golden garlands to ensnare mortals in delicious *amour.* Notice how a painted garland goes "out" the bottom of the central painting, becomes a golden garland held by a satyr, transforms into a gilded wood garland, and then turns back into a painting again. Baroque artists loved to mix their media to fool the eye. Another illusion is in the paintings at both ends of the room—the painted columns match the room's real ones, and so extend this grand room into mythical courtyards.

Don't let the statue of a confident Louis XIV as a Roman emperor fool you. He started out as a poor little rich kid with a chip on his shoulder. His father died before Louis was old enough to rule, and, during the regency period, the French Parliament treated little Louis and his mother like trash. They were virtual prisoners, humiliated in their home (at that time, the Royal Palace was the Louvre in Paris) with bland meals, hand-me-down leotards, and pointed shoes. Once Louis XIV attained power and wealth, there was one topic you never discussed in his presence—poverty. Maybe Versailles was his way of saying, "Living well is the best revenge."

Diana Room

Here in the billiards room, Louis and his men played on a table that stood in the center of the room, while ladies sat surrounding them on Persian-carpet cushions, and music wafted in from the next room. Louis was a good pool player, a sore loser, and a king—he rarely lost.

The famous bust of Louis by Giovanni Lorenzo Bernini (in the center) shows a handsome, dashing, 27-year-old playboy-king. His gaze is steady amid his windblown cloak and hair. Young Louis loved life. He hunted animals by day (notice Diana the Huntress on the ceiling) and chased beautiful women at night.

Games were actually an important part of Louis' political strategy, known as "the domestication of the nobility." By distracting the nobles with the pleasures of courtly life, he was free to run the government his way. Billiards, dancing, and concerts were popular, but the biggest distraction was gambling, usually a card game similar to blackjack. Louis lent money to the losers, making them even more indebted to him. The good life was an addiction, and Louis kept the medicine cabinet well-stocked.

As you move into the next room, notice the fat walls that hid thin servants, who were to be at their master's constant call—but out of sight when not needed.

Mars Room

Also known as the Guard Room (as it was the room for Louis' Swiss bodyguards), it's decorated with a military flair. On the ceiling, there's Mars, the Greek god of war, in a chariot pulled by wolves. The bronze cupids in the corners are escalating from love arrows to heavier artillery. But it's not all war. The painting of David playing his harp is a reminder that Louis loved music and played his guitar or enjoyed a concert here nearly every evening.

Out the window are sculpted gardens in the style of a traditional Italian villa—landscaped symmetrically, with trimmed hedges and cone-shaped trees lining walkways that lead to fountains.

Mercury Room

Louis' life was a work of art, and Versailles was the display case. Everything he did was a public event designed to show his subjects how it should be done. This room served as Louis' official (not actual) bedroom, where the Sun King would ritually rise each morning to warm his subjects.

From a canopied bed (like this 18th-century one), Louis would get up, dress, and take a seat for morning prayer. Meanwhile, the nobles would stand behind a balustrade, in awe of his piety, nobility, and clean socks. At breakfast, they murmured with delight as he deftly decapitated his boiled egg with a knife. And when Louis went to bed at night, the dukes and barons would fight over who got to hold the candle while he slipped into his royal jammies. Bedtime, wake-up, and meals were all public rituals.

Apollo Room

This was the grand throne room. Louis held court from a 10-foot-tall, silver-canopied throne on a raised platform placed in the center of the room. (Notice the metal rings in the ceiling that once supported the canopy.)

Everything in here reminds us that Louis XIV was not just any ruler, but the Sun King, who lit the whole world with his presence. On the ceiling, the sun god Apollo drives his chariot, dragging the sun across the heavens to warm the four corners of the world (counterclockwise from above the exit door): 1) Europe, with a sword; 2) Asia, with a lion; 3) Africa, with an elephant; and 4) good old America, an Indian maiden with a crocodile. Notice the ceiling's beautifully gilded frame and *Goldfinger* maidens.

The famous portrait by Hyacinthe Rigaud over the fireplace gives a more human look at Louis XIV. He's shown in a dancer's pose, displaying the legs that made him one of the all-time dancing fools of kingery. At night, they often held parties in this room, actually dancing around the throne.

Louis XIV (who was 63 when this was painted) had more than 300 wigs like this one, and he changed them many times a day. This fashion first started when his hairline began to recede, then sprouted all over Europe, and even to the American colonies in the time of George Washington.

Louis XIV may have been treated like a god, but he was not an overly arrogant man. His subjects adored him because he was a symbol of everything a man could be, the fullest expression of the Renaissance Man. Compare the portrait of Louis XIV with the one across the room of his last successor, Louis XVI—same arrogant pose, but without the inner confidence to keep his head on his shoulders.

The War Room

"Louis Quatorze was addicted to wars," and France's success made other countries jealous and nervous. At the base of the ceiling (in semi-circular paintings), we see Germany (with the double eagle), Holland (with its ships), and Spain (with a red flag and roaring lion) ganging up on Louis XIV. But Lady France (center of

ceiling), protected by the shield of Louis XIV, hurls thunderbolts down to defeat them. The stucco relief on the wall shows Louis XIV on horseback, triumphing over his fallen enemies.

Versailles was good propaganda. It showed the rest of the world how rich and powerful France was. A visit to the palace and gardens sent visitors reeling. And Louis XIV's greatest triumph may be the next room, the one that everybody wrote home about.

The Hall of Mirrors

No one had ever seen anything like this hall when it was opened. Mirrors were still a great luxury at the time, and the number and size of these monsters were astounding. The hall is nearly 250 feet long. There are 17 arched mirrors, matched by 17 windows reflecting that breathtaking view of the gardens. Lining the hall are 24 gilded candelabras, eight busts of Roman emperors, and eight classical-style statues (7 of them ancient). The ceiling decoration chronicles Louis' military accomplishments, topped off by Louis himself in the central panel (with cupids playing cards at his divine feet), doing what he did best—triumphing. Originally, two huge carpets mirrored the action depicted on the ceiling.

Imagine this place lit by the flames of thousands of candles, filled with ambassadors, nobles, and guests dressed in silks and powdered wigs. At the far end of the room sits the king, on the canopied throne moved in temporarily from the Apollo Room. Servants glide by with silver trays of hors d'oeuvres, and an orchestra fuels the festivities. The mirrors reflect an age when beautiful people loved to look at themselves. It was no longer a sin to be proud of good looks and fine clothes, or to enjoy the good things in life: laughing, dancing, eating, drinking, flirting, and watching the sun set into the distant canal.

From the center of the hall, you can fully appreciate the epic scale of Versailles. The huge palace (by architect Louis Le Vau), the fantasy interior (by Charles Le Brun), and the endless gardens (by André Le Nôtre) made Versailles *le* best. In 1871, after the Prussians defeated the French, Otto von Bismarck declared the establishment of the German Empire in this room. And in 1919, Germany and the Allies signed the Treaty of Versailles, ending

World War I (and, some say, starting World War II) right here, in the Hall of Mirrors.
• *From the Hall of Mirrors, a short detour takes you to the actual heart of the palace, the...*

King's Bedroom and Council Rooms
Look out the window and notice how this small room is at the exact center of the immense horse-shoe shaped building, overlooking the main courtyard and—naturally—facing the rising sun in the east. Imagine the humiliation on that day in 1789 when Louis XVI was forced to stand here and acknowledge the angry crowds that filled the square demanding the end of the divine monarchy. While this was his bedroom, he also worked here and the rooms on either side were for top council meetings.
• *Returning to the Hall of Mirrors, finish hiking through it and, at the far corner, enter the small...*

Peace Room
By the end of Sun King's long life, he was tired of fighting. In this sequel to the War Room, peace is granted to Germany, Holland, and Spain as cupids play with the discarded cannons, armor, and swords. Louis XIV advised his great-grandson to "be a peaceful king."

The oval painting above the fireplace shows 19-year-old Louis XV bestowing an olive branch on Europe. Beside him is his Polish wife, Marie Leszczynska, cradling their baby twin daughters.

The Peace Room marks the beginning of the queen's half of the palace. The Queen's Wing is a mirror image of the King's Wing. While the King's Wing was mostly ceremonial and used as a series of reception rooms, the Queen's Wing is more intimate. For instance, on Sundays, the queen held chamber-music concerts in this room for family and friends (notice the gilded music motifs).
• *Enter the first room of the Queen's Wing, with its canopied bed.*

The Queen's and Nobles' Wing
The Queen's Bedchamber
It was here that the queen rendezvoused with her husband. Two queens died here. This is where 19 princes were born. The chandelier is where two of them were conceived. (Just kidding.) Royal babies were delivered in public to prove their blue-bloodedness.

True, Louis XIV was not the most faithful husband. There was no attempt to hide the fact that the Sun King warmed more

than one bed, for he was above the rules of mere mortals. Adultery became acceptable—even fashionable—in court circles. The secret-looking door on the left side of the bed was for Louis' late-night liaisons—it led straight to his rooms.

Some of Louis XIV's mistresses became more famous and powerful than his rather quiet queen, but he was faithful to the show of marriage and had genuine affection for his wife. Their private apartments were connected, and Louis XIV made a point of sleeping with the queen as often as possible, regardless of whose tiara he tickled earlier in the evening.

This room looks like it did in the days of the last queen, Marie-Antoinette, who substantially redecorated the entire wing. That's her bust over the fireplace, and the double eagle of her native Austria in the corners. The big chest to the left of the bed held her jewels.

The queen's canopied bed is a reconstruction. The bed, chair, and wall coverings switched with the seasons. This was the cheery summer pattern.

Salon of the Nobles

The queen's circle of friends met here, seated on the stools, under paintings by Boucher—popular with the queen for their pink-cheeked rococo exuberance. Discussions ranged from politics to gossip, food to literature, fashion to philosophy. The Versailles kings considered themselves enlightened monarchs who promoted the arts and new ideas. Folks such as Voltaire—a political radi-cal—and the playwright Molière participated in the Versailles court. Ironically, these discussions planted the seeds of liberal thought that would grow into the Revolution.

Queen's Antechamber

The royal family dined here publicly, while servants and nobles fluttered around them, admired their table manners, and laughed at the king's jokes like courtly Paul Shaffers. A typical dinner con-sisted of four different soups, two whole birds stuffed with truffles, mutton, ham slices, fruit, pastries, compotes, and preserves.

The central portrait is of luxury-loving, "let-them-eat-cake" Marie-Antoinette, who became a symbol of decadence to the peas-ants. The portrait at the far end is a public-relations attempt to soften her image by showing her with three of her children.

Queen's Guard Room

On October 6, 1789, a mob of revolutionaries—appalled by their queen's taste in wallpaper—stormed the palace. They were fed up with the ruling class leading a life of luxury in the countryside while they were starving in the grimy streets of Paris.

The King's Vegetable Garden
(Le Potager du Roi)

When Louis XIV demanded fresh asparagus in the middle of winter, he got it, thanks to his vegetable garden. Located a few blocks from the château (see map on page 425), the 22-acre garden—still productive—is open to visitors. Stroll through symmetrically laid-out plots planted with vegetables both ordinary and exotic, among thousands of fruit trees. The garden is surrounded by walls and sunk below street level to create its own microclimate. Overseeing the central fountain is a statue of the agronomist Jean de la Quintinie, who wowed Louis XIV's court with Versailles-sized produce. Even today, the garden sprouts 20 tons of vegetables and 50 tons of fruit a year, which you can buy in season (€4.50 on weekdays, €6.50 on weekends, April–Oct daily 10:00–18:00, closed Nov–March, 10 rue du Maréchal Joffre).

The king and queen locked themselves in. Some of the revolutionaries gained access to this upper floor. They burst into this room where Marie-Antoinette was hiding, overcame her bodyguards, and dragged her and her husband off. (Some claim that, as they carried her away, she sang, "Louis, Louis, oh-oh...we gotta go now.")

The enraged peasants then proceeded to ransack the place as revenge for the years of poverty and oppression they'd suffered. (The stripped palace was refurnished a decade later under Napoleon and turned into a national museum.) Marie-Antoinette and Louis XVI were later taken to the place de la Concorde in Paris, where they knelt under the guillotine and were made a foot shorter at the top.

Did the king and queen deserve it? Were the revolutionaries destroying civilization or clearing the decks for a new and better one? Was Versailles a symbol of progress or decadence?

Coronation Room

No sooner did they throw out a king than they got an emperor. The Revolution established democracy, but it was shaky in a country that wasn't used to it. In the midst of the confusion, the upstart general Napoleon Bonaparte took control, and soon held dictatorial powers. This room captures the glory of the Napoleon years, when he conquered most of Europe. In the huge canvas on the left-hand wall, we see him crowning himself emperor of a new, revived "Roman" Empire. (While also painted by the master, Jacques-Louis David, this is a lesser-quality version of the famous one hanging in the Louvre.)

Turn and face the windows to see the portrait (between the windows) of a dashing, young, charismatic Napoleon in 1796, when he was just a general in command of the Revolution's army in Italy. Compare this with the adjacent portrait from 10 years later—looking less like a revolutionary and more like a Louis. Above the young Napoleon is a portrait of Josephine, his wife and France's empress. In David's *Distribution of Eagles* (opposite the *Coronation*), the victorious general, in imperial garb, passes out emblems of victory to his loyal troops. In *The Battle of Aboukir* (opposite the window), Joachim Murat, Napoleon's general and brother-in-law, looks bored as he slashes through a tangle of dark-skinned warriors. His horse, though, has a look of, "What are we doing in this mob? Let's get out of here!" Let's.

• *Before leaving, consider stopping by the **Hall of Battles**. This nearly 400-foot-long hall (even longer then the Hall of Mirrors) celebrates the great French battles from the 6th century to 1830 with 33 grand paintings and piles of busts of military big shots. This is open sporadically (if there is available staff) and worth a wander for historians.*

The exit staircase puts you outside on the left (south) side of the palace, opposite the WC. Turn left under the colonnade to enter the gardens, turn right to leave the château.

The Gardens—Controlling Nature

Louis XIV was a divine-right ruler. One way he proved it was by controlling nature like a god. These lavish grounds—elaborately planned out, pruned, and decorated—showed everyone that Louis was in total command. Louis loved his gardens and, until his last days, presided over their care. He

personally led VIPs through them and threw his biggest parties here. With the Greco-Roman themes and their incomparable beauty, the gardens further illustrated his immense power. (For a fine and free explanation, pick up the palace's *Garden and Groves* flier.)

• *Entering the gardens, with the palace to your back, go left to the stone railing. You'll pass through flowers and cookie-cutter patterns of shrubs and green cones. Stand at the railing overlooking the courtyard below and the Louis-made lake in the distance.*

The Orangerie

The warmth from the Sun King was so great that he could even grow orange trees in chilly France. Louis XIV had a thousand of these to amaze his visitors. In winter, they were kept in the greenhouses (beneath your feet) that surround the courtyard. On

sunny days, they were wheeled out
in their silver planters and scattered around the grounds.

*• From the stone railing, turn about-
face and walk to the back side of the
palace, with two large pools of water.
Sit on the top stair and look away
from the palace.*

View Down the Royal Drive

This, to me, is the most stunning spot in all of Versailles. With
the palace behind you, the grounds stretch out—it seems—forever.
Versailles was laid out along an eight-mile axis that included the
grounds, the palace, and the town of Versailles itself, one of the
first instances of urban planning since Roman times and a model
for future capitals, such as Washington, D.C. and Brasilia.

Looking down the Royal Drive (also known as "The Green
Carpet"), you see the round Apollo fountain far in the distance.
Just beyond that is the Grand Canal. The groves on either side of
the Royal Drive were planted with trees from all over, laid out in
an elaborate grid, and dotted with statues and fountains. Of the
original 1,500 fountains, 300 remain.

Looking back at the palace, you can see the Hall of Mirrors—
it's the middle story, with the arched windows.

*• Stroll down the steps to get a good look at the frogs and lizards that fill
the round...*

Latona Basin

Everything in the garden has a symbolic meaning. The theme of
Versailles is Apollo, the god of the sun, associated with Louis XIV.
This round fountain tells the story of the birth of Apollo and his
sister, Diana. On top of the fountain are Apollo and Diana as little
kids with their mother, Latona (they're facing toward the Apollo
fountain). Latona, an unwed mother, was insulted by the local
peasants. She called on the king of the gods, Zeus (the children's
father), to avenge the insult. Zeus swooped down and turned all
the peasants into the frogs and lizards that ring the fountain.

*• As you walk down past the basin toward the Royal Drive, you'll
pass by "ancient" statues done by 17th-century French sculptors. The
Colonnade is hidden in the woods on the left-hand side of the Royal
Drive, about three-fourths of the way to the Apollo Basin.*

The Colonnade

Versailles had no prestigious ancient ruins, so the king built his
own. This prefab Roman ruin is a 100-foot circle of 64 marble columns supporting arches. Beneath the arches are small birdbath

Getting Around the Gardens

It's a 30-minute hike from the palace, down to the canal, past the two Trianon Palaces to the Hamlet—this chapter's self-guided tour. The fast-looking, slow-moving **tram** for tired tourists leaves from behind the château (north side) and serves the Grand Canal and the Trianon Palaces. You can hop on and off as you like (€5, free with One-Day Pass, 4/hr, 4 stops but not the Hamlet, commentary is nearly worthless). A **horse carriage** also departs from the north side of the palace. The lazy can rent **golf carts** (€20/hr, pick up at Orangerie side of palace) for a fun drive through the gardens. The cart, which comes with music and a relaxing commentary, is carefully restricted—it won't even drive if you get off the prescribed route. Be warned: To make the entire route out to the Hamlet and back in an hour, you'll need to put the pedal to the metal without stops...or you'll pay extra. Renting a **bike** (€6/hr, near the Grand Canal) gives you the most freedom to explore the gardens effortlessly, freely, and economically.

fountains. Nobles would picnic in the shade to the tunes of a string quartet and pretend that they were the enlightened citizens of the ancient world.

The Apollo Basin

The fountains of Versailles were its most famous attraction, a marvel of both art and engineering. This one was the centerpiece, showing the sun god—Louis XIV—in his sunny chariot, as he starts his journey across the sky. The horses are half submerged, giving the impression, when the fountains play, of the sun rising out of the mists of dawn. Most of the fountains were only turned on when the king walked by, but this one played constantly for the benefit of those watching from the palace.

All the fountains are gravity-powered. They work on the same principle as blocking a hose with your finger to make it squirt. Underground streams (pumped into Versailles by Seine River pressure) feed into smaller pipes at the fountains, which shoot the water high into the air.

Looking back at the palace from here, realize that the distance you just walked is only a fraction of this vast complex of buildings, gardens, and waterways. Be glad you don't have to mow the lawn.

The Grand Canal

Why visit Venice when you can just build your own? In an era before virtual reality, this was the next best thing to an actual trip. Couples in gondolas would pole along the waters accompanied by

barges with orchestras playing "O Sole Mio." The canal is actually cross-shaped; you're looking at the longest part, one mile from end to end. Of course, this, too, is a man-made body of water with no function other than to please. Originally, actual gondoliers, imported with their boats from Venice, lived in a little settlement next to the canal.

The Trianon Area—Retreat from Reality

Versailles began as an escape from the pressures of kingship. But in a short time, the palace became as busy as Paris ever was. Louis XIV needed an escape from his escape and built a smaller palace out in the boonies. Later, his successors retreated still farther into the garden and built a fantasy world of simple pleasures, allowing them to ignore the real world that was crumbling all around them.

• *You can rent a bike or golf cart, or catch the pokey tourist train, but the walk is half the fun. It's about a 30-minute walk from here to the end of the tour, plus another 30-minute walk back to the palace.*

Grand Trianon

This was the king's private residence away from the main palace. Louis usually spent a couple of nights a week here, but the two later Louises spent more and more time retreating. While the main palace of Versailles was a screen separating French reality from the royal utopia, the Trianon Palaces were engulfed in the royals' fantasy world, and therefore favored.

The facade of this one-story building is a charming combination of pink, yellow, and white, a cheery contrast to the imposing Baroque facade of the main palace. Ahead, you can see the gardens through the columns. The king's apartments were to the left of the columns.

The flower gardens were changed daily for the king's pleasure—for new color combinations and new "nasal cocktails."

Walk around the palace (to the right), if you'd like, for a view of the gardens and rear facade.

• *Facing the front, do an about-face. The Summer House is not down the driveway but about 200 yards away, along the smaller pathway at about 10 o'clock.*

Summer House of the French Garden

This small, white building with four rooms fanning out from the center was one more step away from the modern world. Here, the queen spent summer evenings with family and a few friends, listening to music or playing parlor games. She and her friends explored all avenues of *la douceur de vivre,* the sweetness of living.

To the left are the buildings of the ménagerie, where her servants bred cows, goats, chickens, and ducks.

• *Continue frolicking along the path until you run into the...*

Petit Trianon

Louis XV developed an interest in botany. He wanted to spend more time near the French Gardens, but the Summer House just wasn't big enough. He built the Petit Trianon (the "Small" Trianon), a masterpiece of neoclassical architecture. This gray,

cubical building has four distinct facades, each a perfect and harmonious combination of Greek-style columns, windows, and railings. Walk around it and find your favorite.

Louis XVI's wife, Marie-Antoinette, made this her home base. Despite her bad public reputation, Marie-Antoinette was a sweet girl from Vienna who never quite fit in with the fast, sophisticated crowd at Versailles. Here at the Petit Trianon, she could get away and recreate the simple home life she remembered from her childhood. On the lawn outside, she installed a merry-go-round.

• *Five minutes more will bring you to the...*

Temple of Love

A circle of 12 marble Corinthian columns supports a dome, decorating a path where lovers would stroll. Underneath, there's a statue of Cupid making a bow (to shoot arrows of love) out of the club of Hercules. It's a delightful monument to a society where the rich could afford that ultimate luxury, romantic love. When the Revolution came, I bet they wished they'd kept the club.

• *And finally, you'll reach...*

The Hamlet (Le Hameau)

Marie-Antoinette longed for the simple life of a peasant. Not the hard labor of real peasants—who sweated and starved around her—but the fairy-tale world of simple country pleasures. She built this complex of 12 buildings as her own private village.

This was an actual working farm with a dairy, a water mill, and domestic animals. The harvest was served at Marie-Antoinette's table. Marie-Antoinette didn't do much work herself, but she "supervised," dressed in a plain white muslin dress and a straw hat.

The Queen's House is the main building, actually two buildings connected by a wooden gallery. Like any typical peasant

farmhouse, it had a billiard room, library, elegant dining hall, and two living rooms.

Nearby was the small theater. Here, Marie-Antoinette and her friends acted out plays, far from the rude intrusions of the real world....

• *The real world and the main palace are a 30-minute walk to the southeast. Along the way, stop at the Neptune Basin near the palace, an impressive miniature lake with fountains, and indulge your own favorite fantasy.*

SLEEPING

For a laid-back alternative to Paris within easy reach of the big city by RER train (5/hr, 30 min), Versailles, with easy, safe parking and reasonably priced hotels, can be a good overnight stop. Park in the château's main lot while looking for a hotel, or leave your car there overnight (free 19:30–8:00). Get a map of Versailles at your hotel or at the TI.

$$ Hôtel de France*, in an 18th-century townhouse, offers four-star value, with air-conditioned, appropriately royal rooms, a pleasant courtyard, comfy public spaces, a bar, and a restaurant (Db-€145, Tb-€180, Qb-€240, just off parking lot across from château, 5 rue Colbert, tel. 01 30 83 92 23, fax 01 30 83 92 24, www.hotelfrance-versailles.com, hotel-de-france -versailles@wanadoo.fr).

$ Hôtel le Cheval Rouge, built in 1676 as Louis XIV's stables, now houses tourists. It's a block behind the place du Marché in a quaint corner of town on a large, quiet courtyard with free parking and crisp, sufficiently comfortable rooms, many with open beams (Sb-€66, Db with shower-€70, Db with tub-€85, Tb-€90–100, Qb-€106, 18 rue André Chénier, tel. 01 39 50 03 03, fax 01 39 50 61 27, www.chevalrouge.fr.st, chevalrouge@club-internet.fr).

$ Hôtel Ibis Versailles offers fair value and modern comfort, with 85 air-conditioned rooms but no character (Db-€60 Fri–Sun, €90 Mon–Thu, extra bed-€10, across from RER station, 4 avenue du Général de Gaulle, tel. 01 39 53 03 30, fax 01 39 50 06 31, h1409@accor-hotels.com).

$ Hôtel du Palais, facing the RER station, rents 24 clean, basic rooms—the cheapest I list in this area. Ask for a quiet room off the street (Db-€55, piles of stairs, 6 place Lyautey, tel. 01 39 50 39 29, fax 01 39 50 80 41, hotelpalais@ifrance.com).

$ Hôtel d'Angleterre, away from the frenzy, is a tranquil old place with smiling, Polish-born Madame Kutyla in control. Rooms

---

Sleep Code

(€1 = about $1.20, country code: 33)
S = Single, **D** = Double/Twin, **T** = Triple, **Q** = Quad, **b** = bathroom,
s = shower only. Everyone speaks English and accepts credit
cards.

---

are comfortable and spacious. Park in the nearby château lot (one
D-€46, Db-€68–75, family Qb-€90–100, extra bed-€15, just below
palace to the right as you exit, 2 rue de Fontenay, tel. 01 39 51 43
50, fax 01 39 51 45 63, hotel.angleterre.versailles@wanadoo.fr).

EATING

In the pleasant town center, around place du Marché Notre-Dame,
you'll find a variety of reasonably priced restaurants, cafés, and a
few cobbled lanes (market days Sun, Tue, and Fri until 13:00; see
map on page 427). The square is a 15-minute walk from the château (veer left when you leave château). From the place du Marché,
consider shortcutting to Versailles' gardens by walking 10 minutes
west down rue de la Paroisse. The château will be to your left after
entering, with the main gardens, Trianon Palaces, and Hamlet
straight ahead. The quickest way to the château's front door is
along avenue de St. Cloud and rue Colbert.

On or near Place du Marché Notre-Dame: This square is lined
with colorful and inexpensive eateries. I particularly like these
two: **La Bœuf à la Mode,** right on the square, is a bistro with traditional cuisine and a passion for red meat (2-course *menu*-€21,
3-course *menu*-€26, open daily, 4 rue au Pain, tel. 01 39 50 31 99).
A la Côte Bretonne is your best bet for crêpes in a friendly, cozy
setting. Yann-Alan and his family have served up the cuisine of
their native Brittany region since 1951 (€4–10 crêpes from a fun and
creative menu, fine indoor and outdoor seating, daily 12:00–14:30
& 19:00–22:30, a few steps off the square on traffic-free rue des
Deux Portes at #12, tel. 01 39 51 18 24).

On Rue Satory: This pedestrian-friendly street is on the south
side of the château, near Hôtel d'Angleterre (10-min walk, angle
right out of the château). The street is lined with a rich variety of
restaurants, ranging from cheap ethnic to more pricey and formal
French (such as Le Limousin, at #4).

CHARTRES CATHEDRAL DAY TRIP

Some of the children who watched the old church burn to the ground on June 10, 1194, grew up to build Chartres cathedral and attend the dedication Mass in 1260. That's astonishing, considering that other Gothic cathedrals, such as Paris' Notre-Dame, took hundreds of years to build. Having been built so quickly, Chartres is arguably Europe's best example of pure Gothic, with a unity of architecture, statues, and stained glass that captures the spirit of the Age of Faith.

Chartres itself, an easy day trip from Paris, offers a pleasant small-town break. Its pleasing, cobbled old center is overshadowed by its great cathedral. Discover the picnic-friendly park behind the cathedral and wander the quiet alleys and peaceful squares. For accommodations and eateries, see the end of this chapter.

ORIENTATION

Cost: Church entry free; climbing the north tower takes 300 steps and costs €6.10 (free for those under 18).

Hours: Church open daily 8:30–19:30. Tower open May–Aug Mon–Sat 9:30–12:00 & 14:00–17:30, Sun 14:00–17:30, Sept–April closes at 16:30 (last entry 30 min before closing, entrance inside church after bookstore on left). Mass: Mon–Fri at 11:45 and 18:15; Sat at 11:45 and 18:00; Sun at 9:15 (Gregorian), 11:00, and 18:00 (in crypt).

Getting There: Chartres is a one-hour train trip from Paris' Gare Montparnasse (about €12.50 one-way, 10/day; figure on a round-trip total of 3 hrs from Paris to cathedral doorstep and back). Upon arrival in Chartres, jot down times when the train returns to Paris (last train generally departs Chartres around 21:00). Leaving the train station, you'll see

the cathedral dominating the town, a five-minute walk uphill (TI at cathedral).

Combining with Versailles: TER trains link Versailles and Chartres frequently (up to 30 a day), on the route from Paris to Le Mans. In Versailles, this train runs from the Chantiers station (that's "Versailles C.H.")—not the Versailles R.G., or Rive Gauche, station listed in this book's Versailles visit (see page 423). If you're going from Chartres to Versailles, it means a longer walk from the Versailles C.H. station to the château (figure about 25 min; station agents have little maps, but the walk is easy—just ask locals, "Château?").

Bring: Binoculars, if you got 'em.

Information: The helpful TI offers a free map with basic information on the town and cathedral, as well as audioguides for the town only (described below; open April–Sept Mon–Sat 9:00–19:00, Sun 9:30–17:30; Oct–March Mon–Sat 10:00–18:00, Sun 10:00–13:00 & 14:30–16:30; located 100 yards in front of church, tel. 02 37 18 26 26, www.chartres-tourisme.com). The church has two bookstores, one inside near the entrance, the other—called Le Crypte—is outside near the south porch (church tel. 02 37 21 59 08, www.diocese-chartres.com).

Cathedral Tours by Malcolm Miller: This fascinating English scholar moved here nearly 50 years ago, and has made the study this cathedral—and sharing its wonder through his guided walks—his life's work. His 75-minute tours (€10, offered Mon–Sat at 12:00 and 14:45, just show up) are worthwhile, even if you've taken my self-guided tour (below). Some take both tours, as every tour is different. Tours begin at the bookstore inside the church. He also offers private tours (tel. 02 37 28 15 58, fax 02 37 28 33 03, millerchartres@aol.com). For a detailed look at Chartres' windows, sculpture, and history, pick up Malcolm Miller's two guidebooks (sold at cathedral).

Audioguides: You can rent audioguides from the cathedral bookstore. Routes include the cathedral (€4, 45 min), the choir only (€3, 25 min), or both (€6, 70 min). If you are staying the night in Chartres, consider renting an audioguide for a tour of the so-often-missed old town (€5.50, €8.50 for 2 people, about 2 hrs, available only at the TI). You'll need to leave your passport as a deposit.

The Crypt: Under the Baroque altarpiece, whose artist was clearly inspired by Bernini, is the crypt. The crypt (which means "hidden") is the foundation of the previous, ninth-century church. The precious veil of Mary was once kept here. While worshippers could look at it through windows, they couldn't actually go in. Today, these foundations can be visited only

as part of a guided tour in French (with an English handout). You'll see remnants of the earlier churches, a modern copy of the old wooden Mary-and-baby statue, and hints of the old well and Roman wall...but not Mary's veil, which is no longer displayed (€2.60, 4/day April–Oct, 2/day Nov–March, 30-min tours start in La Crypte bookstore, located outside church near south porch, tel. 02 37 21 75 02).

Length of This Tour: One hour, but Chartres is an all-day excursion from Paris.

THE CHARTRES GENERATION—THE 1200s

• *Kill train time by reading this.*

From king to bishop and knight to pawn, French society was devoted to the Christian faith. It inspired knights to undertake the formidable Crusades, artists to re-create heaven in statues and stained glass, and architects to build skyscraping cathedrals filled with the mystic light of heaven. They aimed for a golden age, blending faith and reason. But misguided faith often outstripped reason, resulting in very un-Christian intolerance and violence.

Timeline

1194 The old cathedral burns down.

c. 1200 The University of Paris is founded, using human reason to analyze Christian faith. Borrowing from the pagan Greek philosopher Aristotle, scholars described the Christian universe as a series of concentric rings spinning around the Earth in geometrical perfection.

1202 The pope calls on all true Christians to rescue the Holy Land from Muslim "infidels" in the Fourth Crusade (1202–1204). This crusade ends disastrously in the sacking of Constantinople, a Christian city.

1206 Chartres' cornerstone is laid. The style is *opus francigenum* ("French-style work")—which is what the people in Gothic times called Gothic. Chartres is just one of several great cathedrals under construction in Europe.

1207 Francis of Assisi, a rebellious Italian youth, undergoes a conversion to a life of Christian poverty and love. His open spirit inspires many followers, including France's King Louis IX (a generation later).

1209 France's King Philip Augustus, based in Paris, invades southern France and massacres fellow Christians (the Cathars or Albigensians) as heretics.

1212 Thousands of boys and girls idealistically join the Children's Crusade to save the Holy Land. Most die

in transit or are sold into slavery.

1220 The external structure of Chartres cathedral is nearly finished. Work begins on the statues and stained glass.

1226 Eleven-year-old Louis IX is crowned as *rex et sacerdos,* "King and Priest," beginning a 45-year Golden Age combining church and state. His mother, Blanche of Castile (granddaughter of Eleanor of Aquitaine), is his lifelong mentor.

1230 Most of Chartres' stained glass is completed.

1244 At age 30, Louis IX falls sick and sees a vision in a coma that changes his life. His personal trustworthiness helps unify the nation. He reforms the judicial system along Christian lines, helping the poor.

1245 The last Albigensian heretics are burned at Montségur, in a crusade ordered by Louis IX and his mother, Blanche.

1248 Louis IX personally leads the Seventh Crusade by walking barefoot from Paris to the port of departure. During the fighting, he is captured and ransomed. He later returns home a changed man. Humbled, he adopts the poverty of the Franciscan brotherhood. His devotion earns him the title of St. Louis.

1260 Chartres cathedral is dedicated. The church is the physical embodiment of the Age of Faith, with architecture as mathematically perfect as God's Creation, sculpture serving as sermons in stone, and stained glass lit by the light of God.

Mary's Church ("Notre Dame" = "Our Lady" of Chartres) and Mary's Veil

The church is (at least) the fourth church on this spot dedicated to Mary, the mother of Jesus, who has been venerated here for some 1,700 years. There's even speculation that the pagan Romans dedicated a temple here to a mother-goddess. In earliest times, Mary was honored next to a natural spring of healing waters (not visible today).

In 876, the church acquired the torn, 2,000-year-old veil (or birthing gown) supposedly worn by Mary when she gave birth to Jesus. In A.D. 911, with the city surrounded by Vikings, the bishop hoisted the veil like a battle flag and waved it at the invaders. It scared the bejeezus out of them, and the town was saved.

By the 11th century, Mary (a.k.a. "Queen of All Saints") was hugely popular. God was obscure and scary, but motherhood was accessible, and Mary provided a handy go-between for Christians and their Creator. Chartres, a small town of 10,000 with a prized relic, found itself big time on the pilgrim circuit.

When the fire of 1194 incinerated the old church, the veil was feared lost. Lo and behold, several days later, they found it miraculously unharmed in the crypt (beneath today's choir). The people were so stoked, they worked like madmen to erect this grand cathedral in which to display it. The small town built a big-city church, one of the most impressive structures in all of Europe. Thinkers and scholars gathered here, making it a leading center of learning in the Middle Ages (until the focus shifted to Paris' university).

Until recently, the veil—the main object of adoration for the cult of the Virgin—was on display in the church. But now, for the sake of preservation, it's out of the light and elements except on rare holy days.

The Book of Chartres

Historian Malcolm Miller calls Chartres a picture book of statues, stained glass, and symbolic architecture, telling the entire Christian story—from Creation to Christ's birth (the north side of the church), from Christ and his followers up to the present (south entrance), to the end of time when Christ returns as judge (west entrance).

The Christian universe is a complex web of heaven and earth, angels and demons, and prophets and martyrs. Much of the medieval symbolism is obscure today. Expect to be overwhelmed by the thousands of things to see, but appreciate the perfect unity of this Gothic masterpiece.

You don't go to the library to read all the books, and you don't go to the cathedral to read all the windows. Think of it as the world's biggest comic strip, or the best and most intact library of medieval religious iconography in existence.

THE TOUR BEGINS

❶ The Main Entrance (West Facade), c. 1150

The bases of the two towers (below the mismatched steeples), the three doors, and the rose window are about the only survivors of the intense, lead-melting fire that incinerated the rest of the church in 1194. The church we see today was rebuilt behind this facade in a single generation (1194–1260).

Towers: The right (south) tower, with a stone steeple, is original Romanesque. The left (north) tower lost its wooden steeple in the 1194 fire. In the 1500s, it was topped by a steeple bigger than the tapered lower half was meant to hold.

Chartres Cathedral

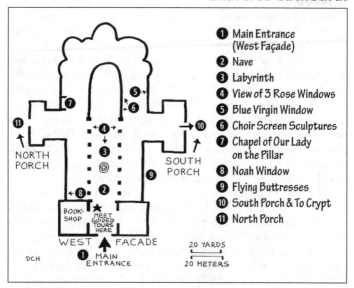

1. Main Entrance (West Façade)
2. Nave
3. Labyrinth
4. View of 3 Rose Windows
5. Blue Virgin Window
6. Choir Screen Sculptures
7. Chapel of Our Lady on the Pillar
8. Noah Window
9. Flying Buttresses
10. South Porch & To Crypt
11. North Porch

NORTH PORCH

SOUTH PORCH

BOOK-SHOP

★ MEET GUIDED TOURS HERE

WEST FAÇADE

1. MAIN ENTRANCE

DCH

20 YARDS
20 METERS

The West Doors: The emaciated column-like statues flanking the three doors are pillars of the faith. These kings of Judah, prophets, and Old Testament big shots foretold the coming of Christ. With solemn gestures and faces, they patiently endure the wait.

What they predicted came to pass, and that story is told above the three doors. History's pivotal event is shown above the **right door,** where Mary (seated) produces baby Jesus from her loins. This Mary-and-baby sculpture is a 12th-century stone version of a wooden statue that burned in 1793. Centuries of pilgrims have visited Chartres to see Mary's statue, gaze at her veil, and ponder the mystery of how God in Heaven became Man on Earth, as He passed through immaculate Mary like sunlight through stained glass.

Over the **central door** is Christ in majesty, surrounded by symbolic animals (symbolizing Matthew, Mark, Luke, and John), and over the **left door** is the Ascension.

• *Enter the church (from a side entrance, if the main one is closed) and wait for your pupils to enlarge.*

❷ Nave

The place is huge. Notice the height of the west (main) doors compared to the tourists. (Do the Boy Scout trick of stacking six-foot links...the doors are 24 feet tall!)

The long, tall central nave, flanked by raised side aisles, was designed for crowd flow, so pilgrims could circle the church without disturbing worshippers. The 12 pillars lining the nave support pointed, crisscrossed arches on the ceiling, which lace together the heavy stone vaulting. The pillars are supported by flying buttresses on the outside of the church (which we'll see later). This skeleton structure was the miracle of Gothic, making it possible to build tall cathedrals with ribbed walls and lots of stained-glass windows (see the big saints in the upper stories of the nave).

Try to picture the church in the Middle Ages—painted in greens, browns, and golds. It was a rough cross between a hostel, a soup kitchen, and a flea market. The floor of the nave slopes in to the center, for easy drainage when hosing down dirty pilgrims who camped here. Looking around the church, you'll see stones at the base of the columns smoothed by centuries of tired pilgrim butts. With all the hubbub in the general nave, the choir (screened-off central zone around the high altar) provided a holy place with a more sacred atmosphere.

• On the floor, midway up the nave, find the...

❸ Labyrinth

The round maze inlaid in black stone on the floor is a spiritual journey. Mazes like this were common in medieval churches. Pilgrims enter from the west rim by foot or on their knees and wind inward, meditating. Treating it much like a rosary, 1,000 feet later, they hope to meet God in the middle. (The chairs are removed on Fridays. To let your fingers do the walking, you'll find a small model of the maze just outside the gift shop, where the tours begin.)

• Walk up the nave to where the transept crosses. As you face the altar, north is to the left.

❹ The Rose Windows—North, South, and West

The three big, round "rose" (floral-shaped) windows over the entrances open like flowers to receive sunlight at different times of day. All three are predominantly blue and red, but each has different "petals," and each tells a different part of the Christian story in a kaleidoscope of fragmented images.

As we've all read, stained glass was a way to teach Bible stories to the illiterate medieval masses...who apparently owned state-of-the-art binoculars. The windows were used many ways: They tell stories, allow parents to teach children simple lessons, help

Surviving the Centuries

Chartres contains the world's largest collection of medieval stained glass, with over 150 early 13th-century windows, about 80 percent still the original glass. Through the centuries, much of the rest of France's stained glass was destroyed by various ideologues: Protestant puritans who disapproved of papist imagery, Revolutionaries who turned churches into "temples of reason" (or stables), Baroque artists who preferred clear windows and lots of light, and the bombs of World War II.

Chartres was spared many (but not all) of these ravages. In World War II, the citizens removed all the windows and piled sandbags to protect the statues. Today, Chartres survives as Europe's best-preserved medieval cathedral.

theologians explain complex lessons, enable worshippers to focus on images as they meditate or pray...and, of course, they light a dark church in a colorful and decorative way.

The brilliantly restored **north rose window** charts history from the distant past up to the birth of Jesus. On the outer rim, murky, ancient (barely visible) prophets foretell Christ's coming. Then (circling inward), there's a ring of red squares with kings who are Jesus' direct ancestors. Still closer, a circle of white doves and winged angels zero in on the central event of history—Mary, the heart of the flower, with her newborn baby, Jesus.

This window was donated by King Louis IX (who built Paris' Sainte-Chapelle) and his mom, Blanche of Castile. See their coats of arms just below the rose—Louis IX's yellow fleur-de-lis on a blue background and Blanche's gold castles on a red background.

The **south rose window** (dark, as it's covered in scaffolding until 2006) tells how the Old Testament prophecies were fulfilled. Christ sits in the center (dressed in blue, with a red background), setting in motion the radiating rings of angels, beasts, and apocalyptic elders who labor to bring history to its close. The five lancet windows below show Old Testament prophets lifting New Testament writers (Matthew, Mark, Luke, and John) on their shoulders (in first window on left, see white-robed Luke riding piggyback on dark-robed Jeremiah). These demonstrated how the ancients prepared the way for Christ—and how the New Testament evangelists had a broader perspective from their lofty perches.

In the center of the **west rose window**, a dark Christ rings in history's final Day of Judgment. Around him, winged angels blow their trumpets and the dead rise, face judgment, and are sent to hell or raised to eternal bliss. The frilly edge of this glorious "rose" is flecked with tiny, clover-shaped dewdrops.

GOD = LIGHT

You can try to examine the details, but a better way to experience the mystery of Chartres is to just sit and stare at these enormous panels, as they float in the dark of empty space like holograms or space stations or the Queen of Heaven's crown jewels. Ponder the medieval concept that God is light.

To the Chartres generation, the church was a metaphor for how God brings his creation to life, like the way light animates stained glass. They were heavy into mysticism, feeling a oneness with all creation in a moment of enlightenment. The Gospel of John (as well as a writer known to historians as the Pseudo-Dionysus) was their favorite. Here are select verses from John 1:1–12 (loosely translated):

In the beginning was The Word.
Jesus was the light of the human race.
The light shines in the darkness, and the darkness
   cannot resist it.
It was the real light coming into the world, the light
   that enlightens everyone.
He was in the world, but the world did not recognize
   Him. But to those who did,
He gave the power to become the children of God.

• *Now walk around the altar to the right (south) side and find the window with a big, blue Mary (2nd one from the right).*

❺ The Blue Virgin Window

Mary, dressed in blue on a rich red background, cradles purple Jesus, while the dove of the Holy Spirit descends on her. With some of the cathedral's oldest stained glass, this window dates from 1150. This was the central window behind the altar of the church that burned in 1194. It survived and was reinserted into this new frame around 1230. The sumptuous blue of Mary's glowing dress is a rare pure cobalt window. The Blue Virgin was one of the most popular stops for pilgrims—especially pregnant ones—of the cult of the Virgin-about-to-give-birth. Devotees prayed, carried stones to repair the church, or donated to the church coffers; Mary rewarded them with peace of mind, easy births, and occasional miracles.

Below Mary, see **Christ being tempted** by a red-faced, horned, smirking devil.

The **Zodiac Window** (2nd window to the left) mixes the 12 signs of the Zodiac (in the right half of the window; read from the bottom up—Pisces, Aries, Gemini in the cloverleaf, Taurus,

Cockroach, Leo, Virgo, etc.) with signs of the months represented by the various labors.
• *Now turn around and look behind you.*

❻ The Choir Screen—Life of Mary

The choir (enclosed area around the altar where church officials sat) is the heart of the church. In French, the choir is called the *coeur*, literally "the heart." A stone screen rings it with **41 statue groups** illustrating Mary's life. Although the Bible says little about the mother of Jesus, legend and lore fleshed out her life.

The work was done by various sculptors over three centuries. As you follow the story around the choir (numbers beneath each scene, see below), notice the art—and fashion—evolve. Scenes #1-12 date from the early 16th century, featuring biblical figures dressed in the styles of the time; scenes #13 and beyond were sculpted earlier during the Renaissance, with figures clothed in more accurate Roman garb. The passion scenes were from the 18th century.

Scene #1 (south side) shows an angel (now missing) telling Mary's dad that Mary is on the way. In #4, Anne has just given birth to Mary, and maidens bathe the new baby. In #6, Mary marries Joseph (sculpted with the features of King François I). Scene #7 is the Annunciation. In #10, she gives birth to Jesus in a manger. Scene #11 shows baby Jesus' circumcision. In #12, the Three Kings—looking like the three musketeers—arrive. Scenes #15–27 show Jesus' life. In #27, Jesus is crucified, and in #28, he lays lifeless in his mother's arms. Scene #29 depicts the Ascension, as Jesus takes off, Cape Canaveral-style, while his awestruck followers look up at the bottoms of his rocketing feet. In #34, the resurrected Jesus appears to his mother and John the Evangelist. In #37, Mary dies; in #39, she's raised by angels into heaven; and in #40, she's crowned Queen of Heaven by the Father, Son, and Holy Ghost.

The **plain windows** surrounding the choir date from the 1770s, when the dark mystery of medieval stained glass was replaced by the open light of the French Enlightenment. The plain windows and the choir are some of the only "new" features. Most of the 13th-century church has remained, despite style changes, Revolutionary vandals, and war bombs.

❼ Chapel of Our Lady on the Pillar

A 16th-century **statue of Mary and baby**—draped in cloth, crowned and sceptered—sits on a 13th-century column in a wonderful carved-wood alcove. This is today's pilgrimage center, built to keep visitors from clogging up the altar area. Modern pilgrims honor the Virgin by leaving flowers, lighting candles, and kissing the column.

• *Return to the west end and find the last window on the right (near the tower entrance).*

❽ The Noah Window

Read Chartres' windows from left to right and bottom to top.

For 800 years, these panes have publicly thanked their **sponsors**. Chartres was a trading center, and its merchant brotherhoods donated money to make 42 of the windows. Most have a proud "this window brought to you by..." pane near the bottom. These offer another fascinating insight into 13th-century life. For example, at the bottom left is a man making a wheel. He's one of the donors of this window. His colleagues to the right are from axe- and barrel-making guilds.

Then comes the story of **Noah** (read from the bottom up): God tells Noah he'll destroy the earth (#1, bottom diamond). Noah hefts an axe to build an ark, while his son hauls wood (diamond #2). Two by two, he loads horses (cloverleaf, above left), purple elephants (cloverleaf, above right), and other animals. The psychedelic ark sets sail (diamond #3). Waves cover the earth and drown the wicked (two cloverleaves). The ark survives (diamond #4), and Noah releases a dove. Finally, up near the top (diamond #7), a rainbow (symbolizing God's promise never to bring another flood) arches overhead, God drapes himself over it, and Noah and his family give thanks.

• *Exit the church (through the main entrance or the door in the south transept) to view its south side.*

❾ South Exterior—Flying Buttresses

On the south side, six flying buttresses (the arches that stick out from the upper walls) push against six pillars lining the nave inside, helping to hold up the heavy stone ceiling and sloped, lead-over-wood roof. The ceiling and roof push down onto the pillars, of course, but also outward (north and south) because of the miracle of Gothic: the pointed arch. These flying buttresses push back, channeling the stress outward to the six vertical buttresses, then down to the ground. The result is a tall cathedral held up by slender pillars buttressed from the outside, allowing the walls to be opened up for stained glass.

The church is built from large blocks of limestone. Peasants trod in hamster-wheel contraptions to raise these blocks into place—a testament to their great faith.

❿ South Porch

The three doorways of the south entrance show the world from Christ to the present, as Christianity triumphs over persecution.

Center Door—Christ and Apostles: Standing between the

double doors, **Jesus** holds a book and raises his arm in blessing. He's a simple, itinerant, bareheaded, barefoot rabbi, but underneath his feet he tramples symbols of evil, the dragon and lion. Christ's face is among the most noble of all Gothic sculpture.

Christ is surrounded by his **apostles,** who spread the good news to a hostile world. **Peter** (to the left as you face Jesus), with curly hair and beard, holds the key to the kingdom of heaven and the slender upside-down cross on which he was crucified. **Paul** (to the right of Jesus) fingers the sword of his martyrdom and contemplates the inevitable loss of his head and the hair upon it. In fact, all of the apostles were killed or persecuted, and their faces are humble, with sad eyes. But their message prevailed, and under their feet, they crush the squirming emperors who once persecuted them.

The final triumph comes above the door in the **Last Judgment.** Christ sits in judgment, raising his hands, while Mary and John beg him to take it easy on poor humankind. Beneath Christ, the souls are judged—the righteous on our left, and the wicked on the right, who are thrown into the fiery jaws of hell. Further to the right (above the statues of Paul and the apostles), horny demons subject wicked women to an eternity of sexual harassment.

Left Door—Martyrs: Eight martyrs flank the left door. **St. Lawrence** (2nd from left) cradles the spit on which he was barbecued alive. His last brave words to the Romans actually were: "You can turn me over—I'm done on this side." **St. George** (far right) wears the knightly uniform of the 1200s, when Chartres was built and King Louis IX was crusading. Depicted beneath the martyrs are gruesome **methods of torture** (e.g., George stretched on the wheel), many of which were used in the 1200s against heretics, Muslims, Jews, and Albigensians (the Cathar sect of southern France).

Right Door—Confessors: Among these eight pillars of the faith, find **Jerome** (3rd from the right), holding the Bible he translated into everyday Latin; and **Gregory** (2nd from the right), the pope who organized church hierarchy and wrote Gregorian chants.

• *Reach the north side by circling around the back end of the church (great views) or by cutting through the church.*

⓫ North Porch

In "the Book of Chartres," the north porch is chapter one, from the Creation up to the coming of Christ.

Center Door: Baby Mary (headless), in the arms of **her**

mother Anne (the statue between the double doors), marks the culmination of the Old Testament world.

History begins in the tiny details in the concentric arches over the doorway. **God creates Adam** (at the peak of the outer arch) by cradling his head in his lap like a child.

Melchizedek (farthest to the left of Mary and Anne), with cap and cup, is the Biblical model of the *rex et sacerdos* (king-priest), the title bestowed on King Louis IX.

Abraham (2nd from left) holds his son by the throat and raises a knife to slit him for sacrifice. Just then, he hears something and turns his head up to see God's angel, who stops the bloodshed. The drama of this frozen moment anticipates Renaissance naturalism by 200 years.

John the Baptist (4th to the right from Mary/Anne), the last Old Testament prophet who prepared the way for Jesus, holds a lamb, the symbol of Christ. John is skinny from his diet of locusts and honey. His body twists and flickers like a flame.

All these **prophets,** with their beards turning down the corners of their mouths, have the sad, wise look of having been around since the beginning of time and having seen it all—from Creation to Christ to Apocalypse. They are some of the last work done on the church, completing the church's stone-and-glass sermon.

Imagine all this painted and covered with gold leaf in preparation for the dedication ceremonies in 1260, when the Chartres generation could finally stand back and watch as their great-grandchildren, carrying candles, entered the cathedral.

CHARTRES TOWN

Chartres is worth a quick stroll. You can rent audioguides from the TI or just wander, following the *circuit touristique* markers that take you on a loop from the cathedral down along the river and back. In medieval times, Chartres was actually two towns—the pilgrims' town around the cathedral and the industrial town along the river, which powered the mills.

Leaving the cathedral, you'll notice streets with evocative names: rue des Changes (pilgrims needed to change money), rue au Lait (milk), rue aux Herbes (before America blessed Europe with tobacco, folks smoked hemp), and place de la Poissonnerie (fish market, today marked by a fine half-timbered building).

As the population grew behind Chartres' protective walls, so did the density. Houses expanded upwards (providing maximum housing and avoiding taxes, which were levied according to square footage on the ground floor).

After a great fire, the town required half-timbered buildings be plastered over for safety. Today, the town government—

Chartres

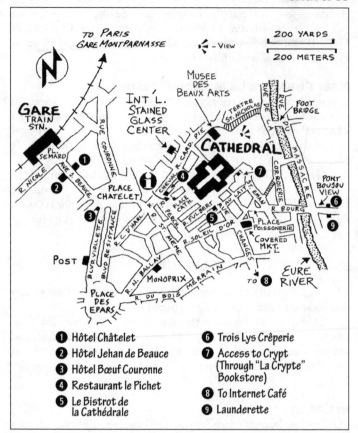

● Hôtel Châtelet
● Hôtel Jehan de Beauce
● Hôtel Bœuf Couronne
● Restaurant le Pichet
● Le Bistrot de la Cathédrale
● Trois Lys Crêperie
● Access to Crypt (Through "La Crypte" Bookstore)
● To Internet Café
● Launderette

interested in pumping up the touristic charm—pays folks to peel away the plaster and re-expose those timbers. Medieval home builders had no time for tidy symmetry. You can identify the oldest buildings—even if plastered—because they're the ones with asymmetrical windows.

The *tertre* (old stepped lanes that linked the upper and lower towns) lead you to the river, once lined with busy mills. This was the industrial town. The worst polluters were kept downstream (dying, tanning, slaughter houses). Notice the names of the riverside lanes: rue du Massacre, rue de la Tannerie.

When the industry moved out to make room for Chartres' growing population, laundry places replaced the old mills. The last riverside laundry (two stories—dry upstairs, where vents allowed the wind to blow through, and washboards lowered by pulley into the river) closed in the 1960s.

When you make your way back up to the cathedral, consider finishing your walk at the International Stained Glass Center (Centre International du Vitrail, €4, Mon–Fri 9:30–12:30 & 13:30–18:00, Sat–Sun 10:00–12:30 & 14:30–18:00, just 50 yards from cathedral, www.centre-vitrail.org).

Near Chartres: La Maison Picassiette

If you have time to burn here and enjoy oddities, walk about 20 minutes to the home created by local artist Raymond Isidore. La Maison Picassiette is covered wall-to-wall (inside and out) with broken pottery mosaics (€4.10, Wed–Fri and Sun–Mon 10:00–12:00 & 14:00–18:00, Sat 14:00–18:00, closed Tue, tel. 02 37 34 10 78).

Getting There: Leave the old town downhill (behind the cathedral, direction Porte Guillaume). Walk straight on rue Faubourg Guillaume, which becomes rue Ste. Chernon. Take a right on rue du Repos. It's at #22. You can also take bus #4 (direction La Madeleine).

SLEEPING

Chartres, a good getaway from Paris, can also be a first or last overnight stop for those flying to/from Orly Airport.

Chartres has a **launderette** (across from recommended Trois Lys Crêperie, near pont Boujou, 15-min walk from cathedral) and **Internet access** (at Tout va Bien, Mon–Sat 8:00–21:00, closed Sun, 2 rue de la Mairie, 5-min walk from cathedral down rue des Changes).

In Chartres

The first two hotels face each other (200 yards straight out of train station, 300 yards below cathedral).

Hôtel Châtelet***, run by friendly Franck and Nathalie, is comfortable, from its welcoming lobby to its spotless, spacious, well-furnished rooms (Sb-€72-86, Db-€80-92, extra bed-€10, streetside rooms are cheaper, parking-€6, 6 avenue Jehan de Beauce, tel. 02 37 21 78 00, fax 02 37 36 23 01, www.hotelchatelet .com, hotel.chatelet@wanadoo.fr).

Hôtel Jehan de Beauce** is basic, clean (despite the shabby hallways), and quiet. Some of its rooms have tiny bathrooms (S-€34, D-€46, Ds-€59, Db-€64, Tb-€64, 19 avenue Jehan de Beauce, tel. 02 37 21 01 41, fax 02 37 21 59 10, jehandebeauce@club-internet.fr).

Hotel Boeuf Couronne** is warmly run by Madame Vinsot, with 21 clean, simple rooms and a handy location (S-€29, Sb-€43–46, D-€33, Db-€54–58, elevator, 15 place Chatelet, tel. 02 37 18 06 06, fax 02 37 21 72 13).

Sleep Code

(€1 = about $1.20, country code: 33)
S = Single, **D** = Double/Twin, **T** = Triple, **Q** = Quad, **b** = bathroom,
s = shower only. Everyone speaks English and accepts credit cards.

Near Chartres

Chambres d'Hote Brossollet, practical only for drivers, is a gorgeous haven of tranquility in Saint-Prest, about four miles from Chartres. This spacious property has an enclosed garden, thatched roofs, two rooms to rent, and kind hosts, Claire and Etienne Brossollet (Db–€55, includes breakfast, tel. 02 37 22 25 31, fax 02 37 22 26 07, claire.etienne.brossollet@libertysurf.fr). Leave Chartres to the north and follow signs to Saint-Prest. Once in the village, continue just over a mile straight through on the main road until you see the thatched roof on your left-hand side.

EATING

Le Pichet, run by friendly Marie-Sylvie and Xavier, is reasonable and homey, with good daily specials (*menus* from €12, closed Tue evening and all day Wed, 19 rue du Cheval Blanc, near TI, tel. 02 37 21 08 35).

Le Bistrot de la Cathédrale is fine for salads and basic bistro fare, but you'll pay for the view (*menus* from €15, daily, south side of cathedral at 1 cloître Notre-Dame, tel. 02 37 36 59 60).

Trois Lys Crêperie makes good, cheap crêpes just across the river on pont Boujou (closed Mon, 3 rue de la Porte Guillaume, across from launderette, tel. 02 37 28 42 02).

MORE DAY TRIPS

- *Grand Châteaux near Paris*
- *Impressionist Excursions: Giverny and Auvers-sur-Oise*
- *Disneyland Paris*

Efficient trains bring oodles of day trips within the grasp of temporary Parisians. Dozens of châteaux, flowery gardens, riverfront villages, and an amusement park await the traveler looking for a refreshing change from urban Paris.

Grand Châteaux near Paris

The region around Paris (Ile de France) is dotted with sumptuous palaces. Paris' booming upper class made it the heartland of European château-building in the 16th and 17th centuries. Most of these châteaux were lavish hunting lodges—getaways from the big city. The only things they defended were noble and royal egos. Try to avoid visiting on weekends, when they are most crowded.

Consider four very different châteaux:

▲▲▲**Versailles**—For its history, grandeur, and accessibility (closed Mon).

▲▲▲**Vaux-le-Vicomte**—For sheer beauty and intimacy (open daily, closed Nov-Feb).

▲▲**Fontainebleau**—For its history, fine interior, and pleasant city (closed Tue).

▲**Chantilly**—For its beautiful setting and fine collection of paintings (closed Tue except in summer).

If you only have time for one château, choose between Vaux-le-Vicomte and Versailles (see tour on page 424). Except for Versailles, these châteaux are quiet on weekdays. Versailles, Fontainebleau, and Chantilly are covered by the Paris Museum Pass (see page 25).

Day Trips from Paris

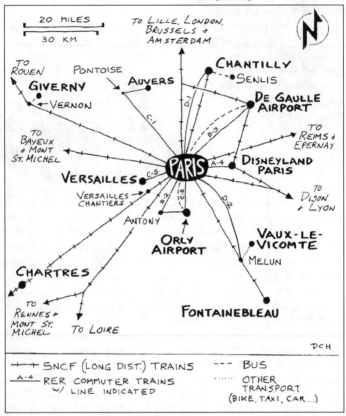

20 MILES
30 KM

TO LILLE, LONDON, BRUSSELS & AMSTERDAM

TO ROUEN
PONTOISE
GIVERNY
VERNON
AUVERS
C-1
CHANTILLY
SENLIS
DE GAULLE AIRPORT
d-1
B-3
TO BAYEUX & MONT ST. MICHEL
PARIS
A-4
TO REIMS & EPERNAY
VERSAILLES
C-5
DISNEYLAND PARIS
VERSAILLES CHANTIERS
B-2
TO DIJON & LYON
IN U
ANTONY
D-2
ORLY AIRPORT
VAUX-LE-VICOMTE
MELUN
CHARTRES
TO RENNES & MONT ST. MICHEL
TO LOIRE
FONTAINEBLEAU

DCH

+ + + SNCF (LONG DIST.) TRAINS   — — — BUS
A-4 RER COMMUTER TRAINS   ...... OTHER TRANSPORT
W/ LINE INDICATED   (BIKE, TAXI, CAR...)

Vaux-le-Vicomte

While Versailles is most travelers' first choice for its sheer historic weight, Vaux-le-Vicomte (voh luh vee-komt) offers a more intimate interior and a better sense of 17th-century château life. Located in a huge forest, with magnificent gardens and no urban sprawl in sight, Vaux-le-Vicomte gave me just a twinge of palace envy.

Vaux-le-Vicomte was the architectural inspiration for Versailles and set the standard for European châteaux to come. The proud owner, Nicolas Fouquet (Louis XIV's finance minister), threw a château-warming party. Louis XIV was so jealous that he arrested his host, took his architect (Louis Le Vau), artist (Charles Le Brun), and landscaper (André Le Nôtre), and proceeded with the construction of the bigger and costlier (but not necessarily more splendid) palace of Versailles. Monsieur Fouquet's party and later arrest feature prominently in the third Musketeer book by

Alexandre Dumas, and at least two versions of *The Man in the Iron Mask* were filmed here.

Vaux-le-Vicomte is more expensive than Versailles to get to (because of cab fare), but a joy to tour. Most rooms have English explanations. For more information, rent a €1.50 audioguide (with a pro-Fouquet perspective) or get a souvenir booklet at the gift shop. Outside the gift shop is a reasonably-priced café (limited menu, daily 11:30–18:00, until 24:00 during candlelit visits).

Start your tour with the fine exhibit of carriages *(équipages)* in the old stables. Wax figures and an evocative soundtrack get you in the proper mood. Next, stroll like a wide-eyed peasant across the stone bridge (any fish down there?) and up the front steps into the château. Turn around to admire the symmetry and elegance of the stables; horses lived well here.

As you wander through Fouquet's dream home, you'll understand Louis XIV's jealousy. Versailles was a simple hunting lodge when this was built. The furniture in Vaux-le-Vicomte is not original—Louis XIV confiscated the real thing for Versailles. You'll see cozy bedrooms upstairs and grand living rooms downstairs (billiards room, library, card room, and dining room; feel free to fast-forward the 90-min audioguide tour). The kitchen and wine cellar are in the basement. Climb the cupola for a great view (€2).

Survey the garden from the back steps of the palace. Landscaper Le Nôtre's first claim to fame, this garden was the cutting edge of sculpted French gardens. He integrated ponds, shrubbery, and trees in a style that would be copied in palaces all over Europe. Take the 30-minute walk (one-way) to the Hercules viewpoint atop the grassy hill far in the distance. Rentable golf carts (Club Cars, 45 min-€14, €125 deposit) make the trip easier, and the funky Nautilles (pedal boats in the shape of water animals, 30 min-€10) are fun for kids. Picnics are not allowed.

Cost and Hours: €12 for gardens, château, and carriage museum, not covered by Museum Pass, audioguide €1.5. Open late March–early Nov daily 10:00–18:00, château closed 13:00–14:00 but gardens remain open, closed early Nov–late March, tel. 01 64 14 41 90, www.vaux-le-vicomte.com. From April through Oct, the impressive fountains run 15:00–18:00 on the second Sat and last Sat of each month.

Candlelit Visits: Two thousand candles and piped-in classical music illuminate the palace May–mid-Oct on Sat and

holiday nights, and June–Aug on Fri nights as well (open 20:00–24:00); call to ask about any upcoming holidays. These *visites aux chandelles* recreate the party thrown in Louis XIV's honor in 1661 and are worth the €15 entry, but remember, it doesn't get really dark until 22:00 in late May, June, and July, and the last train to Paris leaves Melun at about 22:00.

Getting to Vaux-le-Vicomte: To reach Vaux-le-Vicomte by a train-and-taxi combination, take the RER-D train to Melun from Paris' Gare du Nord or Châtelet-Les Halles stations. Faster SNCF *banlieue* trains to Melun leave from the Gare de Lyon (about €7.50 one-way, hourly, 35 min). From Melun's station, taxis make the 15-minute drive to Vaux-le-Vicomte (€15 one-way Mon–Sat, €18 eves and Sun, taxi tel. 01 64 52 51 50, other numbers posted above taxi stand). Ask a staff person at the château to call a cab for your return, or schedule a pickup time with your driver. In either direction, seek others to split the fare with. If you have time to kill before your return train, or just want to make more of your excursion, consider exploring Melun's small medieval center, 10 easy minutes on foot from the station (walk down avenue Gallieni past the ugly concrete buildings, then turn right on rue Thiers and cross the river).

The Paris Vision tour company offers minibus excursions to Vaux-le-Vicomte (www.parisvision.com; see page 34).

By car from Paris, take the A-6 autoroute toward Lyon, then follow signs to Melun. In Melun, follow signs to Meaux (N-36), then Vaux-le-Vicomte.

Adding Fontainebleau: Vaux-le-Vicomte and Fontainebleau can be combined into a full, though manageable, day trip by car, taxi, or train from Paris (except on Tue, when Fontainebleau is closed). Fontainebleau is 12 minutes by train from Melun (allow €35–40 by taxi).

Sleeping near Vaux-le-Vicomte: Modern and unappealing, but handy and cheap, **Ibis Hôtel** is between Melun and the château, just off N-105 (Db-€60, €48 on weekends, tel. 01 60 68 42 45, fax 01 64 09 62 00, www.accorhotels.com, h0620@accor.com). It'd be better to drive 15 minutes to Fontainebleau and sleep at one of the recommended hotels (below).

Château of Fontainebleau

Fontainebleau's history rivals that of more modern Versailles. Many French kings have called this glamorous hunting lodge home. Louis XIII was born here, Louis XV married here, and Napoleon was baptized here. The little emperor also welcomed the pope to this château during his coronation celebration, and it was

here that he abdicated his rule when exiled to Elba in 1814. Many years later, General Patton set up headquarters at this château on his way to Berlin.

While Vaux-le-Vicomte and Versailles are French-designed, Fontainebleau was built a century earlier by an Italian. The palace you see today was largely financed by Renaissance King François I. Inspired by his travels through Renaissance Italy, he hired Italian

artists to build his palaces. He even encouraged one artist to abandon his native Italy and settle in France for the last eight years of his life—Leonardo da Vinci.

Visit the information room to orient yourself using its huge model of the château (first door on your right in the grand courtyard). The palace entry is 50 yards farther down. Your ticket provides access to the Chinese rooms and the main rooms of the château. Napoleon buffs can enjoy the interesting little museum of Napoleonic history, or a visit to his apartments. Both can be visited only with a guided tour in French (some English possible, €3 each, hours vary, call ahead or ask on arrival). The €3 audioguides give good room-by-room descriptions (allow 1 hour), and basic English explanations are posted throughout.

In the main château, start downstairs with the small but impressive Chinese collection of Napoleon III's empress, then climb to the main rooms of the palace. Highlights include the stunning Renaissance hall of François I, the opulent dance hall with piped-in music *(salle de bal)*, Napoleon's throne room, and Diana's Gallery (library). The gardens, designed a century later by the landscaper André Le Nôtre, are worth a stroll. Rent a rowboat for the *étang des carpes* (carp pond), or walk its path for a good view of the château complex.

Cost and Hours: €5.50, covered by Museum Pass, free first Sun of the month. Open Wed–Mon 9:30–17:00, closed Tue; last entry 45 minutes before closing.

Getting to Fontainebleau: Catch a train at the *Grande Ligne* tracks from Paris' Gare de Lyon in the direction of Montereau (about €9 one-way, 40 min) to the Fontainebleau-Avon station. Cross under the tracks and catch the bus to the château (Cars Verts, about €1.50, every 10 min). Get return train times before leaving the station, as there can be big gaps. Your train might make an unscheduled stop in the middle of the forest to drop off hikers. Taxis to the château cost about €7; to nearby Vaux-le-Vicomte, €35–40 (taxi tel. 01 64 22 00 06).

Town of Fontainebleau: Turn right out of the château courtyard and keep right to reach the town center, where cafés and restaurants abound. The helpful **TI** is two blocks across from the château behind Hôtel Londres and has hiking maps and bikes for rent (Mon–Sat 10:00–18:30, Sun 10:00–13:00 & 15:00–17:00, 4 rue Royale, tel. 01 60 74 99 99). When you're ready to catch the bus back to the train station, you'll find bus stops across the street from Hôtel Londres, opposite the château entrance, and at the post office in the city center.

Sleeping and Eating in Fontainebleau: The **Hôtel Londres***** is run by gentle Philippe and Mama, who have left no stone unturned in their zeal to make everything perfect. The rooms are big, immaculate, and *très* country-French. Many have point-blank views of the château (smaller Db-€114, larger Db with château view-€140, 1 place du Général de Gaulle, tel. 01 64 22 20 21, fax 01 60 72 39 16, www.hoteldelondres.com, hdelondres1850@aol.com). **Hôtel Legris et Parc*****is a quiet getaway with a garden, pool, and a country-classy restaurant (*menus* from €28). Rooms are faded, but fine (standard Db-€76, bigger Db-€90, Tb/Qb suites-€145, turn right out of the château entrance and keep right for about 5 blocks to 36 rue Paul Seramy, tel. 01 64 22 24 24, fax 01 64 22 22 05, legris.et.parc@wanadoo.fr).

There are eating options at all prices in Fontainebleau's old city. Here are two of many: **Croquembouche** (*menus* from €20, closed Wed and Sun, 43 rue de France, tel. 01 64 22 01 57) or dine by candlelight under medieval arches at **Caveau des Ducs** (good €20–30 *menus*, open daily, 24 rue de Ferrare, tel. 01 64 22 05 05).

Château of Chantilly

Chantilly (shahn-tee-yee), 30 minutes north of Paris, floats serenely on a reflecting pond amid grand gardens. This extravagant hunting palace is the quintessence of a château—filled with great art, surrounded by a luxurious garden and a moat, and accessed by a drawbridge.

While there are better châteaux to tour, Chantilly's claim to fame is its art collection. Because of the social upheaval in France during the Revolution of 1848, the château's owner, Prince de Conde, fled to England. Twenty years later, when blue blood was safe again in

France, he returned to his château with a fabulous art collection (800 paintings including 3 Raphaels) and book collection. He turned his palace into the museum you see today and willed it to France on the condition that it would be maintained as he left it and the collections would never be loaned to any other museum.

As most of the château was destroyed during the French Revolution, today's château is largely rebuilt in a fanciful 19th-century style. It's divided into two parts: apartments and art gallery. The plush-but-nothing-really-special private apartments require an included guided tour (20 min, leaving every few minutes but generally in French). The painting gallery and library are impressive and come with a free audioguide which gives them meaning. Gallery highlights are paintings by Raphael, Titian, Nicolas Poussin, and Eugène Delacroix. Of the 13,000 books in the prince's library, the most exquisite is the 40-page *Book of Hours* by Jean Fouquet (c. 1460).

The gardens immediately behind the château are formal and austere. With your back to the château, follow the signs to the right to *le Hameau*. This little hamlet, with an enchanting garden café, was the prototype for the more famous *hameau* at Versailles. Just beyond is a small kiosk offering boat trips along the canals.

Cost and Hours: €8, covered by Museum Pass, March–Oct Wed–Mon 10:00–18:00, closed Tue; Nov–Feb Wed–Fri and Mon 10:30–12:45 & 14:00–17:00, Sat–Sun 10:00–18:00, closed Tue, tel. 03 44 62 62 62, www.chateaudechantilly.com.

Live Horse Stables *(Les Ecuries Vivant)*: The Prince de Condé believed he'd be reincarnated as a horse, so he built this opulent horse château for his next go-round (a 5-min walk from château). The museum—with displays on everything from horse medicine to racing to circuses—includes 40 live horses in their stables and daily demonstrations (€8.50, horses prance usually at 11:30, 15:30, and 17:30, in the winter only at 15:30; museum open April–Oct Wed–Mon 10:30–18:30, last ticket sold 1 hour before closing, closed Tue except in May–June; Nov–March Mon and Wed–Fri 14:00–18:00, Sat–Sun 10:30–17:30, closed Tue, tel. 03 44 57 40 40, www.musee-vivant-du-cheval.fr).

Getting to Chantilly: Leave from Paris' Gare du Nord for Chantilly-Gouvieux (on the Creil line). While the RER serves Chantilly, service is faster on the main lines at the *Grandes Lignes* level. Ask any information desk for the next departure (about €7 one-way, covered with railpass, nearly hourly, 30 min). Upon arrival in Chantilly, confirm return times (fewer trips on weekends). The **TI** is across from the station (Mon–Sat 9:30–12:30 & 14:30–17:30, tel. 03 44 67 37 37). To get to the château, get lucky and catch the 4/day bus (marked *le Duc*), or walk 30 minutes (get a map from TI and follow signs, stay on path, turn right before

gas station, cross grassy field, "château" in distance is stables, real château is beyond that); or take a taxi (allow €7, tel. 06 05 45 37 55 or 06 08 22 25 17, they extort people for €17 for a château pickup).

Impressionist Excursions:
Giverny and Auvers-sur-Oise

Giverny

Claude Monet's gardens at Giverny are like his paintings—brightly-colored patches that are messy but balanced. Flowers were his brushstrokes, a bit untamed and slap-dash, but part of a carefully composed design. Monet spent his last (and most creative) years at Giverny (zhee-vayr-nee), the Camp David of Impressionism (1883–1926).

In 1883, middle-aged Claude Monet, his wife Alice, and their eight children from two families settled into a farmhouse here, 50 miles west of Paris. Monet, now a famous artist and happiest at home, would spend 40 years in Giverny, traveling less with each passing year. He built a pastoral paradise complete with a Japanese garden and a pond full of floating lilies.

In the last half of his life (beginning in 1912), Monet—the greatest visionary, literally, of his generation—began to go blind with cataracts. He used larger canvases and painted fewer details. The true subject is not really the famous water lilies, but the changing reflections on the surface of the pond—of the blue sky, white

---

Impressionism

Impressionism was a revolutionary movement in European art—the rage in the 1880s. Artists abandoned photo-realism in favor of a wispy style that captured light, glimmers, feelings, and impressions. Impressionists—capturing nature as a mosaic of short brushstrokes of different colors placed side by side, suggesting shimmering light—were committed to conveying the subtleties of nature. And there is no better nature for an Impressionist ready to paint than Monet's delightful mix of weeping willows, luminous clouds, delicate bridges, reflecting ponds...and lush water lilies.

Giverny

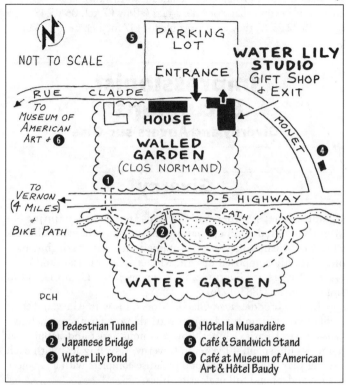

N NOT TO SCALE

PARKING LOT

⑤

ENTRANCE

WATER LILY STUDIO
GIFT SHOP & EXIT

RUE CLAUDE

TO MUSEUM OF AMERICAN ART & ⑥

MONET

HOUSE

WALLED GARDEN (CLOS NORMAND)

④

① TO VERNON (4 MILES) & BIKE PATH

D-5 HIGHWAY

PATH

②

③

WATER GARDEN

DCH

① Pedestrian Tunnel
② Japanese Bridge
③ Water Lily Pond
④ Hôtel la Musardière
⑤ Café & Sandwich Stand
⑥ Café at Museum of American Art & Hôtel Baudy

clouds, and green trees that line the shore.

All kinds of people flock to Giverny. Gardeners admire the earth-moving landscaping and layout, botanists find interesting new plants, and art lovers can see paintings they've long admired come to life. Fans enjoy wandering around the house where Monet spent half his life and seeing the boat he puttered around in, as well as the henhouse where his family got the morning omelets. It's a busy place, so come early or late.

There are two gardens, split by a busy road, plus the house, which displays Monet's prized collection of Japanese prints.

Try to arrive before it opens and be first in line. Buy your ticket and go directly to the Walled Garden (Clos Normand) by the house. Monet cleared this land of pine trees, and laid out symmetrical beds, split down the middle by a "grand alley" covered with iron trellises of climbing roses. He did his own landscaping: flowerbeds of lilies, irises, and clematis, and arbors of climbing roses. The arched trellises form a natural tunnel that leads your eye down the path—an effect exploited in his *Rose Trellis* paintings (on

display in Paris at the Marmottan Museum). In his careless manner, Monet throws together hollyhocks, daisies, and poppies. But
each flowerbed has an overall color scheme that contributes to the
look of the whole garden.

In the far corner of the Walled Garden, you'll find a pedestrian tunnel that leads under the road to the Water Garden. Once
you've crossed under the road, follow the path that leads to the
Japanese bridge, under weeping willows, over the pond filled
with water lilies, and past countless scenes that leave artists ach-
ing for an easel. Monet landscaped like he painted—he built an
Impressionist pattern of blocks of color. Once he'd planted the
gardens, he painted them, from every angle, at every time of day,
in all kinds of weather. Assisted by his favorite daughter, Blanche
(also a painter, who married Monet's son Jean from an earlier marriage), he worked on several canvases at once, moving with the sun
from one to the next. In a series of canvases, you can watch the
sunlight sweep over the gardens from early dawn to twilight.

Back on the other side, continue your visit with a wander
through his mildly interesting home. The jammed gift shop at the
exit is the actual skylighted studio where Monet painted his water-
lily masterpieces (displayed at L'Orangerie Museum in Paris,
scheduled to reopen in the spring of 2006; page 45).

Cost and Hours: €5.50, €4 for gardens only, April–Oct Tue–
Sun 9:30–18:00, last entry 17:30, closed Mon except holidays and
Nov–March, tel. 02 32 51 28 21, www.fondation-monet.com.

Nearby Sights: The Museum of American Art (Musée d'Art
Américain, turn left when leaving Monet's place and walk 100 yards)
is devoted to American artists who followed Claude to Giverny (same
price and hours as Monet's home). Monet and his garden had a great
influence on American artists of his day. This bright, modern gallery—with a good but small Mary Cassatt section—is well-explained
in English, though its most appealing feature might be its garden café
(good if a bit pricey salads and quiches).

If you miss your train back to Paris, pleasant little Vernon is
good for killing an hour while you wait for the next train.

Avoiding Crowds: While lines may be long and tour groups
may trample the flowers, true fans still find magic in the gardens.
Minimize crowds by arriving by 9:15 (get in line, it opens at 9:30),
during lunchtime, or after 16:00. If you're traveling by train, take
the first departure from Paris listed below.

SLEEPING AND EATING

(€1 = about $1.20, country code: 33)
Near Giverny, the cute **Hôtel la Musardière**** is two blocks to the
right out of Monet's home (Db-€56–76, Tb-€78–96, 132 rue Claude

Monet, tel. 02 32 21 03 18, fax 02 32 21 60 00, iraymonde@aol
.com).

You'll find a **café and sandwich stand** near the entrance
to Monet's home and a peaceful **garden café** at the Museum of
American Art (surrounded by gardens Monet would appreciate,
but a little pricey). I also like **Hôtel Baudy's meals** (5-min walk
past American Museum).

TRANSPORTATION CONNECTIONS

By Tour: Big tour companies do a Giverny day trip from Paris for
around €60; ask at your hotel.

By Car: From Paris's Périphérique ring road, follow A-13
toward Rouen, get off at Vernon, follow *Centre Ville* signs, then
signs to Giverny.

By Train: Take the Rouen-bound train from Paris' Gare St.
Lazare station to Vernon (about €22 round-trip, 45 min one-way,
4 miles from Giverny, no baggage check). The schedule from 2005
follows (a few departures require an easy transfer in Mantes la
Jolie, verify 2006 schedule before going!):

Leave Paris for Vernon: Weekdays at 8:16, 11:03, 12:04, 14:23;
Saturday 8:39, 12:04, 12:34, 13:45, 14:23; Sunday 8:06, 9:32, 10:44,
14:25

Leave Vernon for Paris: Weekdays at 10:52, 12:52, 14:57, 15:09,
17:11, 18:04; Saturday 10:52, 12:52, 14:57, 17:32, 17:59, 19:29; Sunday
10:52, 12:41, 15:35, 17:32, 17:59, 19:00.

From Vernon's Train Station to Giverny: From the Vernon
train station to Monet's garden (4 miles one-way), you have four
good options: by bus, taxi, bike, or on foot.

The Vernon-Giverny **bus** meets every train listed above for
the 15-minute run to Giverny (no buses on Mon) and takes you
back to every return train to Paris. If you miss the last bus, find
others to share a taxi (see below). The stop to Giverny is in front
of Vernon's train station, facing Café du Chemin de Fer (don't
dally, the bus leaves soon after your train arrives). The ticket office
at Monet's home in Giverny has bus schedules for the return trip.
The bus stop for the return trip is in the bus parking lot on the
opposite side of the main road, by the roundabout. The stop is
the first one on your right. Look for the white #18 bus marked
Vernon-Giverny Car.

If you take a **taxi**, allow €11 for up to 3, €12 for 4 (tel. 06 07 34
36 68, tel. 06 76 08 50 78, or tel. 02 32 21 31 31). With buses meeting every train, taxis are unnecessary (unless you miss the bus).
Taxis wait in front of the station in Vernon.

You can rent a **bike** at Café du Chemin de Fer opposite the
train station (€12, 30 bikes for rent, you can reserve at tel. 02 32 21

16 01), and follow a paved bike path *(piste cyclable)* that runs from near Vernon along an abandoned railroad right-of-way (figure about 30 min to Giverny). You'll likely get an easy-to-follow map to Giverny with your bike (in case you don't, leave the train station paralleling tracks to your right, take the first left and follow that to the river, cross the river, turn right and meet the bike trail). There's a lovely riverside park on the left side of the bridge after crossing the Seine (where you turn right for the bike path).

You can go on **foot** to Giverny, following the bike instructions above, and take a bus or taxi back.

Auvers-sur-Oise

There's no better place to get a feel for life during the Impressionist era than on the banks of the lazy Oise River, about a 45-minute drive (or 1.5-hour train ride) northwest of Paris.

Auvers-sur-Oise (oh-vehr soor wahz) is famous as the village where Vincent van Gogh committed suicide after relocating from southern France to be near his sympathetic doctor (Paul Gachet). But many other artists enjoyed this peaceful rural retreat, including Charles-François Daubigny, Jean-Baptiste-Camille Corot, Camille Pissarro, and Paul Cézanne.

Today, this modest little town opens doors to visitors with a handful of sights, walking trails leading to scenes painted by the artists (some with copies of the paintings posted), and a tranquil break from the big city. Come for the afternoon (some sights are closed in the morning) and avoid weekends if you can. Auvers has cafés, restaurants, and bakeries with sandwiches. Most sights are closed Mondays and Tuesdays and from November to Easter.

Start at the eager-to-help **TI,** which has good information on all village sights, bus and RER train schedules, a few picnic tables, a rustic WC, and a helpful €0.50 map of Auvers showing the walking routes, with famous art scenes posted (April–Oct Tue–Sun 9:30–12:30 & 14:00–18:00, Nov–March 9:30–12:30 & 14:00–17:00, closed Mon, tel. 01 30 36 10 06).

The skippable **Musée Daubigny**, one floor up from the TI, houses a small collection of works from artists who came to work with Monsieur Daubigny, an ardent defender of the Impressionists (€5, Thu–Sun 14:00–18:00, Nov–March closes at 17:00, closed Mon–Wed, tel. 01 34 48 03 03).

The best way to spend a few hours in Auvers is to wander the streets between the TI and the château and find locations where paintings were set, and to visit the dazzling château.

The town's most worthwhile sight is **Château d'Auvers** (follow *Château* signs along the small road that runs above the TI, 15 min

on foot). The entire château has been transformed into a re-creation of life during the Impressionist years. Elaborate multimedia displays use an audioguide , video screens, and lasers to guide you along the Impressionist route that led from Montmartre to the sea, giving you a keen appreciation of life's daily struggles and pleasures during this time (€10, good family rates, open April–Sept Tue–Sun 10:30–18:00, closed Mon; Oct–March Tue–Sun 10:30–16:30, closed Mon; tel. 01 34 48 48 45, www.chateau-auvers.fr).

You can walk through the same crow-infested wheat fields Vincent did. From the château, return to Auvers along the same road, but veer left when you reach rue Daubigny, then turn right on rue du Montier, and turn right again up a dirt trail. As you stroll through the wheat fields (can be muddy), ponder how amazed the artist would be at his popularity today. You can go as far as the cemetery and visit the tombs of Vincent and his brother Theo (15 min on trail, as you enter cemetery, tombs on left wall halfway down), or take the dirt trail shortcut a few hundred yards before the cemetery, down to the **Church at Auvers** (see painting at Orsay Museum). From here, it's a short walk down to the train station and bus stop to Pontoise.

Some van Gogh fans make a pilgrimage to **Auberge Ravoux** (also called "Maison de Van Gogh"), where Vincent died after shooting himself. Informative English-information plaques in the free courtyard explain Vincent's tragic life. Wooden steps lead to his small room (€5, March–Oct Wed–Sun 10:00–18:00, closed Mon–Tue and Nov–Feb, includes 12-min slideshow and maybe a visit with English commentary, otherwise tour on your own). Food connoisseurs skip the visit and have a tasty lunch in the *auberge's* perfectly preserved restaurant (€28–35 *menu*).

SLEEPING AND EATING

(€1 = about $1.20, country code: 33)
Auvers is a handy first or last stop for drivers using Charles de Gaulle Airport. I can't imagine a better way to begin or end a trip than at **Chambre d'Hôtes la Ramure**, where charming Sylvie opens the doors of her lovely stone home to travelers. The three rooms have fireplaces, oak floors, high ceilings, and real furniture (Db-€60–70, 2 connecting rooms for families-€100, includes breakfast, cash only, 100 yards on road that leads from rear of Auvers' church, look for *Chambre d'Hôtes* sign, tel. 01 30 36 79 32, mobile 06 81 31 30 86, http://perso.club-internet.fr/laramure, laramure@club-internet.fr).

You can sleep luxuriously at the small, friendly, and polished **Hostellerie du Nord***, with modern, spacious rooms and a seriously good restaurant that requires reservations (Db-€98–128,

suites-€188, *menus*-€48–59, a block from train station at 6 rue du Général de Gaulle, tel. 01 30 36 70 74, fax 01 30 36 72 75, www.hostelleriedunord.fr).

The place to eat in Auvers is **Auberge Ravoux,** unchanged (except for its prices) since 1876, when painters would meet here over a good meal (€28-35 *menu,* closed Mon–Tue, below TI on place de la Mairie, tel. 01 30 36 60 60).

TRANSPORTATION CONNECTIONS

Between Paris and Auvers

Frequent trains to Auvers (via Pontoise or St.Ouen) leave from Gare du Nord and Gare St. Lazare, but the easiest trip is via RER-C to Pontoise (catch in Paris at St. Michel, Orsay, Invalides, or Pont de l'Alma stops, 2–3/hr, 40 min, €5). Pontoise is the end of the line.

To get from Pontoise to Auvers, a 10-minute ride away, take the train direction Creil (if it's leaving soon) or hop on bus #95 (runs more frequently than train, catch it to the right out of the station; look for the posted schedule—you're at "Chemin de la Gare" in Pontoise and you want the "Marie" stop in Auvers). Taxis wait outside the Pontoise station to the left (€10 to Auvers, tel. 01 30 75 95 95; for a bit more money the same taxi can pick you up in Auvers for the return).

If you arrive in Auvers by train, you can reach the TI by turning left on the main road leaving Auvers' station (look for signs, TI has bus schedules to Pontoise). For a taxi in Auvers, call 06 71 60 50 06 or 06 08 24 54 88.

By **car,** Auvers is about 45 minutes northwest of Paris, off Autoroute A-15 (exit #7 to N-184, then follow direction: Beauvais).

Disneyland Paris

Europe's Disneyland is a remake of California's, with most of the same rides and smiles. The main difference is that Mickey Mouse speaks French and you can buy wine with your lunch. My kids went ducky. It's easy to get to, and worth a day, if Paris is handier than Florida or California. Saturday, Sunday, Wednesday, public holidays, and any day in July and August are the

most crowded. After dinner, crowds are gone. Food is fun and not outrageously priced. (Still, many smuggle in a picnic.) The free FASTPASS system is a worthwhile timesaver (get FASTPASS card at entry, good for 5 most popular rides, at ride insert card in machine to get a window of time to enter—often within about 45 min). You'll also save time by buying your tickets ahead (at airport TIs, over 100 Métro stations, or along the Champs-Elysées at the TI, Disney Store, or Virgin Megastore). Disney brochures are in every Paris hotel. For Disneyland information and reservations, call 08 25 30 60 30-€.15/min (www.disneylandparis.com).

Walt Disney Studios: This zone, which opened in 2002 next to the original 10-year-old amusement park, has a Hollywood focus geared for an older crowd, with animation, special effects, and movie magic "rides." The Aerosmith Rock 'n' Roller Coaster is nothing special. The highlight is the Stunt Show Spectacular, filling a huge back-lot stadium five times a day for 45 minutes of car chases and thriller filming tips. An actual movie sequence is filmed with stunt drivers, audience bit players, and brash MTV-style hosts.

Cost: Disneyland Paris and Walt Disney Studios charge the same. You can pay separately for each or buy a combined ticket for both, called "Hopper" tickets. A one-day pass to either park is €41 for adults and €33 for kids aged 3-11. There's no charge for kids under 3.

For entry to both parks, adults pay approximately €49 for one day, €90 for two days and €109 for three days. Regular prices are discounted about 25 percent from November through March and promotions are offered occasionally (check www.disneyland.com).

The only budget deal (and, I think, the only way the Walt Disney Studios are worth visiting) is to pay for a full-price Walt Disney Studios ticket, which gets you into the Disneyland Park for free during the last three hours of that day.

Hours: Disneyland is open April–June daily 9:00–20:00, July–Aug daily 9:00–23:00, and Sept–March Mon–Fri 10:00–20:00, Sat–Sun 9:00–20:00. Walt Disney Studios is open 9:00–18:00.

Sleeping at Disneyland: Most are better off sleeping in reality (Paris), though with direct buses and freeways to both airports, Disneyland makes a convenient first- or last-night stop. Seven different Disney-owned hotels offer accommodations at or near the park in all price ranges. Prices are impossible to pin down as they vary by season and by the "package deal" you choose (deals that include park entry are usually a better value). The cheapest

is **Davy Crockett,** but you'll need a car. **Hôtel Santa Fe**** offers the best midrange value, with shuttle service to the park every 12 minutes. The most expensive is **Disneyland Hotel******, right at the park entry, about twice the price of the Santa Fe. To reserve any Disneyland hotel, call 01 60 30 60 30, fax 01 60 30 60 65, or check www.disneylandparis.com. The prices you'll be quoted include entry to the park.

TRANSPORTATION CONNECTIONS

Between Paris and Disneyland Paris

By Train: TGV trains connect Disneyland directly with **Charles de Gaulle airport** (10 min), the **Loire Valley** (1.5 hrs, Tours-St. Pierre des Corps station, 15 min from Amboise), **Avignon** (3 hrs, TGV station), **Lyon** (2 hrs, Part Dieu station), and **Nice** (6 hrs, main station).

By RER: The slick one-hour RER trip is the best way to get to Disneyland from downtown Paris. Take RER line A-4 to Marne-la-Vallée-Chessy (from Charles de Gaulle-Etoile, Auber, Châtelet-Les Halles, or Gare de Lyon stations, about €8 each way, hourly, drops you one hour later right in the park). The last train back to Paris leaves shortly after midnight. Be sure to get a ticket that is good on both the RER and Métro; when returning, remember to use your same RER ticket for your Métro connection in Paris.

By Bus: Both airports have direct shuttle buses to Disneyland Paris (€13, daily 8:30–19:45, every 45 min).

By Car: Disneyland is about 40 minutes (20 miles) east of Paris on the A-4 autoroute (direction Nancy/Metz, exit #14). Parking is €8 per day at the park.

FRENCH HISTORY

Celts and Romans (52 B.C.–A.D. 500)

Julius Caesar conquered the Parisii, turning Paris from a tribal fishing village into a European city. The mix of Latin (southern) and Celtic (northern) cultures, with Paris right in the middle, defined the French character.

Sights
- Cluny Museum (Roman baths)
- Louvre (Roman antiquities)
- Archaeological Crypt (in front of Notre-Dame)

Dark Ages (500–1000)

Roman Paris fell to German pirates ("Franks" = France), and later to the Vikings ("Norsemen" = Normans). During this turbulent time, Paris was just another island state ("Ile de France") in the midst of many warring kingdoms. The lone bright spot was the reign of Charlemagne (A.D. 768–814), who briefly united the Franks, giving a glimpse of the modern nation-state of France.

Sights
- Cluny Museum (artifacts)
- Statue of Charlemagne (near Notre-Dame)

Border Wars with England (1066–1500)

In 1066, the Norman duke William the Conqueror invaded and conquered England. This united England, Normandy, and much of what is today Western France, sparked centuries of border wars, and produced many kings of England who spoke French. In 1328, King Charles IV died without an heir, and the Norman king of England tried to claim the throne of France, which led to

more than 100 years of Franco-Anglo battles, called the Hundred Years' War. Rallied by the teenage visionary Joan of Arc in 1429, the French finally united north and south, and drove the English across the Channel in 1453. Modern France was born, with Paris as its capital.

Sights
- Notre-Dame
- Sainte-Chapelle
- Cluny Museum (tapestries)
- Carnavalet Museum
- The Sorbonne
- The Latin Quarter

Renaissance and Religious Wars (1500s)

A strong, centralized France emerged, with French kings setting Europe's standard. François I made Paris a cultural capital, inviting Leonardo and *Mona Lisa* to visit. Catholics and Protestants fought openly, with 2,000 Parisians slaughtered in the St. Bartholomew's Day Massacre in 1572. The Wars of Religion subsided for a while when the first Bourbon king, Henry IV, took the throne in 1589 after converting to Catholicism. (In 1598, he signed the Edict of Nantes, which instituted freedom of worship.)

Sights
- Louvre (palace and Renaissance art)
- Pont Neuf
- Place des Vosges
- Fontainebleau

Louis XIV, the Absolute Monarch (1600s)

Louis XIV solidified his power, neutered the nobility, revoked the Edict of Nantes, and moved the capital to Versailles, which also became the center of European culture. France's wealth sparked "enlightened" ideas that became the seeds of democracy.

Sights
- Versailles
- Vaux-le-Vicomte
- Les Invalides
- Paintings by Nicolas Poussin and Claude Lorrain

Decadence and Revolution (1700s)

This was the age of Louis XV, Louis XVI, Marie-Antoinette, Voltaire, Jean-Jacques Rousseau, Maximilien de Robespierre, and Napoleon. A financial crunch from wars and royal excess drove the

French people to revolt. On July 14, 1789, they stormed the Bastille. A couple of years later, the First French Republic arrested and then beheaded the king and queen. Thousands lost their heads—guillotined if suspected of hindering progress. A charismatic commoner rose amid the chaos, promising stability—Napoleon Bonaparte.

Sights
- Versailles
- Place de la Concorde
- Place de la Bastille
- Conciergerie
- Paintings by Antoine Watteau, François Boucher, Jean-Honoré Fragonard, and Jacques-Louis David

Elected Emperors and Constitutional Kings (1800s)

Napoleon conquered Europe, crowned himself emperor, invaded Russia, was defeated on the battlefields of Waterloo, and ended up exiled to an island in the Atlantic. The monarchy was restored, but rulers toed the democratic line—or were deposed in the popular uprisings of 1830 and 1848. The latter resulted in the Second French Republic, whose first president was Napoleon's nephew. He rewrote the constitution with himself as Emperor Napoleon III, and presided over a wealthy, middle-class nation with a colonial empire in slow decline. The disastrous Franco-Prussian War in 1870 ended his reign, leading to the Third Republic. France's political clout was fading, even as Paris remained the world's cultural center during the belle époque, or beautiful age.

Sights
- Arc de Triomphe
- Baron Haussmann's wide boulevards
- Eiffel Tower
- Les Invalides and Napoleon's Tomb
- Pont Alexandre III
- Grand Palais
- Petit Palais (slated to reopen in spring of 2006)
- Montmartre
- Opéra Garnier
- Paintings by Jean-Auguste-Dominique Ingres and Eugène Delacroix (Louvre)
- Impressionist and Post-Impressionist paintings (Edouard Manet, Claude Monet, Pierre-Auguste Renoir, Edgar Degas, Henri de Toulouse-Lautrec, Paul Cézanne, and so on) at the Orsay, Marmottan, and L'Orangerie (scheduled to reopen in 2006).

War and Depression (1900–1950)

France began the turn of the 20th century as top dog, but two world wars with Germany (and the earlier Franco-Prussian War) wasted the country. France lost millions of men in World War I, sank into an economic depression, and was easily overrun by Hitler in World War II. Paris, now dirt cheap, attracted foreign writers and artists.

This was the age of Pablo Picasso, Maurice Ravel, Claude Debussy, Erik Satie, Igor Stravinsky, Vaslav Nijinsky, Ernest Hemingway, F. Scott Fitzgerald, Gertrude Stein, Ezra Pound, Jean-Paul Sartre, Edith Piaf, and Maurice Chevalier.

Sights
- Picasso Museum
- Deportation Memorial
- Pompidou Center (art from this period)

Postwar France (1950–Present)

After the war, France reestablished a democracy with the Fourth Republic. But France's colonial empire dissolved after bitter wars in Algeria and Vietnam, which helped mire an already unsteady government. Wartime hero Charles de Gaulle was brought back in 1958 to assist with France's regrowth. He rewrote the constitution, beginning the Fifth (and current) Republic. Immigrants from former colonies flooded Paris. The turbulent '60s, progressive '70s, socialist-turned-conservative '80s, and the middle-of-the-road '90s bring us to the *début de siècle,* or the beginning of the century.

Sights
- Montparnasse Tower
- La Défense
- Louvre's pyramid
- Pompidou Center (modern art)

Contemporary Politics in France

The key political issues in France today are high unemployment (about 9 percent), high taxes (about 45 percent of Gross Domestic Product), a steadily increasing percentage of ethnic minorities (almost 10 percent of France's population is Muslim), the need to compete in a global marketplace, and what to do about the European Union. The challenge is to address these issues while maintaining the social benefits the French expect from their government. As a result, national policies seem to conflict with each other (e.g., France supports the lean economic policies of the European Union, and yet reduced the official work-week to 35 hours for many workers—though that decision is being reconsidered).

The unification of Europe has been powered by France and Germany. The European Union's constitution was negotiated by former French president Valery Giscard d'Estaing, and represents a serious step in the unification of Europe. It is designed to simplify decision-making and to provide a more consistent and coordinated foreign policy for member states. The 25-member European Union was well on its way to becoming a "United States of Europe" (having successfully dissolved borders and implemented the single currency, or euro)—until French citizens voted resoundingly against the constitution in the summer of 2005. While the major political parties in France supported the treaty, voters felt it gave too many concessions to other countries (such as Britain) and would ultimately result in a loss of job security and social benefits (a huge issue in France). Because of France's important role in establishing the European Union, progress on further unification has stalled.

French national politics are even more complex than European politics. While only two parties dominate American politics, France has seven major parties and several smaller ones. From left to right, the major parties include the Ligue Communiste Révolutionnaire (LCR, headed by Olivier Besançenot), which is as far-left as you get in France; the more moderate reformed Communists (PCF-Parti Communiste Français); the environmental party (Les Verts, "The Greens"); the middle-of-the-road Socialists (PS-Parti Socialiste); the aristocratically conservative UDF (Union pour la Démocratie Française); the center-right UMP (Union pour la Majorité Présidentielle); and the racist, isolationist Front National. In general, the UDF and UMP split the conservative middle ground, and the Socialists dominate the liberal middle ground. But in France, unlike in the U.S., informal coalitions are generally necessary for any party to "rule."

You've likely read about the Front National party, led by Jean-Marie Le Pen. Le Pen's "France for the French" platform calls for the expulsion of ethnic minorities and broader police powers. Although the Front National has a staunch voter base of about 15 percent, the recent rise in unemployment and globalization worries have increased its following, allowing Le Pen to nudge the political agenda to the right. On the far left, the once powerful Communists (PCF) draw only about 5 percent of the popular vote, forcing them to work more flexibly with the less radical Socialists and the environmental party (Les Verts). This left end of the political spectrum in France sees its fortunes rise when the economy is strong, and fall when it's weak.

While the French president is elected by popular vote every five years, he is more of a figurehead than his American counterpart. The more powerful prime minister is chosen by the president, then confirmed by the parliament (Assemblée Nationale). With

five major parties, a single majority is rare—it takes a coalition to elect a prime minister. While the right had been more successful in marshaling its supporters under Chirac (President Jacques Chirac and Prime Minister Dominique de Villepin are both conservatives), recent election results have demonstrated a resounding preference for Socialist candidates. The next presidential election, in 2007, should be a fascinating contest.

APPENDIX

Let's Talk Telephones

Here are general instructions for making phone calls. For information specific to France, see "Telephones" in the Introduction.

Making Calls within a European Country: About half of all European countries use area codes (like we do); the other half uses a direct-dial system without area codes.

To make calls within a country that uses a direct-dial system (France, Belgium, the Czech Republic, Denmark, Italy, Portugal, Norway, Spain, and Switzerland), you dial the same number whether you're calling across the country or across the street.

In countries that use area codes (such as Austria, Britain, Croatia, Finland, Germany, Hungary, Ireland, the Netherlands, Poland, Slovakia, Slovenia, and Sweden), you dial the local number when calling within a city, and you add the area code if calling long-distance within the country.

Making International Calls: You always start with the international access code (011 if you're calling from America or Canada, or 00 from anywhere in Europe), then dial the country code of the country you're calling (see chart below).

What you dial next depends on the phone system of the country you're calling. If the country uses area codes, drop the initial 0 of the area code, then dial the rest of the number.

Countries that use direct-dial systems (no area codes) vary in how they're accessed internationally by phone. For instance, if you're making an international call to the Czech Republic, Denmark, Italy, Norway, Portugal, or Spain, simply dial the international access code, country code, and phone number. But if you're calling France, Belgium, or Switzerland, drop the initial 0 of the phone number.

European Calling Chart

Just smile and dial, using this key:
AC = Area Code, LN = Local Number.

European Country	Calling long distance within ...	Calling from the U.S.A./ Canada to ...	Calling from a European country to ...
Austria	AC + LN	011 + 43 + AC (without the initial zero) + LN	00 + 43 + AC (without the initial zero) + LN
Belgium	LN	011 + 32 + LN (without initial zero)	00 + 32 + LN (without initial zero)
Britain	AC + LN	011 + 44 + AC (without initial zero) + LN	00 + 44 + AC (without initial zero) + LN
Croatia	AC + LN	011 + 385 + AC (without initial zero) + LN	00 + 385 + AC (without initial zero) + LN
Czech Republic	LN	011 + 420 + LN	00 + 420 + LN
Denmark	LN	011 + 45 + LN	00 + 45 + LN
Finland	AC + LN	011 + 358 + AC (without initial zero) + LN	00 + 358 + AC (without initial zero) + LN
France	LN	011 + 33 + LN (without initial zero)	00 + 33 + LN (without initial zero)
Germany	AC + LN	011 + 49 + AC (without initial zero) + LN	00 + 49 + AC (without initial zero) + LN
Greece	LN	011 + 30 + LN	00 + 30 + LN
Hungary	06 + AC + LN	011 + 36 + AC + LN	00 + 36 + AC + LN
Ireland	AC + LN	011 + 353 + AC (without initial zero) + LN	00 + 353 + AC (without initial zero) + LN
Italy	LN	011 + 39 + LN	00 + 39 + LN

European Country	Calling long distance within ...	Calling from the U.S.A./ Canada to ...	Calling from a European country to ...
Netherlands	AC + LN	011 + 31 + AC (without initial zero) + LN	00 + 31 + AC (without initial zero) + LN
Norway	LN	011 + 47 + LN	00 + 47 + LN
Poland	AC + LN	011 + 48 + AC (without initial zero) + LN	00 + 48 + AC (without initial zero) + LN
Portugal	LN	011 + 351 + LN	00 + 351 + LN
Slovakia	AC + LN	011 + 421 + AC (without initial zero) + LN	00 + 421 + AC (without initial zero) + LN
Slovenia	AC + LN	011 + 386 + AC (without initial zero) + LN	00 + 386 + AC (without initial zero) + LN
Spain	LN	011 + 34 + LN	00 + 34 + LN
Sweden	AC + LN	011 + 46 + AC (without initial zero) + LN	00 + 46 + AC (without initial zero) + LN
Switzerland	LN	011 + 41 + LN (without initial zero)	00 + 41 + LN (without initial zero)
Turkey	AC (if no initial zero is included, add one) + LN	011 + 90 + AC (without initial zero) + LN	00 + 90 + AC (without initial zero) + LN

- The instructions above apply whether you're calling a fixed phone or mobile phone.
- The international access codes (the first numbers you dial when making an international call) are 011 if you're calling from the U.S.A./Canada, or 00 if you're calling from anywhere in Europe.
- To call the U.S.A. or Canada from Europe, dial 00, then 1 (the country code for the U.S.A. and Canada), then the area code and number. In short, 00 + 1 + AC + LN = Hi, Mom!

Country Codes

After you've dialed the international access code (00 if calling from Europe, 011 if calling from the U.S. or Canada), then dial the code of the country you're calling.

Austria—43	Italy—39
Belgium—32	Morocco—212
Britain—44	Netherlands—31
Canada—1	Norway—47
Croatia—385	Poland—48
Czech Rep.—420	Portugal—351
Denmark—45	Slovakia—421
Estonia—372	Slovenia—386
Finland—358	Spain—34
France—33	Sweden—46
Germany—49	Switzerland—41
Gibraltar—350	Turkey—90
Greece—30	U.S.A.—1
Ireland—353	

Useful French Phone Numbers

Directory Assistance for Paris and France (some English spoken): tel. 12

Collect Calls to the U.S.: tel. 00 00 11

Lost Property (Bureau des Objets Trouvés, at the police station): Open Tue and Thu 8:30–20:00, 36 rue des Morillons, Mo: Convention, tel. 01 55 76 20 20

Emergency/Medical Needs

Police: tel. 17

Emergency Medical Assistance: tel. 15

American Hospital: 63 boulevard Victor Hugo, in Neuilly suburb, Mo: Porte Maillot, then bus #82, tel. 01 46 41 25 25

English-Speaking Pharmacy: tel. 01 45 62 02 41 (Pharmacie les Champs, 24 hrs, 84 avenue des Champs-Elysées, Mo: Georges V)

Chiropractic Centers: tel. 01 43 54 26 25 or 01 43 87 81 62

SOS Doctors: tel. 01 47 07 77 77 or 01 48 28 40 04

SOS Help: This anonymous telephone hotline runs a crisis/suicide prevention listening service in English (daily 15:00–23:00)—tel. 01 46 21 46 46

Rape Crisis Hotline: 24-hr tel. 08 00 05 95 95

Ambulance: tel. 01 45 67 50 50

Consulates/Embassies

U.S. Consulate: Passport services Mon–Fri 9:00–13:00, 2 rue St. Florentin, Mo: Concorde, tel. 01 43 12 22 22, www.amb-usa.fr

English-Language Churches in Paris

American Church (interdenominational): Reception open Mon–Sat 9:30–13:00 & 14:00–22:30, Sun 9:00–14:00 & 15:00–19:00; 65 quai d'Orsay, Mo: Invalides, tel. 01 40 62 05 00, www.acparis.org; for more information, see page 24.

American Cathedral (Episcopalian): 23 avenue George V, Mo. George V, tel. 01 42 17 04 16

Unitarian Universalist Fellowship: 7 bis rue du Pasteur Wagner, Mo: Bastille, tel. 01 30 82 75 33

Scots Kirk (Church of Scotland): 17 rue Bayard, Mo: Franklin D. Roosevelt, tel. 01 48 78 47 94

St. George's Anglican Church: 7 rue Auguste Vacquerie, tel. 01 47 20 22 51

St. Joseph's Church (Roman Catholic): 50 av Hoche, tel. 01 42 27 28 56

St. Michael's Church (Anglican): 5 rue d'Aguesseau, tel. 01 47 42 70 88

U.S. Embassy: 2 avenue Gabriel (to the left as you face Hôtel Crillon), Mo: Concorde, tel. 01 43 12 22 22

Canadian Consulate and Embassy: Mon–Fri 9:00–12:30 & 14:00–16:00, 35 avenue Montaigne, Mo: Franklin D. Roosevelt, tel. 01 44 43 29 00, www.amb-canada.fr

Australian Consulate: Mon–Fri 9:15–12:00 & 14:00–16:30, 4 rue Jean Ray, Mo: Bir-Hakeim, tel. 01 40 59 33 00

Tourist Info, Transportation, and Banking

Paris Tourist Information: tel. 08 92 68 30 00 (recorded info with long menu)

Ile de France Tourist Information (covers Paris area, including Fontainebleau, Vaux-le-Vicomte, and Chantilly): tel. 01 42 60 28 62

Train (SNCF) Information: tel. 3635 (some English usually spoken)

Bus and Métro (RATP) Information: tel. 08 36 68 77 14 (French only)

American Express: 11 rue Scribe, Mo: Opéra, tel. 01 47 77 77 07

Sunday Banks: 115 and 154 avenue des Champs-Elysées

Lost or Stolen Credit Cards

For more information, see the sidebar on page 11.

Visa: tel. 08 00 90 11 79

MasterCard: tel. 08 00 90 13 87

American Express: tel. 01 47 77 72 00

Diner's Club: Call U.S. collect 00-1-702-797-5532

Cheap Flights
Access Voyages: 128 quai de Jemmapes, Mo: République, tel. 08 92 89 38 92
Anyway: 46 rue des Lombards, Mo: Châtelet or Hôtel de Ville, tel. 08 92 89 20 92
Booking Service (for hotels, restaurants, and other tourist activities): tel. 01 43 59 12 12, www.ely1212.com

Airports
Charles de Gaulle: general info tel. 01 48 62 22 80, lost luggage tel. 01 48 62 10 46
Orly: tel. 01 49 75 15 15

Airlines
Aer Lingus: tel. 01 70 20 00 72
Air Canada: tel. 08 25 88 08 81
Air France: tel. 08 20 82 08 20
Alitalia: tel. 08 02 31 53 15
American Airlines: tel. 01 55 17 43 41 or 08 10 87 28 72
BMI British Midlands: tel. 01 41 91 87 04
British Airways: tel. 08 25 82 54 00
Continental: tel. 01 42 99 09 09
Delta: tel. 08 00 35 40 80
Iberia: tel. 08 20 07 50 75
Icelandair: tel. 01 44 51 60 51
KLM: tel. 08 90 71 07 10
Lufthansa: tel. 08 20 02 00 30
Northwest: tel. 08 90 71 07 10
Olympic: tel. 01 44 94 58 58
SAS: tel. 08 25 32 53 35
Swiss: tel. 08 20 04 05 06
United: tel. 08 10 72 72 72
US Airways: tel. 08 10 63 22 22

French Language Classes
American University of Paris: tel. 01 40 62 07 20, fax 01 47 05 34 32, www.aup.edu
Ecole France Langue: tel. 01 45 00 40 15, fax 01 45 00 53 41, www.france-langue.fr

Cooking Schools
These schools have demonstration courses.
Le Cordon Bleu: 8 Rue Léon Delhomme, tel. 01 53 68 22 50, fax 01 48 56 03 96, paris@cordonbleu.edu
Ritz Escoffier Ecole de Gastronomie Française: 15 Place Vendôme, Mo: Madeleine, tel. 01 43 16 30 50, fax 01 43 16 31 50

2006

JANUARY

S	M	T	W	T	F	S
1	2	3	4	5	6	7
8	9	10	11	12	13	14
15	16	17	18	19	20	21
22	23	24	25	26	27	28
29	30	31				

FEBRUARY

S	M	T	W	T	F	S
			1	2	3	4
5	6	7	8	9	10	11
12	13	14	15	16	17	18
19	20	21	22	23	24	25
26	27	28				

MARCH

S	M	T	W	T	F	S
			1	2	3	4
5	6	7	8	9	10	11
12	13	14	15	16	17	18
19	20	21	22	23	24	25
26	27	28	29	30	31	

APRIL

S	M	T	W	T	F	S
						1
2	3	4	5	6	7	8
9	10	11	12	13	14	15
16	17	18	19	20	21	22
23/30	24	25	26	27	28	29

MAY

S	M	T	W	T	F	S
	1	2	3	4	5	6
7	8	9	10	11	12	13
14	15	16	17	18	19	20
21	22	23	24	25	26	27
28	29	30	31			

JUNE

S	M	T	W	T	F	S
				1	2	3
4	5	6	7	8	9	10
11	12	13	14	15	16	17
18	19	20	21	22	23	24
25	26	27	28	29	30	

JULY

S	M	T	W	T	F	S
						1
2	3	4	5	6	7	8
9	10	11	12	13	14	15
16	17	18	19	20	21	22
23/30	24/31	25	26	27	28	29

AUGUST

S	M	T	W	T	F	S
		1	2	3	4	5
6	7	8	9	10	11	12
13	14	15	16	17	18	19
20	21	22	23	24	25	26
27	28	29	30	31		

SEPTEMBER

S	M	T	W	T	F	S
					1	2
3	4	5	6	7	8	9
10	11	12	13	14	15	16
17	18	19	20	21	22	23
24	25	26	27	28	29	30

OCTOBER

S	M	T	W	T	F	S
1	2	3	4	5	6	7
8	9	10	11	12	13	14
15	16	17	18	19	20	21
22	23	24	25	26	27	28
29	30	31				

NOVEMBER

S	M	T	W	T	F	S
			1	2	3	4
5	6	7	8	9	10	11
12	13	14	15	16	17	18
19	20	21	22	23	24	25
26	27	28	29	30		

DECEMBER

S	M	T	W	T	F	S
					1	2
3	4	5	6	7	8	9
10	11	12	13	14	15	16
17	18	19	20	21	22	23
24/31	25	26	27	28	29	30

Public Holidays and Festivals

Paris is lively with festivals throughout the summer and fall. Kicking off the season in late May is the month-long **Festival of St. Denis** in that Parisian suburb, featuring musicians from around the world at various venues (tel. 01 48 13 06 07, www.festival -saint-denis.fr). Paris celebrates the solstice (June 21) at its **Music Festival** (Fête de la Musique), with concerts throughout the city. In July, the prestigious **Tour de France** bicycle race begins and ends in Paris (starts on Ile de France, www.letour.fr). **Bastille Day**, France's National Day (July 14), brings fireworks, dancing, and revelry countrywide (see sidebar on page 110). From mid-July to mid-August is the **Paris Neighborhoods Festival**, featuring theater, dance, and concerts around the city. **La Villette Jazz Festival** brings a week of outdoor jazz concerts to this Parisian park in early- to mid-September. The first Saturday of October, Montmartre celebrates the **grape harvest** with a parade and

festivities. The **Festival of Autumn** (www.festival-automne.com) runs through autumn, with theater, dance, film, and opera performances. For more information on festivals, see www.franceguide .com, www.whatsonwhen.com, and www.festivals.com.

National Holidays in 2006

These national holidays (when many sights close) are observed throughout France. Note that this isn't a complete list; holidays can strike without warning. For more information, check www .whatsonwhen.com.

Jan 1:	New Year's Day
Jan 6:	Epiphany
April 16:	Easter Sunday
May 1:	Labor Day
May 8:	V-E Day
May 28:	Ascension
June 4:	Pentecost
July 14:	Bastille Day
Aug 15:	Assumption of Mary
Nov 1:	All Saints' Day
Nov 11:	Armistice Day
Dec 25:	Christmas Day

Numbers and Stumblers

- Europeans write a few of their numbers differently than we do. 1 = 1, 4 = 4, 7 = 7. Learn the difference or miss your train.
- In Europe, dates appear as day/month/year, so Christmas is 25/12/06.
- Commas are decimal points and decimals commas. A dollar and a half is 1,50, and there are 5.280 feet in a mile.
- When pointing, use your whole hand, palm down.
- When counting with fingers, start with your thumb. If you hold up your first finger to request one item, you'll probably get two.
- What Americans call the second floor of a building is the first floor in Europe.
- When using escalators and moving sidewalks, Europeans keep the left "lane" open for passing. Keep to the right.

Paris' Climate Chart

First line, average daily low; second line, average daily high; third line, days of no rain.

J	F	M	A	M	J	J	A	S	O	N	D
34°	34°	39°	43°	49°	55°	58°	58°	53°	46°	40°	36°
43°	45°	54°	60°	68°	73°	76°	75°	70°	60°	50°	44°
14	14	19	17	19	18	19	18	17	18	15	15

Converting Temperatures: Fahrenheit and Celsius

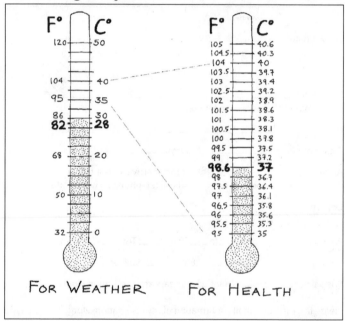

Europe takes its temperature using the Celsius scale, while we opt for Fahrenheit. For weather, remember that 28°C is 82°F—perfect. For health, 37°C is just right.

Metric Conversion (approximate)

1 inch = 25 millimeters
1 foot = 0.3 meter
1 yard = 0.9 meter
1 mile = 1.6 kilometers
1 centimeter = 0.4 inch
1 meter = 39.4 inches
1 kilometer = 0.62 mile

32° F = 0° C
82° F = about 28° C
1 ounce = 28 grams
1 kilogram = 2.2 pounds
1 quart = 0.95 liter
1 square yard = 0.8 square meter
1 acre = 0.4 hectare

Making Your Hotel Reservation

Most hotel managers know basic "hotel English." Faxing or e-mailing are the preferred methods for reserving a room. They're more accurate than telephoning and much faster than writing a letter. Use this handy form for your fax or find it online at www.ricksteves.com/reservation. Photocopy and fax away.

One-Page Fax

To: _____ @ _____
              hotel   *fax*

From: _____@ _____
              name   *fax*

Today's date: _____ / _____ / _____
                 day   *month*   *year*

Dear Hotel _____ ,
Please make this reservation for me:

Name: _____

Total # of people:_____ # of rooms: _____ # of nights: _____

Arriving: _____ / _____ / _____   My time of arrival (24-hr clock): _____
              day   *month*   *year*   (I will telephone if I will be late)

Departing: ____ / ____ / ____
               day   *month*   *year*

Room(s): Single _____ Double ____ Twin _____ Triple ____ Quad _____

With: Toilet _____ Shower _____ Bath _____ Sink only _____

Special needs: View ____ Quiet ____ Cheapest ____ Ground Floor ____

Please fax, mail, or e-mail confirmation of my reservation, along with the type of room reserved and the price. Please also inform me of your cancellation policy. After I hear from you, I will quickly send my credit-card information as a deposit to hold the room. Thank you.

_____
Signature

_____
Name

_____
Address

_____
City   *State*   *Zip Code*   *Country*

_____
E-mail Address

French Pronunciation Guide for Paris

Nasalize the underlined "n" if you can (let the sound come through your nose).

Arc de Triomphe ark duh tree-ohnf

arrondissement ah-rohn-dees-mohn

Art Nouveau art noo-voh

Auvers-sur-Oise oh-vehr-sur-wahz

Bateaux Mouches bah-toh moosh

Bon Marché bohn mar-chay

boulangerie boo-lahn-zheh-ree

Carnavalet kar-nah-val-eh

Champ de Mars shahn duh mar

Champs-Elysées shahn-zay-lee-zay

Chantilly shahn_-tee-yee

charcuterie shar-koo-tuh-ree

Chartres shar-truh

château(x) shah-toh

Cité see-tay

Cité des Sciences see-tay day see-ahns

Conciergerie kon-see-ehr-zhuh-ree

Contrescarpe kohn-truh-scarp

droguerie droh-guh-ree

Ecole Militaire eh-kohl mee-lee-tehr

Egouts ay-goo

Fauchon foh-shohn

Fontainebleau fohn-tehn-bloh

fromagerie froh-mah-zhuh-ree

Galeries Lafayette gah-luh-ree lah-fay-yet

gare gar

Gare d'Austerlitz gar doh-ster-leets

Gare de l'Est gar duh less

Gare de Lyon gar duh lee-ohn

Gare du Nord gar dew nor

Gare St. Lazare gar sahn lah-zar

Garnier gar-nee-ay

Giverny zhee-vehr-nee

Grand Palais grahn pah-lay

Grande Arche de la Défense grahnd arsh duh lah day-fahns

Hôtel de Sully oh-tehl deh soo-lee

Hôtel Salé oh-tehl sah-lay

Ile de la Cité eel duh lah see-tay

Ile St. Louis eel sahn loo-ee

Jacquemart-André zhahk-mar-ahn-dray

jardin zhar-dan

Jardin des Plantes zhar-dan day plahnt

Jeu de Paume juh duh pohm

La Madeleine lah mah-duh-lehn

La Marseillaise lah mar-seh-yehz

Le Hameau luh ah-moh

Les Halles lay ahl

Les Invalides lay-zan-vah-leed

Loire lwar

L'Orangerie loh-rahn-zhuh-ree

Louvre loov-ruh

Marais mah-ray

marché aux puces mar-chay oh poos

Marmottan mar-moh-tahn

Métro may-troh

Monge mohnzh

Montmartre mohn-mart

Montparnasse mohn-par-nas

Moulin Rouge moo-lan roozh

musée mew-zay

Musée de l'Armée mew-zay duh lar-may

Musée d'Orsay mew-zay dor-say

Notre-Dame noh-truh-dahm

orangerie oh-rahn-zhuh-ree

Orsay or-say

palais pah-lay

Palais de Justice pah-lay duh zhew-stees

Palais Garnier pah-lay gar-nee-ay

Palais Royal pah-lay roh-yahl

Parc de la Villette park duh la vee-leht

Parc Monceau park moh<u>n</u>-soh
Père Lachaise pehr lah-shehz
Petit Palais puh-tee pah-lay
Pigalle pee-gahl
place plahs
Place Dauphine plahs doh-feen
Place de la Bastille plahs duh lah bah-steel
Place de la Concorde plahs duh lah koh<u>n</u>-kord
Place de la République plahs duh lah ray-poo-bleek
Place des Vosges plahs day vohzh
Place du Tertre plahs dew tehr-truh
Place St. André-des-Arts plahs sah<u>n</u> tah<u>n</u>-dray day zart
Place Vendôme plahs vah<u>n</u>-dohm
Pompidou poh<u>n</u>-pee-doo
pont poh<u>n</u>
Pont Alexandre III poh<u>n</u> ah-leks-ah<u>n</u>-druh twah
Pont Neuf poh<u>n</u> nuhf
Promenade Plantée proh-moh<u>n</u>-ahd plah<u>n</u>-tay
quai kay
Rive Droite reeve dwaht
Rive Gauche reeve gohsh
Rodin roh-da<u>n</u>
rue rew

Rue Cler rew klehr
Rue Daguerre rew dah-gehr
Rue des Rosiers rew day roz-ee-ay
Rue Montorgueil rew moh<u>n</u>-tor-goy
Rue Mouffetard rew moof-tar
Rue de Rivoli rew duh ree-voh-lee
Sacré-Cœur sah-kray-koor
Sainte-Chapelle sah<u>n</u>t-shah-pehl
Samaritaine sah-mah-ree-tehn
Seine sehn
Sèvres-Babylone seh-vruh-bah-bee-lohn
Sorbonne sor-buhn
St. Germain-des-Prés sah<u>n</u> zhehr-ma<u>n</u>-day-pray
St. Julien-le-Pauvre sah<u>n</u> zhew-lee-ah<u>n</u>-luh-poh-vruh
St. Séverin sah<u>n</u> say-vuh-ra<u>n</u>
St. Sulpice sah<u>n</u> sool-pees
Tour Eiffel toor ee-fehl
Trianon tree-ah<u>n</u>-oh<u>n</u>
Trocadéro troh-kah-day-roh
Tuileries twee-lah-ree
Vaux-le-Vicomte voh-luh-vee-koh<u>n</u>t
Venus de Milo vuh-new duh mee-loh
Versailles vehr-sigh

French Survival Phrases

When using the phonetics, try to nasalize the n̲ sound.

English	French	Phonetics
Good day.	Bonjour.	bohn̲-zhoor
Mrs. / Mr.	Madame / Monsieur	mah-dahm / muhs-yur
Do you speak English?	Parlez-vous anglais?	par-lay-voo ahn̲-glay
Yes. / No.	Oui. / Non.	wee / nohn̲
I understand.	Je comprends.	zhuh kohn̲-prahn̲
I don't understand.	Je ne comprends pas.	zhuh nuh kohn̲-prahn̲ pah
Please.	S'il vous plaît.	see voo play
Thank you.	Merci.	mehr-see
I'm sorry.	Désolé.	day-zoh-lay
Excuse me.	Pardon.	par-dohn̲
(No) problem.	(Pas de) problème.	(pah duh) proh-blehm
It's good.	C'est bon.	say bohn̲
Goodbye.	Au revoir.	oh vwahr
one / two	un / deux	uhn̲ / duh
three / four	trois / quatre	twah / kah-truh
five / six	cinq / six	sank̲ / sees
seven / eight	sept / huit	seht / weet
nine / ten	neuf / dix	nuhf / dees
How much is it?	Combien?	kohn̲-bee-an̲
Write it?	Ecrivez?	ay-kree-vay
Is it free?	C'est gratuit?	say grah-twee
Included?	Inclus?	an̲-klew
Where can I buy / find...?	Où puis-je acheter / trouver...?	oo pwee-zhuh ah-shuh-tay / troo-vay
I'd like / We'd like...	Je voudrais / Nous voudrions...	zhuh voo-dray / noo voo-dree-ohn̲
...a room.	...une chambre.	ewn shahn̲-bruh
...a ticket to ___.	...un billet pour ___.	uhn̲ bee-yay poor
Is it possible?	C'est possible?	say poh-see-bluh
Where is...?	Où est...?	oo ay
...the train station	...la gare	lah gar
...the bus station	...la gare routière	lah gar root-yehr
...tourist information	...l'office du tourisme	loh-fees dew too-reez-muh
Where are the toilets?	Où sont les toilettes?	oo sohn̲ lay twah-leht
men	hommes	ohm
women	dames	dahm
left / right	à gauche / à droite	ah gohsh / ah dwaht
straight	tout droit	too dwah
When does this open / close?	Ça ouvre / ferme à quelle heure?	sah oo-vruh / fehrm ah kehl ur
At what time?	À quelle heure?	ah kehl ur
Just a moment.	Un moment.	uhn̲ moh-mahn̲
now / soon / later	maintenant / bientôt / plus tard	man̲-tuh-nahn̲ / bee-an̲-toh / plew tar
today / tomorrow	aujourd'hui / demain	oh-zhoor-dwee / duh-man̲

In the Restaurant

I'd like / We'd like...	**Je voudrais / Nous voudrions...**	zhuh voo-dray / noo voo-dree-oh<u>n</u>
...to reserve...	**...réserver...**	ray-zehr-vay
...a table for one / two.	**...une table pour un / deux.**	ewn tah-bluh poor uh<u>n</u> / duh
Non-smoking.	**Non fumeur.**	noh<u>n</u> few-mur
Is this seat free?	**C'est libre?**	say lee-bruh
The menu (in English), please.	**La carte (en anglais), s'il vous plaît.**	lah kart (ah<u>n</u> ah<u>n</u>-glay) see voo play
service (not) included	**service (non) compris**	sehr-vees (noh<u>n</u>) kohn-pree
to go	**à emporter**	ah ah<u>n</u>-por-tay
with / without	**avec / sans**	ah-vehk / sah<u>n</u>
and / or	**et / ou**	ay / oo
special of the day	**plat du jour**	plah dew zhoor
specialty of the house	**spécialité de la maison**	spay-see-ah-lee-tay duh lah may-zoh<u>n</u>
appetizers	**hors-d'oeuvre**	or-duh-vruh
first course (soup, salad)	**entrée**	ah<u>n</u>-tray
main course (meat, fish)	**plat principal**	plah pra<u>n</u>-see-pahl
bread	**pain**	pa<u>n</u>
cheese	**fromage**	froh-mahzh
sandwich	**sandwich**	sah<u>n</u>d-weech
soup	**soupe**	soop
salad	**salade**	sah-lahd
meat	**viande**	vee-ah<u>n</u>d
chicken	**poulet**	poo-lay
fish	**poisson**	pwah-soh<u>n</u>
seafood	**fruits de mer**	frwee duh mehr
fruit	**fruit**	frwee
vegetables	**légumes**	lay-gewm
dessert	**dessert**	duh-sehr
mineral water	**eau minérale**	oh mee-nay-rahl
tap water	**l'eau du robinet**	loh dew roh-bee-nay
milk	**lait**	lay
(orange) juice	**jus (d'orange)**	zhew (doh-rah<u>n</u>zh)
coffee	**café**	kah-fay
tea	**thé**	tay
wine	**vin**	va<u>n</u>
red / white	**rouge / blanc**	roozh / blah<u>n</u>
glass / bottle	**verre / bouteille**	vehr / boo-teh-ee
beer	**bière**	bee-ehr
Cheers!	**Santé!**	sah<u>n</u>-tay
More. / Another.	**Plus. / Un autre.**	plew / uh<u>n</u> oh-truh
The same.	**La même chose.**	lah mehm shohz
The bill, please.	**L'addition, s'il vous plaît.**	lah-dee-see-oh<u>n</u> see voo play
tip	**pourboire**	poor-bwar
Delicious!	**Délicieux!**	day-lee-see-uh

For more user-friendly French phrases, check out *Rick Steves' French Phrase Book and Dictionary* or *Rick Steves' French, Italian & German Phrase Book.*

INDEX

CREDITS

Researcher

To help update this book, Rick relied on the assistance of…

Kristen Kusnic

Kristen Kusnic, lover of all things French, leads tours and researches guidebooks for Rick Steves. She lived for a year each in the south of France and Berlin, becoming fluent in French, German, and red wine. When she's not in Europe, Kristen calls Seattle home.

Start your trip at
www.ricksteves.com

Rick Steves' website is packed with over 3,000 pages of timely travel information. It's also your gateway to getting FREE monthly travel news from Rick—and more!

Free Monthly European Travel News

Fresh articles on Europe's most interesting destinations and happenings. Rick will even send you an e-mail every month (often direct from Europe) with his latest discoveries!

Timely Travel Tips

Rick Steves' best money-and-stress-saving tips on trip planning, packing, transportation, hotels, health, safety, finances, hurdling the language barrier...and more.

Travelers' Graffiti Wall

Candid advice and opinions from thousands of travelers on everything listed above, plus whatever topics are hot at the moment (discount flights, packing tips, scams...you name it).

Rick's Annual Guide to European Railpasses

The clearest, most comprehensive guide to the confusing array of railpass options out there, and how to choo-choose the railpass that best fits your itinerary and budget. Then you can order your railpass (and get a bunch of great freebies) online from us!

Great Gear at the Rick Steves Travel Store

Enjoy bargains on Rick's guidebooks, planning maps and TV series DVDs—and on his custom-designed carry-on bags, wheeled bags, day bags and light-packing accessories.

Rick Steves Tours

Every year more than 6,000 lucky travelers explore Europe on a Rick Steves tour. Learn more about our 30 different one-to-three-week itineraries, read uncensored feedback from our tour alums, and sign up for your dream trip online!

Rick on Radio and TV

Read the scripts and run clips from public television's "Rick Steves' Europe" and public radio's "Travel with Rick Steves."

Respect for Your Privacy

Ordering online from us is secure. When you buy something from us, join a tour, or subscribe to Rick's free monthly travel news e-mails, we promise to never share your name, information, or e-mail address with anyone else. You won't be spammed!

Have fun raising your Travel I.Q. at
www.ricksteves.com

Travel smart...carry on!

The latest generation of Rick Steves' carry-on travel bags is easily the best—benefiting from two decades of on-the-road attention to what really matters: maximum quality and strength; practical, flexible features; and no unnecessary frills. You won't find a better value anywhere!

Convertible, expandable, and carry-on-size:
Rick Steves' Back Door Bag $99

This is the same bag that Rick Steves lives out of for three months every summer. It's made of rugged water-resistant 1000 denier Cordura nylon, and best of all, it converts easily from a smart-looking suitcase to a handy backpack with comfortably-curved shoulder straps and a padded waistbelt.

This roomy, versatile 9" x 21" x 14" bag has a large 2600 cubic-inch main compartment, plus three outside pockets (small, medium and huge) that are perfect for often-used items. And the cinch-tight compression straps will keep your load compact and close to your back—not sagging like a sack of potatoes.

Wishing you had even more room to bring home souvenirs? Pull open the full-perimeter expando-zipper and its capacity jumps from 2600 to 3000 cubic inches. When you want to use it as a suitcase or check it as luggage (required when "expanded"), the straps and belt hide away in a zippered compartment in the back.

Attention travelers under 5'4" tall: This bag also comes in an inch-shorter version, for a compact-friendlier fit between the waistbelt and shoulder straps.

Convenient, expandable, and carry-on-size:
Rick Steves' Wheeled Bag $129

At 9" x 21" x 14" our sturdy Rick Steves' Wheeled Bag is rucksack-soft in front, but the rest is lined with a hard ABS-lexan shell to give maximum protection to your belongings. We've spared no expense on moving parts, splurging on an extra-long button-release handle and big, tough inline skate wheels for easy rolling on rough surfaces.

Wishing you had even more room to bring home souvenirs? Pull open the full-perimeter expando-zipper and its capacity jumps from 2600 to 3000 cubic inches.

Rick Steves' Wheeled Bag has exactly the same three-outside-pocket configuration as our Back Door Bag, plus a handy "add-a-bag" strap and full lining.

Our Back Door Bags and Wheeled Bags come in black, navy, blue spruce, evergreen and merlot.

For great deals on a wide selection of travel goodies, begin your next trip at the Rick Steves Travel Store!

Visit the Rick Steves Travel Store at
www.ricksteves.com

Rick Steves

More *Savvy*. More *Surprising*. More *Fun*.

COUNTRY GUIDES 2006

England
France
Germany & Austria
Great Britain
Ireland
Italy
Portugal
Scandinavia
Spain
Switzerland

CITY GUIDES 2006

Amsterdam, Bruges & Brussels
Florence & Tuscany
London
Paris
Prague & The Czech Republic
Provence & The French Riviera
Rome
Venice

BEST OF GUIDES

Best of Eastern Europe
Best of Europe

As the #1 authority on European travel, Rick gives you inside information on what to visit, where to stay, and how to get there—economically and hassle-free.

www.ricksteves.com

PHRASE BOOKS & DICTIONARIES

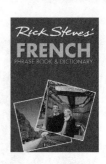

French
French, Italian & German
German
Italian
Portuguese
Spanish

MORE EUROPE FROM RICK STEVES

Easy Access Europe
Europe 101
Europe Through the Back Door
Postcards from Europe

RICK STEVES' EUROPE DVDs

All 43 Shows 2000-2005
Britain
Eastern Europe
France & Benelux
Germany, The Swiss Alps & Travel Skills
Ireland
Italy
Spain & Portugal

PLANNING MAPS

Britain & Ireland
Europe
France
Germany, Austria & Switzerland
Italy
Spain & Portugal

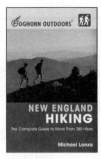
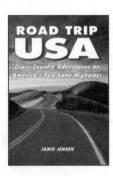